T0296021

The Economics of Poverty Traps

A National Bureau
of Economic Research
Conference Report

The Economics of Poverty Traps

Edited by **Christopher B. Barrett,
Michael R. Carter,
and Jean-Paul Chavas**

The University of Chicago Press

Chicago and London

The University of Chicago Press, Chicago 60637
The University of Chicago Press, Ltd., London
© 2019 by The National Bureau of Economic Research
All rights reserved. No part of this book may be used or reproduced
in any manner whatsoever without written permission, except in the
case of brief quotations in critical articles and reviews. For more
information, contact the University of Chicago Press, 1427 E. 60th St.,
Chicago, IL 60637.
Published 2019
Printed in the United States of America

28 27 26 25 24 23 22 21 20 19   1 2 3 4 5

ISBN-13: 978-0-226-57430-1 (cloth)
ISBN-13: 978-0-226-57444-8 (e-book)
DOI: https://doi.org/10.7208/chicago/9780226574448.001.0001

Library of Congress Cataloging-in-Publication Data

Names: Barrett, Christopher B. (Christopher Brendan), editor. | Carter,
    Michael R., editor. | Chavas, Jean-Paul, editor.
Title: The economics of poverty traps / edited by Christopher B.
    Barrett, Michael R. Carter, and Jean-Paul Chavas.
Other titles: National Bureau of Economic Research conference report.
Description: Chicago ; London : The University of Chicago Press,
    2018. | Series: National Bureau of Economic Research conference
    report | Includes bibliographical references and index.
Identifiers: LCCN 2018006264 | ISBN 9780226574301 (cloth : alk.
    paper) | ISBN 9780226574448 (e-book)
Subjects: LCSH: Poverty. | Public welfare. | Transfer payments. |
    Marginality, Social.
Classification: LCC HC79.P6 E355 2018 | DDC 339.4/6—dc23
LC record available at https://lccn.loc.gov/2018006264

Scripture quotations are from New Revised Standard Version Bible,
© 1989 National Council of the Churches of Christ in the United
States of America. Used by permission. All rights reserved worldwide.

♾ This paper meets the requirements of ANSI/NISO Z39.48-1992
(Permanence of Paper).

National Bureau of Economic Research

Officers

Karen N. Horn, *chair*
John Lipsky, *vice chair*
James M. Poterba, *president and chief executive officer*
Robert Mednick, *treasurer*

Kelly Horak, *controller and assistant corporate secretary*
Alterra Milone, *corporate secretary*
Denis Healy, *assistant corporate secretary*

Directors at Large

Peter C. Aldrich
Elizabeth E. Bailey
John H. Biggs
John S. Clarkeson
Kathleen B. Cooper
Charles H. Dallara
George C. Eads
Jessica P. Einhorn

Mohamed El-Erian
Jacob A. Frenkel
Robert S. Hamada
Peter Blair Henry
Karen N. Horn
Lisa Jordan
John Lipsky
Laurence H. Meyer

Karen Mills
Michael H. Moskow
Alicia H. Munnell
Robert T. Parry
James M. Poterba
John S. Reed
Marina v. N. Whitman
Martin B. Zimmerman

Directors by University Appointment

Timothy Bresnahan, *Stanford*
Pierre-André Chiappori, *Columbia*
Alan V. Deardorff, *Michigan*
Ray C. Fair, *Yale*
Edward Foster, *Minnesota*
John P. Gould, *Chicago*
Mark Grinblatt, *California, Los Angeles*
Bruce Hansen, *Wisconsin–Madison*
Benjamin Hermalin, *California, Berkeley*

George Mailath, *Pennsylvania*
Marjorie B. McElroy, *Duke*
Joel Mokyr, *Northwestern*
Cecilia Rouse, *Princeton*
Richard L. Schmalensee, *Massachusetts Institute of Technology*
Ingo Walter, *New York*
David B. Yoffie, *Harvard*

Directors by Appointment of Other Organizations

Jean-Paul Chavas, *Agricultural and Applied Economics Association*
Martin J. Gruber, *American Finance Association*
Philip Hoffman, *Economic History Association*
Arthur Kennickell, *American Statistical Association*
Jack Kleinhenz, *National Association for Business Economics*

Robert Mednick, *American Institute of Certified Public Accountants*
Peter L. Rousseau, *American Economic Association*
Gregor W. Smith, *Canadian Economics Association*
William Spriggs, *American Federation of Labor and Congress of Industrial Organizations*
Bart van Ark, *The Conference Board*

Directors Emeriti

George Akerlof
Jagdish Bhagwati
Don R. Conlan
Franklin Fisher

George Hatsopoulos
Saul H. Hymans
Rudolph A. Oswald
Andrew Postlewaite

John J. Siegfried
Craig Swan

Relation of the Directors to the
Work and Publications of the
National Bureau of Economic Research

1. The object of the NBER is to ascertain and present to the economics profession, and to the public more generally, important economic facts and their interpretation in a scientific manner without policy recommendations. The Board of Directors is charged with the responsibility of ensuring that the work of the NBER is carried on in strict conformity with this object.

2. The President shall establish an internal review process to ensure that book manuscripts proposed for publication DO NOT contain policy recommendations. This shall apply both to the proceedings of conferences and to manuscripts by a single author or by one or more coauthors but shall not apply to authors of comments at NBER conferences who are not NBER affiliates.

3. No book manuscript reporting research shall be published by the NBER until the President has sent to each member of the Board a notice that a manuscript is recommended for publication and that in the President's opinion it is suitable for publication in accordance with the above principles of the NBER. Such notification will include a table of contents and an abstract or summary of the manuscript's content, a list of contributors if applicable, and a response form for use by Directors who desire a copy of the manuscript for review. Each manuscript shall contain a summary drawing attention to the nature and treatment of the problem studied and the main conclusions reached.

4. No volume shall be published until forty-five days have elapsed from the above notification of intention to publish it. During this period a copy shall be sent to any Director requesting it, and if any Director objects to publication on the grounds that the manuscript contains policy recommendations, the objection will be presented to the author(s) or editor(s). In case of dispute, all members of the Board shall be notified, and the President shall appoint an ad hoc committee of the Board to decide the matter; thirty days additional shall be granted for this purpose.

5. The President shall present annually to the Board a report describing the internal manuscript review process, any objections made by Directors before publication or by anyone after publication, any disputes about such matters, and how they were handled.

6. Publications of the NBER issued for informational purposes concerning the work of the Bureau, or issued to inform the public of the activities at the Bureau, including but not limited to the NBER Digest and Reporter, shall be consistent with the object stated in paragraph 1. They shall contain a specific disclaimer noting that they have not passed through the review procedures required in this resolution. The Executive Committee of the Board is charged with the review of all such publications from time to time.

7. NBER working papers and manuscripts distributed on the Bureau's web site are not deemed to be publications for the purpose of this resolution, but they shall be consistent with the object stated in paragraph 1. Working papers shall contain a specific disclaimer noting that they have not passed through the review procedures required in this resolution. The NBER's web site shall contain a similar disclaimer. The President shall establish an internal review process to ensure that the working papers and the web site do not contain policy recommendations, and shall report annually to the Board on this process and any concerns raised in connection with it.

8. Unless otherwise determined by the Board or exempted by the terms of paragraphs 6 and 7, a copy of this resolution shall be printed in each NBER publication as described in paragraph 2 above.

Contents

Acknowledgments

This volume grew out of a conference held June 28–29, 2016, in Washington, DC, hosted by the National Bureau of Economic Research (NBER). We thank the NBER, and in particular Jim Poterba for his strong support for this conference and project, Carl Beck and Lita Kimble for their outstanding work organizing the conference, and Helena Fitz-Patrick for her expert guidance during the publication process. Sophie Javers at the University of California, Davis created and produced video interviews with conference participants that are available on the BASIS website. Liz Bageant at Cornell University handled much of the background organization of the conference and volume on behalf of the editors.

This book, and the conference that preceded it, were made possible by the generous support of the American people through the United States Agency for International Development (USAID) under grant AID-OAA-L-12-00001 to the BASIS Assets and Market Access Feed the Future Innovation Lab. The Agricultural and Applied Economics Association provided valuable travel support that enabled younger professionals to participate in the conference. The editorial board of the *Economics That Really Matters* blog and contributing authors Mohamad Alloush, Liz Bageant, Julia Berazneva, Jennifer Denno Cissé, Kibrom Tafere Hirfrfot, Nathan Jensen, Jeong Hyun Lee, Linden McBride, Emilia Tjernström, and Joanna Upton summarized the papers and discussions at the conference on social media.

Conference participants provided excellent feedback on the papers, including an excellent talk by Oriana Bandiera, whose paper was unfortunately already committed to be published elsewhere. Makhtar Diop gave an inspiring lunchtime address, and Kaushik Basu and Greg Collins offered excellent summary comments on policymaker perspectives on the papers and discussions. We thank them and all of the contributors—who also served as single-blind peer reviewers on one another's papers—for making this volume possible. The contents of this volume do not necessarily reflect the views of USAID or the United States government. Any remaining errors are our sole responsibility.

Introduction

Christopher B. Barrett, Michael R. Carter, and
Jean-Paul Chavas

The world has seen much progress in economic growth and poverty reduction over the last few decades. At the same time, extreme poverty continues to persist, and its increased concentration in specific places, in particular sub-Saharan Africa, has stimulated renewed interest in the microfoundations of economic growth. While it is clear that asset accumulation (broadly defined to include social, physical, natural, human, and financial capitals) can improve household living standards—as can adoption of improved technologies or participation in more remunerative markets that increase the returns to existing asset holdings—it is also clear that incentives to accumulate assets, adopt new technologies, or participate in new market opportunities vary significantly across households, locations, and time.

These observations draw our attention to understanding how households accumulate assets and increase their productivity and earning potential, as well as the conditions under which some individuals, groups, and economies struggle to escape poverty, and when and why adverse shocks have persistent welfare consequences. While much research has investigated these issues, our

Christopher B. Barrett is the Stephen B. and Janice G. Ashley Professor of Applied Economics and Management, professor of economics, and International Professor of Agriculture at Cornell University, where he also serves as deputy dean and dean of academic affairs at the SC Johnson College of Business. Michael R. Carter is professor of agricultural and resource economics at the University of California, Davis, and directs the Feed the Future Innovation Lab for Assets and Market Access and the Index Insurance Innovation Initiative (I4). He is a fellow of BREAD (Bureau for Research and Economic Analysis of Development) and the American Agricultural Economics Association and a research associate of the National Bureau of Economic Research. Jean-Paul Chavas is the Anderson-Bascom Professor of Agricultural and Applied Economics at the University of Wisconsin–Madison and a member of the board of directors of the National Bureau of Economic Research.

For acknowledgments, sources of research support, and disclosure of the authors' material financial relationships, if any, please see http://www.nber.org/chapters/c13828.ack.

understanding of the complexities of asset and well-being dynamics and their intrinsic heterogeneity across households remains disturbingly incomplete. Further scholarly review and evaluation are needed of the factors affecting (multidimensional) capital formation and resulting productivity and income dynamics. The goal of this volume is to think through the mechanisms that can trap households (and, intergenerationally, families) in poverty, paying particular attention to the interactions between tangible, material assets and general human capabilities, including psychological assets.

The need to better understand the economics of asset accumulation and poverty traps is especially pressing given world leaders' commitment to eliminate "extreme poverty" by 2030 as part of the sustainable development goals. The World Bank defines the "extreme" poor as those who live on US$1.90/day per person or less in 2011 purchasing power parity (PPP)-adjusted terms. The bank's most recent (2013) estimates indicate that 766 million people worldwide live in extreme poverty, just under 11 percent of the global population and 12.6 percent of the world's developing regions.[1] Extreme poverty has fallen quickly and dramatically. One generation earlier, in 1993, the comparable rates were 33 percent of world population and more than 40 percent within developing regions. Global progress over the past generation has been nothing short of remarkable, with pro-poor economic growth doing the "heavy lifting," as Ravallion (2017) remarks.

Progress against poverty remains, however, uneven. As Ravallion (2017) goes on to observe, there is ample scope for direct interventions intended to improve the well-being of those left behind. Ultrapoverty (a standard of living below US$0.95/day in 2011 PPP-adjusted terms) has likewise fallen sharply from 1993 to 2013, from 9.6 percent to just 2.6 percent of the population of developing world regions. But ultrapoverty has also become extremely spatially concentrated, with more than 83 percent of the world's ultrapoor residing in sub-Saharan Africa, up from just 33 percent in 1993. The absolute number of the ultrapoor in sub-Saharan Africa decreased just 13 percent from 1993 to 2013. It is possible that this spatial concentration merely represents average growth from lower initial conditions, thus necessarily taking longer to cross a fixed, global extreme (or ultra) poverty line. But that seems an overly simplistic explanation given that sub-Saharan Africa was at least as wealthy as Asia a half century ago and given the region's slow progress relative to even the ultrapoverty line.

The destitution reflected by ultrapoverty commonly correlates strongly with a range of other indicators of ill-being: poor physical and mental health, limited education, weak political representation, high rates of exposure to

---

1. These and other figures are available through the World Bank's PovcalNet data portal (http://iresearch.worldbank.org/PovcalNet/home.aspx). The World Bank defines the developing regions as: East Asia and Pacific, Europe and Central Asia, Latin America and the Caribbean, Middle East and North Africa, South Asia, and sub-Saharan Africa.

crime, violence, disease and uninsured risks, and so forth. The problem of poverty transcends limited monetary income. Deprivation manifests itself along multiple dimensions including financial, human, manufactured, natural, and social capital that people can accumulate or decumulate. This multidimensionality also reflects the correspondence among flow indicators—for example, of income, expenditures, nutrient intake, cognitive performance—and stock measures—for example, anthropometric scores, wealth, educational attainment—that is intrinsic to any dynamic system.

Furthermore, the poorest populations typically live their entire lives in abject deprivation, suffering chronic or persistent poverty. This is not true across the income spectrum, as reflected by patterns of economic growth observed in many countries over the last few decades or centuries. For example, during the early 1990s recession, poverty in the United States was remarkably transitory, with a median spell length in poverty—the duration of time between falling into and exiting poverty—of just 4.5 months (Naifeh 1998).[2] By contrast, spell lengths in extreme poverty remain poorly understood in the low-income world. In most longitudinal data sets, we have not yet seen half the population exit extreme poverty (Barrett and Swallow 2006).

The depth and persistence of extreme poverty raises the prospect of poverty traps, which arise if poverty becomes self-reinforcing when the poor's equilibrium behaviors perpetuate low standards of living. This can happen when income dynamics are nonlinear and generate multiple equilibria, with a low-level equilibrium corresponding to poverty. But the analysis grows in complexity in the presence of unanticipated shocks. The welfare effects of shocks can vary with the nature and magnitude of the shocks and the ability of decision makers to adjust. Firms and households that can recover quickly from adverse shocks are termed "resilient." But the ability to escape low-income scenarios can vary across households. This stresses the need to distinguish between transitory poverty and persistent poverty, to examine scenarios where households may find it difficult to escape poverty, and to evaluate economic and policy strategies that may stimulate economic growth among the poor.

The poverty traps hypothesis has major policy implications. As Ghatak (comment, chapters 9 and 10, this volume) emphasizes, if no traps exist and poverty is transitory, then costly and imperfectly targeted interventions may impede rather than accelerate escapes from poverty.[3] However, the strength

---

2. The Great Recession of the past decade may well represent a shift in the balance between persistent and transitory poverty in high-income economies, but we know of no compelling evidence on this point to date.

3. Poverty may be transitory if it is due to temporary, adverse income shocks (Baulch and Hoddinott 2000) resulting in what Carter and May (2001) term "stochastic poverty," or if poverty can be easily escaped through migration (Kraay and McKenzie 2014). Alternatively, transitory poverty may simply reflect a slow ascent form poor initial conditions.

of the argument for intervention rises with the strength of the evidence of poverty traps. If a poverty trap exists and makes it difficult for some households to escape poverty, then a strong economic and moral argument exists to experiment with interventions and to implement and scale interventions demonstrated to generate sustained improvements in standards of living. Of course, complex political economy considerations are associated with policies targeted effectively to marginalized populations, and in sun-setting policies that are needed for only a fixed period of time. But where poverty arises due to the existence of multiple equilibria, making some poverty unnecessary and avoidable, policy response will often prove both ethically compulsory and economically attractive (Barrett and Carter 2013).

The chapters in this volume, which were first presented at a National Bureau of Economic Research conference in Washington, DC, in June 2016, extend the range of the mechanisms hypothesized to generate poverty traps, and offer empirical evidence that highlights both the insights and limits of a poverty traps lens on the contemporary policy commitment to achieve zero extreme poverty by 2030. In this introductory essay we aim to frame these contributions in an integrative model meant to capture the key features of the chapters that follow. Mechanisms include poor nutrition and (mental and physical) health, endogenous behavioral patterns (e.g., risk and time preferences), poorly functioning capital markets, large uninsured risk exposure, and weak natural resource governance institutions. The chapters in this book examine these factors in detail. The empirical analyses many of the chapters offer inform us about the factors affecting the prospects for household productivity and income growth, with a special focus on how and why these effects can be heterogeneous across household types and economic/policy environments. They also offer important findings on the effectiveness of programs and policies designed to address persistent extreme poverty, such as cash transfers and microfinance.

Toward an Integrative Theory of Poverty Traps

As Ghatak (comment, chapters 9 and 10, this volume) and several other contributors emphasize, it is essential to have a clear theoretical framework to help identify the relationships between specific antipoverty programs and particular mechanisms that cause poverty to persist. Economists' interest in the topic of poverty traps has waxed and waned over the decades. Economists have long known that coordination failures and market failures can each lead to situations of multiple equilibria characterized by both locally increasing returns that are conducive to capital accumulation and rapid income growth, as well as regions of rapidly diminishing returns where people face weak incentives to invest. A range of largely unintegrated theories exist to explain patterns of differential investment that lead to persistent poverty in equilibrium (Nelson 1956; Mazumdar 1959; Stiglitz 1976; Loury

1981; Dasgupta and Ray 1986, 1987; Banerjee and Newman 1993; Dasgupta 1993; Barham et al. 1995; Zimmerman and Carter 2003).[4] Whatever the theorized mechanism, the essence of a poverty trap is that equilibrium behavior leads predictably to expected poverty indefinitely, given preferences and the constraints and incentives an agent faces, including the set of markets and technologies (un)available to her. Azariadis and Stachurski (2005) therefore define a poverty trap as a "self-reinforcing mechanism, which causes poverty to persist."

One such mechanism is simply low levels of wages and productivity (born perhaps of an unforgiving natural environment and few technological options) such that even in equilibrium all or most individuals are poor. Labeled a single equilibrium poverty trap by Barrett and Carter (2013), and a geographic poverty trap by Kraay and McKenzie (2014), fundamental technological change or out-migration appear as one of the few options for combatting chronic poverty born of this mechanism.[5]

The contributions to this volume focus on mechanisms and feedback loops that can trap people who are not initially poor, but who become chronically poor only following an adverse event or shock. Most of these mechanisms enrich the understanding that can be gained even from a single equilibrium or geographic poverty trap model. These mechanisms are

- biophysical feedback loops in which an initial environmental shock and the poverty it induces undercut the productive capacity of natural resource systems, trapping previously nonpoor individuals in persistent poverty;
- psychological feedback loops in which an economic shock induces depression, undercuts cognitive functioning or prosocial behavior, or reduces aspirations or otherwise changes preferences in such a way that formerly nonpoor individuals become chronically poor through loss of human capability or desire;
- direct loss of human capital, or shock-induced reductions in health and education investments, that pushes previously nonpoor families into perpetual intergenerational poverty; and
- imperfect financial markets that can create multiple equilibrium systems that can trap previously nonpoor families in a situation of persistent poverty following a one-off shock that pushes families' productive assets and abilities below the critical levels needed to strive toward a nonpoor equilibrium.

4. For reasonably complete reviews of the poverty traps literature through early in the twenty-first century, see Azariadis and Stachurski (2005). Barrett, Garg, and McBride (2016) provide an updated summary of the literature.

5. Bryan, Chowdhury, and Mobarak (2014) study interventions that relax constraints to (seasonal) out-migration and show that small cash inducements to migrate seasonally can substantially and sustainably increase household consumption, consistent with a model in which migration is risky and some prospective migrants close to a subsistence constraint choose not to migrate in order to minimize catastrophic risk exposure.

The chapters in this volume offer an array of theoretical reflection and empirical evidence on these various mechanisms, and in several cases evaluate the impacts of policies and programs intended to reduce persistent poverty through various lenses.

A Poverty Trap Model with Endogenous Capabilities

The four mechanisms above, the interactions among them, and the potential impacts of policy that targets chronic poverty, can be most easily explained using a theoretical framework that encompasses the models used in several contributions to this volume. First, consider the following model of income generation for an individual, household, or dynasty[6] i in time period t:

$$(1) \qquad y_{it} = f_I(\alpha_{it}, k_{it} \mid N_t),$$

where y_{it} is output, k_{it} is a tangible productive asset—buildings, land, livestock, machinery, money in the bank, or other forms of capital—and α_{it} is human capability, a term we use to be general enough to encompass such concepts as skill, human capital, and perceived self-efficacy.[7] We assume that capabilities and tangible assets are complements in production. Finally, the conditioning variable N_t measures the stock of natural capital that enhances the productivity of tangible assets and human capabilities.

Absent financial markets and informal transfers between households, household consumption in every time period t is restricted to be no more than cash on hand (the value of current income and productive assets):

$$(2) \qquad c_{it} \le k_{it} + y_{it}.$$

Finally, we introduce stochasticity into the model by assuming that productive assets are subject to a random shock, θ_{it}, which occurs at the beginning of every time period such that

$$(3) \qquad k_{it+1} = [k_{it} + y_{it} - c_{it}][1 + \delta_0 + \delta_1(\theta_{it+1})].$$

Note that the first square bracket measures the amount of productive capital that the household carries forward from the prior time period. The second square bracket measures the net capital growth or loss the household

6. We ask the reader's forbearance as we move somewhat elastically between these terms depending on the context. We use the household as the main unit of analysis, fully recognizing that we abstract here from important issues of intrahousehold bargaining. Since most microdata on poverty exist at household level, we use this terminology to maximize correspondence with the empirical evidence offered in this volume and elsewhere. However, when discussing psychological attributes that are clearly individual, we use that term. Finally, because we also want to consider changes in human capabilities that occur intergenerationally, we will also use the term dynasty to refer to a multigenerational sequence of biologically related individuals or households.

7. It is, of course, the decision maker's perception of their capabilities that matter, a factor stressed by de Quidt and Haushofer in their chapter in this volume.

experiences, where δ_0 is the natural rate of growth, or depreciation, of productive assets, and $\delta_1(\theta_{it+1}) \leq 0$ is the stochastic asset depreciation or destruction driven by the random variable, θ_{it+1}, which captures the exogenous shocks that may affect the household in any time period.[8]

Assembling these pieces, we assume that the ith household makes decisions according to the optimization problem

(4)
$$\text{Max}_{c_{it},k_{it}} \; E_\theta \sum_{t=0}^{\infty} \beta^t u(c_{it})$$

subject to

$$c_{it} \leq k_{it} + y_{it}$$

$$y_{it} = f_i(\alpha_{it}, k_{it}, \theta_{it} \mid N_t)$$

$$k_{it+1} = [k_{it} + y_{it} - c_{it}][1 + \delta_0 + \delta_1(\theta_{it+1})]$$

$$\alpha_{it+1} = \alpha_{it} = \alpha_i$$

$$k_{it} \geq 0$$

where E is the expectation operator, c_{it} represents consumption of a numeraire composite good, $u(c_{it})$ is the utility function representing the household preferences, and β is the discount factor. We assume for the moment that capabilities, α_{it}, do not evolve and are fixed at an initial endowment level for each dynasty, α_i. Models of this sort have been analyzed by Deaton (1991) and Zimmerman and Carter (2003).

Figure I.1 allows us to capture the implications of this model and begin to frame the contributions of the different chapters in this volume. Given heterogeneity in nontradable human endowments, α_{it}, optimal steady-state capital holding, $k_\ell^*(\alpha \mid N_t)$, is increasing in human capabilities, as shown in the figure. Treating capabilities as fixed, this model implies a type of conditional convergence, with the more capable enjoying a higher optimal steady-state level of capital and income than the less capable. Foreshadowing later discussion, note that a deterioration in capabilities (e.g., through a deterioration in psychological assets) will reduce optimal capital, forming what might be termed an internal barrier to capital accumulation, as distinct from the external barrier associated with financial market failures.

To relate this discussion to poverty, define the locus $y^p(\alpha, k \mid N_t)$ as combinations of α and k that given a stock of natural capital, N_t, yield an income

---

8. Stochasticity could also be introduced by applying the shock directly to the production process. What matters for the decision-making problem is that cash on hand is stochastic. Assigning the shock to assets rather than incomes simplifies the graphical discussion. Following McPeak (2004), separate, imperfectly correlated shocks could be assigned to both income flows and asset stocks. We here abstract away from that additional complexity.

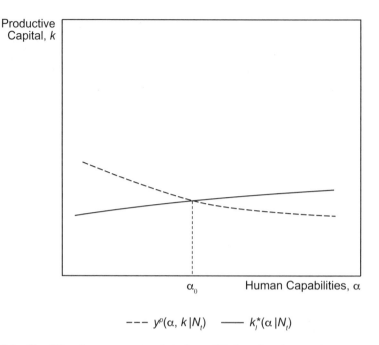

Fig. I.1   Conditional convergence and single equilibrium chronic poverty

equal to an (arbitrary) money metric income poverty line, y^p. Note that $y^p (\alpha, k \mid N_t)$ will be downward sloping in α, k space, as shown. To the southwest of the locus, a household will be poor, while to the northeast they will not be. For a relatively poor and unproductive economy, we might expect y^p to cut the steady capital curve, k_i^*, from above as shown in figure I.1.[9]

For those with capabilities above α_0, a shock that temporarily reduces their stocks of productive assets will at most make them temporarily poor as they would be expected to save and strive to reach their nonpoor, steady-state position. In contrast, those with $\alpha_i < \alpha_0$ will be chronically poor, trapped by their own low level of capabilities in this conditional convergence model. Cash or other forms of nonhuman capital alone cannot free the household from poverty over time, as the Buera, Kaboski, and Shin and the Ikegami, Carter, Barrett, and Janzen chapters highlight. The barriers can arise as well due to sociocultural limits imposed on human capabilities, for example, race (Fang and Loury 2005) or caste (Naschold 2012). This poverty trap mechanism exemplifies a single equilibrium poverty trap.

9. Ikegami, Carter, Barrett, and Janzen (chapter 6, this volume) describe in greater detail the model and computational methods used to generate figures such as those used illustratively in this chapter.

Note that if the underlying technology is or becomes less productive, the poverty locus shifts northward and (under fairly general conditions) the steady-state capital holdings ($k_i^*(\alpha \mid N_t)$) go south. For a given distribution of the population along the capabilities continuum, these shifts of course imply that α_0 moves right and that an increasing fraction of the population will be poor at their steady-state positions. Individuals occupying this economy would be lodged in a geographic poverty trap.

Similarly, a shock to the stock of natural capital will shift these curves and induce an increase in chronic poverty if the natural capital stock does not recover. In his contribution to this volume, Chavas econometrically explores precisely this mechanism in the case of the US Dust Bowl of the 1930s. The dynamic stochastic system Chavas explores, with multiple time-varying assets, quickly becomes complex and nonlinear. As Chavas explains, stochastic dynamical systems lend themselves to distinct zones defined by the current state of asset holdings, (α_{it}, k_{it}), with some zones undesirable and difficult to escape (a poverty trap), others undesirable but relatively easy to escape (poor but resilient), and others desirable (nonpoor). Identifying those zones in data, however, is a terribly complex task (Barrett and Carter 2013). While Chavas finds no evidence that the Dust Bowl created a long-lived poverty trap, he suggests that it was public policy that allowed the stock of natural capital to recover and avoid the less desirable outcomes.

The discussion so far has treated capabilities as fixed and exogenous to realized shocks. In other words, we have so far only considered north-south movements in the α, k space that defines figure I.1. However, as studied by a number of contributions to this volume, households and dynasties can also move in the east-west direction through both voluntary and involuntary mechanisms. Opening this model up to changes in capabilities, α_{it}, expands the array of potential poverty trap mechanisms.

Akin to equation (3) for the evolution of tangible capital assets, we can replace the fourth constraint in the maximization problem above with a law of motion for human capabilities:

$$(5) \qquad \alpha_{it+1} = [\alpha_{it}][1 + \xi_0\,(c_{it}) + \xi_1\,(\theta_{it})],$$

where $\xi_0(c_{it})$ captures the deterioration of capabilities based on shock-induced consumption choices (e.g., reduced educational expenditures for children), while $\xi_1(\theta_{it}) \leq 0$ represents the direct destruction of capabilities due to shocks. Either mechanism could create a scenario in which a single shock could move an individual from nonpoor to a chronically poor position were capabilities to fall below the critical α_0 level shown in figure I.1.

While the direct impact of shocks on human capabilities is a relatively new area of study within economics, such impacts can take place through both physiological and psychological mechanisms. Garg, Jagnani, and Taraz (2017), and the references therein, examine various physiological mechanisms by which shocks can undercut capabilities (e.g., temperature spikes can damage brain development and the future capabilities of the yet unborn). Several contributions to this volume examine how shocks can operate through psychological mechanisms to reduce human capabilities. The chapter by de Quidt and Haushofer on the economics of depression raises the possibility that an economic shock can induce depression, which in turn reduces individuals' perceived capabilities (moving them westward in figure I.1) and thereby reducing investment and labor market participation incentives. These changes in turn reinforce and perpetuate the initial decline in living standards. While the empirical challenges to identifying this underlying simultaneous causal structure are notable, in panel data from South Africa Alloush (2017) estimates that these mechanisms are in play and that an initial economic shock can trap a near-poor individual in an extended poverty spell.

The chapter by Dean, Schilbach, and Schofield raises the possibility that economic shocks and low living standards can directly impede cognitive functioning. Similar to the de Quidt and Haushofer work, their work also raises the possibility that shocks can directly reduce capabilities, at least creating the prospect that a one-off shock can induce a prolonged poverty spell.

A third psychological mechanism is highlighted by the chapters by Lybbert and Wydick and Macours and Vakis. Both chapters provide empirical evidence that improved economic prospects can endogenously shift preferences through what they term an aspirational mechanism.[10] While neither provides direct evidence on the deterioration of aspirations when economic prospects are gloomy, such a mechanism is presumably in play if positive interventions boost aspirations and shift preferences relative to a control group. A particularly provocative contrast emerges between the findings of Macours and Vakis—who show that when aspirations are lifted, women sustain investment in child health and education long after the program ends—and the chapter by Araujo, Bosch, and Schady—which shows that the impacts of a standard cash transfer program dissipate over the longer term.

In addition to their direct psychological effects, shocks and low living standards more generally can also influence capabilities via household consumption choices. In their chapter, Frankenberg and Thomas explore the impact of two megashocks that hit Indonesia (the 1998 Asian financial crisis and the 2004 tsunami). In contrast to some studies that suggest that shocks of this magnitude result in irreversible losses in human capabilities, they find that despite some short-term deterioration in child health and education,

---

10. Other recent contributions examine the impact of shocks on other deep preference parameters (risk aversion and time horizons) that can depress investment in ways similar to a decrease in α in the model here. Examples include Rockmore, Barrett, and Annan (2016), who show that posttraumatic stress in postconflict Uganda increases risk aversion and Moya (2018), who finds a similar phenomenon for victims of violence in Colombia. Laajaj (2017) provides a theoretical model and empirical evidence that shifts around the poverty line influence time horizons.

households (and multigeneration dynasties) proved remarkably able to shield themselves from medium-term deterioration in human capital, as measured by schooling and anthropometric measures. Recent work by Adhvaryu et al. (2017) indicates that social safety net schemes, such as Mexico's PROGRESA program, can augment households' coping capacity and shield child human capital from the deleterious consequences of environmental shocks.

While the Indonesia study signals the remarkable range of coping mechanisms that families can employ, Frankenberg and Thomas note that their finding does not imply that shocks do not have more deleterious consequences in other instances, and that even the recovery of linear growth in shock-exposed children may mask longer-term consequences in terms of lost cognitive capacity. In his contribution to this volume, Hoddinott stresses this latter point, citing a range of medical studies that caution that shocks can result in long-term damage to capabilities even among individuals who suffered no long-term loss of physical stature.

A Multiple Equilibrium Poverty Trap Model with Endogenous Capabilities

The basic model above becomes richer if we add a second, higher productivity technology, f_h, which is characterized by fixed costs or a minimum project size such that $f_h > f_l \forall k > \hat{k}$.[11] The nonconvex production set for the household thus becomes

$$(6) \qquad y_{it} = max\left[f_l\left(\alpha_{it}, k_{it} \mid N_t\right), f_h(\alpha_{it}, k_{it} \mid N_t)\right]$$

and we denote as $k_h^*(\alpha \mid N_t)$ the steady-state capital values implied by the intertemporal optimization problem above for those households that choose to accumulate capital beyond $\hat{k}$. As noted by Skiba (1978), this kind of nonconvex production set can lead to multiple equilibria with an individual choosing to accumulate to $k_l^*(\alpha \mid N_t)$ or $k_h^*(\alpha \mid N_t)$ depending on her initial endowment of capital. Subsequently, other authors have generalized this class of model to include skill heterogeneity (Buera 2009) and skill heterogeneity and risk (Carter and Ikegami [2009], and the chapters in this volume by Ikegami, Carter, Barrett, and Janzen [chapter 6] and Santos and Barrett [chapter 7]).

Figure I.2 illustrates the richer set of equilibrium possibilities that emerge when the basic model is augmented with the nonconvex production set in equation (6) above.[12] This model, with the embedded financial market failures discussed in the simpler model above, generates two critical skill values, denoted $\underline{\alpha}$ and $\overline{\alpha}$ in the figure. Individuals below $\underline{\alpha}$ will find it optimal to

11. Zimmerman and Carter (2003) show that many properties of this model with a nonconvex production set also hold if there is a nonconvexity in the utility function (e.g., a subsistence penalty).
12. The Ikegami et al. chapter in this volume analyzes exactly this model using stochastic dynamic programming techniques.

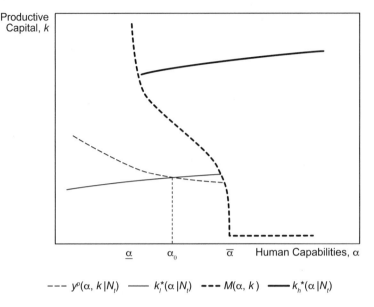

Fig. I.2 Nonconvex technology and coexisting single and multiple equilibrium poverty traps

move to the low-technology steady state irrespective of their initial capital endowment. Above $\bar{\alpha}$, high-capability individuals will always strive for the high-technology steady state, k_h^*, again irrespective of their endowment of productive capital. In between ($\underline{\alpha} < \alpha < \bar{\alpha}$), "middle-ability" individuals will split depending on whether they find themselves below or above the downward-sloping "Micawber Frontier," denoted $M(\alpha, k)$ in figure I.2.[13] As discussed in greater detail in Carter and Ikegami (2009), an increase in risk will shift $\underline{\alpha}$ and $\bar{\alpha}$ to the east and the Micawber Frontier, $M(\alpha, k)$, to the northeast.

Those in the middle-ability group thus face what Barrett and Carter (2013) call a multiple equilibrium poverty trap. Treating capabilities as fixed, those born either above α_h or to the northeast of $M(\alpha, k)$ will place themselves on an optimal trajectory to reach k_h^*. However, a sufficiently large negative shock to the current wealth of those in the middle-ability group may push them below $M(\alpha, k)$ and into a permanently poor standard of living at $k_l^*(\alpha)$. Indeed, as the chapter by Ikegami et al. illustrates, those above $M(\alpha, k)$ will only probabilistically approach the high equilibrium, with

13. This usage, inspired by Lipton (1993) and adopted to the context of poverty trap models by Zimmerman and Carter (2003), harkens to asset levels below which it is not optimal to strive to save and become nonpoor, belying the folk wisdom of Charles Dickens's fictional character Wilkins Micawber who urged David Copperfield and others to supersede their poor circumstances through careful capital accumulation.

that probability increasing in their distance above the Micawber Frontier. The Santos and Barrett chapter in this volume provide empirical evidence of this mixed structure in the risk-prone, semiarid rangelands of southern Ethiopia. A key implication of this kind of multiple equilibrium poverty trap mechanism is what the Ikegami et al. chapter calls the "paradox of social protection." Specifically, they show that targeting some of a fixed social protection budget at the vulnerable nonpoor can result in enhanced well-being of the poor in the medium term as it prevents the ranks of the poor from growing by preventing the vulnerable from joining the ranks of the chronically poor.

With the exception of Carter and Janzen (2018), there has been little exploration of the endogenous skills or capabilities (as represented by equation [3] above) in the context of this type of multiple equilibrium poverty trap model. Their theoretical model shows that the fraction of the initial endowment space that absorbs households into long-term poverty expands when capabilities deteriorate in the face of shocks.[14] A similar impact would be expected from the psychological feedback loops discussed in the chapters by de Quidt and Haushofer, by Dean, Schilbach, and Scho-field, and by Lybbert and Wydick. As already summarized above, these authors discuss how stress, depression, and poverty itself may affect prefer-ences, cognitive function, and thus earnings, resulting in low income that in turn reinforces stress and depression, leading to a stable, low-level equilib-rium standard of living.

In the presence of such reinforcing feedback, exogenous shocks and endog-enous consumption behaviors can jointly influence individuals' psycho-logical state—feelings of depression or hope—and cognitive and physical functioning, which in turn affect future productivity and optimal invest-ment behaviors. For example, negative shocks may lead to overly pessimistic assessments of the return to effort, leading to lower effort and investment, which leaves one worse off and more vulnerable to further shocks (de Quidt and Haushofer, chapter 3, this volume). In terms of figure I.2, these feed-back loops suggest that a material shock that initially moves the household to the south in the figure may result in induced changes in capabilities that then move the household to the west, with attendant declines in productivity and incomes. Consistent with the theoretical model of Carter and Janzen (2018), one can easily imagine scenarios in which a modest shock to the tangible assets of a middle-ability household induces a deterioration in the

14. In contrast to equation (3), Carter and Janzen (2018) only explore the indirect effects of shocks through their impacts on low consumption. Formally, these authors assume that households choose consumption levels ignoring their long-term consequences for the human skills or capabilities of the dynasty. The findings of Frankenberg and Thomas (chapter 1, this volume) suggest that households or multigeneration dynasties have intrahousehold degrees of freedom to protect the education and capabilities of the next generation at the cost of the well-being of the older generation.

household's capabilities, which places it to the southwest of the Micawber Frontier, sentencing it to a state of chronic poverty.

The central problem, from an economic perspective, is the nontradability of human capabilities. One cannot simply buy hope or (mental or physical) health or cognitive capacity. The possibility of absorbing states—for example, blindness, permanent amnesia or paralysis, death—implies nonstationary stochastic processes that naturally lead to multiple steady states if human capabilities are essential complements to nonhuman capital in income generation. The same multiplicity of equilibria arise with tradable forms of capital in the presence of multiple financial markets failures. The crucial difference is that the cognitive, psychological, sociocultural (e.g., gender, race), and even some physical elements of human capabilities are intrinsically internal constraints on human agency, in contrast to the external constraints posed by market failures that may impede accumulation of other financial or physical assets.

One reason empirical analysis is challenging is that if people recognize the dynamic consequences of shocks, then households may alter behaviors so as to protect productive human and nonhuman assets and thereby defend future productivity and consumption, even if it entails some short-run sacrifice. Such "asset smoothing" behaviors arise endogenously in the presence of systems with feedback and multiple equilibria (Hoddinott 2006; Carter and Lybbert 2012; Barrett and Carter 2013). Such behaviors stand in striking juxtaposition to the familiar consumption smoothing that prevails when income follows a stationary stochastic process, leading to a single dynamic equilibrium.

Shocks can degrade nonhuman capital as well as human capabilities. Since most of the world's extreme poor live in rural areas and work in agriculture, exogenous shocks to agricultural productivity—due to extreme weather and other phenomena—can be especially important. Rosenzweig and Binswanger (1993) and Carter (1997) showed how risk preferences can induce poor agricultural households that lack access to credit and insurance markets to choose low-risk, low-return livelihoods as a way of self-insuring against weather risk. Unfortunately, those choices can also trap them in chronic poverty.

The experience of shocks to the natural capital, N_t (such as soils and rangeland vegetation), can also strongly influence accumulation of capital, k_{it}, as described in both the Santos and Barrett chapter on East African pastoralists and the Chavas contribution on the resilience of farmers in the US Midwest following the Dust Bowl experience of the 1930s. A Micawber Threshold may exist in natural capital space, for example, in soils that become excessively degraded, making investment in fertilizer application or conservation structures unprofitable (Marenya and Barrett 2009; Barrett and Bevis 2015). As Barbier's commentary (comment, chapters 7 and 8, this volume) emphasizes, the environmental and geographic conditions faced by poor households fundamentally shape investment incentives, especially in fragile agroecosystems subject to extreme external environmental shocks.

The model sketched out in this introductory chapter has abstracted away from social interconnections among individuals. If multiple financial market failures are a central obstacle to asset accumulation, then social connections can mitigate the effects of those market failures. As the chapter by Frankenberg and Thomas demonstrates, extended family and other social support networks can cushion the blow of shocks that might otherwise drive vulnerable people into poverty traps. Social networks might also matter to individuals' self-efficacy, as both the Lybbert and Wydick and Macours and Vakis chapters suggest. Given that material poverty may affect prosocial behavior and social connectivity (Adato, Carter, and May 2006; Andreoni, Nikiforakis, and Stoop 2017), there may be significant social spillover effects of interventions (Mogues and Carter 2005; Chantarat and Barrett 2011; Macours and Vakis, this volume).[15] As Macours and Vakis (chapter 9, this volume) demonstrate in their evaluation of the medium-term impacts of a short-term transfer program in Nicaragua, the possibility of nontrivial social multiplier effects may matter to the effectiveness of interventions, especially if it is difficult to target individuals appropriately due to incomplete information.

This integrative framework also helps us to recognize the many settings where poverty traps are less likely to occur. Where financial markets are largely accessible at reasonable cost to most people, where social protection programs effectively safeguard the mental and physical health of poor populations and ensure the development of children's human capital through their formative years, and where geographic and intersectoral migration is feasible at reasonably low cost, the likelihood of a poverty trap is far smaller. Moreover, history is not necessarily destiny. Forward-looking behaviors can obviate the adverse effects of even massive shocks. Many poor populations prove amazingly resilient, as the chapters by Frankenberg and Thomas and by Chavas so nicely demonstrate. The aim of poverty traps research is to help render the concept increasingly irrelevant.

Implications for Policy and Project Design

The stylized integrative model we offer not only reflects several crucial features outlined in the mechanism-specific chapters that make up most of this volume, it also captures several key policy implications of the emergent poverty traps literature.

First, it underscores the challenge of targeting poverty-reduction programs in systems where multiple mechanisms that perpetuate poverty coex-

---

15. Social connections can likewise generate the opposite sort of reinforcing feedback through the ecology of infectious diseases (Bonds et al. 2010; Ngonghala et al. 2014).

ist. It is not enough to know that someone is poor. We need to know *why* they are poor in order to target effective interventions. For some, whose human capabilities are permanently compromised ($\alpha_{it} < \alpha_0 \ \forall \ t$), persistent poverty may be the only possibility going forward in the absence of an on-going social safety net that provides regular transfers to supplement their meager earnings. By contrast, other poor people may be able to pull themselves out of poverty through asset accumulation and thereafter maintain a nonpoor standard of living if given a brief boost and some protection against catastrophic shocks. With fixed budgets, policymakers face trade-offs between these two poor subpopulations, which leads to the "social protection paradox" explained in the chapter by Ikegami et al. Spending on short-term poverty reduction may aggravate longer-term poverty, even for near-term beneficiaries, if inadequate attention is paid to preventing the collapse of the vulnerable nonpoor beneath the Micawber Frontier and into chronic poverty.

Second, the multiplicity of mechanisms potentially in play can also lead to striking heterogeneity in the impact of programs and interventions that target financial markets, physical assets, human capabilities, and even aspirations or preferences. For households with midrange capabilities, microfinance interventions that relax financial market constraints may open a pathway from poverty. But for others, who suffer internal or capabilities constraints, such programs may be ineffective, signaling the kind of impact heterogeneity found by Buera, Kaboski, and Shin (chapter 5, this volume). Moreover, as Laajaj's (comment, chapters 3 and 4, this volume) thoughtful commentary underscores, the risk-reward profile of different interventions may not be similar. Interventions can easily have adverse unintended consequences, perhaps especially those that aim to relieve internal psychosocial constraints on asset accumulation.

A third key policy implication is that, to the extent that market failures are the root cause of poverty traps, systemic interventions that address the underlying structural causes of poverty traps are likely to generate indirect, general equilibrium benefits—for example, in wage labor markets—that almost surely dominate the direct effects of small-scale interventions that benefit just a few direct program participants. Bandiera et al. (2017) find that an asset-building program for poor women in Bangladesh increased the low-skill wages received by nonprogram participants. Whether the dominant poverty trap mechanism revolves around fundamentally nontradable human attributes like hope or depression—for which market failures appear insurmountable—or originates from credit and insurance market failures that impede accumulation of physical assets like livestock or machinery, the core challenge to escaping persistent poverty boils down to overcoming the market failures that impede the accumulation of assets. It is easy to lose sight of the structural underpinnings of persistent poverty in the rush to generate cleanly identified reduced-form impacts of interventions.

Fourth, many of the contributions to this volume emphasize the importance of feedback loops between changes in living standards and preferences, psychological health, and even the health of the supporting natural resource system. Such feedback loops can create vicious circles that perpetuate poverty, but they can also create virtuous circles that can surprisingly eradicate it. The integrative framework put forward here underscores why multifaceted interventions—so-called poverty graduation programs—exhibit consistently large impacts (e.g., Banerjee et al. 2015; Bandiera et al. 2017; Gobin, Santos, and Toth 2017). The interdependence of coevolving human capabilities and capital stocks, each potentially impeded by financial (and other) market failures, means that graduation programs that couple asset transfers with skills training, the strengthening of social networks, and psychological "coaching" become especially promising. Conceptually, these programs move individuals to the northeast in figure I.2 as they bolster both tangible and psychological assets. Indeed, in practice, most graduation programs follow the original BRAC model (Hulme and Moore 2008) and build capabilities and psychological assets first, and then transfer tangible productive assets.

While research has yet to unpack exactly what these coaching interventions change in the psychological realm (aspirations, self-efficacy, or mental health?), the longevity and magnitude of their impacts stand out. In contrast, pure cash interventions, even when conditioned on behaviors such as keeping children in school, may have only small and short-term results, as Araujo, Bosch, and Schady (chapter 10, this volume) find in their study of the multiyear effects of Ecuador's conditional cash transfer program.[16]

Fifth, the emphasis so many of the chapters place on shocks, whether these are economic, environmental, or psychological, underscores the critical role safety nets play in poverty reduction. As Smith (comment, chapters 5 and 6, this volume) eloquently puts it, "as we move toward fully addressing the zero-poverty goal of the sustainable development goals, as also embraced by the World Bank, USAID, and other key development agencies, there is likely to be an enhanced focus on preventing people from falling into poverty. At least from a poverty head count or income shortfall perspective, ultimately we may view this as equally important to pulling people out of poverty." This is the "paradox of social protection," that Ikegami et al. highlight. Attending to the dynamics of poverty by promoting the resilience of the nonpoor can have substantial impacts on the long-term extent and depth of poverty.

Finally, the interdependent laws of motion of different forms of (financial, human, natural, physical, and social) capital necessitate multidimen-

16. As stressed earlier, it is important not to overlook the role that safety nets can play in insulating households from shocks that might otherwise compromise child health and education (Adhvaryu et al. 2017).

sional thinking in policy deliberations. Familiar models with a single-state variable (unidimensional capital) lend themselves to overly simplistic diagnoses and prescriptions that fail to capture many of the ways in which deprivation manifests in the lives of the poor. Just as the conference where the chapters in this volume originated forced all of us in attendance to grapple simultaneously with these complexities, so too we hope the slightly more nuanced framework we advance here helps readers of this volume think in more integrative ways about the challenges facing the world's poorest populations today and about how best to design, target, and evaluate interventions targeted at the poor.

References

Adato, M., M. R. Carter, and J. May. 2006. "Exploring Poverty Traps and Social Exclusion in South Africa Using Qualitative and Quantitative Data." *Journal of Development Studies* 42 (2): 226–47.

Adhvaryu, A., T. Molina, A. Nyshadham, and J. Tamayo. 2017. "Helping Children Catch Up: Early Life Shocks and the *Progresa* Experiment." Working paper, University of Michigan.

Alloush, M. 2017. "Income, Psychological Well-Being, and the Dynamics of Poverty: Evidence from South Africa." Working paper, University of California, Davis.

Andreoni, J., N. Nikiforakis, and J. Stoop. 2017. "Are the Rich More Selfish Than the Poor, or Do They Just Have More Money? A Natural Field Experiment." NBER Working Paper no. 23229, Cambridge, MA.

Azariadis, C., and J. Stachurski. 2005. "Poverty Traps." In *Handbook of Economic Growth*, vol. 1A, edited by P. Aghion and S. Durlauf. Amsterdam: Elsevier.

Bandiera, O., R. Burgess, N. Das, S. Gulesci, I. Rasul, and M. Sulaiman. 2017. "Labor Markets and Poverty in Village Economies." *Quarterly Journal of Economics* 132 (2): 811–70.

Banerjee, A., E. Duflo, N. Goldberg, D. Karlan, R. Osei, W. Parienté, J. Shapiro, B. Thuysbaert, and C. Udry. 2015. "A Multifaceted Program Causes Lasting Progress for the Very Poor: Evidence from Six Countries." *Science* 348 (6236). https://doi.org/10.1126/science.1260799.

Banerjee, A. V., and A. F. Newman. 1993. "Occupational Choice and the Process of Development." *Journal of Political Economy* 101 (2): 274–98.

Barham, V., R. Boadway, M. Marchand, and P. Pestieau. 1995. "Education and the Poverty Trap." *European Economic Review* 39 (7): 1257–75.

Barrett, C. B., and L. E. M. Bevis. 2015. "The Reinforcing Feedback between Low Soil Fertility and Chronic Poverty." *Nature Geoscience* 8 (12): 907–12.

Barrett, C. B., and M. R. Carter. 2013. "The Economics of Poverty Traps and Persistent Poverty: Empirical and Policy Implications." *Journal of Development Studies* 49 (7): 976–90.

Barrett, C. B., T. Garg, and L. McBride. 2016. "Well-Being Dynamics and Poverty Traps." *Annual Review of Resource Economics* 8:303–27.

Barrett, C. B., and B. M. Swallow. 2006. "Fractal Poverty Traps." *World Development* 34 (1): 1–15.

Baulch, B., and J. Hoddinott. 2000. "Economic Mobility and Poverty Dynamics in Developing Countries." *Journal of Development Studies* 36 (6): 1–24.

Bonds, M. H., D. C. Keenan, P. Rohani, and J. D. Sachs. 2010. "Poverty Trap Formed by the Ecology of Infectious Diseases." *Proceedings of the Royal Society of London B: Biological Sciences* 277 (1685): 1185–92.

Bryan, G., S. Chowdhury, and A. M. Mobarak. 2014. "Underinvestment in a Profitable Technology: The Case of Seasonal Migration in Bangladesh." *Econometrica* 82 (5): 1671–748.

Buera, F. J. 2009. "A Dynamic Model of Entrepreneurship with Borrowing Constraints: Theory and Evidence." *Annals of Finance* 5 (3): 443–64.

Carter, M. R. 1997. "Environment, Technology, and the Social Articulation of Risk in West African Agriculture." *Economic Development and Cultural Change* 45 (3): 557–90.

Carter, M. R., and M. Ikegami. 2009. "Looking Forward: Theory-Based Measures of Chronic Poverty and Vulnerability." In *Poverty Dynamics: Interdisciplinary Perspectives*, edited by T. Addison, D. Hulme, and R. Kanbur, 128–53. Oxford: Oxford University Press.

Carter, M. R., and S. A. Janzen. 2018. "Social Protection in the Face of Climate Change: Targeting Principles and Financing Mechanisms." *Environment and Development Economics* 23:369–89.

Carter, M. R., and T. J. Lybbert. 2012. "Consumption versus Asset Smoothing: Testing the Implications of Poverty Trap Theory in Burkina Faso." *Journal of Development Economics* 99 (2): 255–64.

Carter, M. R., and J. May. 2001. "One Kind of Freedom: Poverty Dynamics in Post-apartheid South Africa." *World Development* 29:1987–2006.

Chantarat, S., and C. B. Barrett. 2011. "Social Network Capital, Economic Mobility and Poverty Traps." *Journal of Economic Inequality* 10 (3): 299–342.

Dasgupta, P. 1993. *An Inquiry into Well-Being and Destitution.* New York: Oxford University Press.

Dasgupta, P., and D. Ray. 1986. "Inequality as a Determinant of Malnutrition and Unemployment: Theory." *Economic Journal* 96 (384): 1011–34.

———. 1987. "Inequality as a Determinant of Malnutrition and Unemployment: Policy." *Economic Journal* 97 (385): 177–88.

Deaton, A. 1991. "Saving and Liquidity Constraints." *Econometrica* 59 (5): 1221–48.

Fang, H., and G. C. Loury. 2005. "Dysfunctional Identities Can Be Rational." *American Economic Review* 95 (2): 104–11.

Garg, T., M. Jagnani, and V. Taraz. 2017. "Effects of Heat Stress on Physiology and Livelihoods: Implications for Human Capital Accumulation." Working paper, University of California, San Diego.

Gobin, V. J., P. Santos, and R. Toth. 2017. "No Longer Trapped? Promoting Entrepreneurship through Cash Transfers to Ultra-poor Women in Northern Kenya." *American Journal of Agricultural Economics* 99 (5): 1362–83.

Hoddinott, J. 2006. "Shocks and Their Consequences across and within Households in Rural Zimbabwe." *Journal of Development Studies* 42 (2): 301–21.

Hulme, D., and K. Moore. 2008. "Assisting the Poorest in Bangladesh: Learning from BRAC's 'Targeting the Ultra-poor' Programme." In *Social Protection for the Poor and Poorest*, edited by Armando Barrientos and David Hulme, 194–210. New York: Palgrave Macmillan.

Kraay, A., and D. McKenzie. 2014. "Do Poverty Traps Exist? Assessing the Evidence." *Journal of Economic Perspectives* 28 (3): 127–48.

Laajaj, Rachid. 2017. "Endogenous Time Horizons and Behavioral Poverty Trap: Theory and Evidence from Mozambique." *Journal of Development Economics* 127:187–208.

Lipton, Michael. 1993. *Growing Points in Poverty Research: Labour Issues.* Geneva: International Institute for Labour Studies.

Loury, G. C. 1981. "Intergenerational Transfers and the Distribution of Earnings." *Econometrica* 49 (4): 843–67.

Marenya, P. P., and C. B. Barrett. 2009. "State Conditional Fertilizer Yield Response on Western Kenyan Farms." *American Journal of Agricultural Economics* 91 (4): 991–1006.

Mazumdar, Dipak. 1959. "The Marginal Productivity Theory of Wages and Disguised Unemployment." *Review of Economic Studies* 26 (3): 190–97.

McPeak, J. 2004. "Contrasting Income Shocks with Asset Shocks: Livestock Sales in Northern Kenya." *Oxford Economic Papers* 56 (2): 263–84.

Mogues, T., and M. R. Carter. 2005. "Social Capital and the Reproduction of Economic Inequality in Polarized Societies." *Journal of Economic Inequality* 3 (3): 193–219.

Moya, Andres. 2018. "Violence, Psychological Trauma, and Risk Attitudes: Evidence from Victims of Violence in Colombia." *Journal of Development Economics* 131 (March): 15–27.

Naifeh, M. 1998. "Dynamics of Well-Being, Poverty 1993–94: Trap Door? Revolving Door? Or Both?" Current Population Reports, Household Economic Studies, Washington, DC, US Census Bureau.

Naschold, F. 2012. "'The Poor Stay Poor': Household Asset Poverty Traps in Rural Semi-arid India." *World Development* 40 (10): 2033–43.

Nelson, Richard R. 1956. "A Theory of the Low-Level Equilibrium Trap in Underdeveloped Economies." *American Economic Review* 46 (5): 894–908.

Ngonghala, C. N., M. M. Pluciński, M. B. Murray, P. E. Farmer, C. B. Barrett, D. C. Keenan, and M. H. Bonds. 2014. "Poverty, Disease, and the Ecology of Complex Systems." *PLOS Biology* 12 (4): e1001827. https://doi.org/10.1371/journal.pbio.1001827.

Ravallion, Martin. 2017. "Direct Interventions against Poverty in Poor Places." WIDER Annual Lecture 20. https://www.wider.unu.edu/sites/default/files/Publications/Annual-lecture/PDF/AL20-2016.pdf.

Rockmore, M., C. B. Barrett, and J. Annan. 2016. "An Empirical Exploration of the Near-Term and Persistent Effects of Conflict on Risk Preferences." HiCN Working Paper no. 239, Households in Conflict Network.

Rosenzweig, M. R., and H. P. Binswanger. 1993. "Wealth, Weather Risk, and the Composition and Profitability of Agricultural Investments." *Economic Journal* 103 (416): 56–78.

Skiba, A. K. 1978. "Optimal Growth with a Convex-Concave Production Function." *Econometrica* 46 (3): 527–39.

Stiglitz, J. E. 1976. "The Efficiency Wage Hypothesis, Surplus Labour, and the Distribution of Income in LDCs." *Oxford Economic Papers* 28 (2): 185–207.

Zimmerman, F. J., and M. R. Carter. 2003. "Asset Smoothing, Consumption Smoothing and the Reproduction of Inequality under Risk and Subsistence Constraints." *Journal of Development Economics* 71 (2): 233–60.

I

Nutrition, Health, and Human Capital Formation

Human Capital and Shocks
Evidence on Education, Health, and Nutrition

Elizabeth Frankenberg and Duncan Thomas

1.1 Introduction

Capabilities, including nutrition, health, and human capital, play a key role in the literature on poverty traps and are central to the model laid out in the introduction. The nutrition wage hypothesis posits that agricultural workers could earn a wage that was so low they would be trapped in a recurring cycle of poverty in which they were unable to feed themselves sufficiently well to sustain the productivity necessary to be able to climb out of the poverty trap. The model was among the early descriptions of poverty traps and underlies the larger literature on the efficiency wage hypothesis (Liebenstein 1957; Mazumdar 1959; Shapiro and Stiglitz 1984). Investments in human capital, broadly defined to include nutrition, health, education, and cognition, have been shown to be central mechanisms through which an individual, family, community, and state may be lifted out of poverty and out of enduring poverty traps.

A large theoretical and empirical literature links shocks to poverty and poverty traps. The loss of resources because of an unanticipated negative shock

Elizabeth Frankenberg is professor of sociology and public policy and director of the Carolina Population Center, University of North Carolina, Chapel Hill, and a faculty research fellow of the National Bureau of Economic Research. Duncan Thomas is the Norb F. Schaefer Professor of International Studies and professor of economics, global health, and public policy at Duke University and a research associate and director of the Development Economics Program at the National Bureau of Economic Research.

The comments of Chris Barrett, Michael Carter, Jean-Paul Chavas, and John Hoddinott have been very helpful. Financial support from the National Institute on Aging (R01 AG031266), the Eunice Kennedy Shriver National Institute of Child Health and Development (R01 HD052762), and the Wellcome Trust award 106853/Z/15/Z is gratefully acknowledged. For acknowledgments, sources of research support, and disclosure of the authors' material financial relationships, if any, please see http://www.nber.org/chapters/c13829.ack.

results in a spiral down into ever greater poverty because of a loss of earnings capacity (due to, for example, a health shock), a greater debt burden (to cover the costs of the losses associated with the shock), or the loss of a productive asset that an individual simply cannot replace (because of a lack of liquidity or credit markets or because the asset is not worth the replacement cost).

The goal of this research is to evaluate some of the evidence on the links between shocks, on one hand, and health and human capital outcomes, on the other hand. Specifically, we focus on the impact of shocks on human capital during early life and examine the extent to which the human capital of populations and population subgroups display resilience in the face of a large-scale unanticipated shock.

Three main points emerge. First, it is very hard to identify shocks that are unanticipated and uncorrelated with other factors that affect human capital investments and outcomes. One reason is that investing in child human capital is universally recognized as important, and individuals and families are likely to attempt to mitigate the impact of shocks on the health and human capital of the next generation. This is our second point: establishing generalizable evidence on the impacts of a shock is complicated by the fact that there may be behavioral responses to mitigate the impacts and the nature, and effectiveness of those behaviors will vary with the context in ways that are not straightforward to predict or model. Third, even in cases that seem relatively straightforward to model, the impacts of shocks on child human capital outcomes in the short and longer term may differ precisely because of the behavioral changes of individuals, families, and communities in response to the shock. As a result, drawing inferences about the longer-term impacts based on negative impacts in the short term can be very misleading. In some cases, short-term effects will understate the longer-term consequences (such as when health problems emerge only after a long lag); in other contexts, the longer-term consequences will be modest relative to the short-term consequences.

It is important to underscore that these results pertain to the health and human capital of children exposed to the shocks and not to adults exposed to the same shocks. These shocks have been shown to affect the physical and psychological health as well as cognitive performance of adults (Thomas and Frankenberg 2007; Friedman and Thomas 2009). Moreover, the same shocks had large negative impacts on consumption, wages, income, and wealth (Thomas et al. 1999; Friedman and Levinsohn 2002; Frankenberg, Smith, and Thomas 2003). By focusing on the human capital of children, the goal of this research is to place the spotlight on the impact of shocks on poverty and poverty traps in future generations.

1.2   Early Life Shocks and Human Capital in Later Life

Many studies have investigated impacts of early life shocks on later life outcomes. The earliest shocks an individual will experience, those that occur in utero, have been linked to health in adulthood. Building on a foundation in biology, and drawing on evidence from animal and human models, in a very creative body of research, Barker describes the impact on the fetus of nutrition insults at specific times during the pregnancy. As an example, he elucidates pathways from a shock at the time when arteries are being developed in utero to hardened arteries and coronary heart disease in midlife (Barker 1995). Links between in utero shocks, birth weight, adult health, and premature mortality have all been widely documented.

For example, influential research has exploited the timing of ration restrictions because of the Nazi occupation of the Netherlands during the Second World War to establish the impact of nutrition shocks on health and well-being in adulthood. Critically important for this research on the Dutch Hunger is that rations were restricted in areas where the resistance was active but rations were not changed in other areas, so that women who were pregnant and living in the resistance areas experienced a negative nutrition shock while pregnant women in other areas served as controls. The restriction of rations in the resistance areas was not anticipated and short-lived; there was very limited scope for moving to avoid the restrictions. Assuming women who were pregnant at the time and living in the resistance areas are exchangeable with pregnant women living in other areas in the Netherlands, it is possible to identify a casual effect of in utero nutrition shocks through comparisons of birth and later health outcomes of those who were in utero at the time.

Moreover, as predicted by Barker, the precise timing of the nutrition insults plays a key role. Research on the impact of the Dutch Hunger finds those who were exposed early during the fetal period were at elevated risks of obesity, lipid dysregulation, cardiovascular disease, and premature mortality. They were also less likely to be working in their fifties, although there does not appear to have been any impact on earnings of those who were working. In contrast, those who were exposed only toward the end of the gestation period were more likely to be born small, but there is little evidence that adult health or economic outcomes were affected (Ravelli et al. 1998; Ravelli et al. 1999; Roseboom et al. 2001; Rooij et al. 2010; Scholte, van den Berg, and Lindeboom 2015).

This evidence is consistent with programming in utero to develop a "thrifty phenotype" as an adaptive response to nutrition insults (Hales and Barker 1992). Nutrition deprivation early during gestation programs the fetus to adapt to the environment and extract all the nutrients possible from the placenta. Having been programmed in utero, the body continues to maximize nutrient absorption after birth, which results in poor health outcomes in later life. Nutrition deprivation toward the end of gestation does not cause the same type of reprogramming.

Many studies have investigated the longer-term consequences of in utero insults using, for example, variation in rainfall, famines, infectious disease prevalence or virulence (such as Zika, Ebola, or influenza), terrorist attacks, civil conflicts, and weather-related and other natural disasters. The key issue with any natural experiment is that the variation underlying identification of the causal effect must be outside the control of the mother, her family, and society more broadly. In some cases, this calls for strong assumptions.

As an example, studies have exploited the timing of Ramadan, the month of fasting in the Muslim calendar, to identify a causal effect of nutrition deprivation in utero (Almond and Mazumder 2011; Almond, Mazumder, and van Ewijk 2015; van Ewijk 2011). There are at least three concerns with this line of inquiry. First, Ramadan occurs on an established calendar and, give or take a day or two, its timing is known years in advance. In societies where contraception is widespread, pregnancy timing is, at least in part, a choice. Second, it is permissible for pregnant women not to fast if their own health or that of their baby is at risk. It is, therefore, difficult to test whether the assumptions underlying the identification strategy of a causal impact of in utero calorie restriction are met in the study populations. This is important because, in general, studies in this literature report intent-to-treat estimates, and if adherence to fasting is not universal, it is not clear how to generalize the results. Moreover, the majority of these studies use census or register data and thus examine very large samples, in which case it is not clear that it is appropriate to rely on a classical testing strategy that fixes the probability of rejecting the null when it is correct at, say, 5 percent, so that the probability of rejecting the alternate when it is correct becomes infinitesimally small. If these studies were to adopt an information-based criterion for model selection that trades off Type I and Type II errors, such as the Schwarz criterion (Schwarz 1978), then the estimated effects of Ramadan are typically not statistically significant. Taking this and the fact that estimated effects tend to be modest in magnitude, the evidence that Ramadan affects later life cognition or education may not be as strong as suggested by the literature.

In a widely cited and very influential study, Almond (2006) examines the impact of in utero exposure to the 1918 influenza pandemic on education, work, and income in adulthood among those born in the United States. The study combines the unanticipated nature of the influenza pandemic in the fall of 1918 with census data and compares outcomes of birth cohorts exposed to the pandemic in utero with surrounding birth cohorts. Almond concludes that males who were exposed in utero completed fewer years of education, had lower income, poorer socioeconomic status, received more in public transfers, and were more likely to have physical disabilities. Studies conducted in other countries have drawn similar conclusions.

A difficulty with this identification strategy is that there may be other, unobserved differences between the affected cohort and the surrounding cohorts. This would seem plausible given that the fall of 1918 was also the end of World War I. This point is made in Brown and Thomas (2018), who demonstrate that the fathers of those who were in utero in the United States at the time of the influenza pandemic tend to be of lower socioeconomic status than the fathers of the surrounding birth cohorts. They also show that the same pattern is observed in other countries and likely explains at least some of those results.

These examples are not intended to imply that there are no long-term consequences of in utero shocks. Clearly, there are. Rather, the point is that even seemingly well-identified studies may not be as well identified as they appear. Importantly, whereas several scientific animal and human studies have convincingly established that early life shocks have long-term consequences on adolescent and adult health, establishing that in utero shocks have long-term impacts on education and socioeconomic status, and, thus on poverty, has proven to be somewhat more difficult to establish.

1.3   Financial Shocks, Human Capital, and Behavioral Responses

A second concern that arises with interpreting results of studies of the impact of shocks on human capital outcomes is that even if a shock is truly unanticipated and did not coincide with other events that affected human capital, the impact of the shock may be mitigated by behavioral responses of individuals, their families, and their communities. This is important since there is considerable evidence that children who are born into disadvantaged environments are not necessarily destined to have poor human capital outcomes in adulthood. (See, e.g., Heckman 2006.)

There are at least two concerns with inferences drawn under the assumption that there are no behavioral responses to a shock. First, if individuals and their families invest in behaviors that mitigate the impact of the shock on, say, human capital of the next generation, the finding that the shock had no impact on child human capital outcomes in the immediate term may be misleading if the mitigating behaviors affect future investments. For example, if a household liquidates assets when prices are relatively low in order to keep a child in school, it is possible that the reduced long-run wealth will have negative impacts on future capabilities and, therefore, well-being. The implications of shocks for the dynamic path of capabilities over the life course and across generations have not been established and likely vary across contexts. It is, therefore, important to trace out these types of responses in order to develop a fuller understanding of the impacts of shocks on human capital and well-being in the immediate and longer term.

Second, if some individuals and families are more able to smooth the impact of a shock than others, distributional impacts of the shock on human capital outcomes at a point in time may not be informative about the incidence of the initial impact of the shock or about the longer-term consequences of the shock.

These concerns are illustrated using empirical evidence from one example of the global financial crisis that occurred at the end of the twentieth century. Specifically, we focus on Indonesia, the country that experienced

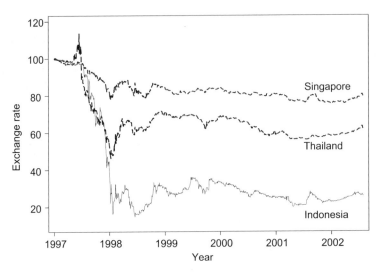

Fig. 1.1A   US$ exchange rates for Singapore, Thailand, and Indonesia, 1997–2002
Note: Jan. 1997 = 100.

the most disruption as a result of the East Asian financial crisis and draw on longitudinal data that we collected specifically to measure the immediate impact of the crisis on individual, household, and family behavior as well as trace out behavioral responses to the crisis. Using later waves of the same longitudinal survey, we investigate the longer-term impacts of the financial crisis on child human capital. For a discussion of other external shocks and child nutrition outcomes see, for example, Darnton-Hill and Cogill (2010).

1.3.1   The 1998 Indonesian Financial Crisis

After almost three decades of sustained economic growth, of all the East Asian countries, Indonesia was hit the hardest by the 1997 financial crisis. As shown in figure 1.1A, the Indonesian rupiah came under pressure in the last half of 1997 when the exchange rate began showing signs of weakness. The rupiah fell from around 2,400 per US$ in the middle of the year to about 4,800 per US$ by the end of 1997. In January 1998, the rupiah collapsed. Over the course of a few days, the exchange rate fell by a factor of three to Rp 15,000 per US$. Although it soon recovered, by the middle of the year the rupiah had slumped back to the lows of January 1998. By the end of 1998, the rupiah had strengthened to around Rp 8,000 per US$. No other East Asian country experienced as deep or as prolonged a decline in the exchange rate.

Interest rates in Indonesia behaved much like the exchange rate: they spiked in August 1997—when they quadrupled—and they remained extremely vol-

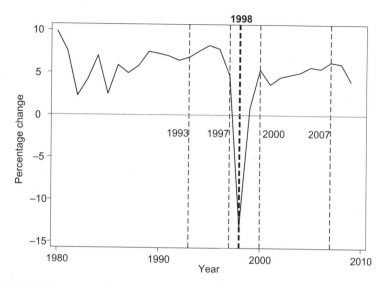

Fig. 1.1B   Percentage change in per capita GDP in Indonesia, 1980–2010, and timing of IFLS

atile through all of 1998. Chaos reigned in the banking sector, and several major banks were taken over by the Indonesian Bank Restructuring Agency. All of this turmoil has wreaked havoc with both the confidence of investors and the availability of credit. Asset prices collapsed—both in the stock market and for real assets such as land.

Simultaneously, there was dramatic transformation in the political sector. Protests across the country that began in January 1998 culminated in May 1998 with Suharto's resignation after three decades in power. Uncertainty in the country was widespread and while the incoming president, Habibie, declared that multiparty elections would be held, it was very difficult to predict whether the elections would, in fact, be held, whether the outcome would result in further turmoil, and whether there would be any fundamental change in the political sphere. It turned out that Suharto's resignation presaged the ushering in of democracy in Indonesia—an outcome that few predicted at the time (Fisman 2001).

The 1998 financial and political crisis was a major shock. Overall, per capita gross domestic product (GDP) in 1998 was about 15 percent below its level in 1997 (figure 1.1B). This downturn is about the same magnitude as the Great Depression in the United States; by contrast, GDP per capita declined by less than 5 percent during the 2008 Great Recession. The Indonesian crisis was not only large, it was also largely unanticipated and, certainly, its severity was a shock both inside and outside the country.

In January 1998, the International Monetary Fund (IMF) described Indonesia's economic situation as "worrisome" (IMF 1999) and, at the same,

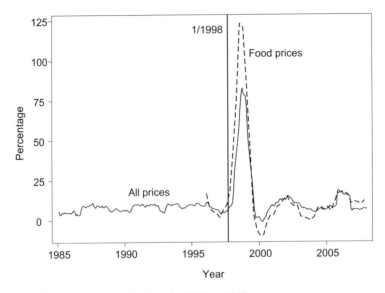

Fig. 1.2   Annual inflation in Indonesia, 1985 to 2007
Note: All prices measured monthly; food prices measured quarterly.

the Indonesian government announced policies to address the situation, predicting economic growth for 1998 would be zero. Indeed, the president of the World Bank summed up the situation in July 1998 saying "we were caught up in the enthusiasm of Indonesia. I am not alone in thinking that 12 months ago, Indonesia was on a very good path."

One way to summarize the impact of the crisis on the lives of Indonesians is through its impact on prices. Prices of many commodities spiraled upward during the first three quarters of 1998. As shown in figure 1.2, according to Statistics Indonesia, annual inflation was between 5 and 10 percent from the early 1980s to 1997. In 1998 inflation rocketed to an unprecedented 80 percent in a matter of months. Subsidies were removed from several key goods, most notably rice, oil, and fuel, the prices of which were pegged by the government at levels below world prices. As the rupiah collapsed, those subsidies became unsustainable and were scaled back along with other public expenditures. Food prices, driven primarily by the rise in the price of the staple, rice, rose by 120 percent, which is about 50 percent more than the general price index.

Net food consumers were severely impacted by the crisis, whereas net food producers either received some protection or possibly benefited from the crisis. The financial crisis provided new opportunities in the export sector, but it was a major negative shock for those on fixed incomes and those outside the tradable sector.

1.3.2   Immediate Impacts on Child Health and Education

To provide empirical evidence on the immediate impacts of the shock on human capital outcomes, we draw on data from the Indonesia Family Life Survey (IFLS) that were specifically designed to provide evidence on this question along with subsequent survey waves. The second wave, IFLS2, was fielded between August 1997 and February 1998. The main fieldwork was completed by mid-December 1997 and a small number of very difficult tracking cases were completed in January and February 1998. Because of the political and financial crisis, we decided to conduct a special rapid-response survey, IFLS2+, between August and December 1998 in order to provide a snapshot of the immediate impact of the shock (Frankenberg and Thomas 2000).

It was imperative to put IFLS2+ in the field without delay in order to measure the impact of the onset of the crisis. Since it was not possible to mount an entire wave of IFLS in a short time frame, for IFLS2+ we selected a sample of one in four enumeration areas that were included in the 1993 IFLS baseline. The IFLS2+ collected information from all the respondents who were living in those enumeration areas at the baseline, including those who had moved away. This is important because migration was a potential response to the crisis.

The IFLS2 returned to the baseline enumeration area and interviewed every member of the baseline households in the community. Baseline respondents who had moved were tracked and interviewed in the new location, along with the members of their new household. The IFSL2 reinterviewed at least one member of 94 percent of the baseline households (Thomas, Frankenberg, and Smith 2001).

The IFLS2+ followed the same protocols, returning to the location of each household interviewed in IFLS2, interviewing all members and tracking movers to their new locations. The IFLS2+ interviewed at least one member of over 99 percent of the households interviewed in IFLS2 and over 96 percent of all baseline households (Frankenberg, Thomas, and Beegle 1999).

Data from IFLS2 and IFLS2+ provide a useful description of the magnitude of the shock that households experienced. The International Labour Organization predicted that millions would join the ranks of the unemployed because of the crisis and called for public works programs. Wage employment did decline—but only by 2 percent—and it was more than offset by an increase in the number of people working in self-employment, particularly females who joined family businesses. With the dramatic increase in the price of rice, the number of people working in the agricultural sector rose, and there was considerable migration from urban to rural areas. While the drama of the crisis was not reflected in employment, it was reflected in hourly earnings.

Between 1986 and 1997, in the market sector, real hourly wages grew by over 40 percent on average. In 1998, all of those gains were wiped out: real wages declined by 40 percent because nominal wages did not keep up with rising prices. In the self-employed sector, hourly earnings declined by 40 percent in urban areas. In rural areas, hourly earnings of females declined by 40 percent, but those of males were little changed. To some extent, this reflects the impact of the price of rice (and food) and also the contributions of unpaid family workers (who contributed more work on the farm in 1998, on average, than in 1997). Overall, household income declined by 30 percent between 1997 and 1998, a substantively very large and statistically significant change (Smith et al. 2002).

There is some evidence that households smoothed these real income declines as real household per capita expenditure (PCE) declined 23 percent, with the biggest declines occurring among those who were best off prior to the crisis. Using the PCE distribution from 1993, the households at the 75th percentile reduced PCE by 30 percent, whereas the decline was 15 percent for the households at the 25th percentile of the 1993 PCE distribution. The crisis appears to have hit PCE of those who were better off the most although, to be sure, the declines are very large and statistically significant throughout the precrisis distribution of PCE (Frankenberg, Smith, and Thomas 2003).

What was the impact on human capital of children over the short term? We first examine anthropometric outcomes and then turn to education. Anthropometry is measured for all household respondents in IFLS. Figure 1.3 displays the z-score of height for age (in the upper panel) and weight for height (in the lower panel) of all children age nine and under measured in IFLS2, before the onset of the financial crisis, and in IFLS2+, after the onset of the financial crisis. Height for age is a longer-run indicator of nutritional status and an important marker of health in and of itself. In addition, length during the first few years of life has been shown to be affected by health and disease-related shocks, and it is thought that length by around twenty-four or thirty months is a very good predictor of attained adult height which, in turn, is predictive of longevity, improved health, educational attainment, and socioeconomic success. Weight for height is a measure of shorter-run nutritional status and is likely to reflect the impact of recent health inputs, including food intake and disease insults (Martorell and Habicht 1986; Alderman, Hoddinott, and Kinsey 2006; Hoddinott et al. 2008; Maluccio et al. 2009; Hoddinott et al. 2013).

There is no evidence that child height for age was deleteriously impacted by the financial crisis. Specifically, there are no significant differences in height for age for any of the age groups, although the sample size for the very youngest and arguably the most vulnerable, is too small to be informative. The evidence on weight for height is less clear for children under thirty-six months of age, who have lower weight, given height, in the 1998 survey relative to the 1997 survey. The difference, however, is not statistically significant

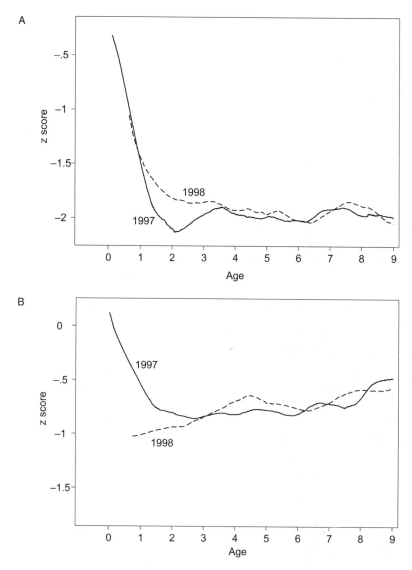

Fig. 1.3   Child anthropometry by age, before and after onset of the 1998 Indonesian crisis. *A*, height for age; *B*, weight for height.

and, importantly, the deficits in weight for height for the youngest children are not evident in height for age.

Figure 1.3 is based on all children in both surveys, including new entrants into the 1998 survey in order to capture new births and mitigate the costs of the relatively small sample size. There were few new entrants and with 99 percent recontact, attrition is ignorable. The figures restricted to panel

Table 1.1   School enrollment and the 1998 Indonesian financial crisis (percentage of children not enrolled in school in 1997 and 1998, by age group and level of household PCE, both measured in 1997)

	1997 (%)	1998 (%)	%Δ
Children age 13–16	25.6	25.1	−2
Children age 7–12			
All	3.1	5.9	90
Poor children (bottom quartile of PCE in 1997)	4.9	10.7	118

Source: Thomas et al. (2004).
Notes: IFLS2 and IFLS2+.

children are essentially the same. While the samples are small, separating rural from urban households does not suggest differential effects across these sectors in anthropometric outcomes.

Results for school enrollment are displayed in table 1.1. Among children who, in 1997, were age thirteen to sixteen years old, 25.6 percent were not enrolled in school in 1997, whereas in 1998, 25.1 percent of the children in that age group were not enrolled; with the onset of the crisis, the fraction not in school decreased by 2 percent. However, among children age seven to twelve, 3.1 percent were not enrolled in school in 1997 and 5.9 percent were not enrolled in 1998—a 90 percent increase in nonenrollment. This gap was largest for the poorest households: for the households in the bottom quartile of PCE (in 1997), 4.9 percent of the children were not enrolled in school in 1997 and 10.7 percent were not enrolled in 1997, an almost 120 percent increase in nonenrollment. Further, for poor children in this age group, having an older sibling who was enrolled in school was associated with a greater chance of not being enrolled. And, conversely, older poor children whose younger siblings who were not in school in 1998 were themselves more likely to be enrolled in 1998. We find no differences between urban and rural children or between male and female children (Thomas et al. 2004).

Why would older children in the poorest households stay in school when their younger siblings were not enrolled? There are at least two plausible reasons. First, if a thirteen- to sixteen-year-old does not enroll in school in a year, that child is not likely to return to school in the future. However, for younger children, being out of school for a year, say, is less likely to have long-term consequences because dispersion in the ages of children in each grade in Indonesia is enormous and so reentering when the child is a year older is not difficult. This reflects the combination of a great deal of variation in the age at which children start school and the high rates of repetition of grades in primary school. Second, the labor market returns to primary school education are very low in Indonesia, whereas the returns to secondary school and college are substantial and thus the long-term economic costs of not completing secondary school likely weighed on family decision-making. It turned out that keeping older children in school was a good choice: by 1999, a scholarship program had been implemented so that the costs of enrollment were forgiven if families were unable to afford them. These included the costs of fees, uniforms, transport costs, and examination charges. By 2000, enrollment rates and disparities across the income distribution had all returned to their precrisis levels (and disparities had been reduced).

Intrahousehold substitution favoring school enrollment of older children over younger children is one mechanism that families used to mitigate the impact of the shock on human capital. There is evidence that adults literally tightened their belts to assure that the growth of the young children did not falter in the face of the crisis. Figure 1.4 displays the body mass index (BMI), which is weight (in kgs) divided by the square of height (in m) of males (in the upper panel) and females (in the lower panel) by age in 1997 and 1998. Body mass index rises with age until around the midforties and then declines. Height does not change for prime-age adults, and so this reflects changes in weight. The remarkable result is the dramatic decline in BMI across the entire age distribution for males and females between 1997 and 1998. On average, the declines are slightly smaller among adults who were living in rural areas prior to the crisis. However, overall, it is the oldest females whose weight declined the most: among females age sixty and older in 1997, weight declined by 15 percent in one year. This is unlikely to reflect the impact of energy expenditure and so we conclude that these women reduced their food intake of favor of their grandchildren. Block et al. (2004) draw similar conclusions that child nutritional status was protected at the expense of the nutritional status of female adults using data collected in rural Central Java.

Over and above drawing on the health and education of family members, how did households mitigate the impact of this large, negative shock to resources? There are four key mechanisms. First, people moved. Urban dwellers moved to the rural sector. As the rupiah collapsed, the nontradable sector took the greatest toll with construction and other services being especially hard hit. Workers in those sectors were more likely to be in urban areas. In contrast, the tradable sector was a relative beneficiary with the farming sector benefiting from the very large increase in the price of food (particularly rice). Thus, relative to the urban sector, the rural sector was to some extent protected from the impact of the crisis and so urban workers moved to the rural sector where there were opportunities to earn income from working on a farm. In addition, since the cost of living is lower in the rural sector, family members who were not working also moved from the urban to the rural sector. Furthermore, extended family members moved in together to benefit from economies of scale of living arrangements. As shown in table 1.2, overall, household size increased significantly from 4.33 to 4.53 members, with the increase being slightly (and not significantly) greater in rural areas (because of urban-to-rural migration). This is an example of a key

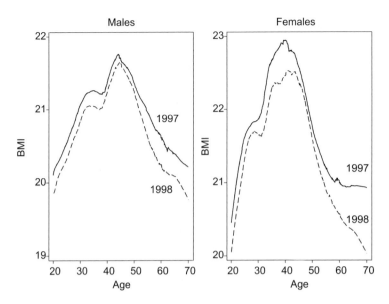

Fig. 1.4   Adult BMI before and after onset of the 1998 Indonesian crisis

social safety net as spatially separated family members provided support to one another through shared living arrangements and providing work opportunities in sectors that benefited from the financial crisis such as rice farming.

Second, whereas, on average, the percentage decline in real household PCE was 23 percent, food expenditures were protected and the average percentage decline was 9 percent. This reflects the combination of reduced food intake and increased price of food. Households cut spending on two classes of goods. First, spending on clothing, furniture, and ceremonies was reduced by 35 percent; we call these items "deferrable" because delaying spending on these items for the short term is unlikely to have the same impact on welfare as reduced spending on, for example, staples. (See Browning and Crossly 2009 for a discussion of deferred spending.) Second, spending on health and education fell by 37 percent. The reduction in education spending reflects the combination of young children not attending school and parents cutting back on school expenditures (including paying fees). The reduction in spending on health is reflected in a dramatic reduction in use of health care during the year after the onset of the financial crisis relative to before the crisis. Whether these cuts in spending have longer-term consequences for welfare depends on the longevity of the cut, whether delayed care will have result in poor health in the future, and whether the child's schooling is affected over the longer term. All of these changes in spending are statistically significant.

Third, households are likely to draw down savings or sell off assets to mitigate the impact of the crisis (Deaton 1992; Browning and Lusardi 1996).

Table 1.2   Consumption patterns and the 1998 Indonesian financial crisis (household composition, household consumption, and composition of consumption)

1997 Rp000s	1997	1998	Percent change
1. Household size	4.33	4.53	7
	(0.05)	(0.04)	(0.8)
2. Per capita household consumption	176	117	−23
	(12)	(9)	(2)
3. Composition of per capita household consumption			
A. Food	79.7	68.9	−9
	(4.9)	(7.4)	(2)
B. Nonfoods	95.2	48.4	−34
	(10.2)	(2.2)	(2)
C. Deferrable items	9.1	6.4	−35
(clothing, furniture, and ceremonies)	(0.4)	(0.4)	(3)
E. Human capital investments	9.0	5.7	−37
(health and education)	(0.6)	(0.3)	(3)

Source: Frankenberg et al. (2003).

Notes: Consumption measured in thousands of 1995 rupiah; 1,971 households interviewed in 1997 and 1998 included in sample.

The value of that strategy was limited by the fact that many assets collapsed in value. Savings in cash lost value as inflation rocketed. The Jakarta stock exchange had lost 75 percent of its precrisis value by the middle of 1998. Land and housing markets dried up along with credit markets. One important asset rose in value: gold. The price of gold is set in world terms and so as the rupiah fell to below half its precrisis level, the value of gold more than doubled. There is an active market for gold, which is sold by weight, and according to the IFLS community survey there is a gold seller within half an hour travel time of every IFLS community. In 1997, over half the households owned gold and the vast majority of this gold was in the hands of women. By 1998, a substantial fraction of the gold had been sold. In regression models of that link changes in budget shares to precrisis assets, we find that spending on health and education are protected the most by gold ownership, an effect that is not only statistically significant but also substantively important (Frankenberg, Smith, and Thomas 2003).

Fourth, households drew on other safety nets. These included community-based support that sought to provide income-earning opportunities for residents, in some cases drawing on resources for employment creation from the central government. The central government introduced several social safety net programs after the onset of the crisis. An emergency food program that delivered rice at subsidized prices to poor households, Beras untuk Rakyat Miskin (Raskin), was introduced in 1998. It became permanent and turned into the largest social assistance program in Indonesia. A scholarship program provided cash for school-age children in poor households. Neither program was in place in the year of the crisis, when IFLS2+ was in the field, and so the short-term effects of the crisis that we document are unlikely to have been affected by these programs. These programs likely mitigated deleterious effects of the crisis on longer-term outcomes.

We conclude that even in the face of a very large financial shock, Indonesian households and families sought to protect the human capital of the next generation through every means possible: they migrated, moved in together, took up work, particularly in family businesses, cut spending, especially on deferrable items, reduced spending on some members in favor of others, and spent down savings, primarily gold. They also drew on informal and formal social safety nets. In so doing, the immediate and longer-term impacts of the financial crisis on the nutrition and schooling of children were minimized.

1.3.3   Longer-Term Impacts on Child Health and Education

While there is little evidence of large, negative impacts of the financial crisis in the short term, the fact that households sold assets, particularly gold, and shifted spending to sustain human capital investments suggests that over the longer term the crisis may have resulted in worse health and education outcomes for those that were affected. The IFLS is a long-term panel study that has followed the same respondents since the financial crisis with the third wave conducted in 2000, the fourth wave in 2007/08 and the fifth wave in 2014/15 (Strauss, Beegle, Dwiyanto, et al. 2004; Strauss, Beegle, Sikoki, et al. 2004; Strauss et al. 2009; Strauss et al. 2016).

Using data from the 2000 and 2007/08 waves, it is possible to trace the evolution of nutritional status of children exposed to the financial crisis. The relationships between height for age and age of the child at the time of the survey are displayed in figure 1.5 for all children in panel A, and separated by whether the child was living in an urban or rural area in 1997, prior to the crisis, in panel B. Sector of residence is a proxy for the magnitude of the negative shock, which took a greater toll on urban households.

Height for age of children prior to the crisis in 1997 is displayed by the solid line. Children at greatest risk of being stunted in the long run are those who were age thirty months or younger at the time of the crisis (the thin dashed line) and would be age two through four and a half years old in the 2000 wave (the thick dashed line). Children in this age group are not only taller than those of the same age in 1998, but even those of the same age in 1997, prior to the crisis. This is true for all children in the age group (in the upper panel) and for urban and rural children, separately (in the lower panel), indicating that the crisis did not have a negative impact on linear growth of this cohort. Height for age eight years later in 2008 (in the dashed-dotted line) is greater for every age than in any other year. For the cohort that was exposed to the financial crisis in the first thirty months of life (age nine through eleven and a half years at the time of the 2008 survey), height for age is the same as its level in 2000 as would be expected if height for

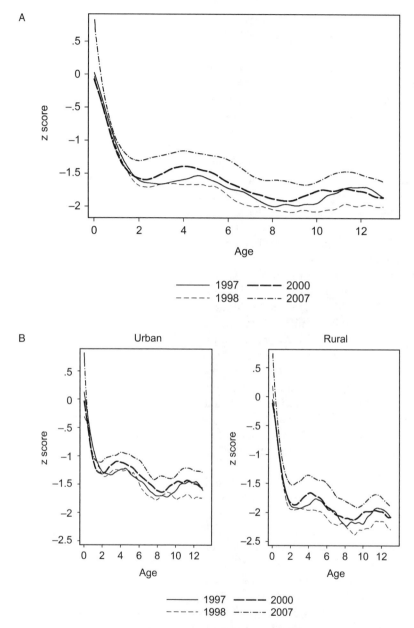

Fig. 1.5   Child height for age in Indonesia, 1997 through 2007. *A*, all Indonesian children; *B*, by sector of residence of parents in 1997, before the financial crisis.

age is largely determined by thirty months. Since height in 2008 is likely to be a very good predictor of attained height as an adult, we conclude there is no evidence that height of children was deleteriously impacted by the financial crisis and the short-run evidence indicating that child height was protected by family responses carries through to the longer term.

Figure 1.6 displays results for BMI for the same cohorts of children. In this case, it is not only those children age less than thirty months who are at risk of being impacted by reduced resources because of the crisis since, unlike height, weight does vary over the entire life course depending on current net energy intake and nutrient absorption. The relationship between BMI and age is remarkably similar for all children in the 1997, 1998, and 2000 waves of IFLS. By 2008, children in every age are heavier, given height. We conclude that nutrition outcomes were also not deleteriously affected by the financial crisis over the longer term (see also Strauss, Beegle, Dwiyanto, et al. 2004; Thomas and Frankenberg 2007).

Exploiting the long-term panel dimension of IFLS, we investigate completed years of education in 2014, sixteen years after the onset of the financial crisis, of respondents who were interviewed in IFLS2 in 1997, before the crisis. We focus on respondents who were age five through twenty-one in 1997 and thus age twenty-two through thirty-eight in 2014. The vast majority of these respondents will have completed their schooling by 2014 and so the number of completed years of education at that time is indicative of the human capital the respondents will carry with them for the rest of their lives.

As discussed above, and shown in table 1.1, children age thirteen through sixteen were no less likely to be enrolled in school in 1998 relative to 1997, but young children age seven through twelve, and especially those from poor households (from the bottom quartile of the distribution of PCE), were significantly less likely to be in school. What were the longer-run consequences for education?

Figure 1.7 displays mean years of completed schooling in 2014 for each age cohort stratified by sector of residence and level of household resources, all measured in 1997. The respondents are separated into those who were living in households in the bottom quartile of PCE and those living in other households. As shown by the linear trends in age, estimated separately for each of the four groups, completed years of schooling has risen for each successive birth cohort included in the figure. While children from the poorest households complete less schooling than those from better-off households, the gap has remained approximately constant for rural dwellers, but in urban areas the rate of growth is faster among the poorest children and so those children in the youngest cohort have almost caught up with their same age peers in better-off urban households.

There is no evidence that educational attainment of children who were age seven through twelve years and living in the poorest households in 1997 was lower than predicted by the linear trend; in fact, they completed slightly more

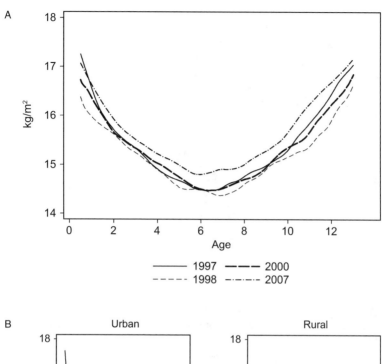

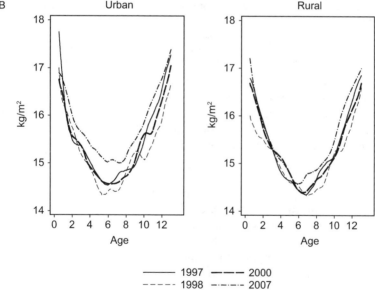

Fig. 1.6 Child body mass index in Indonesia, 1997 through 2007. *A*, all Indonesian children; *B*, by sector of residence of parents in 1997, before the financial crisis.

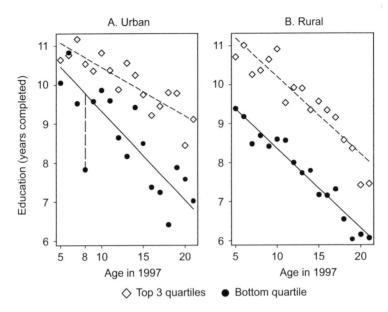

Fig. 1.7   **Completed years of education (in 2014) of Indonesian children age five through twenty-one (in 1997), by sector of residence and quartile of household PCE (both measured in 1997)**
Note: Figure displays mean years of completed education for each age and linear trend for children living in households in the bottom quartile of household PCE (solid line and circles) and the top three quartiles of PCE (dashed line and diamonds) in urban and rural areas.

education than predicted.[1] Nor is there evidence that protection of thirteen-to sixteen-year-olds at the time of the financial crisis resulted in significantly higher levels of completed education on average for that cohort.[2]

It is clear from the figure, however, that there is one birth cohort for whom completed schooling deviates from its predicted level: those age eight years living in households in the lowest quartile of PCE in urban areas in 1997. The gap, almost two years of education, is both large in magnitude and statistically significant (the standard error is 0.6 years of education) and pushes this cohort back to the same level of education as the cohort born eight years earlier.

This evidence is summarized in panel 1 of table 1.3, which reports the relationship between completed years of schooling and age with indica-

1. On average, seven- to twelve-year-olds in the poorest households completed 0.002 years of education more than predicted (standard error = 0.17) and the same-age children in better-off households completed 0.04 years more education than predicted (standard error = 0.14).
2. Children age thirteen to sixteen years in 1997 in the poorest households completed 0.06 (se = 0.18) more years of schooling and those in better-off households completed 0.16 (se = 0.12) more years of schooling. Neither effect is large or statistically significant.

Table 1.3   **Completed schooling and the 1998 Indonesian financial crisis**

Sector of residence	A. Urban			B. Rural		
Quartile of PCE	Bottom (1)	Top 3 (2)	Diff. (3)	Bottom (4)	Top 3 (5)	Diff. (6)
1. No HH controls						
Linear trend in age	−0.23	−0.13	−0.10	−0.20	−0.20	−0.01
	(0.04)	(0.02)	(0.04)	(0.02)	(0.02)	(0.03)
(1) if resp. was 8 years old	−1.95	−0.15	−1.82	−0.08	−0.23	0.16
	(0.63)	(0.38)	(0.73)	(0.31)	(0.34)	(0.46)
2. Control HH PCE and demographics						
(1) if resp. was 8 years old	−2.09	−0.24	−1.86	−0.03	−0.26	0.23
	(0.66)	(0.41)	(0.77)	(0.35)	(0.35)	(0.49)
3. Control HH fixed effects						
(1) if resp. was 8 years old	−1.24	0.19	−1.34	−0.23	−0.43	−0.03
	(0.69)	(0.31)	(0.78)	(0.29)	(0.31)	(0.42)
Sample size		5,900			6,644	

Sources: IFLS2 and IFLS5.

Notes: Completed years of education (measured in 2014) of Indonesians age five to twenty-one (in 1997). Trend for all children and deviation from trend for respondents age eight in 1997. By quartile of household PCE and sector of residence (both measured in 1997). Mean years of education measured for each respondent in 2014 based on characteristics measured in 1997. Standard errors in parentheses take into account heteroscedasticity and clustering of the survey design.

tor variables for the cohort age eight years old in 1997 and gender of the child. The rate of growth in educational attainment by birth cohort is displayed in the first row of panel 1 of the table and the difference from the expected education and actual education for the eight-year-old cohort is in the second row. In contrast with eight-year-olds in poor urban households, those in better-off urban households and those in rural households were not disadvantaged by the financial crisis. Since there is no evidence that the education of children from urban households in the top three quartiles of PCE at the time of the financial crisis was disrupted by the financial crisis, those children provide a useful comparison group for the poorest urban children. The gap in educational attainment between the poorest and better-off children in urban areas is displayed in column (3) of the table: it is also significant. An additional contrast is drawn between the poorest and better-off eight-year-olds in rural areas: there is no difference in their educational attainment. (The difference-in-difference between poorer and better-off eight-year-olds in urban and rural areas is large and statistically significant; it is 1.97 years with a standard error of 0.87 years.)

Household composition and resources mattered for schooling at the time of the crisis. In panel 2 of the table, the models include ln(PCE) and detailed controls for the number of household members in fine age groups (for children) and larger age groups (for adults). The estimated differences between eight-year-olds and other children are little changed.

It is possible that there are other household characteristics that are not included in the model that drive this difference and so, in panel 3 of the table, the models include household fixed effects. The gap for eight-year-olds is reduced by 40 percent and significant at only a 10 percent size of test (which is also the case for the difference between the better-off and poorest urban children). This suggests that there are time-varying household-level characteristics that enabled the families to smooth the educational attainment of eight-year-olds in the poorest urban households.

These results suggest that among the children who were most likely to be out of school at the time of the financial crisis, specifically those children who were age seven to twelve years and living in the poorest households in 1997, the vast majority have not been deleteriously affected in terms of their educational attainment in 2014. The only exception is eight-year-olds in poor, rural households, who account for one in six of children age seven through twelve in poor households and, even among these children, the evidence suggests that the deleterious impact on their education was mitigated by time-varying household-level characteristics or behaviors related to those characteristics. The modest impact of the financial crisis on educational attainment of poor children in Indonesia may be a reflection of the temporary scholarship program that was instituted soon after the financial crisis.[3]

The extent of resilience of child human capital outcomes after a shock that rivals the Great Depression in the United States in magnitude and occurred in a low-income setting is nothing short of remarkable. This is not to argue that the shock had no welfare consequences for children and their families; it did. Poverty rates rose, wealth declined, the physical and psychosocial health of adults worsened, and it took several years for Indonesia to regain the lost ground. The impacts on human capital of children, however, are at most, muted.

1.4   Natural Disasters and Human Capital

In some cases, shocks are so devastating that mitigating their impact in the short term is beyond the reach of even the most resourceful families. It is useful to contrast the immediate and longer-term impact on health and human capital of children of such shocks relative to shocks like the financial crisis. The 2004 Indian Ocean earthquake and tsunami provides a platform for this investigation.

3. None of these inferences is affected taking into account multiple hypothesis testing following Hochberg (1988) or Hommel (1988).

1.4.1   2004 Indian Ocean Earthquake and Tsunami

The 2004 Sumatra-Andaman earthquake occurred at 8:00 a.m. on Sunday, December 26, 2004, and registered 9.3 on the Richter scale. One of the strongest earthquakes in recorded history, it shifted the North Pole by several centimeters, caused a 1,200 km rupture along the floor of the Indian Ocean, and resulted in a tsunami that was felt across the entire Indian Ocean. The epicenter of the earthquake was about 150 kilometers off the west coast of the province of Aceh on the northern tip of the island of Sumatra, Indonesia. Since the tsunami surge was greater than 800 km/hour, its impact was felt along the Acehnese coast within fifteen minutes of the earthquake.

At the time, the Indian Ocean was not thought to be prone to tsunamis and there were no warning buoys or an early warning system (in contrast to the Pacific Ocean). According to archaeological data, there had not been a tsunami on the coast of Aceh for over 600 years.

The impact of the tsunami depended on a combination of the wave height, which reached up to fifteen meters in some areas, the wave direction, and the topography of the land. Areas that were low lying (such as river basins) that faced the wave were devastated: in some areas water and mud reached up to six kilometers inland. Nearby areas that were higher up (because of a cliff, for example) or were protected from the wave by a promontory were not directly affected.

In the SUSENAS survey conducted by Statistics Indonesia in February/March 2004, about ten months before the tsunami, fewer than 3 percent of all respondents in Aceh thought that it was likely they would experience a natural disaster such as an earthquake, tsunami, or volcanic eruption and that fraction did not differ depending on whether their community was in fact directly affected by the tsunami. In sum, the tsunami was unanticipated; it was impossible to predict where it would hit along the Acehnese coast, and few people living in Aceh expected a large-scale natural disaster.

The tsunami was not only unanticipated, it was also a major shock. It is estimated that in Aceh the earthquake and tsunami killed about 170,000 people, which is about 5 percent of the total population of the province. About three-quarters of a million people (about 20 percent of the population) were displaced because their homes were destroyed or damaged. In addition to the loss of homes, there was massive physical destruction. Roads and infrastructure were severely damaged and over 40,000 hectares of agricultural land were affected, with crop destruction and death of livestock. The World Bank estimated there was about $4.5 billion in property damage (Doocy et al. 2007; Frankenberg et al. 2008; Frankenberg et al. 2011; Gray et al. 2014; Cossée, Hermes, and Mezhoud 2006).

There are at least three important dimensions to the shock from the perspective of examining the impact on child human capital. First, many lost assets, livelihoods, and members of their networks as their income-earning opportunities were wiped out and as family members were killed in the tsunami. Second, the destruction to roads and bridges reduced access to markets, which resulted in increases in the price of food, and the loss of housing resulted in increased rents. On both counts, those who were net sellers of food or housing benefited from the shock. Third, the loss of family and friends in the tsunami and the destruction and loss of livelihoods affected the psychosocial health and well-being of the population (Frankenberg et al. 2008). It is difficult to credibly disentangle the income (and asset) shock, price shock, and psychosocial (stress) shock.

The tsunami was followed by the largest influx of aid after a natural disaster in any developing country up to that point. It is estimated that the combination of domestic and international aid from government and non-government sources totaled some $7.2 billion in assistance that was directed to recovery efforts in Aceh and North Sumatra. Initially, aid efforts focused on providing food and temporary shelter and it took several months for regular provision systems to be put in place. Food had to be transported by air or ship to reach many of the most devastated communities as the roads were impassable. Camps were constructed and a small number of displaced moved into camps within three months of the disaster, but the vast majority of camps were not constructed until later in 2005. After these needs were met, aid efforts focused on infrastructure investments—roads, bridges, public building, and housing. The goal was to "build back better."

In short, in December 2004, there was a major shock that affected the lives of those living along the coast of Aceh at the time. It was followed by one of the most successful recovery programs conducted in a developing country that was designed to provide a broad safety net to help the affected populations get back on their feet. How did child human capital fare?

To answer this question, we draw on data from the Study of the Tsunami Aftermath and Recovery (STAR). The baseline sample is drawn from the 2004 SUSENAS conducted ten months before the tsunami and includes all respondents who were living at the time in a kabupaten (district) along the coast of Aceh. The SUSENAS is designed to be population representative at the kabupaten level and so the baseline is representative of the pretsunami population that was affected, to varying degrees, by the tsunami. There are over 25,000 respondents in more than 6,000 households in some 400 communities.

We conducted the first follow-up of the SUSENAS respondents between May 2005 and June 2006 and we refer to that survey as STAR B. Thereafter, we conducted four additional annual follow-ups (STAR C, D, E, and F) and have completed a ten-year follow-up (STAR G). In the first follow-up, finding and interviewing every survivor was critically important and extremely difficult. We have determined the survival status of over 98 percent of the baseline respondents. In most cases, we have found one or more of the surviving baseline household members and obtained survival status from those respondents. In some cases, however, no one in the household survived and in those cases we used multiple reports from neighbors, community leaders, and service providers (in the health and education sectors) to assure that our designations are correct.

Posttsunami follow-up of survivors has been very challenging. On the one hand, in areas that were severely damaged, all (or in some cases almost all) the survivors were displaced with about half moving to camps and the other half moving to private homes. Lack of infrastructure and damage to roads compounded the difficulty of tracking and interviewing the survivors. Over 98 percent of the survivors have been interviewed in at least one of the STAR follow-ups.

The SUSENAS does not collect data on height of respondents. Given the complexity of the fieldwork, identifying, finding, and interviewing surviving respondents in the first follow-up, we chose to not also burden the enumerators with the equipment necessary to measure height and weight and conduct other health assessments in that follow-up. Measurement of anthropometry along with the collection of other biomarkers was added in the second follow-up, STARC, which was in the field between July 2006 and June 2007. Anthropometry was measured in all subsequent waves. Those data are used in our analyses of child nutrition. (See Frankenberg et al. [2018] for more details.)

1.4.2   In Utero Exposure to the Tsunami and Child Height

We focus on the height for age of children who were in utero at the time of the tsunami and exclude all children born in areas that were very heavily damaged by the tsunami and where there were very high death tolls because of the tsunami. There are very few births in the nine months following the tsunami among women who were living in those areas and so the exclusion of those births has no perceptible impact on the estimates discussed below. Their exclusion assures that none of the results are contaminated by selective survival of the strongest mothers since women who were pregnant were much more likely to have died when they were swept away by the water than were women who were not pregnant.

The average height given age of this cohort at the time of the second follow-up when the child was, on average, about fifteen months old is 1.76 standard deviations below the norm set by the Centers for Disease Control and Prevention (CDC). We compare the height for age of this cohort with the cohort born in 2002 since, according to the nutrition literature, the growth trajectory of the height of those children is thought to be largely determined by the time of the tsunami. Conception date is not known for children in STAR, and so we examine children by quarter of birth and assume that those born in the first quarter of 2005 were in the third trimester at the time of the tsunami, those born in the second quarter were in the second trimester, and those born in the third quarter were in the first trimester. Each birth cohort is

Table 1.4   **Linear growth of children in Aceh after the 2004 Indian Ocean tsunami**

Date of measurement	2006/07 (1)	2009/10 (2)	Growth (3)
Birth cohort			
2005:Q1	−0.18	0.41	0.44
	(0.21)	(0.15)	(0.22)
2005:Q2	−0.70	0.31	1.09
	(0.20)	(0.14)	(0.20)
2005:Q3	0.05	0.34	0.62
	(0.21)	(0.14)	(0.21)
Sample size	5,260	5,795	4,456
R^2	0.09	0.11	0.07
F (joint significance)	15.6	12.8	19.6
p-value	0.000	0.000	0.000

Source: Frankenberg et al. (2017).

Notes: Height-for-age z-scores by year of measurement and growth in height-for-age z-scores for children who were in utero at time of the December 2004 tsunami. Dependent variable is standardized height-for-age z-score using CDC standards. Reference cohort is 2002 same quarter of birth. All models include controls for gender, birth order, and month of interview. Standard errors in parentheses take into account clustering at enumeration-area level and heteroscedasticity.

compared with the same quarter of birth cohort in the reference cohort.[4] The gap in the z-score of height for age of those exposed to the tsunami in utero in the second STAR follow-up (in 2006/07) is displayed in the first column of table 1.4. All models also control gender of the child, month of interview, and birth order. Children in the second or third trimesters of the pregnancy at the time of the tsunami are shorter than the reference cohort, and the gap is large and statistically significant for those born in the second quarter of 2005 (taking into account multiple testing). Based on this evidence, the unanticipated shock of the tsunami resulted in reduced linear growth of the children who were in utero at the time of the tsunami by the time they were, on average, eighteen months old. This likely reflects the combination of the nutrition shock (because of the rise in the price of food and access to markets), the income shock (because of the loss of livelihoods), and the stress shock (associated with exposure to the horror of the tsunami).

One year later the estimated gaps are smaller, and after two years none of the gaps between the exposed and reference cohort is significantly different from zero. As shown in column (2), five years after the tsunami, the cohort exposed to the tsunami in utero is taller than the 2002 cohort and the differences are statistically significant for those born in the first and third

---

4. It is important to note that it is likely that more of the children who were in utero at the time of the tsunami were born prematurely relative to the reference cohort, and this effect is captured in the comparison of height for age.

quarters of the year. Growth in height for age between 2006/07 and 2009/10, relative to the reference cohort, is displayed in the third column of the table, restricting attention to those children measured in both waves: all of the exposed children have grown much faster, relative to the CDC norms, than the reference cohort and the growth is greatest for those who had the largest disadvantage in 2006/07, those born in the second quarter. That group of children has grown over one standard deviation more than the reference cohort.[5] Posttsunami growth is statistically significant for all cohorts and, taking into account multiple testing, for the cohorts born in the second and third quarters.

It is possible that the growth trajectory of the reference cohort was affected by the tsunami; children in the reference cohort were born in 2002 and so were, on average, age thirty months at the time of the tsunami. The 2001 birth cohort was potentially affected by the 1998 financial crisis, and so comparison with that cohort may be compromised. Results using this cohort as the reference are not substantially different from those in table 1.4.

Nutrition and stress insults in utero are likely to have resulted in some fetuses being miscarried. It is possible to investigate this issue by comparing the impact of the in utero exposure to the tsunami on males and females. Overall, miscarriages are more common for males, largely because males are far more likely to be miscarried early in the pregnancy whereas females are more likely to be miscarried later in the pregnancy. Thus, males who were in the first or second trimester of the pregnancy at the time of the tsunami are more likely to have been miscarried, relative to males in the third trimester, and so we expect the impact of the tsunami to be greatest on third-trimester males who are most likely to be born in the first quarter of 2005. For females, those in the third trimester are more likely to be miscarried and so, among these fetuses, only the strongest are likely to have survived. Impacts of the tsunami are likely to be greatest on the fetuses exposed earlier in the pregnancy. These predictions are consistent with the data. The impact of in utero exposure is greatest for males in the third trimester of the pregnancy and females in the first and second trimesters at the time of the tsunami. There are two main conclusions. First, this establishes that miscarriage plays an important role and the estimated effects of the tsunami on child height should be interpreted with this in mind. Second, the fact that the evidence is consistent with the predictions of a biological model of miscarriage suggests that the results are unlikely to be driven by unobserved differences between the cohorts. It is, however, possible to test that hypothesis by estimating dose-response effects that compare the heights of children whose mothers had different exposures to the tsunami.

5. Results using the World Health Organization (WHO) norms are essentially identical. Recall that comparisons are made between standardized height for age of the exposed cohort with standardized height for age of the reference cohort.

In the first posttsunami survey, adults were asked a battery of questions about their exposure to the tsunami including, for example, whether they saw people die in the tsunami, whether they were swept away by the water, and whether they saw or heard the water: two-thirds of mothers who survived the tsunami saw or heard the water and one-third did not. The children of mothers who saw or heard the water and were born in the second quarter of 2005 are about a standard deviation shorter than the reference cohort two to three years after the tsunami and are the same height as the reference cohort three to four years later. Among children in the second trimester whose mother did not see or hear the water, two to three years after the tsunami they are slightly but not significantly shorter than the reference cohort and three years later they are taller than the reference cohort. They are also taller than children in the same birth cohort whose mothers were exposed to the water. This evidence is consistent with a dose-response impact of exposure to the tsunami on length at birth and that the children whose mothers were most exposed have an enduring deficit in height for age.

In many contexts, those families with more resources at the time of a shock tend to mitigate the deleterious impact of the shock. We find no evidence that pretsunami resources—measured by household PCE, paternal education, or maternal education—is predictive of the magnitude of the height deficit two to three years after the tsunami or growth in height in the ensuing years.

There are several factors that potentially contribute to the fact that cohort that was in utero at the time of the tsunami grew faster than the reference cohorts. First, the success of the posttsunami recovery effort resulted in rapid economic growth across all Aceh, providing new earnings opportunities for many families. These opportunities included reconstruction-related work such as construction and repair of roads, bridges, and buildings; the opportunities also included the provision of services to the workers and firms involved in the reconstruction such as food preparation, logistics, housing, and transportation. The fact that growth rates were no different for children whose mothers saw or heard the water and those who did not is consistent with the observation that the reconstruction effort benefited all the communities along the coast of Aceh rather than only those communities that were hardest hit. This reflects two forces: on the one hand, road and bridge reconstruction was spread across most of the coast of the province; on the other hand, there was substantial migration in response to the reconstruction effort.

The second factor that potentially contributed to the rapid posttsunami growth of the affected cohort is that as parents rebuilt their livelihoods, they invested heavily in their surviving children. This would be consistent with evidence on investments by Indonesian families in the face of the 1998 financial crisis. Third, it is possible that some of the faster growth can be attributed to postuterine growth of premature births, although much of that catch-up growth is likely to have occurred in the first few months of life and would not be reflected in the catch-up eighteen months through sixty months after birth documented in this study.

We have investigated whether there are differences in the weight for height of the exposed cohort and the reference cohort and find none. Nor do we find any differences depending on the magnitude of exposure. These results are not surprising: the tsunami is likely to have affected the weight of all cohorts. In fact, it is precisely because we are drawing on the biology of human growth and assume that the height of the reference cohort is not much affected by exposure to the tsunami, at least relative to the cohort exposed in utero, that it is possible to identify the causal impact of the tsunami on longer-term child nutrition. We have not examined the growth of children born after the tsunami because there was a very large fertility boom in the months of the tsunami and the mothers of those children tend to be younger and better educated than the mothers of the children conceived before the tsunami (Nobles, Frankenberg, and Thomas 2015). That research, as well as related work on children who lost one or both parents in the tsunami and evidence on financial transfers, illustrates another important source of social safety net resources that likely contributed to mitigating the impact of the tsunami on child health: non-coresident family members and members in the community who contribute to rebuilding the lives of the entire population (Cas et al. 2014; Frankenberg et al. 2015; Frankenberg et al. 2018).

In sum, the Indian Ocean tsunami was a large, unanticipated shock that caused unprecedented disruption in the lives of people living along the coast of Aceh at the time. The shock took a substantial toll on the height of children who were in utero at the time of the tsunami. Had we not followed these children, we would have concluded that the tsunami likely had a significant longer-term impact on the health and well-being of the population. However, the deleterious impacts were for most of the children short-lived and the cohort that was in utero at the time of the tsunami appear to have substantially benefited from the reconstruction effort. Evidence from STAR documents that large-scale, unanticipated shocks have consequences for child growth, there is scope for catch-up growth, and the evidence suggests that increased resource availability because of the reconstruction efforts played a role in mitigating the consequences of these shocks.

1.5 Conclusions

Measurement of the casual impact of shocks on health and human capital is extremely difficult. This is not a novel insight. The goal of this research has been to provide examples of the impact of shocks on health and human capital that turn out to be much more complicated to interpret than a prima facie description of the shock would suggest.

First, it is not straightforward to identify shocks that are, in fact, shocks. Many of the events that are treated as shocks in the literature are anticipated or at least potentially anticipated. Even if the exact timing may be hard to predict, the expectation that there will be, for example, a poor agricultural season periodically complicates interpretation of a poor season as a shock. It is likely that those people who are affected by a poor season will invest in behaviors that mitigate the impact of the poor season. In some cases, a shock is correlated with other changes in the environment or possibly behaviors that contaminate interpretation of estimated effects of the shock. This arises, for example, in the analysis of the 1918 influenza pandemic that occurred at the same time as World War I ended.

Second, the assumption that as shocks unfold, individuals and those in their networks, broadly defined, do not respond to the shock is not consistent with the core tenets of economics. We have shown that in the face of a large financial and political crisis in Indonesia that resulted in huge declines in resources, individuals, families, and communities demonstrated extraordinary resilience and adaptability and sought to mitigate the longer-term impacts of the crisis, even as the magnitude and longevity of the crisis was being revealed. Indonesians are not unique in this regard. Stillman and Thomas (2008) establish that in the face of the collapse of oil prices and, therefore, a massive income shock in Russia, households substantially cut into food spending by switching from more expensive calories and protein to less expensive calories and protein. While spending on food declined by about 25 percent, calorie and protein intake hardly changed and there is no evidence of a change in BMI.

Third, some shocks are so devastating that responses in the short term are limited. However, as the example from the Indian Ocean earthquake and tsunami establishes, drawing conclusions from short-term impacts can be substantially misleading. Over and above evidence on the impacts on child height, we have investigated the impact of the death of one or both parents on the human capital of children who were not killed by the tsunami. Studies of parental death have established that the children of those parents tend to complete fewer years of education (Case, Paxson, and Ableidinger 2004; Beegle, De Weerdt, and Dercon 2010; Evans and Miguel 2007). The majority of those studies are conducted in settings where parental death is due to HIV/AIDS and is treated as if it were a shock. It is not clear that assumption is correct: neither is the death likely to be a shock if there was an illness prior to the death nor are the parents who contract HIV necessarily exchangeable with those who do not. We investigate the impact of an arguably exogenous parental death (from the tsunami) on the education of children age nine to fourteen and, separately, on outcomes of children age fifteen to seventeen at the time of the tsunami (Cas et al. 2014). For young children (age nine to fourteen), we find no impact of parental death of education outcomes: the evidence suggests that other family members and also members of the community rallied to the aid of these children. For older children, however, the story is completely different. Males who lost one or both parents left school earlier and started working earlier than males in the same communities who did not lose a parent. Females also left school earlier and married earlier if one or both parents died. With the new earnings opportunities that accompanied reconstruction, the longer-term consequences of these choices are not obvious; they can only be investigated with data from further follow-ups of the STAR respondents.

In sum, the picture of remarkable resilience that emerges from investigating the impacts of major shocks on child health and human capital in Indonesia is nothing short of stunning. The evidence clearly indicates that individuals, families, and communities respond in manifold ways to mitigate the short- and the longer-term impacts of the shocks on the next generation. To be sure, these mitigation responses have a cost as measured by other dimensions of well-being and the evidence marshaled in this research indicates the responses also impose a substantial burden on the well-being of other family members, including parents, grandparents, and, in some cases, siblings. Taking into account all the evidence on the impact of the 1998 financial crisis and 2004 earthquake and tsunami, it appears that individuals, households, families, and communities do everything they can to either avoid falling into poverty traps or to pull themselves out of poverty, even in the face of large-scale and unanticipated adversity.

References

Alderman, H., J. Hoddinott, and B. Kinsey. 2006. "Long-Term Consequences of Early Childhood Malnutrition." *Oxford Economic Papers* 58 (3): 450–74.

Almond, D. 2006. "Is the 1918 Influenza Pandemic Over? Long-Term Effects of *In Utero* Influenza Exposure in the Post-1940 U.S. Population." *Journal of Political Economy* 114 (4): 672–712.

Almond, D., and B. Mazumder. 2011. "Health Capital and the Prenatal Environment: The Effect of Ramadan Observance during Pregnancy." *American Economic Journal: Applied Economics* 3 (4): 56–85.

Almond, D., B. Mazumder, and R. van Ewijk. 2015. "In Utero Ramadan Exposure and Children's Academic Performance." *Economic Journal* 125 (589): 1501–33.

Barker, D. J. P. 1995. "Fetal Origins of Coronary Heart Disease." *British Medical Journal* 311:171–74.

Beegle, K., J. De Weerdt, and S. Dercon. 2010. "Orphanhood and Human Capital Destruction: Is There Persistence into Adulthood?" *Demography* 47:163–80.

Block S., L. Kiess, P. Webb, S. Kosen, R. Moench-Pfanner, M. Bloem, and P. Timmer. 2004. "Macro Shocks and Micro Outcomes: Child Nutrition during Indonesia's Crisis." *Economics and Human Biology* 2:21–44.

Brown, R., and D. Thomas. 2018. "On the Long-Term Effects of the 1918 U.S. Influenza Pandemic." Working paper, Duke University.

Browning, M., and T. E. Crossley. 2009. "Shocks, Stocks and Socks: Smoothing Consumption over Temporary Income Loss." *Journal of the European Economic Association* 7 (6): 1169–92.

Browning, M., and A. Lusardi. 1996. "Household Saving: Micro Theories and Micro Facts." *Journal of Economic Literature* 34 (4): 1797–855.

Cas, A., E. Frankenberg, W. Suriastini, and D. Thomas. 2014. "The Impact of Parental Death on Child Well-Being: Evidence from the Indian Ocean Tsunami." *Demography* 51 (2): 437–57.

Case, A., C. Paxson, and J. Ableidinger. 2004. "Orphans in Africa: Parental Death, Poverty and School Enrollment." *Demography* 43:401–20.

Cossée, O., R. Hermes, and S. Mezhoud. 2006. *Real Time Evaluation of the FAO Tsunami Response.* Rome: FAO.

Darnton-Hill, I., and B. Cogill. 2010. "Maternal and Young Child Nutrition Adversely Affected by External Shocks Such as Increasing Global Food Prices." *Journal of Nutrition* 140:162S–69S.

Deaton, A. 1992. *Understanding Consumption.* Oxford: Clarendon Press.

Doocy, S., Y. Gorokhovich, G. Burnham, D. Balk, and C. Robinson. 2007. "Tsunami Mortality Estimates and Vulnerability Mapping in Aceh, Indonesia." *American Journal of Public Health* 97:S146–51.

Evans, D., and E. Miguel. 2007. "Orphans and Schooling in Africa: A Longitudinal Analysis." *Demography* 44:35–57.

Fisman, R. 2001. "Estimating the Value of Political Connections." *American Economic Review* 91 (4): 1095–102.

Frankenberg, E., J. Friedman, T. Gillespie, N. Ingwersen, R. Pynoos, I. Rifai, B. Sikoki, A. Steinberg, C. Sumantri, W. Suriastini, and D. Thomas. 2008. "Mental Health in Sumatra after the Tsunami." *American Journal of Public Health* 98 (9): 1671–77.

Frankenberg, E., J. Friedman, N. Ingwersen, and D. Thomas. 2015. "Transfers in Response to a Massive Shock: Interactions between Family and Public Support." Working paper, Duke University.

———. 2018. "Child Health after a Natural Disaster." Working paper, Duke University.

Frankenberg, E., N. Gardner, C. Sumantri, and D. Thomas. 2018. "The Impact of Parental Death on Child Well-Being over the Long-Term." Working paper, Duke University.

Frankenberg, E., T. Gillespie, S. Preston, B. Sikoki, and D. Thomas. 2011. "Mortality, the Family and the Indian Ocean Tsunami." *Economic Journal* 121 (554): F162–82.

Frankenberg, E., J. P. Smith, and D. Thomas. 2003. "Economic Shocks, Wealth and Welfare." *Journal of Human Resources* 38 (2): 280–321.

Frankenberg, E., and D. Thomas. 2000. *The Indonesia Family Life Survey (IFLS): Study Design and Results from Waves 1 and 2.* RAND DRU-2238, Santa Monica, CA.

Frankenberg, E., D. Thomas, and K. Beegle. 1999. "The Real Costs of Indonesia's Economic Crisis: Preliminary Findings from the Indonesia Family Life Surveys." RAND DRU-2064, Santa Monica, CA. https://www.rand.org/pubs/drafts/DRU2064.html.

Friedman J., and J. Levinsohn. 2002. "The Distributional Impacts of Indonesia's Financial Crisis on Household Welfare: A Rapid Response Methodology." *World Bank Economic Review* 16 (3): 397–423.

Friedman J., and D. Thomas. 2009. "Mental Health before, during and after an Economic Crisis: Results from Indonesia 1993–2000." *World Bank Economic Review* 23 (1): 57–76.

Gray, C., E. Frankenberg, T. Gillespie, C. Sumantri, and D. Thomas. 2014. "Studying Displacement after a Disaster Using Large-Scale Survey Methods: Sumatra after the 2004 Tsunami." *Annals of the Association of American Geographers* 104 (3): 594–612.

Hales, C., and D. Barker. 1992. "Type 2 (Non-Insulin-Dependent) Diabetes Mellitus: The Thrifty Phenotype Hypothesis." *Diabetologia* 35:595–601.

Heckman, J. J. 2006. "Skill Formation and the Economics of Investing in Disadvantaged Children." *Science* 312 (5782): 1900–1902.

Hochberg, Y. 1988. "A Sharper Bonferroni Procedure for Multiple Tests of Significance." *Biometrika* 75 (4): 800–802.

Hoddinott, J., J. Behrman, J. Maluccio, P. Melgar, A. Quisumbing, M. Ramirez-Zea, A. Stein, K. Yount, and R. Martorell. 2013. "Adult Consequences of Growth Failure in Early Childhood." *American Journal of Clinical Nutrition* 98 (5): 1170–78.

Hoddinott, J., J. A. Maluccio, J. R. Behrman, R. Flores, and R. Martorell. 2008. "Effect of a Nutrition Intervention during Early Childhood on Economic Productivity in Guatemalan Adults." *Lancet* 371:411–16.

Hommel, G. 1988. "A Stepwise Rejective Multiple Test Procedure Based on a Modified Bonferroni Test." *Biometrika* 82 (2): 383–86.

International Monetary Fund (IMF). 1999. *World Economic Outlook, May 1999: International Financial Contagion*, World Economic Financial Surveys. Washington, DC: International Monetary Fund.

Liebenstein, H. 1957. "The Theory of Underemployment in Densely Populated Backward Areas." In *Efficiency Wage Models of the Labor Market*, edited by G. Akerlof and J. Yellen. New York: Cambridge University Press.

Maluccio, J., J. Hoddinott, J. Behrman, R. Martorell, A. Quisumbing, and A. Stein. 2009. "The Impact of Improving Nutrition during Early Childhood on Education among Guatemalan Adults." *Economic Journal* 119:734–63.

Martorell, R., and J. P. Habicht. 1986. "Growth in Early Childhood in Developing Countries." In *Human Growth: A Comprehensive Treatise*, vol. 3, edited by F. Falkner and J. M. Tanner. New York: Plenum Press.

Mazumdar, D. 1959. "The Marginal Productivity Theory of Wages and Disguised Unemployment." *Review of Economic Studies* 26:190–97.

Nobles, J., E. Frankenberg, and D. Thomas. 2015. "The Effects of Mortality on Fertility: Population Dynamics after a Natural Disaster." *Demography* 52 (1): 15–38.

Ravelli, A. C. J., Jan H. P. van der Meulen, R. P. J. Michels, C. Osmond, D. Barker, C. N. Hales, and O. P. Bleker. 1998. "Glucose Tolerance in Adults after Prenatal Exposure to Famine." *Lancet* 351:173–77.

Ravelli, A. C. J., Jan H. P. van der Meulen, C. Osmond, D. Barker, and O. P. Bleker. 1999. "Obesity at the Age of 50 Years in Men and Women Exposed to Famine Prenatally." *American Journal of Clinical Nutrition* 70:811–16.

Rooij, W. H., J. E. Yonker, R. C. Painter, and T. J. Roseboom. 2010. "Prenatal Under-nutrition and Cognitive Function in Late Adulthood." *Proceedings of the National Academy of Sciences* 107:16881–86.

Roseboom, Tessa J., Jan H. P. van der Meulen, Clive Osmond, David J. Barker, and Otto P. Bleker. 2001. "Adult Survival after Prenatal Exposure to the Dutch Famine 1944–1945." *Paedeatric and Perinatal Epidemiology* 15:220–25.

Scholte, R., G. van den Berg, and M. Lindeboom. 2015. "Long-Run Effects of Gestation during the Dutch Hunger Winter Famine on Labor Market and Hospitalization Outcomes." *Journal of Health Economics* 39:17–30.

Schwarz, G. 1978. "Estimating the Dimension of a Model." *Annals of Statistics* 6 (2): 461–64.

Shapiro, C., and J. Stiglitz. 1984. "Equilibrium Unemployment as a Worker Discipline Device." *American Economic Review* 74 (3): 433–44.

Smith, J. P., D. Thomas, K. Beegle, E. Frankenberg, and G. Teruel. 2002. "Wages,

Employment and Economic Shocks: Evidence from Indonesia." *Journal of Population Economics* 15:161–93.

Stillman, S., and D. Thomas. 2008. "Nutritional Status during an Economic Crisis: Evidence from Russia." *Economic Journal* 118 (531): 1385–417.

Strauss, J., K. Beegle, A. Dwiyanto, Y. Herawati, D. Pattinasarany, E. Setiawan, B. Sikoki, Sukamdi, and F. Witoelar. 2004. *Indonesian Living Standards before and after the Financial Crisis: Evidence from the Indonesia Family Life Survey*. Singapore: Institute of Southeast Asian Studies.

Strauss, J., K. Beegle, B. Sikoki, A. Dwiyanto, Y. Herawati, and F. Witoelar. 2004. *The Third Wave of the Indonesia Family Life Survey (IFLS4)*. RAND Report no. 144, Santa Monica, CA.

Strauss, J., F. Witoelar, and B. Sikoki. 2016. *The Fifth Wave of the Indonesia Family Life Survey (IFLS5)*. RAND Report no. 1143, Santa Monica, CA.

Strauss, J., F. Witoelar, B. Sikoki, and A. M. Wattie. 2009. *The Fourth Wave of the Indonesia Family Life Survey (IFLS4)*. RAND Report no. 675, Santa Monica, CA.

Thomas, D., K. Beegle, E. Frankenberg, B. Sikoki, J. Strauss, and G. Teruel. 2004. "Education in a Crisis." *Journal of Development Economics* 74 (1): 53–85.

Thomas, D., and E. Frankenberg. 2007. "Household Responses to the Financial Crisis in Indonesia: Longitudinal Evidence on Poverty, Resources, and Well-Being." In *Globalization and Poverty*, edited by A. Harrison. Cambridge: Cambridge University Press.

Thomas, D., E. Frankenberg, K. Beegle, and G. Teruel. 1999. "Household Budgets, Household Composition and the Crisis in Indonesia: Evidence from Longitudinal Survey Data." Working paper, RAND Labor and Population Program, Santa Monica, CA.

Thomas, D., E. Frankenberg, and J. P. Smith. 2001. "Lost But Not Forgotten: Attrition in the Indonesia Family Life Survey." *Journal of Human Resources* 36 (3): 556–92.

van Ewijk, R. 2011. "Long-Term Health Effects on the Next Generation of Ramadan Fasting during Pregnancy." *Journal of Health Economics* 30 (6): 1246–60.

2

Poverty and Cognitive Function

Emma Boswell Dean, Frank Schilbach, and
Heather Schofield

2.1 Introduction

Economic growth has lifted billions out of poverty in the span of a few generations. Despite these positive trends, poverty remains entrenched for millions around the globe. One long-standing explanation for poverty's persistence is the possibility of poverty traps, or self-reinforcing cycles of poverty. Theoretical models of such poverty traps—often centered on nutrition in the earliest cases—have been central in the development literature for over half a century (Leibenstein 1957; Mirrlees 1975; Stiglitz 1976; Bliss and Stern 1978; Dasgupta and Ray 1986). This literature has expanded in many directions to consider the varying potential underlying forces such as geographic characteristics, pecuniary externalities, and even cultural forces, as well as both theoretical and policy implications of such traps, ranging from intergenerational transmission of poverty to equilibrium unemployment (Jalan and Ravallion 2002; Sachs 2005; Fang and Loury 2005; Currie and Almond 2011; Barrett and Carter 2013; Sachs 2014; Kraay and Raddatz 2007).

Emma Boswell Dean is assistant professor at the University of Miami. Frank Schilbach is assistant professor of economics at the Massachusetts Institute of Technology, a JPAL affiliate, and a faculty research fellow of the National Bureau of Economic Research. Heather Schofield is assistant professor in the Perelman School of Medicine and the Wharton School of the University of Pennsylvania.

We thank participants at the NBER conference, John Hoddinott, Joshua Dean, and our anonymous referee for insightful comments and suggestions. We are also grateful for excellent research assistance from Jordan Browne, Stephanie Chan, Sarah Quinn, and Alicia Weng. We also thank Emily Gallagher and Lesley Fowler for their meticulous editing and helpful suggestions. All remaining errors are our own. For acknowledgments, sources of research support, and disclosure of the authors' material financial relationships, if any, please see http://www.nber.org/chapters/c13830.ack.

Despite the extensive literature in this area and the policy appeal of potentially instigating virtuous and self-reinforcing cycles of income growth and wealth, the empirical evidence that such traps exist remains mixed (Banerjee and Duflo 2011; Kraay and McKenzie 2014; Barrett, Garg, and McBride 2016). Moreover, even in the instances where actual evidence is consistent with such traps, their exact mechanisms remain unclear (Banerjee et al. 2015; Bandiera et al. 2015). This chapter focuses on one potential underlying mechanism that has yet to be explored in depth, cognitive function.

Poverty may affect cognitive function in a variety of ways. Evidence is beginning to accumulate that cognitive functions are limited resources that can be strained by living in poverty (Schilbach, Schofield, and Mullainathan 2016). Being forced to make constant trade-offs with limited resources can act as a "load" on cognitive function (Mullainathan and Shafir 2013). Further, poverty can affect economic behavior via psychological effects including stress and negative affective states, such as depression (Haushofer and Fehr 2014). In addition to directly capturing individuals' minds, poverty often entails a number of material deprivations that may further impede cognitive function. Perhaps most well known among these deprivations is malnutrition. One in seven individuals around the world remain below recommended levels of caloric intake (Food and Agricultural Organization of the United Nations et al. 2011). Moreover, in many settings, the poor are exposed to sleep deprivation, physical pain, and substance abuse at alarming levels. While research is still in progress, to date we have found that the poor in Chennai, India, sleep just over five hours per night, with more than twenty disruptions on average, using objective measurements from wristwatch-like actigraphs. Similarly remarkable, a survey of 1,200 low-income informal labor market participants revealed an average pain level of 5 at the end of the workday, on a 0 to 10 scale. Moreover, the majority of male low-income workers in Chennai drink daily, consuming an average of over five standard drinks per day and spending over 20 percent of their daily labor incomes on alcohol (Schilbach 2017). Each of these correlates of poverty have been shown to tax cognitive resources (Schofield 2014; Lim and Dinges 2010; Moriarty, McGuire, and Finn 2011; Steele and Josephs 1990).

The resulting reductions in these cognitive resources may have broad feedback effects on earnings and wealth, ranging from occupational choice to technology adoption, consumption patterns, and risk and time preferences. In other words, the relationship between cognitive function and poverty could be bidirectional, generating the potential for feedback loops, reduced mobility, and—if the resulting effects are large enough—poverty traps. The goal of this chapter is to highlight the potential interplay between cognitive function and poverty and, in doing so, to facilitate further study of this potential bidirectional mechanism by providing a "primer for economists" on areas of cognitive function, their measurement, and their potential implications for poverty.

Despite the potential importance of cognitive function in the lives of the poor, there are several challenges for understanding its causes and consequences. First, both the factors impeding cognitive function and the downstream effects of reduced cognitive function are likely to be diffuse, making measurement of channels and feedback effects challenging. Second, while some of the impacts of poverty on cognitive function are immediate (e.g., via acute physical pain), other impacts (e.g., via sleep deprivation or nutrition) are slow-moving and cumulative, making them even more challenging to detect, both for researchers and individuals themselves. Third, existing measurements of many of the channels discussed in this chapter are limited. For instance, data on sleeping patterns in developing countries is scarce and often limited to self-reports, which are likely to be inaccurate (Lauderdale et al. 2008). Yet, although these challenges exist, careful design and improved measurement technologies make them surmountable, opening the door to a wide variety of high-value studies.

Beyond a potential role in creating feedback loops that increase the persistence of poverty, an enhanced understanding of the psychological or cognitive lives of the poor is, in and of itself, of substantial value. Improved understanding of the financial lives of the poor over the previous few decades has generated many insights; for example, the wealth of data from financial diaries has shed light on the incredible complexity of the financial lives of the poor—with those in poverty often balancing a dizzying array of transactions, income streams, and debts. These data have helped to greatly enhance our understanding of financial behaviors among the poor. Similarly, as methods to study cognitive function at scale improve, and as there is increased acceptance of the idea that limits on cognition may influence economic decision-making, there is significant potential to improve our understanding of the psychological lives of the poor, with many broad consequences across countless aspects of lives of the poor.

The remainder of this chapter is structured as follows. Section 2.2 begins with a concise overview of cognitive functions for economists, including definitions and descriptions of four key areas with potential importance for economic decision-making. In addition, this section discusses how to measure the different aspects of cognitive function in order to quantify potential effects of poverty and to facilitate further research in this area. Section 2.3 then summarizes the existing evidence for the potential impact of poverty on cognitive function and economic behavior via various channels, including malnutrition, alcohol consumption, monetary concerns, physical pain, sleep deprivation, environmental factors, stress, and depression. Section 2.4 shifts focus to the impact of different areas of cognitive function on economic outcomes, and more broadly to future income, wealth, decision-making, and poverty. Finally, section 2.5 concludes by highlighting open questions and high-value areas of future research in the relationship between cognitive function and poverty.

2.2   Cognitive Functions

This section begins with a brief overview of cognitive functions crucial to economic outcomes and decision-making. Following this overview we will discuss four key aspects of cognitive function in detail, as well as canonical tests to measure them. Additional detail on the cognitive functions we consider here can be found in Lyon and Krasnegor (1996), Suchy (2009), and Diamond (2013).

2.2.1   Overview of Cognitive Functions

The brain and its many functions have been studied by researchers in psychology, neuroscience, and other fields for many decades. Each of its roles—for example, movement, sensory input, and interpretation—is essential to daily life. There is, however, one set of functional areas that is of particular relevance and interest to decision-making and economic life. Termed "cognitive function" or "executive function" in the cognitive psychology literature, these are broadly defined as mental processes that control one's attention, dictate one's ability to work with information, and are required for deliberate activity. Cognitive functions are crucial to task performance and decision-making, and carry longer-term impacts such as literacy and school performance (Borella, Carretti, and Pelegrina 2010; Duncan et al. 2007).

Cognitive functions are top-down processes, initiated from the prefrontal cortex of the brain, that are required for deliberate thought processes such as forming goals, planning ahead, carrying out a goal-directed plan, and performing effectively (Lezak 1983; Miller and Cohen 2001). Although most researchers agree on this general understanding of cognitive functions, there is a wide array of views on details such as how to categorize its subcomponents, which neurological brain circuits are required for different areas of functioning, and whether there exists one unifying mechanism underlying all cognitive functions, also known as the "Theory of Unity" (Kimberg et al. 1997; de Frias, Dixon, and Strauss 2006; Godefroy et al. 1999; Jurado and Rosselli 2007).

Although beliefs are wide-ranging, most researchers would agree that there is no one unifying mechanism, and broad classification of subcomponents is possible (Miyake et al. 2000). In this chapter, we will utilize this classification system of subcomponents of functioning, focusing on four aspects of cognitive functions that are both generally agreed upon by cognitive psychologists and that we consider central to understanding economic behavior and outcomes. This list is not fully exhaustive, and the complexity of and overlap in cognitive functions make many categorizations possible, especially for higher-order functions. However, in order to keep this introduction to the topic a tractable reference, we focus on a limited number of subcomponents with stronger agreement in their categorization and direct relevance to economic choices.

I. Attention is the ability to focus on particular pieces of information by engaging in a selection process that allows for further processing of incoming stimuli. This process can happen voluntarily or involuntarily. For instance, attention alerts us to sudden loud noises (involuntarily) or enables us to comprehend a bullet point on a presentation slide (voluntarily).

II. Inhibitory Control is the ability to control impulses and minimize interference from irrelevant stimuli. It is used to block out distractions, to control impulsive urges, and to override prepotent responses. For example, an application of inhibitory control is stopping yourself from reaching for a chocolate cookie on the table when you are exhausted after a long day.

III. Memory is the ability to recall, recognize, and utilize previously learned information. Of particular interest in this chapter is working memory, the ability to evaluate new information as it enters, to manipulate the information if necessary, and to delete or update irrelevant existing information. For example, the use of working memory enables us to remember a conversation with another conference attendee, and then to revisit the topic later and update a draft paper.

IV. Higher-Order Cognitive Functions involve one or more of the basic cognitive functions highlighted above and are therefore considered more complex. This chapter will discuss three higher-order cognitive functions: cognitive flexibility, intelligence, and planning.

Cognitive flexibility is a higher-order ability that involves switching between tasks, rules, or mental sets (Lezak, Howieson, and Loring 2004). For example, if a small business owner decides to implement a new bookkeeping system, adjusting to this change requires a combination of inhibiting existing habits, attending to the old and new rules, and actively adopting the new system—a more involved process compared to one that merely relies on a single cognitive function. Cognitive flexibility is also used interpersonally, helping us to understand others' perspectives in situations of potential conflict.

Intelligence is commonly separated into fluid and crystallized intelligence. The former refers to the ability to solve novel problems and the latter involves the ability to use learned languages, subjects, skills, and so forth. Both forms of intelligence involve a combination of core functions such as attention and memory, rendering them "higher order," that is, more complex cognitive functions (Cattell and Horn 1966).

Planning—also sometimes known as "sequencing"—is the ability to generate a strategy, including the sequencing of steps, which meets intended goal(s). This function is central to many economic activities. For example, just to open for the day, the manager of a restaurant must anticipate demand, contract with the necessary suppliers, and organize staff schedules—all tasks that involve sequencing steps appropriately to meet an intended goal.

Each of these broad constructs has the potential to help shape our understanding of the relationship between poverty, decision-making, and productivity. Each has direct relevance to a variety of types of economic decision-making, as well as the potential to be shaped by poverty and its correlates. Such effects, if large enough, may in turn lead to reduced socioeconomic mobility or potentially even poverty traps. Before discussing the potential relationship between these areas of cognitive function and economic outcomes, we provide a more thorough description of each area of cognitive function, as well as examples of ways to measure them, in order to facilitate their integration into economic studies. Appendix table 2A.1 provides a summary of tasks that can be used to measure cognitive function, including some of their advantages and disadvantages for use in development economics.

2.2.2   Attention

Definition and Description of Attention

Given its fundamental nature underlying several other cognitive functions and its relevance to decision-making, attention has garnered exceptional interest among both psychologists and economists (Pashler 1998). This interest has generated a wide-ranging and deep literature in psychology, with many active debates and disagreements about the precise definition, role, and boundaries of attention. This chapter aims to define attention in a manner consistent with the prevailing views in cognitive psychology, while noting some of the most substantial disagreements with that view. Notably, we focus only on *conscious* attention for the purposes of this chapter, as opposed to aspects of attention, such as priming, that could happen subconsciously.

At its most basic level, attention is the selection of information for further processing. A key feature of attention is that it is limited (Broadbent 1958). It is not possible to attend to and encode the millions of stimuli encountered each day. That is, attention filters information into or out of processing mechanisms, enabling us to focus more effectively on the things we care about (Sternberg and Sternberg 2011; Treisman and Gelade 1980; Cohen 2014). Given this filtering role, and because one usually attends to a stimulus before being able to retain or recall information, the early and still prevailing view is that attention is a key component of memory (Yates 1966; Phelps 2006).

Within the realm of attention, researchers have made significant headway in understanding the mechanisms underlying attention by separating it into categorical types:

Internal versus External Attention. One such categorical distinction is the separation between internal and external attention (Chun, Golomb, and Turk-Browne 2011). Internal attention is the selection, modulation, and maintenance of internally generated information. For instance, a use of internal attention would be thinking about the upcoming deadline for a journal submission. In contrast, external attention is the selection and modulation of incoming stimuli from your surroundings, for example, viewing images as they appear on a television screen.

Narrow versus Broad Attention. A second categorical distinction of attention is narrow versus broad attention (Wachtel 1976). In broad attention, a person pays attention to many stimuli or attributes of stimuli simultaneously, whereas in narrow attention, the person excludes irrelevant information, allowing for a limited focus. This categorization of attention is considered to coexist with internal and external attention. The theory of attention developed by Nideffer (1976), and the scale developed from it (the Test of Attention and Interpersonal Style), states that attention is a two-factor process, measured by both breadth (narrow versus broad) *and* direction (internal versus external), and that people use combinations of these two factors of attention depending on the task at hand. For instance, a student solving a math problem on an exam would be using narrow internal attention, whereas that same student would use broad external attention when arriving at a party later that night to scan the room, see who is present, and decide who to begin talking to.

Simple versus Complex Attention. Related to narrow versus broad attention, but less well known, is the classification of simple versus complex attention, as proposed by Lim and Dinges (2010). Simple attention refers to attending to one stimulus, whereas complex attention refers to attending to multiple stimuli at the same time. While this categorization is not very common among psychologists, tasks devised to measure cognitive functions can be to a large extent related to either simple or complex attention. As such, this categorization provides a straightforward structure to understand attention and, in particular, to study the potential relationship between poverty and cognitive function.

Other classifications are arguably less informative when considering downstream effects such as economic decision-making and productivity. For example, posterior and anterior attention studied in neuroscience focus on the specific neurotransmitters that are active in the brain when attending to different stimuli and investigate in depth the particular brain cells at play (Peterson and Posner 2012). Due to our focus on the relationship between cognitive function and economic outcomes of interest, these discoveries are not our primary focus; therefore, we proceed with the simple versus complex attention categorization. The next section provides examples of tests measuring simple and complex attention.

Measuring Attention

One of the areas of attention with potentially significant consequences to human behavior is "sustained attention," also commonly referred to as "vigilance" or "attentional vigilance" (Egeland, Johansen, and Ueland 2009). This skill is the general ability to detect a stimulus during times of habituation and/or tiredness (Mackworth 1968; Robertson et al. 1997). A common example of this skill is driving, especially while fatigued. In lab and field settings, measuring vigilance usually involves identifying a target signal from a pool of otherwise continuous and repetitive nontarget stimuli. This section describes canonical tasks used to measure this skill, in both its simple and complex forms.

I. Psychomotor Vigilance Task. Within simple attention, one widely used task to measure attentional vigilance is the Psychomotor Vigilance Task (PVT). The PVT is especially popular among sleep researchers (Basner and Dinges 2011; Basner, Mollicone, and Dinges 2011; Dinges et al. 1997). In this task, researchers ask participants to press a button when a stimulus, such as a light or a colored dot, appears. The task measures reaction time and accuracy—in other words, how quickly the participant (correctly) presses the button when the stimulus appears, and how often she presses the button when no stimulus appears (a false response). In a review by Basner and Dinges (2011), the most common outcome metric of the PVT is the number of "lapses," reported by around two-thirds of published studies. Lapses are usually defined as a reaction time of longer than 500 milliseconds and are understood as breaks in one's attention (Lim and Dinges 2008). Other commonly used metrics are mean reaction time, inverse reaction time, fastest 10 percent of reaction times, and median reaction time. The PVT collects extremely granular data, as it is administered on a computer (or other electronic device) and records time on a millisecond scale. Researchers can easily adjust factors such as interstimulus interval—the time and regularity of gaps between the appearance of two stimuli, a feature that impacts task difficulty. Participants exhibit limited learning effects in this task, making it ideal for repeated use in within-subject designs (Dorrian, Rogers, and Dinges 2005). The task does, however, require electronic administration, which can make it inconvenient in certain field settings. Increasing the duration of the task generally increases error rates, especially when implemented along with a battery of other cognitive tasks (Lim et al. 2010).

II. Concentration Endurance Test. In contrast to simple attention tasks, complex attention tasks involve more than one stimulus and/or more than one rule. The Concentration Endurance Test, also known as the "d2 Test of Attention," is a task that aims to measure sustained attention (Bates and Lemay 2004). Participants view a continuous list of letters *p* and *d*, with up to two marks above and up to two marks below each of the letters. The participants then identify and cross out each case of the letter *d* that has two associated marks. Common outcome variables include the total number of correct cancellations, errors, and the distribution of errors. The task requires participants to recognize the letter "d," making literate participants more easily able to complete the task, but it can be administered using similar shapes as opposed to letters for nonliterate participants or participants whose native language does not use the Latin alphabet. Notably, the task requires accurate visual scanning, which can be impeded not only by poor attention, but also by poor eyesight, a common concern in developing countries.

2.2.3   Inhibitory Control

Definition and Description of Inhibitory Control

Inhibitory control is a top-down mental process that blocks out distractions, controls impulsive urges, and overrides prepotent responses (Rothbart and Posner 1985). It is sometimes used interchangeably with self-control, and is also referred to as "selective attention," "attentional control," "attentional inhibition," and "executive attention" (Lavie et al. 2004; Kane and Engle 2002; Kaplan and Berman 2010). The ability to control impulses has been studied extensively in child development (Carlson and Moses 2001; Diamond and Taylor 1996; Mischel, Shoda, and Rodriguez 1989) as well as among adults (Ward and Mann 2000; Dempster 1992). This important aspect of cognitive functioning enables people to perform well socially, physically, at work, and in society. For example, discipline and self-control are required to refrain from eating when on a diet (Shiv and Fedorikhin 1999), or to inhibit socially inappropriate responses when mentally drained (von Hippel and Gonsalkorale 2005).

One notable model of self-control proposes that self-control is governed by a limited resource that can be depleted over time (Baumeister et al. 1998; Muraven, Tice, and Baumeister 1998). This model, known as the "ego-depletion" model, has been empirically tested, with meta-analyses finding small effect sizes. But more recent replications of the task used to study this phenomena have called this conclusion into question, with a preregistered trial involving twenty-three labs and over 2,000 participants finding no significant effect (Hagger et al. 2016).

However, there is better evidence that situational factors can have a significant effect on self-control. In addition to individual differences, variable factors in one's environment or life circumstances such as fatigue or cognitive load may also affect the availability of this limited mental resource (Inzlicht and Schmeichel 2012; Muraven and Baumeister 2000). For example, it is much more difficult to suppress one's impulses after exposure to stress (Glass, Singer, and Friedman 1969) or when working in a crowded space (Sherrod 1974), both prevalent conditions faced by the urban poor. Empirically, recent prominent work on self-control has focused on exploring the consequences of depleted self-control and ways to overcome this depletion (Baumeister 2002; Hofmann, Rauch, and Gawronski 2007; Hofmann, Friese, and Strack 2009).

Measuring Inhibitory Control

This section describes a subset of the many cognitive tasks used to measure inhibitory control. Researchers have applied the tests discussed below in a wide range of settings and populations, providing a useful guide for designing future experimental studies related to inhibitory control.

I. Hearts and Flowers Task. This task, previously known as the Dots Task, shows participants a screen that is divided into two panels where either a heart or a flower appears on one side of the screen.[1] In the first round, participants are shown only hearts and are asked to click a button on the same side as the heart whenever it appears. In the second round, only flowers appear and participants are asked to click on the opposite side of the screen as the flower. Finally, in the third round, individuals see both hearts and flowers, and the goal is to click on the appropriate side of the screen according to the rule for each stimulus. Round 2 and in particular round 3 measure inhibitory control, as they require individuals to override their natural tendency to press on the same side whenever flowers appear on the screen. While this test does require inhibitory control, it has been critiqued as also requiring working memory (Diamond 2013). A different version of this test, using arrows instead of symbols, is particularly effective at separating inhibitory control from other cognitive functions (Davidson et al. 2006).[2] The test can be made more difficult by decreasing the amount of time individual stimuli appear on the screen. Though this task is most effectively administered electronically, it is well suited for economic development research. It is quick, easy to explain, and does not require specific background knowledge or a specific education level, making it applicable in a wide range of settings.

II. Eriksen Flanker Task. In this task, participants are shown a set of five stimuli, of which they are supposed to respond only to the middle stimulus (Eriksen and Eriksen 1974; Mullane et al. 2009). A common version of this task uses an arrow as the target (middle) stimulus. Respondents have two buttons—one left and one right—and are asked to press the button corresponding to the direction of the target arrow. The target stimulus can be flanked by congruent stimuli (e.g., arrows pointing in the same direction as the target), incongruent stimuli (e.g., arrows pointing in the opposite direction of the target), or neutral stimuli (e.g., squares flanking the target arrow). Incongruent stimuli require participants to use top-down control to focus on the middle stimulus (Diamond 2013). Using an arrow as the stimulus for this task minimizes memory requirements from participants, as the arrows indicate where the participant is supposed to respond. This task is best performed electronically, and researchers have limited ability to manipulate its difficulty. When conducted using arrows as described above, however, the test does not require any background knowledge or educational attainment

1. The Hearts and Flowers Task is quite similar to an older task known as the Simon task. This task has two rules: press left for one stimulus, and press right for a second stimulus. The stimulus can appear on the right or left side of the screen. While the side of the screen on which the stimuli appear is irrelevant, respondents tend to be quicker when the stimuli appear on the same side as their associated response (this is termed the Simon effect) (Lu and Proctor 1995).

2. As it only requires participants to hold one rule in mind at a time it does not require working memory.

level, and more effectively separates inhibitory control from other cognitive functions such as working memory.

III. Stroop Test. While there are a number of versions of the Stroop Test, we detail two in this chapter: the Classic Stroop Test and the Spatial Stroop Test.

The Classic Stroop Test displays a list of words that spell out the names of colors (Stroop 1935). The congruent condition occurs when the word matches the ink color (e.g., the word "blue" is displayed in blue ink). Conversely, the incongruent condition occurs when the word is displayed in a different color ink (e.g., the word "blue" displayed in green ink). The goal of the task is to name the color of the ink as opposed to the word, for instance, blue in the congruent condition and green in the incongruent condition (MacLeod 1991).[3] Although it is a common test in developed countries, the Stroop Test has several disadvantages for development researchers. In particular, most versions require literacy, and different educational levels are likely to affect performances. A numeric version of the task can overcome the literacy barrier, although it may still be problematic if numeracy is also low. The test is also typically conducted electronically (though it can be done with paper and a stopwatch), and there is little researchers can do to manipulate its difficulty other than shorten the response time.

The Spatial Stroop Test relies on the same basic concept as the Classic Stroop Test, but measures spatial rather than verbal and visual incompatibility. Researchers show participants both relevant and irrelevant dimensions of a stimulus, which are similar and can influence responses. For example, in one variant, participants are shown an arrow that points left or right (in another variant they are shown the words "LEFT" or "RIGHT") and that is displayed on either the left or right side of the computer screen. Participants are asked to press the button on the side the arrow is pointing to, ignoring the location of the arrow on the computer screen. While the side of the screen on which the stimuli appear is irrelevant, respondents tend to be quicker when the stimuli appear on the same side as their associated response. This version of the task has an advantage over the Classic Stroop Test in that it does not require literacy when using the arrow stimuli. Though generally administered electronically, this task is otherwise well suited to field settings, as it is both quick and easy to explain. Researchers can also alter the difficulty of the task easily by adjusting its speed.

2.2.4 Memory

Definition and Description of Memory

Memory is the ability to encode, store, retain, and retrieve information and previous experiences (Kandel, Schwartz, and Jessell 2000). This ability

---

3. Although the classic Stroop Test is a prototypical test of inhibitory control (Miyake et al. 2000), MacLeod et al. (2003) argue that the "Stroop effect" or "Stroop interference"—a delayed response when ink color differs from that of the displayed word—may not measure inhibition.

to retain and use previous knowledge supports relationship building and is essential to learning. Memory has multiple components; for instance, auditory memory is the ability to process and retain oral information (information given "out loud"), whereas visual memory is the ability to remember what one has seen. Short-term memory describes the brain's ability to retain information for a short amount of time. Information can then be stored for long-term usage via rehearsal or active processing. Closely connected to short-term memory is working memory, which describes a person's ability to simultaneously store and manipulate (work with) information. More information on short-term, long-term, and working memory follows.

Short-Term Memory and Long-Term Memory. Research on memory has explored the relationship and interactions between what we commonly and intuitively refer to as "short-term memory" and "long-term memory" (James 1890). Short-term memory is defined as information that enters into conscious memory through a sensory registry such as through the eyes or sense of touch. Information then resides for a short period of time in the conscious memory but will be forgotten if not deliberately rehearsed or managed. Scientists generally agree that the capacity of short-term memory is limited, with seven plus or minus two considered to be the typical number of items one can hold in short-term memory at the same time (Miller 1956). Following extensive rehearsal and active processing, information solidifies and moves into long-term memory, where it is retained for future use. When people's actions, decisions, and speech require them to retrieve information from long-term memory, the memory or information moves back into short-term memory for active use. Compared with the limited capacity in the short-term store, researchers hypothesize that the capacity of the long-term store is unlimited (Cowan 2008).

Working Memory. Research in recent decades has largely replaced the concept of short-term memory with an integrated, multicomponent classification known as working memory (Baddeley and Hitch 1974). Working memory refers to the set of cognitive processes involved in the temporary storage *and* manipulation of information (Diamond 2013). For example, a waitress taking orders at a dining table could use working memory to remember all the orders without writing anything down. She might also manipulate the "data" in her mind by grouping all the appetizers, all the drink orders, and so on. This combination of temporary storage and manipulation is the core of working memory. As with short-term memory capacity, individuals' working memory capacity is limited. There is some disagreement among researchers in psychology about how working memory fits into the broader category of cognitive function. In particular, working memory and inhibitory control are often difficult to parse completely. One possibility, which is popular within computational modeling, is to group inhibitory control with working memory (Hasher and Zacks 1998, 2006; Miller and Cohen 2001; Munakata et al. 2011). However, although there is some overlap, here we treat working memory and inhibitory control as distinct due to their differential impacts on economic outcomes, as we will outline in section 2.4.

Measuring Memory

Cognitive psychologists have devised numerous tasks to measure short-term and working memory. We discuss four such tasks, including their relevant variations.

I. Digit Span Tasks. To measure short-term memory, researchers often use the Forward Digit Span Task, in which participants are read a list of numbers and then asked to repeat these numbers in the same order (Daneman and Carpenter 1980, 1983). Participants with a lower level of numeracy may be at a disadvantage in this task, so researchers can substitute simple items or words in place of numbers as needed. One also can modify this task to have participants listen to and repeat nonnumerical items and reorganize them. For instance, modifications might include providing participants with a series of letters to list back in alphabetical order (requires literacy) or a series of objects to list back in order of size (requires background knowledge of items, which may differ across settings). This task is easy to implement in the field—it does not require any equipment other than what is needed to record participants' responses. Outcomes for this study are accuracy and the longest correctly remembered span. It is easy to make this test more challenging by increasing the number of digits or objects the participants are asked to remember. Closely related to the Forward Digit Span Task is the Reverse Digit Span Task. Intuitively, the task asks participants to listen to a list of numbers and repeat them in reverse order. Similar to the modifications of the task discussed above, this version of the task is commonly used as a measure of working memory because it requires some manipulation of information instead of mere repetition. This task has the same implementation challenges as the Forward Digit Span Task, but similar modifications can be implemented. Both the forward and reverse digit span tasks are sometimes implemented asking the participant to reorder the digits numerically. However, this version of the task is less desirable in contexts where numeracy is low.

II. Corsi Block Test. The Corsi Block Test (Corsi 1972) is well suited to measure visual-spatial memory (Lezak 1983). Participants view a series of spatially separated blocks, which individually change colors in a random sequence. They then tap or click the series of blocks in the order in which they changed color. In an alternative version of this task, a researcher will tap individual blocks and participants are then asked to tap these blocks in the same order as the researcher. The sequence typically starts out with a small number of blocks (e.g., each series will consist of two flashing blocks) and then becomes more and more difficult as the number of blocks in the series increases. As initially designed, the Corsi Block Test does not require mental manipulation, which categorizes it as a short-term memory test rather than a working memory test. However, the Reverse Corsi Block Test, in which participants reverse the order of the indicated blocks, measures working memory. The Corsi Block Test is also relatively easy to implement in the field; it can be administered on paper or electronically, and a tablet version, eCorsi, has been developed (Brunetti, Del Gatto, and Delogu 2014). The task also does not require any particular background (such as numeracy), making it particularly well suited for research in development economics. Furthermore, researchers can easily increase the test's difficulty by increasing the number of blocks respondents must remember.

III. N-Back Task. The N-Back Task is a commonly used test of working memory. In this task, participants are presented with a series of stimuli. They are then asked to press a button or otherwise indicate if the current stimuli matches the stimuli presented n stimuli prior (Kirchner 1958). Both accuracy and speed are measured as outcomes of interest. This task can take a visual form, in which a series of objects are shown on a screen, or an auditory form, where a participant listens to a series of words. A third variant of the task, the "dual-task" version, uses a similar framework but presents two independent, simultaneous sequences—typically one visual and one auditory, to which respondents must respond (Jaeggi et al. 2003). While N-Back is widely used, its validity as a test of working memory has been questioned by studies finding that its results are only weakly correlated with other well-accepted measures of working memory (Jaeggi et al. 2010; Kane et al. 2007). In its general form, the test generally does not require literacy or numeracy, unless words, letters, or numbers are used as stimuli. It can be made more or less difficult by adjusting the n parameter or speed of the stimuli.

IV. Self-Ordered Pointing Task. This test measures nonspatial or spatial working memory (Petrides et al. 1993; Petrides and Milner 1982). Participants are shown three to twelve objects (in the form of boxes with line drawings or other identifiable stimuli), and are then asked to touch one item at a time, without repeating items, until each object has been touched. However, the test randomly scrambles the locations of the objects in between turns. A modification of this task that measures spatial working memory also includes an identical set of objects that remain stationary throughout the task (Diamond et al. 2007; Wiebe, Lukowski, and Bauer 2010). One can manipulate the difficulty by increasing the number of items. The task can be carried out either electronically or using physical objects (or paper drawings). It does not require participants to have a specific background or a certain level of education, making it appropriate in a wide range of settings.

2.2.5   Higher-Order Cognitive Functions

Definition and Description of Higher-Order Cognitive Functions

In the previous sections we presented attention, inhibitory control, and memory as unidimensional cognitive functions because researchers attempting to understand the human mind typically focus on one specific aspect of functioning while controlling for or mitigating the influence of unrelated areas in order to obtain the cleanest results. However, as described previously, attention, inhibitory control, and memory are all interrelated and difficult to fully disentangle because they utilize the same region in the brain (Stuss and Alexander 2000).[4]

In fact, real-life human behavior rarely relies on one cognitive domain alone and instead usually requires a combination of these underlying functions. For example, think about the seemingly simple act of crossing a road. All of the core cognitive functions are at play here. First, you pay attention to the traffic light and the passing vehicles. Looking at the cars, you use working memory to calculate their speed and distance and contemplate whether jaywalking seems safe enough. However, you decide to suppress your impulse to jaywalk because the young child next to you is patiently waiting for the green light and you want to set a good example; you exert inhibitory control. This example illustrates the complexity involved in almost every decision or action we take, even those that appear mundane on the surface. Instead of using a unidimensional cognitive function, our actions and decisions typically require a multidimensional approach, combining several of the cognitive functions discussed so far. In this section, we discuss the more advanced types of cognitive functions, which we refer to as "higher-order cognitive functions," focusing on cognitive flexibility, intelligence, and planning, three key areas with the potential to greatly impact economic outcomes.

Cognitive Flexibility. The ability to adapt to changing circumstances is referred to as cognitive flexibility (Friedman et al. 2006; Andrewes 2001). This mental process is used when a situation is altered and there is a need to adapt to the new context by updating procedures to reflect new circumstances, rules, or environments. Cognitive psychologists hypothesize that cognitive flexibility is composed of three steps (Martin and Rubin 1995; Martin and Anderson 1998). The first is an awareness that there are options and alternatives available in a given situation. The second is a willingness to be flexible and adapt to a given situation. The third is the decision to make the switch and modify behavior or beliefs given the situation. Researchers argue that all three steps are critical because one cannot adapt to a new rule without an awareness of it, and similarly, one would not successfully adapt to the new rule without the willingness and ability to change. Cognitive flexibility is also referred to as set shifting, task or attention switching/ shifting, cognitive shifting, and mental flexibility (Tchanturia et al. 2012; Canas et al. 2002).

Fluid and Crystallized Intelligence. General intelligence is typically considered to have two components: fluid intelligence and crystallized intelligence (Horn and Cattell 1967). *Fluid intelligence* refers to the ability to

---

4. Diamond (2013, figure 4) is an excellent summary of the interrelation of cognitive functions.

solve novel problems and to adapt to new situations. Frequently abbreviated as *gF* in the literature, researchers believe fluid intelligence exists independently of acquired skills and knowledge (Cattell 1963). Individuals who use logic such as deductive reasoning to solve a puzzle or think about problems abstractly employ fluid intelligence. As a higher-order cognitive function, it is most often associated with memory, in particular, working memory, which involves updating and manipulating information. In contrast, *crystallized intelligence*, commonly abbreviated as gC, relies on acquired skills and knowledge from one's schooling and/or upbringing. Crystallized intelligence can be formed from experience or information and also relies on memory, in particular, long-term memory (Knox 1997). Notably, intelligence measures are often used interchangeably with other decision-making activities. For example, many researchers view reasoning and problem solving as synonymous with fluid intelligence (Diamond 2013); others group reasoning and crystallized intelligence together as a closely related construct (Lim and Dinges 2010).

Planning is a higher-order construct that captures the ability to think strategically about how best to sequence steps in order to obtain a goal. In order to plan well, individuals must consider multiple hypothetical sequences of events and actions that could be used to reach an intended outcome and then assess which will most efficiently and effectively help them reach the intended outcome (Carlin et al. 2000). This construct is also sometimes referred to as "sequencing." There is less direct agreement on how to categorize and define planning given the large number of underlying aspects of cognitive function required, including some higher-order functions, but its direct relevance to economic choices and actions make it worthwhile to consider nonetheless (Miyake et al. 2000; Beshears, Milkman, and Schwartzstein 2016). In the context of this chapter—considering both psychological approaches and economic approaches—it is important to note that there is a key distinction between the ability to plan and the act of undertaking planning. The psychological approach to planning focuses more on planning *ability*. We will follow this approach here as a useful first step. However, the economic approach to planning would also want to consider whether an individual chooses to make a plan and follow through on it. Since those choices also draw on other domains, we will limit our discussion to measuring planning ability for the purposes of this chapter.

Measuring Higher-Order Cognitive Functions

This section describes tasks used to measure higher-order cognitive functions. We divide the tests into four categories: (a) cognitive flexibility, (b) fluid intelligence, (c) crystallized intelligence, and (d) planning.

I. Wisconsin Card Sorting Task. Measuring cognitive flexibility often involves a series of set-shifting tasks. A prominent example is the Wisconsin Card Sort Task, in which participants are provided with a deck of cards, each of which can be sorted by color, shape, or number (Berg 1948; Grant and Berg 1948). The objective here is for participants to learn the correct sorting criterion based on feedback provided by the experimenter as to whether they have sorted the card correctly. In this task, however, the rules change periodically and without notification, such that participants must learn to change the sorting rule based on the feedback they receive, which requires cognitive flexibility. In its standard form, the task requires the ability to read and understand numbers. However, it can be adjusted to only include color and shape.[5] On the other hand, it is easy to explain and can be conducted electronically or with paper cards, making it practical in field settings.

II. Raven's (Progressive) Matrices Test. The most common and universally accepted measure of fluid intelligence (and a frequent component of IQ tests) is the Raven's Matrices Test, developed by the British psychologist John Raven almost eighty years ago (Raven 1936, 2000). In this test, researchers ask participants to consider a main figure that is missing a section. The goal of the task is to choose the missing piece that will complete the figure with a logical pattern from a set of (typically eight) options. Easier versions of Raven's Matrices involve simple matching tasks such as identifying the shape that matches the other shapes in the figure, while more difficult puzzles require participants to solve an analytical problem or apply multiple logical rules (Prabhakaran et al. 1997). While the traditional Raven's Matrices set contains sixty such trials, more recent studies that use this task as part of a larger battery of tests use fewer trials (Mani et al. 2013; Raven 2000). Researchers can alter the difficulty of a Raven's Matrices task by increasing the number of multiple choice options available or the complexity of the rules participants must deduce to complete the puzzle.

III. Wechsler Adult Intelligence Scale (WAIS). Researchers frequently use this test to measure both fluid and crystallized intelligence. Composed of eleven subtests, the WAIS consists of both a "verbal" and a "performance" component (Lichtenberger and Kaufman 2009; Wechsler 2008). The verbal sections include vocabulary, digit span, comprehension, and arithmetic. The performance sections include picture completion and arrangement, object assembly, and so forth. There are three variants of Wechsler Intelligence Tests, designed for (a) adults, (b) young children, and (c) older children, each of varying difficulty. As described above, tasks that measure crystallized intelligence rely on previous knowledge. As a result, performance on subtests that involve vocabulary or sentence completion can be limited by language skills, making implementation and interpretation difficult in many developing-country settings. The test has been translated into over twenty languages to date.

---

5. See, for instance, "Berg's Card Sorting Test," the Psychology Experiment Building Language (PEBL) computerized version of the Wisconsin Card Sorting Task.

IV. Tower of London Task. The Tower of London Task is among the most common tasks used to measure planning ability. In this task, participants are presented with two configurations of three stacks of small colored disks arranged on pegs. The first configuration of the disks is the target or goal arrangement and the second configuration of the disks is the starting arrangement. The participant's task is to reach the goal arrangement from the starting arrangement in the fewest possible moves of disks (Banich 2009). To complete the task by moving the disks from the starting arrangement to the goal arrangement, participants must follow a number of different rules. The specifics of the rules may vary to alter the difficulty of the task, but typically fall into three categories: (a) the number of disks that can be moved at one time—typically just one disk can be moved at a time; (b) which disks can be moved—typically only the top disk in the stack; and (c) limits on the number of disks that can be placed on a single peg—typically either the same across all pegs or descending with the height of the peg (e.g., three disks on the tallest peg, two on the peg of intermediate height, and only one on the shortest peg).

As the goal of the task is to capture planning ability, the participants are asked to plan ahead mentally before carrying out the task physically. Participants typically undertake a large (e.g., twenty) number of trials of varied difficulty to more precisely capture the individual's ability. The complexity of the task can be increased by (a) increasing the number of colored disks used in the trial or (b) increasing the required number of moves to correctly complete the puzzle with a fixed number of disks. Outcome measures include the total number of moves, the number of trials solved in the fewest possible moves (considered to be "correct"), the time taken to plan in advance of starting to move the disks, and time taken to move the disks (Unterrainer et al. 2004).

2.2.6   Practical Concerns

Most of the tasks described above exhibit several useful features that promote ready utilization across a variety of domains. These features include ease of administration, broad applicability, and ease of instruction, as described in more detail in Schilbach, Schofield, and Mullainathan (2016). Yet, important caveats remain in order to successfully integrate these tasks into randomized trials or surveys. First among these is the importance of careful piloting of the task in the relevant population. As described above, there are often a variety of ways to adjust the difficulty of each task and piloting provides the opportunity to make appropriate adjustments for the population of interest. Selection of the task settings that are most appropriate for the context will help the researcher to avoid both floor and ceiling effects. In addition, integrating at least one and sometimes several practice rounds before starting the actual posttreatment trials to be used as outcome measures will reduce the variance unrelated to the treatment across participants. Piloting the task is typically necessary to identify the appropriate number of practice rounds to provide accurate measures and ensure comprehension of the task. Finally, piloting also provides an opportunity to fine-tune instructions in the local language and ensure that surveyors are providing complete and accurate instruction both via direct observation and via analysis of pilot data for variation in performance by the surveyor conducting the test.

Another important consideration in utilizing these tasks is the selection of appropriate outcome measures. In contexts with repeated measurement, participants increase proficiency, potentially leading to a significant fraction of participants reaching the maximal performance. This issue is particularly likely to arise for measures with a natural maximum (e.g., accuracy rates). It is possible to avoid this concern by considering measures without a natural maximum and with greater potential variation, such as reaction times. Some researchers have also used even more granular measurements of speed and accuracy, such as fastest 10 percent reaction times (Basner and Dinges 2011). Alternatively, another approach that can be effective in avoiding such concerns is to design the task to include multiple rounds of increasing difficulty.

2.2.7   Identifying Alternative Tasks

The tasks described here provide merely an overview of a few potential tasks that can be used to capture different elements of cognitive function. Many other tasks can also be used to measure these (and other) aspects of cognitive functions but were omitted for brevity. A number of websites provide resources to implement additional tasks, though they vary in the areas of cognitive functions targeted, as well as in flexibility and quality of implementation, instructions, and outcome data. A few such examples are provided below. In addition, although not yet finalized, the authors will post software and instructions for a number of the tasks described above to their websites shortly. This software is free of charge and is intended specifically for use in research, with flexible settings and comprehensive data collection.

Additional Resources for Cognitive Tasks:

1. ICAR: http://icar-project.org/. See also: http://icar-project.org/papers /ICAR2014.pdf.
2. Kikolabs: https://www.kikolabs.com/.
3. Cognitive Fun!: cogfun.net.

2.3   Impact of Poverty on Cognition and Economic Behavior

Although it may seem counterintuitive that a person's fundamental cognitive "capacity" can be altered by his or her circumstances, there is a small but growing literature that demonstrates poverty can and does impact cognitive function in a variety of ways. This section briefly discusses some of the factors associated with poverty that have been shown to impact cognitive function and economic behaviors. Moreover, it provides a nonexhaustive introduction to other aspects of life in poverty for which the evidence is more limited but suggestive of potential negative impacts and warrant further investigation. For each of the factors described below, a growing body of evidence of its impact on cognitive function and economic behaviors exists. However, much more evidence is needed to fully understand such impacts. Moreover, we have only very limited evidence regarding individuals' awareness of these potential effects.

2.3.1   Malnutrition

Throughout history, malnutrition has been associated with poverty. This relationship is still present today. One-seventh of the world's population is below the level of caloric intake recommended by health professionals, and the vast majority of these individuals are among the poor in developing countries (Food and Agricultural Organization of the United Nations et al. 2011). Economists have studied this relationship for over sixty years, modeling nutrition as both consumption and an input into physical productivity (Leibenstein 1957; Bliss and Stern 1978; Stiglitz 1976; Dasgupta and Ray 1986). However, in recent years, the possibility of such traps has been discounted due to good evidence that liquidity is unlikely to constrain investment in calories. Hence, a revealed preference argument suggests that despite the apparently low consumption, any productivity gains from additional caloric intake are likely to be relatively small—less than the discount rate. Yet, there are both behavioral and structural reasons why this argument may not hold and, to date, a potentially critical aspect of this relationship may have been overlooked: too little food may impact not only physical function, but also mental function: thoughts may become lethargic, attention difficult to sustain, and temptations harder to resist (Fonseca-Azevedo and Herculano-Houzel 2012; Gailliot et al. 2007; Danziger, Levav, and Avnaim-Pesso 2011; Baumeister and Vohs 2007; US Army Institute of Environmental Medicine 1987).

Schofield (2014) tests this idea with a randomized trial that examines the impact of additional calories on measures of cognitive function among low-BMI cycle-rickshaw drivers in India over a five-week period. Study participants undertook a battery of both physical and cognitive tasks at the beginning and end of the study, in addition to reporting their labor supply and earnings daily throughout the study. The increased caloric intake improved not only labor market outcomes, but also cognitive outcomes; treated individuals showed a 12 percent improvement in performance on the laboratory-based cognitive tasks. This gain occurred almost immediately and was sustained at the fifth week. In addition, these changes also manifested in a real-world effort discounting task in which participants could choose to provide no labor and earn nothing, to take a journey with a lighter load today, or to take a journey with a heavier load tomorrow, with both trips earning the same payment tomorrow. In this decision, treated participants were 25 percent more likely to opt to take the journey today instead of delaying at the cost of a more difficult trip tomorrow, suggesting a meaningful reduction in discount rates for effort in their work.

2.3.2 Excessive Alcohol Consumption

Excessive alcohol consumption has been associated with poverty at least since Fisher (1930), yet the underlying causal channels of this relationship remain largely unknown. Some aspects of poverty such as physical or mental pain might increase individuals' demand for alcohol by enhancing its short-term benefits. However, poverty might also be caused or deepened by excessive alcohol consumption. By impeding mental and physical function, alcohol consumption might distort decision-making and lower productivity. More specifically, Steele and Josephs (1990) posit in their "alcohol myopia" theory that alcohol's narrowing effect on attention causes individuals to focus on simple, present, and salient cues, which may in turn lead to short-sighted behaviors.

In a three-week randomized field experiment in Chennai, India, Schilbach (2017) tests whether such cognitive effects can translate into economically meaningful real-world consequences. In this study, financial incentives reduced daytime drinking among low-income workers in Chennai, India. Higher sobriety due to the incentives caused a large increase in individuals' daily savings as measured by their daily deposits into a personal savings box at the study office. Since the incentives for sobriety caused only minor changes in alcohol expenditures and labor market earnings, the impact of increased sobriety on savings behavior appears to be due to changes in myopia rather than due to purely mechanical effects via increased income net of alcohol expenditures. Similarly, in a completely different context, Ben-David and Bos (2017) provide complementary evidence on the negative impact of alcohol availability on credit-market behavior in Sweden.

Many open questions regarding the role of alcohol consumption in the lives of the poor remain. First, much more work is needed to understand the causal impact of alcohol consumption on individuals and their families, including labor market behaviors, family resources, decision-making, violence, and well-being among women and children. Second, the underlying determinants of the demand for alcohol remain largely unknown. In particular, we do not know whether factors associated with poverty such as physical and mental pain, depression, or sleep deprivation contribute to the demand for alcohol. Third, little is known about the effectiveness of different interventions to curb undesired drinking in developing countries. Of particular interest could be the evaluation of government policies such as increased taxes or even prohibition on consumption of alcohol and its substitutes, as well as on potential downstream consequences of heavy drinking including poverty levels.

2.3.3   Physical Pain

Heavy physical labor, uncomfortable living conditions, and limited access to adequate health care and pain-management tools all contribute to a disproportionate burden of physical pain in the lives of the world's poor (Poleshuck and Green 2008; Case and Deaton 2015). This inequality may be further compounded by disparate perceptions of pain; recent evidence suggests that economic insecurity in itself may increase perceived physical pain and lead to reduced pain tolerance (Chou, Parmar, and Galinsky 2016). Not surprisingly to those who have experienced physical pain, pain has been shown to negatively affect various cognitive domains including attention, learning, memory, speed of information processing, psychomotor ability, and capacity to self-regulate (Moriarty, McGuire, and Finn 2011; Nes, Roach, and Segerstrom 2009). Interference with one's thought process at inopportune moments can also make it difficult for individuals to focus, potentially competing for limited cognitive resources (Eccleston and Crombez 1999).

Such impacts on cognitive function have the potential to also affect economic decision-making, labor supply, and earnings. However, to date, few studies have investigated such effects. In one study, Kuhnen and Knutson (2005) found that people make more suboptimal financial decisions and are more risk averse after the anterior insula, the part of the brain that reacts to pain, is activated. Further, acute pain has been shown to increase shortsighted behavior as well as risk seeking when conditions involve potential gains (Koppel et al. 2017). Kilby (2015) considers the impact of changes in policies regarding prescription opioid pain relievers and finds increases in missed days for injured and disabled individuals. These studies underline the potential importance of a better understanding of the role of physical pain in the lives of the poor. However, much more evidence is needed to learn about the impact of physical pain on economic behavior and well-being among the poor as well as about potential policies to help individuals to alleviate their pain in a sustainable way.

2.3.4   Sleep Deprivation

While inadequate sleep is a widespread problem across the globe, the poor in particular may not sleep well (Patel et al. 2010; Centers for Disease Control 2015). Urban environments and developing countries are particularly prone to interfere with individuals' sleep due to the higher prevalence of ambient noise, heat, light, mosquitoes, stress, overcrowding, and overall uncomfortable physical conditions (Grandner et al. 2010; Patel et al. 2010). Moreover, suboptimal sleeping conditions may also hinder deep sleep, which is essential to cognitive functioning (Sadeh, Gruber, and Raviv 2002; Roehrs et al. 1994). Although not yet published, our data collected using small wristwatch-like actigraphs (which accurately measure sleep) worn by over 200 individuals for two weeks per person among the poor in Chennai, India, supports this idea. Individuals in our sample sleep just over five hours per night. This limited sleep may be further exacerbated by poor sleep quality, with more than twenty disruptions per night on average. Further, because the impacts of sleep deprivation increase with the cumulative extent of the deprivation, these impacts may be especially far-reaching among those with few options for "catching up" on sleep given poor sleep environments (Van Dongen, Mullington, and Dinges 2003; Basner et al. 2013).

A robust body of evidence demonstrates that sleep deprivation and low-quality sleep impair cognitive function, including reduction in attention and vigilance and impairments to memory and logical reasoning (Lim and Dinges 2010; Killgore 2010; Philibert 2005; Scott, McNaughton, and Polman 2006). Moreover, Baumeister and coauthors hypothesize that willpower is replenished overnight via sleep (Baumeister 2002). Similar to the literature on pain, much less work has been done to document the impact of these cognitive changes on economic decision-making and labor market outcomes. Notable exceptions include a series of papers by Dickinson and coauthors that demonstrate that acute sleep deprivation (such as a full night without sleep) has mixed effects on risk preferences (McKenna et al. 2007), reduces trust and trustworthiness (Dickinson and McElroy 2016), and reduces iterative reasoning in a p-beauty game in US populations (Dickinson and McElroy 2010). In addition, although the channels through which the effects operate are not explored, research utilizing shift work, shifts in sunset time, and child sleep quality as sources of quasi-exogenous variation in sleep find significant negative impacts of limited sleep on productivity (Gibson and Shrader 2015; Czeisler, Moore-Ede, and Coleman 1982; Costa-Font and Flèche 2017). However, much work remains to fully understand the productivity and decision-making consequences of sleep deprivation, particularly in developing-country contexts.

2.3.5 Monetary Concerns

One obvious consequence of being poor is having less money to buy things and improve one's environment. Less obviously, being poor also means having to spend more of one's cognitive resources managing what little money is available. The poor must manage sporadic income and constantly make difficult trade-offs between expenses. Even outside of financial decision-making, preoccupation with money and budgeting can act as a distraction, in effect taxing mental resources.

Mani et al. (2013) use two distinct but complementary research designs to establish the causal link between poverty and mental function. In the first study, the authors experimentally induce participants to think about everyday financial demands. For the rich participants, these thoughts are not worries. Yet for the poor, inducing these thoughts can trigger concern and distraction, with corresponding negative impacts on cognitive performance. Complementing this more "laboratory-style" study, the second study uses quasi-experimental variation in actual wealth over time among Indian farmers. Agricultural income is highly variable, with sugarcane farmers receiving income just once a year at harvest time. Because it is difficult to smooth their consumption across the year, these farmers experience cycles of poverty—poorer before harvest and richer after—generating the opportunity to compare the cognitive capacity of a given individual across both "rich" and "poor" states (the authors rule out competing explanations, such as nutrition or work effort). Both studies produce consistent effects, with large and direct negative impacts of poverty on cognitive function; when living in poverty, economic challenges also manifest as cognitive challenges.

While the effects found in Mani et al. (2013) are striking, they are yet to be replicated in other settings. In fact, in the US context Carvalho, Meier, and Wang (2016) find no changes in cognitive function or decision-making around paydays among low-income workers using a pre-post design. For both studies, important identification concerns remain, which emphasizes the need for additional well-identified studies. Moreover, the existing work has not considered real-world economic behaviors. As a result, it remains an open question whether poverty impedes cognitive function in ways that translate into meaningfully large effects on economic outcomes such as labor supply, productivity, or savings behavior.

2.3.6   Environmental Factors

A variety of environmental factors including noise, heat, and air pollution may also tax cognitive function. These environmental irritants may have direct and indirect impacts on the poor, especially in the developing world and in particular in urban areas where exposure to these environmental irritants is often high (World Bank 2015). While we focus only on specific noise and air pollution below, other types of pollution, such as water contaminants, could also potentially have an impact on cognitive function and decision-making either through direct chemical channels or through other channels such "disgust."[6]

Noise Pollution. In urban and developing environments, frequent noise pollution from car horns honking, dogs barking, or crowds chattering can make it difficult to focus and perform any given task at hand. Studies of noise levels in cities in developing countries have found noise levels significantly above World Health Organization (WHO)-recommended levels (Jamir, Nongkynrih, and Gupta 2014; Jamrah, Al-Omari, and Sharabi 2006; Zannin, Diniz, and Barbosa 2002; Oyedepo and Saadu 2009; Mehdi et al. 2011). In lab and field settings, increases in noise may not only induce anxiety and affect mood, but may also impair performance on cognitive tasks,

6. Emotions, such as disgust, can impact decision-making. For example, disgust has been shown in lab studies to decrease risk taking (Fessler, Pillsworth, and Flamson 2004) and reduce both sale and choice prices (Lerner, Small, and Loewenstein 2004).

particularly those that require attention and memory (Szalma and Hancock 2011; Hygge, Boman, and Enmarker 2003; Boman, Enmarker, and Hygge. 2003; Enmarker, Boman, and Hygge 2006). Noise can increase the mental workload needed for a particular situation by acting as an annoyance or stressor, in effect limiting the available cognitive resources (Becker et al. 1995). Children are at an additionally increased risk of the negative impact of noise exposure and show impairments in reading comprehension, attention, and memory when exposed to noise (Stansfeld et al. 2005; Clark and Stansfeld 2007; Hygge, Evans, and Bullinger 2002). Though rigorous evidence on the effects of long-term exposure to noise pollution is scarce, there are a few studies that suggest that impacts may continue to exist despite individuals becoming accustomed to this noise. Irgens-Hansen et al. (2015) find that increased noise is associated with slower response times to a visual attention task among employees on board Royal Norwegian Navy vessels, where noise-exposure levels are consistently higher than recommended levels. Stansfeld et al. (2005) study the effect of chronic exposure to aircraft and road traffic noise on cognitive function in children and find associations between long-term exposure to aircraft noise and reading comprehension and recognition memory impairments, though they find no association with sustained attention. Further, there is suggestive evidence that prolonged exposure to noise may impact working memory (Hockey 1986; Szalma and Hancock 2011). However, lab evidence suggests that with longer exposure to continuous noise, agents can develop coping strategies that allow them to mitigate the effects of this noise (Szalma and Hancock 2011). Despite the above indications of impacts on cognitive function, there is a dearth of evidence regarding the potential downstream impacts of noise pollution on decisions and productivity.

Heat. Similarly, excessive heat has the potential to impede cognitive function and impair motivation. However, evidence to this effect is mixed (Gaoua 2011). This factor and its potential impacts are particularly relevant to life in developing countries, where the tropical environments and the lack of air conditioning make oppressive heat a near constant for many individuals.[7] Existing evidence suggests that when exposed to an uncomfortably high temperature, reaction time and accuracy on attention, vigilance, and inhibitory control tasks are compromised (Simmons et al. 2008; Mazloumi et al. 2014). Moreover, exposure to excessive heat can impact productivity in manual work when the body is unable to maintain the appropriate core temperature (Kjellstrom, Holmer, and Lemke 2009). At the macro level, countries in hot climates have lower total agricultural output and economic growth, which

7. Given the long-term exposure to heat among those living in tropical regions, individuals do acclimatize to heat, which improves their physiological responses to heat exposure (Cheung and McLellan 1998; Fox et al. 1967). Radakovic et al. (2007) found that acclimation to heat did not improve performance on attention tasks; however, it did improve performance on more complex tests of cognitive function.

could be partially explained by workers' reduced cognitive functioning (Dell, Jones, and Olken 2012). As global climate shifts continue to occur, studying these causal impacts will become even more central, with the majority of the burden borne by those in developing countries (Intergovernmental Panel on Climate Change 2014). Although few studies to date map the entire causal chain from extreme heat to economic decisions and outcomes, recent research explores the effects of oppressive heat on downstream effects such as reduced worker productivity in developing-country settings (Adhvaryu, Kala, and Nyshadham 2016; Burke, Hsiang, and Miguel 2015; Dell, Jones, and Olken 2012; Jones and Olken 2010; Hsiang 2010) and to an extent in developed-country settings as well (Deryugina and Hsiang 2014; Cachon, Gallino, and Olivares 2012).

Air Pollution. The prevalence of less energy-efficient technologies and the lack of strong enforcement mechanisms for pollution regulations make high levels of air pollution common for many individuals living in urban developing environments (McGranahan and Murray 2003). Not only do pollutants harm physical health (Seaton et al. 1995; Pope 2000; Ghio, Kim, and Devlin 2000) and decrease life expectancy (Greenstone et al. 2015; WHO 2014; Lim et al. 2012), but there is also suggestive evidence that air pollution may be linked to reduced worker productivity (Chang et al. 2016a, 2016b; Adhvaryu, Kala, and Nyshadham 2014; Graff Zivin and Neidell 2012) and cognitive impairments in domains including attention, processing speed, and memory (Tzivian et al. 2015; Lavy, Ebenstein, and Roth 2014; Weuve et al. 2012; Power et al. 2011; Franco Suglia et al. 2008). Air pollution has also been shown to decrease performance on high-stakes academic tests (Ebenstein, Lavy, and Roth 2016; Ham, Zweig, and Avol 2011). Though further research needs to be conducted to establish a causal link, recent research studies have also found a correlation between exposure to air pollution and rates of dementia and Alzheimer's disease (Cacciottolo et al. 2017; Chen et al. 2017).

2.3.7   Stress and Depression

While other channels are likely operating as well, poverty might also affect cognitive function and economic behavior via its impacts on stress and depression. Stress and depression are widely prevalent across the globe. An estimated 350 million people globally suffer from depression (WHO 2016). Moreover, there is reason to believe that the poor are disproportionately likely to suffer from these ailments. Income and socioeconomic status have well-known correlations with stress and anxiety (Chen, Cohen, and Miller 2010; Fernald and Gunnar 2009; Evans and English 2002; Lupien et al. 2001), with levels of the stress hormone cortisol (Cohen, Doyle, and Baum 2006; Li et al. 2007; Saridjana et al. 2010), and with depression (Lund et al. 2010; WHO 2001). Recent research using both natural experiments and randomized field experiments provides evidence that this relationship is causal, that is, that low income increases stress levels. For instance, using random rainfall shocks in Kenya, Chemin, de Laat, and Haushofer (2016) find that negative income shocks raise stress levels as measured by increases in the stress hormone cortisol. Randomized controlled trials support these findings, showing that a reduction in poverty caused by cash transfers reduces both stress and depression (Haushofer and Shapiro 2016; Baird, De Hoop, and Özler 2013; Ozer et al. 2011; Fernald and Gunnar 2009).

A growing body of evidence considers the role of mental health in the lives of the poor. Among them, a number of studies show that inducing stress in laboratory settings can increase risk aversion (Kandasamya et al. 2013; Mather, Gorlick, and Lighthall 2009; Porcelli and Delgado 2009; Cahlíková and Cingl 2017; Lighthall, Mather, and Gorlick 2009). In contrast, the evidence on stress's impact on time discounting is mixed (Cornelisse et al. 2014; Haushofer et al. 2013; Haushofer, Jang, and Lynham 2015). Furthermore, chronic stress in childhood is inversely related to working memory in adults (Evans and Schamberg 2009). Researchers have only recently begun to study the effects of depression on economic decision-making, with several studies currently in the field. While these initial results focused primarily on short-run impacts of stress and depression are interesting, much more evidence is needed to understand the how these factors affect economic outcomes outside of laboratory settings. Moreover, most research to date considers the impact of short-term changes in stress. However, individuals often live in poverty for extended periods, suggesting that studies to understand the longer-term impact of chronic stress and depression on economic outcomes are particularly promising avenues of research.

2.4   Impact of Cognitive Functions on Economic Outcomes

Building on the previous section, which highlighted links from poverty to changes in cognitive function, this section discusses the reverse linkages from cognitive function to economic outcomes. Considering linkages in both directions highlights the significant potential for feedback loops, or cycles of poverty centered on changes in bandwidth.

With subsections dedicated to each of the areas of cognitive function covered in section 2.2, we begin by discussing the existing evidence, both theoretical and empirical, for such impacts. Then we provide conceptual background on how changes in that area of cognitive function may impact economic outcomes and poverty in ways that have yet to be studied. Importantly, these discussions are not exhaustive; the number of potential pathways is sufficiently vast that we can only highlight a select set of illustrative examples in each area.

2.4.1   Attention

Attention, and its role in economic life, has generated growing interest in recent years. Economists have recognized that attention is a scarce resource, creating very real trade-offs. We first briefly review four modeling approaches of attention in economics as examples of this literature and discuss the existing empirical evidence bearing on the predictions of each model. We then outline other outcomes that may be the result of attentional constraints, making them particularly promising directions for future research.

Theory

Four main strands of research modeling the role of attention in shaping economic behaviors have been developed. To the best of our knowledge, however, direct tests of these models—for example, by considering the impact of increases or decreases in attention on the outcomes of interest—have not been conducted to date.

I. Rational Inattention. Consistent with evidence from cognitive psychology research, the rational inattention literature considers attention to be a limited resource. Optimizing agents subject to attentional constraints allocate their available attention among competing sources of differing value. Most prominent in this literature, Sims (1998, 2003) proposes a model of limited attention as an information flow with a bound, where information is quantified as a reduction in uncertainty that comes at a cost. This model has widespread applicability to many decisions. Among other topics, Sims's rational inattention model has been applied to price setting (Woodford 2012; Maćkowiak and Wiederholt 2009; Matějka 2016), consumption versus savings problems with constant (Sims 2006; Luo 2008) and variable interest rates (Maćkowiak and Wiederholt 2015), portfolio management (Van Nieuwerburgh and Veldkamp 2009; Mondria 2010), political campaigns (Gul and Pesendorfer 2012), and discrimination (Bartoš et al. 2016).

II. Sparsity. Gabaix (2014, 2016) presents a model of bounded rationality in which individuals "sparsely maximize" or only pay attention to certain attributes. In this framework, an agent faces a choice of actions and must choose among them to maximize her utility, with her optimal action dependent on multiple variables. The agent uses a two-step algorithm to choose her utility-maximizing action. First, she chooses a "sparse" model of the world by ignoring many of the variables that could affect her optimal action. Second, she chooses a boundedly rational action with this endogenously chosen sparse model of the world. For each decision a person faces, there may be hundreds of relevant attributes, and it would be difficult, if not impossible, to take each of these into account. While there are likely other factors at play as well, one potential consequence of a consumer choosing a "sparse" model of the world is the "stickiness" of choices and individuals' propensity to follow default options, for instance, in organ donation (Johnson and Goldstein 2003) or retirement savings decisions (Madrian and Shea 2001; Choi et al. 2006; Beshears et al. 2009), and in insurance markets (Handel 2013; Handel and Kolstad 2015; Bhargava, Loewenstein, and Sydnor 2015), even when other potentially dominating options become available.

III. Salience. A third strand of theory directly models the salience of different attributes (prices, product characteristics, etc.) for different options in an agent's choice set and environment. In these models, salient attributes are defined as attributes that consumers disproportionately focus on and therefore overweight in their decision-making process. The key questions in such models are then what influences which attributes individuals focus on and which attributes are salient in different environments. Three approaches of modeling salience have been proposed to date (Bordalo, Gennaioli, and Shleifer 2012, 2013; Kőszegi and Szeidl 2013; Bushong, Rabin, and Schwartzstein. 2016). However, the empirical literature is yet to provide conclusive evidence testing the predictions of these theories against each other.

IV. Selective Attention. In a fourth strand of the economics literature on inattention, Schwartzstein (2014) details how selective attention can have *persistent* effects on belief formation and learning. Underlying Schwartzstein's model is the idea that what an agent attends to today is dependent on his or her current beliefs. Following from this, what the agent attends to today will then also affect his/her beliefs in the future. Accordingly, given an agent's incorrect initial beliefs or model of the world, this attentional strategy can lead to a failure to recognize important predictors or patterns (those outside the agent's existing model of the world), leading individuals to overlook key factors in their decision-making consistently and over long periods.

Empirical Evidence

To date, there is only limited empirical evidence directly testing the predictions of the above models, and in particular, evidence that can help to distinguish between the predictions of these models. As a result, it is likely too early to clearly predict how decreases in attentional constraints affect individuals' choices. However, one natural hypothesis is that an increase in attention (e.g., due to improved sleep) reduces biases in choice that the models discussed above predict and hence improves decision-making.

Empirical evidence for models centered on the role of attention can be found in a number of realms. We provide a few illustrative examples, but these effects are likely to apply much more broadly to areas such as savings, education, and health choices as well.

Technology Adoption. Hanna, Mullainathan, and Schwartzstein (2014) apply Schwartzstein's model to technology adoption in seaweed farming and demonstrate that even when people have repeated experience with a decision they may fail to notice important product attributes, and thus may fall continuously away from the production frontier. Similarly, Datta and Mullainathan (2014) note that programs to encourage the adoption of technology often fail and that it is essential that new users are attentive to certain features of the technology to use it effectively. Further, the selective-attention model has been used to explain low usage or nonadoption of technology or best practices. For instance, historically, there was delayed recognition of the importance of sterilizing operating rooms to prevent infections despite access to relevant data (Gawande 2004; Nuland 2004). Doctors had false beliefs about other causes of infection that prevented them from considering, or paying attention to, a simple, effective intervention such as hand washing. In a similar manner, Bloom et al. (2013) show that managers failed to adopt best practices in the Indian textile industry despite natural variation, which should permit learning about the importance of the attributes that contribute to best practices. However, to the best of our knowledge, there is no direct evidence linking changes in attention to changes in technology adoption.

Shrouded Attributes and Salience. A number of studies find that consumers pay only limited attention to taxes or certain product characteristics, often referred to as "shrouded attributes" (Gabaix and Laibson 2006). Accordingly, increasing or decreasing salience of these attributes can significantly affect sales (Chetty, Looney, and Kroft 2009; Gallagher and Muehlegger 2011), labor supply, and earnings behavior (Chetty and Saez 2013). In a study of commodity tax salience, Chetty, Looney, and Kroft (2009) find that a small increase in tax that is included in posted prices reduces demand more than when that tax is added to the price at the register. Although consumers are aware that the taxes exist (based on survey data), they fail to attend fully to these less-salient taxes at the time of purchase.

Other Potential Pathways

Despite the fact that attention receives more focus in the economics literature than most areas of cognitive function, there remain many unexplored ways in which constraints on attention may impact the lives of the poor.

Productivity. Existing theoretical work also links attention to poverty traps. Banerjee and Mullainathan (2008) present a model of poverty and attention based on the idea of attention scarcity. The authors note that wealthier individuals are likely to have access to goods that can reduce the attention required at home—for instance, water piped into their home or reliable childcare. The poor, who do not have access to distraction-limiting goods, are therefore more distracted at work, whereas the wealthier are able to devote more attention to work with less worry about problems at home, and thus the rich are more productive than the poor. While this is an intriguing hypothesis, direct empirical evidence of such effects is scarce.

Workplace and Traffic Accidents. Accidents are substantial concerns among the poor and are potentially driven in part by lapses in attention. The consequences of such attentional lapses may be larger for the poor, who often lack the safety nets or precautions that exist in more developed economies. Imagine a worker on a factory assembly line monotonously operating a machine, whose mind wanders off for a split second at the wrong moment. In many resource-poor settings, such a lapse often results in a serious accident. Similarly, consider the dire consequences of a driver who loses focus on a highway after hours of commuting every day. In fact, 41 percent of car crashes in the United States are estimated to be the result of recognition errors, including inattention (USDT 2008). Yet these lapse rates are likely to be significantly higher in developing countries where factors causing lapses, such as sleep deprivation or noise, are more prevalent and where the mechanisms to prevent accidents or mitigate their impacts, such as rumble strips, are less likely to be present.

Home Production and Childcare. Inattention to matters at home can have enormous consequences—for instance, not realizing a child is becoming sick or that a household good, such as water or kerosene, is running low. Lapses in attention can also cause more subtle and long-term consequences. For example, consider attending to one's children to ensure that they complete their homework, or that they stay healthy and safe. Although a single lapse may not have significant consequences, the effects are likely to compound and may have severe long-run welfare effects for the child, including increasing the likelihood of intergenerational transmission of poverty.

2.4.2 Inhibitory Control

An important aspect of inhibitory control is self-control—the ability to regulate one's behavior when faced with impulses and temptations in order to follow through on an intended plan. The study of self-control problems continues to receive enormous attention in the economics literature, including both theoretical and empirical work. Several excellent reviews survey this large body of work (Frederick, Loewenstein, and O'Donoghue 2002; DellaVigna 2009; Bryan, Karlan, and Nelson 2010).

Theory

To date, the two main strands of theoretical work on self-control that have been most influential are hyperbolic discounting and dual-self models.

Quasi-hyperbolic Discounting. Quasi-hyperbolic discounting theory is based on empirical findings that discounting is not time-invariant: individuals tend to put more weight on the immediate present than on the future (Frederick, Loewenstein, and O'Donoghue 2002). Laibson (1997) and O'Donoghue and Rabin (1999) formalize quasi-hyperbolic discounting models of these observed preferences, building on work by Strotz (1956), Phelps and Pollak (1968), and Akerlof (1991). These models have two parameters governing intertemporal preferences—δ, the standard long-run discount factor, and β, the short-run parameter that represents the desire for immediate gratification. When $\beta < 1$, discounting between the present and future periods is higher than between future time periods and the agent's preferences are time-inconsistent. A decision maker's awareness of his or her future preferences can have important effects on behavior. O'Donoghue and Rabin (1999, 2001) model expectations of future time preferences, and define three types of agents: (a) sophisticated agents who know they will exhibit present bias in the future; (b) naive agents, who falsely believe their future self is not present-biased; and (c) partially naive agents who know that they exhibit self-control issues, but underestimate the extent of the bias, causing these agents to be overconfident about their future level of self-control.

Dual-Self Models. The other prominent strand of theoretical work on self-control focuses on dual-self models (Fudenberg and Levine 2006; Gul and Pesendorfer 2001, 2004). Dual-self models differ in structure, but they all include a short-run self and a long-run self, which often find themselves in conflict. The short-run doer is myopic and mostly concerned with the present, while the long-run planner is concerned with lifetime utility (Thaler and Shefrin 1981). The long-run planner can exert influence over the short-run doer, but this comes at a cost (Fudenberg and Levine 2006). In a different type of dual-self model, the temptation-preference model of Gul and Pesendorfer (2001, 2004), agents consider preferences among choice sets. While most models of intertemporal choice assume that options not chosen are irrelevant to utility, Gul and Pesendorfer's model posits that agents experience disutility from not choosing the most tempting current option. Thus agents can avoid temptation, but there is an associated cost to this avoidance. Therefore, agents can benefit when they remove tempting options from their choice sets.

Empirical Evidence

A large empirical literature has considered how self-control problems influence economic behavior. However, cleanly identified evidence of the causal impact of income, wealth, or other factors that affect bandwidth on self-control and time preferences is scarce. More generally, we only have a limited understanding of the underlying determinants of self-control problems and causes of differences in self-control across people and within people over time. Moreover, to the best of our knowledge, no studies to date have considered the underlying determinants of individuals' naïveté regarding future self-control problems.

Borrowing, Saving, and Investing. A body of evidence suggests that self-control problems interfere with low-income individuals' intertemporal choices.[8] A number of studies detail instances in which the poor fail to take advantage of small and divisible high-return investment opportunities. Moreover, the poor are more likely to borrow at high interest rates, taking out loans routinely rather than only for emergencies (Aleem 1990; Karlan and Mullainathan 2010; Banerjee and Mullainathan 2010). Several studies find evidence that self-control impacts individuals' consumption-savings choices. Ashraf, Karlan, and Yin (2006) report high take-up rates and significantly increased savings due to a commitment savings product in the Philippines, revealing a causal impact of self-control problems on savings behavior. Dupas and Robinson (2013) find that study participants in a field

8. See Haushofer and Fehr (2014) for a discussion of poverty and time discounting.

experiment in Kenya increase savings and benefit from access to simple, safe, savings accounts, as well as from earmarked savings accounts and Rotating Savings and Credit Associations (ROSCAs). However, among study participants with time-inconsistent preferences, access to a simple savings account and earmarked savings account did not increase savings, while access to ROSCAs did. This evidence suggests that providing access to safe savings technologies may not be sufficient to increase savings. Other factors—external societal pressure or commitment devices—might aid those with time-inconsistent preferences in achieving their desired long-run savings goals.

Consumption Choices. Beyond distortions in intertemporal choice, there is also evidence that self-control problems interfere with individuals' consumption choices across periods. Such evidence exists in particular for addictive goods. In line with Gruber and Kőszegi (2001), Giné et al. (2010) find demand for a voluntary commitment product for smoking cessation in the Philippines, which produced moderate improvements in long-term smoking cessation. In a field study among low-income workers in India, Schilbach (2017) finds that about half of study participants exhibit demand for commitment to increase their sobriety, again revealing self-control problems. Moreover, about a third of participants were willing to give up at least ten percent of their daily incomes in order to receive incentives to remain sober.

Productivity. People who recognize that they suffer from self-control problems may seek commitment devices to improve their productivity. Ariely and Wertenbroch (2002) run experiments in which students are allowed to preemptively set due dates for school assignments, and find that students are willing to self-impose costly deadlines. While these self-imposed deadlines did improve overall performance, these deadlines were not set optimally. In a real-world work setting, Kaur, Kremer, and Mullainathan (2015) find evidence that self-control problems interfere with worker productivity. Employees at a data entry firm were offered weakly dominated "commitment" contracts, which paid less than the standard piece rate if a production target was not met, and the standard piece rate if the production target was met. The authors find substantial demand for commitment among the workers. Moreover, workers who were *offered* such commitment contracts were significantly more productive and enjoyed higher earnings.

Other Potential Pathways

While the study of self-control in poverty is already extensive, there are many ways in which potential cognitive changes that alter self-control can impact the lives of the poor. Health, education, and crime are potential channels that could be explored further. First, in addition to refraining from addictive substances that can harm health, self-control is essential for other health factors, such as attending yearly checkups at the doctor or maintaining a healthy weight. Rates of overweight and obesity are rising rapidly in many developing countries. As calories become less expensive and more readily and consistently available, individuals will require substantial self-control in order to regulate intake and maintain a healthy weight. Second, self-control might have important implications for educational attainment. Students need to exercise self-control to be able to get up in the morning to attend class, pay attention to the teacher, study new material, and complete homework assignments. Deficiencies in self-control are likely to impact academic attendance, performance, and eventual achievement. Third, one prominent theory on crime, the "self-control" or "general" theory of crime, posits that low levels of individual self-control are the main factor driving criminal behavior (Gottfredson and Hirschi 1990). This view has received empirical support in the criminology literature (Pratt and Cullen 2000), as well as from recent research on cognitive behavior therapy (CBT) in Liberia (Blattman, Jamison, and Sheridan 2017).

As in the case of attention, lapses in self-control could be more costly for those living in poverty. Splurging on a tasty snack item or a new item of clothing is hardly a life-changing event for the wealthy. Among the poor, however, lapses in self-control can have far-reaching consequences, such as expensive cycles of debt as described above. Moreover, the self-control available might be systematically different for poorer individuals if they are exposed to more temptations in their everyday lives than the rich. However, while intriguing, there is no direct causal evidence of this hypothesis. Much more work in this area is needed.

2.4.3   Memory

There is a small but growing theoretical literature on the relationship between memory and economic outcomes. After briefly reviewing this literature, we discuss the related empirical evidence, which mainly focuses on memory's impacts on health and savings.

Theory

While economic theory on memory is less developed than the literature on attention or inhibitory control, a number of models do exist. We discuss three of these approaches.

Rehearsal and Associativeness. Mullainathan (2002) provides an economic model of memory limitations that can explain certain biases and empirical puzzles (e.g., over- or underreaction to news in financial markets). In doing so, Mullainathan (2002) draws on two constructs from the psychological and biological literatures on memory: *rehearsal*, the idea that it is easier to remember an event after having remembered it once before, and *associativeness*, the idea that it is easier to recall an event that is similar to current events. Both of these concepts affect how accessible a given memory is and can thus be explanations for observed behavioral biases.

The Cost of Keeping Track. Haushofer (2015) shows that keeping track of incomplete tasks generates costs to the agent in the form of financial consequences (e.g., late fees) and/or psychological consequences of keeping the task in mind. Haushofer models these costs as a lump sum, and shows that such costs can lead people to "pre-crastinate," or incur a loss in the present rather than in the future. Haushofer provides empirical support for his model using experimental evidence from Kenya. Haushofer notes that this model of memory can be valuable in many settings within development economics—for example, by providing options that do not require people to pay the cost of keeping track—such as providing chlorine at the place where water is collected rather than in the home, which has been shown to improve usage (Kremer et al. 2009).

Memory and Procrastination. Ericson (2017) describes how reminders can have significant effects on actions, yet deadlines—which should prompt agents to overcome present bias and act—are often ignored, even when such actions lead to substantial losses.[9] Ericson shows that the interaction of present bias and memory can explain these phenomena. His model suggests that anticipated reminders, such as deadlines, can induce procrastination, while unexpected reminders might bring welfare-inducing actions to the top of mind, spurring action.

Empirical Evidence

A relatively large body of evidence demonstrates the importance of memory to economically important outcomes by providing evidence that reminders can effectively alter agents' behaviors. However, we are not aware of research that considers the direct impact of interventions to improve memory on economic outcomes.

Health. A large share of the evidence on reminders stems from the medical literature, in particular the literature on medical adherence (see Haynes et al. [2008] and Vervloet et al. [2012] for overviews). A relatively robust finding from this literature is that reminders typically have a modest but meaningful impact on healthful behaviors including smoking cessation (Free et al. 2011), adherence to medication and treatment regimens (Pop-Eleches et al. 2011; Dulmen et al. 2007; Krishna, Boren, and Balas 2009), and preventive health behaviors such as sunscreen use (Armstrong et al. 2009).

Savings. Conducting an experiment with commitment savings customers in Bolivia, Peru, and the Philippines, Karlan et al. (2016) show that reminders can increase savings. The authors vary reminders sent to customers and find that reminders increase savings and that reminders of specific future goals, which often require a high lumpy expense, are particularly effective at increasing savings. This evidence shows that memory and recall are partially responsible for low savings and suggests that reminding people of long-term

---

9. For example, King (2004) finds that students fail to apply for financial aid by the deadlines, and Pechmann and Silk (2013) find that people do not submit rebates prior to their expiration.

goals can effectively alter behavior. Significant effects of reminders have also been found for loan repayments (Karlan, Morten, and Zinman, forthcoming; Cadena and Schoar 2011).

Other Potential Pathways

Memory also plays a central role in a wide range of other economic behaviors, as evidenced by the effectiveness of reminders in a wide variety of domains beyond the health applications above. Examples include donations (Damgaard and Gavert 2014), appointment sign-ups (Altmann and Traxler 2012) and show-ups (Guy et al. 2012), and rebate claims (Letzler and Tasoff 2014), among others. However, memory is central to economic outcomes beyond simply remembering to undertake tasks. In particular, working memory plays an important role in understanding language, doing mental math, updating information or actions, and considering alternatives. As such, improving working memory might affect a range of important behaviors and decisions, ranging from technology adoption among small-scale farmers to shopkeepers' inventory choices and low-income workers' decisions to (not) migrate to cities during lean seasons. Moreover, impediments to working memory are associated with higher discount rates and impulsiveness (Hinson, Jameson, and Whitney 2003). The ability to consider alternatives and make prudent, rather than impulsive, decisions is essential for sound long-run decision-making.

Although to the best of our knowledge unstudied to date, low levels of literacy may interact with memory in important ways. On the one hand, individuals with low literacy are forced to rehearse their memory on a daily basis as they are not able to write down instructions, directions, or other key information, which might improve their memory capacity. However, being forced to keep a lot of information in mind ties up existing mental resources, which in turn may reduce the cognitive capacity available to be devoted to other decisions and tasks. Take, for example, a farmer learning about a new fertilizer or seed variety. Remembering the advice of an agricultural extension agent for a number of months and then recalling it at the appropriate time might drain cognitive resources, which in turn may distort other important choices or result in a loss of other potentially valuable information. Such burdens are largely shouldered by the poor due to their lower levels of literacy and numeracy.

2.4.4   Higher-Order Executive Functions

Compared to other components of cognitive function, economic theory and empirical evidence on higher-order executive functions are less developed. We posit a number of areas where these functions may play an important role in behavior and decision-making and provide some suggestive empirical evidence on these effects.

Theory

Economists would likely all agree with the notion that intelligence and planning affect economic outcomes in important ways. However, the economic theory machinery to map changes in higher-order executive functions into economic behavior is yet to be developed. We therefore focus on existing empirical evidence.

Empirical Evidence

Below we outline the existing empirical evidence regarding the role of cognitive flexibility, intelligence, and planning in shaping economic behavior.

Optimization Behavior. Traditional economic theory posits that agents optimize their choices based on their preferences, beliefs, and constraints. Therefore, given the same choice set with the same preferences and information, agents should make the same utility-optimizing choices. However, research shows that this is not always the case and that in certain situations decision-making is inconsistent (Famulari 1988; Sippel 1997; Février and Visser 2004). Recent research shows that cognitive ability, measured using a variation of the Raven's matrices test and the Cognitive Reflection Test (Frederick 2005), may also be related to inconsistent or seemingly random decision-making (Andersson et al. 2016). Choi et al. (2014) test for consistency in utility maximization and find that consistency scores vary significantly within and across socioeconomic groups, with consistency particularly strongly related to wealth. Poorer individuals exhibit lower consistency even when controlling for unobserved constraints, preferences, and beliefs. However, we do not know whether this relationship is causal. There exists no direct evidence that increasing income or wealth (for instance, via cash transfers) improves choice consistency.

Innovation and Creativity. Psychologists widely regard cognitive flexibility to be an important aspect of both innovation and creativity (Chi 1997; Jaušovec 1991, 1994; Runco and Okuda 1991; Thurston and Runco 1999; Torrance 1974). Cognitive flexibility can facilitate creativity, and thereby increase innovation by helping individuals see a problem from a new perspective and shift strategies to more efficiently solve a problem (Thurston and Runco 1999; Okuda, Runco, and Berger 1991). Higher-order thinking can also enable individuals to switch between conceptual ideas and thus avoid getting stuck on one piece of a problem.

Labor Market Outcomes. There is a wide body of literature that highlights the importance of cognitive skills, often measured by intelligence scores, in predicting wages (Murnane, Willett, and Levy 1995), on-the-job performance and training success (Bishop 1991), and schooling (Cawley, Heckman, and Vytlacil 2001). Assessing the effects of general intelligence on future labor market success is difficult given that it is so strongly and inextricably correlated with educational attainment, making measurement of the separate effects of these factors difficult or impossible (Cawley, Heckman, and Vytlacil 2001; Heckman and Vytlacil 2001). However, even controlling for educational attainment, Judge, Hurst, and Simon (2009) find that general mental ability (as measured by a battery of tests including Raven's matrices and the Wechsler Intelligence Test) has a significant direct effect on income levels. Further, the authors find that general mental ability has significant indirect effects on income through its impact on education and self-esteem. Results from developing countries are more mixed. Psacharopoulos and Velez (1992) find that intelligence—as measured by Raven's matrices test—accounts for a small portion of the return to education on wages in Colombia. Fafchamps and Quisumbing (1999) find that, controlling for education, intelligence as measured by the Raven's matrices test, has an insignificant effect on earnings from crops, livestock, and nonfarm labor in rural Pakistan. Vogl (2014) studies the height premium on wages in Mexico—the additional wages associated with being taller—and finds that cognitive ability, as measured by the Raven's matrices test, accounts for only a small share of the height premium, while educational attainment and occupational selection account for approximately half this premium. However, Vogl suggests that cognitive ability may play an important role through its indirect effects on educational attainment and occupational sorting.

Other Potential Pathways

In addition to the empirical evidence outlined above, we hypothesize that higher-order executive functions may play a role in other areas of economic interest.

Technology Adoption. To be willing to adopt a given technology, agents must be willing and able to see themselves and their surroundings in other states of the world. For instance, a farmer considering the adoption of a new crop must foresee and plan how to sell the crop in the subsequent season. Such flexibility and planning is essential as the investment needed to adopt a new technology generally takes place prior to the realization of benefits. In short, it is necessary to be able to imagine the potential costs and benefits of the technology prior to adopting it. Moreover, the ability to accurately learn about the costs and benefits of new technologies likely directly depends on higher-order cognitive functions and, in particular, fluid intelligence.

Resilience. Cognitive flexibility is a key component of resilience. It allows individuals to reframe or reappraise a situation instead of getting stuck in a particular mind-set, providing more potential solutions to a problem. Further, cognitive flexibility enables individuals to reevaluate and adjust their perceptions of difficult and traumatic events, which can help them to understand the trauma and recover from it. For example, after surviving a traumatic event, cognitive flexibility can enable an individual to maintain the belief that he or she will prevail despite the difficulties of life.

Cooperation. Cognitive flexibility even has the potential to effect cooperation and interpersonal relationships. Consider interpersonal disagreements or conflicts—the ability to see the world through the eyes of others is often helpful in order to resolve conflict when there are different preferences or opinions. This, in turn, could have potential implications in models of household bargaining, social cohesion and trust, and workplace relationships.

2.5   Open Questions and Future Research Directions

Cognitive function and its implications for human behavior and economic outcomes are not poverty-specific—they are applicable in a much broader range of settings and across many income levels. However, understanding the relationship between cognitive function and economic behavior is particularly relevant to the study of economic development and poverty because poverty may be both a cause and a consequence of changes in cognitive function. An adult's cognitive ability is traditionally considered fixed. However, recent evidence shows that it is variable and can be affected by circumstances. Poverty has associated hardships—lack of nutritious food, limited access to medical care, difficult working conditions, and the stress of paying bills—which all have the potential to impair cognitive ability. Shifts in cognitive ability, in turn, can lead to diminished productivity and impaired decision-making, thus potentially deepening poverty and creating a feedback loop that may even generate the potential for poverty traps.

Although some evidence of this potential exists, much remains unknown regarding the exact nature of the bidirectional relationships between areas of cognitive function and poverty. This relative paucity of knowledge generates an open and valuable area of research to pursue. How do poverty and environment shape cognitive function, and how does cognitive function shape economic outcomes? There are specific components of poverty that have already been studied and shown to affect cognitive ability, such as scarcity (Mani et al. 2013) and poor nutrition (Schofield 2014). Yet numerous other components and correlates of poverty may affect cognitive function in ways that are not yet well understood, such as lack of sleep, chronic pain, or noise and air pollution. Beyond these relationships, there are many other valuable directions of inquiry in this area to understand these relationships comprehensively, and in doing so, potentially inform both basic knowledge and policy. For example, does long-run exposure to aspects of poverty (e.g., chronic physical pain or sleep deprivation) increase or decrease the associated impacts on cognitive function and economic behavior? Should policies target poverty, leading to improvements in cognitive function, or should they target improvements in cognitive function to reduce poverty? Are there important interaction effects between different aspects of life in poverty? Are individuals aware of the effects of poverty and do they adjust their behavior accordingly (e.g., by avoiding to make important choices while being tired or in pain)? What is the correlation of different aspects of cognitive function between and within individuals? Is bandwidth an asset that can be accumulated, generating a reserve?

Seeking a deeper, more nuanced understanding of cognitive function has enormous potential to help us understand the causes and consequences of poverty. Although a broad topic with many overlapping aspects, cognitive function does consist of measurable and reasonably distinct components. In this chapter we have outlined four components of cognitive function that are important to economics—attention, inhibitory control, memory and working memory, and higher-order executive functions, which include cognitive flexibility, fluid and crystallized intelligence, and planning. While we know a fair amount about how to measure cognitive function, we know far less about its influence on productivity and decision-making. Now that the tools are available, there is a lot more to be learned.

Appendix

Table 2A.1   Summary table of cognitive tasks

Task name	Description	Background needed	Manipulation of difficulty	Modes of administration
	Simple attention			
Psychomotor Vigilance Task (PVT)	A task that measures the accuracy and reaction time of participants responding to a stimulus.	No	Yes	Electronic only
	Complex attention			
Concentration Endurance Test	A task that requires participants to view a continuous list of letters p and d, with up to two markings above and/or two markings below the letter. The participant has to cross out d's that are surrounded by exactly two markings. Can be adjusted for respondents who are illiterate or whose native language does not use the Latin alphabet.	In some forms affected by literacy	No	Paper or electronic
	Inhibitory control			
Hearts and Flowers Task	This task requires participants to learn two rules, and then switch between them flexibly. Specifically, the screen is divided into two panels and either a heart or a flower is flashed onto one side of the screen. Participants are first shown only hearts and are asked to click on the same side of the screen as the heart. They are then only shown flowers and are asked to click on the opposite side of the screen as the flowers. In a third trial, they are shown both hearts and flowers and must click on the appropriate side according to the stimulus.	No	Yes	Electronic only
Eriksen Flanker Task	Participants are shown stimuli and are asked to only respond to the central stimuli, ignoring the stimuli surrounding it.	In certain forms, literacy is required	Limited	Electronic only

(continued)

Table 2A.1 (continued)

Task name	Description	Background needed	Manipulation of difficulty	Modes of administration
Classic Stroop Test	A task in which participants see the name of a color printed in a different ink color, and the participant is asked to name the ink color (e.g., the word "green" is written in red ink and the participant is expected to reply with "red").	Literacy required	No	Paper or electronic
Spatial Stroop Test	Participants are shown stimuli with both relevant and irrelevant dimensions, and are told only to respond to the relevant dimension. One common version has participants respond to arrows shown on different sides of a screen, and press in the direction the arrow is pointing.	No	Yes	Electronic only
Short-term memory				
Forward Digit Span Task	Participants are asked to listen to a list of numbers and repeat them back in the same order. Can be modified for subjects without numeracy to include objects in place of numbers.	Numeracy required in traditional version	Yes	Verbal or electronic
Corsi Block Test	Participants are shown a series of blocks, which are indicated one at a time by a change of color or pointing in a random sequence. Participants are then asked to click on or point to the blocks in the sequence just shown. A modified version of this task requires subjects to reorder the blocks, which measures working memory.	No	Yes	Paper or electronic
Working memory				
Backward Digit Span Task	Participants are asked to listen to a list of numbers and repeat them in numerical or reverse-numerical order. Can be modified for subjects without numeracy to include objects in place of numbers.	Numeracy required in traditional version	Yes	Verbal or electronic
N-Back Task	Participants are shown a series of stimuli and asked to respond if the current stimuli match the stimuli shown n steps previously. This task can be presented orally, visually, or as both modes simultaneously.	No	Yes	Electronic and/or auditory

Task	Description			
Self-Ordered Pointing Task	Participants are shown a number of items (e.g., physical items or different drawings or symbols) and asked to touch one item at a time, in any order, without repeating a choice while the items are scrambled in between turns.	No	Yes	Using physical items, paper, or electronic
Cognitive flexibility				
Wisconsin Card Sorting Task	Participants are provided with a deck of cards, each of which can be sorted by color, shape, or number. Participants attempt to learn the correct sorting criterion based on feedback and are expected to switch sorting rules if they receive feedback that the rules have changed. The task can be modified for subjects without numeracy.	Numeracy required in traditional form	No	Paper or electronic
Fluid intelligence and crystallized intelligence				
Raven's (Progressive) Matrices Test	Participants are shown visual geometric designs missing one piece and are given six to eight choices and asked to pick the one that represents the missing piece.	No	Yes	Paper or electronic
Wechsler Adult Intelligence Scale (WAIS)	Participants complete a verbal section covering vocabulary, digit span, comprehension, and arithmetic, and a performance section including picture completion/arrangement, object assembly, and so forth.	Literacy and numeracy required, education can affect outcomes	Yes	Paper or electronic
Planning				
Tower of London Task	Participants are tasked with configuring one stack of colored disks to match a second goal configuration in as few moves as possible.	No	Yes	Physical objects or electronic

References

Adhvaryu, Achyuta, Namrata Kala, and Anant Nyshadham. 2014. "Management and Shocks to Worker Productivity: Evidence from Air Pollution Exposure in an Indian Garment Factory." Working paper, Department for International Development.
———. 2016. "The Light and the Heat: Productivity Co-benefits of Energy-Saving Technology." Working paper, University of Michigan.
Akerlof, George. 1991. "Procrastination and Obedience." *American Economic Review Papers and Proceedings* 81 (2): 1–19.
Aleem, Irfan. 1990. "Imperfect Information, Screening, and the Costs of Informal Lending: A Study of a Rural Credit Market in Pakistan." *World Bank Economic Review* 4 (3): 329–49.
Altmann, Steffan, and Christian Traxler. 2012. "Nudges at the Dentist." IZA Discussion Paper no. 6699, Institute of Labor Economics.
Andersson, Ola, Håkan J. Holm, Jean-Robert Tyran, and Erik Wengström. 2016. "Risk Aversion Relates to Cognitive Ability: Preferences or Noise?" *Journal of the European Economic Association* 14 (5): 1129–54.
Andrewes, David G. 2001. *Neuropsychology: From Theory to Practice*, 2nd ed. East Sussex, UK: Psychology Press.
Ariely, Dan, and Klaus Wertenbroch. 2002. "Procrastination, Deadlines, and Performance: Self-Control by Precommitment." *Psychological Science* 13 (3): 219–24.
Armstrong, April W., Alice J. Watson, Maryanne Makredes, Jason E. Frangos, Alexandra B. Kimball, and Joseph C. Kvedar. 2009. "Text-Message Reminders to Improve Sunscreen Use: A Randomized, Controlled Trial Using Electronic Monitoring." *Archives of Dermatology* 145 (11): 1230–36.
Ashraf, Nava, Dean Karlan, and Wesley Yin. 2006. "Tying Odysseus to the Mast: Evidence from a Commitment Savings Product in the Philippines." *Quarterly Journal of Economics* 121 (2): 635–72.
Baddeley, Alan D., and Graham Hitch. 1974. "Working Memory." In *The Psychology of Learning and Motivation*, vol. 8, edited by Gordon H. Bower, 47–89. Cambridge, MA: Academic Press.
Baird, Sarah, Jacobus De Hoop, and Berk Özler. 2013. "Income Shocks and Adolescent Mental Health." *Journal of Human Resources* 48 (2): 370–403.
Bandiera, Oriana, Robin Burgess, Narayan Das, Selim Gulesci, Imran Rasul, and Munshi Sulaiman. 2015. "Labor Markets and Poverty in Village Economies." STICERD-Economic Organisation and Public Policy Discussion Papers Series no. 058, Suntory and Toyota International Centres for Economics and Related Disciplines.
Banerjee, Abhijit, and Esther Duflo. 2011. *Poor Economics: A Radical Rethinking of the Way to Fight Global Poverty*. New York: PublicAffairs.
Banerjee, Abhijit, Esther Duflo, Nathanael Goldberg, Dean Karlan, Robert Osei, William Parienté, Jeremy Shapiro, Bram Thuysbaert, and Christopher Udry. 2015. "A Multifaceted Program Causes Lasting Progress for the Poor: Evidence from Six Countries." *Science* 348 (6236). https://doi.org/10.1126/science.1260799.
Banerjee, Abhijit, and Sendhil Mullainathan. 2008. "Limited Attention and Income Distribution." *American Economic Review Papers & Proceedings* 98 (2): 489–93.
———. 2010. "The Shape of Temptation: Implications for the Economic Lives of the Poor." NBER Working Paper no. 15973, Cambridge, MA.
Banich, Marie T. 2009. "Executive Function: The Search for an Integrated Account." *Current Directions in Psychological Science* 18 (2): 89–94.

Barrett, Christopher B., and Michael R. Carter. 2013. "The Economics of Poverty Traps and Persistent Poverty: Empirical and Policy Implications." *Journal of Development Studies* 49 (7): 976–90.

Barrett, Christopher B., Teevrat Garg, and Linden McBride. 2016. "Well-Being Dynamics and Poverty Traps." *Annual Review of Resource Economics* 8:303–27.

Bartoš, Vojtěch, Michal Bauer, Julie Chytilová, and Filip Matějka. 2016. "Attention Discrimination: Theory and Field Experiments with Monitoring Information Acquisition." *American Economic Review* 106 (6): 1437–75.

Basner, Mathias, and David F. Dinges. 2011. "Maximizing Sensitivity of the Psychomotor Vigilance Test (PVT) to Sleep Loss." *Sleep* 34 (5): 581–91.

Basner, Mathias, Daniel Mollicone, and David F. Dinges. 2011. "Validity and Sensitivity of a Brief Psychomotor Vigilance Test (PVT-B) to Total and Partial Sleep Deprivation." *Acta Astronautica* 69 (1): 949–59.

Basner, Mathias, Hengyi Rao, Namni Goel, and David F. Dinges. 2013. "Sleep Deprivation and Neurobehavioral Dynamics." *Current Opinion in Neurobiology* 23 (5): 854–63.

Bates, Marsha E., and Edward P. Lemay. 2004. "The d2 Test of Attention: Construct Validity and Extensions in Scoring Techniques." *Journal of the International Neuropsychological Society* 10 (3): 392–400.

Baumeister, Roy F. 2002. "Yielding to Temptation: Self-Control Failure, Impulsive Purchasing, and Consumer Behavior." *Journal of Consumer Research* 28 (1): 670–76.

Baumeister, Roy F., Ellen Bratslavsky, Mark Muraven, and Dianne M. Tice. 1998. "Ego Depletion: Is the Active Self a Limited Resource?" *Journal of Personality and Social Psychology* 74 (5): 1252–65.

Baumeister, Roy F., and Kathleen D. Vohs. 2007. "Self-Regulation, Ego Depletion, and Motivation." *Social and Personality Psychology Compass* 1 (1): 115–28.

Becker, Ami B., Joel S. Warm, William N. Dember, and Peter A. Hancock. 1995. "Effects of Jet Engine Noise and Performance Feedback on Perceived Workload in a Monitoring Task." *International Journal of Aviation Psychology* 5 (1): 49–62.

Ben-David, Itzak, and Marieke Bos. 2017. "Impulsive Consumption and Financial Wellbeing: Evidence from an Increase in the Availability of Alcohol." NBER Working Paper no. 23211, Cambridge, MA.

Berg, Esta A. 1948. "A Simple Objective Technique for Measuring Flexibility in Thinking." *Journal of General Psychology* 39:415–22.

Beshears, John, James J. Choi, David Laibson, and Brigitte C. Madrian. 2009. "The Importance of Default Options for Retirement Saving Outcomes: Evidence from the United States." In *Social Security Policy in a Changing Environment*, edited by Gary Burtless, 167–95. Chicago: University of Chicago Press.

Beshears, John, Katherine L. Milkman, and Joshua Schwartzstein. 2016. "Beyond Beta-Delta: The Emerging Economics of Personal Plans." *American Economic Review* 106 (5): 430–34.

Bhargava, Saurabh, George Loewenstein, and Justin Sydnor. 2015. "Do Individuals Make Sensible Health Insurance Decisions? Evidence from a Menu with Dominated Options." NBER Working Paper no. 21160, Cambridge, MA.

Bishop, John H. 1991. "The Impact of Academic Competencies on Wages, Unemployment and Job Performance." CAHRS Working Paper no. 91-34, Center for Advanced Human Resource Studies, Cornell University.

Blattman, Christopher, Julian C. Jamison, and Margaret Sheridan. 2017. "Reducing Crime and Violence: Experimental Evidence from Cognitive Behavioral Therapy in Liberia." *American Economic Review* 107 (4): 1165–206.

Bliss, Christopher, and Nicholas Stern. 1978. "Productivity, Wages, and Nutrition: Part I: The Theory." *Journal of Development Economics* 5 (4): 331–62.

Bloom, Nicholas, Benn Eifert, Aprajit Mahajan, David McKenzie, and John Roberts. 2013. "Does Management Matter? Evidence from India." *Quarterly Journal of Economics* 128:1–51.

Boman, Eva, Ingela Enmarker, and Staffan Hygge. 2003. "Strength of Noise Effects on Memory as a Function of Noise Source and Age." *Noise & Health* 7 (27): 11–26.

Bordalo, Pedro, Nicola Gennaioli, and Andrei Shleifer. 2012. "Salience Theory of Choice under Risk." *Quarterly Journal of Economics* 127 (3): 1243–85.

———. 2013. "Salience and Consumer Choice." *Journal of Political Economy* 121 (5): 803–43.

Borella, Erika, Barbara Carretti, and Santiago Pelegrina. 2010. "The Specific Role of Inhibition in Reading Comprehension in Good and Poor Comprehenders." *Journal of Learning Disabilities* 43 (6): 541–52.

Broadbent, Donald. 1958. *Perception and Communication*. London: Pergamon Press.

Brunetti, Riccardo, Claudia Del Gatto, and Franco Delogu. 2014. "eCorsi: Implementation and Testing of the Corsi Block-Tapping Task for Digital Tablets." *Frontiers in Psychology* 5:1–8.

Bryan, Gharad, Dean Karlan, and Scott Nelson. 2010. "Commitment Devices." *Annual Review of Economics* 2:671–98.

Burke, Marshall, Solomon M. Hsiang, and Edward Miguel. 2015. "Global Nonlinear Effect of Temperature on Economic Production." *Nature* 527:235–39.

Bushong, Ben, Matthew Rabin, and Josh Schwartzstein. 2016. "A Model of Relative Thinking." Working paper, Harvard Business School, Harvard University.

Cacciottolo, Mafalda, Xinhui Wang, Ira Driscoll, Nicholas Woodward, Arian Saffari, Jeanette Reyes, Mark L. Serre, et al. 2017. "Particulate Air Pollutants, APOE Alleles and their Contributions to Cognitive Impairment in Older Women and to Amyloidogenesis in Experimental Models." *Translational Psychiatry* 7:1–8.

Cachon, Gerard P., Santiago Gallino, and Marcelo Olivares. 2012. "Severe Weather and Automobile Assembly Productivity." Columbia Business School Research Paper no. 12-37, Columbia University.

Cadena, Ximena, and Antoinette Schoar. 2011. "Remembering to Pay? Reminders vs. Financial Incentives for Loan Payments." NBER Working Paper no. 17020, Cambridge, MA.

Cahlíková, Jana, and Lubomir Cingl. 2017. "Risk Preferences under Acute Stress." *Experimental Economics* 20 (1): 209–36.

Canas, Jose J., Jose F. Quesada, Adoracion Antoli, and Inmaculada Fajardo. 2002. "Cognitive Flexibility and Adaptability to Environmental Changes in Dynamic Complex Problem-Solving Tasks." *Ergonomics* 46 (5): 482–501.

Carlin, Danielle, Joy Bonerba, Michael Phipps, Gene Alexander, Mark Shapiro, and Jordan Grafman. 2000. "Planning Impairments in Frontal Lobe Dementia and Frontal Lobe Lesion Patients." *Neuropsychologia* 38 (5): 655–65.

Carlson, Stephanie M., and Louis J. Moses. 2001. "Individual Differences in Inhibitory Control and Children's Theory of Mind." *Child Development* 72 (4): 1032–53.

Carvalho, Leandro, Stephan Meier, and Stephanie Wang. 2016. "Poverty and Economic Decision-Making: Evidence from Changes in Financial Resources at Payday." *American Economic Review* 106 (2): 260–84.

Case, Anne, and Angus Deaton. 2015. "Rising Morbidity and Mortality in Midlife among White Non-Hispanic Americans in the 21st Century." *Proceedings of the National Academy of Sciences USA (PNAS)* 112 (49): 15078–83.

Cattell, Raymond B. 1963. "Theory of Fluid and Crystallized Intelligence: A Critical Experiment." *Journal of Educational Psychology* 54 (1): 1–22.

Cattell, Raymond B., and John L. Horn. 1966. "Refinement and Test of the Theory of Fluid and Crystallized General Intelligence." *Journal of Educational Psychology* 57 (5): 253–70.

Cawley, John, James Heckman, and Edward Vytlacil. 2001. "Three Observations on Wages and Measured Cognitive Ability." *Labour Economics* 8 (4): 419–42.

Centers for Disease Control and Prevention. 2015. "Quickstats: Percentage of Adults Who Average ≤6 Hours of Sleep, by Family Income Group and Metropolitan Status of Residence, National Health Interview Survey, United States, 2013." Accessed September 5, 2016. http://www.cdc.gov/mmwr/preview/mmwrhtml/mm6412a10.htm.

Chang, Tom, Joshua Graff Zivin, Tal Gross, and Matthew Neidell. 2016a. "The Effect of Pollution on Worker Productivity: Evidence from Call-Center Workers in China." NBER Working Paper no. 22328, Cambridge, MA.

———. 2016b. "Particulate Pollution and the Productivity of Pear Packers." *American Economic Journal: Economic Policy* 8 (3): 141–69.

Chemin, Matthieu, Joost de Laat, and Johannes Haushofer. 2016. "Negative Rainfall Shocks Increase Levels of the Stress Hormone Cortisol among Poor Farmers in Kenya." Working paper. Available at https://papers.ssrn.com/sol3/papers.cfm?abstract_id=2294171.

Chen, Edith, Sheldon Cohen, and Gregory E. Miller. 2010. "How Low Socioeconomic Status Affects 2-Year Hormonal Trajectories in Children." *Psychological Science* 21 (1): 31–37.

Chen, Hong, Jeffrey C. Kwong, Ray Copes, Karen Tu, Paul J. Villeneuve, Aaron van Donkelaar, Perry Hystad, et al. 2017. "Living Near Major Roads and the Incidence of Dementia, Parkinson's Disease, and Multiple Sclerosis: A Population-Based Cohort Study." *Lancet* 389 (10070): 718–26.

Chetty, Raj, Adam Looney, and Kory Kroft. 2009. "Salience and Taxation: Theory and Evidence." *American Economic Review* 99 (4): 1145–77.

Chetty, Raj, and Emmanuel Saez. 2013. "Teaching the Tax Code: Earnings Responses to an Experiment with EITC Recipients." *American Economic Journal: Applied Economics* 5 (1): 1–31.

Cheung, Stephen S., and Tom M. McLellan. 1998. "Heat Acclimation, Aerobic Fitness, and Hydration Effects on Tolerance during Uncompensable Heat Stress." *Journal of Applied Physiology* 84 (5): 1731–39.

Chi, Michelene T. H. 1997. "Creativity: Shifting across Ontological Categories Flexibly." In *Creative Thought: An Investigation of Conceptual Structures and Processes*, edited by Thomas B. Ward, Steven M. Smith, and Jyotsna Vaid, 209–34. Washington, DC: American Psychological Association.

Choi, James, David Laibson, Brigitte Madrian, and Andrew Metrick. 2006. "Saving for Retirement on the Path of Least Resistance." In *Behavioral Public Finance*, edited by Edward McCaffrey and Joel Slemrod, 304–52. New York: Russell Sage.

Choi, Syngjoo, Shachar Kariv, Wieland Müller, and Dan Silverman. 2014. "Who Is (More) Rational?" *American Economic Review* 104 (6): 1518–50.

Chou, Eileen Y., Bidhan L. Parmar, and Adam D. Galinsky. 2016. "Economic Insecurity Increases Physical Pain." *Psychological Science* 27 (4): 1–12.

Chun, Marvin M., Julie D. Golomb, and Nicholas B. Turk-Browne. 2011. "A Taxonomy of External and Internal Attention." *Annual Review of Psychology* 62 (1): 73–101.

Clark, Charlotte, and Stephen A. Stansfeld. 2007. "The Effect of Transportation Noise on Health and Cognitive Development: A Review of Recent Evidence." *International Journal of Comparative Psychology* 20 (2): 145–58.

Cohen, Ronald A. 2014. *The Neuropsychology of Attention*, 2nd ed. New York: Springer US.

Cohen, Sheldon, William J. Doyle, and Andrew Baum. 2006. "Socioeconomic Status Is Associated with Stress Hormones." *Psychosomatic Medicine* 68 (3): 414–20.

Cornelisse, Sandra, Vanessa van Ast, Johannes Haushofer, Maayke Seinstra, and Marian Joëls. 2014. "Time-Dependent Effect of Hydrocortisone Administration on Intertemporal Choice." Working paper. Available at https://papers.ssrn.com /sol3/papers.cfm?abstract_id=2294189.

Corsi, Philip M. 1972. "Human Memory and the Medial Temporal Region of the Brain." *Dissertation Abstracts International* 34:819B.

Costa-Font, Joan, and Sarah Flèche. 2017. "Parental Sleep and Employment: Evidence from a British Cohort Study." CEP Discussion Paper no. dp1467, Centre for Economic Performance.

Cowan, Nelson. 2008. "What Are the Differences between Long-Term, Short-Term, and Working Memory?" *Progress in Brain Research* 169: 323–38.

Currie, Janet, and Douglas Almond. 2011. "Human Capital Development before Age Five." *Handbook of Labor Economics* 4:1315–486.

Czeisler, Charles A., Martin C. Moore-Ede, and Richard H. Coleman. 1982. "Rotating Shift Work Schedules That Disrupt Sleep Are Improved by Applying Circadian Principles." *Science* 217 (4558): 460–63.

Damgaard, Mette, and Christina Gavert. 2014. "Now or Never! The Effect of Deadlines on Charitable Giving: Evidence from a Natural Field Experiment." Economics Working Paper no. 2014-03, Department of Economics and Business Economics, Aarhus University.

Daneman, Meredyth, and Patricia A. Carpenter. 1980. "Individual Differences in Working Memory and Reading." *Journal of Verbal Learning and Verbal Behavior* 19 (4): 450–66.

———. 1983. "Individual Differences in Integrating Information between and within Sentences." *Journal of Experimental Psychology: Learning, Memory, and Cognition* 9 (4): 561–84.

Danziger, Shai, Jonathan Levav, and Liora Avnaim-Pesso. 2011. "Extraneous Factors in Judicial Decisions." *Proceedings of the National Academy of Sciences USA (PNAS)* 108 (7): 6889–92.

Dasgupta, Partha, and D. Ray. 1986. "Inequality as a Determinant of Malnutrition and Unemployment: Theory." *Economic Journal* 96 (384): 1011–34.

Datta, Saugato, and Sendhil Mullainathan. 2014. "Behavioral Design: A New Approach to Development Policy." *Review of Income and Wealth* 60 (1): 7–35.

Davidson, Matthew C., Dima Amso, Loren C. Anderson, and Adele Diamond. 2006. "Development of Cognitive Control and Executive Functions from 4 to 13 Years: Evidence from Manipulations of Memory, Inhibition, and Task Switching." *Neuropsychologia* 44 (11): 2037–78.

de Frias, Cindy M., Roger A. Dixon, and Esther Strauss. 2006. "Structure of Four Executive Functioning Tests in Healthy Older Adults." *Neuropsychology* 20 (2): 206–14.

Dell, Melissa, Benjamin F. Jones, and Benjamin A. Olken. 2012. "Temperature Shocks and Economic Growth: Evidence from the Last Half Century." *American Economic Journal: Macroeconomics* 4 (3): 66–95.

DellaVigna, Stefano. 2009. "Psychology and Economics: Evidence from the Field." *Journal of Economic Literature* 47 (2): 315–72.

Dempster, Frank N. 1992. "The Rise and Fall of the Inhibitory Mechanism: Toward a Unified Theory of Cognitive Development and Aging." *Developmental Review* 12 (1): 45–75.

Deryugina, Tatyana, and Solomon M. Hsiang. 2014. "Does the Environment Still Matter? Daily Temperature and Income in the United States." NBER Working Paper no. 20750, Cambridge, MA.

Diamond, Adele. 2013. "Executive Functions." *Annual Review of Psychology* 64:135–68.

Diamond, Adele, W. Steven Barnett, Jessica Thomas, and Sarah Munro. 2007. "Preschool Program Improves Cognitive Control." *Science* 318:1387–88.

Diamond, Adele, and Colleen Taylor. 1996. "Development of an Aspect of Executive Control: Development of the Abilities to Remember What I Said and to 'Do as I Say, Not as I Do.'" *Developmental Psychobiology* 29 (4): 315–34.

Dickinson, David L., and Todd McElroy. 2010. "Rationality around the Clock: Sleep and Time-of-Day Effects on Guessing Game Responses." *Economics Letters* 108 (2): 245–48.

———. 2016. "Sleep Restriction and Time-of-Day Impacts on Simple Social Interaction." IZA Discussion Paper no. 9673, Institute of Labor Economics.

Dinges, David F., Frances Pack, Katherine Williams, Kelly A. Gillen, John W. Powell, Geoffrey E. Ott, Caitlin Aptowicz, and Allan I. Pack. 1997. "Cumulative Sleepiness, Mood Disturbance, and Psychomotor Vigilance Performance Decrements during a Week of Sleep Restricted to 4–5 Hours per Night." *Sleep* 20 (4): 267–77.

Dorrian, Jillian, Naomi L. Rogers, and David F. Dinges. 2005. "Psychomotor Vigilance Performance: A Neurocognitive Assay Sensitive to Sleep Loss." In *Sleep Deprivation: Clinical Issues, Pharmacology and Sleep Loss Effects*, edited by Clete Kushida, 39–70. New York: Marcel Dekker.

Dulmen, Sandra, Emmy Sluijs, Liset Dijk, Denise Ridder, Rob Heerdink, and Jozien Bensing. 2007. "Patient Adherence to Medical Treatment: A Review of Reviews." *BMC Health Services Research* 7 (1): 55–68.

Duncan, Greg J., Chantelle J. Dowset, Amy Claessens, Katherine Magnuson, Aletha C. Huston, Pamela Klebanov, Linda S. Pagani, et al. 2007. "School Readiness and Later Achievement." *Developmental Psychology* 43 (6): 1428–46.

Dupas, Pascaline, and Jonathan Robinson. 2013. "Why Don't the Poor Save More? Evidence from Health Savings Experiments." *American Economic Review* 103 (4): 1138–71.

Ebenstein, Avraham, Victor Lavy, and Sefi Roth. 2016. "The Long-Run Economic Consequences of High-Stakes Examinations: Evidence from Transitory Variation in Pollution." *American Economic Journal: Applied Economics* 8 (4): 36–65.

Eccleston, Chris, and Geert Crombez. 1999. "Pain Demands Attention: A Cognitive-Affective Model of the Interruptive Function of Pain." *Psychological Bulletin* 125 (3): 356–66.

Egeland, Jens, Susanne Nordby Johansen, and Torill Ueland. 2009. "Differentiating between ADHD Sub-types on CCPT Measures of Sustained Attention and Vigilance." *Scandinavian Journal of Psychology* 50 (1): 347–54.

Enmarker, Ingela, Eva Boman, and Staffan Hygge. 2006. "Structural Equation Models of Memory Performance across Noise Conditions and Age Groups." *Scandinavian Journal of Psychology* 47:449–60.

Ericson, Keith Marzilli. 2017. "On the Interaction of Memory and Procrastination: Implications for Reminders, Deadlines and Empirical Estimation." *Journal of the European Economic Association* 5 (3): 692–719.

Eriksen, Barbara A., and Charles W. Eriksen. 1974. "Effects of Noise Letters upon the Identification of a Target Letter in a Nonsearch Task." *Perception and Psychophysics* 16 (1): 143–49.

Evans, Gary W., and Kimberly English. 2002. "The Environment of Poverty: Multiple Stressor Exposure." *Child Development* 73 (4): 1238–48.

Evans, Gary W., and Michelle A. Schamberg. 2009. "Childhood Poverty, Chronic Stress, and Adult Working Memory." *Proceedings of the National Academy of Sciences USA (PNAS)* 106 (16): 6545–49.

Fafchamps, Marcel, and Agnes R. Quisumbing. 1999. "Human Capital, Productivity, and Labor Allocation in Rural Pakistan." *Journal of Human Resources* 34 (2): 369–406.

Famulari, Melissa. 1988. "A Household-Based, Nonparametric Test of Demand Theory." *Review of Economics and Statistics* 77 (2): 372–82.

Fang, Hanming, and Glenn C. Loury. 2005. "Dysfunctional Identities Can Be Rational." *American Economic Review* 95 (2): 104–11.

Fernald, Lia, and Megan R. Gunnar. 2009. "Effects of a Poverty-Alleviation Intervention on Salivary Cortisol in Very Low-Income Children." *Social Science & Medicine* 68 (12): 2180–89.

Fessler, Daniel M. T., Elizabeth G. Pillsworth, and Thomas J. Flamson. 2004. "Angry Men and Disgusted Women: An Evolutionary Approach to the Influence of Emotions on Risk Taking." *Organizational Behavior and Human Decision Processes* 95:107–23.

Février, Philippe, and Michael Visser. 2004. "A Study of Consumer Behavior Using Laboratory Data." *Experimental Economics* 7 (1): 93–114.

Fisher, Irving. 1930. *The Theory of Interest, as Determined by Impatience to Spend Income and Opportunity to Invest It.* New York: MacMillan.

Fonseca-Azevedo, Karina, and Suzana Herculano-Houzel. 2012. "Metabolic Constraint Imposes Trade-Off between Body Size and Number of Brain Neurons in Human Evolution." *Proceedings of the National Academy of Sciences USA (PNAS)*, 109 (45): 18571–76.

Food and Agricultural Organization of the United Nations, International Fund for Agricultural Development, and World Food Programme. 2011. *The State of Food Insecurity in the World 2011. How does International Price Volatility Affect Domestic Economies and Food Security?* Rome: Food and Agriculture Organization Publications.

Fox, R. H., R. Goldsmith, I. F. G. Hampton, and T. J. Hunt. 1967. "Heat Acclimatization by Controlled Hyperthermia in Hot-Dry and Hot-Wet Climates." *Journal of Applied Physiology* 22 (1): 39–46.

Franco Suglia, Shakira, Charis Gryparis, Robert O. Wright, Joel Schwartz, and R. John Wright. 2008. "Association of Black Carbon with Cognition among Children in a Prospective Birth Cohort Study." *American Journal of Epidemiology* 167 (3): 280–86.

Frederick, Shane. 2005. "On the Ball: Cognitive Reflection and Decision-Making." *Journal of Economic Perspectives* 19 (4): 25–42.

Frederick, Shane, George Loewenstein, and Ted O'Donoghue. 2002. "Time Discounting and Time Preference: A Critical Review." *Journal of Economic Literature* 40 (2): 351–401.

Free, Caroline, Rosemary Knight, Steven Robertson, Robyn Whittaker, Phil Edwards, Weiwei Zhou, Anthony Rodgers, John Cairns, Michael G. Kenward, and Ian Roberts. 2011. "Smoking Cessation Support Delivered via Mobile Phone Text Messaging (txt2stop): A Single-Blind, Randomised Trial." *Lancet* 378 (9785): 49–55.

Friedman, Naomi P., Akira Miyake, Robin P. Corley, Susan E. Young, John C. DeFries, and John K. Hewitt. 2006. "Not All Executive Functions Are Related to Intelligence." *Psychological Science* 17 (2): 172–79.

Fudenberg, Drew, and David K. Levine. 2006. "A Dual-Self Model of Impulse Control." *American Economic Review* 96 (5): 1449–76.

Gabaix, Xavier. 2014. "A Sparsity-Based Model of Bounded Rationality." *Quarterly Journal of Economics* 129 (4): 1661–710.

———. 2016. "Behavioral Macroeconomics via Sparse Dynamic Programming." NBER Working Paper no. 21848, Cambridge, MA.

Gabaix, Xavier, and David Laibson. 2006. "Shrouded Attributes, Consumer Myopia, and Information Suppression in Competitive Markets." *Quarterly Journal of Economics* 121 (2): 505–40.

Gailliot, Matthew T., Roy F. Baumeister, C. Nathan DeWall, Jon K. Maner, E. Ashby Plant, Dianne M. Tice, Lauren E. Brewer, and Brandon J. Schmeichel. 2007. "Self-Control Relies on Glucose as a Limited Energy Source: Willpower Is More Than a Metaphor." *Journal of Personality and Social Psychology* 92 (2): 325–36.

Gallagher, Kelly Sims, and Erich Muehlegger. 2011. "Giving Green to Get Green? Incentives and Consumer Adoption of Hybrid Vehicle Technology." *Journal of Environmental Economics and Management* 61 (1): 1–15.

Gaoua, Nadia. 2011. "The Effects of Heat Exposure on Cognitive Performance." *Scandinavian Journal of Medicine & Science in Sports* 20 (3): 60–70.

Gawande, Atul. 2004. "On Washing Hands." *New England Journal of Medicine* 350:1283–86.

Ghio, Andrew J., Chong Kim, and Robert B. Devlin. 2000. "Concentrated Ambient Air Particles Induce Mild Pulmonary Inflammation in Healthy Human Volunteers." *American Journal of Respiratory and Critical Care Medicine* 162 (3.1): 981–88.

Gibson, Matthew, and Jeffrey Shrader. 2015. "Time Use and the Labor Market: The Wage Returns to Sleep." Department of Economics Working Paper no. 2015-17, Department of Economics, Williams College.

Giné, Xavier, Dean Karlan, and Jonathan Zinman. 2010. "Put Your Money Where Your Butt Is: A Commitment Contract for Smoking Cessation." *American Economic Journal: Applied Economics* 2:213–35.

Glass, David C., Jerome E. Singer, and Lucy N. Friedman. 1969. "Psychic Cost of Adaptation to an Environmental Stressor." *Journal of Personality and Social Psychology* 12 (3): 200–210.

Godefroy, Olivier, Maryline Cabaret, Violaine Petit-Chenal, Jean-Pierre Pruvo, and Marc Rousseaux. 1999. "Control Functions of the Frontal Lobes. Modularity of the Central-Supervisory System?" *Cortex* 35 (1): 1–20.

Gottfredson, Michael R., and Travis Hirschi. 1990. *A General Theory of Crime.* Palo Alto, CA: Stanford University Press.

Graff Zivin, Joshua, and Matthew Neidell. 2012. "The Impact of Pollution on Worker Productivity." *American Economic Review* 102 (7): 3652–73.

Grandner, Michael A., Nirav P. Patel, Philip R. Gehrman, Dawei Xie, Daohang Sha, Terri Weaver, and Nalaka Gooneratne. 2010. "Who Gets the Best Sleep? Ethnic and Socioeconomic Factors Related to Sleep Complaints." *Sleep Medicine* 11:470–78.

Grant, David A., and Esta A. Berg. 1948. "A Behavioral Analysis of Degree of Reinforcement and Ease of Shifting to New Responses in Weigl-Type Card-Sorting Problem." *Journal of Experimental Psychology* 38:404–11.

Greenstone, Michael, Janhavi Nilekani, Rohini Pande, Nicholas Ryan, Anant Sudarshan, and Anish Sugathan. 2015. "Lower Pollution, Longer Lives: Life Expectancy Gains If India Reduced Particulate Matter Pollution." *Economic & Political Weekly* 1 (8): 40–46.

Gruber, Jonathan, and Botond Kőszegi. 2001. "Is Addiction Rational? Theory and Evidence." *Quarterly Journal of Economics* 116:1261–303.

Gul, Faruk, and Wolfgang Pesendorfer. 2001. "Temptation and Self-Control." *Econometrica* 69:1403–35.

———. 2004. "Self-Control, Revealed Preferences and Consumption Choice." *Review of Economic Dynamics* 7 (2): 243–64.

———. 2012. "The War of Information." *Review of Economic Studies* 79 (2): 707–34.

Guy, Rebecca, Jane Hocking, Handon Wand, Sam Stott, Hammad Ali, and John Kaldor. 2012. "How Effective Are Short Message Service Reminders at Increasing Clinic Attendance? A Meta-analysis and Systematic Review." *Health Services Research* 47 (2): 614–32.

Hagger, Martin S., Nikos L. D. Chatzisarantis, H. Alberts, C. O. Anggono, C. Batailler, A. R. Birt, R. Brand, et al. 2016. "A Multilab Preregistered Replication of the Ego-Depletion Effect." *Perspectives on Psychological Science* 11 (4): 546–73.

Ham, John C., Jacqueline S. Zweig, and Edward Avol. 2011. "Pollution, Test Scores and the Distribution of Academic Achievement: Evidence from California Schools 2002–2008." http://www.iza.org/conference_files/TAM2012/ham_j1496.pdf.

Handel, Benjamin R. 2013. "Adverse Selection and Inertia in Health Insurance Markets: When Nudging Hurts." *American Economic Review* 103 (7): 2643–82.

Handel, Benjamin R., and Jonathan T. Kolstad. 2015. "Health Insurance for Humans: Information Frictions, Plan Choice, and Consumer Welfare." *American Economic Review* 105 (8): 2449–500.

Hanna, Rema, Sendhil Mullainathan, and Joshua Schwartzstein. 2014. "Learning through Noticing: Theory and Evidence from a Field Experiment." *Quarterly Journal of Economics* 129 (3): 1311–53.

Hasher, Lynn, and Rose T. Zacks. 1998. "Working Memory, Comprehension, and Aging: A Review and a New View." In *The Psychology of Learning and Motivation: Advances in Research and Theory*, edited by G. H. Bower, 193–225. San Diego, CA: Academic.

———. 2006. "Aging and Long-Term Memory: Deficits Are Not Inevitable." In *Lifespan Cognition: Mechanisms of Change*, edited by Ellen Bialystock and Fergus I. M. Craik, 162–77. New York: Oxford University Press.

Haushofer, Johannes. 2015. "The Cost of Keeping Track." Working paper, Princeton University.

Haushofer, Johannes, Sandra Cornelisse, Maayke Seinstra, Ernst Fehr, Marian Joëls, and Tobias Kalenscher. 2013. "No Effects of Psychosocial Stress on Intertemporal Choice." *PLOS One* 8 (11): e78597.

Haushofer, Johannes, and Ernst Fehr. 2014. "On the Psychology of Poverty." *Science* 344 (6186): 862–67.

Haushofer, Johannes, Chaning Jang, and John Lynham. 2015. "Stress and Temporal Discounting: Do Domains Matter?" Working paper, Princeton University.

Haushofer, Johannes, and Jeremy Shapiro. 2016. "The Short-Term Impact of Unconditional Cash Transfers to the Poor: Experimental Evidence From Kenya." *Quarterly Journal of Economics* 131 (4): 1973–2042.

Haynes, R. Brian, Elizabeth Ackloo, Navdeep Sahota, Heather Pauline McDonald, and Xiaomei Yao. 2008. "Interventions for Enhancing Medication Adherence." *Cochrane Database of Systematic Reviews* 16 (2). https://doi.org/10.1002/14651858.CD000011.pub3.

Heckman, James, and Edward Vytlacil. 2001. "Identifying the Role of Cognitive Ability in Explaining the Level of and Change in the Return of Schooling." *Review of Economics and Statistics* 83 (1): 1–12.

Hinson, John M., Tina L. Jameson, and Paul Whitney. 2003. "Impulsive Decision Making and Working Memory." *Journal of Experimental Psychology: Learning, Memory, and Cognition* 29 (2): 298–306.

Hockey, G. Robert J. 1986. "Changes in Operator Efficiency as a Function of Environmental Stress, Fatigue, and Circadian Rhythms." In *Handbook of Human Perception and Performance: Vol. 2. Cognitive Processes and Performance*, edited by Kenneth R. Boff, Lloyd Kaufman, and James P. Thomas, 1–49. New York: Wiley.

Hofmann, Wilhelm, Malte Friese, and Fritz Strack. 2009. "Impulse and Self-Control from a Dual-Systems Perspective." *Perspectives on Psychological Science* 4 (2): 162–76.

Hofmann, Wilhelm, Wolfgang Rauch, and Bertram Gawronski. 2007. "And Deplete Us Not into Temptation: Automatic Attitudes, Dietary Restraint and Self-Regulatory Resources as Determinants of Eating Behavior." *Journal of Experimental Social Psychology* 43 (1): 497–504.

Horn, John L., and Raymond B. Cattell. 1967. "Age Differences in Fluid and Crystallized Intelligence." *Acta Psychologica* 26 (1): 107–29.

Hsiang, Solomon M. 2010. "Temperatures and Cyclones Strongly Associated with Economic Production in the Caribbean and Central America." *Proceedings of the National Academy of Sciences USA (PNAS)* 107 (35): 15367–72.

Hygge, Staffan, Eva Boman, and Ingela Enmarker. 2003. "The Effects of Road Traffic Noise and Meaningful Irrelevant Speech on Different Memory Systems." *Scandinavian Journal of Psychology* 44:13–21.

Hygge, Staffan, Gary W. Evans, and Monika Bullinger. 2002. "A Prospective Study of Some Effects of Aircraft Noise on Cognitive Performance in Schoolchildren." *Psychological Science* 13 (5): 469–74.

Intergovernmental Panel on Climate Change. 2014. "Summary for Policymakers." In *Climate Change 2014: Impacts, Adaptation, and Vulnerability. Part A: Global and Sectoral Aspects. Contribution of Working Group II to the Fifth Assessment Report of the Intergovernmental Panel on Climate Change*, edited by C. B. Field, V. R. Barros, D. J. Dokken, K. J. Mach, M. D. Mastrandrea, T. E. Bilir, M. Chatterjee, et al., 1–32. Cambridge: Cambridge University Press.

Inzlicht, Michael, and Brandon J. Schmeichel. 2012. "What Is Ego Depletion? Toward a Mechanistic Revision of the Resource Model of Self-Control." *Perspectives on Psychological Science* 7 (5): 450–63.

Irgens-Hansen, Kaja, Hilde Gundersen, Erlend Sunde, Valborg Baste, Anette Harris, Magne Bråtveit, and Bente E. Moen. 2015. "Noise Exposure and Cognitive Performance: A Study on Personnel on Board Royal Norwegian Navy Vessels." *Noise & Health* 17 (78): 320–27.

Jaeggi, Susanne M., Martin Buschkuehl, Walter J. Perrig, and Beat Meier. 2010. "The Concurrent Validity of the N-Back Task as a Working Memory Measure." *Memory* 18 (4): 394–412.

Jaeggi, Susanne M., Ria Seewer, Arto C. Nirkko, Doris Eckstein, Gerhard Schroth, Rudolf Groner, and Klemens Gutbrod. 2003. "Does Excessive Memory Load Attenuate Activation in the Prefrontal Cortex? Load-Dependent Processing in Single and Dual Tasks: Functional Magnetic Resonance Imaging Study." *Neuroimage* 19 (2): 210–25.

Jalan, Jyotsna, and Martin Ravallion. 2002. "Geographic Poverty Traps? A Micro Model of Consumption Growth in Rural China." *Journal of Applied Econometrics* 17 (4): 329–46.

James, William. 1890. *The Principles of Psychology*. New York: Henry Holt.

Jamir, Limalemla, Baridalyne Nongkynrih, and Sanjeev Kumar Gupta. 2014. "Community Noise Pollution in Urban India: Need for Public Health Action." *Indian Journal of Community Medicine* 39 (1): 8–12.

Jamrah, Ahmad, Abbas Al-Omari, and Reem Sharabi. 2006. "Evaluation of Traffic Noise Pollution in Amman, Jordan." *Environmental Monitoring and Assessment* 120 (1): 499–525.

Jaušovec, Norbert. 1991. "Flexible Strategy Use: A Characteristic of Gifted Problem Solving." *Creativity Research Journal* 4 (4): 349–66.

————. 1994. *Flexible Thinking: An Explanation for Individual Differences*. New York: Hampton Press.

Johnson, Eric J., and Daniel Goldstein. 2003. "Do Defaults Save Lives?" *Science* 302 (5649): 1338–39.

Jones, Benjamin F., and Benjamin A. Olken. 2010. "Climate Shocks and Exports." *American Economic Review* 100 (2): 454–59.

Judge, Timothy A., Charlice Hurst, and Lauren S. Simon. 2009. "Does It Pay to Be Smart, Attractive, or Confident (or All Three)? Relationships among General Mental Ability, Physical Attractiveness, Core Self-Evaluations, and Income." *Journal of Applied Psychology* 94 (3): 742–55.

Jurado, María Beatriz, and Mónica Rosselli. 2007. "The Elusive Nature of Executive Functions: A Review of Our Current Understanding." *Neuropsychology Review* 17 (3): 213–33.

Kandasamya, Narayanan, Ben Hardy, Lionel Page, Markus Schaffner, Johann Graggaber, Andrew S. Powlson, Paul C. Fletcher, Mark Gurnell, and John Coates. 2013. "Cortisol Shifts Financial Risk Preferences." *Proceedings of the National Academy of Sciences USA (PNAS)* 111 (9): 3608–13.

Kandel, Eric, James H. Schwartz, and Thomas Jessell. 2000. *Principles of Neural Science*. New York: McGraw-Hill.

Kane, Michael J., Andrew R. A. Conway, Timothy K. Miura, and Gregory J. H. Colflesh. 2007. "Working Memory, Attention Control, and the N-Back Task: A Question of Construct Validity." *Journal of Experimental Psychology: Learning, Memory, and Cognition* 33 (3): 615–22.

Kane, Michael J., and Randall W. Engle. 2002. "The Role of Pre-frontal Cortex in Working-Memory Capacity, Executive Attention, and General Fluid Intelligence: An Individual-Differences Perspective." *Psychonomic Bulletin and Review* 9 (4): 637–71.

Kaplan, Stephen, and Marc G. Berman. 2010. "Directed Attention as a Common Resource for Executive Functioning and Self-Regulation." *Perspectives on Psychological Science* 5 (1): 43–57.

Karlan, Dean, Margaret McConnell, Sendhil Mullainathan, and Jonathan Zinman. 2016. "Getting to the Top of Mind: How Reminders Increase Saving." *Management Science*. https://doi.org/10.1287/mnsc.2015.2296.

Karlan, Dean, Melanie Morten, and Jonathan Zinman. Forthcoming. "A Personal Touch: Text Messaging for Loan Repayment." *Behavioral Science and Policy*.

Karlan, Dean, and Sendhil Mullainathan. 2010. "Debt Cycles." Unpublished manuscript.

Kaur, Supreet, Michael Kremer, and Sendhil Mullainathan. 2015. "Self-Control at Work." *Journal of Political Economy* 123 (6): 1227–77.

Kilby, Angela. 2015. "Opioids for the Masses: Welfare Tradeoffs in the Regulation of Narcotic Pain Medications." Job Market Paper, Department of Economics, Massachusetts Institute of Technology. http://economics.mit.edu/files/11150.

Killgore, William D. S. 2010. "Effects of Sleep Deprivation on Cognition." *Progress in Brain Research* 185:105–29.

Kimberg, Daniel Y., Mark D'Esposito, and Martha J. Farah. 1997. "Cognitive Functions in the Prefrontal Cortex: Working Memory and Executive Control." *Current Directions in Psychological Science* 6 (6): 185–92.

King, Jacqueline. 2004. "Missed Opportunities: Students Who Do Not Apply for Financial Aid." American Council on Education Issue Brief. http://www.acenet.edu/news-room/Pages/Missed-Opportunities-Students-Who-Do-Not-Apply-for.aspx.

Kirchner, Wayne K. 1958. "Age Differences in Short-Term Retention of Rapidly Changing Information." *Journal of Experimental Psychology* 55 (4): 352–58.

Kjellstrom, Tord, Ingvar Holmer, and Bruno Lemke. 2009. "Workplace Heat Stress, Health and Productivity—An Increasing Challenge for Low and Middle-Income Countries during Climate Change." *Global Health Action* 2 (1). https://doi .org/10.3402/gha.v2i0.2047.

Knox, Alan B. 1997. *Adult Development and Learning.* San Francisco: Jossey-Bass.

Koppel, Lina, David Andersson, India Morrison, Kinga Posadzdy, Daniel Västfjäll, and Gustav Tinghög. 2017. "The Effect of Acute Pain on Risky and Intertemporal Choice." *Experimental Economics* 20 (4): 878–93.

Kőszegi, Botond, and Adam Szeidl. 2013. "A Model of Focusing in Economic Choice." *Quarterly Journal of Economics* 128 (1): 53–104.

Kraay, Aart, and David McKenzie. 2014. "Do Poverty Traps Exist? Assessing the Evidence." *Journal of Economic Perspectives* 28 (3): 127–48.

Kraay, Aart, and Claudio Raddatz. 2007. "Poverty Traps, Aid, and Growth." *Journal of Development Economics* 82 (2): 315–47.

Kremer, Michael, Edward Miguel, Sendhil Mullainathan, Clair Null, and Alix P. Zwane. 2009. "Making Water Safe: Price, Persuasion, Peers, Promoters, or Product Design." Unpublished manuscript.

Krishna, Santosh, Suzanne Austin Boren, and E. Andrew Balas. 2009. "Healthcare via Cell Phones: A Systematic Review." *Telemedicine and e-Health* 15 (3): 231–40.

Kuhnen, Camelia M., and Brian Knutson. 2005. "The Neural Basis of Financial Risk Taking." *Neuron* 47 (5): 763–70.

Laibson, David. 1997. "Golden Eggs and Hyperbolic Discounting." *Quarterly Journal of Economics* 112 (2): 443–78.

Lauderdale, Diane S., Kristen L. Knutson, Lijing L. Yan, Kiang Liu, and Paul J. Rathouz. 2008. "Self-Reported and Measured Sleep Duration: How Similar Are They?" *Epidemiology* 19 (6): 838–45.

Lavie, Nilli, Aleksandra Hirst, Jan W. de Fockert, and Essi Viding. 2004. "Load Theory of Selective Attention and Cognitive Control." *Journal of Experimental Psychology* 133 (3): 339–54.

Lavy, Victor, Avraham Ebenstein, and Sefi Roth. 2014. "The Impact of Short Term Exposure to Ambient Air Pollution on Cognitive Performance and Human Capital Formation." NBER Working Paper no. 20648, Cambridge, MA.

Leibenstein, Harvey. 1957. "The Theory of Underemployment in Backward Economies." *Journal of Political Economy* 65 (2): 91–103.

Lerner, Jennifer S., Deborah A. Small, and George Loewenstein. 2004. "Heart Strings and Purse Strings: Carryover Effects of Emotions on Economic Decisions." *Psychological Science* 15 (5): 337–41.

Letzler, Robert, and Joshua Tasoff. 2014. "Everyone Believes in Redemption: Nudges and Overoptimism in Costly Task Completion." *Journal of Economic Behavior & Organization* 107:107–22.

Lezak, Muriel D. 1983. *Neuropsychological Assessment.* New York: Oxford University Press.

Lezak, Muriel D., Diane B. Howieson, and David W. Loring. 2004. *Neuropsychological Assessment*, 4th ed. New York: Oxford University Press.

Li, Leah, Chris Power, Shona Kelly, Clemens Kirschbaum, and Clyde Hertzman. 2007. "Life-Time Socio-economic Position and Cortisol Patterns in Mid-life." *Psychoneuroendocrinology* 32:824–33.

Lichtenberger, Elizabeth O., and Alan S. Kaufman. 2009. *Essentials of WAIS-IV Assessment.* Hoboken, NJ: John Wiley.

Lighthall, Nichole R., Mara Mather, and Marissa A. Gorlick. 2009. "Acute Stress Increases Sex Differences in Risk Seeking in the Balloon Analogue Risk Task." *PLOS One* 4 (7): e6002.

Lim, Julian, and David Dinges. 2008. "Sleep Deprivation and Vigilant Attention." *Annals of the New York Academy of Sciences* 1129 (1): 305–22.

———. 2010. "A Meta-analysis of the Impact of Short-Term Sleep Deprivation on Cognitive Variables." *Psychological Bulletin* 136 (3): 375–89.

Lim, Julian, Wen-Chau Wu, Jiongjiong Wang, John A. Detre, David F. Dinges, and Hengyi Rao. 2010. "Imaging Brain Fatigue from Sustained Mental Workload: An ASL Perfusion Study of the Time-on-Task Effect." *Neuroimage* 49 (4): 3426–35.

Lim, Stephen S., Theo Vos, Abraham D. Flaxman, Goodarz Danaei, Kenji Shibuya, Heather Adair-Rohani, and Markus Amann. 2012. "A Comparative Risk Assessment of Burden of Disease and Injury Attributable to 67 Risk Factors and Risk Factor Clusters in 21 Regions, 1990–2010: A Systematic Analysis for the Global Burden of Disease Study 2010." *Lancet* 380 (9859): 2224–60.

Lu, Chen-Lui, and Robert W. Proctor. 1995. "The Influence of Irrelevant Location Information on Performance: A Review of the Simon and Spatial Stroop Effects." *Psychonomic Bulletin and Review* 2 (2): 174–207.

Lund, Crick, Alison Breen, Alan J. Flisher, Ritsuko Kakuma, Joanne Corrigall, John A. Joska, Leslie Swartz, and Vikram Patel. 2010. "Poverty and Common Mental Disorders in Low and Middle Income Countries: A Systematic Review." *Social Science & Medicine* 71 (3): 517–28.

Luo, Yulei. 2008. "Consumption Dynamics under Information Processing Constraints." *Review of Economic Dynamics* 11 (2): 366–85.

Lupien, Sonia J., Suzanne King, Michael J. Meaney, and Bruce S. McEwan. 2001. "Can Poverty Get under Your Skin? Basal Cortisol Levels and Cognitive Function in Children from Low and High Socioeconomic Status." *Developmental Psychopathology* 13:651–74.

Lyon, G. Reid, and Norman A. Krasnegor. 1996. *Attention, Memory, and Executive Function*. Baltimore: Paul H. Brookes Publishing.

Maćkowiak, Bartosz, and Mirko Wiederholt. 2009. "Optimal Sticky Prices under Rational Inattention." *American Economic Review* 99 (3): 769–803.

———. 2015. "Business Cycle Dynamics under Rational Inattention." *Review of Economic Studies* 82 (4): 1502–32.

Mackworth, Jane F. 1968. "Vigilance, Arousal, and Habituation." *Psychological Review* 75 (4): 308–22.

MacLeod, Colin M. 1991. "Half a Century of Research on the Stroop Effect: An Integrative Review." *Psychological Bulletin* 109 (2): 163–203.

MacLeod, Colin M., Michael D. Dodd, Erin D. Sheard, Daryl E. Wilson, and Uri Bibi. 2003. "In Opposition to Inhibition." In *The Psychology of Learning and Motivation*, vol. 43, edited by Brian H. Ross, 163–214. Amsterdam: Elsevier Science.

Madrian, Brigitte C., and Dennis F. Shea. 2001. "The Power of Suggestion: Inertia in 401(k) Participation and Savings Behavior." *Quarterly Journal of Economics* 116 (4): 1149–87.

Mani, Anandi, Sendhil Mullainathan, Eldar Shafir, and Jiaying Zhao. 2013. "Poverty Impedes Cognitive Function." *Science* 341:976–80.

Martin, Matthew M., and Carolyn M. Anderson. 1998. "The Cognitive Flexibility Scale: Three Validity Studies." *Communication Reports* 11 (1): 1–9.

Martin, Matthew M., and Rebecca B. Rubin. 1995. "A New Measure of Cognitive Flexibility." *Psychological Reports* 76:623–26.

Matějka, Filip. 2016. "Rationally Inattentive Seller: Sales and Discrete Pricing." *Review of Economic Studies* 83 (3): 1125–55.

Mather, Mara, Marissa A. Gorlick, and Nichole R. Lighthall. 2009. "To Brake or Accelerate When the Light Turns Yellow? Stress Reduces Older Adults' Risk Taking in a Driving Game." *Psychological Science* 20 (2): 174–76.

Mazloumi, Adel, Farideh Golbabaei, Somayeh M. Khani, Zeinab Kazemi, Mostafa Hosseini, Marzieh Abbasinia, and Somayeh F. Dehghan. 2014. "Evaluating Effects of Heat Stress on Cognitive Function among Workers in a Hot Industry." *Health Promotion Perspectives* 4 (2): 240–46.

McGranahan, Gordon, and Frank Murray, eds. 2003. *Air Pollution and Health in Rapidly Developing Countries*. Abingdon-on-Thames, UK: Routledge.

McKenna, Benjamin, David L. Dickinson, Henry J. Orff, and Sean Drummond. 2007. "The Effects of One-Night Sleep Deprivation on Known-Risk and Ambiguous-Risk Decisions." *Journal of Sleep Research* 16 (3): 245–52.

Mehdi, Mohammed Raza, Minho Kim, Jeong Chang Seong, and Mudassar Hassan Arsalan. 2011. "Spatio-temporal Patterns of Road Traffic Noise Pollution in Karachi, Pakistan." *Environment International* 37 (1): 97–104.

Miller, Earl K., and Jonathan D. Cohen. 2001. "An Integrative Theory of Prefrontal Cortex Function." *Annual Review of Neuroscience* 24 (1): 167–202.

Miller, George A. 1956. "The Magic Number Seven, Plus or Minus Two: Some Limits on Our Capacity for Processing Information." *Psychological Review* 63 (2): 81–97.

Mirrlees, James A. 1975. *A Pure Theory of Underdeveloped Economies, Using a Relationship between Consumption and Productivity*. New Haven, CT: Yale University Press.

Mischel, Walter, Yuichi Shoda, and Monica L. Rodriguez. 1989. "Delay of Gratification in Children." *Science* 244 (4907): 933–38.

Miyake, Akira, Naomi P. Friedman, Michael J. Emerson, Alexander H. Witzki, Amy Howerter, and Tor D. Wager. 2000. "The Unity and Diversity of Executive Functions and Their Contributions to Complex 'Frontal Lobe' Tasks: A Latent Variable Analysis." *Cognitive Psychology* 41 (1): 49–100.

Mondria, Jordi. 2010. "Portfolio Choice, Attention Allocation, and Price Comovement." *Journal of Economic Theory* 145 (5): 1837–64.

Moriarty, Orla, Brian E. McGuire, and David P. Finn. 2011. "The Effect of Pain on Cognitive Function: A Review of Clinical and Preclinical Research." *Progress in Neurobiology* 93 (3): 385–404.

Mullainathan, Sendhil. 2002. "A Memory-Based Model of Bounded Rationality." *Quarterly Journal of Economics* 117 (3): 735–74.

Mullainathan, Sendhil, and Eldar Shafir. 2013. *Scarcity: Why Having Too Little Means So Much*. New York: Henry Holt.

Mullane, Jennifer C., Penny V. Corkum, Raymond M. Klein, and Elizabeth McLaughlin. 2009. "Interference Control in Children with and without ADHD: A Systematic Review of Flanker and Simon Task Performance." *Child Neuropsychology* 15 (4): 321–42.

Munakata, Yuko, Seth A. Herd, Christopher H. Chatham, Brendan E. Depue, Marie T. Banich, and Randall C. O'Reilly. 2011. "A Unified Framework for Inhibitory Control." *Trends in Cognitive Science* 15 (10): 453–59.

Muraven, Mark, and Roy F. Baumeister. 2000. "Self-Regulation and Depletion of Limited Resources: Does Self-Control Resemble a Muscle?" *Psychological Bulletin* 126 (2): 247–59.

Muraven, Mark, Dianne M. Tice, and Roy Baumeister. 1998. "Self-Control as a Limited Resource: Regulatory Depletion Patterns." *Journal of Personality and Social Psychology* 74 (3): 774–89.

Murnane, Richard J., John B. Willett, and Frank Levy. 1995. "The Growing Importance of Cognitive Skills in Wage Determination." *Review of Economics and Statistics* 2:251–66.

Nes, Lise S., Abbey R. Roach, and Suzanne C. Segerstrom. 2009. "Executive Functions, Self-Regulation, and Chronic Pain: A Review." *Annals of Behavioral Medicine* 37 (2): 173–83.

Nideffer, Robert M. 1976. "Test of Attentional and Interpersonal Style." *Journal of Personality and Social Psychology* 34:394–404.

Nuland, Sherwin B. 2004. *The Doctors' Plague: Germs, Childbed Fever, and the Strange Story of Ignac Semmelweis.* New York: W. W. Norton.

O'Donoghue, Ted, and Matthew Rabin. 1999. "Doing It Now or Later." *American Economic Review* 89 (1): 103–24.

———. 2001. "Choice and Procrastination." *Quarterly Journal of Economics* 116 (1): 121–60.

Okuda, Shawn M., Mark A. Runco, and Dale E. Berger. 1991. "Creativity and the Finding and Solving of Real-World Problems." *Journal of Psychoeducational Assessment* 9 (1): 45–53.

Oyedepo, Olayinka S., and Abdullahi A. Saadu. 2009. "A Comparative Study of Noise Pollution Levels in Some Selected Areas in Ilorin Metropolis, Nigeria." *Environmental Monitoring and Assessment* 158:155–67.

Ozer, Emily, Lia Fernald, Ann Weber, Emily Flynn, and Tyler VanderWeele. 2011. "Does Alleviating Poverty Affect Mothers' Depressive Symptoms? A Quasi-experimental Investigation of Mexico's Oportunidades Programme." *International Journal of Epidemiology* 40 (6): 1565–76.

Pashler, Harold. 1998. *The Psychology of Attention.* Cambridge, MA: MIT Press.

Patel, Nirav P., Michael A. Grandner, Dawei Xie, Charles C. Branas, and Nalaka Gooneratne. 2010. "'Sleep Disparity' in the Population: Poor Sleep Quality Is Strongly Associated with Poverty and Ethnicity." *BMC Public Health* 10:1–11.

Pechmann, Cornelia, and Tim Silk. 2013. "Policy and Research Related to Consumer Rebates: A Comprehensive Review." *Journal of Public Policy & Marketing* 32 (2): 250–70.

Peterson, Steven, and Michael I. Posner. 2012. "The Attention System of the Human Brain: 20 Years After." *Annual Review of Neuroscience* 35 (1): 73–89.

Petrides, Michael, Bessie Alivisatos, Alan C. Evans, and Ernst Meyer. 1993. "Dissociation of Human Mid-dorsolateral from Posterior Dorsolateral Frontal Cortex in Memory Processing." *Proceedings of the National Academy of Sciences USA (PNAS)* 90:873–77.

Petrides, Michael, and Brenda Milner. 1982. "Deficits on Subject-Ordered Tasks after Frontal- and Temporal-Lobe Lesions in Man." *Neuropsychologia* 20:249–62.

Phelps, Edmund S., and Robert A. Pollak. 1968. "On Second-Best National Saving and Game-Equilibrium Growth." *Review of Economic Studies* 35 (2): 185–99.

Phelps, Elizabeth A. 2006. "Emotion and Cognition: Insights from Studies of the Human Amygdala." *Annual Review of Psychology* 57 (1): 27–53.

Philibert, Ingrid. 2005. "Sleep Loss and Performance in Residents and Nonphysicians: A Meta-analytic Examination." *Sleep* 28 (11): 1392–402.

Poleshuck, Ellen L., and Carmen R. Green. 2008. "Socioeconomic Disadvantage and Pain." *Pain* 136:235–38.

Pope, C. Arden. 2000. "Epidemiology of Fine Particular Air Pollution and Human Health: Biologic Mechanisms and Who's at Risk?" *Environmental Health Perspectives* 108 (4): 713–23.

Pop-Eleches, Cristian, Harsha Thirumurthy, James P. Habyarimana, Joshua G. Zivin, Markus P. Goldstein, Damien de Walque, Leslie MacKeen, et al. 2011. "Mobile Phone Technologies Improve Adherence to Antiretroviral Treatment in a Resource-Limited Setting: A Randomized Controlled Trial of Text Message Reminders." *AIDS* 25 (6): 825–34.

Porcelli, Anthony J., and Mauricio R. Delgado. 2009. "Acute Stress Modulates Risk Taking in Financial Decision Making." *Psychological Science* 20 (3): 278–83.

Power, Melinda C., Marc G. Weisskopf, Stacey E. Alexeeff, Brent A. Coull, Avron Spiro III, and Joel Schwartz. 2011. "Traffic-Related Air Pollution and Cognitive Function in a Cohort of Older Men." *Environmental Health Perspectives* 119 (5): 682–87.

Prabhakaran, Vivek, Jennifer A. L. Smith, John E. Desmond, Gary H. Glover, and John D. E. Gabrieli. 1997. "Neural Substrates of Fluid Reasoning: An fMRI Study of Neocortical Activation during Performance of the Raven's Progressive Matrices Test." *Cognitive Psychology* 33 (1): 43–63.

Pratt, Travis C., and Francis T. Cullen. 2000. "The Empirical Status of Gottfredson and Hirschi's General Theory of Crime: A Meta-analysis." *Criminology* 38 (3): 931–64.

Psacharopoulos, George, and Eduardo Velez. 1992. "Does Training Pay Independent of Education? Some Evidence from Colombia." *International Journal of Educational Research* 17 (6): 629–43.

Psychology Experiment Building Language (PEBL). 2008–2010. Berg's Card Sorting Test. http://pebl.sourceforge.net/wiki/index.php/Berg's_Card_Sorting_Test.

Radakovic, Sonja S., Jelena Maric, Maja Surbatovic, Slavica Radjen, Elka Stefanova, Nebojsa Stankovic, and Nikola Filipovic. 2007. "Effects of Acclimation on Cognitive Performance in Soldiers during Exertional Heat Stress." *Military Medicine* 172 (2): 133–36.

Raven, John C. 1936. "Mental Tests Used in Genetic Studies: The Performance of Related Individuals on Tests Mainly Educative and Mainly Reproductive." Master's thesis, University of London.

———. 2000. "The Raven's Progressive Matrices: Change and Stability over Culture and Time." *Cognitive Psychology* 41 (1): 1–48.

Robertson, Ian H., Tom Manly, Jackie Andrade, Bart T. Baddeley, and Jenny Yiend. 1997. "'Oops!': Performance Correlates of Everyday Attentional Failures in Traumatic Brain Injured and Normal Subjects." *Neuropsychologia* 35 (6): 747–58.

Roehrs, Timothy, Lori Merlotti, Nancie Petrucelli, Edward Stepanski, and Thomas Roth. 1994. "Experimental Sleep Fragmentation." *Sleep* 17 (5): 438–43.

Rothbart, Mary K., and Michael I. Posner. 1985. "Temperament and the Development of Self-Regulation." In *The Neuropsychology of Individual Differences: A Developmental Perspective*, edited by Lawrence C. Hartlage and Cathy F. Tezrow, 93–123. New York: Springer US.

Runco, Mark A., and Shawn M. Okuda. 1991. "The Instructional Enhancement of the Flexibility and Originality Scores of Divergent Thinking Tests." *Applied Cognitive Psychology* 5 (5): 435–551.

Sachs, Jeffrey. 2005. *The End of Poverty: Economic Possibilities for Our Time.* New York: Penguin.

———. 2014. "The Case for Aid." *Foreign Policy*, Jan. 21. http://foreignpolicy.com /2014/01/21/the-case-for-aid/.

Sadeh, Avi, Reut Gruber, and Amiram Raviv. 2002. "Sleep, Neurobehavioral Functioning, and Behavior Problems in School-Age Children." *Child Development* 73 (2): 405–17.

Saridjana, Nathalie S., Anja C. Huizink, Jitske A. Koetsier, Vincent W. Jaddoe, Johan P. Mackenbach, Albert Hofman, Clemens Kirschbaum, Frank C. Verhulst, and Henning Tiemeier. 2010. "Do Social Disadvantage and Early Family Adversity Affect the Diurnal Cortisol Rhythm in Infants? The Generation R Study." *Hormones and Behavior* 57 (2): 247–54.

Schilbach, Frank. 2017. "Alcohol and Self-Control: A Field Experiment in India." Working paper, Department of Economics, Massachusettes Institute of Technology.

Schilbach, Frank, Heather Schofield, and Sendhil Mullainathan. 2016. "The Psychological Lives of the Poor." *American Economic Review Papers & Proceedings* 106 (5): 435–40.

Schofield, Heather. 2014. "The Economic Costs of Low Caloric Intake: Evidence from India." Working paper, Harvard University.

Schwartzstein, Joshua. 2014. "Selective Attention and Learning." *Journal of the European Economic Association* 12 (6): 1423–52.

Scott, Jonathon P. R., Lars R. McNaughton, and Remco C. J. Polman. 2006. "Effects of Sleep Deprivation and Exercise on Cognitive, Motor Performance, and Mood." *Physiology and Behavior* 87 (2): 396–408.

Seaton, Anthony, William MacNee, Ken Donaldson, and David Godden. 1995. "Particulate Air Pollution and Acute Health Effects." *Lancet* 345 (8943): 176–78.

Sherrod, Drury R. 1974. "Crowding, Perceived Control, and Behavioral Aftereffects." *Journal of Applied Social Psychology* 4 (2): 171–86.

Shiv, Baba, and Alexander Fedorikhin. 1999. "Heart and Mind in Conflict: The Interplay of Affect and Cognition in Consumer Decision Making." *Journal of Consumer Research* 26 (3): 278–92.

Simmons, Shona E., Brian K. Saxby, Francis P. McGlone, and David A. Jones. 2008. "The Effect of Passive Heating and Head Cooling on Perception, Cardiovascular Function and Cognitive Performance in the Heat." *European Journal of Applied Physiology* 104 (2): 271–80.

Sims, Christopher A. 1998. "Stickiness." *Carnegie-Rochester Conference Series on Public Policy* 49 (1): 317–56.

———. 2003. "Implications of Rational Inattention." *Journal of Monetary Economics* 50:665–90.

———. 2006. "Rational Inattention: Beyond the Linear-Quadratic Case." *American Economic Review Papers and Proceedings* 96 (2): 158–63.

Sippel, Reinhard. 1997. "An Experiment on the Pure Theory of Consumer's Behaviour." *Economic Journal* 107 (444): 1431–44.

Stansfeld, Stephen A., Birgitta Berglund, Charlotte Clark, Isabel Lopez-Barrio, Peter Fischer, Evy Ohrstrom, Mary M. Haines, J. Head, Staffan Hygge, Irene van Kamp, and Bernard F. Berry. 2005. "Aircraft and Road Traffic Noise and Children's Cognition and Health: A Cross-National Study." *Lancet* 365 (9475): 1942–49.

Steele, Claude M., and Robert A. Josephs. 1990. "Alcohol Myopia: Its Prized and Dangerous Effects." *American Psychologist* 45 (8): 921–33.

Sternberg, Robert J., and Karin Sternberg. 2011. *Cognitive Psychology*, 6th ed. Boston: Cengage Learning.

Stiglitz, Joseph E. 1976. "The Efficiency Wage Hypothesis, Surplus Labour, and the Distribution of Income in LDCs." *Oxford Economic Papers* 28 (2): 185–207.

Stroop, John Ridley. 1935. "Studies of Interference in Serial Verbal Reactions." *Journal of Experimental Psychology* 18 (6): 643–62.

Strotz, Robert. 1956. "Myopia and Inconsistency in Dynamic Utility Maximization." *Review of Economic Studies* 23 (3): 165–80.

Stuss, Donald T., and Michael P. Alexander. 2000. "Executive Functions and the Frontal Lobes: A Conceptual View." *Psychological Research* 63 (1): 289–98.

Suchy, Yana. 2009. "Executive Functioning: Overview, Assessment, and Research Issues for Non-neuropsychologists." *Annals of Behavioral Medicine* 37 (2): 106–16.

Szalma, James L., and Peter A. Hancock. 2011. "Noise Effects on Human Performance: A Meta-analytic Synthesis." *Psychological Bulletin* 137 (4): 682–707.

Tchanturia, Kate, Helen Davies, Marion Roberts, Amy Harrison, Michiko Nakazato, Ulrike Schmidt, Janet Treasure, and Robin Morris. 2012. "Poor Cognitive

Flexibility in Eating Disorders: Examining the Evidence Using the Wisconsin Card Sorting Task." *PLOS One* 7 (1): e28331.

Thaler, Richard, and Hersh M. Shefrin. 1981. "An Economic Theory of Self-Control." *Journal of Political Economy* 89 (2): 392–406.

Thurston, Becky J., and Mark A. Runco. 1999. "Flexibility." In *Encyclopedia of Creativity*, edited by Mark A. Runco and Steven R. Pritzker, 729–31. San Diego, CA: Academic Press.

Torrance, E. Paul. 1974. *Torrance Tests of Creative Thinking: Norms and Technical Manual*. Bensenville, IL: Scholastic Test Services.

Treisman, Anne M., and Garry Gelade. 1980. "A Feature-Integration Theory of Attention." *Cognitive Psychology* 12:97–136.

Tzivian, Lilian, Angela Winkler, Martha Dlugaj, Tamara Schikowski, Mohammad Vossoughi, Kateryna Fuks, Gudrun Weinmayr, and Barbara Hoffmann. 2015. "Effect of Long-Term Outdoor Air Pollution and Noise on Cognitive and Psychological Functions in Adults." *International Journal of Hygiene and Environmental Health* 218 (1): 1–11.

Unterrainer, Josef M., Benjamin Rahm, Christoph P. Kaller, Rainer Leonhart, C. Meier, C. Müller, K. Quiske, K. Hoppe-Seyler, and U. Halsband. 2004. "Planning Abilities and the Tower of London: Is This Task Measuring a Discrete Cognitive Function?" *Journal of Clinical and Experimental Neuropsychology* 26 (6): 846–56.

US Army Institute of Environmental Medicine. 1987. "Nutritional Status and Physical and Mental Performance of Special Operations Soldiers Consuming the Ration, Lightweight, or the Meal, Ready-to-Eat Military Field Ration during a 30-Day Field Training Exercise." Technical Report no. T7-87, AD A179 553, Natick, MA, US Army Research Institute of Environmental Medicine.

US Department of Transportation (USDT). 2008. National Motor Vehicle Crash Causation Survey. US Department of Transportation, National Highway Traffic Safety Administration, DOT HS 811 059: 1–31.

Van Dongen, Greg M., Janet M. Mullington, and David F. Dinges. 2003. "The Cumulative Cost of Additional Wakefulness: Dose-Response Effects on Neurobehavioral Functions and Sleep Physiology from Chronic Sleep Restriction and Total Sleep Deprivation." *Sleep* 26 (2): 117–26.

Van Nieuwerburgh, Stijn, and Laura Veldkamp. 2009. "Information Immobility and the Home Bias Puzzle." *Journal of Finance* 64 (3): 1187–215.

Vervloet, Marcia, Annemiek J. Linn, Julia C. M. van Weert, Dinny H. de Bakker, Marcel L. Bouvy, and Liset van Dijk. 2012. "The Effectiveness of Interventions Using Electronic Reminders to Improve Adherence to Chronic Medication: A Systematic Review of the Literature." *Journal of the American Medical Informatics Association* 19:696–704.

Vogl, Tom S. 2014. "Height, Skills, and Labor Market Outcomes in Mexico." *Journal of Development Economics* 107:84–96.

von Hippel, William, and Karen Gonsalkorale. 2005. "'That Is Bloody Revolting!'—Inhibitory Control of Thoughts Better Left Unsaid." *Psychological Science* 16 (7): 497–500.

Wachtel, Paul L. 1976. "Conceptions of Broad and Narrow Attention." *Psychological Bulletin* 68 (6): 417–29.

Ward, Andrew, and Traci Mann. 2000. "Don't Mind If I Do: Disinhibited Eating under Cognitive Load." *Journal of Personality and Social Psychology* 78 (4): 753–63.

Wechsler, David. 2008. *Wechsler Adult Intelligence Scale*, 4th ed. San Antonio, TX: Psychological Corporation.

Weuve, Jennifer, Robin C. Puett, Joel Schwartz, Jeff D. Yanosky, Francine Laden, and Francine Grodstein. 2012. "Exposure to Particulate Air Pollution and Cognitive Decline in Older Women." *Archives of Internal Medicine* 172 (3): 219–27.

Wiebe, Sandra A., Angela F. Lukowski, and Patricia J. Bauer. 2010. "Sequence Imitation and Reaching Measures of Executive Control: A Longitudinal Examination in the Second Year of Life." *Developmental Neuropsychology* 35:522–38.

Woodford, Michael. 2012. "Inattentive Valuation and Reference-Dependent Choice." Working paper, Columbia University.

World Bank. 2015. *World Development Indicators.* Washington, DC: World Bank.

World Health Organization (WHO). 2001. *World Health Report 2001: Mental Health: New Understanding, New Hope.* Geneva: World Health Organization.

———. 2014. "Seven Million Premature Deaths Annually Linked to Air Pollution." Accessed September 5, 2016. http://www.who.int/mediacentre/news/releases/2014 /air-pollution/en/.

———. 2016. "Fact Sheet on Depression." Accessed September 5, 2016. http://www .who.int/mediacentre/factsheets/fs369/en/.

Yates, Frances A. 1966. *The Art of Memory.* Chicago: University of Chicago Press.

Zannin, Paulo Henrique Trombetta, Fabiano Belisário Diniz, and Wiliam Alves Barbosa. 2002. "Environmental Noise Pollution in the City of Curitiba, Brazil." *Applied Acoustics* 63 (4): 351–58.

Comment on Chapters 1 and 2

John Hoddinott

The chapters by Emma Dean, Frank Schilbach, and Heather Schofield and by Elizabeth Frankenberg and Duncan Thomas are thoughtful, well-written studies by researchers with deep knowledge of their subject matter. But beyond that, a first impression would suggest that they are chapters with radically different objectives and analyses. The Dean, Schilbach, and Schofield chapter provides economists with a solid understanding of the interplay between aspects of cognitive function and economic behavior, including its implications for poverty. By contrast, Frankenberg and Thomas provide a careful empirical analysis of the impact of two shocks, the 1998 Indonesian financial crisis and the 2004 Indian Ocean tsunami, on children's human capital. Nor is it immediately clear what links these chapters make with the broader themes of this book. Once past their respective introductions, the phrase "poverty traps" occurs only three times in the Dean, Schilbach, and Schofield chapter and not at all in Frankenberg and Thomas.

But these first impressions are misleading. Both chapters are deeply relevant to current research agenda on poverty traps and they complement each other in at least three ways. In this comment, I provide a brief summary of these chapters before outlining these complementarities.

Summary

Frankenberg and Thomas use two high-quality data sets from Indonesia to examine the impact of early life shocks on health and human capital out-

John Hoddinott is the H. E. Babcock Professor of Food and Nutrition Economics and Policy at Cornell University.

For acknowledgments, sources of research support, and disclosure of the author's material financial relationships, if any, please see http://www.nber.org/chapters/c13952.ack.

comes. Using multiple rounds of the Indonesian Family Life Survey (IFLS), they show that the severe 1998 financial crisis had no effect on child anthropometric status as measured by height ten years after the crisis had passed. Nor were there impacts on grade attainment. Using multiple rounds of the STAR (Study of the Tsunami Aftermath and Recovery) surveys, Frankenberg and Thomas find that in utero exposure to the tsunami during the second trimester has a large initial adverse effect on height-for-age z-scores, but that this diminishes over time. Based on these findings, Frankenberg and Thomas note that public and private responses to shocks can be effective in blunting their malign consequences. Short-term shocks do not necessarily translate into long-term adverse consequences. History is not destiny.

There are, however, some caveats to their findings. In their introductory remarks, Frankenberg and Thomas comment that looking at aggregate effects may mask impacts that differ across income or other distributions. This is an important and correct point, but one that does not receive as much attention as one might like. They document recovery from the tsunami but offer relatively little in the way of explanation about why this occurs. And a case could be made for making their conclusions more nuanced. Over the time frames and outcomes they consider, there are no measurable impacts of these shocks on children's health and human capital outcomes. But this does not mean that there are *no* effects; it may be that more time must pass before these begin to manifest themselves. This was true of the Dutch Famine discussed in their introduction and is an issue I return to below.

Dean, Schilbach, and Schofield provide a terrific introduction to the literature on the measurement and interpretation of cognitive function; appendix table 2A.1 provides a useful summary of these. They provide a state-of-the-art assessment of how poverty in its various manifestations can affect cognitive function; the discussion of the effect of the physical environment (noise, heat, air pollution) being especially noteworthy. They note that poor cognitive function can contribute to poverty through the adverse consequences of lowered attention, poorer inhibitory control, memory, and poorer higher-order executive function. As they provide more than fifteen pages of references—a testament to the thoroughness of their research—it is a little churlish to ask for more discussion of certain points. But with that caveat, there are three areas where further discussion would be helpful:

- While they provide an excellent summary of various measures of cognitive function, there is much less discussion of the magnitudes of these measures. Does poverty in its various guises have linear or nonlinear effects on these? Does cognitive function have linear impacts on the outcomes considered or are there threshold effects? How much of a change in any of these can be considered a "big" effect?
- How feasible is it to take these out of the lab and into the field? Would it be helpful to do so, for example, in order to obtain population-level

assessments of these aspects of cognitive function? If this is not feasible, does this limit our ability to assess the interplay between poverty (and possibly poverty traps) and cognitive function?

- The discussion of the determinants of cognitive function seems to focus heavily on contemporaneous causes. To what extent are these a function of early life experiences? Are they transmitted intergenerationally? Once individuals reach adulthood, how malleable are these and what do the answers to these questions imply for poverty and poverty traps?

Complementarities

There are two straightforward complementarities in the Frankenberg and Thomas and Dean, Schilbach, and Schofield chapters. First, both provide immensely helpful overviews of the literatures that they nest their work within. They emphasize that identification of effects is challenging. They stress that making progress on these difficult topics requires economists to "raise their game," including long-term data collection efforts such as the Indonesia Family Life Surveys and by engaging more substantively with other disciplines. Second, much of the literature on asset poverty traps sees assets in terms of financial resources, machinery and equipment, and land and livestock (Carter and Barrett 2006). As both chapters make clear, research on poverty traps can be enriched through expanding the set of assets to include health and cognitive function.

The third complementarity, and arguably the most important, is more subtle. Various dimensions of undernutrition in early life have neurological consequences that lead to cognitive impairments. Prado and Dewey (2014) provide a recent review of this literature, updating an older review by Levitsky and Strupp (1995). This earlier work showed that the prefrontal cortex may be especially vulnerable to undernutrition as well as reduced myelination of axon fibers, thus reducing the speed at which signals are transmitted (Levitsky and Strupp 1995); that undernourished children score poorly on tests of attention, fluency, and working memory is consistent with this (Kar, Rao, and Chandramouli 2008). Undernutrition adversely affects the hippocampus by reducing dendrite density (Blatt et al. 1994; Mazer et al. 1997; Ranade et al. 2008) and by damaging the chemical processes associated with spatial navigation, memory formation (Huang et al. 2003), and memory consolidation (Valadares and de Sousa Almeida 2005). Chronic undernutrition damages the occipital lobe and the motor cortex (Benítez-Bribiesca, De la Rosa-Alvarez, and Mansilla-Olivares 1999), producing dentrites with fewer spines and greater numbers of abnormalities, thus leading to delays in the evolution of locomotor skills (Barros et al. 2006) with adverse consequences for learning. Levitsky and Strupp (1995) note that early life undernutrition decreases the number of neurons in the locus coeruleus, which plays a role in signaling the need to inhibit the production of cortisol. Thus, early life malnutrition diminishes the ability to exhibit down regulation and handle stressful situations.

Do these malign effects have persistent effects on attention, inhibitory control, memory, and higher-order cognitive function—the four areas identified by Dean, Schilbach, and Schofield? Galler et al. (2005), using case control cohort data, report that children who suffered from kwashiorkor in their first year of life had, relative to well-nourished peers, poorer socialization skills at ages five to eleven years, a greater propensity for aggressive behavior at ages nine to fifteen, and a greater likelihood of attentional deficits (60 percent versus 15 percent for controls) at age eighteen. Particularly relevant, given the findings of Frankenberg and Thomas of no discernable effects on anthropometry in their Indonesian studies, is the fact that the malnourished children in the Galler et al. study were treated for kwashiorkor and recovered, exhibiting neither chronic nor acute undernutrition subsequently. Galler et al. (2012) find that these attentional deficits persist into mid-adulthood (ages thirty-seven to forty-three), and Galler et al. (2013) find that, as adults, these malnourished children were more likely to exhibit anxiety, lowered sociability, less intellectual curiosity, a more egocentric rather than altruistic orientation, and a lowered sense of efficacy. Hoddinott et al. (2013) find that children who were chronically undernourished at age two years scored lower on tests of vocabulary, reading, and fluid intelligence. That said—and as discussed in a different way by Frankenberg and Thomas—Prado and Dewey (2014) emphasize that the timing of nutrient deficiency, the form and degree of the deficiency, and the potential for environmental factors (such as compensating public or parental investments) all play a role in attenuating or accentuating the effect of shocks on cognitive function.

These biomedical literatures—which receive too little attention from economists—suggest a deep complementarity between the chapters by Frankenberg and Thomas and Dean, Schilbach, and Schofield. Frankenberg and Thomas provide a guide to the literature on the impact of shocks in early life and a cautionary case study in over interpreting the short-run impact of these. The biomedical literature tells us, however, that depending on environmental responses, these short-run shocks can have adverse consequences for cognitive function, some of which may not become apparent until adulthood. Dean, Schilbach, and Schofield give economists the tools to assess many of these as well as an understanding of how they link to lowered living standards in adulthood. Together, they suggest that early life shocks that result in undernutrition, whether temporary or permanent, can contribute to poverty traps in adulthood through their effect on reduced cognitive function. But our evidence base on the magnitude and extent of such contributions is limited; this represents an important area for future research.

References

Barros, K. M., R. Manhães-De-Castro, S. Lopes-De-Souza, R. J. Matos, T. C. Deiró, J. E. Cabral-Filho, and F. Canon. 2006. "A Regional Model (Northeastern Brazil) of Induced Malnutrition Delays Ontogeny of Reflexes and Locomotor Activity in Rats." *Nutritional Neuroscience* 9:99–104.

Benítez-Bribiesca L., I. De la Rosa-Alvarez, and A. Mansilla-Olivares. 1999. "Dendritic Spine Pathology in Infants with Severe Protein-Calorie Malnutrition." *Pediatrics* 104:e21–27.

Blatt, G. L., C. J. Chung, D. L. Rosene, L. Volicer, and J. R. Galler. 1994. "Prenatal Protein Malnutrition Effects on the Serotonergic System in the Hippocampal Formation: An Immunocytochemical, Ligand Binding, and Neurochemical Study." *Brain Research Bulletin* 34:507–18.

Carter, M. R., and C. B. Barrett. 2006. "The Economics of Poverty Traps and Persistent Poverty: An Asset-Based Approach." *Journal of Development Studies* 42 (2): 178–99.

Galler, J. R., C. P. Bryce, M. L. Zichlin, G. Fitzmaurice, G. D. Eaglesfield, and D. P. Waber. 2012. "Infant Malnutrition Is Associated with Persisting Attention Deficits in Middle Adulthood." *Journal of Nutrition* 142 (4): 788–94.

Galler, J., C. Bryce, M. Zichlin, D. Waber, N. Exner, G. Fitzmaurice, and P. Costa. 2013. "Malnutrition in the First Year of Life and Personality at Age 40." *Journal of Child Psychology and Psychiatry* 54 (8): 911–19.

Galler, J. R., D. P. Waber, R. Harrison, and F. Ramsey. 2005. "Behavioral Effects of Childhood Malnutrition." *American Journal of Psychiatry* 162 (9): 1760–61.

Hoddinott, J., J. Maluccio, J. Behrman, R. Martorell, Paul Melgar, Agnes R. Quisumbing, Manuel Ramirez-Zea, Aryeh D. Stein, and Kathryn M. Yount. 2013. "Adult Consequences of Growth Failure in Early Childhood." *American Journal of Clinical Nutrition* 98:1170–78.

Huang L. T., M. C. Lai, C. L. Wang, C. A. Wang, C. H. Yang, C. S. Hsieh, C. W. Liou, and S. N. Yang. 2003. "Long-Term Effects of Early-Life Malnutrition and Status Epilepticus: Assessment by Spatial Navigation and CREB (Serine-133) Phosphorylation." *Developmental Brain Research* 145:213–18.

Kar, B. R., S. L. Rao, and B. A. Chandramouli. 2008. "Cognitive Development in Children with Chronic Protein Energy Malnutrition." *Behavioral and Brain Functions* 4:1–31.

Levitsky, D., and B. Strupp. 1995. "Malnutrition and the Brain: Changing Concepts, Changing Concerns." *Journal of Nutrition* 125 (Suppl. 8): 2212S–20S.

Mazer, C., J. Muneyyirci, K. Taheny, N. Raio, A. Borella, and P. Whitaker-Azmitia. 1997. "Serotonin Depletion during Synaptogenesis Leads to Decreased Synaptic Density and Learning Deficits in the Adult Rat: A Possible Model of Neurodevelopmental Disorders with Cognitive Deficits." *Brain Research* 760:68–73.

Prado, E., and K. G. Dewey. 2014. "Nutrition and Brain Development in Early Life." *Nutrition Reviews* 72 (4): 267–84.

Ranade, S. C., A. Rose, M. Rao, J. Gallego, P. Gressens, and S. Mani. 2008. "Different Types of Nutritional Deficiencies Affect Different Domains of Spatial Memory Function Checked in a Radial Arm Maze." *Neuroscience* 152:859–66.

Valadares, C. T., and S. de Sousa Almeida. 2005. "Early Protein Malnutrition Changes Learning and Memory in Spaced but Not in Condensed Trials in the Morris Water-Maze." *Nutritional Neuroscience* 8:39–47.

II

Psychology of Poverty, Hope, and Aspirations

Depression through the Lens of Economics
A Research Agenda

Jonathan de Quidt and Johannes Haushofer

3.1 Introduction

Major depressive disorder (MDD; henceforth simply "depression") is one of the leading causes of disease burden worldwide, second only to lower back pain in terms of years lost to disability (Vos et al. 2012). The cross-sectional prevalence is an estimated 4 to 5 percent of the global population at a given time (Vos et al. 2012; Steel et al. 2014), and lifetime prevalence averages 13 percent across a sample of eighteen countries (Bromet et al. 2011; see Kessler and Bromet 2013 for a review). The economic costs of depression from lost productivity have been estimated at around €76 billion in Europe (Sobocki et al. 2006) and $31 billion in the United States (Stewart et al. 2003).

Depression is intimately linked to poverty for two reasons: first, prevalence among low-income populations is higher than among high-income populations (Bromet et al. 2011; Lund et al. 2010; Lund et al. 2011). Second, low-income individuals have significantly less access to treatment than high-income populations: the World Health Organization (WHO) reports that low-income countries on average have 2.1 psychiatric beds (a proxy for the capacity of the mental health system as a whole) per 100,000 individuals, while high-income countries have 90.9.

Jonathan de Quidt is assistant professor at the Institute for International Economic Studies. Johannes Haushofer is assistant professor of psychology and public affairs at Princeton University and a faculty research fellow of the National Bureau of Economic Research.

We thank Jim Reisinger, John Kramer, and Benedetta Lerva for excellent research assistance, and Rachid Laajaj, Yves Le Yaouanq, Gautam Rao, Frank Schilbach, Heather Schofield, Justin Wolfers, Bruce Wydick, and seminar participants at the NBER conference and AEA annual meetings for helpful comments. De Quidt acknowledges support from Handelsbanken's Research Foundation, grant no. B2014-0460:1. For acknowledgments, sources of research support, and disclosure of the authors' material financial relationships, if any, please see http://www.nber.org/chapters/c13831.ack.

Given this high prevalence, especially among the poor, the significant economic cost, and economists' interest in other psychiatric conditions such as substance abuse (Becker and Murphy 1988), it is perhaps surprising that depression has not received greater attention in the economics literature. In this chapter we seek to make three contributions. First, we describe the canonical symptoms of depression in the language of economics and discuss what these symptoms imply for economic outcomes. Second, we present descriptive evidence illustrating the relationships between depression and important economic variables. Third, we discuss two main approaches to how economic theory might model depression. Together, our hope is to signpost ways that economics, and in particular economic theory, can take toward understanding depression.

Our first exercise is to describe depression in the language of economics. In doing so, we follow the classification of the symptoms of depression provided by Aaron Beck, one of the foremost theorists on depression in psychiatry, as well as the diagnostic criteria laid out in the standard diagnostic manual, the *DSM-5*. Beck grouped the symptoms of depression broadly into four categories, which he termed cognitive, motivational, emotional, and somatic, respectively (Beck 1967). We argue that many symptoms can be thought of as capturing distorted beliefs about the returns to effort, informed by shocks that the decision maker experiences, or distortions in preferences, for example, by shocks that affect marginal utility. Specifically, many depressed patients exhibit pessimistic beliefs about the future, themselves, and the world (this classic group of symptoms is known as Beck's "cognitive triad"), suggesting a change in beliefs. In addition, they are frequently unable to derive pleasure from otherwise enjoyable activities, suggesting a change in preferences. These features of depression are reflected in economic outcomes: depressed individuals reduce labor supply, consumption, and investment, increase temptation good spending, and have altered eating and sleeping patterns.

Our second contribution is to illustrate the economic characteristics of depression using cross-sectional data from the Indonesia Family Life Survey (IFLS-5), which surveyed 50,148 individuals in 16,204 households. We show that depressed individuals indeed have lower labor supply and consumption than nondepressed individuals, their educational investment is lower, they spend more money on temptation goods, and they have altered sleeping patterns. This correlational analysis fulfills two purposes. First, the economic correlates of depression provide a first plausibility check on our description of depression in terms of economic primitives described above. Second, the analysis, together with existing literature, provides a list of stylized facts to be accounted for by theory.

Our final contribution is to propose a research agenda for modeling depression using standard economic analysis. Specifically, we discuss two possible modeling approaches. The first is to model depression with distorted beliefs about the returns to effort as a result of a shock, such as a stressful negative life event. We suggest that such a shock to beliefs can generate several of the sets of features of depression described above: pessimism about the future; reduction in labor supply, income, and consumption; and changes in sleeping and eating patterns. The second approach is based on changes to preferences: if shocks lead to distortions of marginal utility, or beliefs about marginal utility, this in turn could generate the emotional symptoms of depression described above, especially the inability to derive pleasure from everyday activities.

We do not presume to have all the answers. The tradition of applied economic research, exemplified by the work of Becker and Murphy (1988) on addiction, is to reduce complex environments to a small number of mechanisms—in our case, shocks to beliefs and preferences. We do not claim that simple theories will explain every nuance of the causes, symptoms, or consequences of depression. We nevertheless find it a valuable exercise to identify key economic mechanisms and behaviors among the psychological evidence. We think of this chapter as a first step toward a richer economic approach to thinking about depression, both theoretically and empirically.

The remainder of the chapter is organized as follows. Section 3.2 attempts to describe the symptoms of depression in the language of economics. Section 3.3 presents empirical data illustrating the relationships predicted by the model. Section 3.4 discusses potential avenues for a description of depression in terms of economic theory. Section 3.5 concludes.

3.2   Describing Depression in the Language of Economics

In this section, we make an attempt to describe the symptoms of depression in the language of economics. The goal of this exercise is to see to what extent we can distill the complex symptomatology of depression down to economic primitives, in particular, beliefs and preferences. We mainly use the comprehensive list of symptoms provided by Beck (1967), and in the entire following section we paraphrase heavily from his exposition. Beck's list of symptoms was originally compiled by generating a list of candidate symptoms from textbooks and monographs, conducting a pilot test comparing the presence of the individual symptoms in fifty depressed patients and thirty nondepressed patients, constructing an inventory consisting of items relevant to depression and pretesting it on 100 patients, and, finally, presenting the revised inventory to 966 psychiatric patients, of whom 224 had no depression and 297, 360, and 85 patients had mild, moderate, and severe depression, respectively.[1]

1. Beck leaves open the question of how these patients were diagnosed as depressed and how severity was assessed; the standard tool is the clinical interview that tests for the presence of depression symptoms, so it is likely that there is a degree of circularity in the list of symptoms.

The other obvious candidate list of depression symptoms are the diagnostic criteria presented in standard diagnostic manuals, such as the *DSM-5* in the United States. However, these symptoms are a subset of those described by Beck; we therefore focus on his more comprehensive list, and mention in our discussion which of these symptoms are also used as diagnostic criteria. In addition, the *DSM-5* diagnostic criteria are listed in the appendix.

3.2.1   "Cognitive" Symptoms

The *cognitive* symptoms of depression describe a set of negative beliefs and attitudes toward oneself and the environment, distorted "notions of causality" in which patients blame themselves for problems, and indecisiveness. Specifically, Beck describes five such symptoms: First, depressed individuals have *low self-evaluation* or self-esteem; that is, they feel that they are inadequate and not performing well, including in their financial lives, for example, feeling that they are impoverished. Second, they have *negative expectations* about the future, "a pattern of expecting the worst and rejecting the possibility of any improvement." Third, patients engage in *self-blame and self-criticism* because their "egocentric notions of causality" cause them to "ascribe adverse occurrences to some deficiency in themselves."[2] Fourth, patients exhibit *indecisiveness*, that is, are unable to make even simple decisions. The reason for this inability is that "[d]epressed patients anticipate making the wrong decision: whenever they consider one of various possibilities they tend to regard it as wrong and think they will regret making that choice." Finally, patients suffer from *distortion of body image*, thinking that they are unattractive. For instance, a man might "worr[y] incessantly about the beginnings of hair loss, convinced that women find him unattractive."

These cognitive symptoms are closely congruous with the idea that depressed patients have pessimistic beliefs about their returns to effort. Specifically, a patient with negative expectations about the future and egocentric notions of causality would believe precisely that her actions led to undesirable outcomes. This, in turn, would generate self-blame and self-criticism and result in low self-evaluation. Such beliefs could lead to indecisiveness because patients are worried about their actions leading to bad outcomes. Finally, the distortion of body image, for example, the belief that one is unattractive, could be conceived of as a pessimistic belief about the returns to investment in one's own physical appearance.

3.2.2   "Motivational" Symptoms

The motivational symptoms of depression are mainly characterized by withdrawal from activities, escapist tendencies and avoidance of responsi-

---

2. Evidence on the predictors of depression onset suggests that shocks in domains where individuals believe outcomes are under their control are particularly predictive of depression (Kendler, Karkowski, and Prescott 1999).

bility, the assumption of a childlike rather than an adult's role, and a focus on "immediate but transient gratification instead of delayed but prolonged gratifications." Specifically, Beck describes four symptoms in this category: First, patients have *paralysis of the will*, that is, they "have a major problem in mobilizing themselves to perform even the most elemental and vital tasks." Beck identifies as the reason for this paralysis that "although they can define for themselves what they should do, they do not experience any internal stimulus to do it." Second, patients show *avoidance, escapist, and withdrawal wishes*: they want to shirk from their duties and want to withdraw into other activities. Third, patients exhibit increased *dependency* on others, in the sense that they want others to perform tasks for them. Finally, depressed patients often have *suicidal wishes*.

Most of these motivational symptoms can be understood as direct consequences of the core cognitive symptom described above, that is, pessimistic beliefs about oneself. In particular, when an individual believes that their actions lead to negative outcomes, she may naturally want others to perform tasks for them instead. Relatedly, if she believes that her own efforts will not amount to anything, she may choose not to undertake them in the first place, which presents itself as paralysis of the will to the observer. Similar reasoning could be implicated in avoidance, escapist, and withdrawal wishes, that is, individuals with negative beliefs about the consequences of their actions may avoid having to perform these actions in the first place and instead withdraw from life. Finally, suicidal wishes may be an extreme manifestation of the escapist tendencies described above; for instance, they could occur when people believe that efforts generate *negative* returns.

3.2.3 "Emotional" Symptoms

The emotional symptoms of depression mainly consist of dysphoria, that is, low mood and an inability to feel pleasure, and related symptoms. Specifically, depressed patients experience *dejected mood*, that is, they feel "sad," "hopeless," or "miserable." They also exhibit a *reduction in gratification*, in the sense that they are unable to derive pleasure from activities they usually enjoy. This inability extends to both professional and personal contexts, and includes basic activities such as eating and sex. Third, patients experience *negative feelings toward themselves*, blaming themselves for mistakes and believing that they "can't do anything right." Fourth, the inability to derive pleasure from previously enjoyable activities is accompanied by a *loss of emotional attachment*, that is, a "decline in interest in particular activities or in affection or concern for other persons," including one's job, family, and friends. Fourth, depressed patients show a *loss of the mirth response*, that is, their sense of humor: they still understand the point of jokes, but do not find them funny. Finally, they frequently experience *crying spells*.

Dejected mood and crying spells may be thought of as consequences of the reduction in income and overall experienced utility that results from the behaviors above. Similarly, negative feelings toward oneself are a natural consequence of this effect to the extent one assumes blame (which depressed individuals often do; recall the "egocentric notions of causality" described above).

In contrast, loss of emotional attachment, reduction in gratification, and loss of mirth response are, in our view, best understood as consequences of a *low marginal utility of consumption of experiences, relationships, and humor.* This subgroup of emotional symptoms is the leading set of symptoms that is difficult to conceptualize as resulting from pessimistic beliefs. Put differently, these symptoms appear to be about *preferences* rather than *beliefs.*

3.2.4   Delusions, Hallucinations, and Somatic Symptoms

Depressed people frequently suffer from delusions. Beck describes five main categories: delusions of worthlessness; delusions of having committed crimes; nihilistic delusions, for example, thinking that the world is "empty"; somatic delusions, for example, believing that one's body is decaying; and delusions of poverty, that is, believing that one is impoverished. Depressed patients also frequently report hallucinations, for example, of voices that condemn them. Delusions and hallucinations are more difficult to fit into a framework of beliefs and preferences, but several of them are plausibly extreme consequences of pessimistic beliefs. Most prominently, the belief that one is or will be impoverished may be a natural consequence of such beliefs.

Not covered in Beck's description of the symptoms of depression, but contained in the *DSM-5* diagnostic criteria, are two important somatic symptoms. Specifically, depressed individuals often display either hypersomnia or insomnia, that is, excessive sleeping or an inability to sleep. Second, they frequently suffer from either a lack of appetite or overeating. Such nonmonotonicities provide interesting restrictions on the form economic theories can take. Theories in which people face conflicting internal and external motives (for example, they need to sleep eight hours to be productive, but their "natural tendency" is to sleep more or less) may be able to fit these facts. In these cases, distortions to beliefs or preferences might alter the trade-offs between motives: a negative shock to beliefs about the returns to labor provision, for instance, would shift the optimum level of food and sleep from the "productive" optimum to the "consumption" optimum. As a consequence, the observed levels of eating and sleeping may either rise or fall, depending on whether the consumption optima lie below or above the production optima.

3.3   Stylized Facts

In this section, we briefly present a number of empirical stylized facts about depression that our model attempts to predict. Owing to the dearth of

Table 3.1   CESD correlations: economic variables

	CESD total raw score (1)	CESD total z-score (2)	N (3)
HH business shut down in last 18 months	0.8077*** (0.2367)	0.1902*** (0.0557)	13,095
Experienced natural disaster or civil strife	0.3967*** (0.0695)	0.0934*** (0.0164)	31,401
Experienced economic disruption	0.5800*** (0.0703)	0.1366*** (0.0166)	31,401

Notes: Each row is a separate regression of depression on the variable listed on the left. Each regression includes controls for sex and age. Standard errors are clustered at the household level and are reported in parentheses below the coefficient estimate.
***Significant at the 1 percent level.

good causal evidence on the consequences of depression, we mainly do this by presenting correlations between depression and other variables. We rely on the 2014–2015 wave of the Indonesia Family Life Survey (IFLS-5), which surveyed 50,148 individuals in 16,204 households. Depression is measured using the Center for Epidemiologic Studies Depression Scale (CESD), a widely used and validated self-report instrument for measuring depression. We emphasize that the usual disclaimers about correlational evidence apply, and that future work should tease out the direction and strength of causality in the relationships we describe below.

We begin by noting that, in our data, economic shocks are associated with depression. We present in table 3.1 the relationship between CESD scores and indicator variables for whether the household had a business that closed in the past eighteen months, experienced natural disaster or civic strife, or experienced any economic disruption. We find moderately sized and highly significant associations between depression scores and all three variables, with the largest point estimate, a 0.19 standard deviations difference in depression scores, for households with a business that recently shut down. Thus, depression is associated with economic shocks. In addition, quasi-experimental evidence suggests that economic shocks in the form of floods, droughts, or job loss lead to increases in mental disorders, including depression (Amstadter et al. 2009; Goenjian et al. 2001; Mendolia 2009; see Rataj, Kunzweiler, and Garthus-Niegel 2016 for a review). Conversely, randomized controlled trials and natural experiments have shown that poverty alleviation interventions such as unconditional cash transfers lead to reductions in depression (Haushofer and Shapiro 2016). Recent work by Alloush (2017) uses panel GMM estimation to show that the relationship between income and depression is bidirectional, which is consistent with the mechanisms we describe in this chapter. More broadly, programs like health insurance, pensions, microfinance, and access to water lead to improvements in overall mental health and psychological well-being (Devoto et al. 2012; Ssewamala, Han, and Neilands 2009; Ssewamala et al. 2012; Finkelstein et al. 2012; Rosero and Oosterbeek 2011; Tseng and Petrie 2012).

We next ask how depression relates to economic choice variables such as labor supply and expenditure decisions. Panels A–D of figure 3.1 illustrate relevant relationships in the Indonesia data using local linear regressions. Pessimistic beliefs about returns would suggest that labor supply should correlate negatively with depression, by weakening the incentives to supply labor. Indeed, we find a strong negative overall relationship between depression and the number of hours the individual works in a typical week. The relationship is not completely monotonic at low levels of labor supply: below about twenty-two working hours per week, it has a shallow positive association with depression scores. However, over most of the distribution, the relationship is strongly negative.

Next we consider investment and temptation goods, whose consumption might be affected by belief or preference change. In the Indonesia data, we find negative relationships between depression and total expenditure and spending on education; conversely, we find a positive relationship with spending on tobacco.[3] This finding is supported by correlations between depression and changes in tobacco consumption within individuals (Taylor et al. 2014). The causal relationship between depression and tobacco use has been the subject of intense debate in the medical literature, with authors arguing both that smoking precedes and precipitates depression (Munafò et al. 2008; Boden, Fergusson, and Horwood 2010), and that depression increases smoking (Windle and Windle 2001); however, we are not aware of rigorously causally identified studies of the effect of changes in depression status on smoking.

Finally, we highlighted a nonmonotonic relationship between depression and food intake, and between depression and sleep. The diagnostic criteria suggest that depressed individuals suffer from either increased or decreased appetite, and increased or decreased sleep. In our data, we proxy increased or decreased food intake with body mass index (BMI; measured in kg/m^2), and sleep with the number of hours the individual slept in the preceding night. Panels E–F of figure 3.1 show that indeed we find nonmonotonic relationships between these variables and depression scores: high depression scores are associated with both very short and very long sleep duration, and with both high and low BMI. The upward-sloping relationship between BMI and depression at the upper end of the BMI distribution is not very pronounced, possibly because in this sample, the BMI distribution does not have much support at high levels of BMI.

---

3. Spending on another important temptation good, alcohol, is not shown because Indonesia is a Muslim country and therefore the vast majority of our sample does not consume any alcohol.

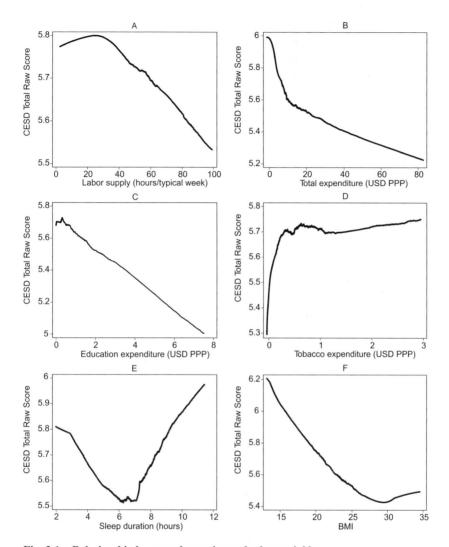

Fig. 3.1 Relationship between depression and other variables

Notes: Local linear regressions of depression (CESD) scores on other variables. The raw CESD score ranges from 0 (not depressed) to 60 (severely depressed), with a cutoff of 16 for depression. Labor supply is measured in hours of labor supplied by the respondent in their main income-generating activity in a typical week; we exclude individuals who supplied zero or more than 100 hours of labor. Total expenditure and spending on tobacco and education is measured in USD PPP. Sleep duration is measured through self-report in hours for the preceding night. BMI is imputed from self-reports of height and weight. In each regression we first use the Frisch-Waugh theorem to create residuals from a regression of the variables of interest on gender, age, their square terms, and the interactions; we then create a new variable by adding the unconditional mean. Local linear regressions use a tricube weighting function and have a bandwidth of 0.8.

On the whole, we find good correlational support for the associations between depression and economic variables. We stress again that these relationships are not causal, and can therefore only be suggestive. In particular, it is likely that in several cases causality runs from the other variables to depression; for example, being unable to work, being overweight or underweight, or having a sleep disorder can plausibly lead to depression. Future work could investigate the causal effect from depression to these variables.

3.4   Avenues for Economic Theory

The goal of this section is to suggest directions for new theoretical work on depression. The symptoms outlined above suggest a core set of mechanisms that we believe are amenable to economic modeling.

We see three main benefits of using economic theory to study depression. First and foremost, depression and mental health more broadly raise first-order welfare concerns, and translating the core of the symptomatology and evidence for driving mechanisms into economic theory can give economists a richer language and terminology with which to discuss these issues. Second, formal models of depression would allow it to be incorporated into other applied analyses, for instance into macroeconomic modeling or policy analysis. Third, theoretical analysis may deliver new insights for understanding mechanisms underlying depression, predicting new behaviors caused by depression and even guiding potential new approaches to treatment.

In the following, we discuss two main approaches for capturing the symptoms of depression in economic models: belief-based and preference-based models. As mentioned above and further discussed below, a number of features of depression lend themselves to a description in terms of distorted beliefs, while others (in particular, emotional symptoms) are more readily captured by changes in preferences. We do not view these mechanisms as mutually exclusive.

3.4.1   Beliefs

In the following, we outline a simple model of belief-driven depression (de Quidt and Haushofer 2017). The core mechanism at the heart of the model is that external shocks can lead people to hold negative beliefs about themselves. This mechanism is analogous to the first pillar of Beck's cognitive triad, and turns out to predict several of the stylized facts described above. Consider a decision maker who maximizes utility from consumption and makes productive decisions to generate income by supplying labor. In each period, the decision maker chooses labor effort, then observes her income realization. Based on this, she forms a (Bayesian) belief about her returns to effort, which feeds into choices next period. In the model, we take as a benchmark the optimal choices that would be made if the agent had correct beliefs, and study what happens when her beliefs become distorted following shocks.

This very simple model can fit a number of the key facts. It generates pessimistic beliefs following negative shocks, which lead to withdrawal of labor effort. In addition, inputs into production that are complementary to beliefs, such as food and sleep, are not optimally chosen: because these variables are both consumption and inputs into production, decreases in one's beliefs about the returns to effort will lead to changes in food intake and sleep away from the production-optimal allocations toward the consumption-optimal allocations, which will decrease output. Income and consumption are also therefore lower among the depressed, and food and sleep patterns are altered. Investment, for example, in education, would be reduced for similar reasons, and spending on temptation goods, which can be thought of as negative investment, would increase. Thus, a simple model of pessimistic beliefs about the returns to effort has the potential to capture many of the stylized facts.

Role of Non-Bayesian Updating

A natural starting point for any modeling effort is that agents learn about their returns to effort via Bayesian updating, and in a sense become depressed "rationally." Modeling belief formation as Bayesian has many attractive theoretical properties—it is familiar to economists, captures the key intuition needed (essentially, that beliefs become more negative following a shock), and is tractable and parsimonious.

But Bayesian belief formation also raises questions. Is it reasonable to think of depression as "rational"? We suspect many would find this at least highly controversial. Moreover, is it calibrationally realistic? Individuals have a whole lifetime to learn about their returns to effort, so for a single unemployment shock to be sufficient to convince them their returns are much lower than they previously thought may not be quantitatively consistent with Bayesian updating.[4]

Promising directions for future work could involve use of models of non-Bayesian updating. A number of papers study models of "motivated cognition" in which decision makers distort or selectively remember information to arrive at biased beliefs.[5] A key empirical finding is overconfidence, potentially arrived at by asymmetric updating after positive and negative information (see, e.g., Eil and Rao 2011; Möbius et al. 2011). But there is some evidence of "depressive realism," that depressed people hold more accurate

---

4. A related calibration point: in discussion at the AEA meetings, Justin Wolfers pointed out that while depressed people in the United States have somewhat lower incomes than nondepressed people, the drop in life satisfaction associated with depression is considerably larger than would be expected from income alone.

5. See, for example, the review in Bénabou and Tirole (2016).

beliefs about the world, thus appearing *relatively* pessimistic (Alloy and Abramson 1979). As for calibration issues, one possibility is that depressed people tend to focus "too much" on recent negative news, overweighting it relative to the past. Underweighting of prior information is referred to as the "base-rate fallacy" (Bar-Hillel 1980).

In sum, a potential force driving the onset of depression is changes to the belief-updating process, to become more selectively negative, or to focus too much on recent shocks and events.

Poverty Traps

The flip side of becoming overly pessimistic in response to recent bad news is a tendency for spells of depression to persist and recur. In the model sketched above, this could lead to a "depression poverty trap," in which pessimistic beliefs cause people to withdraw effort and stop learning about returns. This can lead to multiple equilibria, where a poverty trap equilibrium is one in which effort is inefficiently low but the depressed person does not learn.[6] An important mechanism in models in which learning depends on choice is the extent to which the decision maker is sophisticated about future learning. For example, a depressed person who is aware that her beliefs might be overly pessimistic might continue to take exploratory actions so as to ascertain whether that is the case. The extent to which depressed people are sophisticated in this manner is, to our knowledge, unknown.

3.4.2   Preferences

Shocks to Marginal Utility

The experience of dysphoria as discussed under "emotional" symptoms most naturally lends itself to a preference-driven explanation. Something about the preferences of depressed people changes to reduce the satisfaction from once-pleasurable activities. One possible source of this effect is that pessimistic expectations of the future diminish the pleasure of consumption today, perhaps even as a form of protection against future disappointment. Such behavior might be well captured in a reference-dependent model, relating to, for example, Kőszegi and Rabin (2006, 2009). Hermalin and Isen (2007) also present a model in which preferences are influenced by mood, which depends on past outcomes.

A simple way to capture dysphoria is to distort marginal utilities. For example, depression could be characterized as a decrease in the marginal

6. Related mechanisms exist in other models, for example, Piketty (1995), Ali (2011), and Warren and Wilkening (2012). Conceptually, the problem is related to bandit problems (Robbins 1952; Bergemann and Valimaki 2006). See also Dalton, Ghosal, and Mani (2015) on aspirations-based poverty traps.

utility of nonfood consumption. Such a lower marginal utility of nonfood consumption reduces the incentive to earn income, and also distorts the trade-off between consumption and production motives in food and sleep. It literally captures the notion that consumption delivers "less utility" than before. While such a mechanism is less congruent with symptoms related to a negative view of the self, it aligns well with pessimistic beliefs about the future if the individual expects that future consumption will also be less satisfying and pleasurable.

Beliefs about Marginal Utility

A further potential avenue for research is a model that links preferences to beliefs.[7] In particular, suppose that utility is subject to a shock. The decision maker is uncertain about the marginal utility of consumption, and learns about it over time by observing consumption and experienced utility. A negative utility shock (for example, a stressful life event) that enters may be (incorrectly) partially attributed to the marginal utility of consumption, leading the agent to become more pessimistic about her future ability to generate utility and resulting in the behavior changes described above. For example, anticipating lower marginal utility in the future might reduce earning incentives and decrease the incentive to choose "production optimal" food and sleep consumption.

Substitutes in the Utility Function

The medical literature largely mentions self-medication as the motivation for temptation good consumption in depression (Khantzian 1985). Partly this may be because of psychoactive properties of nicotine, alcohol, and other drugs, which might directly interact with the belief or preference distortions induced by depression. It could also be that depression changes trade-offs in the utility function, and that such goods become more attractive substitutes when the returns to other forms of consumption diminish.

3.5 Conclusion

The goal of this chapter was to make first steps in understanding depression through the lens of economic analysis. In particular, we have described the core symptoms of depression in terms of economic primitives, and present correlational data illustrating the relationship between depression and important economic variables. Finally, we have discussed two possible modeling approaches for depression: belief-based and preference-based theories. In this conclusion, we briefly discuss the relative merits of both.

---

7. We thank Yves Le Yaouanq for this suggestion.

The virtue of belief-based theories is that they have the potential to capture a large number of the core symptoms of depression described at the outset of the chapter. In addition, belief-based theories of depression resonate with prominent psychological and psychiatric theories of depression, and the therapeutic approaches to which they gave rise. An early account of depression in the tradition of the behaviorist B. F. Skinner was provided by the psychologist Charles Ferster, who argued that depression resulted from an overexposure to negative reinforcement and underexposure to positive reinforcement in the environment (Ferster 1973). This view led to the development of behavioral activation therapy, which focuses on exposing the patient to positive reinforcement. While today's treatment approaches are different, Ferster's account of the etiology of depression is closely aligned with analysis that emphasizes the importance of exposure to negative shocks.

When the cognitive revolution in psychology shifted the focus from simple stimulus-response contingencies in the tradition of Skinner to the cognitive processes that mediate an individual's responses, the classic work of the psychiatrist Aaron Beck suggested that a core reason for depression is distorted thinking (Beck 1967). Correcting such distorted thoughts is still a central element in the standard therapeutic tool to treat depression, cognitive behavioral therapy (CBT). Inaccurate beliefs about the returns to effort are an example of such distorted beliefs, and the focus of CBT on correcting such beliefs may explain its effectiveness. An equally important component of CBT—correcting distorted behaviors—might also be effective by exposing individuals to more opportunities to learn that their beliefs are overly pessimistic.

However, while beliefs may be a suitable target for therapeutic efforts, a description of the symptomatology and etiology of depression purely in terms of beliefs falls short of capturing reality. The emotional symptoms of depression are especially difficult to characterize as resulting from pessimistic beliefs. Instead, they call for a preference-based account of depression, such as the one outlined above. Nevertheless, while preference distortions caused by depression seem well aligned with some of the facts, they provide a less satisfying and potentially less helpful account than belief-based models. In particular, it is unclear how preference shocks could come about, and how practitioners might be able to treat "distorted marginal utility." In contrast, the causal chain from shock to belief to behavior is very clear, and offers good targets for treatment. Future work may be able to provide richer psychological and economic foundations to preference change induced by and inducing depression, and to gather new evidence to separate preference and belief-based explanations of depression. Together, our hope is that this approach will enable economists to advance our understanding of depression in particular, and mental health in general.

Appendix

Major Depressive Disorder: *DSM-5* Diagnostic Criteria

A. Five (or more) of the following symptoms have been present during the same two-week period and represent a change from previous functioning: at least one of the symptoms is either (a) depressed mood or (b) loss of interest or pleasure.

Note: Do not include symptoms that are clearly attributable to another medical condition.

(a) Depressed mood most of the day, nearly every day, as indicated by either subjective report (e.g., feels sad, empty, hopeless) or observation made by others (e.g., appears tearful). (**Note:** In children and adolescents, can be irritable mood.)

(b) Markedly diminished interest or pleasure in all, or almost all, activities most of the day, nearly every day (as indicated by either subjective account or observation).

(c) Significant weight loss when not dieting or weight gain (e.g., a change of more than 5 percent of body weight in a month), or decrease or increase in appetite nearly every day. (**Note:** In children, consider failure to make expected weight gain.)

(d) Insomnia or hypersomnia nearly every day.

(e) Psychomotor agitation or retardation nearly every day (observable by others, not merely subjective feelings of restlessness or being slowed down).

(f) Fatigue or loss of energy nearly every day.

(g) Feelings of worthlessness or excessive or inappropriate guilt (which may be delusional) nearly every day (not merely self-reproach or guilt about being sick).

(h) Diminished ability to think or concentrate, or indecisiveness, nearly every day (either by subjective account or as observed by others).

(i) Recurrent thoughts of death (not just fear of dying), recurrent suicidal ideation without a specific plan, or a suicide attempt or a specific plan for committing suicide.

B. The symptoms cause clinically significant distress or impairment in social, occupational, or other important areas of functioning.

C. The episode is not attributable to the physiological effects of a substance or to another medical condition.

Note: Criteria A–C represent a major depressive episode.

Note: Responses to a significant loss (e.g., bereavement, financial ruin, losses from a natural disaster, a serious medical illness or disability) may include the feelings of intense sadness, rumination about the loss, insomnia, poor appetite, and weight loss noted in Criterion A, which may resemble a depressive episode. Although such symptoms may be understandable or considered appropriate to the loss, the presence of a major depressive episode in addition to the normal response to a significant loss should also be carefully considered. This decision inevitably requires the exercise of clinical judgment based on the individual's history and the cultural norms for the expression of distress in the context of loss.[8]

D. The occurrence of the major depressive episode is not better explained by schizoaffective disorder, schizophrenia, schizophreniform disorder, delusional disorder, or other specified and unspecified schizophrenia spectrum and other psychotic disorders.

E. There has never been a manic episode or a hypomanic episode.

   Note: This exclusion does not apply if all of the manic-like or hypomanic-like episodes are substance-induced or are attributable to the physiological effects of another medical condition.

Diagnostic Features

The criterion symptoms for major depressive disorder must be present nearly every day to be considered present, with the exception of weight change and suicidal ideation. Depressed mood must be present for most of the day, in addition to being present nearly every day. Often insomnia or fatigue is the presenting complaint, and failure to probe for accompanying depressive symptoms will result in underdiagnosis. Sadness may be denied at first, but may be elicited through interview or inferred from facial expression and demeanor. With individuals who focus on a somatic complaint, clinicians should determine whether the distress from that complaint is associated with specific depressive symptoms. Fatigue and sleep disturbance are present in a high proportion of cases; psychomotor disturbances are much less common but are indicative of greater overall severity, as is the presence of delusional or near-delusional guilt.

The essential feature of a major depressive episode is a period of at least two weeks during which there is either depressed mood or the loss of interest

---

8. In distinguishing grief from a major depressive episode (MDE), it is useful to consider that in grief the predominant affect is feelings of emptiness and loss, while in MDE it is persistent depressed mood and the inability to anticipate happiness or pleasure. The dysphoria in grief is likely to decrease in intensity over days to weeks and occurs in waves, the so-called pangs of grief. These waves tend to be associated with thoughts or reminders of the deceased. The depressed mood of MDE is more persistent and not tied to specific thoughts or preoccupations. The pain of grief may be accompanied by positive emotions and humor that are uncharacteristic of the pervasive unhappiness and misery characteristic of MDE. The thought content associated with grief generally features a preoccupation with thoughts and memories of the deceased, rather than the self-critical or pessimistic ruminations seen in MDE. In grief, self-esteem is generally preserved, whereas in MDE feelings of worthlessness and self-loathing are common. If self-derogatory ideation is present in grief, it typically involves perceived failings vis-à-vis the deceased (e.g., not visiting frequently enough, not telling the deceased how much he or she was loved). If a bereaved individual thinks about death and dying, such thoughts are generally focused on the deceased and possibly about "joining" the deceased, whereas in MDE such thoughts are focused on ending one's own life because of feeling worthless, undeserving of life, or unable to cope with the pain of depression.

or pleasure in nearly all activities (Criterion A). In children and adolescents, the mood may be irritable rather than sad. The individual must also experience at least four additional symptoms drawn from a list that includes changes in appetite or weight, sleep, and psychomotor activity; decreased energy; feelings of worthlessness or guilt; difficulty thinking, concentrating, or making decisions; or recurrent thoughts of death or suicidal ideation or suicide plans or attempts. To count toward a major depressive episode, a symptom must either be newly present or must have clearly worsened compared with the person's preepisode status. The symptoms must persist for most of the day, nearly every day, for at least two consecutive weeks. The episode must be accompanied by clinically significant distress or impairment in social, occupational, or other important areas of functioning. For some individuals with milder episodes, functioning may appear to be normal but requires markedly increased effort.

The mood in a major depressive episode is often described by the person as depressed, sad, hopeless, discouraged, or "down in the dumps" (Criterion A1). In some cases, sadness may be denied at first but may subsequently be elicited by interview (e.g., by pointing out that the individual looks as if he or she is about to cry). In some individuals who complain of feeling "blah," having no feelings, or feeling anxious, the presence of a depressed mood can be inferred from the person's facial expression and demeanor. Some individuals emphasize somatic complaints (e.g., bodily aches and pains) rather than reporting feelings of sadness. Many individuals report or exhibit increased irritability (e.g., persistent anger, a tendency to respond to events with angry outbursts or blaming others, an exaggerated sense of frustration over minor matters). In children and adolescents, an irritable or cranky mood may develop rather than a sad or dejected mood. This presentation should be differentiated from a pattern of irritability when frustrated.

Loss of interest or pleasure is nearly always present, at least to some degree. Individuals may report feeling less interested in hobbies, "not caring anymore," or not feeling any enjoyment in activities that were previously considered pleasurable (Criterion A2). Family members often notice social withdrawal or neglect of pleasurable avocations (e.g., a formerly avid golfer no longer plays, a child who used to enjoy soccer finds excuses not to practice). In some individuals, there is a significant reduction from previous levels of sexual interest or desire.

Appetite change may involve either a reduction or increase. Some depressed individuals report that they have to force themselves to eat. Others may eat more and may crave specific foods (e.g., sweets or other carbohydrates). When appetite changes are severe (in either direction), there may be a significant loss or gain in weight, or, in children, a failure to make expected weight gains may be noted (Criterion A3).

Sleep disturbance may take the form of either difficulty sleeping or sleeping excessively (Criterion A4). When insomnia is present, it typically takes the form of middle insomnia (i.e., waking up during the night and then having difficulty returning to sleep) or terminal insomnia (i.e., waking too early and being unable to return to sleep). Initial insomnia (i.e., difficulty falling asleep) may also occur. Individuals who present with oversleeping (hypersomnia) may experience prolonged sleep episodes at night or increased daytime sleep. Sometimes the reason that the individual seeks treatment is for the disturbed sleep.

Psychomotor changes include agitation (e.g., the inability to sit still, pacing, handwringing; or pulling or rubbing of the skin, clothing, or other objects) or retardation (e.g., slowed speech, thinking, and body movements; increased pauses before answering; speech that is decreased in volume, inflection, amount, or variety of content, or muteness) (Criterion A5). The psychomotor agitation or retardation must be severe enough to be observable by others and not represent merely subjective feelings.

Decreased energy, tiredness, and fatigue are common (Criterion A6). A person may report sustained fatigue without physical exertion. Even the smallest tasks seem to require substantial effort. The efficiency with which tasks are accomplished may be reduced. For example, an individual may complain that washing and dressing in the morning are exhausting and take twice as long as usual.

The sense of worthlessness or guilt associated with a major depressive episode may include unrealistic negative evaluations of one's worth or guilty preoccupations or ruminations over minor past failings (Criterion A7). Such individuals often misinterpret neutral or trivial day-to-day events as evidence of personal defects and have an exaggerated sense of responsibility for untoward events. The sense of worthlessness or guilt may be of delusional proportions (e.g., an individual who is convinced that he or she is personally responsible for world poverty). Blaming oneself for being sick and for failing to meet occupational or interpersonal responsibilities as a result of the depression is very common and, unless delusional, is not considered sufficient to meet this criterion.

Many individuals report impaired ability to think, concentrate, or make even minor decisions (Criterion A8). They may appear easily distracted or complain of memory difficulties. Those engaged in cognitively demanding pursuits are often unable to function. In children, a precipitous drop in grades may reflect poor concentration. In elderly individuals, memory difficulties may be the chief complaint and may be mistaken for early signs of a dementia ("pseudodementia"). When the major depressive episode is successfully treated, the memory problems often fully abate. However, in some individuals, particularly elderly persons, a major depressive episode may sometimes be the initial presentation of an irreversible dementia.

Thoughts of death, suicidal ideation, or suicide attempts (Criterion A9) are common. They may range from a passive wish not to awaken in the morning or a belief that others would be better off if the individual were dead, to transient but recurrent thoughts of committing suicide, to a specific suicide plan. More severely suicidal individuals may have put their affairs in order (e.g., updated wills, settled debts), acquired needed materials (e.g., a rope or a gun), and chosen a location and time to accomplish the suicide. Motivations for suicide may include a desire to give up in the face of perceived insurmountable obstacles, an intense wish to end what is perceived as an unending and excruciatingly painful emotional state, an inability to foresee any enjoyment in life, or the wish to not be a burden to others. The resolution of such thinking may be a more meaningful measure of diminished suicide risk than denial of further plans for suicide.

The evaluation of the symptoms of a major depressive episode is especially difficult when they occur in an individual who also has a general medical condition (e.g., cancer, stroke, myocardial infarction, diabetes, pregnancy). Some of the criterion signs and symptoms of a major depressive episode are identical to those of general medical conditions (e.g., weight loss with untreated diabetes, fatigue with cancer, hypersomnia early in pregnancy, insomnia later in pregnancy or postpartum). Such symptoms count toward a major depressive diagnosis except when they are clearly and fully attributable to a general medical condition. Nonvegetative symptoms of dysphoria, anhedonia, guilt or worthlessness, impaired concentration or indecision, and suicidal thoughts should be assessed with particular care in such cases. Definitions of major depressive episodes that have been modified to include only these nonvegetative symptoms appear to identify nearly the same individuals as do the full criteria.

Associated Features Supporting Diagnosis

Major depressive disorder is associated with high mortality, much of which is accounted for by suicide; however, it is not the only cause. For example, depressed individuals admitted to nursing homes have a markedly increased likelihood of death in the first year. Individuals frequently present with tearfulness, irritability, brooding, obsessive rumination, anxiety, phobias, excessive worry over physical health, and complaints of pain (e.g., headaches; joint, abdominal, or other pains). In children, separation anxiety may occur.

Although an extensive literature exists describing neuroanatomical, neuroendocrinological, and neurophysiological correlates of major depressive disorder, no laboratory test has yielded results of sufficient sensitivity and specificity to be used as a diagnostic tool for this disorder. Until recently, hypothalamic-pituitary-adrenal axis hyperactivity had been the most extensively investigated abnormality associated with major depressive episodes, and it appears to be associated with melancholia, psychotic features, and risks for eventual suicide. Molecular studies have also implicated peripheral factors, including genetic variants in neurotrophic factors and proinflammatory cytokines. Additionally, functional magnetic resonance imaging studies provide evidence for functional abnormalities in specific neural systems supporting emotion processing, reward seeking, and emotion regulation in adults with major depression.

Summary of the Literature on Economic Causes of Depression

The related economics literature almost exclusively studies mental well-being as an outcome, often as a component of a more holistic view of well-being than conventional measures such as income or consumption. We provide a brief review of that literature here, discussing studies of the effects of unemployment, fear of unemployment, wealth shocks, crime and fear of crime, and social comparisons. For brevity, we focus on the studies that explicitly seek causal identification through use of panel data techniques, natural experiments, instrumental variables, or field experiments. Most studies use composite measures of mental well-being, but we highlight those that specifically measure depression prevalence or incidence.

Unemployment and Fear of Unemployment

It is well documented that depression rates are much higher among the unemployed, but causality could run in both directions. In our theory, we would interpret an unemployment shock (or fear of unemployment) as a shock to an individual's perceived future returns to her labor.

Clark (2003) uses the British Household Panel Survey (BHPS) (from 1991/92–1997/98) and studies the GHQ-12 composite measure of mental well-being, which includes questions on depression, as well as "feelings of strain," and insomnia. Mental well-being is significantly lower among the unemployed and among those whose partner is unemployed. In fixed-effects regressions he shows that mental well-being falls when an individual moves into unemployment and increases when he/she moves into employment.

Marcus (2013) uses the German Socio-Economic Panel (2002–2010) to study the impact of plant closures on composite mental health, measured by the Mental Component Summary Scale (MCS). Households that experienced a job loss due to plant closure during the period are matched on observables to households that did not, and the plant closure effect estimated by difference-in-differences. He finds approximately equal negative effects on mental health from own or spouse's unemployment—only in seven households did both members become unemployed, so he cannot study the interaction considered by Clark (2003) (see below). Our framework focuses on private returns of a representative agent and cannot directly speak to depression induced by shocks to a close family member, except to the extent that they induce pessimism about own returns.

Farré, Fasani, and Mueller (2015) use the Spanish Health Survey (2006 and 2011 waves) to estimate the causal effect of job loss on mental health. They exploit the collapse of the Spanish construction industry since 2007 as a source of exogenous negative to both short- and long-run employment for construction workers.[9] Key outcomes of interest are diagnoses of, and self-reported, mental disorders (depression or chronic anxiety). In addition, they study responses to the GHQ-12 questions. The identification strategy is instrumental variables, with location-specific exposure to construction as the instrument. They find a statistically significant 1.1 standard deviation in mental disorder diagnoses, and a 0.9 standard deviation in mental health as measured by GHQ-12. Closely in line with our theory, they write "[the shock] led to long unemployment spells, hopelessness and feelings of uselessness."

Colantone, Crinò, and Ogliari (2015) use the BHPS (2001–2007) to study the effect of import competition in an individual's industry on his/her mental distress, measured using GHQ-12. Using individual fixed-effects regressions, they find that a one standard deviation increase in import competition (defined as the ratio of imports to national consumption) in the individual's industry leads to a decline of 0.13 standard deviations in the GHQ-12 index. Splitting out the components, they find particularly large effects on anxiety and depression. Analyzing mechanisms, they use a two-step procedure to study how import competition feeds through to final mental health outcomes. They find support for the effect working through decreased job security, lower wage growth, and lower job satisfaction particularly regarding workload. We interpret these findings as closely aligned with our theory.

Wealth Shocks

While our theory only considers wealth shocks that operate through the return to labor, the link we invoke from anticipated future consumption to mood also naturally carries over to shocks to nonlabor income. We highlight two studies of the effect of stock market losses on the mental health of retirees.

McInerney, Mellor, and Nicholas (2013) study the effect of wealth shocks on mental health in the US Health and Retirement Study (HRS), exploiting exogenous variation in interview dates: some individuals in the 2008 wave were surveyed before the October stock market crash, and some after. They find that antidepressant use and self-reported measures of depression and mental health worsened after the crash. Notably, the effect was strongest for individuals with high stock holdings. However, clinically validated measures based on the CESD showed no systematic effects.

Schwandt (2014) also uses the HRS to study wealth shocks, extending the analysis to the 1998–2011 waves. He constructs individual-specific exposure to stock market shocks by measuring individual stock market participa-

9. They argue that a key advantage of this natural experiment (as opposed to plant closures) is that it enables the study of long-run effects since it was very hard for unemployed, low-education construction workers to re-enter employment, while those laid off because of a plant closure might reenter employment differentially according to their (mental) health status.

tion. He finds strong negative effects on both physical health and depression (using the CESD).

Crime and Fear of Crime

One interpretation in line with our theory is that recent crime experience or exposure induces fear of future crime and either directly reduces the return to labor effort (through theft or destruction of property) or indirectly because of lost productivity caused by the crime event, particularly when violence is involved.

Cornaglia, Feldman, and Leigh (2014) use the Household, Income and Labour Dynamics in Australia (HILDA) survey from 2002 to 2006, and measure mental health outcomes using subsets of the 36-Item Short Form Health Survey (SF-36). We are primarily interested in their mental health scale, using five questions that focus on depression and nervousness. In individual fixed-effects regressions, they find a negative relationship between recent experience of violent crime and mental health, and also between local crime rates and mental health. They find smaller, not significant effects from property crime.

Dustmann and Fasani (2016) study the BHPS, focusing also on the GHQ-12 index that they divide into separate components, including an anxiety and depression component. In individual fixed-effects regressions they find that increases in the local crime rate harm mental health, including anxiety and depression. In contrast with Cornaglia, Feldman, and Leigh (2014), and closer in spirit to our theory, the effect of property crime is statistically significant while violent crime is not. Dustmann and Fasani (2016) also use data from the English Longitudinal Study of Ageing (ELSA) of individuals age fifty and older, which contains a direct measure of depression, the Psychosocial Health Module (PSH) based on the CESD, which we also use. They find that increases in local crime rates, both violent and property crime, lead to increases in depression rates.

Socioeconomic Environment

We highlight two sets of studies that can be thought of as analyzing the effects of changes to peer-group composition or outcomes on own mental health.

Katz, Kling, and Liebman (2001) study the two-year impacts of the well-known Moving to Opportunity program (at the Boston site), in which poor households were randomly assigned subsidies to move to low-poverty neighborhoods or rent subsidies that could be used in any neighborhood. Income and employment did not change relative to control, but the predicted probability of a major depressive episode[10] fell by 5 to 10 percentage points (not

---

10. A measure constructed from the Composite Diagnostic Interview Short Form (CIDI-SF).

statistically significant) from a baseline of 25 to 35 percent. Medium-run effects (four to seven years), studied in Kling, Liebman, and Katz (2007), are more positive—poverty rates declined and mental health outcomes, both for depression specifically, as well as composite measures, improved substantially. The effect on mental health is also shown to be larger the lower is the poverty rate of the new neighborhood. Finally, Ludwig et al. (2012) study long-run effects (ten to fifteen years), finding persistently lower poverty rates and (marginally significant) improvements in composite mental health. We note also that an additional channel discussed in these papers is through the fear of crime, and that fear of crime declined after moving to better neighborhoods.

In contrast with these positive effects of low relative socioeconomic status on mental health outcomes, a second set of studies suggests negative effects. Luttmer (2005) studies the relationship between neighbors' average earnings on individuals' self-reported happiness and finds a negative effect, holding constant the individual's own income. Similarly, Baird, de Hoop, and Özler (2013) and Haushofer, Reisinger, and Shapiro (2015) provide evidence of negative spillovers of cash transfer programs in Malawi and Kenya on neighbors' psychological well-being. Clark (2003), discussed above, studies the interaction between own unemployment and unemployment in three reference groups: the spouse or partner, household members, and the region. He finds a moderating effect: the mental well-being of the unemployed is higher when the unemployment rate among plausible reference groups is higher (spouse or partner, household members, region).

The two sets of findings seem to conflict—the Moving to Opportunity experiment decreased the relative standing of the treated households relative to their neighbors and increased mental well-being, while the remainder of the studies suggest an opposite effect of peer comparisons. However, Moving to Opportunity also improved the *absolute* prospects of the treated households as seen in the poverty and crime exposure results, and this may have outweighed the relative effects.

References

Ali, S. Nageeb. 2011. "Learning Self-Control." *Quarterly Journal of Economics* 126 (2): 857–93.

Alloush, M. 2017. "Unpacking the Causal Relationships between Income and Psychological Well-Being." Working paper, University of California, Davis.

Alloy, L. B., and L. Y. Abramson. 1979. "Judgment of Contingency in Depressed and Nondepressed Students: Sadder but Wiser?" *Journal of Experimental Psychology General* 108 (4): 441–85.

Amstadter, Ananda B., Ron Acierno, Lisa K. Richardson, Dean G. Kilpatrick, Daniel F. Gros, Mario T. Gaboury, Trinh Luong Tran, et al. 2009. "Posttyphoon

Prevalence of Posttraumatic Stress Disorder, Major Depressive Disorder, Panic Disorder, and Generalized Anxiety Disorder in a Vietnamese Sample." *Journal of Traumatic Stress* 22 (3): 180–88.

Baird, Sarah, Jacobus de Hoop, and Berk Özler. 2013. "Income Shocks and Adolescent Mental Health." *Journal of Human Resources* 48 (2): 370–403.

Bar-Hillel, Maya. 1980. "The Base-Rate Fallacy in Probability Judgments." *Acta Psychologica* 44 (3): 211–33.

Beck, Aaron T. 1967. *Depression: Causes and Treatment*. Philadelphia: University of Pennsylvania Press.

Becker, Gary S., and Kevin M. Murphy. 1988. "A Theory of Rational Addiction." *Journal of Political Economy* 96 (4): 675–700.

Bénabou, Roland, and Jean Tirole. 2016. "Mindful Economics: The Production, Consumption, and Value of Beliefs." *Journal of Economic Perspectives* 30 (3): 141–64.

Bergemann, Dirk, and Juuso Valimaki. 2006. "Bandit Problems." Cowles Foundation Discussion Paper no. 1551. Available at https://ssrn.com/abstract=877173.

Boden, Joseph M., David M. Fergusson, and L. John Horwood. 2010. "Cigarette Smoking and Depression: Tests of Causal Linkages Using a Longitudinal Birth Cohort." *British Journal of Psychiatry* 196 (6): 440–46.

Bromet, E., L. H. Andrade, I. Hwang, N. A. Sampson, J. Alonso, G. de Girolamo, R. de Graaf, et al. 2011. "Cross-National Epidemiology of DSM-IV Major Depressive Episode." *BMC Medicine* 9 (1): 90.

Clark, Andrew E. 2003. "Unemployment as a Social Norm: Psychological Evidence from Panel Data." *Journal of Labor Economics* 21 (2): 323–51.

Colantone, Italo, Rosario Crinò, and Laura Ogliari. 2015. "The Hidden Cost of Globalization: Import Competition and Mental Distress." CESifo Working Paper no. 5586, Center for Economic Studies, Munich.

Cornaglia, Francesca, Naomi E. Feldman, and Andrew Leigh. 2014. "Crime and Mental Well-Being." *Journal of Human Resources* 49 (1): 110–40.

Dalton, Patricio S., Sayantan Ghosal, and Anandi Mani. 2015. "Poverty and Aspirations Failure." *Economic Journal* 126 (590): 165–88.

de Quidt, Jonathan, and Johannes Haushofer. 2017. "Depression for Economists." NBER Working Paper no. 22973, Cambridge, MA.

Devoto, Florencia, Esther Duflo, Pascaline Dupas, William Parienté, and Vincent Pons. 2012. "Happiness on Tap: Piped Water Adoption in Urban Morocco." *American Economic Journal: Economic Policy* 4 (4): 68–99.

Dustmann, Christian, and Francesco Fasani. 2016. "The Effect of Local Area Crime on Mental Health." *Economic Journal* 126 (593): 978–1017.

Eil, David, and Justin M. Rao. 2011. "The Good News–Bad News Effect: Asymmetric Processing of Objective Information about Yourself." *American Economic Journal: Microeconomics* 3 (2): 114–38.

Farré, Lidia, Francesco Fasani, and Hannes Felix Mueller. 2015. "Feeling Useless: The Effect of Unemployment on Mental Health in the Great Recession." Working Paper no. 774, School of Economics and Finance, Queen Mary University of London.

Ferster, C. B. 1973. "A Functional Analysis of Depression." *American Psychologist* 28 (10): 857–70.

Finkelstein, Amy, Sarah Taubman, Bill Wright, Mira Bernstein, Jonathan Gruber, Joseph P. Newhouse, Heidi Allen, Katherine Baicker, and the Oregon Health Study Group. 2012. "The Oregon Health Insurance Experiment: Evidence from the First Year." NBER Working Paper no. 17190, Cambridge, MA.

Goenjian, Armen K., Luis Molina, Alan M. Steinberg, Lynn A. Fairbanks, Maria Luisa Alvarez, Haig A. Goenjian, and Robert S. Pynoos. 2001. "Posttraumatic

Stress and Depressive Reactions among Nicaraguan Adolescents after Hurricane Mitch." *American Journal of Psychiatry* 158 (5): 788–94.

Haushofer, Johannes, James Reisinger, and Jeremy Shapiro. 2015. "Is Your Gain My Pain? Psychological Externalities of Wealth Changes." Working paper, Princeton University.

Haushofer, Johannes, and Jeremy Shapiro. 2016. "The Short-Term Impact of Unconditional Cash Transfers to the Poor: Experimental Evidence from Kenya." *Quarterly Journal of Economics* 131 (4): 1973–2042.

Hermalin, Benjamin E., and Alice M. Isen. 2007. "A Model of the Effect of Affect on Economic Decision Making." *Quantitative Marketing and Economics* 6 (1): 17–40.

Katz, Lawrence F., Jeffrey R. Kling, and Jeffrey B. Liebman. 2001. "Moving to Opportunity in Boston: Early Results of a Randomized Mobility Experiment." *Quarterly Journal of Economics* 116 (2): 607–54.

Kendler, K. S., L. M. Karkowski, and C. A. Prescott. 1999. "Causal Relationship between Stressful Life Events and the Onset of Major Depression." *American Journal of Psychiatry* 156 (6): 837–41.

Kessler, Ronald C., and Evelyn J. Bromet. 2013. "The Epidemiology of Depression across Cultures." *Annual Review of Public Health* 34:119–38.

Khantzian, Edward J. 1985. "The Self-Medication Hypothesis of Addictive Disorders: Focus on Heroin and Cocaine Dependence." *American Journal of Psychiatry* 142 (11): 1259–64.

Kling, Jeffrey R., Jeffrey B. Liebman, and Lawrence F. Katz. 2007. "Experimental Analysis of Neighborhood Effects." *Econometrica* 75 (1): 83–119.

Kőszegi, Botond, and Matthew Rabin. 2006. "A Model of Reference-Dependent Preferences." *Quarterly Journal of Economics* 121:1133–65.

———. 2009. "Reference-Dependent Consumption Plans." *American Economic Review* 99 (3): 909–36.

Ludwig, Jens, Greg J. Duncan, Lisa A. Gennetian, Lawrence F. Katz, Ronald C. Kessler, Jeffrey R. Kling, and Lisa Sanbonmatsu. 2012. "Neighborhood Effects on the Long-Term Well-Being of Low-Income Adults." *Science* 337 (6101): 1505–10.

Lund, Crick, Alison Breen, Alan J. Flisher, Ritsuko Kakuma, Joanne Corrigall, John A. Joska, Leslie Swartz, and Vikram Patel. 2010. "Poverty and Common Mental Disorders in Low and Middle Income Countries: A Systematic Review." *Social Science & Medicine* 71 (3): 517–28.

Lund, Crick, Mary De Silva, Sophie Plagerson, Sara Cooper, Dan Chisholm, Jishnu Das, Martin Knapp, and Vikram Patel. 2011. "Poverty and Mental Disorders: Breaking the Cycle in Low-Income and Middle-Income Countries." *Lancet* 378 (9801): 1502–14.

Luttmer, Erzo F. P. 2005. "Neighbors as Negatives: Relative Earnings and Well-Being." *Quarterly Journal of Economics* 120 (3): 963–1002.

Marcus, Jan. 2013. "The Effect of Unemployment on the Mental Health of Spouses— Evidence from Plant Closures in Germany." *Journal of Health Economics* 32 (3): 546–58.

McInerney, Melissa, Jennifer M. Mellor, and Lauren Hersch Nicholas. 2013. "Recession Depression: Mental Health Effects of the 2008 Stock Market Crash." *Journal of Health Economics* 32 (6): 1090–104.

Mendolia, S. 2009. "The Impact of Job Loss on Family Mental Health." UNSW Working Paper, University of New South Wales.

Möbius, Markus, Muriel Niederle, Paul Niehaus, and Tanya Rosenblat. 2011. "Managing Self-Confidence: Theory and Experimental Evidence." NBER Working Paper no. 17014, Cambridge, MA.

Munafò, Marcus R., Brian Hitsman, Richard Rende, Chris Metcalfe, and Raymond Niaura. 2008. "Effects of Progression to Cigarette Smoking on Depressed Mood in Adolescents: Evidence from the National Longitudinal Study of Adolescent Health." *Addiction* (Abingdon, England) 103 (1): 162–71.

Piketty, Thomas. 1995. "Social Mobility and Redistributive Politics." *Quarterly Journal of Economics* 110 (3): 551–84.

Rataj, Elisabeth, Katharina Kunzweiler, and Susan Garthus-Niegel. 2016. "Extreme Weather Events in Developing Countries and Related Injuries and Mental Health Disorders—A Systematic Review." *BMC Public Health* 16:1020.

Robbins, Herbert. 1952. "Some Aspects of the Sequential Design of Experiments." *Bulletin of the American Mathematical Society* 55:527–35.

Rosero, Jose, and Hessel Oosterbeek. 2011. "Trade-Offs between Different Early Childhood Interventions: Evidence from Ecuador." Tinbergen Institute Discussion Paper no. 11-102/3, Tinbergen Institute.

Schwandt, Hannes. 2014. "Wealth Shocks and Health Outcomes: Evidence from Stock Market Fluctuations." IZA Discussion Paper no. 8298, Institute for the Study of Labor.

Sobocki, Patrik, Bengt Jönsson, Jules Angst, and Clas Rehnberg. 2006. "Cost of Depression in Europe." *Journal of Mental Health Policy and Economics* 9 (2): 87–98.

Ssewamala, Fred M., Chang-Keun Han, and Torsten B. Neilands. 2009. "Asset Ownership and Health and Mental Health Functioning among AIDS-Orphaned Adolescents: Findings from a Randomized Clinical Trial in Rural Uganda." *Social Science & Medicine* (1982) 69 (2): 191.

Ssewamala, Fred M., Torsten B. Neilands, Jane Waldfogel, and Leyla Ismayilova. 2012. "The Impact of a Comprehensive Microfinance Intervention on Depression Levels of AIDS-Orphaned Children in Uganda." *Journal of Adolescent Health: Official Publication of the Society for Adolescent Medicine* 50 (4): 346–52.

Steel, Zachary, Claire Marnane, Changiz Iranpour, Tien Chey, John W. Jackson, Vikram Patel, and Derrick Silove. 2014. "The Global Prevalence of Common Mental Disorders: A Systematic Review and Meta-analysis 1980–2013." *International Journal of Epidemiology* 43 (2): 476–93.

Stewart, Walter F., Judith A. Ricci, Elsbeth Chee, Steven R. Hahn, and David Morganstein. 2003. "Cost of Lost Productive Work Time among US Workers with Depression." *Journal of the American Medical Association* 289 (23): 3135–44.

Taylor, Gemma, Ann McNeill, Alan Girling, Amanda Farley, Nicola Lindson-Hawley, and Paul Aveyard. 2014. "Change in Mental Health after Smoking Cessation: Systematic Review and Meta-analysis." *British Medical Journal* 348:g1151.

Tseng, Fu-Min, and Dennis Petrie. 2012. "Handling the Endogeneity of Income to Health Using a Field Experiment in Taiwan." Dundee Discussion Papers in Economics no. 263, Economic Studies, University of Dundee, February.

Vos, Theo, Abraham D. Flaxman, Mohsen Naghavi, Rafael Lozano, Catherine Michaud, Majid Ezzati, Kenji Shibuya, et al. 2012. "Years Lived with Disability (YLDs) for 1160 Sequelae of 289 Diseases and Injuries 1990–2010: A Systematic Analysis for the Global Burden of Disease Study 2010." *Lancet* 380 (9859): 2163–96.

Warren, Patrick L., and Tom S. Wilkening. 2012. "Regulatory Fog: The Role of Information in Regulatory Persistence." *Journal of Economic Behavior & Organization* 84 (3): 840–56.

Windle, M., and R. C. Windle. 2001. "Depressive Symptoms and Cigarette Smoking among Middle Adolescents: Prospective Associations and Intrapersonal and Interpersonal Influences." *Journal of Consulting and Clinical Psychology* 69 (2): 215–26.

Hope as Aspirations, Agency, and Pathways
Poverty Dynamics and Microfinance in Oaxaca, Mexico

Travis J. Lybbert and Bruce Wydick

4.1 Introduction

Much research in development economics has been devoted recently to the study of poverty dynamics. The possibility of multiple equilibria in economic outcomes and, thereby, poverty traps has been particularly compelling as both a research focus and a motivation for development policy and program design. The majority of the research on poverty traps has concentrated on dynamics arising from external constraints such as missing credit, labor, and land markets or structural features such as locally increasing returns to scale in production. Recent work in behavioral economics, however, has illuminated the potential for development traps based on internal psychological phenomena. These phenomena may take the form of culturally imposed internal constraints (Sen 1999) that create a belief that one is incapable of engaging successfully in certain types of economic activities or domains of economic life. They may also take the form of a recursive trap

Travis J. Lybbert is professor of agricultural and resource economics at the University of California, Davis. Bruce Wydick is professor of economics and international studies at the University of San Francisco.

We thank the directors and staff of Fuentes Libres in Oaxaca, Mexico, for their partnership and collaboration. We are grateful to Johannes Haushofer, Chris Barrett, Paolo Carozza, Michael Carter, Alessandra Cassar, Jonathan de Quidt, Paul Glewwe, José Maria Gonzales, Karen Macours, Daniel Prudencio, Irvin Rojas, Phillip Ross, Laine Rutledge, seminar participants at the University of California at Davis, San Jose State University, University of Gothenberg, University of Notre Dame, Hope College, the University of California at Berkeley, the 2016 Pacific Conference for Development Economics at Stanford University, and the NBER conference for assistance and helpful comments related to this research. Scripture quotations are from New Revised Standard Version Bible, copyright © 1989 National Council of the Churches of Christ in the United States of America. Used by permission. All rights reserved worldwide. For acknowledgments, sources of research support, and disclosure of the authors' material financial relationships, if any, please see http://www.nber.org/chapters/c13832.ack.

in which low income produces feelings of helplessness that then result in feelings of low self-efficacy that reduce effort and reinforce the cycle of low income and a continued or deepened sense of helplessness.

In this research, we address the subject of hope, which may form a key component to breaking cycles of poverty. While hope has played a central role in understanding multiple equilibria and low-equilibrium traps in macroeconomics, usually articulated contextually as *confidence* or *expectations* (e.g., Diamond 1982; Murphy, Shleifer, and Vishny 1988), it is less often invoked in microeconomics. And although development practitioners routinely reference the importance of hope in work among the poor, microeconomists have only recently engaged hope as a subject worthy of serious research.

Understanding the role hope plays in shaping poverty dynamics is a daunting pursuit because the two subjects are nuanced and complex even when viewed in isolation. Yet, even a fleeting reflection suggests that the interactions and interdependency between hope and poverty dynamics are potentially potent and therefore deserving of attention from development economists. This complex relationship will only be understood though the accumulation of careful theoretical and empirical study. The work described in this chapter constitutes an initial offering in this direction.

One must begin with clear working definitions of the concept of hope— definitions that can be operational in the context of poverty interventions. As we will argue subsequently, hope has a number of components that may operate both individually and jointly in breaking cycles of poverty. Furthermore, it is important to understand whether hope as a phenomenon is a substitute or complement to more concrete and conventional interventions in areas such as health, schooling, and finance. We favor the latter. That is, there must be a tangible basis for hope that stems from reality, but at the same time, reality may not create its own hope. In other words, patterns of hopelessness may persist even when an intervention that relieves real economic constraints offer the potential for economic advancement—and if such an intervention is not accompanied by elevated aspirations or an expanded vision of what is possible, its impacts are unlikely to be fully realized. Throughout this chapter, we explore the complementarity between hope and more standard economic interventions.

Our inquiry into the economics of hope is structured in four parts: In section 4.2, we provide an introduction to the psychological literature on hope and related concepts. In section 4.3 we review the theoretical and empirical literature in development economics related to hope, which has largely been reduced to material aspirations. In section 4.4 we summarize a simple economic model of hope we develop in Lybbert and Wydick (2018) that uses a reference-dependent utility framework to incorporate three essential elements of hope from the positive psychology literature: aspirations, agency, and pathways. We use this simple model to differentiate aspirations from the broader concept of hope and to show how hope shapes economic development outcomes and the impact of different types of interventions. We then illustrate how recent empirical results in development economics can be more clearly understood in this hope framework. In section 4.5, we present one-month follow-up results from a randomized controlled trial among microfinance borrowers. In the Oaxaca Hope Project, we experimentally test the effects of an intervention that includes all three components of hope. Results show the intervention significantly raised aspirations and had a positive but yet statistically insignificant impact on short-term small business outcomes. In section 4.6, we conclude with reflections on the complex interplay of hope and poverty dynamics.

4.2   The Psychology of Hope

Psychology began to explore the concept of hope systematically in the 1950s with the emergence of positive psychology as a new field of study within the discipline. In response to complaints that the field had focused too much on pathologies and had overlooked positive psychological phenomena (Menninger 1959), a branch of psychology took up this challenge to understand hope and other "healthy" psychological attributes as part of what would ultimately become defined as the subfield of positive psychology (Seligman and Csikszentmihalyi 2000). This new branch of psychology proved to be the fertile ground that ultimately gave rise to new thinking about the psychology of hope.

As described in Froh (2004), positive psychology initially developed around the study of human virtues and attributes such as happiness, courage, love, forgiveness, and hope. An individual's influence over the factors that shape one's life, and more specifically the perception of this influence, has formed a key component of positive psychology. Rotter (1954) was instrumental in pioneering the notion of an individual's "locus of control," the belief of individuals regarding the factors that shape their lives (Rotter 1954, 1966; Lefcourt 1982). An individual's locus of control is conceptualized along a continuum ranging from internal to external according to the individual's perception of the forces that shape experiences and outcomes. The more an individual assigns influence to personal initiative and responsibility, the more internal her locus of control. The more influence she attributes to other people and forces out of one's control, the more external her local of control. While it is generally defined as a forward-looking assessment of the determinants of future outcomes, locus of control clearly reflects past experiences and lessons learned from these experiences. Locus of control also tends to betray a broader view of the forces that shape outcomes for everyone; thus, an individual with an external (internal) locus of control may believe that nobody (anybody) can succeed on the basis of significant personal effort alone. A smallholder farmer, for example, who views a successful harvest as purely the fortuitous result of weather, fate, or luck (external locus of control) may also ascribe external forces as the dominant explanation of other farmers' performance as well.

Building on Rotter, Bandura (1977) developed the concept of "self-efficacy," a person's perception of his competence in achieving goals and objectives.[1] In contrast to locus of control, self-efficacy is individually focused more than representing a global view and is often domain-specific, such as one's perceived ability to solve math problems (see Wuepper and Lybbert [forthcoming] for additional discussion of these and other related concepts). Both self-efficacy and the locus of control are powerful explanatory mechanisms by which an individual explains cause and effect of their experiences, forming one's so-called attributional style. How we assign causality to the events that happen around us is directed by our attributional style. One student, for example, might explain a bad grade as caused by an unkind teacher, while another may explain it by a lack of study effort. Attributional style is fundamental to our perception of causal relationships and of the "production functions" that govern the outcomes we care about. It shapes, at the deepest levels, the internal narrative through which we make sense of our lives and formulate our broader worldview. Thus, our actions and reactions in daily life often bear the fingerprints of our individual attributional style.

Snyder expands on these ideas to conceptualize *hope* as consisting of three key elements: goals, agency, and pathways. An individual must have a goal, see a pathway to reaching that goal, and believe that she is able to achieve the goal by progressing along this pathway. This understanding of hope nests the concepts of locus of control and self-efficacy within the agency component (Wuepper and Lybbert, forthcoming), yet the causal relationship between the three components of hope is less than straightforward. A greater sense of personal agency and the ability to conceptualize pathways in pursuit of a goal create the basis for the formation of aspirations, but aspirations may also motivate the conceptualization of pathways and a desire to increase agency in a particular domain. Snyder's version of aspirational hope thus differentiates itself strongly from a kind of "wishful hope" that is optimistic, but embodies low agency and views positive change as originating from external forces.

4.3   Hope and Aspirations in Development Economics

Traditionally, development economics has conceptualized poverty as primarily the product of *external* constraints such as credit, education, health,

1. Judge et al. (2002) argue that these two concepts along with the other two that compose the four dimensions of core self-evaluations (neuroticism and self-esteem) measure the same, single factor. The concept is referred to interchangeably as "perceived self-efficacy" and "self-efficacy."

infrastructure, and technology. Based on this approach, poverty alleviation hinges on relieving these external constraints. With greater appreciation for the role of internal constraints that arise from one's self-efficacy, agency, and aspirations, relaxing these external constraints may be insufficient. Moreover, relieving internal constraints may require a broader set of interventions that are less conventional and more creative than standard economic interventions. This growing awareness forms the basis of an exciting new literature in development economics that tries to break new ground in the understanding of the root causes of poverty traps.

Economic research related to hope and aspirations has its origin in the work of anthropologist Arjun Appadurai (2004). In this framework, aspiring to an improved standard of living first requires the "capacity to aspire." Appadurai (2004) considers this capacity to be fundamentally shaped by social forces in the sense that aspirations form as part of the ethos, possibilities, and norms of an individual's reference community. While economists might capture some of this capacity to aspire by adding parameters or constraints to utility functions, this fails to reflect the richness of the idea that aspirations in the framework of Appadurai are jointly determined and shaped through time, suggesting direct social influences on individual preferences. Appadurai argues that the target, intensity, and composition of aspirations in any given community reflect the dominant worldviews and ideologies about the nature of worldly possessions and their relative value to social relations, as well as deeper ideas about the meaning of life, family, community, and death. Appadurai's work laid the basis for the development of economic models that have sought to better understand the role that aspirations play in economic development such as Ray (2006), Bogliacino and Ortoleva (2013), Genicot and Ray (2014), and Dalton, Ghosal, and Mani (2016) and for promising new efforts to provide quantitative measures of hope such as in Bloem et al. (forthcoming).

Ray (2006) expands Appadurai's conception of aspirations to introduce several concepts that help to structure both theoretical and empirical research on the topic: *aspirations window*, the *aspirations gap*, and *aspirations failure*. One's *aspirations window* consists of the people one perceives to be similar enough to oneself that they provide a useful benchmark for formulating one's own aspirations. This set of persons establishes boundaries around and reference points regarding future possibilities. The similarly that is the basis of the aspirations window may hinge on capability and capacity, including salient traits such as skin color, ethnicity, gender, religion, or socioeconomic class. The degree of social mobility strongly influences the breadth of one's aspirations window. Ray's concept of an *aspirations gap* is the difference between the standard of living to which one aspires and one's present circumstances. If the aspirations gap is too narrow, rewards to productive effort are low. If it is too wide, the gap can make the aspiration seem unattainable, leading to frustration. *Aspirations failure* occurs when an individual's effort is stymied by limited aspirations rather than structural constraints. Thus in the presence of aspirations failure, internal constraints may bind before external constraints.

By adapting aspirations and other psychological concepts to the poverty literature in anthropology and economics, Appadurai and Ray offer an excellent point of departure for exploring the complementarity between hope and poverty traps. Such an exploration may be treacherous, as one must always exert care in transporting terms and ideas across disciplines and cultures. For example, the context in which much psychological theory is developed, tested, and practiced differs greatly from most of the developing world. The constraints people face and their adaptations to these constraints differ in substantive ways. As a result, bridging from Snyder to the Appadurai and Ray (and beyond) is complicated by semantic and even philosophical differences. We nevertheless believe there are great potential insights from this effort.

Building on the conceptual and theoretical work of Appadurai and Ray, empirical analysis of the determinants and impact of aspirations has become one of the liveliest research areas in applied development economics. In our review of this emerging literature, our objective is not to provide a comprehensive survey of this work, but rather to summarize a few of the studies that have become—or are likely to become—influential in this area of inquiry.

Interesting new evidence appears to show that role modeling plays a significant role in driving aspirations among the poor. Beaman et al. (2012), for example, use a natural experiment in West Bengal to study the impact of role modeling and its effect on aspirations of young girls and of their parents for the lives of their young girls. In their study area of West Bengal, one-third of all elected chief councilors of villages, the "Pradhan," must be reserved for females. The researchers surveyed 8,453 adolescents age eleven to fifteen and their parents in 495 villages, where questions included in the survey strongly focused on aspirations, and the closing of the aspirations gap between boys and girls. Questions included asking if the parent would like (a) the child to at least graduate from secondary school; (b) the child to marry at an age above eighteen; (c) the child to have an occupation different than housewife or what the in-laws prefer; (d) whether the desired occupation is a doctor, engineer, scientist, teacher, or a legal career; and (e) the child to become the Pradhan. The same aspirations questions were asked to the children themselves. The randomized nature of the village-district set-aside policy allowed for an estimation of causal effects from the existence of a female Pradhan to the aspirations of young girls in that particular village district. In villages assigned to a female leader for two election cycles, exposure to a female Pradhan caused the gender gap in aspirations in these districts to close by 25 percent for parents and 32 percent for adolescents. The gender gap in adolescent educational attainment was closed completely, and girls in villages with a female Pradhan spent less time on household chores.

In another study in India, Jensen and Oster (2009) study the impact of cable television in households and its effect on women's aspirations. They use a three-year panel data set on individuals and find that exposure to cable television causes increases in school enrollment for younger children, decreases in the adult acceptability of domestic violence toward women, and increases in women's autonomy. The introduction of cable TV is even associated with decreases in adult women's fertility. Jensen and Oster also find that differences in attitudes and behaviors between urban and rural areas decreased between 45 and 70 percent within two years of the introduction of cable TV.

Glewwe, Ross, and Wydick (forthcoming) carry out an experiment in Indonesia among 526 children living in the slums of Jakarta, about half of whom were internationally sponsored through Compassion, one of the leading child sponsorship organizations worldwide. Children sponsored through Compassion are provided with school tuition, school uniforms, nutritious meals, health care, and have access to an after-school tutoring program that focuses not only on supplemental academic training, but on spiritual development, character growth, socioemotional skills, self-esteem, and aspirations. In addition to direct questions on self-esteem and aspirations, children were given a new box of twenty-four colored pencils and asked to "draw a picture of yourself in the rain," a standard technique in child psychology.[2]

In this study, identification of causal impacts is based on an age-eligibility rule, which dictated that only children nine years old and younger were eligible for sponsorship when the program was rolled out into the local neighborhood. Factor analysis was used to generate three factors identified as happiness, hopelessness, and self-efficacy, based on their correlations with survey questions and mainly with drawing characteristics. Ordinary least squares (OLS) and instrumental variable (IV) estimations found that child sponsorship significantly raises sponsored children's levels of happiness (0.42 standard deviations), self-efficacy (0.29 standard deviations), and hope (0.66 standard deviations). Here we see evidence of substantial impacts from a program with an intervention comprising not only tangible economic interventions (that affect avenues and agency), but interventions intended to augment noncognitive skills, character, self-esteem, grit, and aspirations.

What is the impact of augmented aspirations? Wydick, Glewwe, and Rutledge (2013) carry out a six-country study on the long-term impact of Compassion's sponsorship program through a survey obtaining data on

---

2. The use of children's drawings has been well developed in the clinical psychology literature (see, e.g., Koppitz 1968; Thomas and Silk 1990; Furth 2002). A detailed psychology literature has shown that drawings can reveal the minds and feelings of children. This literature empirically correlates children's self-portraits that have missing facial features, fingers, and feet, for example, with extreme shyness and insecurity. Those drawn with a dark color or single colors are indicative of depression, hopelessness, and anxiety, and tiny figures are associated with hopelessness and low self-esteem. Monster figures are correlated (not surprisingly) with aggression.

10,144 adults, 1,860 of whom began sponsorship from 1980 to 1992. A similar age-eligibility rule existed during this period (where a child had to be age twelve or younger to be sponsored instead of nine years old as in Indonesia) that facilitated identification of causal effects from the program. Although it is difficult to separately identify the relative impacts of the tangible interventions that are a part of sponsorship with the higher aspirations in childhood created by the program, impacts of sponsorship in adulthood are found to be substantial. Sponsorship resulted in an increase in schooling completion of 1.03–1.46 years, a 12–18 percentage point increase in secondary school completion (over a baseline rate of 44.5 percent), and an increase in the probability of white-collar employment in adulthood of 6.6 percentage points over a baseline rate of 18.7 percent. Sponsored children were also more likely in adulthood to be community and church leaders. In a separate paper studying economic impacts on income and wealth and demographic impacts on marriage and childbearing, Wydick, Glewwe, and Rutledge (2017) find sponsorship resulting in an increase in monthly income of $13–19 over an untreated baseline of $75, mainly from higher labor market participation, positive impacts on adult dwelling quality in adulthood, and increased probability of mobile phone ownership. There is also some evidence of modest effects on childbearing later in adulthood among those sponsored earlier in the program's history when baseline birthrates were higher.

In a cash transfer program in Nicaragua, Macours and Vakis (2014) utilized a two-stage randomized intervention that combined conditional transfers with other interventions aimed at protecting the asset base of the rural poor in six municipalities in the northwest part of the country. Both participants and leaders among the 3,000 subjects were randomly assigned to one of three different group interventions within randomly selected treatment communities. The three interventions consisted of a conditional cash transfer, the conditional cash transfer plus a scholarship for occupational training, and a productivity treatment that combined a grant for productive investments with the conditional cash transfer. Macours and Vakis find that the higher the share of female leaders to a household's proximity, the larger the impacts of an array of outcomes were on that particular household within the productivity intervention. Leaders were not allocated equally among program assemblies during program rollout, although there was an average of four leaders per assembly. Having one additional leader (given the productive investment package) increased household income from nonagricultural activities by about US$3.30, and the value of the animal stock by roughly US$12.00. Interestingly, like child sponsorship, the intervention Macours and Vakis study is one that not only may improve agency (in this case through learning from group leaders) but also impact aspirations through the inspiration and role-modeling effects of leaders, and an intervention that yields large impacts.

In their follow-up research, Macours and Vakis (chapter 9, this volume) find that even two years after the conditional cash transfers stopped, the former beneficiaries of the transfers who lived in close proximity to these influential leaders continued to display significantly higher investments in the education and nutrition of their children as well as higher expectations and aspirations for them. As a result there is evidence that exposure to those who can augment aspirations may exhibit long-term impacts that are complementary to a tangible intervention such as cash transfers.

In some cases it may be that the mere articulation of an aspiration is able to establish a new reference point for enterprise activity that stimulates higher effort and economic outcomes. Cassar et al. (2016) carry out an experiment in Colombia in which randomly selected microfinance borrowers were assigned to combinations of treatments, the first of which included setting an intermediate goal for their training or enterprise.[3] Each of the goals was accompanied by a strict verification procedure and rated in terms of difficulty. Other crosscut treatments included being part of a goal-realization support group and the receipt of a small prize from the experimenter if a goal was realized. The combination of these treatments together constitutes the approach of the Family Independence Initiative (FII) pioneered by Maurice Lim Miller, recipient of a MacArthur genius grant for the implementation of this model among low-income households in Oakland, California. Subjects formed into groups representing combinations of the above treatments were tracked over a six-month period. Results indicate that all of the treatments, including the support group and the prize, had significant impacts on enterprise outcomes, and that combined in the full FII package had large and significant impacts on enterprise revenues. But perhaps most interestingly, the mere articulation of the goal, the synthetic creation of aspirations, among subjects had by far the most significant impact on the economic outcomes of subjects.

In work that lays an important foundation for our own experimental results we present here, Bernard et al. (2013) study aspirations through a field experiment in Ethiopia. In this project, researchers contracted with film producers to create four fifteen-minute documentaries featuring families telling their personal narrative of escape from poverty. From a total of sixty-four villages, experimenters selected eighteen households from each village, and each of these eighteen households were allocated to one of three groups: a treatment group (that watched the documentary), a placebo group

3. Subjects could choose from a menu of attending a marketing workshop, creating a business plan, implementing accounting practices, paying off an outstanding debt, purchasing a piece of business equipment, implementing a marketing strategy, obtaining one of six different licenses to legalize the enterprise, attending a job fair, saving 15,000 Colombian pesos every week (US$8), making a payment to improve credit score, purchasing a durable good for the home, applying for an education grant, attending an adult literacy course, or joining the health security system.

(that watched standard Ethiopian TV entertainment), and a control group that was only surveyed. Local social network data was obtained to study peer effects of the intervention.

Bernard et al. found, after six months since the intervention at baseline, that the documentary had a significant impact on an aspirations index with components consisting of income, wealth, social status, and educational aspirations for children, both in direct effects and from the number of friends who had attended the documentary. They also reported positive impacts on future-oriented *behaviors* six months after the screening, including changes in savings, time spent in business relative to leisure, demand for microfinance, and investments in children's education. Bernard et al. found no direct impact on educational enrollments or expenditures on children's education, but reported evidence of school enrollment and expenditures based on every additional friend in the village who viewed the documentary. While there are some caveats to the results of the study related to overtesting, Bernard et al. provide some early evidence that it may be possible to increase aspirations through the kind of direct intervention we carry out through our field research in Oaxaca, Mexico.

4.4 Oaxaca Hope Project: Theoretical Framework

As an initial exploration into the economics of hope, we conducted a randomized controlled trial in collaboration with a microfinance lender in Oaxaca, Mexico. This experimental work was structured within a modeling framework that we develop and present in greater detail in Lybbert and Wydick (2018).

The model we present serves a number of purposes in relationship to our experiment. First, it rigorously defines Snyder's psychological components of hope in the context of a formal economic model. Second, it demonstrates how these different components may each work to yield better development outcomes. Third, it explores the relationships of these components, both with each other and with tangible interventions such as microfinance, and how they may yield complementary effects with one another and with the tangible economic interventions focused primarily on relieving external constraints. Note that while we believe the model adequately serves these three purposes and motivates the structure of the microfinance experiment we evaluate empirically, it is not designed to generate predictions that are directly tested in our subsequent empirical analysis.

The model is derived from the components of aspirational hope developed in Snyder (1994): goals, agency, and pathways. We find that Snyder's conception of hope lends itself nicely to economic modeling, where some of the more basic ideas can be captured in a (nontraditional) utility maximization subject to productivity parameters and constraints. A simple extension of the model can account not just for actual agency (productivity) and constraints (closed pathways), but the *perception* of agency (self-efficacy) and pathways.

While goals form the central component of the Snyder framework, we broaden this notion through the development of an aspirations-based utility function. Following Appadurai (2004), we assume that aspirations are exogenous and shaped by household context, culture, and history. Aspirations may be in discrete space (a secondary school degree) or form a reference point in continuous space (microenterprise sales of 1,000 pesos).

In Lybbert and Wydick (2018) we propose that an aspirations-based utility function should satisfy four properties: (a) discontinuity at the aspiration, where marginal utility is higher just below it than above it; (b) convexity in the utility function below the aspiration and concavity above it; (c) gains in utility become increasingly a function of whether an aspiration is realized as aspirations grow in importance; and (d) utility is increasing in higher realized aspirations.

These four properties are satisfied by the following, where $u(Y \mid A)$ is an aspirations-based utility function over a continuous outcome Y and an aspiration A, $\alpha \in [0,1]$ denotes the strength of aspirations in utility, and where $1(\cdot)$ is the indicator function.

$$(1) \qquad u(Y \mid A) = A \left(\frac{Y}{A}\right)^{[1/(1-\alpha)]} \cdot 1(Y < A) + A \left(\frac{Y}{A}\right)^{(1-\alpha)} \cdot 1(Y \geq A).$$

At intermediate values of α, the function generates a parameterized version of the Kahneman and Tversky (1979) value function where the aspiration A serves as a reference point. A handy property of this function is that it can be seen as a generalization of a neoclassical utility function that allows for aspirations: If the strength of aspirations is allowed to vary such that α_1 reflects the strength of aspirations below A and α_2 above A, then in the case where $\alpha_2 = \alpha_1 / (\alpha_1 - 1)$, it simplifies to the standard concave neoclassical utility function. This allows for the potential testing of utility against its deviation from the standard neoclassical form in cases where structural estimation of the function is possible.

In the most basic formulation of Lybbert and Wydick (2018), Snyder's component of agency is modeled as productivity and the blockage of a pathway is modeled by an output constraint for a given activity. Effort at time t is given as e_t and, along with a random shock in the next period v_{t+1}, produces the outcome Y_{t+1} at time $t + 1$, or $Y_{t+1} = \pi e_t + \pi_v v_{t+1}$, where the coefficients π and π_v indicate the respective contributions of effort and the random shock to total production. Pathways in the model are the absence of constraints on Y. Beyond an outcome constraint, $\bar{Y}$, marginal product of effort becomes zero. While the possibility exists that $Y_{t+1} > \bar{Y}$, this cannot occur through individual agency, but only via high realizations of the random shock v such that $E[Y_{t+1}] = \begin{cases} \pi e_t & \text{if } e_t < \bar{e} \\ \bar{Y} & \text{if } e_t \geq \bar{e} \end{cases}$, where $\pi \bar{e} = \bar{Y}$. The final component to the model is a function that gives the cost of effort, $c(e_t)$, where effort is costly at an increasing rate, that is, $c'(e_t) > 0$, $c''(e_t) > 0$, and $c(0) = 0$. The agent then solves the problem. Individuals thus choose optimal effort to maximize $E[u_{t+1}] - c(e_t)$.

While an optimal aspiration $A*$ can be derived as endogenous to the model, we do not assume that individuals choose aspirations optimally. This is based on evidence that aspirations in large measure are established exogenously by local context (Appadurai 2004). However, we do allow for the idea that aspirations can be altered exogenously through an intervention.

An important extension to the model, which is key to the intervention in our experimental work, allows not just for *actual* agency and pathways, but the individual's *perception* of agency (self-efficacy) and *perception* of pathway blockage (what Sen [1999] calls "internal constraints"). Indeed, even in Snyder's conceptualization of hope, it is not just agency that is relevant, but the perception of agency in a given domain that is important. Snyder likewise understands the perception of pathways in their constraints to be equally important to behavior as what is actual. These distinctions are important because traditional approaches in development economics have focused on increasing productivity (e.g., schooling, vocational and business training) and relieving real economic constraints (e.g., microcredit, land reclamation, construction of infrastructure), and in the model these interventions could very well lead to greater levels of effort and economic welfare. However, the model helps illustrate that interventions that increase self-efficacy and that remove internal constraints may have equal or greater impact if it is the latter rather than the former that are binding.

Consider the impact of a conventional economic intervention in figure 4.1. Here a constraint is released (a pathway is opened), but where aspirations lie below these constraints. Because aspirations represent the binding constraint (rather than the more obvious economic constraint), effort, outcomes, expected utility, and net expected utility remain unchanged. In the case where an intervention that relaxes an economic constraint is released when aspirations are high, this may result in substantial impacts in the form of greater effort, higher outcomes, higher expected utility, and higher net expected utility. But when aspirations (or self-efficacy) is low, release of the economic constraint fails to affect these welfare measures.

In figure 4.2, however, we depict an intervention that increases self-efficacy and internal constraints in the context of an intervention in which economic constraints have been released. A primary example of this may be some form of child sponsorship (Wydick, Glewwe, and Rutledge 2013, 2017) in which the intervention not only increases agency through an after-school tutoring program (and avenues through the provision of tuition, uniforms, and other materials so that children may continue in school), but intentionally devotes resources to increasing aspirations about educational and vocational outcomes. Some practitioners refer to this kind of multifaceted intervention as "integral (or integrated) development," programs designed

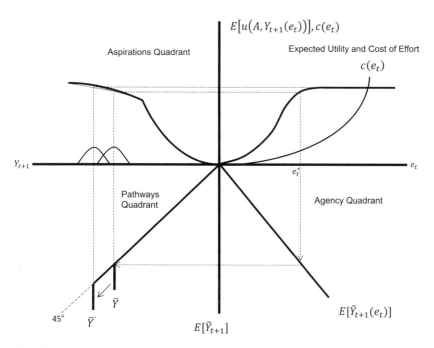

Fig. 4.1 **A new pathway opens, such as releasing a credit constraint, but this fails to have substantial impacts due to low aspirations**

to exploit complementarities between economic, psychological, spiritual, and social interventions.[4] Our hope intervention in Oaxaca takes just such an approach in the context of a group of women who have had economic constraints ostensibly released via access to microfinance loans, but at least anecdotally have realized only very small impacts from microcredit.

4.5   Short-Term Effects in the Oaxaca Hope Project

Here we present one-month follow-up results from a microfinance experiment in Oaxaca, Mexico, that follows from the theoretical framework outlined above. A presentation of the longer-term impacts of the intervention will be forthcoming in subsequent work. Our experiment was implemented with our field partner, Fuentes Libres, a nonprofit, faith-based organization affiliated with the Evangelical Covenant Church that is engaged in a number of activities to promote justice and economic opportunity for impoverished women of all faith backgrounds in the state of Oaxaca, Mexico.

---

4. The United Nations Development Programme, the Organization of American States, Save the Children, World Vision, and Compassion International are several of many development organizations that espouse an integrated-development approach.

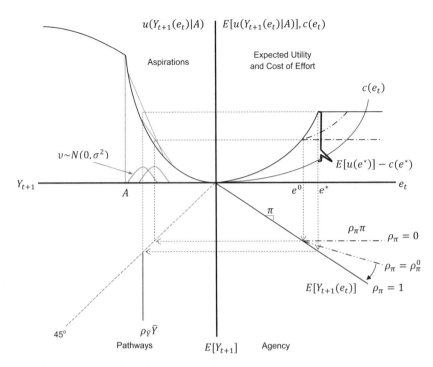

Fig. 4.2   Graphical depiction of the economic model of hope

Note: Optimal effort (e^*) with "pathways" constraint binding below aspiration and optimal expected utility net of cost of effort depicted by $E[u] - c$. Increased perception of self-efficacy drives the individual from a low-effort trap to a higher effort and higher utility.

Part of the work of Fuentes Libres involves the operation of fifty-two community banks in the state of Oaxaca. About 60 percent of these community banks are located near the Mexican Isthmus that separates the Caribbean from the Pacific Ocean in the southern part of the country, with the remaining 40 percent located in and around the periurban regions of the state capital of Oaxaca City. All of the roughly 600 community bank members are female. Meetings in the community banks occur weekly, where women pay off current loans and make savings deposits. A minimum savings contribution of twenty pesos per week is required of each community bank member. The size of the fifty-two community banks range from about six to thirty members, the median size being thirteen members.

We carried out a stratified cluster randomization using pairwise matching. Groups were matched into pairs by a hierarchical process based on focus group interviews with loan officers to rank factors in order of the importance to community bank performance. To form matched pairs, community banks were first clustered by loan officer, then among those with the same loan officer, and banks were matched by size. When there were more than two banks of nearly identical size, community banks were then matched by number of loan cycles, then if close similarities continued to exist, respectively by age of members, and then by similarity of microenterprises within the group until twenty-six matching pairs consisting of A and B groups were formed. A single coin was then flipped to determine whether the twenty-six A-banks or twenty-six B-banks would be selected into treatment status, with the other chosen for control. In total, 601 community bank members took part in the experiment, 326 in the 26 treatment banks and 275 in the 26 control banks. Table 4.1 shows that treatment and control were well-balanced over twenty-four variables at baseline.

The baseline survey obtained data on basic control variables such as age, marital status, and education. It also contains sets of five questions each on aspirations, agency, and conceptualization of avenues out of poverty.[5] These questions were designed to create indices capturing changes in Snyder's three components of hope. The survey also contained questions obtaining subjective measures of well-being and happiness, optimism, future orientation, risk aversion, and spiritual questions oriented toward ascertaining an individual's perception of locus of control. Subjects also filled out a 3×3 matrix of hypothetical levels of sales based on interactions of three levels of work effort (high, medium, low) and three levels of "luck" (good, normal, and bad). Variation in sales across levels of effort relative to the total variation in the matrix yields a measure of self-efficacy or agency from an ANOVA-type calculation on the ratio of the variation in sales due to changes in effort over the total variation in sales within the matrix.

4.5.1 Treatment

There are three aspects to the hope intervention carried out among the community banks selected for treatment. First, a film crew from Sacramento State University produced a documentary on four of the women who were deemed by the directors and loan officers to have been among the most successful in using their microloans to expand their enterprises. The thirty-five-minute documentary was filmed in Oaxaca and produced and edited in Sacramento, California, under the direction of film studies

---

5. Questions to gauge aspirations included "It is better learn to accept the reality of things than to dream for a better future"; "It is better to have aspirations for your family than to accept each day as it comes"; "I am satisfied with the current sales and profits from my business"; "It is wiser to establish business goals than to address situations as they arrive"; and "I have specific goals and plans for the future growth of my business." Questions regarding agency included "On a scale of 0 to 10, how important is *hard work/being lucky* to prospering in business? hard work____ being lucky____"; "My future is shaped mainly by my own actions rather by than the actions of others"; "I often have difficulty leading and influencing my friends and neighbors"; and "Women like me can help bring about positive change in our community." Questions addressing pathways out of poverty included "I can find a way to solve most problems"; "If my business sales are low, I know how to explore new markets"; "I become discouraged easily when I encounter obstacles in my business"; "If my current business fails, I could start a new business selling a different product"; and "I understand the different ways to succeed in business."

Table 4.1   Means and balancing tests

Variables	Age (1)	Education (2)	Religion (3)	Number of children (4)	Number of children < 18 (5)	Bank leader (6)	Clothing business (7)	Food business (8)
Hope group	2.670*	0.547	−0.068	0.099	−0.282**	−0.024	0.022	0.073*
	(1.350)	(0.601)	(0.062)	(0.218)	(0.130)	(0.028)	(0.037)	(0.042)
Baseline control group mean	41.0	7.31	0.27	2.91	1.34	0.28	0.13	0.30

Variables	Grocery business (9)	Hope-3 index (10)	Hope-7 index (11)	Happiness index (12)	Optimism index (13)	Aspirations index (14)	Agency index (15)	Avenues index (16)
Hope group	−0.013	0.068	0.025	−0.022	−0.070	−0.047	−0.002	0.089
	(0.024)	(0.131)	(0.125)	(0.160)	(0.169)	(0.118)	(0.130)	(0.134)
Baseline control group mean	0.064	−0.34	−0.054	8.68	8.62	−0.010	0.041	−0.112

Variables	Future orient. (17)	Spiritual obv. index (18)	Business hours (19)	Weekly sales (20)	Weekly profits (21)	Weekly savings (22)	Employees (23)	Plans for employees (24)
Hope group	−0.044	0.005	−0.181	85.478	100.423	17.279	−0.001	−0.056
	(0.123)	(0.109)	(3.319)	(317.135)	(121.387)	(11.041)	(0.039)	(0.060)
Baseline control group mean	−0.004	−0.062	35.3	2,274.1	827.2	46.5	0.106	0.543

Note: Regression of variable on treatment only. Clustered standard errors in parentheses.

**Significant at the 5 percent level.

*Significant at the 10 percent level.

DIOS ME DA ESPERANZA...

1. ASPIRACIONES:
"Pon tu delicia en el Señor y El te dará las peticiones de tu corazón." (Salmos 37:4)

2. HABILIDADES:
"Todo lo puedo en Cristo que me fortalece." (Filipenses 4:13)

3. AVENIDAS:
"Reconócele en todos tus caminos, y El enderezará tus sendas." (Proverbios 3:6)

MIS METAS:

VENTAS SEMINALES:_____ AHORROS SEMINALES:_____ MI META DE FUTURO:_____

GOD GIVES ME HOPE...

1. ASPIRATIONS:
"Take delight in the LORD,
and he will give you the desires of your heart." (Psalm 37:4, NRSV)

2. ABILITIES:
"I can do all things through him who strengthens me." (Philippians 4:13, NRSV)

3. AVENUES:
"In all your ways acknowledge him,
and he will make straight your paths." (Proverbs 3:6, NRSV)

MY GOALS:

WEEKLY SALES:_____ WEEKLY SAVINGS:_____ MY FUTURE GOAL:_____

Fig. 4.3   Original Spanish text and English translation of the goal-setting magnet provided to women in treated groups

Note: English versions of Bible verses are from the New Revised Standard Version Bible, © 1989 National Council of the Churches of Christ in the United States of America. Used by permission. All rights reserved worldwide.

professor and documentary producer Robert Machoian. The documentary film was screened to treatment banks immediately after the baseline survey was carried out in these locations. Initial impressions were that the women took pleasure in seeing the film, and focus groups carried out after the film indicated that women found the film to be highly inspiring to them.

After viewing the documentary, the borrowers in the twenty-six treatment groups received a three-by-eight-inch refrigerator magnet, articulating Snyder's three components of hope, which were translated as *Aspiraciones, Habilidades,* and *Avenidas* in Spanish. Congruent with the faith-based nature of the nongovernmental organization, an inspirational scripture verse was given under each of these three words (see figure 4.3). At the bottom of the refrigerator magnet there were three spaces for women to write in personal goals for weekly sales in their enterprise, weekly savings in the community bank, and a long-term goal. Common goals were leasing a stall in a market, sending a son or daughter to high school or college, or adding a room to the house.

The third aspect of the intervention was a four-week "hope curriculum," in which each of the components of hope were discussed for approximately half an hour during the weekly community bank meeting, and a fourth week consisted of the discussion of several case studies. In these case studies women had to learn how to apply the different components of hope to practical microenterprise problems. The curriculum, however, was designed as much as possible to be scrubbed of any traditional type of business or financial training. Only the "soft skills" of developing goals and aspirations, enhancing self-efficacy, and the practice of visualizing pathways from poverty were emphasized in the curriculum.

To enhance the quality of our microenterprise data, loan officers carried out a short review of basic accounting and bookkeeping with *both* treatment and control groups approximately two months before the experiment. However, the intervention carried out during the treatment carefully avoided imparting any such hard business skills to the women in treated community banks. Based on the strong compliance with this design feature, we are confident that any differences between the groups at end line are either idiosyncratic or are due to the hope intervention.

Five weeks after the baseline survey and the completion of the hope curriculum, we conducted a follow-up survey that was virtually identical to the baseline survey. We present ANCOVA regressions that estimate impact at one month (more specifically five weeks) after the intervention is estimate impacts on psychological and business variables. We estimate intervention impacts using ANCOVA due to its greater efficiency than difference-in-differences using experimental data with baseline and follow-up surveys (McKenzie 2012). Our specification is

$$y_{ijt} = \alpha + \tau \text{Treat}_j + \theta y_{ijt-1} + X_i'\beta + \varepsilon_{it},$$

where $X_i'\beta$ are a vector of variables that include controls for age, education, religion, number of children, children under age eighteen, bank leader, dwelling index, loan officer, type of business, and missing baseline data. The ANCOVA estimates also control for the baseline value of the impact variable. The coefficient τ measures impact. The results we present are for only the first (one-month) follow-up survey.

4.5.2   Results

We created indices of our variables based on Kling, Liebman, and Katz (2007) in which the dependent variables are de-meaned and standardized to give them equal weighting in an index that is also then standardized to give it mean zero and unit variance to provide a more comparable interpretation for impacts.

Table 4.2   **ANCOVA estimations: psychology**

Variables	Happiness (1)	Optimism (2)	Aspirations (3)	Agency (4)	Pathways (5)
Hope group	0.099	0.098	0.244***	0.054	0.036
	(0.094)	(0.077)	(0.077)	(0.073)	(0.084)
Observations	555	555	555	555	555
R-squared	0.096	0.118	0.206	0.191	0.237

Variables	Future orientation (6)	Risk-aversion reduction (7)	ANOVA agency (8)	Hope-3 index (9)	Hope-7 index (10)
Hope group	0.125*	0.031	−0.005	0.149*	0.174**
	(0.073)	(0.092)	(0.021)	(0.074)	(0.085)
Observations	555	592	548	555	555
R-squared	0.148	0.173	0.073	0.298	0.291

Note: ANCOVA regressions include controls for baseline value of impact variable, age, education, religion, number of children, children under age eighteen, bank leader, dwelling index, loan officer, type of business, and missing baseline data. Clustered standard errors at community group level in parentheses.
***Significant at the 1 percent level.
**Significant at the 5 percent level.
*Significant at the 10 percent level.

Our first results show impacts on psychological variables and are given in table 4.2 and figure 4.4. Our intervention clearly strongly impacted aspirations, and our aspirations index increased by 0.24σ, significant at the 0.01 percent level. Point estimates point to increases in agency and pathways, but these are much smaller (0.054σ and 0.036σ) and not statistically significant, roughly half the size of their standard error. Columns (1) and (2) in table 4.2 show point estimates indicating that happiness and optimism increased approximately 0.10σ under treatment, but the 95 percent confidence intervals of these estimates contain zero. Future orientation increases among the treated by 0.13σ, significant at the 10 percent level. Smaller point estimate increases are seen in risk-aversion reduction (0.03σ) and our ANOVA-based measure of agency actually shows a slight reduction (-0.005σ).

Nevertheless, our Hope-7 index (which includes all seven of our variables potentially related to hope: aspirations, agency, avenues, happiness, optimism, future orientation, and risk-aversion reduction) increases significantly (at the 5 percent level) by 0.17σ and our Hope-3 index (which contains only Snyder's three components—aspirations, agency, and pathways) increases by 15σ. The increase in the overall hope indices, however, is due to two factors: first, that nearly every hope-related factor displayed positive point estimates, and second that the impact on aspirations was substantial. Indeed, the overall impact on hope was driven largely by increases in aspirations. It seems that, at least in the short term, it is easier to raise aspirations

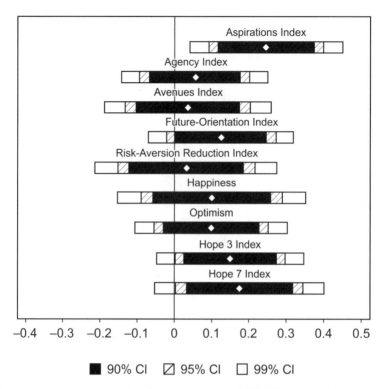

Fig. 4.4   Impact estimates from hope intervention, ANCOVA estimations, one-month follow-up

than it is to increase self-efficacy or conceptualization of pathways out of poverty. Impacts on small enterprise outcomes of the women in our study are shown in table 4.3 and figure 4.5. We expected the number of hours per week that women dedicated to her business to increase with increased aspirations, however, our point estimates indicate a negative impact here, although statistically insignificant. Our ANCOVA point estimates find positive impacts on log sales (increase of 17.7 percent), log profits (increase of 19.1 percent), and log community bank savings (increase of 14.2 percent), although the 95 percent confidence interval for all of these includes zero. As we suspected after only a little more than a month after treatment, we find no increase in employees, or even plans for new employees. A standardized business performance index increases by 0.095σ, but is statistically insignificant.

In summary, we find some evidence that after one month our intervention increased aspirations and future orientation among women in treated community banks who received the hope intervention, but less evidence that

Table 4.3	ANCOVA estimations: business outcomes			
Variables	Business hours (1)	Log weekly sales (2)	Log weekly profits (3)	Log weekly savings (4)
Hope group	−1.104	0.177	0.191	0.142
	(1.800)	(0.150)	(0.134)	(0.091)
Observations	550	551	549	544
R-squared	0.352	0.280	0.271	0.167
Variables	Employees (5)	Plans for employees? (6)	Bus. perform. index (7)	Anderson BP index (8)
Hope group	−0.006	−0.005	0.095	0.085
	(0.025)	(0.041)	(0.091)	(0.088)
Observations	550	549	555	555
R-squared	0.354	0.242	0.336	0.335

Note: ANCOVA regressions include controls for baseline value of impact variable, age, education, religion, number of children, children under age eighteen, bank leader, dwelling index, loan officer, type of business, and missing baseline data. Clustered standard errors at community group level in parentheses.

other important psychological variables, such as agency, were impacted by the treatment. We find modest evidence for positive impacts on business performance, where point estimates are quite large, but cannot reject the null hypothesis of no impact at this early stage of follow-up.

Could these effects have been created by other aspects of our intervention than augmenting aspirations, agency, and illuminating pathways out of poverty? While our experiment targeted only these phenomena in the design of the documentary, the reminder, and the hope curriculum, as is the case with many experiments it is possible that women in treated groups exerted more effort in their businesses simply because they felt that someone else cared about their performance or through other types of Hawthorne effects. While we cannot rule out such confounding effects, the design and implementation of the experiment attempted to avoid introducing such differences. Specifically, data collection and the weekly group meetings with loan officers were identical in both treated and control groups. Any such Hawthorne effects would have to come from the implementation of the hope treatment itself.

Our hope intervention continued for twelve months, during which subjects in treatment continued to engage in goal-setting exercises, self-esteem development, and exercises in conceptualizing pathways out of poverty via their microenterprises. In future work we will report one-year impacts from this longer-term intervention.

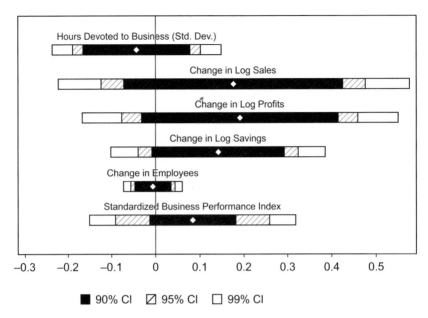

Fig. 4.5   **Impact estimates from hope intervention, ANCOVA estimations, one-month follow-up**

4.6   Reflections on Hope and Poverty Dynamics

Can hopelessness among the poor create poverty traps? We have explored potential answers to this question throughout this chapter by considering potential complementarities between hope and poverty dynamics. A small but growing evidence base provides some support for an affirmative answer. Hopelessness can, it seems, create a vicious cycle in which pessimistic beliefs create a self-fulfilling prophecy leading to prolonged episodes of poverty. Indeed, in this volume (chapter 3), Haushofer and de Quidt present a model in which depression induced by a negative shock makes an individual so pessimistic regarding returns to any effort that effort is reduced to zero, creating a poverty trap dynamic. Hope is directly related to escape from this kind of trap in that hope creates optimism about the returns to effort. But while hope embodies optimism, aspirational hope as defined in modern positive psychology is different from optimism. Aspirational hope is a much richer concept that embodies not only optimism about the returns to effort through perceived agency and self-efficacy, but is characterized first by a clear direction of intended and desired progress in the form of goals and aspirations and by the ability to visualize achieving these aspirations through specific and realistic pathways of progress.

Whether it is possible to break poverty traps by raising this kind of aspirational hope is an important question—to which our microfinance experiment aims to contribute. We believe hope may play an important role in poverty dynamics in general, but a few caveats are worth noting. Relieving internal constraints should rarely be viewed as a substitute for relieving external constraints. In many cases, internal and external constraints are likely to be strong complements, but in others it may be that external constraints are binding and that interventions targeting internal constraints will have little impact at all. Well-intentioned practitioners and organizations have frequently implemented interventions to relieve external constraints with little effect on the intended beneficiaries. While there are many potential explanations for ineffective interventions, internal constraints may play an important role. Such internal constraints may reflect long periods of pessimism and "learned helplessness" that have developed over protracted periods of poverty and deprivation. This is the situation, at least anecdotally described to us by practitioners, that has existed among many indigenous women in Oaxaca, who have enjoyed access to resources such as microcredit for many years, but have realized very little real gain from these interventions.

As such, the ability to diagnose different varieties of poverty traps in practice is a critical but underappreciated skill among both development economists and practitioners. Learning to differentiate between poverty traps in which psychological factors or strictly economic factors constitute the binding constraint is fertile new ground for development economists and practitioners alike. Thus, the first question we as development economists should ask when poverty traps are invoked as an explanation of low standards of living is, "What is the structural, social or behavioral force behind the welfare dynamics that produce this presumed poverty trap?" The small but growing and exciting literature on the economics of hope may enhance our ability to address this critical question—and, through an improved understanding of the underlying forces at play, induce greater creativity in formulating policies and interventions that create integrative models of development aimed at alleviating chronic poverty in such cases. We intend this work to inroads into these research topics and questions at the intersection of behavioral and development economics.

References

Appadurai, A. 2004. "The Capacity to Aspire: Culture and the Terms of Recognition." In *Culture and Public Action*, edited by V. Rao and M. Walton, 59–84. Palo Alto, CA: Stanford University Press.
Bandura, A. 1977. "Self-Efficacy: Toward a Unifying Theory of Behavioral Change." *Psychological Review* 84:191.
Beaman, E., E. Duflo, R. Pande, and P. Topalova. 2012. "Female Leadership Raises Aspirations and Educational Attainment for Girls: A Policy Experiment in India." *Science* 335 (6068): 582–86.

Bernard, T., S. Dercon, K. Orkin, and A. S. Taffesse. 2013. "Learning with Others: A Field Experiment on the Formation of Aspirations in Rural Ethiopia." Working paper, Oxford University.

Bloem, J., D. Boughton, K. Htoo, A. Hein, and E. Payongayong. Forthcoming. "Measuring Hope: A Quantitative Approach with Validation in Rural Myanmar." *Journal of Development Studies.*

Bogliacino, F., and P. Ortoleva. 2013. "The Behavior of Others as a Reference Point." Research Paper no. 13-55, Columbia Business School, Columbia University.

Cassar, A., P. Aguinaga, J. Graham, L. Skora, and B. Wydick. 2016. "Goals, Incentives and Support Groups to Improve Economic Conditions: A Field Experiment in Medellin, Colombia." Working paper, University of San Francisco.

Dalton, P. S., S. Ghosal, and A. Mani. 2016. "Poverty and Aspirations Failure." *Economic Journal* 126 (590): 165–88.

Diamond, P. A. 1982. "Aggregate Demand Management in Search Equilibrium." *Journal of Political Economy* 90 (5): 881–94.

Froh, J. J. 2004. "The History of Positive Psychology: Truth Be Told." *NYS Psychologist* 16:18–20.

Furth, Gregg. M. 2002. *The Secret World of Drawings: A Jungian Approach to Healing through Art.* Toronto: Inner City Books.

Genicot, G., and D. Ray. 2014. "Aspirations and Inequality." NBER Working Paper no. 19976, Cambridge, MA.

Glewwe, P., P. Ross, and B. Wydick. Forthcoming. "Developing Hope among Impoverished Children: Using Children's Self-Portraits to Measure Program Impacts." *Journal of Human Resources.* https://doi.org/10.3368/jhr.53.2.0816-8112R1.

Jensen, R., and E. Oster. 2009. "The Power of TV: Cable Television and Women's Status in India." *Quarterly Journal of Economics* 124 (3): 1057–94.

Judge, T. A., A. Erez, J. E. Bono, and C. J. Thoresen. 2002. "Are Measures of Self-Esteem, Neuroticism, Locus of Control, and Generalized Self-Efficacy Indicators of a Common Core Construct?" *Journal of Personality and Social Psychology* 83 (3): 693–710.

Kahneman, D., and A. Tversky. 1979. "Prospect Theory: An Analysis of Decision under Risk." *Econometrica* 47 (2): 263–92.

Kling, J., J. Liebman, and L. Katz. 2007. "Experimental Analysis of Neighborhood Effects." *Econometrica* 75:83–119.

Koppitz, E. M. 1968. *Psychological Evaluation of Children's Human Figure Drawings.* New York: Grune and Stratton.

Lefcourt, H. M. 1982. *Locus of Control: Current Trends in Theory and Research,* 2nd ed. New York: Psychology Press.

Lybbert, T., and B. Wydick. 2018. "Poverty, Aspirations, and the Economics of Hope." *Economic Development and Cultural Change.* https://doi.org/10.1086/696968.

Macours, K., and R. Vakis. 2014. "Changing Households' Investment Behaviour through Social Interactions with Local Leaders: Evidence from a Randomized Transfer Program." *Economic Journal* 124:607–33.

McKenzie, D. 2012. "Beyond the Baseline and Follow-Up: The Case for More T in Experiments." *Journal of Development Economics* 99 (2): 210–21.

Menninger, K. 1959. "The Academic Lecture Hope." *American Journal of Psychiatry* 116:481–91.

Murphy, K., A. Shleifer, and R. Vishny. 1988. "Industrialization and the Big Push." NBER Working Paper no. 2708, Cambridge, MA.

Ray, D. 2006. "Aspirations, Poverty, and Economic Change." In *Understanding Poverty,* edited by Abhijit Vinayak Banerjee, Roland Bénabou, and Dilip Mookherjee, 409–21. Oxford: Oxford University Press.

Rotter, J. B. 1954. *Social Learning and Clinical Psychology*. Englewood Cliffs, NJ: Prentice-Hall.

———. 1966. "Generalized Expectancies for Internal versus External Control of Reinforcement." *Psychological Monographs: General and Applied* 80 (1): 1–28.

Seligman, M. E., and M. Csikszentmihalyi. 2000. "Positive Psychology: An Introduction." *American Psychologist* 55 (1): 5–14.

Sen, A. 1999. *Development as Freedom*. Oxford: Oxford University Press.

Snyder, C. R. 1994. *The Psychology of Hope: You Can Get There from Here*. New York: Simon and Schuster.

Thomas, G., and M. J. Silk. 1990. *An Introduction to the Psychology of Children's Drawings*. New York: New York University Press.

Wuepper, D., and T. J. Lybbert. Forthcoming. "Perceived Self-Efficacy, Poverty and Economic Development." *Annual Review of Resource Economics*.

Wydick, B., P. Glewwe, and L. Rutledge. 2013. "Does Child Sponsorship Work? A Six-Country Study of Impacts on Adult Life Outcomes." *Journal of Political Economy* 121 (2): 393–426.

———. 2017. "Does Child Sponsorship Pay Off in Adulthood? An International Study of Impacts on Income and Wealth." *World Bank Economic Review* 31 (2): 434–58.

Comment on Chapters 3 and 4

Rachid Laajaj

Psychology has gone a long way in the analysis of personality, emotions, and mental states that can lead individuals to make decisions that classical economics would consider irrational. Economics provides a number of tools that allow the analysis of how such phenomena might affect poverty dynamics. A first step necessary to make progress in this area is for economists to assimilate the rich literature from psychology and other fields before integrating such insights into economic models.

This comment provides a discussion of the two preceding chapters, "Depression for Economists," by Jonathan de Quidt and Johannes Haushofer and "Hope as Aspirations, Agency, and Pathways: Poverty Dynamics and Microfinance in Oaxaca, Mexico," by Travis J. Lybbert and Bruce Wydick. De Quidt and Haushofer and Lybbert and Wydick both develop particularly valuable insights from psychology on depression and hope, respectively, in a language very understandable and relevant to economists. Each chapter also includes an analytical framework, some strengths and weaknesses of which this comment discusses. I also provide a broader discussion of the condition under which a behavioral poverty trap might emerge, and of future steps necessary to better understand the issue and to design policies that can address it.

Socioemotional Skills and Behavioral Poverty Traps

As explained by Barrett, Carter, and Chavas (introduction, this volume) as well as Azariadis and Stachurski (2005), a poverty trap arises when

Rachid Laajaj is assistant professor of economics at the University of the Andes.
For acknowledgments, sources of research support, and disclosure of the author's material financial relationships, if any, please see http://www.nber.org/chapters/c13953.ack.

poverty becomes self-reinforcing. A drop in capital leads to a reduction in productivity or wealth accumulation that perpetuates the low equilibrium. A central role of this volume is to enrich this approach by understanding that it can apply to multiple forms of capital, including skills broadly defined.

Many economists have given a central role to physical capital accumulation as a driver of economic growth (Harrod 1939; Solow 1956) before better incorporating human capital (Mankiw, Romer, and Weil 1992). The latter was initially narrowed to health and education before being refined to a whole set of cognitive and socioemotional skills that determine people's decisions and thus their generation and accumulation of wealth. The research in anthropology, psychology, and behavioral economics provides some mechanisms through which such skills can be affected by one's conditions (Appadurai 2004; Ray 2006; Laajaj 2017; Moya 2015; Carter 2016; Dalton, Ghosal, and Mani 2016). The bidirectional effect between skills (broadly defined) and economic conditions raises the possibility of a behavioral poverty trap, defined as a situation where poverty reduces some aspects of the skills of the agent, which in turn perpetuates the situation of poverty.

A number of conditions are required for a behavioral poverty trap to emerge:

1. There are at least two possible dynamically stable equilibria;[1] for simplicity we will consider the case with two equilibria.
2. Individuals who behave optimally/rationally[2] would always find themselves in the high equilibrium (even if they start in the neighborhood of the low equilibrium).
3. The individual's skills are affected by her economic environment.
4. The skills that result from the low-equilibrium behaviors are such that it leads the person to decisions that perpetuate the low equilibrium.

De Quidt and Haushofer and Lybbert and Wydick both fit within this framework. De Quidt and Haushofer claim that negative economic shocks lead to depression, which is associated with pessimistic beliefs about the returns to individual effort, which can thereby generate a poverty trap if the individual reduces effort, thereby confirming and reinforcing the pessimistic beliefs. Lybbert and Wydick present a model where a lack of hope affects both one's preferences (via the utility function) and perceived return to effort, also causing a behavioral poverty trap.

1. Some other researchers have included single equilibrium situations as poverty traps (Carter and Barrett 2006). Whether one decides to include this in the concept of poverty traps is mostly a semantic debate. In this case we call it a trap only if there is a possible exit in the sense that another equilibrium is possible within the model.
2. Here rationality does not incorporate many forms of bounded rationality, or the fact that an optimum might incorporate psychological costs (e.g., the cost of having high hopes that go unsatisfied).

Depression for Economists: Should Depression Adapt to Economists or Economists Adopt Depression?

De Quidt and Haushofer do a fantastic job at defining and explaining major depressive disorder (MDD; hereafter, "depression") and its symptoms, in a language very understandable for economists, which is extremely valuable. They also propose a model where individuals derive utility from consumption, food, and sleeping, and where a strong negative shock lowers the beliefs about the returns to effort. As a result, individuals tend to revert to their natural tendencies in food or sleeping. This explains why depressed individuals often display either hypersomnia or insomnia and they tend to either overeat or lack appetite. The proposed model is intuitive and efficient in the sense that it explains a number of behaviors within a simple framework.

The main shortcoming of the analysis comes from the attempt to interpret the wide set of conditions that characterize depression within the limited framework of beliefs about the return to one's effort. Although many syndromes do fit very well, others seem to affect elements other than beliefs: negative expectations may simply be a general pessimism (if pessimism is "neutral to effort," expected future utility may fall holding the return to effort constant), reduction in gratification can be expressed with a flattening of the utility function without changing return to effort, and paralysis of the will and indecisiveness may reflect a higher cost of effort (or a consequence of the flattened utility). Hence as much as beliefs about the returns to one's effort can, by itself, predict many observed behaviors, the whole range of effects may lead to a more complete understanding of depression and how it affects decisions.

The set of symptoms mentioned also map nicely with a number of socioemotional skills: locus of control, self-efficacy, optimism, and tenacity are all skills that seem to be affected by depression and have been found to be good predictors of decisions and economic outcomes. It is also conceivable that the emotional effects of depression are likely to reduce patience and the ability to undertake risk. I used data from a skills-measurement exercise among 960 farmers in rural Kenya (Laajaj and Macours 2017) to look at correlations between depression and different socioemotional skills. Our analysis shows the numerous challenges related to the measurement of socioemotional skills, but also points at the Center for Epidemiologic Studies Depression (CESD) scale (a measure of depression) as one of the most consistent measures. Among the thirteen other socioemotional skills, CESD best correlates with (starting from the highest bivariate correlation coefficient estimate) neuroticism, metacognition, locus of control, and self-confidence,[3]

---

3. Neuroticism is a personality trait characterized by anxiety, moodiness, and frustration. Metacognition, sometimes defined as "thinking about thinking," refers to the extent to which a person is aware of herself as a thinker and a learner. Locus of control is internal when an individual believes that she has a strong influence on what happens to her, but external when she believes it is mostly driven by factors outside of her control. Self-confidence can be defined as the trust in one's abilities, qualities, and judgments.

which is very much in line with the symptoms highlighted by de Quidt and Haushofer. Depression may play a key role as a determinant of multiple skills and provide a key tool for understanding the mental processes under which skills might be affected. Further research in this area holds great potential for our understanding of the interactions between psychological factors and poverty dynamics.

The de Quidt and Haushofer model is a story about optimal behavior under imperfect information about the returns to one's effort. Under these conditions, a negative shock may lead to underinvestment as a consequence of Bayesian updating, and in extreme cases it might discourage the individual enough that she will not invest in effort anymore and thus not learn anymore and thereby remain in the low equilibrium. However, depression is diagnosed precisely when an attitude is excessively pessimistic with respect to one's experience. In practice, effort is multidimensional, and a failure in one type of effort may lead to the learning that this type of effort is ineffective. But complete discouragement of any form of effort may come from the "egocentric notions of causality" of depressed people (mentioned by de Quidt and Haushofer). This tells us first that a fully rational framework may miss fundamental elements of the concept of depression; its effects go beyond a Bayesian update, taking people away from the optimal reaction (under imperfect information). Furthermore, it raises fundamental questions: Why would some individuals associate the failure to a particular form of effort, and others to themselves and be discouraged? Is there an underlying skill such as emotional resilience that makes some individuals more prone to depression than others (in particular, depression triggered by a negative, exogenous event)? Could this skill be a common factor that explains the level and stability of multiple socioemotional skills, which themselves independently affect poverty dynamics? The introduction of this volume emphasizes the importance of understanding the determinants of resilience. The extent to which some individuals' skills are more or less affected by an adverse shock may play an important role in the persistence of poverty and is an area that remains relatively unexplored by economists.

Hope as Aspirations, Agency, and Pathways: Can Hope Bring New Exit Solutions to Poverty Traps?

Lybbert and Wydick provide a particularly useful review of the psychological literature on hope and its three main components: aspirations, agency, and pathways. This maps again with some traditional socioemotional skills such as locus of control and self-efficacy. The authors propose a model where hope affects effort decisions in multiple ways: the goal setting affects utility, while agency and pathways affect beliefs. It shows how a lack of hope might generate internal constraints to development and potential poverty traps.

One may think of a number of alternative ways in which hope could be modeled: (a) given that "falling short of aspirations may be experienced psychologically as a shock" (as mentioned by the authors), then a discontinuity in the utility function at the level of the goal could represent the added satisfaction that comes from reaching one's goal; (b) the time dimension is very important in the role of hope: the anticipation before reaching a goal generates utility or disutility (Loewenstein 1987; Laajaj 2017) that should be a function of aspiration, just like the utility at the time of achievement and after it, all leading to more complex utility functions and effects that will be affected by the lag between an effort and its potential reward; and (c) an alternative way to represent pathways would allow individuals to have multiple draws of π_v, the random shock of total production: this would mean that an individual with high pathways is less subject to random shocks because of her ability to find alternative solutions when facing a negative external shock.

I do not claim that the proposed alternatives are better, merely that they are also intuitive ways to model hope. This highlights a fundamental issue about the literature on internal constraints: given that utility functions and beliefs are never perfectly observable, we need to be cautious about results that require a model with specific, strong assumptions. Because it is infeasible to check the robustness of the conclusion to any viable alternative model, it may be preferable to start with models that are as broad as possible, and relatively minimalist in their assumptions.

On the other side, recent progress in survey methods are offering nonnegligible improvements in the estimation of utility functions and beliefs, even among populations with relatively low education. The authors' estimation of locus of control, asking for expected sales under different scenarios of luck and work effort, is a good example of innovative survey methods to estimate beliefs and locus of control. There is, however, a fundamental issue that affects many measures of socioemotional skills. According to Lybbert and Wydick's measure, a greater locus of control is inferred when the respondent's answers show that she believes that sales are affected by her effort more than by luck. It is certainly true that the measure captures the respondent's subjective perception (and thus agency). But it also captures exogenous reality; the respondent may be selling in a street where the demand is particularly low, have no access to credit, or any other external constraint that truly reduces the return to her effort. Hence the questions proposed capture not only the locus of control, but also external constraints that can prevent effort. Similar concerns apply to self-efficacy, of which standard questions broadly ask whether the person believes that she has many qualities. But one person may answer no because of some realism about a low level of education and cognitive skills, in which case, this is rather a standard lack of human capital constraint. But it would be attributed to psychological constraints if one jumps to the conclusion that it is capturing only socioemotional skills. Amartya Sen (1990) defines low development as the lack of capabilities, that is, the number of things that a person can be and do in her life. By definition, even without internal constraints, underdevelopment is associated with a reduced set of options. In order for the claim that internal constraints can cause poverty traps to gain credibility, this literature absolutely needs to find ways to distinguish this effect from a realistic observation by the poor of their reduced opportunities.

Following a new trend in the literature (Bernard et al. 2013), Lybbert and Wydick propose an intervention that directly targets aspirations. Their intervention includes videos, sessions, and magnets all aimed at encouraging hope. The immediate follow-up shows significant changes in aspirations and positive but not statistically significant impact on agency, pathways, and economic decisions and outcomes such as working hours, sales, savings, and so forth. One great potential of the study is that the results from this round and upcoming follow-up can tell us a lot about the dynamic evolution of hope, from early changes in aspirations levels to changes in behavior, and perhaps followed by changes in agency and pathways.

The existence of a vicious cycle between psychological factors and economic conditions lead to two types of interventions, depending on whether they affect psychology or economic conditions. Even though Lybbert and Wydick certainly have the best of intentions in their attempt to directly raise hope, their approach raises a number of concerns. Most theoretical models on the topic (including the one of the authors or, e.g., Genicot and Ray [2014]) find that aspirations are set at a given level for good reasons that include adjustments to a difficult reality or the reduction of frustrations or other psychological costs. Hence, at least for some individuals, an increase in hope may have negative effects. A video showing the most successful cases may inspire some, but it may also mislead others. It may push some people with lower skill or opportunities to invest and lose their money, and/or reach greater levels of frustration. Psychology research has shown the importance of treating people who suffer from depression. However, treating everyone for depression without prior testing of who suffers from it may generate mixed consequences. Interventions that focus on internal constraints can be received negatively by a population who may see it as a lack of consideration of the real constraints that they face. For these reasons internal constraints certainly deserve to be studied, but researchers and policymakers should be cautious before implementing interventions or policies that aim at directly changing psychological factors. It may be more effective and less risky for the populations if interventions first address external constraints and measure resulting behavioral changes and estimate the multiplier effects that might be generated. Research that documents aspirational effects of leadership within a community may also help design interventions that enhance this positive effect while limiting the risks mentioned (Beaman et al. 2012; Macours and Vakis 2014). Empirical research that combines credible exogenous variation in economic conditions with rich measures of socioemotional skills and studies the changes resulting from an intervention remain quite scarce and offer a rich avenue for future research on the dynamic between economic and psychological changes in the path out of poverty traps.

References

Appadurai, A. 2004. "The Capacity to Aspire: Culture and the Terms of Recognition." In *Culture and Public Action*, edited by V. Rao and M. Walton, 59–84. Palo Alto, CA: Stanford University Press.

Azariadis, C., and J. Stachurski. 2005. "Poverty Traps." In *Handbook of Economic Growth*, vol. 1A, edited by P. Aghion and S. Durlauf. Amsterdam: Elsevier.

Beaman, E., E. Duflo, R. Pande, and P. Topalova. 2012. "Female Leadership Raises Aspirations and Educational Attainment for Girls: A Policy Experiment in India." *Science* 335 (6068): 582–86.

Bernard, T., S. Dercon, K. Orkin, and A. S. Taffesse. 2013. "Learning with Others: A Field Experiment on the Formation of Aspirations in Rural Ethiopia." Working paper, Oxford University.

Carter, M. R. 2016. "What Farmers Want: The 'Gustibus Multiplier' and Other Behavioral Insights on Agricultural Development." *Agricultural Economics* 47 (S1): 85–96.

Carter, M. R., and C. B. Barrett. 2006. "The Economics of Poverty Traps and Persistent Poverty: An Asset-Based Approach." *Journal of Development Studies* 42 (2):178–99.

Dalton, P. S., S. Ghosal, and A. Mani. 2016. "Poverty and Aspirations Failure." *Economic Journal* 126 (590): 165–88.

Genicot, G., and D. Ray. 2014. "Aspirations and Inequality." NBER Working Paper no. 19976, Cambridge, MA.

Harrod, R. F. 1939. "An Essay in Dynamic Theory." *Economic Journal* 49 (193): 14–33.

Laajaj, R. 2017. "Endogenous Time Horizon and Behavioral Poverty Trap: Theory and Evidence from Mozambique." *Journal of Development Economics* 127:187–208.

Laajaj, R., and K. Macours. 2017. "Measuring Skills in Developing Countries." Policy Research Working Paper no. 8000, Washington, DC, World Bank. https://openknowledge.worldbank.org/handle/10986/26250.

Loewenstein, G. 1987. "Anticipation and the Valuation of Delayed Consumption." *Economic Journal* 97 (387): 666–84.

Macours, K., and R. Vakis. 2014. "Changing Households' Investment Behaviour through Social Interactions with Local Leaders: Evidence from a Randomised Transfer Programme." *Economic Journal* 124:607–33.

Mankiw, N. G., D. Romer, and D. N. Weil. 1992. "A Contribution to the Empirics of Economic Growth." *Quarterly Journal of Economics* 107 (2): 407–37.

Moya, A. 2015. "Violence, Psychological Disorders, and Risk Attitudes in Colombia." Unpublished manuscript.

Ray, D. 2006. "Aspirations, Poverty, and Economic Change." In *Understanding Poverty*, edited by Abhijit Vinayak Banerjee, Roland Bénabou, and Dilip Mookherjee, 409–21. Oxford: Oxford University Press.

Sen, A. K. 1990. "Development as Capability Expansion." In *Readings in Human Development*, edited by Sakiko Fukuda-Parr and A. K. Shiva Kumar. Oxford: Oxford University Press.

Solow, R. M. 1956. "A Contribution to the Theory of Economic Growth." *Quarterly Journal of Economics* 70 (1): 65–94.

III

Imperfect and Incomplete Financial Markets

5

Taking Stock of the Evidence on Microfinancial Interventions

Francisco J. Buera, Joseph P. Kaboski,
and Yongseok Shin

5.1 Introduction

Microfinancial interventions are often designed as responses to poverty traps, where the poor cannot invest because they lack wealth, but this poverty persists without investment. The past decade of empirical development research has produced a host of highly insightful, well-identified evaluations of the impacts of microfinancial interventions. These interventions include microcredit programs, asset grants to microentrepreneurs, and small asset transfers to the very poor, regardless of their entrepreneurial status. The aim of this chapter is to take stock of the state of our knowledge.

The process involves at least two parts. A necessary part of taking stock is the review of these findings that attempts to crystallize the salient patterns. Another equally necessary part of taking stock is to assess our understanding of these empirical patterns through the lens of economic theory. Reflecting on the policy lessons of the East Asian miracles, Robert E. Lucas Jr. once observed "If we understand the process of economic growth—or of anything else—we ought to be capable of demonstrating this knowledge by

Francisco J. Buera is the Sam B. Cook Professor of Economics at Washington University in St. Louis. Joseph P. Kaboski is the David F. and Erin M. Seng Foundation Professor of Economics at the University of Notre Dame and a research associate of the National Bureau of Economic Research. Yongseok Shin is professor of economics at Washington University in St. Louis, a research fellow of the Federal Reserve Bank of St. Louis, and a faculty research fellow of the National Bureau of Economic Research.

We thank our discussant, Stephen Smith, as well as Oriana Bandiera, Michael Carter, and the other conference participants for useful comments and suggestions. All errors remain our own. The views expressed here do not necessarily reflect the position of the Federal Reserve Banks of Chicago and St. Louis or the Federal Reserve System. For acknowledgments, sources of research support, and disclosure of the authors' material financial relationships, if any, please see http://www.nber.org/chapters/c13833.ack.

creating it in these pen and paper (and computer-equipped) laboratories of ours. If we know what an economic miracle is, we ought to be able to make one" (Lucas 1993, 271). The same is true for poverty traps and financial interventions. If we truly understand why an intervention works, we ought to be able to recreate the empirical patterns in our theories. Such an understanding is necessary to design our policy interventions, apply them with confidence in new contexts, and make projections for larger-scale programs that will have macroeconomic consequences.

Toward the first step, this chapter reviews the lessons from the empirical literature on microinterventions. At least three general lessons arise consistently. First, no policies produce large-scale miracle escapes from poverty traps. That is, although some of the policies have led to sustained gains, none has been shown to lead to permanent increases in income or consumption well beyond poverty levels nor to extended and sizable increases in *the rate of growth of* income, consumption, and capital that predict such escapes. Second, take-up rates for microcredit are typically low, while those of asset transfer programs are understandably much higher. Third, heterogeneous responses to policies are evident in almost all studies, where impacts vary by initial wealth, size of intervention, gender, ability, entrepreneurial status, financial access, and time frame. Variation in measurement and context (e.g., rural vs. urban, the degree of preexisting financial development) may also play a role.

The most interesting patterns emerge from a comparison across interventions. Although individual-level microcredit interventions can lead to increases in credit, entrepreneurial activity, and investments, they have been much less successful in leading to higher income or consumption. Among these interventions, only the two studies of village funds microcredit interventions uncovered gains to income and possibly consumption. They often show relatively larger impacts on existing or marginal entrepreneurs. Small asset grants of less than $200 at purchasing power parity (PPP) to entrepreneurs often lead to stronger increases in capital and profits with typically high returns on assets. Grants to "ultrapoor" households often have led to changes in income-generating activities, higher asset levels and capital, and increases in consumption of up to 30 percent.

The natural question is what leads to such very different outcomes, and what do they say about the relevant economic mechanisms at play. Even to replicate the outcomes of these different policies in varying contexts, we need an understanding of these mechanisms. Lucas (1993, 252) is again much more eloquent: "simply advising a society to 'follow the Korean model' is a little like advising an aspiring basketball player to 'follow the Michael Jordan model.' To make use of someone else's successful performance at any task, one needs to be able to break this performance down into its component parts so that one can see what each part contributes to the whole, which aspects of this performance are imitable and, of these, which are worth imitating. One needs, in short, a theory." A purely qualitative theory is useful in terms of organizing ideas and checking the internal consistency of one's reasoning, but we also want to know how well such a theory can *quantitatively* explain our observations, which is undoubtedly a higher hurdle.

Toward the second step, we review existing quantitative theory of financially constrained entrepreneurial decisions. A representative model in this literature incorporates much of what seems a priori essential in the economics involved: ex ante heterogeneity in wealth and ability, entrepreneurial decisions on both the extensive (entry) and intensive margins (scale), stochastic shocks, "necessity" entrepreneurs, and financial constraints that interact with wealth and ability. The combination of heterogeneity, intensive margins, and stochastic shocks provide enough smoothness and mixing so that poverty traps at the level of an individual (where investment decisions and asset and income paths depend critically on initial wealth levels) become irrelevant at the level of the economy (where a unique stationary equilibrium exists). Using this model, we simulate analogues of microcredit interventions and the asset grants targeted toward the poor and small entrepreneurs. Within our microcredit interventions we further vary the interest rates faced by borrowers. Some of these simulations reproduce results from our earlier work (Buera, Kaboski, and Shin 2012, 2014), while others are unique to this chapter.

We show that the model captures many of the qualitative and quantitative patterns observed empirically in the interventions, but we also learn lessons from where it fails. For asset grants, the model shows that marginal entrepreneurs enter, and that capital, income, and consumption increase, while assets tend to decline over time. However, the model does not generate the large increases in income, and we conjecture that the model fails to account for increases in labor supply in certain economic situations (e.g., where market labor is limited for women). Moreover, the training components of such interventions might increase the effective ability of livestock "entrepreneurs," or the real-world projects may somehow target the higher-ability people (i.e., marginal entrepreneurs).[1] Indeed, we show that marginal products of capital to poor existing entrepreneurs are quite high in the model. For microcredit, the simulations capture low take-up rates, borrowing and impacts that are concentrated in the higher end of the ability distribution, and small increases in entrepreneurship mostly due to the entry of marginal entrepreneurs. The baseline model somewhat overpredicts the increases in investment. However, with realistically higher interest rates on microloans, the model limits microcredit along the extensive and intensive margins and dampens the impacts of microcredit.

Several key lessons from the simulations involve the long-run and general equilibrium implications, however. First, although microfinancial interven-

---

1. Business training interventions have not proven particularly effective, but the training in these programs involves technical training regarding livestock rearing.

tions can have substantial steady-state and transitional impacts on development measures (income, consumption, productivity, etc.), no escape from aggregate poverty traps operating through wealth distributions and general equilibrium effects occurs in the simulations, since these traps do not exist. In this sense, we are unable to "make a miracle." Second, the simulations show that one-time redistribution in the form of asset grants alone tends to have only short-run aggregate and distributional impacts, as eventually infused assets are depleted over time. In contrast, microfinance—at least subsidized low-interest microfinance—has potentially longer-run impacts because of its permanent availability and general equilibrium impact through wages. The cost-effectiveness of smaller but sustained subsidies to microfinance versus one-time asset grants is therefore of interest. It also suggests the importance of proper targeting and technical training for asset grant programs to have persistent effects.[2]

5.2   Microempirical Estimates

In this section, we review the evidence on asset grants to microentrepreneurs and the ultrapoor, and on microcredit interventions. We then hypothesize about potential explanations for the patterns that emerge.

5.2.1   Asset Grants to Microentrepreneurs

Field experiments involving asset grants to microentrepreneurs have been undertaken in multiple countries: for example, Sri Lanka, Mexico, Ghana, and Nigeria. With one exception, all studies found significant profit increases from these asset grants. These findings are important experimental evidence for the long-held conjecture that at least some microentrepreneurs can generate above-market returns to capital, which in turn is evidence of the existence of financial constraints. We summarize these studies in table 5.1.

The Sri Lanka study (de Mel, McKenzie, and Woodruff 2008) identified about 400 nonemployer entrepreneurs in urban areas of Sri Lanka, and gave them small one-time grants either in kind (inventories or equipment) or in cash. They randomized between small and large grants equaling 460 or 920 PPP dollars, or roughly three to six months of average profits for these entrepreneurs. The impacts on investment were sizable: capital had increased by 70–130 percent of the grant at twenty-four months (i.e., roughly the size of the grant), and monthly profits increased by 4–6 percent of the original grant. The implied monthly return on the grant was substantially above market interest rates, and would imply recovery of the original amount after

---

2. Kaboski and Townsend (2011) compares asset grants to village funds, and finds that the latter are more cost-effective overall. This model has indivisibilities, but only an intensive investment margin, and is partial equilibrium.

Table 5.1   Studies of grants to microentrepreneurs

Study	De Mel, McKenzie, and Woodruff (2008)	McKenzie and Woodruff (2008)	Fafchamps et al. (2013)	Karlan, Knight, and Udry (2015)	McKenzie (2016)
Country	Sri Lanka	Mexico	Ghana	Ghana	Nigeria
Sample	408, nonemployer	198, self-employed	793, self-employed	160, tailors employing three or fewer	1,831, young applicants, "ordinary merit" winners
Intervention	$460–920 PPP (cash or in kind)	$210 (cash or in kind)	$280 (cash or in kind)	$370 (cash), plus consulting	$98,200 (cash), plus business training
Time horizon (months)	24	12	12	14	12
Profit (chg. rel. to grant) (%)	4–6 per month	20–33 per month	15 per month	−67	23
Capital (chg. rel. to grant) (%)	70–130	n/a	20–105	−250	n/a

1.5–2 years, if it were a loan. Moreover, the timing of the growth could be characterized as immediate and stable. Indeed, the point estimates of the follow-up work in de Mel, McKenzie, and Woodruff (2012) shows stability of higher profits even after five years, and the results are statistically significant. The sizable returns are evidence of potential financial frictions limiting profitable investments, but the fact that these impacts are stable over time, rather than leading to virtuous cycles of ever more reinvestment and growth indicate that the gains to relaxing these constraints may be limited. The Mexican study by McKenzie and Woodruff (2008) is a similar study lending further support to these findings. The study is smaller than the Sri Lankan study both in the sample size (about 200) and in the grant size (210 PPP dollars). They found extremely large returns to these small grants, between 20–33 percent *per month* at about one year, but acknowledged that sample attrition rate of 35 percent was potentially problematic.

Although returns may be high, the original Sri Lanka study also emphasized the strong heterogeneity in returns to capital, however. In particular, they found that the impacts were driven by those with disproportionally low levels of wealth or those with higher ability (measured by education attainment or through digit recall tests). Consistent with the wealth results, they found smaller returns on larger grants. Moreover, they were driven overwhelmingly by grants to men rather than to women. Fafchamps et al. (2013) further examine the impact on women. They granted about 280 PPP dollars to about 800 microentrepreneurs in Ghana and also found large impacts on monthly profits, which increased by about 15 percent of the original grant. These again imply high rates of return, but in contrast to the Sri Lankan study, they found that in-kind grants yielded larger impacts than cash grants. Moreover, the in-kind grants generated increases in profits among female entrepreneurs, which the Sri Lankan grants did not.

A study in Ghana provides a reminder that high returns to microentrepreneurs are not always and everywhere, however. Karlan, Knight, and Udry (2015) found that grants significantly decreased profits, as much as by 67 percent of the size of the initial grant. Their study experimented with a two-by-two intervention of grants and consulting, and neither intervention proved effective. They found some positive short-run changes, which quickly reversed their course. A few ways in which this study differs from the Fafchamps et al. (2013) study should be noted, however. First, the sample size of 160 entrepreneurs was much smaller, about one-fifth of the size of the other study. Given the multiple branches of the sample, it may simply be that the control group was a statistical anomaly. Second, the grants were cash, while the impacts in the Fafchamps et al. (2013) were larger for in-kind grants. Third, this study focused on a particular occupation, tailors, and perhaps the industry differs from the typical microentrepreneur industry. Finally, their targeting rule allowed for slightly larger entrepreneurs with up to three employees. In practice, the differences were not large as their entrepreneurs averaged 0.35 employees and 0.86 apprentices. In addition, baseline profits were larger, so that their larger grants of 370 PPP dollars amounted to about six weeks of profit, comparable to the grant size in the other study.

Only one study has looked at the impacts of larger grants on larger firms. McKenzie (2016) examines the impacts of large grants, averaging nearly 100,000 PPP on young, aspiring entrepreneurs. The experiment stems from a Nigerian entrepreneurship competition, in which applicants submitted business plans and received business training, and the randomization was among a middle group of 1,200 applicants who were deemed of "ordinary merit"—a selected group of applicants, but not the most promising. Profits increased by 23 percent, implying a monthly rate of return of 1–2 percent, somewhat lower than in other studies but comparable to market rates for small and medium enterprises in Nigeria. Thus, with more financial access, the control group should have been able to invest in principle.

In summary, the bulk of the evidence shows sizable returns to capital grants of modest sizes, equaling up to six months of profits on existing microentrepreneurs. On average, these grants lead to higher investment and profits, though the impacts are heterogeneous. The returns are somewhat lower for the wealthy, the less able, and female entrepreneurs.

5.2.2   Asset Grants to the Ultrapoor

Microentrepreneurs are often not the poorest of the poor, those living on only a few PPP dollars per day. A natural question for poverty alleviation is whether asset grants could have substantial impacts on this population. Many of the ultrapoor are only involved in subsistence agriculture, where the results for existing microentrepreneurs are less relevant. On the one hand, the wealth results from the entrepreneur studies might make us expect high returns, but the results for low-ability and female entrepreneurs suggest otherwise. In any case, a wide set of recent studies has given us strong evidence on the impact of asset grants to rural, ultrapoor households with female heads. We summarize them in table 5.2.

Several of the studies focus on a standardized program developed in Bangladesh by BRAC (Building Resources Across Communities, formerly Bangladesh Rural Advancement Committee) and exported to other countries. The studies focused on households headed by a female, and experimented with in-kind transfers of livestock, amounting to roughly four to eight goats or one to two cattle/buffaloes. In PPP terms, the value of these assets are in the ballpark of the microentrepreneur grants described above, but they are somewhat larger, and certainly larger as a fraction of the recipients' income. More important, the program is not a simple asset grant but is instead the lead part of a set of services offered to the participant households that together are designed as a microlevel "big push." These other services can include required or encouraged savings, technical assistance often in the area of livestock rearing, and a consumption supplement. One key purpose is to

Table 5.2   Studies of grants to the ultrapoor

Study	Bandiera et al. (2017)	Banerjee, Duflo, Goldberg, et al. (2015), ex. India[a]	Banerjee et al. (2011)	Morduch, Ravi, and Bauchet (2012)	Blattman, Fiala, and Martinez (2014)	Blattman et al. (2016)	Haushofer and Shapiro (2013)
Country Sample	Bangladesh 6,700, women	Five countries 9,500 (900 to 2,600 per country), women	India (WB) 800, women	India (AP) 3,500, women	Uganda 1,900, younger adults	Uganda 1,800, younger women	Kenya 1,380, men and women
Randomization level	Village	Village and individual	Individual	Village	Groups of 10–40	Village	Village and individual
Intervention	$520 PPP or two cows, plus technical training	$450–1,280, plus consumption support	$330, plus consumption support, technical training, forced saving	$510, plus technical training, forced saving, health service, group building	$1,310, plus artisan training	$380, plus business training, group building	$404–1,520, plus mobile money access
Time horizon (months)	48	36	18	18	47	16	≤ 4
Income change	+44%	Sig. positive	+39%	Insignificant	+43%	+70–150%	+34%
Income activity	Specialized self-emp. +15 pp, self-emp. hours +106%	Sig. increase in productive asset in ETH, GHA, PAK; sig. increase in hours in ETH (17%)	48% increase in hours worked, income from business labor	Increase in livestock income	Non-agri. hours +56%, overall labor supply +19%	Hours +60%, non-agri. hours +100%	Business, agri. expenses rise
Increase in assets	137% of grant	Sig. in ETH (83% of grant), PAK (14%)	Sig. positive	No impact, except the prob. of owning livestock	34% of transfer, 68% of original investment	Sig. positive	35% of grant
Consumption change	10%	Sig. in ETH (18%), GHA (10%)	29%	Insignificant	Sig. positive	30%	23%

[a] Banerjee, Duflo, Goldberg, et al. (2015) consider programs in six countries, one of which (India) is analyzed in depth in Banerjee et al. (2011). Since we report on Banerjee et al. (2011) separately in this table, we show the results on the other five countries in Banerjee, Duflo, Goldberg, et al. (2015).

lower the chances that the household would need to liquidate the livestock assets for short-term needs.

Bandiera et al. (2017) evaluate the ultrapoor program in the setting where it was developed, Bangladesh.[3] Their results are the most impressive of these programs. Randomizing at the village level, they report experimental results up to four years after the livestock grants with a sample of 6,700 households. Four years out, the treatment has higher assets that exceed the original value of the asset grant by 40 percent. The fraction of women specializing in self-employment increased by 15 percentage points, and labor hours in self-employment doubled. Income is 44 percent higher as well. Putting this into perspective, this amounts to an extra income equivalent to 22 percent of the initial asset grant *per month*, comparable to the very high returns found with microentrepreneurs in Mexico. However, the program also involved technical assistance costs.[4] Moreover, they find that consumption is 10 percent higher. Looking at the dynamics between two and four years, they find growth in assets, income, and consumption, but labor supply remains stable.

The largest and broadest study is Banerjee, Duflo, Goldberg, et al. (2015), which presents experimental results for Ethiopia, Ghana, Honduras, Pakistan, and Peru (and West Bengal, which we discuss below). The samples in these countries range from 900 to 2,600, and over 10,000 households are involved in the analysis combined. They evaluate the impacts three years out and find that assets are higher, but by less than the initial asset transfer. There is a great deal of variation across countries. Assets are significantly higher in Pakistan and Ethiopia, but the point estimates constitute 14 and 83 percent of the initial transfer, respectively. The study combines multiple measures into indices, which allows for more statistical power in terms of finding significant tendencies but makes it difficult to compare the magnitudes they report to other studies or theory. Nonetheless, they find statistically significant increases in their income index in productive assets in Ethiopia, Ghana, and Pakistan, and a significant 17 percent increase in hours in Ethiopia. They find significant increases of 18 percent in Ethiopia and 10 percent in Ghana.

The results in Banerjee, Duflo, Goldberg, et al. (2015) are reported in more depth in Banerjee et al. (2011). In a sample of 800, where individual rather than village randomization was used, they find a substantial increase in assets, income, and consumption at eighteen months. The measured increase in income of 39 percent amounts to a monthly return of 12 percent on the value of the asset. Here the cost of the program involves not only the

3. Emran, Robano, and Smith (2014) find very similar results for the BRAC program in Bangladesh based on earlier data, but using nonexperimental methods to account for selection bias.
4. In conversations, the authors also reported the presence of food supplements and savings encouragement.

grant and technical assistance, but also up to nine months of food supplements (tantamount to per capita consumption) and a saving requirement of three dollars per month. Nevertheless, the returns are sizable. Moreover, the program led to an increase in consumption of 29 percent. Because measured consumption exceeds measured income, as is typical in survey data from developing countries, the absolute increase in consumption exceeds the increase in income. The consumption increase is thus financed not only by increased income-generating activities, but also by sales of assets.

A larger study in another Indian state (Andhra Pradesh) finds less promising results, however. In a sample of 3,500 households, Morduch, Ravi, and Bauchet (2012) find no significant effects on income or consumption. They find increases in livestock and livestock income, but these are offset by lower levels of labor income. Like the Bengali program, this program incorporated technical assistance and mandatory savings, but it also differed in that it had a health component but no food supplement.

Looking across these studies, there is a pattern of sizable increases in income and consumption going together with increases in hours. In Bangladesh, West Bengal, and Ethiopia are the countries with the most promising results, and all showed increases in labor supply. In Andhra Pradesh, where jobs were widely available because of the presence of the National Rural Employment Guarantee Act (NREGA), there was no increase in income or consumption, but only movements from labor income to self-employed agricultural income. Bandiera et al. (2017) build a model where labor supply plays a key role, and it may be that such a model is only relevant in particular economic environments. Indeed, it is interesting to note that the two places with the largest observed gains, Bangladesh and West Bengal, have strong affinities, both cultural and socioeconomic.

Other asset grant programs in East Africa exhibit positive yet relatively modest impacts. Blattman, Fiala, and Martinez (2014) examine transfers targeted toward young adults (age eighteen to thirty-five) rather than women. The grants were cash and sizable, on average (1,310 PPP dollars), especially relative to the recipients' income. The grants were made at the group level, and in part they were used to finance artisanal training. Four years after the grant, the grantees had higher assets, with the difference being 34 percent of the original transfer or 68 percent of the original asset investment. Nonetheless, income was 43 percent higher, and this additional income constituted a monthly increase of about 5 percent, comparable to the returns to Sri Lankan entrepreneurs. The grantees had 19 percent higher labor supply on average, and 56 percent higher labor supply in nonagricultural/ skilled labor activities.

As mentioned, the additional assets four years out are only a fraction of the original transfer. Indeed, the program had larger effects two years out. After four years, nearly half of the recipients no longer practiced their trade. Although the program did not have a gender focus, the decline between years two and four is driven overwhelmingly by men. Nonetheless, the program is estimated to have a positive net present value.

Blattman et al. (2016) examine another program in Uganda, but this targets women in war-torn areas of the country. The cash grants were considerably smaller (380 PPP dollars) and constituted just 17 percent of the total costs of the program, which included business-skills training, follow-up supervision, and group-building activities. The program was evaluated at sixteen months, and the recipients had 60 percent higher labor supply and nearly twice as many hours in nonagriculture as those in the control, and their consumption was 30 percent higher. The increase in monthly income amounted to 7 percent of the initial transfer, again comparable to the Sri Lankan returns.

A final study is Haushofer and Shapiro (2013), which examines a program in Kenya offering grants averaging about 800 PPP dollars. The study had multiple levels of randomization including the size of total grants, the gender of recipients, and the timing of payments. Smaller grants were made over nine months, while larger grants were made over sixteen months. In principle, the drawn-out payments might help households that struggle with inconsistent intertemporal preference unless a lump sum is needed for an indivisible, illiquid investment. The overall time horizon is much shorter, however, averaging about four months, which overlaps with the payment schedule. Over this short run, the program led to increases in income and consumption, but the monthly increase in income constitutes just 2 percent of the average total transfer, somewhat lower than the other studies. Using both a village and individual-level design, they find no evidence of spillovers to nonparticipants, which is in harmony with the other studies.

In sum, the asset grant programs to poor, rural, usually female-headed households lead to substantial increases in assets, income, and consumption. With the exception of the Bangladesh study, the existing evidence shows the initial increase in assets dissipating over time, however.[5]

5.2.3   Microcredit Evaluations

The high apparent marginal returns on assets among portions of micro-entrepreneurs and the ultrapoor suggest that financial frictions may be prohibitive for these groups, and could motivate microcredit as an alternative program for these populations that could potentially improve on asset grant programs in terms of both cost-effectiveness and identifying those with high returns. Indeed, this is the original, anecdote-based motivation for microcredit as a transformative financial intervention. A host of recent

---

5. This is difficult to assess for the papers like Blattman et al. (2016), who only provide a normalized asset index. Asset transfers of land as in Bleakley and Ferrie (2013) and Keswell and Carter (2014) show long persistence, although Bleakley and Ferrie (2013), perhaps surprisingly, only find it on the right tail of the distribution.

research has given a more nuanced and sober assessment of its impacts, however.

Banerjee, Karlan, and Zinman (2015) report the results of six recent randomized evaluations of microcredit interventions in Bosnia-Herzegovina, Ethiopia, India, Mexico, Mongolia, and Morocco. These are summarized in table 5.3.[6] In PPP terms, the average loans are of similar magnitudes to the asset grants, although somewhat larger. The studies tend to find (a) relatively low take-up rates, (b) increases in credit overall, (c) increases in business activity, but (d) little impact on overall measures of profits, income, or consumption. Together with these studies, table 5.3 also includes two evaluations of village fund programs in China and Thailand, which show more positive results. There are some common findings, but also remarkable differences in both the programs and findings.

The first study (Attanasio et al. 2015) evaluates an expansion of microcredit within villages in Mongolia. Although generally Mongolia has a strong microcredit presence, the villages studied have relatively low baseline usage. The unique aspect of this study is the variation between joint-liability and individual-liability loans. The loans are relatively short term (six months), and after nineteen months they find that roughly half of those surveyed have taken up loans, which is higher than the other studies. The intervention increases the fraction with loans by 26 percentage points and the level of credit overall by 67 percent. They also find an 8 percentage point increase in the fraction of self-employed, and a 57 percent increase in labor supply. This is the lone study of traditional microcredit that finds any evidence of an increase in consumption, an 11 percent increase that seems to be driven by a significant increase in food consumption.

Crépon et al. (2015) and Tarozzi, Desai, and Johnson (2015) study expansions of microcredit programs into rural areas, Morocco and Ethiopia, respectively. In Morocco, the program targeted those already involved in activities other than crops. Thus, it is unsurprising to not see an increase in the fraction of people involved in self-employment activities. After two years, the program still had low take-up, with just 13 percentage points more having borrowed, but that led to a 64 percent increase in credit overall. Capital increased by 29 percent, and there was a decrease in labor supplied to non-self-employment activities. This yielded an increase in profits of 40 percent, which was marginally significant, but no significant impact on consumption.

The Tarozzi, Desai, and Johnson (2015) study involves repeated cross sections of households, but effectively panels of villages and "peasant associations," which are the unit of randomization. The microcredit program was joint with a family-planning intervention that was ex post ineffectual. After three years, the fraction with loans was 25 percentage points higher in treatment villages, and credit had increased by 195 percent. Still, they found

---

6. Some of the information reported comes from the individual papers, while others come from the Banerjee, Karlan, and Zinman (2015) overview article.

Table 5.3   Studies of microcredit

Study	Attanasio et al. (2015)	Crépon et al. (2015)	Tarozzi, Desai, and Johnson (2015)	Banerjee, Duflo, Glennerster, et al. (2015)	Angelucci, Karlan, and Zinman (2015)	Augsburg et al. (2015)	Kaboski and Townsend (2011, 2012)	Cai, Park, and Wang (2016)
Country	Mongolia	Morocco	Ethiopia	India	Mexico	Bosnia and Herzegovina	Thailand	China
Sample	600, rural, women microentrepreneurs	5,600, rural, at least partly self-employed	6,300, rural, poor, potential entrepreneurs	6,900, urban, women	16,600, women	1,000, marginal borrower	1,000, rural, no targeting	1,200, rural, no targeting
Randomization level	Village	Village	Peasant assoc.	Neighborhood	Village, neighborhood	Individual	Village	Village
Average loan size	$700 PPP	$1,080	$500	$600	$450	$1,820	16,700 THB	5,000 CNY
Nominal APR (%)	27	15	12	24	110	22	7	8
Average loan term (months)	6	16	12	12	4	14	12	12
Time horizon (months)	19	24	36	39–42	27	14	24	24
Take-up (%)	50–57	13	31	17	19	99, by design	54	29
Overall credit chg.	+67%	+64%	+195%	+63%	+18 pp (frac. with loan)	+19 pp (frac. with loan)	+50%	+23 pp (frac. with loan)
Change in entrepreneurs	Fraction of entrepreneurs +8 pp	Insignificant, as expected	Livestock revenue and crop exp. rise	Fraction of entrepreneurs +2 pp	Revenue and crop exp. rise	Insignificant	Insignificant	Cash crop land +63%
Change in capital	Insignificant	+29%	Insignificant	+25%	−18%	Insignificant	Insignificant	+47% (in husbandry)
Labor supply change	+57%	Decreased non-self-emp. hours	Insignificant	Insignificant	n/a	Insignificant	n/a	+8%, driven by migrant labor
Profit change	Insignificant	+40%	+68% insignificant point est.	+57% insignificant point est.	Insignificant	+34% insignificant point est.	Income +35%	Income +50% (husbandry income +53%)
Consumption change	+11%	Insignificant	n/a	Insignificant	Insignificant	−16% insignificant point est.	+10%	+8% insignificant point est.

no impacts on businesses, capital, or profits, despite the program targeting potential entrepreneurs. The survey did not measure consumption.

Banerjee, Duflo, Glennerster, et al. (2015) evaluate an urban expansion of microcredit in India, while Angelucci, Karlan, and Zinman (2015) combine both rural and urban expansions in Mexico. They find take-up rates below 20 percent. Both programs find substantial increases in credit and its prevalence, and different measures of business activity, but neither finds a significant effect on profits (although the point estimate for India is sizable) or consumption. India shows an increase in assets, while Mexico shows a substantial decline. The Mexico intervention is unique in that the loans were very short term (averaging four months).

The Bosnia-Herzegovina study (Augsburg et al. 2015) stands apart in several ways. First, it randomized at the individual level, targeting marginal borrowers who otherwise would not have qualified for loans.[7] Second, the loan amounts were substantially higher, averaging 1,820 PPP dollars. By design, the take-up rate approaches 100 percent. Still, they only find significant impacts on credit and nothing on entrepreneurship, profits, or consumption. Naturally, marginal borrowers make a unique sample, which may partially explain the none result.

The two remaining studies examine village fund interventions and yield somewhat more positive results. Village funds differ in that they are largely independent of existing microfinance institutions and instead involve a transfer of funds to a village in order to set up its own quasi-formal institution. Kaboski and Townsend (2011, 2012) study introduction of village funds in Thailand. Although they lack a randomized control, the fact that the government gave the same amount of funds to all villages, regardless of their size, makes village sizes an effective instrument for the intensity of treatment. In the first two years, they find a near doubling of the level of short-term credit in the villages, a 35 percent increase in income, and a 10 percent increase in consumption. Followed over six years, the increase in credit is stable, but the increases in consumption and income are concentrated in the early years.

Cai, Park, and Wang (2016) examine a similar village fund program in China, but had a randomized introduction at the village level. After two years, there is a 23 percentage point increase in the probability of having a loan, substantial increases in resources going to cash crops and animal husbandry, and a 50 percent increase in income per capita. Interestingly, total working days increase, but this is driven by migrant labor outside of the village (and province) rather than self-employed labor or labor within the village.

The setup of the Cai, Park, and Wang (2016) study allows us to compare the results using the experimental variation with the results using quasi-

---

7. Karlan and Zinman (2010, 2011) follow a similar approach.

experimental variation in village size of Kaboski and Townsend (2011, 2012). The results largely validate the village-size approach, although the standard errors rise, highlighting the improved identification with field experiments.

A few other nuanced findings from the empirical work deserve discussion.

First, impacts tend to be heterogeneous. Kaboski and Townsend (2011) showed that households who are marginal for large indivisible investments benefited the most. Quantile regressions in the *American Economic Journal: Applied* special issue articles above show that impacts are often concentrated among the very highest percentiles. Banerjee, Duflo, Glennerster, et al. (2015) provide further evidence that positive impacts are concentrated among existing entrepreneurs.

Second, Angelucci, Karlan, and Zinman (2015), Crépon et al. (2015), and Cai, Park, and Wang (2016) examine impacts on (expected) nonparticipants and find no spillovers. In contrast, Kaboski and Townsend (2012) find impacts of the Thai village fund intervention on local wages. Interacting the balance sheets of microfinance institutions with government-driven microfinance crisis and subsequent collapse of microfinance in Andhra Pradesh as a source of quasi-experimental variation, Breza and Kinnan (2016) find that day wages declined in areas where microcredit contracted more severely. Whether general equilibrium spillovers are important may depend greatly on the structure of the labor market and the relative importance of microfinance.

Third, the impact of the introduction of the program on the use of other credit products varies by study. Some find that the new intervention has no effect (Attanasio et al. 2015; Tarozzi, Desai, and Johnson 2015), others find that it crowds out other sources (Augsburg et al. 2015; Banerjee, Duflo, Glennerster, et al. 2015; Cai, Park, and Wang 2016), while still others actually find crowding in (Kaboski and Townsend 2011, 2012; Angelucci, Karlan, and Zinman 2015; Crépon et al. 2015; Greaney, Kaboski, and Van Leemput 2016). Even at a more disaggregate level (e.g., bank loans, informal loans), the impacts vary from crowding out to crowding in.

Fourth, the long-term impacts have been examined in two papers with different results. In Thailand, Kaboski and Townsend (2011) find that impacts fluctuate over six years, but are concentrated in the early years. Banerjee et al. (2014) find fluctuations in treatment effects over time but also finds some contrasting results, at least for existing entrepreneurs. They examine the impact of the collapse of microcredit in Andhra Pradesh again, looking at whether the benefits persist even after microcredit has exogenously declined. They find that existing entrepreneurs are more profitable six years later, but the more reluctant entrepreneurs' profitability has declined.

Finally, impacts tend to vary substantially based on program details.[8] Attanasio et al. (2015) found that only joint-liability loans led to positive

---

8. Kaboski and Townsend (2005) is an early paper showing the importance of program policies for impacts in a nonexperimental setting.

impacts. Although Field and Pande (2008) found no impact of moving from weekly to biweekly payment frequency, Field et al. (2013) shows that a two-month delay before the onset of required repayment leads to higher levels of entrepreneurial investments. Finally, Greaney, Kaboski, and Van Leemput (2016) show that the contractual structure of the administrative agents in self-help groups impacts both entrepreneurial activities and group membership.

5.2.4   Taking Stock across Interventions

The evaluations uncover some commonalities, but also strong differences across the interventions.

Among the commonalities, one important theme is that of individual heterogeneity. The entrepreneur grants focused on the dimensions of initial assets, ability, and gender. In many countries, the ultrapoor programs showed broad-based impacts (Banerjee, Duflo, Goldberg, et al. 2015), but even they exhibit a factor of 20 difference in the impacts on income between the 90th and the 10th percentiles. Moreover, while those specializing in wage labor shifted activities toward self-employment, the impacts on earnings were much larger for those already specialized in self-employment (Bandiera et al. 2017). The microcredit work highlighted the low take-up and the concentration of largest impacts near the very top of the distribution.

A second, related generalization is that even among existing entrepreneurs, interventions can increase profitability, indicating constraints along the intensive margin. The intensive-margin impacts of the entrepreneur grants are obvious, but we also find impacts of microcredit and ultrapoor grants among the existing self-employed. On the other hand, the ultrapoor grants also show impacts along the extensive margin of entrepreneurship, perhaps only for the severely constrained, however.

A third common finding was a general lack of sustained growth patterns, at least among the bulk of the population. Among those studies with multiple end lines, impacts were generally realized fairly rapidly, and either remained steady or fell over time. Across the ultrapoor programs, the additional assets at end line were generally smaller than the initial grants. The one exception is the Bangladesh ultrapoor program, which led to increases in assets, income, and consumption even between years two and four.

The key difference across the interventions is the smaller impact of microcredit on income and consumption relative to the grants to entrepreneurs (which impacted profits positively) and to the ultrapoor. We hypothesize several possible reasons for this difference, along with some supportive evidence.

The most obvious explanation is that the burden of repayment limits the impact of microcredit relative to grants. Take-up tends to be low, and so—in the absence of strong spillovers—much of the population is simply not affected. The need to repay could also lower the impact on consumption, even among those who borrow. However, we also see small impacts on income, indicating that this is unlikely to be the only factor. Repayment can impact the income-generating investments themselves. First, by definition, relatively high interest rates make investments less profitable. Second, the need to make immediate repayments may limit investments with longer horizons, even if they are otherwise profitable. Interest rates of 2.5 percent per month are high, certainly higher than the returns exhibited by some in the grants studies.

In considering the burden of repayment, the village fund programs in China and Thailand are of particular interest, since they fall somewhere in between grants and pure microfinance. The fund itself is a grant to the village, but it is channeled to the villagers in the form of loans that need to be repaid. They had lower interest rates (8 and 7 percent, respectively) and longer payment schedules (a single repayment at the end of the loan). They showed relatively high take-up (54 and 29 percent, respectively) and resulted in strong increases in income (in both) and consumption (significant in Thailand). In addition, the microcredit study in Morocco allowed for a two-month grace period for animal husbandry investments, and it was the only pure microcredit study to find any evidence of higher profits. This is again consistent with Field et al. (2013), which documents the impact of a two-month grace period in India.

Another explanation is the difference in the targeted population of microcredit relative to the grant programs. The programs to the poor show that grants can have large impacts on very poor populations (at least in the short run), and the entrepreneurship grants also found larger impacts on those with fewer assets. Microfinance programs, however, often do not lend to the poorest populations. Related, microcredit may be a "small" intervention in the sense that, in many places, those with the most to gain by borrowing may already have access to other forms of credit, and so the interventions are only changing the terms. Those whose investments respond to small changes in terms are likely those with the most marginal returns. This would be a good description of those areas in which significant crowding out was observed.

Another difference is that microcredit programs have often targeted women, and with cash. The entrepreneurship grants found that it was difficult to increase the profitability of women entrepreneurs, at least with cash. They also found that more-educated entrepreneurs exhibited bigger impacts, but women tend to be less educated than men in many developing countries. Here the village fund programs are again an interesting comparison, since they did not target women specifically, and the gender education gap is small in both China and Thailand.

5.3   Taking Stock of Theory

We now turn to evaluating our understanding of these empirical patterns through the lens of quantitative theory. We present the basic model as developed in a series of papers: Buera and Shin (2013) and Buera, Kaboski, and Shin (2011, 2012, 2014). It captures many common elements in the theoretical and quantitative literature, and financial frictions have quantitative bite both in the steady state (Buera, Kaboski, and Shin 2011) and transitionally (Buera and Shin 2013; for a more comprehensive review of this literature, see Buera, Kaboski, and Shin [2015]). We evaluate the theory a priori based on its consistency with many of the common patterns above, discuss its implications on poverty traps, and then assess its ability to predict the variety of interventions.

5.3.1   Basic Model

Consistent with the commonalities discussed above, the quantitative theory has focused on models with (a) extensive entrepreneurship decisions; (b) intensive investments; (c) individual heterogeneity in wealth, productivity/ability, and whether or not their entrepreneurship is simply a matter of necessity; and (d) forward-looking decisions regarding entrepreneurship, investment, and saving. We reproduce this basic model below.

Individuals differ in terms of their productivity as workers x and entrepreneurs z. As entrepreneurs, they produce output using capital k, labor l, and a diminishing returns to scale production function $zk^{\alpha}l^{\theta}$. Worker productivity and entrepreneurial productivity follow Markov processes that are independent of each other. Specifically, with probability γ, the value of the entrepreneurial productivity remains constant from one period to the next, z', and, with probability $1-\gamma$, it is a random draw from a Pareto distribution, $z' = \zeta \sim -\eta\zeta^{-\eta-1}$. The stochastic nature captures the possibility of both positive and negative shocks to business profitability, which we observe in the data.[9] A worker's productivity or efficiency units of labor is assumed to follow a two-state symmetric Markov chain, $x \in \{x_l, x_h\}$, with $x_l < x_h$. The probability of the shocks remaining in its current value is π and $\mathbb{E}[x]$ is normalized to one.

The financial frictions in the model follow a simple yet useful form and stem from limited enforceability of contracts. In particular, by defaulting on their credit contracts, entrepreneurs can keep a fraction $1 - \phi$ of the period's output net of labor costs and the same fraction of the undepreciated capital. Defaulting individuals regain access to credit markets in the following period, and hence the limited commitment constraint has a simple static representation.

Given the interest rate r and the wage per efficiency units of labor at time t, w_t, the problem of an individual with wealth a and worker/entrepreneurial productivity x and z at time t is recursively formulated as

$$v_t(a, x, z) = \max_{c,a',k,l \geq 0, e \in \{0,1\}} \left\{ \frac{c^{1-\sigma}}{1-\sigma} + \beta\mathbb{E}_{x',z'}\left[v_{t+1}(a', x', z') \mid x, z\right] \right\}$$

9. Note that we model shocks to productivity rather than assets as in Ikegami et al. (2016).

s.t. $c + a' + T_t(a) - S_t(a) \leq$

$$e[zk^\alpha l^\theta - (r + \delta)k - w_t l] + (1 - e)xw_t + (1 + r)a$$

and $zk^\alpha l^\theta - w_t l - (r + \delta)k + (1 + r)a$

$$\geq (1 - \phi)[zk^\alpha l^\theta - w_t l + (1 - \delta)k]$$

$$\text{when } e = 1$$

where c is consumption and e is the discrete occupational choice ($e = 1$ for entrepreneur and $e = 0$ for wage worker). The second inequality captures the financial friction for entrepreneurs, which places an upper bound on available capital. Buera, Kaboski, and Shin (2012) shows this reduces to $k \leq \bar{k}(a, z; \phi)$, where $\bar{k}$ is increasing in wealth a, ability z, and ϕ. In our modeling of financial frictions, ϕ is the unique parameter indexing the enforceability of contracts across countries, and so it captures financial development and the availability of credit.[10] As ϕ varies from zero to one, the model spans the spectrum of cases from financial autarky to perfect credit markets.

The basic components of the model can be calibrated quantitatively to key measurables, including the firm-size distribution (which identifies thick-tailed ability distributions), the income distribution (which, given the thick tails, identifies the return-to-scale parameters), and larger firms' exit rates (which identify the frequency of shocks to productivity). The parameters of the labor income process can be calibrated to the autocorrelation and standard deviation of income in rural areas of developing countries, which reflect the dearth of labor market opportunities. Given the distribution of heterogeneous productivities in the population, this model can be aggregated to solve for endogenous levels of financial intermediation, productivity, aggregate capital, and so forth. One can do this within the framework of a partial equilibrium model (where wages and interest rates are taken as given), a small open economy (where the wage is endogenous but the interest rate is given), or a full general equilibrium. Both steady-state and transitional analyses are computationally tractable.

A few words on some implicit modeling assumptions vis-à-vis real-world empirics. First, we follow the quantitative literature in fixing total labor supply (hours worked in business or the labor market) exogenously. Although labor supply was often impacted in the experimental work cited above, this is a reasonable benchmark for looking across programs because the sign of impacts varied across studies. Nonetheless, labor supply seemed to play an important role in the more successful ultrapoor grants to women. Second, occupational choice is binary. Empirically, we often observe households and even individuals whose income and hours are attributed to both

---

10. Buera, Kaboski, and Shin (2015) review alternatives to this form in the literature.

labor and business/self-employment. Nonetheless, we view this as preferable to ignoring the natural indivisibility that comes from minimum efficient scale or fixed costs. Buera, Kaboski, and Shin (2011) models these fixed costs explicitly and emphasizes how they vary across sectors, and Buera, Kaboski, and Shin (2014) argue that such a fixed cost may be necessary to explain the persistent effects on the right tail of the wealth distribution from the land distribution in Bleakley and Ferrie (2013). Similarly, Banerjee et al. (2014) argues that their microfinance results are consistent with a model with fixed costs and technology choice within industries.[11]

One can easily consider the decisions of a single individual taking prices as given, or a full general equilibrium. One can consider either a stationary equilibrium where aggregates and prices are stable or a dynamic equilibrium where these aggregates and prices transition over time. The model therefore holds a theory for both household and aggregate behavior, and the latter allows us to have insight into potential impacts of both scaled up microinterventions and macropolicies.

5.3.2   Financial Frictions and Poverty Traps

When considering the role of poverty traps in the model, it is important to distinguish between individual and aggregate poverty traps. Within the model, we define poverty traps as self-reinforcing differences in steady-state income that result from differences in initial wealth conditions. Without financial frictions, agents with identical productivities would have identical occupational and productive choices regardless of their wealth. Since all individual decisions coincide, aggregate productive behavior (and ultimately aggregate savings behavior) is unaffected by the distribution of wealth.

However, when financial frictions are present, the model can lead to individual-level poverty traps in which agents with identical productivities but different initial wealth levels behave differently and their wealth levels diverge. Buera (2008) and later Banerjee and Moll (2010) show the importance of self-financing in driving these poverty traps. Initial wealth determines how quickly saving to self-finance would pay off, and agents with low initial wealth do not find it optimal to save for so long. At the macro level, financial frictions lower the demand for capital, while self-financing motives increase the supply. Both of these in turn lower equilibrium interest rates, leading those with no intention of becoming entrepreneurs to dissave instead.

We visually demonstrate this in figure 5.1, which plots normalized net worth (a in the model) against unconstrained profits (a linear function of z

---

11. Kaboski, Lipscomb, and Midrigan (2014) develop an explicit quantitative model with this technology/scale choice and assesses the relative role for cash-denominated versus in-kind microfinance.

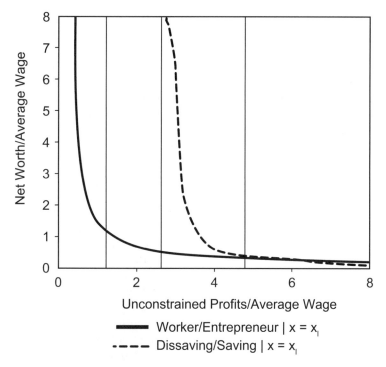

Fig. 5.1   Occupation and saving decision map

in the model). The dashed lines illustrate the occupational-choice decision as a function of individual wealth and productivity. Under financial frictions, it is not only high productivity that leads people to become entrepreneurs, but also high wealth. The solid lines represent the thresholds above which agents save and below which they dissave. For agents with high productivity, the wealthiest agents save while the poorest agents dissave. The intersection of the occupational-choice and poverty trap lines indicate that there are workers who are saving to eventually escape poverty, while there are rich entrepreneurs who are eventually converging to poverty. Of course, shocks to ability can alter these dynamics, so that these "poverty traps" are *not* absorbing states in the long run.

Beyond individual-level poverty traps, however, many stylized theories of entrepreneurial choice predict the possibility that financial frictions can lead to poverty traps for entire economies by distorting entrepreneurship, for example, Banerjee and Newman (1993), Ghatak and Jiang (2002), Aghion and Bolton (1997), and Piketty (1997).[12] Poverty traps arise in these models

---

12. Matsuyama (2011) provides an excellent recent review of these and related results.

because initial distributions affect general equilibrium wages or interest rates, and in turn aggregate dynamics. If few people have the required initial assets to become entrepreneurs, wages and interest rates will be low, which leads to a persistence of a wealth distribution in which few have the resources to become entrepreneurs. The models typically assume small roles for (a) forward-looking, self-financing motives, and (b) intensive margins in the scale of establishments. Both of these should, in principle, respond to the low cost of labor and capital. For example, Banerjee and Newman (1993) and Ghatak and Jiang (2002) lack an intensive margin in the demand for labor that would make the equilibrium wage respond continuously rather than discretely. Piketty (1997) lacks any labor market and, like Aghion and Bolton (1997), also abstracts from an intensive margin for capital that could respond to the interest rate. Moreover, all of these models have warm-glow savings behavior.

Qualitatively, the mechanisms emphasized in the poverty trap literature (lower interest rates and wages due to constrained entrepreneurial borrowing) are present in our benchmark model, and indeed with the self-financing motive, the impact on interest rates can be exacerbated. The benchmark model also contains nonconvexities in production, which could generate multiple equilibria. Nevertheless, quantitative versions of these models, when properly mapped to the data, do not lead to aggregate poverty traps—for example, Giné and Townsend (2004) and Buera, Kaboski, and Shin (2011)—but only slower convergence to a unique stationary distribution, the main point of Buera and Shin (2013).[13] As explained in Buera, Kaboski, and Shin (2014), aggregate poverty traps disappear once one relaxes the above-mentioned simplifying assumptions needed for analytical tractability. In addition to the intensive margins, the productivity shocks assure churning in the distribution of wealth and ability that leads to uniqueness.

5.3.3   Assessing Poverty Interventions

Variants of the above model have been simulated to assess asset grants (Buera, Kaboski, and Shin 2014) and microcredit (Buera, Kaboski, and Shin 2012). We follow those calibrations, which map the model to Indian moments on the firm-size distribution and dynamics (which helps identify the z distribution and the γ shocks to z), wealth concentration (which, together with the z distibution, captures the returns to scale/share of entrepreneurial profits), labor income dynamics (which identify the x shocks), and the level of external finance relative to income (which identifies the ϕ parameter). In these papers, short-run partial equilibrium simulations are compared to some of the above empirical results, and the longer-run, general equilibrium, and macroeconomic implications of the scaling-up of these programs

13. See also Moll (2014) for a theoretical analysis of this point.

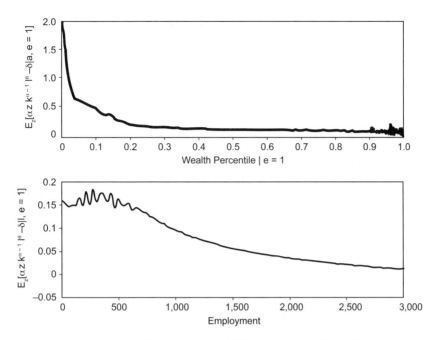

Fig. 5.2   Average marginal product of capital by entrepreneurial wealth and size (employment)

are assessed. We review these results before extending them to evaluate the role of high lending rates on the impacts of microcredit.

Returns to Capital among Entrepreneurs

Before using the quantitative model to assess the aggregate and distributional impacts of poverty interventions, we first illustrate the distribution of the marginal product of capital in the model economy. These returns provide a natural benchmark to compare with the estimates of the return to capital from the asset grants to microentrepreneurs in section 5.2.1. The microestimates on the return to capital provide a natural test of the quantitative theory.

In figure 5.2, we present the marginal product of capital among entrepreneurs. In the top panel, we show the average marginal product of capital among entrepreneurs in a given wealth percentile. For entrepreneurs in the bottom 10 percentiles, the (annual) return to capital net of depreciation is between 25 and 75 percent. The measured returns to capital to large interventions in the Nigeria study (McKenzie 2016) are close to the lower end of this range, while the returns in the Sri Lanka study (de Mel, McKenzie, and Woodruff 2008) are slightly above the upper end of this range. The large returns found in the Mexico study (McKenzie and Woodruff 2008) or the Ghana study (Fafchamps et al. 2013) are only rationalized if they are interpreted as capturing an average return to capital for entrepreneurs in the lowest percentile of the asset distribution. In the bottom panel, we plot the average marginal product of capital among entrepreneurs with a given establishment size, measured by the number of entrepreneurs. Since with few exceptions, the real-world programs relate to the self-employed without employees, the relevant group in the model is nonemployers in the far-right end, whose average annual return exceeds 15 percent. Overall, this figure shows that the return to capital is very heterogeneous among entrepreneurs in the calibrated model.

Asset Grant Programs

Buera, Kaboski, and Shin (2014) assesses the role of asset grant programs in the context of a small open economy with fixed interest rates.[14] In particular, the transitional dynamics following an unexpected redistribution of wealth from the wealthiest toward the poorest are analyzed. The redistribution establishes at that point in time a minimum wealth in the economy equal to double the average annual wage in the initial stationary equilibrium, and is funded in an extreme fashion by instituting a one-time, 100 percent tax on wealth above a particular threshold, $\bar{a}$.[15] The size of the redistribution is fairly comparable to the asset grants to the poor summarized in table 5.2, which is estimated to range from about five months of income to three years of income.[16] The cash grants to entrepreneurs in table 5.1 are a bit smaller in absolute terms, but much smaller as a fraction of reported income of the entrepreneurs (0.5 to 6 months of baseline profits). The exercise in Buera, Kaboski, and Shin (2014) is less comparable to the entrepreneurial grants, however, since they target the poor rather than small-scale entrepreneurs.

In medium-run projections of Buera, Kaboski, and Shin (2014), the impacts dissipate over time but largely remain after four years, but they are substantially smaller than those found in the empirical study. The program matches the empirics in that the fraction of people that pass over the poverty trap thresholds illustrated in figure 5.1 is relatively small. Initially, 17 percent of the treated population switches to entrepreneurship. This compares well with the 15 percentage point increase in Bandiera et al. (2017). In terms of labor hours, it constitutes a roughly 200 percent increase in hours

14. In order to capture the poor saving opportunities in developing countries, we set this interest rate to zero, which is 2 percent lower than the historical average in developed economies.

15. Specifically, we implement in the initial period the wealth grant $S_0(a) = \max\{2w\mathbb{E}[x] - a, 0\}$, which is financed by a one-time tax over the wealthiest individuals, $T_0(a) = \max\{a - \bar{a}, 0\}$, where $\bar{a}$ is chosen to satisfy the static government budget constraint.

16. These calculations are complicated because income may be underestimated (e.g., people underreport noncash income or income of other household members), and also because many studies report household income, which we need to convert into income per working-age household member.

to entrepreneurship for this population, which is greater than the results in table 5.2 that vary between 50 and 110 percent. In this sense, the strict occupational choice may lead to too strong a result with hours.

Qualitatively, the model also predicts an increase in earnings, but quantitatively the effects on earnings are just 4 percent. This is in line with the negligible impact on income reported in Morduch, Ravi, and Bauchet (2012), but substantially smaller than the promising results found in the other studies in table 5.2. Recall that where increases in income and consumption were substantial, they were accompanied by increases in labor supply, and the labor-leisure decision is not considered in the model. Alternatively, perhaps we can interpret these increases in income as resulting from an increase in productivity z as a result of the technical training, which is not in the benchmark model. Thus, the large and sustained increase in earnings that some of the empirical work reports is not really a puzzle for theory.

The model matches most of the studies, with the exception of Bandiera et al. (2017), in having the impacts fall over time, however. After four years, the entrepreneurship rate is just 8 percentage points higher, and earnings are just 3 percent higher. Again, in line with the empirics, the impacts in the model are very heterogeneous across individuals, with the earnings of the treated individuals in the 90th (95th) percentile of the entrepreneurial productivity increasing by 11 (15) percent in the second year. Thus, the model has potential to have somewhat larger impacts for marginal entrepreneurs, but not the large gains reported in table 5.1. In any case, the model is certainly consistent with a lack of a virtuous cycle of growth for the average recipient.

Although the model cannot match the magnitude of the observed income increase, the long-run macroeconomic impacts reported in Buera, Kaboski, and Shin (2014) are still of interest. These aggregate effects include those on both the recipients, nonrecipients, and those taxed by the redistribution. The wealth grants have a positive effect on aggregate total factor productivity (TFP), but a relatively larger negative impact on aggregate capital. The increase in TFP is due to the net entry of productive entrepreneurs and the capitalization of poor entrepreneurs with relatively high marginal products of capital. On impact, the decline in capital arises for the following reasons. The funds for the wealth grants come from rich active entrepreneurs who decrease their capital input by more than the drop in their wealth, since the acquisition of capital is based on leveraging wealth as collateral. This decrease is not completely offset by the grant recipients because not all of them choose to become active entrepreneurs. In a small open economy, the redistribution of wealth therefore leads to a drop in the capital used in production and a capital outflow.

The net effect of the increase in productivity, but decrease in capital on aggregate per capita income, is negative but small. Although these mechanisms may be offset by the larger gains in income experienced by recipients in the empirical work, the capital decline mechanism in the model may still be an important consideration at the macro level.

All of these impacts, however, are transitional. Since the overall distribution of ability remains constant, wealth levels gradually return to their stationary distribution. There is no aggregate poverty trap to begin with, and so in the long run, the one-time wealth redistribution can cause no aggregate escape, and the economy returns to their original state.

Microcredit Programs

Buera, Kaboski, and Shin (2012) reports parallel results for the impacts of microfinance. They model microcredit as a new alternative intermediation technology that allows anyone access to a small level of credit for capital, b^{MF}, regardless of wealth or ability. The financial constraint on capital is thus relaxed to a choice between formal credit and microcredit:

(1) $k \leq \max \left\{ \bar{k}\left(a, z; \phi\right), a + b^{MF} \right\}$

where the second element of the maximum captures the microcredit option. They run alternative models, but we report the results without the labor shock as it provides the simplest benchmark.[17]

Their benchmark analysis sets b^{MF} at 150 percent of annual wages, which implies a maximum microloan size relative to per capita expenditures of one and an average microloan size relative to per capita expenditures of 0.1. This average is comparable to the levels of *average* loan size to income of 6–43 percent reported by Banerjee, Karlan, and Zinman (2015) in all but one of the empirical evaluations in the special issue. In the aggregate, it leads to total microcredit constituting 30 percent of overall credit, somewhat smaller than the 33 percent in Thailand (Kaboski and Townsend 2011, 2012) or the 44 percent in India (Banerjee, Karlan, and Zinman 2015).

The model does well in generating small take-up rates, 11 percent in the population overall, somewhat lower than the empirical estimates in table 5.3, but those microcredit programs targeted marginal populations. The model also does well in predicting heterogeneous impacts, where both take-up and impacts are concentrated in the top decile of the entrepreneurial ability distribution.

In the short-run, partial equilibrium (i.e., small scale) simulations, the model predicts significant impacts on entrepreneurship (an increase of 4 percentage point) overall and investment by borrowers (a 46 percent increase), but small effects on overall consumption (a 1 percent increase). The increase in entrepreneurship is on the high end of the empirical studies, which ranges

---

17. In an extension, they consider a stark calibration of a labor shock where $x_l = 0$ to capture an individual who is forced into entrepreneurship because he has no labor market option. They choose the process of the labor shock to match the high rates of entrepreneurship that are typical in developing countries.

from no impact in several countries to 2 and 8 percentage points in India and Mongolia, and the increase in investment is also larger than in most. The Chinese study shows a 48 percent increase in investment, however, which is comparable to the simulation. The small increase in consumption is in line with the majority of the studies. Thailand and Mongolia show significant increases of roughly 10 percent, while the others exhibit negligible increases. In sum, the model does well in predicting the impact on entrepreneurship and consumption, but somewhat overpredicts the impact on investment.[18]

The aggregate impacts of microcredit are similar to those of the asset grants in the model. Capital decreases as income and resources are redistributed toward the poor who have lower saving rates. The impacts on TFP is positive, but on net, the impacts of microcredit on per capita income are small.[19]

The main long-run impact of microcredit is that it is highly redistributive. Indeed, in contrast to the one-time asset grants, the permanent availability of the microcredit option to poor households has long-run impacts. Despite low take-up, the option to finance entrepreneurship leads to a general equilibrium increase in the wage level, which is consistent with the findings of Kaboski and Townsend (2012) and Breza and Kinnan (2016). When widely available, microcredit can therefore be highly redistributive, even if the take-up rates are low. Of course, these impacts are within a model where microcredit has substantial impacts on entrepreneurship and investment.

5.3.4   New Analysis with Interest Rate Spreads

In section 5.2.4, we conjectured that the interest rate charged on microloans may contribute to the varying impacts both within microfinance interventions and across microcredit and the asset grant interventions. We pursue this formally here within the context of our model. In the model results of the Microcredit Programs section, the interest rate on microcredit was the same as the low rate available to savers and borrowers from formal finance. Here we add microcredit-specific intermediation costs that lead to higher interest rates on microfinance loans. In principle, the variation in these spreads may reflect different rates of subsidies toward microfinance. We simulate each lending rate as its own unique scenario.

In the simulations below, the interest rate on savings is −0.04. Table 5.4 reports results for interest rates charged on microcredit of −0.04, 0.06 (comparable to the low-interest village funds in table 5.3), and 0.36 (toward the higher end of the interest rates reported in table 5.3), where all quantities are normalized by the respective levels in the no-microcredit economy. Focusing

18. In the version of the model in which a sizable fraction of the population faces a lack of labor market opportunities and therefore become necessity entrepreneurs, microcredit has a bigger impact on consumption (a 20 percent increase).

19. In the case with necessity entrepreneurs, the effects on per capita income can be even negative, although consumption increases.

Table 5.4   Simulation with different interest rates on microloans

	Short-run PE			Long-run GE		
MF lending rate	−4%	6%	36%	−4%	6%	36%
Wage		1 by definition		1.05	1.04	1.01
Output	1.07	1.04	1.02	1.02	1.02	1.01
Capital	1.03	1.01	1.01	0.94	0.96	1.00
TFP	1.00	1.03	1.02	1.04	1.03	1.01
Consumption	1.01	1.01	1.01	1.03	1.03	1.00
Avg. z (active entrepreneurs)	1.01	1.02	1.01	1.03	1.04	1.02
Fraction of entrepreneurs[a]	+0.04 p.p.	+0.01 p.p.	+0.00 p.p.	+0.03 p.p.	+0.02 p.p.	+0.00 p.p.

[a] Deviations from the no-microcredit economy. All other quantities are divided by their respective values in the no-microcredit economy.

on the short-run, partial equilibrium results in the first three columns, we see that the interest rates matter considerably. At market interest rates, in the short run, the model predicts a 3 percentage point increase in the fraction of entrepreneurs in the population, a 3 percent increase in capital, and 7 percent increase in output. At the intermediate interest rates, comparable to the village funds, these impacts are smaller, but there is still a 4 percent increase in output and a 1 percentage point increase in the fraction of entrepreneurs. At the high interest rates, the impact on output is just 2 percent and there is no impact on entrepreneurship. In the short run, the increase in consumption—in this model without necessity entrepreneurs—is small across the board, just 1 percent, however.

Focusing on the long-run, general equilibrium impacts, we see the patterns discussed above for the low and moderate interest rates: increases in the wage, reductions in capital accumulation, and increases in TFP leading to small changes in output, but a somewhat larger increase in consumption. For the case with high interest rates, even these modest impacts all but disappear.

Figure 5.3 gives more insights into these patterns. It plots take-up rates, microcredit as a fraction of total credit, and impacts on income and consumption at different percentiles of the entrepreneurial ability (z) distribution for microcredit with different lending rates. The figure crystallizes the heterogeneous impacts in the model. At all interest rates, borrowing and impacts are concentrated near the higher end of the ability distribution, but as interest rates increase, take-up falls and becomes even more concentrated near the top (top-left panel). Microcredit relative to total credit shows even sharper declines as interest rates increase, showing that the intensive margin also responds negatively (top-right panel). The lower panels show that the impacts on income and consumption are even more muted than those on credit.

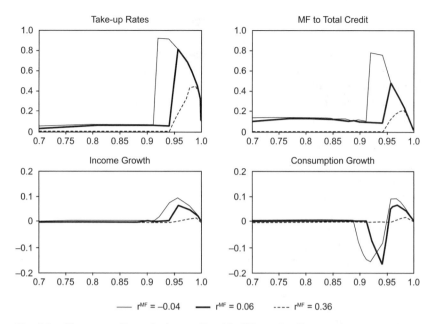

Fig. 5.3   Short-run effect of microcredit with different lending rates

In sum, higher interest rates, as expected, dampen the effects of microfinance, bringing the short-run investment and entrepreneurship predictions closer to the existing empirical evidence on the effect of microfinance reviewed in table 5.3. Another implication is the stronger positive selection in who uses microloans. As shown in figure 5.3, the higher the lending rates, the more concentrated the effect of microfinance at the top of the entrepreneurial ability distribution.

5.4   Concluding Remarks

We first reviewed the empirical evidence on the effect of asset grants and microcredit programs and then showed how these findings, to the extent that a pattern exists, can be explained by a model in which agents make optimal decisions subject to financial frictions. The simplest model underestimated the impact of asset grants in the short run and overestimated that of microfinance, although the microfinance results were more comparable to the estimates from village funds programs. We first conjecture that a modified version of our model with technical training, a common element of real-world asset grant programs, can replicate the empirical evidence on asset grants. We then show that introducing realistic levels of spreads between lending and deposit rates makes the model short-run results align with the empirical evaluations of microfinance. A central finding from both empirical and quantitative research is the lack of dramatic escapes from poverty traps.

Because the empirical studies are small scale relative to the overall economy, and the follow-ups are performed at most a few years after the program implementation, we only learn from them short-run, partial equilibrium outcomes. Having a fully specified equilibrium model allows us to consider the macrolevel effect of scaled up programs and also over a longer time horizon. We find that it would be erroneous to simply extrapolate the short-run, partial equilibrium empirical results to predict long-run, general equilibrium effects. While one-time asset grant programs hold a lot of promise based on the empirical evidence, the model shows that it has negligible longer-run effects, since the economy, absent any other permanent change, will revert eventually to its unique invariant distribution. On the other hand, while microcredit programs in the real world have low take-up rates and small overall impact, the model shows that, once they are scaled up through the increase in wage, even nonborrowers will be positively affected by the programs, consistent with village funds programs that showed local labor market equilibrium effect. Again, neither intervention leads to escapes from poverty traps, even when scaled up to the full economy.

More broadly, we see large gains from trade between micro- and macrodevelopment. The well-established microexperimental evidence helps us enhance theoretical models, while quantitative theory is a natural guide to interpreting the micro evidence and making predictions on what can be expected when existing programs are scaled up over time.

References

Aghion, Philippe, and Patrick Bolton. 1997. "A Theory of Trickle-Down Growth and Development." *Review of Economic Studies* 64 (2): 151–72.
Angelucci, Manuela, Dean Karlan, and Jonathan Zinman. 2015. "Microcredit Impacts: Evidence from a Randomized Microcredit Program Placement Experiment by Compartamos Banco." *American Economic Journal: Applied Economics* 7 (1): 151–82.
Attanasio, Orazio, Britta Augsburg, Ralph De Haas, Emla Fitzsimons, and Heike Harmgart. 2015. "The Impacts of Microfinance: Evidence from Joint-Liability Lending in Mongolia." *American Economic Journal: Applied Economics* 7 (1): 90–122.
Augsburg, Britta, Ralph De Haas, Heike Harmgart, and Costas Meghir. 2015. "The Impacts of Microcredit: Evidence from Bosnia and Herzegovina." *American Economic Journal: Applied Economics* 7 (1): 183–203.
Bandiera, Oriana, Robin Burgess, Narayan Das, Selim Gulesci, Imran Rasul, and Munshi Sulaiman. 2017. "Labor Markets and Poverty in Village Economies." *Quarterly Journal of Economics* 132 (2): 811–70.
Banerjee, Abhijit, Emily Breza, Esther Duflo, Rachel Glennerster, and Cynthia G. Kinnan. 2014. "Does Microfinance Foster Business Growth? The Importance of Entre-

preneurial Heterogeneity." Presentation, Massachusetts Institute of Technology, Columbia University, and Northwestern University. https://www8.gsb.columbia .edu/leadership/sites/leadership/files/CBS%20Presentation%20Breza.pdf.

Banerjee, Abhijit V., Esther Duflo, Raghabendra Chattopadhyay, and Jeremy Shapiro. 2011. "Targeting the Hardcore Poor: An Impact Assessment." Unpublished manuscript, Massachusetts Institute of Technology.

Banerjee, Abhijit, Esther Duflo, Rachel Glennerster, and Cynthia Kinnan. 2015. "The Miracle of Microfinance? Evidence from a Randomized Evaluation." *American Economic Journal: Applied Economics* 7 (1): 22–53.

Banerjee, Abhijit, Esther Duflo, Nathanael Goldberg, Dean Karlan, Robert Osei, William Parienté, Jeremy Shapiro, Bram Thuysbaert, and Christopher Udry. 2015. "A Multifaceted Program Causes Lasting Progress for the Very Poor: Evidence from Six Countries." *Science* 348 (6236). https://doi.org/10.1126/science.1260799.

Banerjee, Abhijit, Dean Karlan, and Jonathan Zinman. 2015. "Six Randomized Evaluations of Microcredit: Introduction and Further Steps." *American Economic Journal: Applied Economics* 7 (1): 1–21.

Banerjee, Abhijit V., and Benjamin Moll. 2010. "Why Does Misallocation Persist?" *American Economic Journal: Macroeconomics* 2 (1): 189–206.

Banerjee, Abhijit V., and Andrew F. Newman. 1993. "Occupational Choice and the Process of Development." *Journal of Political Economy* 101 (2): 274–98.

Blattman, Christopher, Nathan Fiala, and Sebastian Martinez. 2014. "Generating Skilled Self-Employment in Developing Countries: Experimental Evidence from Uganda." *Quarterly Journal of Economics* 129 (2): 697–752.

Blattman, Christopher, Eric P. Green, Julian Jamison, M. Christian Lehmann, and Jeannie Annan. 2016. "The Returns to Microenterprise Support among the Ultrapoor: A Field Experiment in Postwar Uganda." *American Economic Journal: Applied Economics* 8 (2): 35–64.

Bleakley, Hoyt, and Joseph P. Ferrie. 2013. "Up from Poverty? The 1832 Cherokee Land Lottery and the Long-Run Distribution of Wealth." NBER Working Paper no. 19175, Cambridge, MA.

Breza, Emily, and Cynthia Kinnan. 2016. "Measuring the Equilibrium Impacts of Credit: Evidence from the Indian Microfinance Crisis." Unpublished manuscript, Northwestern University.

Buera, Francisco J. 2008. "Persistency of Poverty, Financial Frictions, and Entrepreneurship." Unpublished manuscript, Northwestern University.

Buera, Francisco J., Joseph P. Kaboski, and Yongseok Shin. 2011. "Finance and Development: A Tale of Two Sectors." *American Economic Review* 101 (5): 1964–2002.

———. 2012. "The Macroeconomics of Microfinance." NBER Working Paper no. 17905, Cambridge, MA.

———. 2014. "Macro-perspective on Asset Grants Programs: Occupational and Wealth Mobility." *American Economic Review* 104 (5): 159–64.

———. 2015. "Entrepreneurship and Financial Frictions: A Macrodevelopment Perspective." *Annual Review of Economics* 7:409–36.

Buera, Francisco J., and Yongseok Shin. 2013. "Financial Frictions and the Persistence of History: A Quantitative Exploration." *Journal of Political Economy* 121 (2): 221–72.

Cai, Shu, Albert Park, and Sangui Wang. 2016. "Microfinance Can Raise Incomes: Evidence from a Randomized Control Trial in China." Technical Report, HKUST Institute for Emerging Market Studies.

Crépon, Bruno, Florencia Devoto, Esther Duflo, and William Parienté. 2015. "Estimating the Impact of Microcredit on Those Who Take It Up: Evidence from a Randomized Experiment in Morocco." *American Economic Journal: Applied Economics* 7 (1): 123–50.

de Mel, Suresh, David McKenzie, and Christopher Woodruff. 2008. "Returns to Capital in Microenterprises: Evidence from a Field Experiment." *Quarterly Journal of Economics* 123 (4): 1329–72.

———. 2012. "One-Time Transfers of Cash or Capital Have Long-Lasting Effects on Microenterprises in Sri Lanka." *Science* 335 (6071): 962–66.

Emran, M. Shahe, Virginia Robano, and Stephen C. Smith. 2014. "Assessing the Frontiers of Ultrapoverty Reduction: Evidence from Challenging the Frontiers of Poverty Reduction/Targeting the Ultra-poor, an Innovative Program in Bangladesh." *Economic Development and Cultural Change* 62 (2): 339–80.

Fafchamps, Marcel, David McKenzie, Simon Quinn, and Christopher Woodruff. 2013. "Microenterprise Growth and the Flypaper Effect: Evidence from a Randomized Experiment in Ghana." Technical Report, University of Oxford.

Field, Erica, and Rohini Pande. 2008. "Repayment Frequency and Default in Microfinance: Evidence from India." *Journal of the European Economic Association* 6 (2–3): 501–9.

Field, Erica, Rohini Pande, John Papp, and Natalia Rigol. 2013. "Does the Classic Microfinance Model Discourage Entrepreneurship among the Poor? Experimental Evidence from India." *American Economic Review* 103 (6): 2196–226.

Ghatak, Maitreesh, and Nien-Huei Jiang. 2002. "A Simple Model of Inequality, Occupational Choice, and Development." *Journal of Development Economics* 69 (1): 205–26.

Giné, Xavier, and Robert M. Townsend. 2004. "Evaluation of Financial Liberalization: A General Equilibrium Model with Constrained Occupation Choice." *Journal of Development Economics* 74 (2): 269–307.

Greaney, Brian, Joseph P. Kaboski, and Eva Van Leemput. 2016. "Can Self-Help Groups Really Be 'Self-Help'?" *Review of Economic Studies* 83:1614–44.

Haushofer, Johannes, and Jeremy Shapiro. 2013. "Household Response to Income Changes: Evidence from an Unconditional Cash Transfer Program in Kenya." Technical Report, Abdul Latif Jameel Poverty Action Lab.

Ikegami, Munenobu, Michael R. Carter, Christopher B. Barrett, and Sarah A. Janzen. 2016. "Poverty Traps and the Social Protection Paradox." NBER Working Paper no. 22714, Cambridge, MA.

Kaboski, Joseph P., Molly Lipscomb, and Virgiliu Midrigan. 2014. "The Aggregate Impact of Household Saving and Borrowing Constraints: Designing a Field Experiment in Uganda." *American Economic Review* 104 (5): 171–76.

Kaboski, Joseph, and Robert Townsend. 2005. "Policies and Impact: An Analysis of Village-Level Microfinance Institutions." *Journal of the European Economic Association* 3 (1): 1–50.

———. 2011. "A Structural Evaluation of a Large-Scale Quasi-experimental Microfinance Initiative." *Econometrica* 79 (5): 1357–406.

———. 2012. "The Impact of Credit on Village Economies." *American Economic Journal: Applied Economics* 4 (2): 98–133.

Karlan, Dean, Ryan Knight, and Christopher Udry. 2015. "Consulting and Capital Experiments with Microenterprise Tailors in Ghana." *Journal of Economic Behavior and Organization* 118:281–302.

Karlan, Dean, and Jonathan Zinman. 2010. "Expanding Credit Access: Using Randomized Supply Decisions to Estimate the Impacts." *Review of Financial Studies* 23 (1): 433–64.

———. 2011. "Microcredit in Theory and Practice: Using Randomized Credit Scoring for Impact Evaluation." *Science* 332 (6035): 1278–84.

Keswell, Malcolm, and Michael L. Carter. 2014. "Poverty and Land Distribution." *Journal of Development Economics* 110:250–61.

Lucas, Jr., Robert E. 1993. "Making a Miracle." *Econometrica* 61 (2): 251–72.

Matsuyama, Kiminori. 2011. "Imperfect Credit Markets, Household Wealth Distribution, and Development." *Annual Review of Economics* 3 (1): 339–62.

McKenzie, David J. 2016. "Identifying and Spurring High-Growth Entrepreneurship: Experimental Evidence from a Business Plan Competition." Unpublished manuscript, World Bank.

McKenzie, David, and Christopher Woodruff. 2008. "Experimental Evidence on Returns to Capital and Access to Finance in Mexico." *World Bank Economic Review* 22 (3): 457–82.

Moll, Benjamin. 2014. "Productivity Losses from Financial Frictions: Can Self-Financing Undo Capital Misallocation?" *American Economic Review* 104 (10): 3186–221.

Morduch, Jonathan, Shamika Ravi, and Jonathan Bauchet. 2012. "Failure vs. Displacement: Why an Innovative Anti-poverty Program Showed No Net Impact." CEI Working Paper no. 2012-05, Center for Economic Institutions, Institute of Economic Research, Hitotsubashi University.

Piketty, Thomas. 1997. "The Dynamics of the Wealth Distribution and the Interest Rate with Credit Rationing." *Review of Economic Studies* 64 (2): 173–89.

Tarozzi, Alessandro, Jaikishan Desai, and Kristin Johnson. 2015. "The Impacts of Microcredit: Evidence from Ethiopia." *American Economic Journal: Applied Economics* 7 (1): 54–89.

6

Poverty Traps and the Social Protection Paradox

Munenobu Ikegami, Michael R. Carter, Christopher B. Barrett, and Sarah Janzen

Cash transfer programs, progressively targeted at the poorest, have become a predominant policy for addressing chronic poverty in developing countries. While pioneered by middle-income developing countries (notably Mexico, South Africa, and Brazil), cash transfer programs have spread across the developing world, including the risk-prone pastoral regions of northern Kenya whose economic reality underwrites the analysis in this chapter.[1]

Munenobu Ikegami is professor at Hosei University. Michael R. Carter is professor of agricultural and resource economics at the University of California, Davis, and directs the Feed the Future Innovation Lab for Assets and Market Access and the Index Insurance Innovation Initiative (I4). He is a fellow of BREAD (Bureau for Research and Economic Analysis of Development) and the American Agricultural Economics Association and a research associate of the National Bureau of Economic Research. Christopher B. Barrett is the Stephen B. and Janice G. Ashley Professor of Applied Economics and Management, professor of economics, and International Professor of Agriculture at Cornell University, where he also serves as deputy dean and dean of academic affairs at the SC Johnson College of Business. Sarah Janzen is assistant professor of economics at Kansas State University.

An earlier version of this work circulated under the title "Poverty Traps and Social Protection" (Barrett, Carter, and Ikegami 2013). We thank John Hoddinott, Joe Kaboski, Valerie Kozel, Felix Naschold, and seminar audiences at Cornell, the International Food Policy Research Institute, Namur, Purdue, Wageningen, Wisconsin, and the World Bank for helpful comments on earlier versions of this work. Generous financial support was provided by the Social Protection Division of the World Bank and by a grant from the USAID Office of Poverty Reduction to the BASIS Assets and Market Access Innovation Lab. The ideas expressed are the responsibility of the authors and should not be attributed to either sponsoring organization. For acknowledgments, sources of research support, and disclosure of the authors' material financial relationships, if any, please see http://www.nber.org/chapters/c13834.ack.

1. With the region receiving "emergency" food aid year after year, the Kenyan government in 2009 created a social protection scheme, the Hunger Safety Net Programme (HSNP), built around bimonthly cash transfers targeted at the region's chronically poor and indigent. By regularizing progressively targeted assistance, HSNP had hoped to put households on a pathway out of poverty by enabling asset accumulation and sustained investment in child health and education so as to avert future chronic poverty arising due to economic disability (see the discussion in Hurrell and Sabates-Wheeler [2013]).

There is ample evidence that cash transfers break the liquidity constraints that Loury (1981) argues propagate poverty intergenerationally by limiting parents' health and education investments in their children. However, there is much more modest evidence that these programs enhance the earned incomes of recipient households and affect their living standards once the cash transfers come to an end, despite their theoretical potential to do so.[2] Indeed, policymakers in Latin America now confront the conundrum of former cash transfer recipients who revert to their pretransfer living standards once their transfer eligibility ends. In northern Kenya, the Hurrell and Sabates-Wheeler (2013) impact evaluation of the Hunger Safety Net Programme (HSNP) cash transfer scheme found that while transfers allowed recipient households to economically tread water even as their untreated neighbors sunk under the weight of continuing shocks, it did nothing to help recipient households craft a pathway out of poverty. Similar to Latin American countries, Kenya is now looking to augment its HSNP cash transfer program with a "poverty graduation program."[3]

The apparently weak impact of cash transfer programs on the upward mobility of poor households in at least the medium run has particular salience in risky regions. If cash transfers do little to promote upward mobility in general, their effect on poverty dynamics may be further blunted in risky environments because they do not protect the assets of the nonpoor who are vulnerable to falling into poverty. This omission has two potential effects. First, conventional cash transfers do not stem the downflow of the vulnerable nonpoor into poverty that is driven by shocks (Krishna 2006). Second, by not protecting the assets of the poor and the vulnerable nonpoor, cash transfers in turn do little to enhance the investment incentives of the already poor.[4] Given these two effects, the population of future poor may grow, raising the cost of any antipoverty program.

These observations raise the question whether an alternative social protection scheme can more effectively reduce the extent and depth of poverty when compared to the purely progressive targeting rules of standard cash transfer programs. Using a dynamic stochastic programming

2. The Gertler, Martinez, and Rubio-Codina (2012) study of Mexico's PROGRESA program finds notable investment and income effects from a purely cash transfer program. The Bastagli et al. (2016) review study finds more modest evidence of such effects, unless specific efforts were made by implementers to support planning, investment, and business development. In a similar spirit, the six country studies contained in Maldonado et al. (2016) find some evidence that the potential impacts of cash transfers on earned income are when cash transfers are paired with ancillary business development programs targeted at cash transfer recipients.

3. The current generation of graduation programs takes their inspiration from BRAC's ultrapoor program that recognizes that more than liquidity increments may be needed to reduce chronic poverty. Such programs involve a mix of cash transfers, financial education, confidence building and coaching, and culminate with an asset transfer. Banerjee et al. (2015) summarize evaluations of graduation programs that span both middle- and low-income countries.

4. Indeed, if anything, it might be expected that means-tested cash transfers would discourage accumulation, as successful accumulation could lead to loss of benefits.

model meant to capture key features of a risky rural landscape like that of northern Kenya, this chapter explores the poverty-reduction potential of a hybrid social protection system that combines conventional cash transfers targeted at the poorest with state of the world contingent cash transfers (SWCTs) targeted at the vulnerable nonpoor in the wake of negative shocks.

Our findings include what we call the paradox of social protection. Under the assumption that transfers are unanticipated (i.e., that households do not alter their accumulation strategies in anticipation of social protection benefits), we show that when compared to a standard, progressively targeted scheme, a hybrid policy that diverts some the social protection budget to the vulnerable nonpoor results in lower levels of poverty in the medium term, although poverty rates are higher in the short term. Conventional cash transfer programs thus implicitly make an intertemporal trade-off between the well-being of the poor today versus their well-being in the future. The hybrid program creates the mirror intertemporal trade-off.

We then relax the assumption that transfers are unanticipated and explore the impacts of hybrid social protection when the contingent transfers are anticipated. We show first that anticipation crowds in additional accumulation by the poor, who are incentivized by the fact that SWCTs will protect their assets should they invest and advance to the ranks of the vulnerable nonpoor. This ex ante accumulation effect might be termed a positive moral hazard, as it induces investment and risk taking by the poor that lessens the overall rate of poverty. At the same time, when SWCTs are precisely targeted at the vulnerable as in our model, a new equilibrium appears. Specifically, a subset of agents accumulate only to the point where they are eligible for SWCTs, but not beyond. This new equilibrium reflects a more conventional negative moral hazard, as those at this equilibrium make choices that increase the probability of receiving the insurance-like contingent social protection payments.

Given the trade-offs, expense, and complexities associated with SWCTs and hybrid social protection, we then ask whether the impacts of an SWCT can be achieved with an insurance contract that is cofunded by the government and by the vulnerable nonpoor. Rather than holding the social protection budget fixed, we instead ask how much budget is needed over time to fully close the poverty gap for all poor households and to pay for the government insurance subsidy that is offered to all poor and vulnerable nonpoor households under the hybrid scheme. Drawing on companion work that models the dynamically optimal demand for insurance (Janzen, Carter, and Ikegami 2018), we show that the present value of the required government expenditure stream is lower under the hybrid insurance scheme than it would be under a conventional cash transfer scheme targeted only at the poor. This cost saving is realized without any trade-off between the well-being of the poor in the present and the future.

The remainder of the chapter proceeds as follows. Section 6.1 presents a dynamic stochastic model of household consumption and asset accumulation in which households enjoy heterogeneous endowments of assets and productive skill. Section 6.2 then uses this model to analyze a stylized model of a village economy composed of 300 households distributed randomly over the ability-initial asset space that defines the intertemporal choice model. As a baseline for later analysis of alternative policy regimes, we use dynamic programming methods to simulate the stylized economy over a sixty-year time horizon, tracking the evolution of growth, poverty, and a new measure of "unnecessary deprivation."

Section 6.3 then explores the impact of alternative social protection schemes, one that targets transfers in a purely progressive fashion, and another in which the available budget is targeted according to a triage protocol that prioritizes transfers to households that are vulnerable to slipping into chronic poverty over transfers to already poor households. In this section, we assume that households do not anticipate transfers. It is here where the paradox of social protection emerges. By preventing collapse into poverty by agents vulnerable to asset shocks, the triage scheme ultimately reduces the extent of poverty and leads to greater transfers to and higher welfare for poor households in later years.

Section 6.4 then relaxes the assumption that transfers are unanticipated and explores what happens when agents fully anticipate contingent transfers provided to the vulnerable under the triage scheme. We show that anticipation of these transfers has both positive and negative effects. Finally, we show that implementing the contingent transfers as a partially subsidized insurance contract (with copays required of beneficiaries) eliminates the negative while preserving the positive effects of contingent protection. Section 6.5 concludes.

6.1   Assets, Ability, Risk, and the Multiple Dimensions of Chronic Poverty

Azariadis and Stachurski (2005) define a poverty trap as a "self-reinforcing mechanism which causes poverty to persist." A robust theoretical literature has identified a variety of such mechanisms that may operate at either the macro level—meaning that an entire country or region is trapped in poverty—or at the micro level—meaning that a subset of individuals become trapped in chronic poverty even as others escape (Barrett and Carter [2013], Kraay and McKenzie [2014], Ghatak [2015], and Barrett, Garg, and McBride [2016] provide recent review papers). In this chapter, we explore the implications of a micro poverty trap mechanism for the design of social protection programs, employing a variant of what Barrett and Carter (2013) call the "multiple financial market failure" poverty trap model. This model can generate multiple equilibria in the sense that a given individual may end up at the high or the low equilibrium depending on initial conditions and stochastic realizations.

The semiarid pastoral region of northern Kenya, which motivates this work, is an area of widespread chronic poverty. Multiple studies, using different data sets, have found evidence of bifurcated asset dynamics in this region, with households above a critical level tending to a high equilibrium and those below it tending to a low level (Barrett et al. 2006; Lybbert et al. 2004; McPeak and Barrett 2001; Santos and Barrett 2011; Santos and Barrett, chapter 7, this volume).[5] To explore how social protection might work in this environment, we build on the Buera (2009) nonstochastic model of asset accumulation with two production technologies under credit constraints and heterogeneous agent ability.[6] We extend the Buera model by adding asset shocks to allow for the importance of both ex ante awareness of risk and the ex post experience of shocks as key determinants of poverty dynamics (Elbers, Gunning, and Kinsey 2007).

We show that multiple poverty trap mechanisms emerge in this setting. Low-ability households are innately poor, as they never find the high-return technology attractive and thus they endure low incomes indefinitely. Meanwhile, intermediate-ability households can dramatically change their asset accumulation choices in response to ex ante asset risk and ex post realization of asset shocks. This cohort faces a multiple equilibrium poverty trap of the sort on which the literature has long focused. Finally, there is a high-ability group that may start off poor but will inevitably take up the high-return technology and graduate out of poverty and remain nonpoor (in expectation) in the long run.

6.1.1   A Model of Asset Dynamics and Heterogeneous Ability

Consider an economy in which each individual j is endowed with a level of innate ability (α_j) as well as an initial stock of capital (k_{j0}). Preferences are unrelated to the individual's innate ability. In what follows, we treat α_j as fixed. We conceptualize the agents in this economy as adults and α_j as capturing the predetermined physical stature, cognitive development, and educational attainment with which they entered adulthood and the economy. This approach obviously ignores the origins and evolution of such innate ability. Carter and Janzen (2017) generalize the specification here and allow each

5. Note, these findings do not generalize globally. Broad-based empirical evidence of poverty traps has been mixed (Subramanian and Deaton 1996; Kraay and McKenzie 2014), although Kraay and McKenzie (2014) conclude that the evidence for the existence of structural poverty traps is strongest in rural remote regions like the arid and semiarid lands of East Africa. As Barrett and Carter (2013) note, there is a tendency to sometimes conflate the failure to find a multiple equilibrium poverty trap with the nonexistence of poverty traps. Poverty traps can, of course, be single equilibrium, as in Naschold (2013). For a particularly interesting analysis of the emergence of a multiple equilibrium from a single equilibrium structure, see Kwak and Smith (2013).

6. Related previous papers include Becker and Tomes (1979), Loury (1981), Banerjee and Newman (1991, 1993), Galor and Zeira (1993), Ray and Streufert (1993), Aghion and Bolton (1997), Piketty (1997), Carter and Zimmerman (2000), and Ghatak and Jiang (2002).

dynasty's human capital to evolve intergenerationally through a stochastic process in which ability regresses to the mean level unless compromised by nutritional shortfalls. In this chapter, however, we set aside this additional complexity in order to concentrate on exploring social protection policy design in the presence of poverty traps.

Each period the individual has to choose between two alternative technologies for generating income. Both technologies are capital using and skill sensitive (i.e., for both technologies, more able people can produce more than less able people). One technology (the "high" technology) is subject to a fixed cost, E, such that the technology is not worth using at low amounts of capital. Specifically, we assume that income, f, for individual j in period t is given by

$$f\left(\alpha_j, k_{jt}\right) = \alpha_j \max\left[f_H\left(k_{jt}\right), f_L\left(k_{jt}\right)\right]$$

where $f_L\left(k_{jt}\right) = k_{jt}^{\gamma_L}$, $f_H\left(k_{jt}\right) = k_{jt}^{\gamma_H} - E / \alpha_j$, $E > 0$, and $0 < \gamma_L < \gamma_H < 1$.[7] We denote as $\hat{k}\left(\alpha\right)$ as the value of capital where it becomes worthwhile to switch to the more productive technology (i.e., $\hat{k}\left(\alpha_j\right) = \{k \mid \alpha_j f_L\left(k\right) = \alpha_j f_H\left(k\right)\}$).[8]

If an individual had access to only one technology, she or he would accumulate capital up to a unique steady-state value $k_L^*\left(\alpha_j\right)$ for the low technology or $k_H^*\left(\alpha_j\right)$ for the high technology. The key question is then what happens when the individual has access to both technologies. In the spirit of Skiba (1978), we ask whether an individual, whose initial capital stock is below $\hat{k}\left(\alpha_j\right)$, will gravitate toward the high or the low technology.[9]

Consider the case of an individual who begins life with $k_L^*\left(\alpha_j\right) < k_{j0} < \hat{k}\left(\alpha_j\right)$. Note that because this individual is beyond the low-level steady state, but short of the technology switch point, incremental returns to further investment are low relative to the cost of forgone consumption, discouraging further accumulation. Borrowing constraints and limited income make it impossible for the individual to discretely jump over the region of low returns. Will this individual optimally accumulate assets over time and end up at $k_H^*\left(\alpha_j\right)$ and a nonpoor standard of living? Alternatively, will the individual settle into a poor standard of living with capital stock $k_L^*\left(\alpha_j\right)$? More formally, is there an initial asset threshold, $\tilde{k}\left(\alpha_j\right) < \hat{k}\left(\alpha_j\right)$, below which individuals slip to the low equilibrium (remaining chronically poor), and above which she or he will move to the high equilibrium (eventually becoming nonpoor)?

7. Note that fixed costs do not vary by ability level as the division of E by α_j is canceled out by the premultiplication of the production function by α_j, which allows us to more generally keep the notation simpler.

8. By construction, this formulation favors adoption of the high technology by assuming away information problems and all other obstacles to adoption other than financing. This simplification eliminates inessential factors that would reinforce the effects that are generated here under full information.

9. As first explored by Skiba (1978), with a nonconvex production technology, a bifurcated accumulation strategy could occur around a critical minimum asset level.

We analyze this question with a dynamic model of consumption and investment choice. We rule out borrowing, and hence consumption in every period can be no more than available wealth, or what Deaton (1991) calls cash on hand:

$$c_{jt} \leq k_{jt} + f\left(\alpha_j, k_{jt}\right),$$

The household's stock of accumulated capital evolves over time according to the following rule:

$$k_{jt+1} = (k_{jt} + f(\alpha_j, k_{jt}) - c_t)(\theta_{t+1} - \delta)$$

where δ is the natural asset depreciation rate and $\theta_t \leq 1$ is a random asset shock realized at the beginning of every period t. Note that $\theta = 1$ implies optimal conditions, whereas $\theta < 1$ indicates less favorable conditions or an unfavorable shock that destroys some fraction of wealth. We assume that $(\theta_t - \delta) > 0$. While in principle $\theta > 1$ might be allowed, such events seem unlikely and we will restrict the analysis to the case where only negative shocks are possible.[10] The cumulative density function of θ_t is denoted by $\Omega(\cdot)$ and we assume that every household knows $\Omega(\cdot)$.

In period t households choose their production technology, consumption, and (implicitly) investment based on state variable k_{jt} (asset holdings), α_j (innate ability), and the probability distribution of future asset losses (Ω). Households then observe asset shocks θ_{t+1}, which determine asset losses. The primary timing assumption is that the shocks happen after the household's decision to save or consume, and then once again all the information needed to make the next period's optimal decision is contained in k_{jt}. Assembling these pieces, we can write the decision maker's intertemporal choice problem as

(1)
$$\max_{c_{jt}} E_\theta \sum_{t=0}^{\infty} \beta^t u\left(c_{jt}\right)$$

subject to:

$$c_{jt} \leq k_{jt} + f\left(k_{jt}\right)$$

$$f\left(\alpha_j, k_{jt}\right) = \alpha_j \max\left[f_H\left(k_{jt}\right), f_L\left(k_{jt}\right)\right]$$

$$k_{jt+1} = \left(k_{jt} + f\left(k_{jt}\right) - c_{jt}\right)\left(\theta_{jt+1} - \delta\right)$$

$$k_{jt} \geq 0$$

---

10. While this assumption mechanically implies lower expected returns relative to the case where some shocks are greater than one (holding f fixed), this assumption does not necessarily imply that returns are low. Instead, in the spirit of frontier production analysis, $k + f(\alpha, k)$ can be thought of as the maximum achievable cash on hand assuming good conditions, and less than optimal conditions simply means that returns are some fraction less than what is maximally obtainable.

where E_θ is expectation taken over the distribution of the random shock θ, β is the time discount factor, and $u(\cdot)$ is the utility function defined over consumption c_{jt} and has the usual properties. Denote the investment rule in the presence of asset shocks as $i^*(k_{jt} \mid \alpha_j, \Omega)$.[11]

6.1.2   The Micawber Frontier and the Two Dimensions of Chronic Poverty

As in Skiba (1978) and Buera (2009), this model identifies a critical asset level, denoted $\tilde{k}(\alpha_j)$, around which dynamic behavior bifurcates. An individual with ability level α_j will attempt to accumulate the assets needed to reach the high-technology equilibrium if she enjoys capital stock $k_{jt} > \tilde{k}(\alpha_j)$. Otherwise, she will only pursue the low technology, accumulating the modest stock of capital that it requires. Note that this frontier, a generalization of what Zimmerman and Carter (2003) call the Micawber Threshold, divides those who have the wealth needed to accumulate from those who do not.[12] We label $\tilde{k}(\alpha_j)$ the Micawber Frontier.

The two graphs in figure 6.1, created through numerical analysis of the dynamic programming model 1, present the Micawber Frontier under the parameterization reported in the appendix that we use to implement the model in the remainder of this chapter.[13] Along the horizontal axes are innate ability or skill levels, ranging left to right from least to most able. The vertical axes measure the stock of productive assets. Figure 6.1, panel A graphs the probability that a household occupying each initial endowment position will end up chronically poor, that is, at the low-level equilibrium. Notice that households on the west/southwest side of the figure approach the low-level equilibrium with probability one, indicating that for these endowment positions it is not worthwhile to even attempt the accumulation of the assets required to reach the high equilibrium. As shown in figure 6.1, panel B, we define the Micawber Frontier as the locus of skill and assets where the household, behaving optimally according to model 1, switches to a strictly positive probability of escaping chronic poverty. The solid curve in figure 6.1, panel B graphs this locus. Comparing across the two graphs in figure 6.1, we can see that for endowment positions far enough east and north of the Frontier, the probability of escaping chronic poverty is one. For middle-ability households in the multitoned band just north and east of the Micawber Frontier, the probabilities of escape are modest.

---

11. More precisely, $i^*(k_t \mid \alpha, \Omega)$ is the policy function of the following Bellman equation:

$$V(k_t) \equiv \max_{i_t} \{u(f(\alpha, k_t) - i_t) + \beta E[V(k_{t+1} \mid k_t, i_t)]\}$$

where $E[V(k_{t+1} \mid k_t, i_t)] = \int V(\theta_t[i_t + (1 - \delta)k_t]) d(\theta_t)$.

12. Skiba (1978) less poetically calls the equivalent threshold in his model a critical cutoff point.

13. Buera (2009) provides a formal proof for his nonstochastic model.

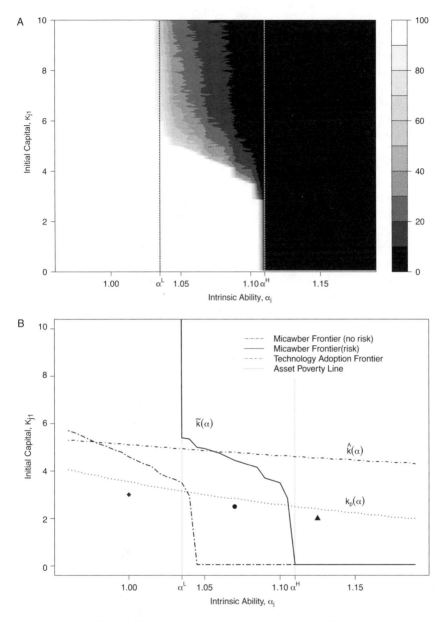

Fig. 6.1 **The Micawber Frontier and chronic poverty.** *A*, probability of chronic poverty (percent); *B*, risk and the Micawber Frontier.

To ease discussion and link it to more conventional poverty analysis, figure 6.1 also includes an "asset poverty line," the dashed downward-sloping line, denoted $k_p(\alpha_j)$. For each ability level, this asset poverty line indicates the stock of assets the individual must have in order to produce a living standard exactly equal to a money metric poverty line, y_p. We define y_p as the level of income that a reference middle-ability person ($\alpha_m = 1.07$ in the numerical analysis) would produce were she in steady-state equilibrium at the *low* technology ($y_p = f(\alpha_m, k_L^*(\alpha_m))$). This assumption is, of course, arbitrary, but it has the rhetorical advantage of allowing us to label most individuals poor unless they craft a pathway to the high technology. This is desirable in our stylized model as it creates a strong linkage between improved technology adoption, income, and poverty measures.

Note that the Micawber Frontier has a behavioral foundation and thus differs from the asset poverty line, which is based on a standard (and therefore arbitrary) income poverty line.[14] Those agents whose initial ability-asset endowments place them above the Micawber Frontier but beneath the asset poverty line will be initially poor. With the positive probabilities illustrated in figure 6.1, panel A, these individuals will prove to only be transitorily poor as they attempt to accumulate their way out of poverty. By contrast, those whose initial endowments situates them beneath the Micawber Frontier but above the asset poverty line will not be poor initially, but will steadily eat into their asset holdings and will eventually become poor. These movements represent structural transitions across the poverty line.

There can also be stochastic movements around the asset poverty line among the subpopulation that finds itself above the Micawber Frontier. For those individuals, small asset shocks may temporarily leave them beneath the asset poverty line without driving them off their growth path toward the high equilibrium. Such individuals would be seen to be "churning," to use the language employed by some poverty analysts. Individuals could find themselves above both the Micawber Frontier and the asset poverty line, in which case they would always be nonpoor assuming they escaped further shocks. Symmetrically, individuals initially below both the Micawber Frontier and the asset poverty line would always register as being poor. This simple depiction of the Micawber Frontier and the asset poverty line captures the full range of conventional static and dynamic poverty measures.[15]

As illustrated in figure 6.1, the numerical analysis identifies three distinct regions in the space of ability and initial asset holdings. Irrespective of their capital endowment, high-skill individuals with $\alpha_j > \alpha^H$ will always move toward the high equilibrium as $\tilde{k}(\alpha_j) = 0 \; \forall \; \alpha_j > \alpha^H$. When they reach the

---

14. As discussed by Carter and Ikegami (2009), this characteristic of the Micawber Frontier makes it an interesting candidate as the base for chronic poverty measures.

15. See Carter and Barrett (2006) for a discussion of distinct generations of poverty analysis that encompass these different ideas.

technology-shift asset threshold $\hat{k}(\alpha_j)$ they will optimally switch to the higher technology. Irrespective of their starting position, these *upwardly mobile* agents steadily converge to the steady-state asset value for the high technology. They may be poor over some extended period as they move toward their steady-state value, but eventually they should become nonpoor by virtue of the optimal accumulation behavior induced by their high-ability endowment. Such individuals do not face a poverty trap.

In contrast, those with an innate ability level below the critical level α^L will never move toward the high technology, irrespective of their initial asset endowment. This critical skill level defines a region of intrinsic chronic poverty, made up of individuals who lack the ability to achieve a nonpoor standard of living in their existing economic context.[16] These individuals face a single equilibrium poverty trap.

Those in the intermediate-skill group with $\alpha^L < \alpha_j < \alpha^H$ have positive but finite values $\tilde{k}(\alpha_j)$. If sufficiently well-endowed with assets ($k_{j0} > \tilde{k}(\alpha)$), these intermediate-ability individuals will attempt to accumulate additional assets over time, and will with some strictly positive probability adopt the high technology and eventually reach a nonpoor standard of living. However, if these same intermediate-skill individuals begin with assets below $\tilde{k}(\alpha_j)$—or if a shock pushes them below that level—they will no longer find the high equilibrium attainable and will settle into a low standard of living. Like those in the region of intrinsic chronic poverty, intermediate-ability individuals initially endowed with less than $\tilde{k}(\alpha_j)$ will be chronically poor. Unlike the intrinsically chronically poor, the chronic poverty of the intermediate-skill individuals represents needless or unnecessary deprivation in the sense that they could be helped to lift themselves out of poverty with appropriate social protection policies, as we discuss below. For a given set of production possibilities, the total number of chronically poor in any society will thus depend on the distribution of households across the ability-wealth space.

Finally note that while some authors (e.g., Barrett and Carter 2013; Kraay and McKenzie 2014) often distinguish between single equilibrium poverty trap models, multiple equilibrium poverty trap models, and models without poverty traps, our model shows that all three possibilities can coexist in a single economy with heterogeneously endowed agents.[17]

6.1.3   The Ex Post and Ex Ante Effects of Asset Shocks

The Micawber Frontier is a function of the economic environment in which individuals find themselves. In particular, the distribution of the

---

16. CPRC (2004, 2008) give examples of individuals who suffer such fundamental disabilities.

17. The econometrics of empirically testing for the existence of poverty traps in the face of this kind of complexity is not fully developed, although Santos and Barrett (chapter 7, this volume) make some important progress in this regard.

stochastic term θ fundamentally shapes investment behavior. We now explore the impact of ex ante risk and ex post shocks on investment and the long-term evolution of poverty.

The ex post effect of realized shocks comes about simply because negative events may destroy assets, knocking people off their expected path of accumulation. For upwardly mobile individuals, such shocks may delay their arrival at the upper-level equilibrium, necessitating a period of additional savings and asset reaccumulation. But it does not set them on a different accumulation path. Similarly, realized shocks have no long-term effect on the equilibrium toward which the low ability, intrinsically chronically poor gravitate.

In contrast, the ex post consequences of shocks can be rather more severe for households of intermediate ability. Consider the case of a household that is initially slightly above the Micawber Frontier. A shock that knocks it below the frontier will banish the household into the ranks of the chronically poor, as in the wake of the shock, the household will alter its strategy and move toward the low equilibrium (divesting itself of assets).

While these ex post effects of shocks are important, the anticipation that they might take place would be expected to generate a "sense of insecurity, of potential harm people must feel wary of—something bad can happen and spell ruin," as Calvo and Dercon (2009) put it. Numerical analysis of the model shows that this sense of impending ruin indeed discourages forward-looking households from making the sacrifices necessary to reach the high equilibrium. The Micawber Frontier shifts to the southwest once asset risk is removed, as shown in figure 6.1, panel B. The dashed curve is the Micawber Frontier in the absence of risk. The boundaries marking the critical skill levels at which households move between the different accumulation regimes also shift out, meaning more intrinsically upwardly mobile households and fewer intrinsically chronically poor households when we eliminate the ex ante effects of risk.

The most dramatic effects of risk are seen by considering a household whose skill and capital endowments place it between the two frontiers. Consider a household whose skill and initial asset endowments are represented by the solid circle in the middle of figure 6.1, panel B. Absent the risk of asset shocks, such a household would strive for the upper equilibrium and eventually escape poverty. In the presence of risk, such a household would abandon this accumulation strategy as futile and settle into a low-level, chronically poor standard of living. In the face of asset risk, the extraordinary sacrifice of consumption[18] required to try to reach the high equilibrium is no longer worthwhile, and the household will optimally pursue the low-level, poverty trap equilibrium. By contrast, the shift has no significant behavioral

---

18. The consumption sacrifice is extraordinary because the immediate returns from incremental accumulation do not outweigh the cost of forgone consumption.

effect on either intrinsically chronically poor households (represented by the solid diamond on the left side of figure 6.1, panel B) or intrinsically upwardly mobile households (the solid triangle on the right side of figure 6.1, panel B).

To explore the differential effects of risk and shocks on these different subpopulations, Carter and Ikegami (2009) use the dynamic choice model above and simulate the income streams it generates in three distinct settings:

- A nonstochastic economy in which agents repeatedly apply the optimal investment rule, $i_n^*(k_{jt} \mid \alpha_j)$;[19]
- an economy characterized by risk without realized shocks in which agents follow the risk-adjusted optimal accumulation rule, $i^*(k_{jt} \mid \alpha_j, \Omega)$, but never actually experience shocks (a scenario that allows us to isolate the ex ante effects of risk); and,
- a fully stochastic economy, meaning that individuals not only follow the risk-adjusted optimal investment rule but each period they are subject to a random asset shock generated in accordance with the probability structure Ω.

Their simulations show that for the intrinsically chronically poor (low α_j) and the upwardly mobile (high α_j) groups, the impact of risk and shocks on the realized stream of utility is relatively modest and attributable almost entirely to the disruptive, ex post effects of asset shocks. In contrast, for the intermediate-ability group, the ex ante behavioral (i.e., investment disincentive) effects of uninsured risk account for most of the welfare effects of risk and shocks. These effects are also large in magnitude for the intermediate-ability group. While the discounted income streams for the other two groups fall only 5–10 percent in the fully stochastic scenario, the drop is approximately 25 percent for the intermediate-ability group, with roughly 90 percent of the losses due to the ex ante risk effect exclusively.[20] The difference arises because while risk slightly reduces the desired steady-state capital stock for low- and high-ability agents, mainly it forces them to occasionally rebuild assets in order to reattain the desired steady-state capital stock. In sharp contrast, intermediate-ability agents may fundamentally shift their investment strategy in the presence of risk, eschewing any attempt at trying to reach the high-level equilibrium open to them, creating added avoidable chronic poverty.

Among other things, these simulations show that in the presence of critical asset thresholds, risk takes on particular importance for those individuals

---

19. The subscript n denotes this nonstochastic world and $i_n^*(k_t \mid \alpha)$ is policy function of the following Bellman equation:

$$V_{nr}(k_t) \equiv \max_{i_t} \{u(f(\alpha, k_t) - i_t) + \beta V_{nr}(k_{t+1}|k_t, i_t)\}$$
$$= \max_{i_t} \{u(f(\alpha, k_t) - i_t) + \beta V_{nr}(i_t + (1 - \delta) k_t)\}.$$

20. Details on these simulation results are available from the authors by request.

subject to multiple equilibria. Conversely, removal of risk (through social protection or insurance schemes) could in principle generate large benefits for intermediate-ability individuals, as we now explore.

6.2   Poverty Dynamics Absent Social Protection

The analysis in the prior section showed that both the anticipation and experience of economic shocks have a fundamental effect on behavior and welfare in the presence of poverty traps, expanding the portion of the endowment space from which people do not escape poverty through their own efforts. This observation suggests that social protection policies have a fundamental role to play in stimulating poverty reduction and economic growth. But how will different social protection policies work in a world with multiple sources of poverty traps? As a first step toward answering this question, this section uses the model of individual decision-making developed above as the basis for analyzing accumulation, growth, and poverty in a stylized economy lacking any social protection policies. Sections 6.3 and 6.4 will then take a careful look at the impact of alternative social protection schemes on this economy.

6.2.1   The Stylized Economy and Measures of Performance

Consider now an economy comprising agents whose livelihood choices are described by the intertemporal maximization problem (1). To keep things simple, we will assume that all shocks are idiosyncratic and that prices in the economy are unaffected by shocks and by individuals' decisions. While these assumptions are clearly at odds with the real world, they permit us in the first instance to clarify basic principles and trade-offs in the design of social protection policies.[21]

For purposes of the numerical analysis, we assume that there are 300 agents, each described by a skill and initial capital stock pair. We allocated agents along the skill continuum, with 25 percent each in the intrinsically chronically poor and upwardly mobile ranges, and half of the agents in the intermediate-ability range where endowments matter to their accumulation and welfare trajectories. Each agent was then assigned a random initial capital stock drawn from a uniform distribution over the zero to ten range. While in any existing economy we would expect there to be a correlation between skill and observed capital stock, this random assignment of capital creates an experimental environment in which to study asset dynamics under alternative social protection schemes.

---

21. When shocks are correlated across households, asset and other prices will begin to covary with household income. The implications of this covariance can be important, as Carter et al. (2007) discuss empirically in the case of Ethiopia. Zimmerman and Carter (2003) theoretically examine the implications of such asset price covariance, showing that it can create another type of poverty trap.

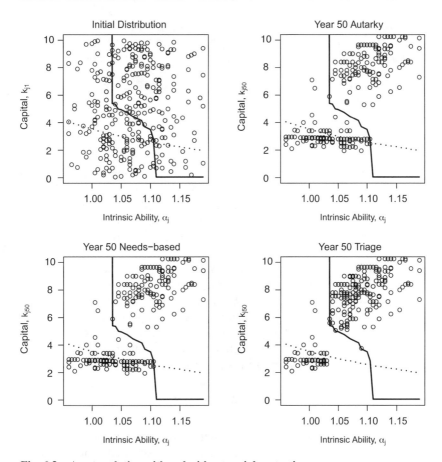

Fig. 6.2   Asset evolution with and without social protection

The diagram in the top left corner of figure 6.2 shows the initial distribution of ability and wealth in this stylized economy. Each symbol on the graph represents the initial position of an individual agent. The solid line is the Micawber Threshold under the stochastic environment, while the dashed line is again the asset poverty line. The other graphs in the figure—to be discussed below—show the evolution of endowment positions under alternative social protection policies.

While we can simply focus on the trajectories of agents given their initial endowment positions, we also employ a set of summary measures to track the performance of the stylized economy under alternative social protection regimes:[22]

22. In work not reported here, we also analyzed the impacts of the different policies using a conventional Benthamite social welfare function as well as the dynamic poverty measures suggested by Calvo and Dercon (2009). The qualitative story told by these measures is similar to that which can be gleaned from the measures discussed here.

1. Gross national income (GNI) defined simply as the sum of the incomes of the 300 agents. Note that this measure will evolve over time based on capital accumulation (or deaccumulation) as well as the shift of households between the low- and high-technology regimes.

2. Standard static poverty measures based on the Foster-Greer-Thorbecke (FGT) family of measures:

(2)
$$P_\gamma^y = \frac{1}{n} \sum_{y_j < y_p} \left(\frac{y_p - y_j}{y_p} \right)^\gamma$$

where n is the total number of individuals, y_p is the income poverty line, y_j is individual j's income, and γ is the usual FGT sensitivity parameter. We will specifically focus on the popular head count (P_0^y) and poverty gap (P_1^y) measures. As discussed above, we set the poverty line y_p at the level of income that a medium-skill individual would produce in steady state if she had access only to the low technology.

3. A novel measure of unnecessary deprivation, D_γ^y. This measure resembles the FGT poverty gap measure, in that it focuses only on those beneath the income poverty line. In addition, D_γ^y focuses only on the subset of the poor who have the skill or human capability to reach the high equilibrium, $\alpha_j > \alpha^L$. Denoting the maximum steady-state income available to individuals with $\alpha_j > \alpha^L$ as $\bar{y}_j^* = \alpha_j f_H(k_H^*(\alpha_j))$, we define the unnecessary deprivation gap as $\bar{y}_j^* - y_j$, and we define our measure of unnecessary deprivation as

(3)
$$D_\gamma^y = \frac{1}{n} \sum_{\substack{y_j < y_p \\ \alpha_j > \alpha^L}} \left(\frac{\bar{y}_j^* - y_j}{\bar{y}_j^*} \right)^\gamma.$$

As with the FGT measure, γ is a sensitivity parameter, with $\gamma = 0$ offering a head count of unnecessary deprivation, $\gamma = 1$ measuring the money metric unnecessary deprivation gap, and $\gamma > 1$ placing greater weight on larger underperformance relative to potential. In our subsequent calculations, we rely on the unnecessary deprivation head count measure.[23]

Together, these economic core measures permit us to track over time both the economic costs (forgone output and unexploited technological opportunities) and the human costs (low standards of living and unnecessary deprivation) of poverty traps.

6.2.2   Baseline Case of No Social Protection

The top right panel of figure 6.2 shows the asset distribution after fifty years of simulated history for our stylized economy. As can be seen, the asset

---

23. Because it relies on knowledge of steady-state capital holdings conditional on unobservable ability, this measure seems impractical in empirical work. It is nonetheless helpful as a conceptual tool for distinguishing unnecessary poverty from that which is unavoidable given individuals' immutable endowments and the economic environment in which they operate.

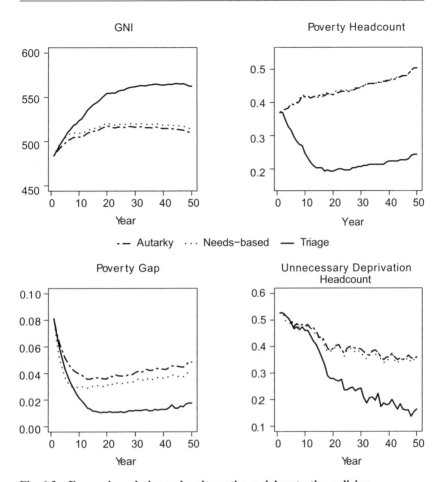

Fig. 6.3   **Economic evolution under alternative social protection policies**

distribution (which was originally randomly distributed independently of the ability distribution) has bifurcated, with a strong positive correlation between innate ability and wealth. One set of individuals has comfortably settled above the Micawber Frontier at the high-technology steady state. The other group is at the low-level steady state, below the asset poverty line. There are quite a few poor individuals in the middle-ability group whose potential to reach the high equilibrium has been blocked by their low initial asset levels, or realized asset shocks that trapped them below the Micawber Frontier.

With no exogenous technical change or growth in productive inputs to stimulate growth and modest investment incentives for a large portion of the population, GNI in this baseline economy is relatively stagnant over time as reflected in the "autarky" line in the top left quadrant of figure 6.3. This reflects the fact that the positive accumulation and associated productivity gains of those above the Micawber Frontier is offset by the lost potential—and wealth deaccumulation and productivity decline—of many of those trapped below it. The decline among some subpopulations is manifested through the disadoption of the high technology, use of which falls from roughly 60 percent to only 40 percent of the population. Further reflection of this economic bifurcation is found in the increasing levels of poverty, measured both as a poverty head count (top right quadrant) as well as by the poverty gap indicator (bottom left quadrant), and our unnecessary deprivation head count measure (bottom right quadrant). Income inequality (not shown) declines modestly over the first decade of the simulations, then increases above the initial level by year twenty-five as households converge on their α-conditional long-run equilibria. The lackluster performance of the base case poverty trap economy illustrates both the human and aggregate economic costs of poverty traps. The next sections consider alternative policy regimes that might lead to better outcomes.

6.3   Poverty Dynamics with Unanticipated Social Protection

This section examines the impact of reactive food aid or unanticipated cash transfers on the stylized economy studied in the prior section. The label "unanticipated" signals that these policies are implemented ex post of shocks and we assume away agents' anticipation of the resulting transfers and the behavioral response that would follow from such anticipation. This simplification is made to help understand more clearly how poverty dynamics shift in response to different sorts of social protection policies. In particular, we seek to illustrate clearly the value of addressing the purely ex post effects of asset shocks, even if agents do not expect transfers. Section 6.4 below will relax the assumption that households fail to anticipate and respond to social protection policies.

For all alternatives, we assume that the social protection agency[24] has access to an annual budget that amounts to 2.5 percent of initial GNI.[25] This arbitrary amount was chosen because it is insufficient to lift all initially poor individuals above the poverty line, though it is enough to substantially close the poverty gap. We further assume that the social protection agency has access to full information, including household ability and asset holdings, realized shocks, and knowledge of the production technology. While these are implausibly strong assumptions, using them to explore targeting

---

24. We use the broad term social protection agency to encompass local or national governments as well as nongovernmental organizations (NGOs) that might respond to shocks.

25. We ignore the source of taxation that generates these resources and the associated distortionary effects on the economy. They could be conceptualized as either external resources (brought in by a donor, an NGO, or a relief agency), or as domestic tax resources transferred from another sector of the national economy.

of this limited assistance budget helps further illustrate the workings of the multiple poverty trap economy.

6.3.1 Poverty and Aid Traps under Progressive, Means-Tested Cash Transfers

Under the progressively targeted or needs-based scenario, the agency uses its budget only for progressively targeted, humanitarian/cash transfers. After each production cycle, it calculates the total poverty shortfall for the economy, $S = \Sigma_{y_j < y_p}(y_p - y_j)$. If the available budget B exceeds the shortfall ($B/S > 1$), then all poor individuals are given transfers to increase their income to the level of the poverty line. If $B/S < 1$, then each poor individual is given transfers that move them to an income level equal to $(B/S)y_p$. Note that this targeting method makes the largest transfers to the least well-off, but as the ranks of the poor grow, S increases and thus each individual poor person's transfer receipt shrinks. The transfer simply adds an increment to the first (budget) constraint in optimization problem (1). Once individuals receive the transfer, they make their consumption versus investment decision according to the same logic of problem (1) above and assume that future transfers will never occur. Section 6.4 relaxes this strong assumption, but for now it helps to understand the different effects of alternative social protection policies.

The impact of this needs-based assistance regime on asset distribution can be seen in the bottom left diagram in figure 6.2. The figure is quite similar to that under autarky (the top right panel), except that asset levels are somewhat higher for those below the poverty line, especially among lower-ability persons, reflecting a transfer rule based on realized income levels and the exogenous injection of resources, B, into the economy that manifest as individual transfers to the current poor. Turning to figure 6.3, we see that the poverty head count and unnecessary deprivation measures follow a trajectory nearly identical to that which emerges absent social protection. While standard cash transfers do not fundamentally alter poverty dynamics, they do reduce the poverty gap. As can be seen in the bottom left graph of figure 6.3, the injection of well-targeted external resources cuts the poverty gap relative to the no social protection policy regime. But, the steady creation of newly poor households over time due to adverse asset shocks causes the FGT(1) to steadily rise after year ten of the simulation because the transfer received by any individual poor household shrinks as more poor people compete for a fixed aid budget, leading to an increasing poverty gap. The GNI is higher in the economy with needs-based transfer, but this is largely an artifact of the exogenous aid resources that are transferred into the economy via the cash transfer mechanism.

In a world where budgets for transfers are available exogenously (e.g., via unrequited transfers associated with overseas development assistance), progressively targeted transfers that flow to the chronically poor plainly reduce income and asset poverty, if only because there are added resources in this scenario. However, these transfers do not fundamentally alter the economy's dynamics. Indeed, the troubling irony is that poverty grows in this economy in spite of these transfers as some agents suffer asset shocks that drop them into poverty, but then receive insufficient transfers to enable them to climb back out of poverty on their own. Transfer policies that are designed to respond to one poverty trap mechanism—low innate ability that leads to chronically low income—systematically fail to address the other poverty trap mechanisms in this economy by failing to prevent more people from inadvertently falling into the trap over time.

These results signal what might be termed a relief trap. By failing to stem the flow of intermediate-ability individuals below the Micawber Frontier, the fixed humanitarian assistance budget becomes less and less able to meet the needs of those below the poverty line. If the social protection agency (or the international community) were intent on holding poverty at, say, year ten levels, then increasing fractions of total public expenditures would need to be devoted to aid budgets to accommodate the inflow of the unnecessarily poor who have suffered severe asset shocks and fallen into the basin of attraction of their low-level equilibrium.[26] We abstract here from the standard public finance problems of raising revenues, but clearly the growing demands for transfers would have to be met either through increasingly distortionary taxation or through reducing funds available for developing new technologies, building schools and infrastructure, or other interventions (not modeled here) that are aimed at boosting productivity. Poverty traps can thus, in a very direct way, create relief traps for purely progressively targeted social protection programs.

6.3.2   State of the World Contingent Cash Transfers

As the prior simulations make clear, asset risk in our model creates an ever increasing amount of unnecessary deprivation that eventually overwhelms the capacity of needs-based cash transfers to provide relief, as seen in the rising poverty gap and head count measures in figure 6.2. This observation suggests that a social protection scheme targeted at the vulnerable in the vicinity of the Micawber Frontier—that is, a safety net designed to stem the increase in unnecessary poverty—can potentially generate a win-win-

26. There is a complex set of changes occurring in these simulations, which begin from an arbitrary distribution of assets across the ability distribution. The decline (but not the elimination) of unnecessary deprivation shows that some individuals are adjusting to a new steady state in which they are not poor. Similarly, some low-ability individuals who were arbitrarily assigned large initial stocks of assets also dissave and eventually become poor over time. Finally, some number of households get pushed below the households when large shocks are realized. This latter group is reflected in the slow but steady increase in the poverty and deprivation measures in the out-years of the simulation suggesting that the pressure for an increasing aid budget moderates, but is not completely eliminated over time as households settle into their new steady states.

win scenario, with higher rates of improved technology adoption and GNI growth, reduced poverty (especially for intermediate-ability groups), and less stress on the social protection budget.

To explore this idea, we initially analyze a harsh "triage" policy regime in which the social protection agency provides transfers to households according to the following rules:

1. Each time period, the available budget, B, is allocated with first priority to individuals pushed below the Micawber Frontier by negative shocks. Denote these threshold-based transfers as SWCTs. An individual j is eligible for a SWCT of amount $\text{SWCT}_j = \tilde{k}(\alpha_j) - \theta_t[i_{jt} + (1 - \delta)k_{jt}]$ if $i_{jt} + (1 - \delta)k_{jt} > \tilde{k}(\alpha_j)$ and $\theta_{jt}[i_{jt} + (1 - \delta)k_{jt}] < \tilde{k}(\alpha_j)$. In words, if an individual was above the Micawber Frontier prior to the most recent asset shock but below it afterward, the agency provides a transfer to move the household back to the Micawber Frontier. If the total budget is no less than the total eligible contingent transfers ($B \geq \Sigma_{j=1}^{J}\text{SWCT}_j$), then all individuals pushed below the threshold are given an asset transfer to lift them exactly back to it. If the budget is insufficient to cover all SWCTs, then it is allocated first to those closest to the Micawber Frontier so as to minimize the increase in the head count of unnecessary deprivation.

2. If there is any remaining budget after step 1 (i.e., if $B > \Sigma_{j=1}^{J}\text{SWCT}_j$), then those middle-ability individuals already below the Micawber Frontier (due to low initial inheritance or prior bad luck not remedied by an SWCT) are given priority for asset transfers that lift them over the Micawber Frontier.[27] Analogous to stage (1), total potential spending on asset transfers is calculated (denote this total amount as CN). If $CN > B - \Sigma_{j=1}^{J}\text{SWCT}_j$, then the budget is again prioritized in order to minimize unnecessary deprivation by first helping the most vulnerable, defined as those closest to the Micawber Frontier.

3. If $B > \text{SWCT} + CN$, then the residual budget is allocated according to the progressive or needs-based formulation discussed in the previous subsection.

This triage policy would be difficult to implement in most places due to the daunting information requirements it imposes—knowing the Micawber Frontier, individual ability, individual-specific shocks, and so forth. We develop this as a thought experiment because it captures clearly the intertemporal trade-offs inherent to a system characterized by multiple poverty mechanisms. Figures 6.2 and 6.3 illustrate the results of this assistance

---

27. Barrett (2005) refers to this kind of asset transfer as a cargo net transfer, as it is intended to lift people above—or help people climb over—thresholds at which accumulation dynamics bifurcate. Note that asset transfers are distinct from SWCT safety net transfers that keep people at or above those same thresholds. Graduation programs centered on asset transfers to the capable poor, like those described in Banerjee et al. (2015) and Gobin, Santos, and Toth (2017), are the real-world analogue to these asset or cargo net transfers.

regime for our stylized poverty trap economy. The results stand in strong contrast to autarky and needs-based assistance simulations. As shown in the bottom right panel of figure 6.3, by year fifty, all most unnecessary deprivation is eliminated and the head count of total poverty levels off at 25 percent, the share of the population that is intrinsically chronically poor by construction. Compared to the standard cash transfer policy, technology adoption is higher, as is GNI. In the longer run, this triage approach to development assistance plainly outperforms needs-based assistance by any of these metrics.

However, the bottom left diagram in figure 6.3 illustrates a core ethical challenge associated with vulnerability-targeted social protection. The FGT(1) poverty gap measure is lower under progressively targeted cash transfers for the first eight to ten years of the simulation because needs-based assistance flows primarily to the least well-off, while the stylized vulnerability-targeted policies are aimed at the vulnerable nonpoor nearest the Micawber Frontier. But, paradoxically, after eight to ten years, those who are poor are better off under the triage design because it reduces the number of people needing assistance, allowing the fixed social protection budget to provide more generous support to those who inevitably need it due to irreversibly low ability. But, prior to that time, individuals who are poor, and especially the poorest, are better off under needs-based targeting. The results for (asset or income) inequality (not shown) are qualitatively similar, with needs-based transfers generating lower inequality in the economy over the first eight to ten years, but threshold-based transfers generating lower inequality over longer horizons. These results underscore the difficult trade-offs inherent to the design of social protection policy, both over time and across subpopulations of the poor. In the presence of multiple poverty trap mechanisms, these trade-offs become especially sharp.[28]

6.4   Moral Hazard and the Design of Anticipated Social Protection

The analysis in section 6.3 revealed the paradoxes and challenges of social protection in an economy characterized by poverty traps that take several forms. That analysis, however, unrealistically assumed that individuals do not anticipate social protection benefits. This lacuna is especially important for SWCTs that are targeted at the vulnerable. Such transfers operate as a form of insurance, and as discussed above, this insurance might alter ex ante

28. In additional simulations not reported here, we considered whether these trade-offs could be mitigated by mixing different kinds of transfers and/or by reallocating budgets intertemporally through borrowing. While these alternatives can reduce the magnitude of the trade-offs reported here somewhat, they cannot be eliminated entirely. This underscores the unavoidable nature of the targeting trade-offs in both cross section (between different subpopulations of the poor and vulnerable) and over time in a multiple poverty trap economy.

investment incentives for households both above and below the Micawber Frontier itself.

In this section, we therefore relax the assumption that contingent transfers are unanticipated and consider households' rational response to them. While we could, in principle, analyze endogenous response to anticipated, progressively targeted cash transfers, we limit our attention here to anticipated vulnerability-targeted social protection schemes.[29]

6.4.1   Positive and Negative Moral Hazard

We expect two kinds of household response to safety net transfers. First, since safety net transfers mitigate asset risk, households are willing to accumulate more assets ceteris paribus. This is canonical moral hazard, in that the provision of some insurance induces increased risk taking.[30] In this model, accumulation of assets subject to stochastic shocks is the only risk-taking behavior available to agents. But asset accumulation is socially desirable in this setting, as it increases productivity and adoption of improved production technologies, increases GNI, and reduces poverty. We therefore call this incentive effect "positive moral hazard."

Second, because the safety net transfers are conditional (on pre- and postshock asset holdings) and given the standard intertemporal trade-off between current consumption and saving for future consumption, ceteris paribus households have an incentive to satisfy the transfer condition as often as possible so as to receive extra resources. If some external agency or government will insure them against falling into a poverty trap, households do not need to self-insure through asset accumulation to the same degree, thereby creating a disincentive to invest beyond the Micawber Frontier that defines eligibility—equivalently, reducing the need for precautionary savings—that runs counter to social objectives. We therefore label this effect "negative moral hazard."

For a middle-ability person with $\tilde{k}(\alpha_j) = 5$, figure 6.4, panel A, shows expected asset losses as a function of level of capital stock held with (the dashed line) and without (the solid line) the SWCT policy. As can be seen, there is zero chance of asset losses exactly at this threshold, and expected asset losses above the threshold will always keep the individual at or above $\tilde{k}$. When these contingent transfers of the vulnerability-targeted social pro-

---

29. This choice is primarily made for analytical convenience. Under the triage policy developed in section 6.3, the magnitude of cash transfer payments is itself uncertain, depending on the vagaries of the weather that dictate the residual budget left for such transfers. Clearly, we would expect cash transfers to discourage private accumulation (Hubbard, Skinner, and Zeldes [1995] give an empirical example showing how means-tested social insurance programs discourage precautionary savings in the United States). By ignoring these disincentive effects, we are thus overstating the possible effectiveness of cash transfers, which only reinforces our broader point.

30. Recognize that risk is increasing in asset holdings because θ is a multiplicative shock and independent of k. Therefore, stochastic losses are greater when k is larger.

tection are anticipated, the individual's optimization problem (1) can be rewritten as follows:

(4)
$$\max_{c_{jt}} E_\theta \sum_{t=0}^{\infty} \beta^t u(c_{jt})$$

subject to:

$$c_{jt} \le k_{jt} + f(k_{jt})$$

$$f(\alpha_j, k_{jt}) = \alpha_j \max[f_H(k_{jt}), f_L(k_{jt})]$$

$$k_{jt+1} = \begin{cases} \tilde{k}(\alpha_j) \text{ if } & \begin{cases} (f(k_{jt}) - c_{jt}) + (1 - \delta)k_t > \tilde{k}(\alpha_j) \text{ and} \\ (k_{jt} + (f(k_{jt}) - c_{jt})(\theta_{jt+1} - \delta) < \tilde{k}(\alpha_j) \end{cases} \\ (k_{jt} + f(k_{jt}) - c_{jt})(\theta_{jt+1} - \delta) \text{ otherwise} \end{cases}$$

$$k_{jt} \ge 0.$$

This is the same as the problem specified in section 6.2, except for the important change in the law of motion governing k_{jt+1} now that households are aware of and respond to the contingent transfers.[31]

Figure 6.5 illustrates the impact of the anticipation of contingent transfers on the probability of chronic poverty. For ease of comparison, figure 6.5, panel A, repeats the probabilities when these transfers are not anticipated (from figure 6.1, panel A). Comparing figure 6.5, panels A and B, we see that substantially fewer endowment positions are likely to end up chronically poor. This additional accumulation induced by the presence of contingent transfers at the (autarky) Micawber Frontier precisely represents positive moral hazard.

While the vulnerability-targeted contingent transfers incentivize upward mobility, they also have a discouraging effect on further accumulation that would take households beyond the safety of $\tilde{k}(\alpha_j)$ where assets are fully protected. A large swath of middle-ability agents end up in long-term equilibrium at exactly $\tilde{k}(\alpha_j)$. This behavior represents classic negative moral hazard as the presence of the implicit insurance provided by the contingent transfer leads individuals to undertake behaviors that make contingent payments more likely.

---

31. The household problem at period t can be represented in Bellman Equation form as

$$V(k_t) \equiv \max_{i_t} \{u(f(\alpha, k_t) - i_t) + \beta E[V(k_{t+1}|k_t, i_t)]\}$$

where $E[V(k_{t+1}|k_t, i_t)] = \int V(k_{t+1}(k_t, i_t, \theta_t, k_g, \delta))d\Omega(\theta_t)$

$$k_{t+1}(k_t, i_t, \theta_t, k_g, \delta) = \begin{cases} k_g \text{ if } i_t + (1 - \delta)k_t > k_g \text{ and } \theta_t[i_t + (1 - \delta)k_t] < k_g \\ \theta_t[i_t + (1 - \delta)k_t] \text{ otherwise.} \end{cases}$$

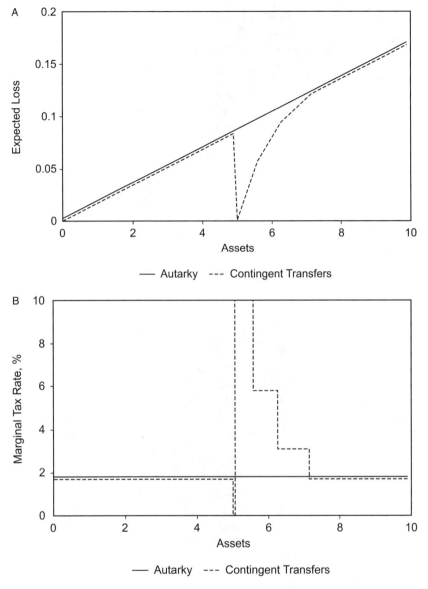

Fig. 6.4   Nature's tax rates under contingent social protection. *A*, expected asset
losses; *B*, marginal tax rates.

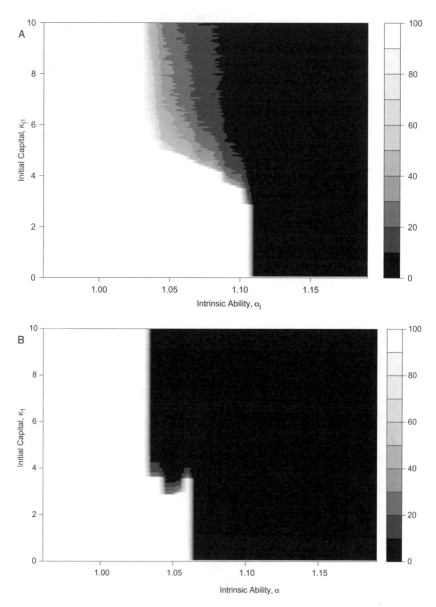

Fig. 6.5 **Ex ante impacts of anticipated social protection.** *A*, prob. low equilibrium under autarky (percent); *B*, prob. low equilibrium under social protection (percent).

Figure 6.4 allows further insight into the emergence of this new insured outcome. Note that nature essentially acts as an unreliable tax collector in this model, probabilistically taking away some fraction of assets every period. Figure 6.4, panel A, shows expected asset losses as a function of the level of capital stock held. The solid line shows these expected losses absent the contingent social protection scheme. Under the multiplicative risk specification, this is linear with a constant expected marginal tax rate of 1.7 percent (under the numerical assumptions used to analyze our model). This marginal tax rate is shown by the corresponding horizontal line in figure 6.4, panel B.

Under the precisely targeted SWCT scheme, expected losses drop to exactly zero at $\tilde{k}(\alpha_j)$, as shown by the dashed line in figure 6.4, panel A. Beyond that asset level expected losses begin to increase, eventually becoming identical to expected losses absent this form of social protection.[32] Figure 6.4, panel B, shows the implied marginal tax rates under this scheme. As can be seen, under the discrete probability structure used to analyze the model, the marginal tax rate abruptly jumps from 0 to 10 percent, and then slowly decreases to the natural tax rate of 1.7 percent as capital stocks accumulate beyond the indemnity payment threshold. This sharp and discontinuous elimination of social protection as the individual moves away from the insured point $\tilde{k}(\alpha_j)$ discourages accumulation and leads to a class of agents who settle in at the new $\tilde{k}(\alpha_j)$ equilibrium.

6.4.2 Using Index Insurance and Copays to Implement State of the World Contingent Social Protection

Negative moral hazard and the attraction of $\tilde{k}(\alpha_j)$ as a new equilibrium reflect in part the extremely precise targeting of the contingent transfers (and sharp jump in marginal tax rates) that define the vulnerability-targeted social protection scheme. However, this kind of precise targeting is of dubious relevance in the real world where neither realized shocks, asset levels, the Micawber Frontier, nor individual skills are easy to observe. Together, these observations raise the question as to whether something akin to SWCTs can be implemented using a market-based microinsurance scheme. Index insurance, which delivers payouts to policyholders on the basis of a predetermined index unaffected by the behavior or skill of the insured, could be particularly useful. Index insurance offers four potential advantages:

1. Payments can be triggered by a relatively cheap-to-observe index that signals shocks;[33]

---

32. With bounded shocks, there will be a capital stock such that even the largest shocks cannot reduce assets to $\tilde{k}(\alpha)$, the level where contingent payments kick in.

33. For the specific case of northern Kenya, see the discussion of an index insurance design in Chantarat et al. (2013).

2. it can rely on self-selection through the purchase of insurance, obviating the need to observe skill;

3. it can require a copayment, which reduces costs, allows the available public budget to stretch further, and enhances individual investment incentives relative to the SWCT case; and,

4. if cost reductions are sufficiently strong, reliance on insurance may eliminate the need for a precisely targeted subsidy that creates the behaviorally perverse sharp discontinuities in the effective marginal tax rate, as explored in section 6.4.1.

Janzen, Carter, and Ikegami (2018) employ a dynamic model similar to that developed here, while ignoring skill heterogeneity. The analysis compares an autarky scenario in which insurance is unavailable, and a targeted insurance subsidy scenario in which the government pays half of the commercial insurance premium (assuming a 20 percent markup) for all households that hold assets less than the level required to generate an average income equal to 150 percent of the poverty line. In all cases, the simulation assumes that households behave optimally based on the price of insurance and the dynamic choice problem displayed above.

The Janzen, Carter, and Ikegami (2018) analysis shows a 50 percent insurance subsidy (offered across the board to all but the wealthiest agents) can induce investment and upward mobility (positive moral hazard), but without the negative moral hazard seen in section 6.4.1. Importantly, they show that under the assumptions of their model,[34] the total social protection budget (defined as funds for the insurance subsidy plus funds for cash transfers needed to close the poverty gap for all poor households) quickly becomes lower under a combined insurance/cash transfer scheme than under a pure cash transfer scheme. As shown in figure 6.6, total costs are in fact higher in the short run under the hybrid scheme, but they become lower as the induced upward mobility eventually reduces the cost of cash transfers. Under their numerical assumptions, the present value of total social protection expenditures is 16 percent lower under the hybrid scheme.

The feasibility of using index insurance to offer contingent protection has been extensively studied in the semiarid regions of northern Kenya. Chantarat et al. (2013) and Mude et al. (2009) describe an initial contract design used in this region, and Jensen, Barrett, and Mude (2017) and Janzen and Carter (2016) report empirical impact evaluation results that are

---

34. The parameters of the model deviate from those used in the other simulations in this chapter. While the results are not directly comparable, the findings are still insightful. Notably, the Janzen, Carter, and Ikegami (2018) model must assume some level of basis risk (the difference between realized losses and the index). The model assumes relatively low basis risk. In practice, this is likely to overestimate the benefits of index insurance if basis risk is high.

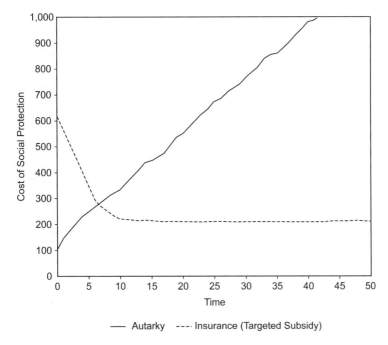

Fig. 6.6   Costs of alternative social protection schemes

consistent with the expected ex ante and ex post effects of contingent social protection that have been explored theoretically in this chapter. Despite these empirical findings, demand for the available insurance in northern Kenya has remained modest. At least partially in response to this puzzle, the government of Kenya has recently launched multiple programs that offer state of the world contingent social protection, including distribution of free livestock insurance through its KLIP (Kenya Livestock Insurance Program). The government also offers a scalable version of its core social protection scheme (the HSNP program), which extends benefits to vulnerable (but not abjectly poor) households when objective indicators signal drought conditions. The impacts of these new programs, and their ability to fundamentally alter poverty dynamics, as this chapter's theoretical analysis suggests, remain to be seen.

6.5   Conclusions

This chapter has put forward a dynamic stochastic model of a stylized poverty trap economy in which asset risk plays a major role and heterogeneity of individual ability creates two types of chronic poverty. Some people are chronically poor because their innate ability condemns them to a low standard of living. Others suffer unnecessary deprivation simply because they inherit insufficient productive capital to reach the critical asset or Micawber Frontier at which it becomes optimal to make the short-term sacrifices necessary to accumulate assets and (probabilistically) escape chronic poverty. Each of these two poverty trap mechanisms invites a different policy response. When both types of chronic poverty coexist, therefore, trade-offs inevitably arise in developing cost-effective poverty-reduction strategies.

Using this framework, we have shown that purely progressively targeted social relief—such as cash transfers—can fall prey to an aid trap because it does nothing to address the root causes of poverty. In particular, it does not protect the assets of those of intermediate ability and wealth who are vulnerable to asset shocks and to becoming poor over time. Members of this latter group steadily fall into avoidable chronic poverty, adding to the pool of individuals suffering unnecessary deprivation and needing income support. As a result, while purely progressively targeted social protection initially reduces the depth of poverty, the lot of the poor deteriorates over time due to increasing competition for limited social protection resources. Moreover, an unadorned, purely progressively targeted system of social protection does not appreciably change the number of poor, nor does it enhance wealth accumulation, economic output, or adoption rates of improved technologies.

We have then shown that a hybrid policy, which issues state of the world contingent cash transfers (SWCTs) to vulnerable-but-not-indigent households, eliminates unnecessary deprivation, empowers upward mobility, and boosts growth through endogenous asset accumulation and adoption of improved technologies. While this hybrid policy still confronts important trade-offs among different poor people and over time, this theoretical exercise establishes the potential gains to social protection that targets vulnerability (not just abject poverty) and thereby creates economic multipliers. However, despite these gains, household anticipation of SWCTs discourages some from accumulating assets beyond the range where they remain eligible for social protection transfers.

A key question then becomes whether the balance between positive and negative moral hazard can be altered by changing the mode of delivering contingent transfers. Drawing on the work of Janzen, Carter, and Ikegami (2018), we have argued that imprecisely targeted partial subsidies for index insurance can achieve the benefits of SWCTs and strike a better balance between positive and negative moral hazard, encouraging upward mobility but not artificially braking it with means-tested cutoffs. While there are challenges to implementing SWCTs via an insurance mechanism in practice, a hybrid social protection system that mixes insurance subsidies and cash transfers in theory appears to be more cost-effective than standard cash transfers as a way to address chronic poverty in risk-prone regions like northern Kenya.

Ultimately, the key finding of this chapter is that poverty traps characterized by multiple equilibria can have a pronounced effect on the performance and design of policies intended to stimulate poverty reduction, economic growth, and uptake of improved production technologies. There are potentially large returns to developing and using knowledge about critical asset thresholds to target assistance to the vulnerable nonpoor. The coexistence of populations facing different sorts of poverty traps, however, also raises unavoidable, thorny trade-offs among distinct cohorts of the poor, as well as difficult intertemporal trade-offs between current and future poverty reduction.

Appendix
Parameters and Other Details for Numerical Simulation

This section provides additional detail on the formal model used to generate the results discussed in the main body of the chapter.

The functional specification for the utility function $u(\cdot)$ is

$$u(c_t) = \frac{c_t^{1-\sigma} - 1}{1 - \sigma}.$$

The probability density of θ_t is assumed to be

$$\text{density of } \theta_t = \begin{cases} 0.90 \text{ if } \theta_t = 1.0 \\ 0.05 \text{ if } \theta_t = 0.9 \\ 0.03 \text{ if } \theta_t = 0.8 \\ 0.02 \text{ if } \theta_t = 0.7. \end{cases}$$

The other structural parameter values are assumed as follows: $\sigma = 1.5$, $\delta = 0.08$, $\beta = 0.95$, $\gamma_L = 0.3$, $\gamma_H = 0.45$, and $E = 0.45$.

We discretize continuous variables k and α as follows: $k = \{0.05, 0.10, \ldots, 15.00\}$ and $\alpha = \{0.960, 0.965, \ldots, 1.190\}$.

For the simulation of the stylized economy of 300 individuals, we draw α from $N(1.070, 0.055^2)$, with the mean and variance chosen so that ex ante proportion of low-, middle-, and high-type individuals (defined relative to the stochastic Micawber Frontier) would be 25 percent, 50 percent, and 25 percent, respectively. We draw k_1 from Uniform[0.1, 10.0] and assume that k_1 and α are statistically independent from each other.

We specify poverty line as follows. The asset level that generates income exactly equal to the poverty line satisfies the following equation:

$$y_p = f(\alpha, k_p),$$

where y_p is income-based poverty line. That asset level obviously depends on α and we denote it by $k_p(\alpha)$. We assume that an intermediate-ability individual would fall below the income poverty line if he used the low technology and thus set poverty line by $k_p(\alpha = 1.070) = 2.8$ and thus $y_p = 1.46$.

References

Aghion, P., and P. Bolton. 1997. "A Theory of Trickle-Down Growth and Development." *Review of Economic Studies* 64 (2): 151–72.

Azariadis, C., and J. Stachurski. 2005. "Poverty Traps." In *Handbook of Economic Growth*, vol. 1, part A, edited by P. Aghion and S. N. Durlauf, 295–384. Amsterdam: Elsevier.

Banerjee, A., E. Duflo, N. Goldberg, D. Karlan, R. Osei, W. Parienté, J. Shapiro, B. Thuysbaert, and C. Udry. 2015. "A Multifaceted Program Causes Lasting Progress for the Very Poor: Evidence from Six Countries." *Science* 348 (6236). https://doil .org/10.1126/science.1260799.

Banerjee, A. V., and A. F. Newman. 1991. "Risk-Bearing and the Theory of Income Distribution." *Review of Economic Studies* 58 (2): 211–35.

———. 1993. "Occupational Choice and the Process of Development." *Journal of Political Economy* 101 (2): 274–98.

Barrett, C. B. 2005. "Rural Poverty Dynamics: Development Policy Implications." In *Reshaping Agriculture's Contributions to Society*, edited by D. Colman and N. Vink. Oxford: Blackwell.

Barrett, C. B., and M. R. Carter. 2013. "The Economics of Poverty Traps and Persistent Poverty: Policy and Empirical Implications." *Journal of Development Studies* 49 (7): 976–90.

Barrett, C. B., M. R. Carter, and M. Ikegami. 2013. "Poverty Traps and Social Protection." Working paper, Department of Agricultural and Resource Economics, University of California, Davis.

Barrett, C., T. Garg, and L. McBride. 2016. "Well-Being Dynamics and Poverty Traps." *Annual Review of Resource Economics* 8:303–27.

Barrett, C. B., P. P. Marenya, J. McPeak, B. Minten, F. Place, J. C. Randrianarisoa, J. Rasambainarivo, and J. Wangila. 2006. "Welfare Dynamics in Rural Kenya and Madagascar." *Journal of Development Studies* 42 (2): 248–77.

Bastagli, F., J. Hagen-Zanker, L. Harman, V. Barca, G. Sturge, and T. Schmidt. 2016. "Cash Transfers: What Does the Evidence Say?" Technical Report, Overseas Development Institute.

Becker, G. S., and N. Tomes. 1979. "An Equilibrium Theory of the Distribution of Income and Intergenerational Mobility." *Journal of Political Economy* 87 (6): 1153–89.

Buera, F. J. 2009. "A Dynamic Model of Entrepreneurship with Borrowing Constraints: Theory and Evidence." *Annals of Finance* 5 (3–4): 443–64.

Calvo, C., and S. Dercon. 2009. "Chronic Poverty and All That: The Measurement of Poverty over Time." In *Poverty Dynamics: Interdisciplinary Perspectives*, edited by T. Addison, D. Hulme, and R. Kanbur, ch. 2. Oxford: Oxford University Press.

Carter, M. R., and C. B. Barrett. 2006. "The Economics of Poverty Traps and Persistent Poverty: An Asset-Based Approach." *Journal of Development Studies* 42 (2): 178–99.

Carter, M. R., and M. Ikegami. 2009. "Looking Forward: Theory-Based Measures of Chronic Poverty and Vulnerability." In *Poverty Dynamics: Interdisciplinary Perspectives*, edited by T. Addison, D. Hulme, and R. Kanbur, ch. 6. Oxford: Oxford University Press.

Carter, M. R., and S. A. Janzen. 2017. "Social Protection in the Face of Climate Change: Targeting Principles and Financing Mechanisms." *Environment and Development Economics* 1 (21). https://doi.org/10.1017/S1355770X17000407.

Carter, M., P. Little, T. Mogues, and W. Negatu. 2007. "Poverty Traps and the Long-Term Consequences of Natural Disasters in Ethiopia and Honduras." *World Development* 35 (5): 835–56.

Carter, M. R., and F. J. Zimmerman. 2000. "The Dynamic Cost and Persistence of Asset Inequality in an Agrarian Economy." *Journal of Development Economics* 63 (2): 265–302.

Chantarat, S., A. G. Mude, C. B. Barrett, and M. R. Carter. 2013. "Designing Index-Based Livestock Insurance for Managing Asset Risk in Northern Kenya." *Journal of Risk and Insurance* 80 (1): 205–37.

Chronic Poverty Research Centre (CPRC). 2004. "Chronic Poverty Report 2004–2005." Chronic Poverty Research Centre. http://www.chronicpoverty.org/resources/cprc_report_2004-2005.html.

———. 2008. "Chronic Poverty Report, 2008–2009, Escaping Poverty Traps." Technical Report, Chronic Poverty Research Centre.

Deaton, A. 1991. "Saving and Liquidity Constraints." *Econometrica* 59:1221–48.

Elbers, C., J. W. Gunning, and B. Kinsey. 2007. "Growth and Risk: Methodology and Micro Evidence." *World Bank Economic Review* 21 (1): 1–20.

Galor, O., and J. Zeira. 1993. "Income Distribution and Macroeconomics." *Review of Economic Studies* 60 (1): 35–52.

Gertler, P. J., S. W. Martinez, and M. Rubio-Codina. 2012. "Investing Cash Transfers to Raise Long-Term Living Standards." *American Economic Journal: Applied Economics* 4 (1): 164–92.

Ghatak, M. 2015. "Theories of Poverty Traps and Anti-poverty Policies." *World Bank Economic Review* 29 (suppl. 1): 77–105.

Ghatak, M., and N. N.-H. Jiang. 2002. "A Simple Model of Inequality, Occupational Choice, and Development." *Journal of Development Economics* 69 (1): 205–26.

Gobin, V., P. Santos, and R. Toth. 2017. "No Longer Trapped? Promoting Entrepreneurship through Cash Transfers to Ultra-poor Women in Northern Kenya." *American Journal of Agricultural Economics* 99 (5): 1362–83.

Hubbard, R. G., J. Skinner, and S. P. Zeldes. 1995. "Precautionary Saving and Social Insurance." *Journal of Political Economy* 103 (2): 360–99.

Hurrell, A., and R. Sabates-Wheeler. 2013. "Kenya Hunger Safety Net Programme Monitoring and Evaluation Component: Quantitative Impact Evaluation Final Report: 2009 to 2012." Technical Report, Oxford Policy Management.

Janzen, S. A., and M. R. Carter. 2016. "After the Drought: The Impact of Microinsurance on Consumption Smoothing and Asset Protection." NBER Working Paper no. 19702, Cambridge, MA.

Janzen, S. A., M. R. Carter, and M. Ikegami. 2018. "Asset Insurance Markets and Chronic Poverty." Working paper, Department of Economics, Montana State University.

Jensen, N. D., C. B. Barrett, and A. G. Mude. 2017. "Index Insurance and Cash Transfers: A Comparative Analysis from Northern Kenya." *Journal of Development Economics* 129:14–18.

Kraay, A., and D. McKenzie. 2014. "Do Poverty Traps Exist? Assessing the Evidence." *Journal of Economic Perspectives* 28 (3): 127–48.

Krishna, A. 2006. "Pathways out of and into Poverty in 36 Villages of Andhra Pradesh, India." *World Development* 34 (2): 271–88.

Kwak, S., and S. Smith. 2013. "Regional Agricultural Endowments and Shifts of Poverty Trap Equilibria: Evidence from Ethiopian Panel Data." *Journal of Development Studies* 49 (7): 955–75.

Loury, G. C. 1981. "Intergenerational Transfers and the Distribution of Earnings." *Econometrica* 49 (4): 843–67.

Lybbert, T. J., C. B. Barrett, S. Desta, and D. Layne Coppock. 2004. "Stochastic Wealth Dynamics and Risk Management among a Poor Population." *Economic Journal* 114 (498): 750–77.

Maldonado, J. H., R. del Pilar Moreno-Sánchez, J. A. Gómez, and V. L. Jurado, eds. 2016. *Protección, Producción, Promoción: Explorando Sinergias entre Protección Social y Fomento Productivo Rural en América Latina.* Rome: International Fund for Agricultural Development.

McPeak, J., and C. B. Barrett. 2001. "Differential Risk Exposure and Stochastic Poverty Traps among East African Pastoralists." *American Journal of Agricultural Economics* 83:674–79.

Mude, A. G., S. Chantarat, C. B. Barrett, M. R. Carter, M. Ikegami, and J. McPeak. 2009. "Insuring against Drought-Related Livestock Mortality: Piloting Index-Based Livestock Insurance in Northern Kenya." Working paper, Nairobi, Kenya, International Livestock Research Institute.

Naschold, F. 2013. "Welfare Dynamics in Pakistan and Ethiopia—Does the Estimation Method Matter?" *Journal of Development Studies* 49 (7): 936–54.

Piketty, T. 1997. "The Dynamics of the Wealth Distribution and the Interest Rate with Credit Rationing." *Review of Economic Studies* 64 (2): 173–89.

Ray, D., and P. A. Streufert. 1993. "Dynamic Equilibria with Unemployment Due to Undernourishment." *Economic Theory* 3 (1): 61–85.

Santos, P., and C. B. Barrett. 2011. "Persistent Poverty and Informal Credit." *Journal of Development Economics* 96 (2): 337–47.

Skiba, A. K. 1978. "Optimal Growth with a Convex-Concave Production Function." *Econometrica* 46 (3): 527–39.

Subramanian, S., and A. Deaton. 1996. "The Demand for Food and Calories." *Journal of Political Economy* 104 (1): 133–62.

Zimmerman, F. J., and M. R. Carter. 2003. "Asset Smoothing, Consumption Smoothing and the Reproduction of Inequality under Risk and Subsistence Constraints." *Journal of Development Economics* 71 (2): 233–60.

Comment on Chapters 5 and 6

Stephen C. Smith

There has arguably become a recent imbalance in development economics, with the pendulum swinging too far away from theory; these two chapters may be seen as part of a trend toward rebalance between theory and empirics.

Comments on Chapter 5

Francisco J. Buera, Joseph P. Kaboski, and Yongseok Shin provide a useful targeted literature review set in context of a formal model. They offer some impressive innovations; in particular in the way they treat heterogeneity, and in making intriguing connections between micro programs and macro outcomes. Although highly stylized, the model has impressive properties, and its generality is one of its strengths. The model is compact and flexible enough to cleverly represent a range of recent empirics and theory, and its formulation provides for great tractability. The model is well deployed to guide intuition at various stages of the arguments. In particular, the authors provide an insightful way to model and study the role of productivity shocks, while allowing for relevant market failures with suitable model interpretation. Despite its flexibility, there are important limits to what the model can represent. However, it is unreasonable to expect one model to span the canon of trap analysis, even with respect to their more limited focus on microenterprise and programs to relax credit constraints.

Stephen C. Smith is professor of economics and international affairs at George Washington University.

I thank Jean-Paul Chavas for excellent editorial comments. Support from the Institute for International Economic Policy (IIEP) is gratefully acknowledged. All errors are my own. For acknowledgments, sources of research support, and disclosure of the author's material financial relationships, if any, please see http://www.nber.org/chapters/c13954.ack.

The literature review is a valuable overview of important papers on the impacts of microfinance interventions, particularly for those not working directly in that area. At the same time, if the authors are able to pursue the themes of this chapter in future research, an alternative framing and organization could provide different perspectives on what can be learned from the model. For example, it may be useful to pull the strands of the literature with a focus on examining commonalities across programmatic themes and specific components of the theory.

The empirical literature on this topic has grown rapidly, so it is necessary to be selective. Standards of evidence for what is to be included in the review are not set out explicitly. This is common in such reviews, but in my opinion it would be an improvement across the literature to state such standards as systematically as reasonably practical. Thus, readers will try to make inferences about what must have underpinned the selections. Most, though not all, papers in the review are based on randomized controlled trials (RCTs). Among RCTs, when they have not been included in the review, plausible criteria could be doubts about external validity or of insufficient study length for robust conclusions. Plausible criteria for when non-RCTs are included could include lack (to date) of availability of RCTs on an important topic, when impacts are not or cannot be well identified by RCTs, or results are similar to related RCT findings, among other things, lending credence to RCTs in which there are doubts about external validity or implementation issues. An explicit statement of standards of evidence may be considered particularly important when reviewing results on a topic for which the literature has not arrived at a consensus that is based on a decisive preponderance of evidence in a large number of studies.

It is worth stating again that the lack of clarity about why some papers are included and others not included extends to a wide range of literature reviews, whether full-fledged review articles or the customary brief reviews near the beginning of research articles. This point is not intended as a criticism of articles included or excluded. However, one strand that might be added concerns research on the impacts of microcredit into which has been integrated one or two additional programs or services that were viewed as having complementary roles, such as literacy training, business education, or maternal health care and education. These types of programs are otherwise relatively conventional (in particular, they provide no asset transfers) and are generally much narrower in their range of interventions than graduation programs (which do not necessarily involve provision of credit per se). Otherwise, this chapter is very impressive in the wide coverage of the research literature that it provides, with nearly fifty citations.

There are always limits to what can be covered in one chapter, but in future work it would be useful to know whether and how widely the model presented can span other relevant poverty trap concepts, including some covered in other parts of this volume. For example, the behavioral trap literature and the literature on complementary traps (such as credit and health) highlight cases in which traps cannot in general be escaped with cash or assets alone. It would be helpful to know whether the general model could be recast to usefully represent at least some of those other cases examined elsewhere in this volume.

Moreover, it would be useful to explain more explicitly whether the cases addressed can be fully modeled with diminishing returns. Some microfinance literature emphasizes input complementarities and features the idea that there is likely to be a range of increasing returns even in a single, standard capital input. There may be some way to explicitly represent more of these cases using the general modeling framework, and it would be of interest to see how this can be addressed.

There are some other questions to consider regarding whether there is special significance to how the transfers are to be financed. At least part of the analysis assumes a transfer financed by a tax on the upper part of the income distribution: a one-time 100 percent tax on wealth above a threshold. Could an alternative revenue source have different effects in a model? For example, in practice, asset transfer programs are often financed through foreign aid. At scale this could have macrolevel effects, and it may be important to know whether these are likely to differ depending upon the method of financing. For example, could other models lead to smaller "dissipation" found in the empirics than in the formal model?

Last, regarding the lack of identified "dramatic" escapes from poverty traps: perhaps such escapes are rare, if not possible, but microfinance institutions and the microenterprises they help finance may represent "transitional institutions" as a necessary step to conventional jobs, and may thus facilitate later structural transformation. In any case, microenterprises—and some vehicle to provide credit to them—apparently will be needed for some time, where modern job growth is proceeding from a very low base.

Comments on Chapter 6

Munenobu Ikegami, Michael R. Carter, Christopher B. Barrett, and Sarah Janzen introduce several substantial points to this literature. First, they model high and low production activity in the presence of more than one type of trap, in particular dividing risk-driven and other poverty traps in a broad framework.

The authors provide a good framework for modeling heterogeneity—that generates their paradox—dividing ability into some types that are (treated as) immutable, and others that are improvable with appropriate interventions.

Their approach raises a possible benefit of triage across types of people who are "vulnerable" to falling into poverty as opposed to those who are already "poor." The vulnerable face a stochastic environment in which they could fall into poverty deeply enough to drop to a worse equilibrium, losing a possible better equilibrium from their set of possible futures. This is addressed through a proposed form of subsidized insurance, in which payouts are based on the difference between preshock and postshock asset holdings. In the process, the authors frame the role of (safety net) insurance mechanisms in the asset-oriented poverty trap literature as a counterpoint to the programmatic approach based upon cash transfers.

The authors challenge cash transfers programs' reputation as a "silver bullet" for at least four reasons: Transfers may fail to lift beneficiaries out of poverty sustainably (recent empirics); relatedly, transfer programs may reduce incentives for the poor to accumulate assets (theory); transfers to the poor do not prevent "vulnerable" populations from falling below an asset threshold that results in chronic poverty; and, given a hard budget constraint for the poverty program, cash transfer programs may result in too-low benefits as the model evolves over time, or an "aid trap" as the total number of poor could grow.

An area for future work is to expand the way cash transfer programs are modeled. In the present chapter, transfers are characterized in ways that differ in some important respects to how many, if not most, such programs are implemented in practice. In particular, the transfer programs in the model provide cash unconditionally to those whose incomes are observed to fall below a poverty line. But many of the recently implemented large programs offer conditional cash transfers (CCTs), for which receipt depends upon behavioral requirements that, often intentionally, may be expected to lead to greater assets for the children of the household (i.e., for the next generation). Yet, this is an important distinction. The CCT programs require children to remain in school, get regular medical care and checkups, and take nutrition supplements when the checkups reveal deficiencies; schooling and childhood nutrition raise the children's productivity (after they grow up). The welfare comparisons may be altered if required behavioral change and consequent intergenerational dynamics are taken into account. Some evidence of the impact of CCT programs on outcomes such as enrollment is actually relatively strong. As the authors already note, a promising strategy in the context of their model is endogenizing α_j; and the impact on α_j could depend upon the type and extent of conditionality.

In addition, there may be distinct "third options" beyond asset insurance versus (conditional or unconditional) cash transfers, which could be at least as cost-effective. This is clearly outside the scope of the chapter, and this is raised only as a caveat to the approach. However, as an example, the most cost-effective solution to geographic poverty traps, such as may be found in mountainous China or semiarid areas in Africa, may be out-migration. Harsh as it may sound, if cost-effectiveness is a key criterion—as it is in this chapter—then using resources to subsidize migration of the poor to cities and facilitate their integration into urban job markets could turn out to be the lowest-cost and most sustainable way to reduce income poverty. Even if this is not presently feasible, it could become so as structural transformation proceeds. In comparisons of even broadly defined and conceptual sets of antipoverty strategies—particularly those that emphasize triage options— we benefit from examining a full consideration of feasible options. This chapter provides an important building block toward that more complete structure.

The authors also innovate in the measurement literature with a proposed indicator of "unnecessary deprivation" of individuals who could be given a boost to "lift themselves out of poverty" through an insurance-based social protection policy. Their measure is analogous in structure to the FGT index, and is based on the difference between current income and the income associated with the model's optimal capital stock (conditional on "innate" skill endowment), absent credit constraints. The authors note this may have more conceptual than practical applied use because of the difficulty of estimating equilibrium capital (and thus potential permanent income), and ability is imperfectly observable. But one could consider developing imperfect, proxy-based estimates based on panel data studies, comparing those who did and did not break out of poverty over a long enough period of observation. Clearly, there will be a lot of noise, and the results will be very far from perfect—but perhaps the exercise would yield results that are much better than nothing.

In any case, the "unnecessary deprivation" measures would benefit from further examination of properties, including precisely what aggregation means, and clearer welfare interpretations. Properties do not transfer obviously from the FGT family of measures (or at least proofs are required). For example, Sen's focus principle does not apply; accordingly, what is called deprivation is not the same concept as income gaps in conventionally accepted poverty measures. If not defined carefully, the measure could give a nonzero value even when current deprived income—and equilibrium income—were both above an income poverty line (although this does not appear to be a concern in the authors' application.) Finally, even if a large part of skill endowment is indeed innate, optimal capital stock is in general a "moving target," as conditions in the local economy including prices and asset productivity evolve over time even in relatively stagnant regions such as northern Kenya (as Kwak and Smith find for Ethiopia).

On welfare comparisons: for those chronically trapped in poverty, it will be useful to show how welfare comparisons in the "triage" may change if they are calculated conforming to the distributional sensitivity principle (and consistent with marginal utility of income increasing as poverty becomes deeper), which can be accomplished by basing calculations on FGT P_2 (poverty severity), rather than just FGT P_1 (poverty depth). But even placing greater welfare weight on poorer people, it may still create more benefits to focus limited resources on observationally better-off people; it is a substantial contribution to show how this protection trade-off can be analyzed rigorously.

Finally, as we move toward fully addressing the zero-poverty goal of the sustainable development goals, as also embraced by the World Bank, USAID, and other key development agencies, there is likely to be an enhanced focus on preventing people from falling into poverty. At least from a poverty head count or income shortfall perspective, ultimately we may view this as equally important to pulling people out of poverty.

In conclusion, both sets of authors have made innovative and stimulating contributions that deserve broad attention and could lead to useful strands in the poverty literature.

IV

Dynamics and Resilience in Natural Resources and Agriculture

7

Heterogeneous Wealth Dynamics
On the Roles of Risk and Ability

Paulo Santos and Christopher B. Barrett

7.1 Introduction

Contemporary policy debates are rife with discussion of "poverty traps" (see, e.g., Sachs 2005; United Nations Millennium Project 2005). Several theoretical models combine some nonconvex technology with some market failure to explain why "the poor stay poor and the rich stay rich."[1] But

Paulo Santos is a Senior Lecturer in the Department of Economics at Monash University. Christopher B. Barrett is the Stephen B. and Janice G. Ashley Professor of Applied Economics and Management, professor of economics, and International Professor of Agriculture at Cornell University, where he also serves as deputy dean and dean of academic affairs at the SC Johnson College of Business.

Fieldwork for this chapter was conducted under the Pastoral Risk Management (PARIMA) project of the Global Livestock Collaborative Research Support Program (GL CRSP), funded by the Office of Agriculture and Food Security, Global Bureau, USAID, under grant no. DAN-1328-G-00-0046-00, and analysis was underwritten by the USAID SAGA cooperative agreement, grant no. HFM-A-00-01-00132-00. Financial support was also provided by the Social Science Research Council's Program in Applied Economics on Risk and Development (through a grant from the John D. and Catherine T. MacArthur Foundation), The Pew Charitable Trusts (through the Christian Scholars Program of the University of Notre Dame), the Fundação para a Ciência e Tecnologia (Portugal), and the Graduate School of Cornell University. Thanks are due to ILRI-Ethiopia for their hospitality and support and to Action for Development (Yabello) for logistical support. A previous version circulated under the title "Safety Nets or Social Insurance in the Presence of Poverty Traps? Evidence from Southern Ethiopia." We thank Ed Barbier, Michael Carter, Stefan Dercon, Andrew Foster, Vivian Hoffman, Bob Myers, Dhushyanth Raju, Wally Thurman, Stephen Younger, and participants at multiple conferences and seminars for comments that greatly improved that paper. We thank Getachew Gebru and our field assistants, Ahmed Ibrahim and Mohammed Ibrahim, for their invaluable assistance in data collection. The views expressed here are those of the authors and do not represent any official agency. Any remaining errors are our own. For acknowledgments, sources of research support, and disclosure of the authors' material financial relationships, if any, please see http://www.nber.org/chapters/c13835.ack.

1. See Azariadis and Stachurski (2005) or Bowles, Durlauf, and Hoff (2006) for earlier reviews of the theoretical and empirical literature on poverty traps.

do poverty traps exist in the data? One prominent strand of the empirical literature that addresses this question focused on searching for a threshold associated with nonlinear growth that would lead to multiple equilibria, with one such equilibrium below a poverty line. Recent reviews of this literature suggest that the support for the existence of such a threshold is quite mixed (see Barrett and Carter 2013; Kraay and McKenzie 2014; Barrett, Garg, and McBride 2016).

In this chapter, we use data from a poor population, Boran pastoralists in southern Ethiopia, where the presence of such a threshold has been previously identified. Among this population, the evolution of livestock (in many cases, the only nonhuman asset held by these households) is characterized by boom-and-bust cycles determined by drought and biological reproduction. Using seventeen-year herd-history data collected by Desta (1999), Lybbert et al. (2004) find herd dynamics that follow an S-shaped curve with two stable dynamic equilibria (at roughly one and thirty-five to forty cattle), separated by an unstable dynamic equilibrium, a threshold at fifteen to twenty cattle.[2] The authors' conjecture is that this threshold results from a minimum critical herd size necessary to undertake migratory herding to deal with spatiotemporal variability in forage and water availability. Further work by Toth (2015) corroborates that herd mobility is sharply increasing in herd size in the neighborhood of the herd-size threshold that Lybbert et al. (2004) identify, while Santos and Barrett (2011) find that informal credit arrangements behave as one would expect in the presence of this threshold, largely excluding the persistently poor from informal insurance. These findings from East African pastoralists are recognized as being among the strongest empirical evidence Kraay and McKenzie (2014) find in support of the threshold-based poverty traps hypothesis.

We build on this work to explore one additional question: If poverty traps exist, do they exist for everyone? We frame this discussion using a general representation of wealth dynamics:

$$(1) \qquad y_{ist} = \begin{cases} g_{sA}^c(y_{it-1} \mid \theta_i) + \varepsilon_{ist} & \text{if } y_{it-1} \geq \gamma^c \\ g_{sB}^c(y_{it-1} \mid \theta_i) + \varepsilon_{ist} & \text{if } y_{it-1} < \gamma^c \end{cases}$$

where y_{ist} is a measure of wealth of individual i, who belongs to cohort c, in state s in period t, and growth dynamics may differ above and below any (possibly cohort-specific) threshold, $\gamma^c > 0$. If a threshold exists, expected dynamics may bifurcate, as reflected in different parameters describing the growth function above (A) and below (B) the threshold. We use this formulation to recognize that multiple mechanisms, in particular, both the individual's characteristics, θ_i, and its initial conditions, y_{it-1}, could be at play simultaneously. This is a more compact representation of the dynamics developed by Ikegami et al. (chapter 6, this volume).

2. Barrett et al. (2006) find similar herd patterns in herd-dynamics data from similar communities in northern Kenya.

This recognition matters because the policy implications differ markedly depending on which mechanism is at play. If poverty is an equilibrium because of immutable individual characteristics, ongoing social transfers may be the only available remedy for an unacceptably low standard of living. But if poverty results from initial asset holdings insufficient to clear a critical asset threshold, then policies such as asset transfers, or financial intermediation to encourage investment or to insure asset holdings, can lead to increases in wealth that move beneficiaries toward a higher-level equilibrium, thereby reducing the need for ongoing transfers (Carter 1998). If both processes are at play within a population, then effective targeting of appropriate interventions depends on identifying the relevant subpopulation to which a given poor household belongs.

Despite the very different policy implications, identifying the mechanisms that underpin persistent poverty is quite difficult methodologically. Barrett and Carter (2013) and Barrett, Garg, and McBride (2016) identify a range of confounding factors that challenge the econometric identification of poverty trap mechanisms, several of which our unusual data let us overcome, as we argue in more detail in the next section. We study a relatively simple system in which a single variable (livestock holdings) serves as an excellent proxy for overall wealth, we have household-level panel data that permit us to establish initial conditions and to estimate herd management ability, and we have data on households' expected herd growth conditional on particular states of nature, which we collected so as to explore the role of shocks and ability in shaping wealth dynamics. These attributes permit a deeper exploration of the genesis of multiple dynamic wealth equilibria than has been feasible previously.

Empirically, we focus on two mechanisms. First, in section 7.3, we confirm the possibility, first suggested in this context by Lybbert et al. (2004), that negative shocks may generate persistent poverty if they drive individuals below the threshold. We analyze data on pastoralists' expectations of herd size one year ahead, given different values of initial herd size. We disaggregate these dynamics as a function of rainfall states and find a nonlinear relation between initial and future wealth only under adverse states of nature. Under favorable rainfall regimes, respondents' subjective perceptions suggest a smooth asset growth process. We use these data to simulate long-run equilibria that we show correspond closely with those identified by Lybbert et al. (2004) in the historical data. We also note considerably larger variation among households in expected herd dynamics under adverse states of nature, which raises the possibility of household or individual characteristics that might generate such cross-sectional variation.

Second, we explore the possibility that characteristics such as skills or ability may explain the observed heterogeneity in expected growth. Perhaps the talented can more easily escape poverty regardless of initial wealth, or better manage their wealth in the face of negative shocks. Of particular relevance to this chapter, Schultz (1975) emphasizes the central importance of individual ability to reallocate scarce resources in response to shocks, what he terms "the ability to deal with disequilibria." He applies the concept to a different setting, with particular reference to technology shocks and the structural transformation of rural economies. But his core concept applies here, as it does to other aspects of that transformation.[3] In section 7.4 we use stochastic frontier estimation to obtain household-specific estimates of technical efficiency, which we use as proxy for herding ability. We use these estimates to address the hypothesis that herder ability conditions wealth dynamics. This appears true in the data. Low-ability herders (which we define as those in the bottom quartile of the efficiency distribution) are expected to slide into poverty regardless of initial wealth; we observe multiple dynamic herd-size equilibria only for the cohort of herders of higher ability. Finally, in section 7.5 we stress the policy implications of these findings with respect to complex wealth dynamics and the centrality of shocks and individual ability to understanding the existence of multiple equilibria in this system and raise some questions for future research. Section 7.6 concludes.

7.2   Data

We use data from a household survey fielded among a random sample of 120 Boran pastoralist households, in the same four communities of southern Ethiopia as those studied by Lybbert et al. (2004), although among different households. These data were collected by the Pastoral Risk Management (PARIMA) project every three months, March 2000–June 2002, and then annually each September–October starting in 2003. The focus of the project, and consequently, of the data collected, was on understanding the importance of shocks as a source of poverty persistence in this context, and the data include rich detail on household composition, migration histories, changes in herds, shocks, informal transfers of assets, and so forth. Barrett et al. (2004) describe the location, survey methods, and available variables. In section 7.4 we use these data, briefly summarized in table 7.1, to estimate herd frontiers, from which we can estimate household-specific ability.

The respondents are, as a rule, male, experienced in herd management and, to a large extent, have not migrated from where they were born. Conditional on owning livestock, cattle represents approximately 85 percent of their total tropical livestock units, and only seven households own more livestock in species other than cattle. An important fraction (close to one in five households) owns no cattle. These households are sedentarized and depend

---

3. See, for example, Feder, Just, and Zilberman (1985) for a review of the importance of human capital in the process of technology adoption.

Table 7.1   **PARIMA data: definition and descriptive statistics**

Variable	Definition	Mean	Std. err.
Cattle	As % of TLU	0.85	0.22
Herd size at t	Herd size at t	9.18	12.87
Herd size at $t-1$	Herd size at $t-1$	8.12	11.35
No cattle at $t-1$	= 1 if owns no cattle at $t-1$, 0 otherwise	0.19	0.39
Herd below threshold at $t-1$	= 1 if $0 <$ herd size at $t-1 < 15$, 0 otherwise	0.68	0.47
Herd above threshold at $t-1$	= 1 if herd size at $t-1 > 15$	0.14	0.35
Labor	Family size at t	5.50	3.36
Land	Land cropped in June 2000	1.12	2.25
Sex	= 1 if male	0.64	0.48
Experience	Years since start of herd management	20.26	14.07
Migrant	= 1 if migrated to where currently lives	0.21	0.41

heavily on relief food distribution in towns. They own few, if any, other nonhuman assets, so even for these stockless households livestock holdings serve as a reasonable proxy for wealth (McPeak, Little, and Doss 2011). An even more important fraction (slightly above two in three households) owns herds that are smaller than fifteen cattle, the accumulation threshold identified in Lybbert et al. (2004), which does not account for possible heterogeneity. During the period for which we have data, the average herd did grow, from an average herd size of 8.1 cattle in 2000 to 9.2 cattle in 2003 (the equivalent of a growth rate of 4.3 percent per year). However, this average masks important heterogeneity in terms of growth experiences: focusing only on households who owned cattle, growth episodes were almost as likely as decreases or stagnation in herd size.

In 2004 we collected data on households' subjective expectations of herd dynamics, designed to complement the data routinely collected by PARIMA. The use of elicited expectations to study decision-making has now been applied extensively for testing economic hypotheses in both developed and developing countries (for reviews, see Manski 2004; Hurd 2009; Delavande 2014; Delavande, Giné, and McKenzie 2011). That said, it is worth explaining in some detail how we elicited these data.

We started by randomly selecting four hypothetical initial herd sizes for each respondent, one from each of the intervals defined by the equilibria identified by Lybbert et al. (2004).[4] Respondents were then asked to characterize their expectations of rainfall during the coming year, choosing between

---

4. The intervals are [1,5), [5, 15), [15, 40) and [40, 60] tropical livestock units (TLU) where 1 TLU = 1 cattle = 0.7 camels = 10 goats or sheep. The TLU measure allows aggregation across species on the basis of animals' average adult metabolic weight. Among the Boran we study, the overwhelming majority of TLU are held in the form of cattle.

good, normal, or bad.[5] Because the data were collected well into the rainy season, these answers should not be interpreted as uninformed priors that could merely reflect differences in optimism.[6] Respondents were also asked to assume a herd of standard composition for the region (in terms of age and sex of the animals). In one site, and in a second separate interview, we additionally asked respondents to consider what would happen to their herd (with an identical randomly allocated initial herd size) in the case of more extreme weather conditions, namely, severe drought and a very good year.[7]

After thus framing the problem, we asked each respondent to define the maximum and the minimum herd size they would expect to have one year later if they themselves started the year with the randomly assigned initial herd size. These bounds provide a natural anchor for the next step, in which we asked respondents to distribute on a board twenty stones among herd sizes between the minimum and the maximum previously elicited, thereby describing their subjective herd-size distribution one year ahead conditional on the randomly assigned initial herd size and the statement about rainfall. Finally, each respondent was asked if s/he had ever managed a herd approximately equal in size to the initial value provided as the random seed. The elicitation of the probability distribution function is an appropriate technique under these circumstances (Morgan and Henrion 1990) and allows us to compute conditional distributions and their moments. In addition, and because hypothetical initial wealth was randomly assigned to the respondent, it eliminates the prospective endogeneity of initial herd size in determining the estimated herd dynamics.

In total, we have 460 observations collected among 115 respondents for rainfall conditions labeled as good/normal or bad. Of these, nineteen do not

5. In this and several other African rangelands ecosystems, pasture biomass covaries strongly with rainfall. In recent years, the density of grazing livestock and wildlife has been insufficient to affect biomass sufficiently to alter herd dynamics, with stocking rates well below carrying capacity outside of a relatively small cluster of overgrazed areas around settlements (McPeak, Little, and Doss 2011). While climate change or a significant increase in human population and stocking rates could change the relationship between herd sizes and range vegetation dynamics, at the current time both appear driven largely by variation in weather. So the rainfall states we study should suffice to capture the stochastic dynamics of interest. This sort of trinomial rainfall characterization is familiar to respondents, as it corresponds to published rainfall forecasts such as those disseminated by the regional Drought Monitoring Centre and government and nongovernmental organization extension officers. See the analysis in Luseno et al. (2003) and Lybbert et al. (2007), who previously studied pastoralists' rainfall expectations.

6. The geographical concentration of pastoralists' expectations regarding rainfall further reinforces this interpretation: in two sites, over 90 percent of the respondents expected bad rainfall, while in the other two sites expectations were equally divided between bad rainfall and good rainfall.

7. In particular, we asked respondents to consider herd evolution "as if" in 1999, the last major drought, or "as if" in a very good year, which we asked them to define based on their own experience.

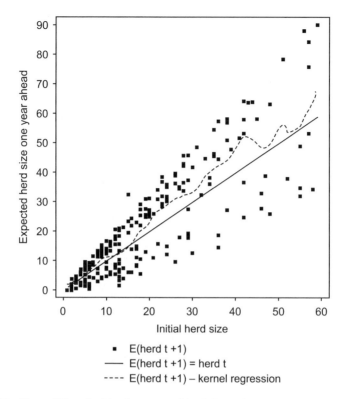

Fig. 7.1   Unconditional subjective expected herd dynamics

include a herd-size prediction, usually because respondents were unable to distribute the stones across the board, a problem that occurred mainly for bigger initial herd sizes when the difference between the maximum and the minimum was sometimes quite large. Of the remaining 441 observations, the respondents had prior personal experience managing a herd of comparable size in 288 cases (65.3 percent). In addition, we have sixty-one similar observations for very good and very bad years.

We finish this brief description of the data we use by presenting in figure 7.1 the scatter plot and kernel regression relating expected herd size one year ahead and initial herd size, conditional on ever having had a herd with a similar size, but *unconditional on weather conditions*.[8] Several points emerge from comparing pastoralists' subjective expectations of one-year-ahead herd dynamics (figure 7.1) with the dynamics revealed by Desta/Lybbert

8. We estimate Nadaraya-Watson nonparametric regressions with the Epanechnikov kernel and bandwidth of 4.545. The value of bandwidth was selected using Silverman (1986) rule of thumb, as determined by the "bounds for Stata" package (Beresteanu and Manski 2000).

et al.'s herd-history data (in particular, the dashed line in figure 4 of Lybbert et al. 2004, which reflects one-year-ahead dynamics).

First, both these data and the prior studies exhibit multiple dynamic equilibria consistent with the notion of a poverty trap. Second, however, the equilibria identified by pastoralists appear to differ markedly from those apparent in herd-history data, both with respect to their location and stability. Notably, herd accumulation occurs for a wider range of initial herd sizes, while herd losses seem a relatively marginal occurrence, contradicting detailed studies of this system (Coppock 1994) and the dynamics suggested by herd-history data.

These casual comparisons invite more disaggregated analysis. Our data on herders' subjective expectations of herd dynamics (figure 7.1) represent only one-year-ahead expectations under necessarily limited variability in rainfall regimes. By contrast, the pattern exhibited in the actual herd-history data used by Desta/Lybbert et al. are the result of a mixture of environmental conditions over a period of seventeen years.[9] These differences are made clear in table 7.2, which summarizes the data on expected herd size one year ahead, conditional on the state of nature and on having had a herd with a similar size, and its representation in figures 7.2 and 7.3, where we present the scatter plot and kernel regression relating expected herd size one year ahead and initial herd size for bad and normal/good years.[10]

These plots, and the summary statistics in table 7.2, suggest two insights. First, the relation between expected and initial herd size is nonlinear only in the case of bad rainfall conditions. Under good or normal climatic conditions (and perhaps unsurprisingly), almost all herders expect herd growth no matter the initial herd size. This disaggregation implies that adverse weather shocks drive the nonlinear dynamics revealed by the analysis of herd-history data.

Second, the dispersion around the expected herd-growth values is much bigger under conditions of bad rainfall than in a normal/good year, as reflected by the max.-min. spreads. Herders exhibit far more heterogeneous beliefs about their ability to deal with adverse states of nature than with favorable ones. If, following Schultz (1975), one interprets this variation as at least partly reflecting pastoralist herding ability then "the ability to deal with disequilibria" seems to play a significant role in wealth dynamics. Put differently, risk and ability may intersect to generate the complex herd dynamics observed in this system.

9. For example, Kamara, Swallow, and Kirk (2004) identify three major droughts (1984/85, 1991/92, and 1995/96) and two periods of excessive rains (1980/81 and 1997/98) in this region over the period covered by the Desta/Lybbert et al. data. To these natural disasters, one may add the generalized ethnic clashes between the Boran and the Gabra in 1992, following the fall of the Derg regime. Barrett and Santos (2014) explore how changing rainfall distributions might affect observed herd dynamics.

10. To conserve space, we omit figures reflecting the data and nonparametric regressions under extreme weather conditions, which show that during severe drought everyone expects to lose cattle.

Table 7.2 Expected herd size, one year ahead: the effect of rainfall and initial wealth

$E(\text{herd})_{t+1}$	Very bad			Bad			Good			Very good		
	Min.	Mean	Max.	Min.	Mean	Max.	Min.	Mean	Max.	Min.	Mean	Max.
$\text{Herd}_t \in [1, 5)$	0	0.6	1.6	0	1.6	5.6	0.8	4.5	6.9	1.8	3.7	6.6
$\text{Herd}_t \in [5, 15)$	0.8	3.5	12	0.3	7.8	15.6	4.5	12.8	21.2	3.3	12.5	21.6
$\text{Herd}_t \in [15, 40)$	1.4	6.0	13.9	5.5	23.3	50.9	14.1	36.3	57.9	18.3	31.9	50.6
$\text{Herd}_t \in [40, 60)$	4.4	13.3	27.7	24.6	42.6	79.1	63.0	74.4	89.9	56.3	64.9	78.4

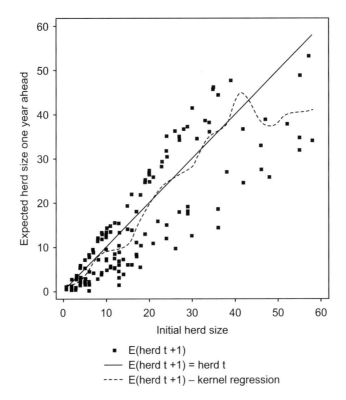

Fig. 7.2 Expected herd dynamics under bad rainfall conditions

7.3   Expected Herd Dynamics in a Stochastic Environment

In order to generate herders' subjective expectations of herd dynamics under a mixture of states of nature, we need to integrate data on herd-growth expectations conditional on rainfall (the elicited expectations data previously described) with historical rainfall data (in practice, monthly rainfall data for the four sites over the period 1991–2001).[11] With this information we can then simulate herd evolution over longer periods than just one year ahead. Since we must predict out-of-sample in simulating herd evolution for large values of initial herd size, we estimate the parametric relation between initial and expected herd sizes (hereafter, $herd_0$ and $herd_1$,

11. Average rainfall was 490 mm/year, with a standard deviation of 152 mm/year. Given the skewness and the kurtosis of this distribution, we cannot reject the null hypothesis that rainfall follows a normal distribution. The minimum annual rainfall over the period was registered in 1999 (259 mm) and the maximum in 1997 (765 mm). The probability of such events is 0.064 and 0.035. Given these results, we assumed, for simulation purposes, a symmetric distribution, with a probability of extreme events (drought; or very good year) equal to 0.10. In a separate analysis (Barrett and Santos 2014) we show that the results are relatively sensitive to changes in the rainfall distribution, reflecting the dependency of this system on rainfall and its vulnerability to climate change.

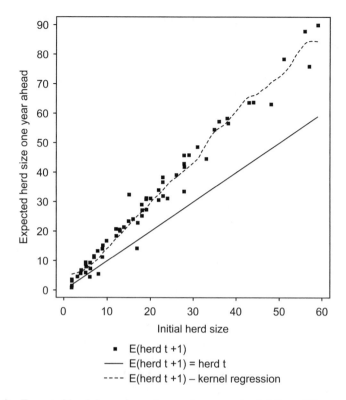

Fig. 7.3   Expected herd dynamics under good or normal rainfall conditions

respectively) conditional on each of the four rainfall scenarios (drought [very bad], bad, normal/good, and very good). We estimate this relation with a respondent fixed effect specification, α_i, taking advantage of having repeated observations, r, across different herd-size intervals for each individual i. We thus estimate

$$(2) \qquad \text{herd}_{1ir} = f\,(\text{herd}_{0ir}) + \alpha_i + \varepsilon_{ir}$$

where $f(\text{herd}_{0ir})$ is a polynomial function of initial herd size.[12] Table 7.3 presents the estimates, which reflect the same results displayed visually in figures 7.2 and 7.3, and suggested in table 7.2: unambiguous linear expected growth under normal/good/very good rainfall conditions, a nonlinear relation between herd_1 and herd_0 under conditions of poor rainfall and drought,

---

12. Besides the assumptions on the functional form of $f(\cdot)$, we also assumed that $\varepsilon_{ir} \sim N(0, \sigma^2)$. Other specifications that replace the fixed effect with other regressors that could affect subjective expectations, such as gender, age, experience, and migrant status, were considered, but none of those variables proved statistically significant, so we omit these results. We omit higher-order polynomial terms in the very good and good/normal year specifications because they added nothing given the good fit already achieved with a simple linear specification with fixed effects.

Table 7.3   Estimates of expected herd dynamics conditional on rainfall

Variable	Very good	Good	Bad	Very bad
$Herd_0$	1.293	1.477	0.528	0.246
	(0.000)	(0.019)	(0.224)	(0.246)
$Herd_0^2$			0.026	0.009
			(0.010)	(0.010)
$Herd_0^3$			−0.00039	−.00017
			(0.0001)	(0.0001)
Constant	0.897	0.179	0.513	−0.575
	(0.448)	(0.416)	(1.185)	(1.083)
N	61	96	192	61
R^2	0.986	0.994	0.792	0.589

Note: Values within parentheses are robust standard errors.

and with considerable dispersion so that the precision of those estimates (as measured by the R^2) is far less than under favorable rainfall regimes.

We then use these estimates to simulate the expected evolution of herd sizes.[13] Figure 7.4 presents the basic structure of the simulation procedure we used, while figure 7.5 presents the mean of ten-year-ahead herd size for 500 replicates of this simulation with initial herd sizes between one and sixty.

The results are remarkably similar to the dynamics revealed by the herd-history data (the solid line in figure 4 of Lybbert et al. 2004), both in the general shape of the curve and in the location of the different equilibria. This strongly suggests that the mismatch between the one-year-ahead transitions predicted by the two data sets that we discussed above arose because of differences in the underlying distribution of the states of nature. Once we account for historical rainfall patterns and simulate the longer-term herd dynamics, it appears that Boran pastoralists' subjective expectations reflect a remarkably accurate understanding of the nature of how their herds have evolved over the past generation. In particular, they expect that, on average, someone with a herd below approximately fifteen cattle will eventually lose almost all of his wealth, collapsing into a destitute equilibrium with just one cow.

Can we be sure that multiple equilibria exist? Given the small sample size, the answer is no; the lower confidence band crosses the equilibrium line only once, from above, at the lower-level equilibrium (one animal). But as we show below, this merely reflects our current assumption that all herders

13. We calibrate these estimates to impose basic biological rules for livestock. More precisely, we do not allow for negative herds and impose that biological growth under good rainfall conditions is delayed by two years, that is, enough for cows to reproduce in accordance with basic gestational patterns. We also constrain the predicted values for initial herd sizes above fifty-two (poor rainfall) and forty-five (drought) to be linear, with a slope of 0.033 and 0.009, respectively, preventing unbelievable predictions due to the parameter estimates at the boundaries of our sample.

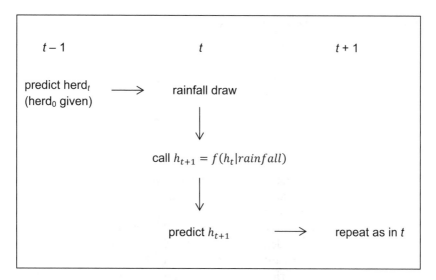

Fig. 7.4 Simulation procedure

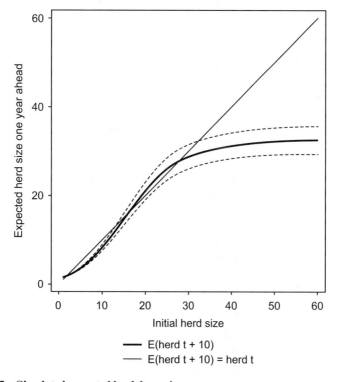

Fig. 7.5 Simulated expected herd dynamics

Table 7.4   Estimated herd size ten-year transition matrix

Herd$_{t+10}$	0–4	5–14	15–39	>40
Herd$_t$				
0–4	0.879	0.113	0.009	0.000
5–14	0.575	0.262	0.133	0.030
15–39	0.204	0.280	0.255	0.261
>40	0.136	0.230	0.291	0.342

follow the same growth path. When we abandon the strong assumption that all herders follow the same dynamics and disaggregate by herder ability, the precision of our estimates improves significantly.

Concentrating on our average estimates, do these nonlinearities lead to a poverty trap? The answer depends, in part, on what one means by a "poverty trap." In table 7.4 we quantify the probability of moving between equilibria over a ten-year period given the stochastic nature of these shocks. There is a positive probability that a herder starting with a herd between one and four cattle will, ten years later, have grown his herd. Indeed, there is even a very small probability (less than 1 percent) that he finishes above the accumulation threshold. Hence, the strictest interpretation of a poverty trap—that initial conditions totally determine future wealth and the system is nonergodic, thus the probability of growing to a higher equilibrium is zero—finds no support in our data. However, the probability of moving out of poverty is quite low (less than 12 percent), suggesting that, in this context, the idea of a poverty trap is most usefully conceptualized as a high probability that agents will remain at lower levels of welfare, a weaker but perhaps more realistic interpretation of the concept in stochastic environments (Azariadis and Stachurski 2005).

Summarizing the results so far, we find that Boran pastoralists accurately perceive long-term herd dynamics characterized by multiple wealth equilibria consistent with the notion of a poverty trap: shocks almost totally prevent wealth accumulation that would allow herders at a low initial wealth level from escaping poverty. However, these dynamics seem entirely the result of heterogeneity in growth rates under different rainfall conditions. Growth is universally expected in good years, while S-shaped dynamics seem to result from wealth-differentiated capacity to deal with bad rainfall conditions.[14]

Our data also show that, even in bad years, not all herders expect their herds to shrink. The considerable dispersion of beliefs about herd dynamics

14. This could explain why, for example, Mogues (2011), studying livestock accumulation in other regions of Ethiopia in the period 2000/03, with no major shocks in between, does not find evidence of such nonlinearities, and why Barrett et al. (2006) find evidence of an S-shaped curve for asset dynamics in the northern Kenya PARIMA sample, which included a major drought ending in 2001.

under adverse states of nature suggests that herder-specific characteristics, which we summarize as ability, may likewise play a central role in conditioning wealth dynamics. The next section investigates this possibility.

7.4   Ability and Expected Herd Dynamics

Herding in semiarid environments is a difficult livelihood. One must know how to treat livestock diseases and injuries, protect cattle against predators, manage their nutrition, navigate to distant grazing and watering sites, assist in difficult calving episodes, and so forth. Not everyone learns and practices these diverse skills equally well. One would expect herders with greater animal husbandry skills to be able to manage larger herds and to be less subject to adverse shocks to herd size than less skilled herders. Put differently, the herd dynamics explored in the historical data and in the previous section may ignore important differences in herder ability.

We explore the impact of differences in herding ability on herd dynamics by using the data coming from three rounds of the PARIMA panel of pastoralist households, described in section 7.2, to estimate herder ability using stochastic parametric frontier estimation methods for panel data (Kumbhakar and Lovell 2000). More precisely, we estimate the herd frontier that explains individual i's herd size at the beginning of period t, h_{it}, conditional on a vector of household attributes, X_{it-1}, and herd size and labor endowments (the two most important inputs for which we have information) at the beginning of the prior period, using a composed error term that includes a normally distributed random component reflecting standard sampling and measurement error, ψ, and a one-sided term reflecting observation-specific but time-invariant inefficiency, $\phi_i \geq 0$, which we assume follows a truncated normal distribution, $N^+ (\mu, \sigma^2)$:

$$(3) \qquad h_{it} = f\left(h_{it-1}, l_{it-1}\right) + \beta X_{it-1} - \phi_i + \psi_{it}.$$

We allow for $f(h_{it-1}, l_{it-1})$ to reflect the possibility of two different growth paths, depending on whether the initial herd is above or below the fifteen-cattle threshold identified by Lybbert et al. (2004).[15]

Since these households were surveyed repeatedly from 2000 to 2003, we can take advantage of multiple observations for each herder to compute consistent herder-specific mean efficiency measures, that is, each pastoralist's proximity to the herd frontier. The inefficiency parameter ϕ_i captures any time-

15. In equation (1) we make clear that there is no necessary equivalence between the threshold identified for the average household—which would correspond to the value estimated by Lybbert et al. (2004)—and a possible cohort-specific threshold. However, given the analysis cited in section 7.1 that seems to suggest changes in household behavior for herd sizes around the average threshold, this value seemed a natural starting point for the analysis. One alternative that we did not pursue would be to agnostically address this problem using a search and testing approach similar to the one suggested in Hansen (2000).

invariant—and period-average time-varying—unobservables associated with systematic deviation from the herd frontier. This parameter can clearly capture factors beyond the herder's unobserved ability, such as the quality of local grazing lands, but ϕ_i is almost surely strongly correlated with ability. Moreover, it is an open question whether it matters for targeting and programming if the features that cause systematic underperformance are intrinsic, immutable individual skills or community-level or slow-changing individual characteristics. The key is that there exist distinct groups of households who routinely outperform or underperform their neighbors, however we understand the structural genesis of those relative performance differences.

The interpretation of these estimates as proxies for ability can still be contested on at least two grounds. First, the lagged values of herd size are clearly related to lagged (and current) ability, hence our estimates of inefficiency are likely inconsistent. This would matter if we were interested in cardinal measures of inefficiency. But we focus only on the ordinal measures, grouping households into low- and high-ability cohorts. So long as the correlation between lagged wealth and ability does not affect the ordering of each observation within the inefficiency distribution, the possible bias in point estimates will be of no consequence for present purposes.

Second, we estimate inefficiency by imposing a specific functional form, a specific distribution for the inefficiency parameter, and a specific accumulation threshold that, from the existing literature (in particular, Lybbert et al. 2004), seems valid for the *average* herder in this setting. These assumptions can introduce misspecification error that may be easily conflated with inefficiency (Sherlund, Barrett, and Adesina 2002). As with the prior concern about inconsistent parameter estimates, our reliance purely on the ordering of the estimates sharply limits the relevance of such concerns. Nonetheless, an alternative approach is to use more flexible, nonparametric efficiency estimation methods, in particular data envelopment analysis, that can easily allow for variable returns to scale without imposing specific assumptions about functional or distributional forms (see Coelli et al. 2005). Our analysis is robust to this alternative way of estimating inefficiency, so we maintain that the ordinal inefficiency estimates we estimate provide a reasonable proxy for relative herder ability/skill and thus serve present purposes well.[16]

Table 7.5 presents estimates of the herd frontier based on 2000–2001, 2001–2002, and 2002–2003 annual observations for the 113 households for which we have complete data on each of the covariates.[17] The results indicate statistically significant (p-value $= 0.053$) differences in the asset dynamics above and below the threshold, with expected herd growth (collapse)

16. The DEA estimates were obtained using the -dea- command in Stata (Ji and Lee 2010). The results are available from the lead author by request.

17. Because one of the households is the successor of an initial household, we only have data for the last two years. Hence, we're using an unbalanced panel with 338 observations.

Table 7.5   **Stochastic parametric herd frontier estimates**

Variable	Coefficient	Std. err.	P-value
Herd size at $t-1$ * above threshold	1.022	0.093	0.000
Herd size at $t-1$ squared * above threshold	0.000	0.001	0.689
Herd size at $t-1$ * below threshold	0.890	0.307	0.004
Herd size at $t-1$ squared * below threshold	−0.009	0.022	0.681
No cattle at $t-1$	−1.126	1.245	0.366
Labor * above threshold	−0.089	0.174	0.611
Labor * below threshold	0.099	0.125	0.427
Land	0.022	0.152	0.885
Sex	1.333	0.702	0.057
Experience	0.137	0.071	0.052
Experience squared	−0.002	0.001	0.174
Migrant	−0.605	0.998	0.544
2000–2001	−0.740	0.531	0.164
2001–2002	1.553	0.525	0.003
Dida Hara	1.870	1.110	0.092
Qorate	0.026	1.229	0.983
Wachille	0.827	1.131	0.465
Constant	13.012	195.554	0.947
μ	14.671	195.551	0.940
N		338	
R^2		0.230	

above (below) the threshold. The estimated frontier is piecewise quadratic, as higher-order polynomial terms of lagged herd size have no statistically significant effect.[18] Household labor and land endowments have no effect at the margin on expected herd size, signaling that these are not limiting in this environment for most households. Male-headed households enjoy significantly larger herd sizes, which may partly capture household composition effects (with male-headed households having more men available to herd, especially on treks away from base camp lasting days or weeks, holding labor availability constant). There exist statistically significant, albeit diminishing, marginal returns to herding experience. And there are marginally significant fixed effects associated with location and year (in particular, for 2001–2002, the year of recovery after the severe 1999–2000 drought), the latter result

18. Table 7.1 defines these variables and presents the descriptive statistics. We also estimated this regression using cubic and quartic terms, but none of the higher-order polynomials were statistically significantly different from zero and one could not reject the null hypothesis that the higher-order terms jointly have no effect on next period's herd size, once one allows for the threshold effect. The variable "no cattle at $t-1$" is included to control for the fact that herd growth is different when one has no cattle—growth can then only occur through purchases or gifts, both of which are very infrequent (Lybbert et al. 2004)—than when one has a positive herd size. Although the point estimate on this variable is not statistically significantly different from zero, when we do not control for this effect the estimated coefficients on lagged herd size and its various interactions become far more imprecise.

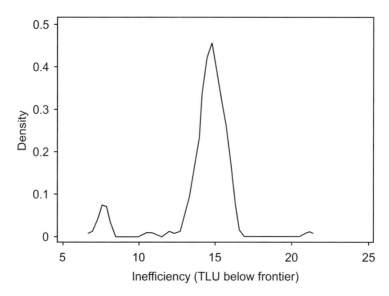

Fig. 7.6   **Empirical density function of herd-size inefficiency estimates**

reinforcing our earlier finding about state-dependent growth. The estimated distribution of the inefficiency estimates (with cattle as the units of measure) is presented in figure 7.6,[19] allowing a visual analysis of the within-sample variation.

Using the predicted value of each herder's estimated inefficiency, we then divide our sample into two subsamples: lower-ability (those in the 4th quartile of the inefficiency estimates with $\phi_i > 15.38$) and a complementary category of higher-ability herders. The observations are concentrated around just a few points ranges of inefficiency estimates, suggesting that there may be little value to further subdivision of the sample.[20] For each of these two classes we reestimate equation (2), obtaining estimates of the parametric models that relate expected and initial herd size for each subsample, after which we performed the same simulation as above.[21] Figure 7.7 shows the nonparametric conditional expectation function (and 95 percent confidence intervals) of ten-year-ahead herd size obtained for 500 replicates with initial

19. Estimated using the Epanechnikov kernel, with a bandwidth of 0.24697.
20. We also experimented with splitting the higher-ability herders into two categories, those of highest ability (the 1st quartile of the inefficiency distribution) and a residual medium-ability class (the 2nd and 3rd quartiles). The qualitative results are similar, so we present the simpler approach here. Results of the most disaggregated analysis are available from the lead author by request.
21. These eight parametric models (four states of nature × two ability classes) are qualitatively similar to the ones presented in table 7.2. To conserve space we omit them here, but they are available from the lead author by request.

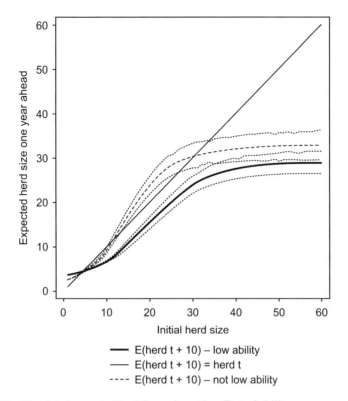

Fig. 7.7   Simulated expected herd dynamics—the effect of ability

herd sizes between one and sixty cattle for each ability class. The results are easily summarized.

Although those in the lowest ability quartile exhibit S-shaped expected herd dynamics, these lie everywhere beneath the dynamic equilibrium line (the solid 45° line in figure 7.7). Thus, low-ability herders are expected to converge toward the low-level dynamic asset equilibrium of one to two head of cattle over time. Recall that all herders expect to grow their herds during good and normal rainfall years. So this expected long-run herd-size collapse arises entirely from low-ability herders' difficulty in managing and recovering from adverse weather shocks.

Higher-ability herders likewise exhibit S-shaped expected herd dynamics. However, they face multiple dynamic equilibria, with an accumulation threshold at eleven to seventeen cattle, similar to the threshold estimated by Lybbert et al. (2004) from the herd-history data. Notice also that, when we allow for different growth paths conditional on ability, we get much more precise estimates of the herd dynamics. In particular, both confidence bands for the higher-ability herders cross the dynamic equilibrium line in three points, two of which represent stable dynamic equilibria, at one to two and twenty-nine to thirty-five cattle, respectively. The implication, reflected in figure 7.7, is that S-shaped herd dynamics characteristic of a multiple equilibrium poverty trap are not followed by all herders. Low-ability herders face a unique dynamic equilibrium at lower levels of welfare, giving rise to a different sort of poverty trap than that faced by herders with higher ability, who expect to accumulate wealth so long as they maintain an herd size above the twelve to seventeen cattle threshold. These results clearly raise important practical questions with respect to any asset redistribution or transfer policy, as ability is not easily and quickly identified in conventional survey methods, at least not by outsiders such as the governmental and nongovernmental agencies that typically provide transfers and public safety net programs.

7.5   The Policy Challenge: Targeting with Imperfectly Known Dynamics

The possibility that multiple mechanisms underpin wealth dynamics poses a challenge for policymakers. To illustrate how an understanding of wealth dynamics might affect the design and performance of an intervention, we explore the effectiveness of herd restocking in this system, as this is perhaps the most common form of postdrought assistance provided to pastoralists by donors and governments in the region.

We simulate the effect of three different scenarios under the maintained assumption that growth does depend on ability (as represented in figure 7.7) and using a constant budget. In Scenario 1, all herds below five cattle (a customary, Boran-defined poverty line) are given animals to boost their herd to five head, irrespective of the recipient herder's ability. This reflects the dominant current paradigm of progressive transfers to the poorest. In our simulations, in aggregate that rule leads to a transfer of thirty-six cattle to seventeen beneficiaries in our 2003 sample of ninety-seven households. Those thirty-six cattle become the fixed "budget" that we maintain in the next two scenarios. In Scenario 2, we simulate the effects of a transfer targeted so as to maximize the number of "viable" herders, that is, those that have a herd that is larger than the estimated minimum accumulation threshold of eleven cattle. Although we assume that growth depends on ability, we also assume that there exists no effective mechanism to elicit herder ability; so, transfers are conditioned solely on observable herd sizes. Then, in Scenario 3, we assume one can accurately identify herder by ability group and, as with Scenario 2, again target transfers so as to maximize asset growth. Scenario 3 involves transfers to sixteen higher-ability herders, with limited overlap in identity with the seventeen recipients under Scenario 1. The main difference between these scenarios is evident in figure 7.8, where we draw the expected herd-size gains associated with the transfer of one cattle, conditional on herder ability.

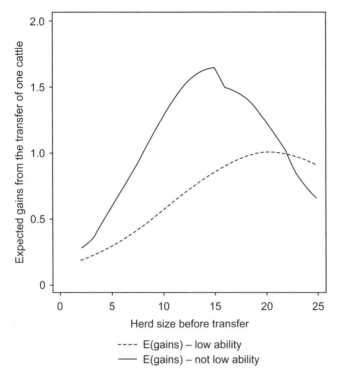

Fig. 7.8   Expected gains from the transfer of one cattle

Given expected herd dynamics over the decade following the hypothesized transfer, the transfer is expected to generate herd growth, net of the one cattle transfer (i.e., expected gains > 1), only for higher-ability recipients with ex ante herd size between nine and twenty-two head. Herders of low ability or, if of higher ability, with the smallest (or largest) herds are expected to lose some of their posttransfer herd over the ensuing decade, signaling negative medium- to long-term growth returns on livestock transfers to the poorest (or wealthiest) herders of higher ability. The expected herd gain is maximized for a transfer to a higher-ability herder with an ex ante herd size of fifteen cattle, a significantly larger herd than is typical of restocking program participants, since such interventions are typically targeted following some poverty-reduction criteria, like Scenario 1.

Table 7.6 presents the results of a comparison among these three different scenarios for targeting herd-restocking transfers that reflect both this discussion and, implicitly, the distribution of low- and high-ability types as a function of pretransfer wealth, as represented in figure 7.9.

As one would expect based on the dynamics of this system, restocking targeted to lower-wealth households (specifically, those fewer than five cattle)

Table 7.6   Expected effects of restocking under different targeting assumptions

| | | | | Expected herd size (2013) | | Expected |
Scenario	Number	Average transfer	Average herd size (2003)	w/ transfer	w/out transfer	gains from transfer
1. Beneficiaries	17	2.12	2.88	4.46	3.63	0.86
2. Beneficiaries	23	2	10	12.20	9.34	2.86
3. Beneficiaries	18	1.94	10.05	13.40	10.09	3.3

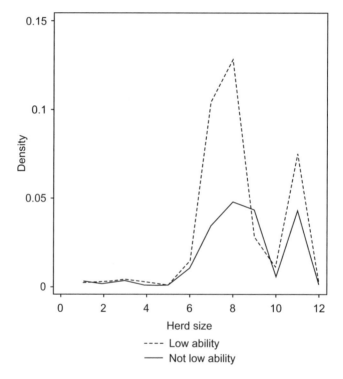

Fig. 7.9   Distribution of high- and low-ability types as a function of initial wealth

fails to promote growth among the poor. After ten years, beneficiaries enjoy an expected gain of 0.86 cattle, but from an average transfer of 2.12 cattle. This implies a −4.4 percent compound annual return on investment in transfer resources, reflecting expected herd losses below the critical herd-size threshold. The growth-promoting impacts of herd restocking become more satisfactory in the other two scenarios that target those who can reach the herd accumulation threshold through transfers rather than the ex ante poorest households. Under Scenario 2, the average net returns to this policy after ten years are 43 percent (3.6 percent annually). These returns significantly increase to 70 percent (5.4 percent annually), under Scenario 3, showing that the payoff to the design of a reliable mechanism for identifying herding ability is potentially considerable, given that ability seems to matter a great deal to wealth dynamics in this system. But targeting the accumulation threshold is the main factor that drives achieving a positive long-run rate of return on transfer resources.

This payoff naturally depends on the distribution of ability types. As shown in figure 7.9 there is, in this system at least, a correlation between ex ante wealth and ability that reflects the joint operation of the dynamics described in this chapter—with low-ability types expected to fall into and remain in poverty regardless of initial wealth—and the insufficiency of informal insurance, particularly among the poor (Santos and Barrett 2011). Roughly half of the herders with less than five cattle are classified as low ability (which, recall, we defined as being in the lower quartile of the distribution of our estimates of technical efficiency). The frequency of low-ability herders then diminishes with wealth: 22 percent of the beneficiaries of transfers under Scenario 2 (with herds between nine and eleven cattle) are classified as low ability, and only little more than 10 percent of the herders with wealth above the accumulation threshold are classified as such. The challenge intrinsic to restocking projects targeted at those with small herds is that it implicitly favors those with the least ability to manage the livestock they receive. This finding lends support to recent policy initiatives in the East African drylands that focus more on cash transfers than livestock transfers to support the poorest community members.

7.6   Conclusions

Using unique data on subjective herd-growth expectations conditional on expected rainfall, we find that southern Ethiopian pastoralists appear to understand the nonstationary herd dynamics that long-term herd-history data suggest characterize their system, corroborating Lybbert et al. (2004) and related results using different data and methods. Moreover, pastoralists' responses reveal that multiple dynamic equilibria arise purely due to adverse shocks associated with low rainfall years and only among pastoralists of higher herding ability. Lower-ability herders appear to converge toward a unique, low-level equilibrium herd size. When adverse weather events strike, they lose livestock and, in expectation, cannot recover quickly enough before the next drought hits. Thus, the data suggest that even among a seemingly homogeneous population in an ethnically uniform region offering effectively only one livelihood option—livestock herding—there exist complex wealth dynamics characterized by distinct convergence clubs defined by individual ability, with multiple dynamic equilibria existing for only a subset of those clubs and a unique, low-level equilibrium for the other club.

These findings carry two main policy implications. First, the need for interventions to lift people out of—or to prevent their collapse into—poverty traps, seems to depend on the nature of the adverse shocks, in particular, whether their severity and frequency is such that growth under favorable states of nature is often and sharply reversed, making accumulation below a critical threshold unlikely (albeit not impossible). Risk mitigation or transfer methods to limit the frequency or magnitude of shocks may be as or more valuable than transfers to facilitate growth among the poorest, a point made as well in Ikegami et al. (chapter 6, this volume). Second, the appropriate design and targeting of social protection in this stochastic environment depend very much on individual characteristics, perhaps including difficult-to-observe characteristics such as ability. Identifying ability may be operationally difficult, but failure to take such characteristics into account may lead to ill-conceived efforts and wasted scarce resources.

Finally, these findings also carry implications in terms of future research. First, the need to understand how important is heterogeneity in poverty dynamics. Recent work analyzing poverty-graduation programs seems to suggest that unobserved heterogeneity matters (see, e.g., Bandiera et al. 2017; Gobin, Santos, and Toth 2017). Second, what can be done to understand what lies under the frequently used, but rarely defined, concept of "ability." In this chapter, we equated ability with the (estimates of) technical efficiency, as the capacity to produce more with the same resources seems an intuitively acceptable approximation of ability. A natural next step is to "reduce the residual" by measuring the skills that, so far and to a large extent, have been left unmeasured. Dean, Schilbach, and Schofield's (chapter 2, this volume) discussion of the potential importance of noncognitive skills such self-control, attention, and memory as psychological determinants of productivity seems a natural starting point, although much needs to be understood regarding the practical difficulties of such measurement (Laajaj and Macours 2017).

References

Azariadis, Costas, and John Stachurski. 2005. "Poverty Traps." In *Handbook of Economic Growth*, edited by Phillipe Aghion and Steven Durlauf. Amsterdam: Elsevier.

Bandiera, Oriana, Robin Burgess, Narayan Das, Selim Gulesci, Imran Rasul, and Munshi Sulaiman. 2017. "Labor Markets and Poverty in Village Economies." *Quarterly Journal of Economics* 132 (2): 811–70.

Barrett, Christopher B., and Michael Carter. 2013. "The Economics of Poverty Traps and Persistent Poverty: Empirical and Policy Implications." *Journal of Development Studies* 49:976–90.

Barrett, Christopher B., Teevrat Garg, and L. McBride. 2016. "Well-Being Dynamics and Poverty Traps." *Annual Review of Resource Economics* 8:303–27.

Barrett, Christopher B., Getachew Gebru, John G. McPeak, Andrew G. Mude, Jacqueline Vanderpluye-Orgle, and Amare T. Yirbecho. 2004. "Codebook for Data Collected under the Improving Pastoral Risk Management on East Africa Rangelands (PARIMA) Project." Unpublished manuscript, Cornell University.

Barrett, Christopher B., Paswel Phiri Marenya, John McPeak, Bart Minten, Festus Murithi, Willis Oluoch-Kosura, Frank Place, Jean Claude Randrianarisoa, Jhon Rasambainarivo, and Justine Wangila. 2006. "Welfare Dynamics in Rural Kenya and Madagascar." *Journal of Development Studies* 42:248–77.

Barrett, Christopher B., and Paulo Santos. 2014. "The Impact of Changing Rainfall Variability on Resource-Dependent Wealth Dynamics." *Ecological Economics* 105:48–54.

Beresteanu, Arie, and Charles F. Manski. 2000. "Bounds for Stata: Draft Version 1.0." Working paper, Department of Economics, Northwestern University.

Bowles, Samuel, Steven Durlauf, and Karla Hoff. 2006. *Poverty Traps*. Princeton, NJ: Princeton University Press.

Carter, Michael R. 1998. "On the Economics of Realizing and Sustaining an Efficient Redistribution of Productive Assets." In *Recasting Egalitarianism: New Rules for Accountability and Equity in Markets, Communities and States*, edited by Erik O. Wright. London: Verso.

Coelli, T. J., D. S. P. Rao, C. J. O'Donnell, and G. E. Battese. 2005. *An Introduction to Efficiency and Productivity Analysis*. New York: Springer.

Coppock, D. Layne. 1994. *The Borana Plateau of Southern Ethiopia: Synthesis of Pastoral Research, Development and Change, 1980–91*, no. 5 in International Livestock Centre for Africa Systems Study. Addis Ababa: ILCA.

Delavande, A. 2014. "Probabilistic Expectations in Developing Countries." *Annual Review of Economics* 6:1–20.

Delavande, A., X. Giné, and D. McKenzie. 2011. "Measuring Subjective Expectations in Developing Countries: A Critical Review and New Evidence." *Journal of Development Economics* 94:151–63.

Desta, Solomon. 1999. "Diversification of Livestock Assets for Risk Management in the Borana Pastoral System of Southern Ethiopia." PhD diss., Utah State University.

Feder, Gershon, Richard E. Just, and David Zilberman. 1985. "Adoption of Agricultural Innovations in Developing Countries: A Survey." *Economic Development and Cultural Change* 33 (2): 255–98.

Gobin, Vilas J., Paulo Santos, and Russell Toth. 2017. "No Longer Trapped? Promoting Entrepreneurship through Cash Transfers to Ultra-poor Women in Northern Kenya." *American Journal of Agricultural Economics* 99 (5): 1362–83.

Hansen, Bruce. 2000. "Sample Splitting and Threshold Estimation." *Econometrica* 68:575–603.

Hurd, M. D. 2009. "Subjective Probabilities in Household Surveys." *Annual Review of Economics* 1:543–62.

Ji, Yong-Bae, and Choonjoo Lee. 2010. "Data Envelopment Analysis." *Stata Journal* 10:267–80.

Kamara, Abdul, Brent Swallow, and Michael Kirk. 2004. "Policies, Interventions and Institutional Change in Pastoral Resource Management in Borana, Southern Ethiopia." *Development Policy Review* 22 (4): 381–403.

Kraay, A., and David McKenzie. 2014. "Do Poverty Traps Exist? Assessing the Evidence." *Journal of Economic Perspectives* 28:127–48.

Kumbhakar, Subal, and C. A. Knox Lovell. 2000. *Stochastic Frontier Analysis*. Cambridge: Cambridge University Press.

Laajaj, Rachid, and Karen Macours. 2017. "Measuring Skills in Developing Countries." World Bank Policy Research Working Paper no. WPS 8000, World Bank.

Luseno, Winnie K., John G. McPeak, Christopher B. Barrett, Getachew Gebru, and Peter D. Little. 2003. "The Value of Climate Forecast Information for Pastoralists: Evidence from Southern Ethiopia and Northern Kenya." *World Development* 31 (9): 1477–94.

Lybbert, Travis, Christopher B. Barrett, Solomon Desta, and D. Layne Coppock. 2004. "Stochastic Wealth Dynamics and Risk Management among a Poor Population." *Economic Journal* 114 (498): 750–77.

Lybbert, Travis, Christopher B. Barrett, John McPeak, and Winnie K. Luseno. 2007. "Bayesian Herders: Asymmetric Updating of Rainfall Beliefs in Response to External Forecasts." *World Development* 35:480–97.

Manski, C. F. 2004. "Measuring Expectations." *Econometrica* 72:1329–76.

McPeak, John, Peter Little, and Cheryl Doss. 2011. *Risk and Social Change in an African Rural Economy*. London: Routledge.

Mogues, Tewodaj. 2011. "Shocks and Asset Dynamics in Ethiopia." *Economic Development and Cultural Change* 60:91–120.

Morgan, M. Granger, and Max Henrion. 1990. *Uncertainty: A Guide to Dealing with Uncertainty in Quantitative Risk and Policy Analysis*. Cambridge: Cambridge University Press.

Sachs, Jeffrey D. 2005. *The End of Poverty: Economic Possibilities for Our Times*. New York: Penguin Press.

Santos, Paulo, and Christopher Barrett. 2011. "Persistent Poverty and Informal Credit." *Journal of Development Economics* 96:337–47.

Schultz, Theodore W. 1975. "The Value of the Ability to Deal with Disequilibria." *Journal of Economic Literature* 13:827–46.

Sherlund, Shane M., Christopher B. Barrett, and Akinwumi A Adesina. 2002. "Smallholder Technical Efficiency Controlling for Environmental Production Functions." *Journal of Development Economics* 69:85–101.

Silverman, B. 1986. *Density Estimation for Statistics and Data Analysis*. London: Chapman & Hall.

Toth, Russell. 2015. "Traps and Thresholds in Pastoralist Mobility." *American Journal of Agricultural Economics* 97:315–32.

United Nations Millennium Project. 2005. *Investing in Development: A Practical Plan to Achieve the Millennium Development Goals*. New York: United Nations Development Program.

8

Agroecosystem Productivity and the Dynamic Response to Shocks

Jean-Paul Chavas

8.1 Introduction

Dynamics is at the heart of economic development and the search for processes that contribute to improving human welfare. But dynamic processes are typically complex, especially under nonlinear dynamics. Indeed, nonlinear dynamic systems can exhibit many patterns. For deterministic systems, this can go from reaching a unique steady state to having multiple steady states, to displaying limit cycles, or even to being chaotic (e.g., May 1976). For stochastic systems the complexity increases further, making it challenging to evaluate the dynamic response to unanticipated shocks. The assessment of such dynamic response is highly relevant in economics. Some shocks are favorable (e.g., good weather, the discovery of new knowledge) with positive impacts on welfare both in the short run and the longer run. But other shocks have a negative impact on human welfare (e.g., drought, disease). The dynamic effects of such shocks has been of great interest to economists and policymakers. Under some scenarios, their adverse effects matter in the short run but dissipate in the longer run. But under other scenarios, their longer-term impacts can be sustained and large. An example is the case of poverty traps, which associate poverty with meager prospects for economic growth (e.g., Dasgupta 1997; Azariadis and Stachurski 2005; Barrett and Carter 2013; Kraay and McKenzie 2014; Barrett and Constas 2014). Another example is from ecology: under some circumstances, an

Jean-Paul Chavas is the Anderson-Bascom Professor of Agricultural and Applied Economics at the University of Wisconsin–Madison and a member of the board of directors of the National Bureau of Economic Research.

For acknowledgments, sources of research support, and disclosure of the author's material financial relationships, if any, please see http://www.nber.org/chapters/c13836.ack.

ecosystem may fail to recover under extreme shocks (e.g., Holling 1973; Common and Perrings 1992; Perrings 1998; Gunderson 2000; Folke et al. 2004; Derissen, Quaas, and Baumgärtner 2011). Other examples include cases of economic collapse with large and lasting adverse effects on society and civilization (e.g., Tainter 1990; Diamond 2005). This includes the case of ancient Egypt, where failures of the Nile floods caused great famines that imperiled Nile civilizations (e.g., Shaw 2000; Marriner et al. 2012). This also includes widespread droughts that contributed to the collapse of Classic Mayan civilization in Central America between 800 to 1000 AD (Gill 2000; Webster 2002; Medina-Elizalde and Rohling 2012). Adverse weather shocks remain relevant today as they threaten food production and food security around the world (e.g., Headey 2011; Nelson et al. 2014; Kalkuhl, von Braun, and Torero 2016). In these examples, the shocks are all undesirable. But the assessment of these situations can be challenging for two reasons: (a) such adverse scenarios are not very common, and (b) the dynamics of the underlying process is often complex and poorly understood. This suggests two useful directions of inquiry. First, we need to refine our tools used in dynamic analysis. Second, we need to explore applications that may provide new insights into economic dynamics. These two directions are key motivations for this chapter.

This chapter studies nonlinear dynamics in economics. It makes three contributions. First, the analysis evaluates the linkages between stochastic dynamics and the characterization of resilience and traps. Resilience means good odds of escaping from undesirable zones of instability toward zones that are more desirable. Traps mean low odds of escaping from zones that are both undesirable and stable. As such, resilience is desirable but traps are not. As noted above, the measurement and evaluation of dynamics associated with traps or resilience remains difficult (e.g., Barrett and Constas 2014). Our analysis focuses on identifying zones of stability/instability that provides a good basis to evaluate the resilience of a system and the presence of traps.

Second, the investigation of resilience and traps requires a refined approach to the study of stochastic dynamics, with a special focus on representations that allow for flexible dynamic response to shocks. The chapter relies on a threshold quantile autoregressive (TQAR) model (Galvao, Montes-Rojas, and Olmo 2011; Chavas and Di Falco 2017). The TQAR model is empirically tractable. And it is flexible: it allows dynamics to vary with both current shocks and past states. As such, a TQAR model can be used to assess how dynamics can differ across situations (as reflected by different shocks and different states). This makes it particularly appropriate for our purpose.

A third contribution is to illustrate the usefulness of our approach in an application to the dynamics of an agroecosystem. Our empirical analysis uses historical data on wheat yield in Kansas during the period 1885–2012. Historically, the western Great Plains have experienced many periods of severe drought (Burnette and Stahle 2013). The worse drought occurred in the 1930s leading to the Dust Bowl, a major American environmental catastrophe (Hornbeck 2012). Coupled with intensive land use, the drought led to major crop failure, wind erosion, and dust storms. The impact was particularly severe in Kansas, where land erosion contributed to significant decrease in land value and agricultural productivity (Hornbeck 2012). The short-run response to the environmental destruction was mostly population migration away from the affected areas, but the long-run effects were major and lasting. Hornbeck (2012) documents that soil erosion due to the Dust Bowl contributed to a decline in land value up to 30 percent in the long term. Wheat being the major crop in Kansas (USDA 2015), studying Kansas wheat yield provides a great case study of the dynamic response to environmental shocks. Of special interest are the effects of extreme shocks both in the short run and in the long run. In the context of wheat yield, our analysis identifies a zone of instability in the presence of successive adverse shocks. It also finds evidence of resilience. We associate the resilience with induced innovations in management and policy in response to adverse shocks. This stresses the importance of management and policy in the dynamic response to shocks.

The chapter is organized as follows. Section 8.2 presents a general model of stochastic dynamics and examines its linkages with traps and resilience. Section 8.3 introduces a threshold quantile autoregressive model and its flexible representation of the dynamic effects of shocks. Section 8.4 presents an econometric application to the dynamics of wheat productivity in Kansas. Implications and discussion of the results are the topic of sections 8.5 and 8.6. Finally, section 8.7 concludes.

8.2   Dynamics, Traps, and Resilience

Consider a dynamic system evolving according to the state equations

$$(1a) \qquad y_t = h(y_{t-1}, \ldots, y_{t-p}, z_t),$$

$$(1b) \qquad z_t = g(y_{t-1}, \ldots, y_{t-p}; z_{t-1}, \ldots, z_{t-p}),$$

where $y_t \in \mathbb{R}$ measures payoff at time t, z_t is a vector of variables affecting the system with dynamics given in equation (1b), and $p \geq 1$. Equations (1a) and (1b) provide a general representation of dynamics, allowing for joint dynamics in payoff y_t and in the state variables z_t. After successive substitutions of equation (1b), note that equation (1a) can be alternatively written as

$$(2) \quad y_t = h\left(y_{t-1}, y_{t-2}, \ldots, g\left(y_{t-1}, y_{t-2}, \ldots; z_{t-1}, z_{t-2}, \ldots\right)\right)$$

$$= h(y_{t-1}, y_{t-2}, \ldots, g(y_{t-1}, y_{t-2}, \ldots; g(y_{t-2}, \ldots; z_{t-2}, \ldots), z_{t-2}, \ldots))$$

$$= \ldots$$

$$= f_0(y_{t-1}, y_{t-2}, \ldots; y_0, z_0)$$

where (y_0, z_0) are initial conditions, which we take as given. Assume that the effects of lagged values of y_{t-j} on y_t in equation (2) become negligible for all $j > m$. It follows that equation (2) can be written as

$$(3) \qquad y_t = f(y_{t-1}, \ldots, y_{t-m}, e_t),$$

and e_t is a random variable representing unobservable effects at time t. We assume that e_t is identically and independently distributed[1] with a given distribution function.

Equation (3) is an mth order stochastic difference equation representing economic dynamics under general conditions. Comparing equations (1) and (3), equations (1a) and (1b) are structural equations describing how the system evolves over time, while equation (3) is a reduced-form equation of the same system. While equation (3) does not reflect structural information about the system, it has two advantages: (a) it provides a valid representation of the system dynamics, and (b) it does not require information about the variables z_t. This is a significant advantage when some of the dynamic factors affecting payoff are not observable. For this reason, our analysis will focus on the reduced-form representation (3).

Note that equation (3) can be written as the first-order difference equation

$$(4) \qquad w_t \equiv \begin{bmatrix} y_t \\ \vdots \\ y_{t-m+1} \end{bmatrix} = \begin{bmatrix} f(y_{t-1}, \ldots, y_{t-m}, e_t) \\ \vdots \\ y_{t-m+1} \end{bmatrix} \equiv H(w_{t-1}, e_t)$$

where $w_t \in \mathbb{R}_+^m$. Equation (4) can be used to characterize the nature of dynamics. Under differentiability, let $DH(w_{t-1}, e_t) = \partial H(w_{t-1}, e_t) / \partial w_{t-1}$ be an $(m \times m)$ matrix. Denote the characteristic roots of $DH(w_{t-1}, e_t)$ by $[\lambda_1(w_{t-1}, e_t), \ldots, \lambda_m(w_{t-1}, e_t)]$ where $|\lambda_1(w_{t-1}, e_t)| \geq \ldots \geq |\lambda_m(w_{t-1}, e_t)|$, $|\lambda_j|$ being the modulus of the jth root, $j = 1, \ldots, m$, and λ_1 being the dominant root.

Where equation (3) is linear in $(y_{t-1}, \ldots, y_{t-m})$, the system exhibits linear dynamics. In this case, the matrix DH is constant and so are its roots $(\lambda_1, \ldots, \lambda_m)$. Consider for a moment a situation where e_t is constant for all t. Then, under linear dynamics, the system is globally stable (in the sense that $\lim_{t \to \infty} y_t = y^e$ for any initial condition y_0) if $|\lambda_1| < 1$ (Hasselblatt and Katok 2003). Alternatively, the system would be unstable if $|\lambda_1| > 1$. When λ_1 is real, the dynamics of y_t has a forward path that is $\{\begin{smallmatrix}\text{exponential} \\ \text{oscillatory}\end{smallmatrix}\}$ when $\lambda_1\{\begin{smallmatrix}>0 \\ <0\end{smallmatrix}\}$. And when λ_1 is complex, then $\lambda_1 = a + b\sqrt{-1}$ and the system exhibits cyclical dynamics, with a cycle of period $[2\pi / arctg(b / a)]$.

In the general case where equation (3) is nonlinear in $(y_{t-1}, \ldots, y_{t-m})$, the system exhibits nonlinear dynamics. Under nonlinear dynamics, the forward path of y_t can exhibit a variety of dynamic patterns. For example, holding

---

1. Note that assuming serial independence of e_t is not restrictive since any serial correlation can be captured by the dynamic equation for z_t in equation (1b).

e_t constant for all t, y_t can eventually reach a unique steady state, it can have multiple steady states, it can exhibit limit cycles, or it can be chaotic (e.g., May 1976). Situations of multiple steady-state equilibria have been of interest. Multiple steady states $(y_1^e, \ldots, y_M^e)$ would arise if $\lim_{t \to \infty} y_t = y_j^e$ when $y_0 \in S_j$, $j = 1, \ldots, M$, where $M > 1$ and $(S_1, \ldots, S_M)$ is a partition of $\mathbb{R}$. In this context, the set S_j is the attractor of point y_j^e, $j = 1, \ldots, M$, as having initial condition y_0 in S_j eventually leads to y_j^e, $j = 1, \ldots, M$. When a steady state y_j^e is identified as being "undesirable," it means that it is good to avoid being in the set S_j. Examples include cases of ecological collapse in ecology (Holling 1973) and poverty trap in economics (Barrett and Carter 2013; Kraay and McKenzie 2014).

Under nonlinear dynamics, both $DH(w_{t-1}, e_t)$ and the dominant root $\lambda_1(w_{t-1}, e_t)$ depend on the evaluation point (w_{t-1}, e_t). In general, $\ln(|\lambda_1(w_{t-1}, e_t)|)$ measures the rate of divergence in y_t along forward paths in the neighborhood of (w_{t-1}, e_t) (Hasselblatt and Katok 2003). In this context, the dynamic properties just discussed still apply but only locally, that is, in the neighborhood of (w_{t-1}, e_t): the dynamics is locally stable if the dominant root satisfies $|\lambda_1(w_{t-1}, e_t)| < 1$, and it is locally unstable if $|\lambda_1(w_{t-1}, e_t)| > 1$. We will make use of these local properties in our empirical analysis below.

The analysis of dynamics becomes more challenging in the stochastic case: the random vector e_t in equation (3) affects the path of y_t over time. This is relevant when e_t represents unanticipated shocks. In this context, a key question is: What is the dynamic response of the system (3) to a shock e_t? This is the essence of the concept of resilience. A resilient system is defined as a system that can recover quickly from a shock (Holling 1973). This gains importance in the presence of adverse shocks (Di Falco and Chavas 2008; Chavas and Di Falco 2017). For example, in ecology, a resilient system would recover quickly from an adverse shock by moving away from undesirable situations and toward more desirable ones, but a nonresilient system may collapse. Similarly, in economics, a resilient household would recover quickly from an adverse income shock, but a nonresilient household would not (e.g., Barrett and Constas 2014). While adverse shocks always have negative short-term effects, resilience means such effects would eventually disappear in the longer term. But nonresilient systems would behave differently: they would see persistent adverse long-term effects.

The dominant root $\lambda_1(w_{t-1}, e_t)$ provides useful insights on system dynamics. We discuss three cases. First, consider the case where $\lambda_1(w_{t-1}, e_t)$ is close to 0 for all (w_{t-1}, e_t). This system would exhibit little dynamics, and any shock would have minor or no long-term effects. In a second case, assume that $|\lambda_1(w_{t-1}, e_t)|$ is positive but less than 1 for all (w_{t-1}, e_t). Then, there would be a dynamic response to any shock. But having $|\lambda_1(w_{t-1}, e_t)| < 1$ means that the impact of a shock would die down over time and eventually disappear in the long term. In this case, the magnitude of the dominant root remains useful. Having $|\lambda_1(w_{t-1}, e_t)|$ close to 0 (close to 1) means a rapid (slow) decay of the temporal effects of a shock. In other words, a rise in $|\lambda_1 (w_{t-1}, e_t)| \in (0, 1)$ corresponds to stronger impacts of a shock in the intermediate term. Third, consider the case where $|\lambda_1 (w_{t-1}, e_t)|$ is greater than 1 for some (w_{t-1}, e_t). As discussed above, this corresponds to local instability in the neighborhood of (w_{t-1}, e_t). A possible situation is that this local instability varies with the neighborhood. To illustrate, consider a system where N_1, N_2, N_3 are three different neighborhoods where $|\lambda_1 (w_{t-1}, e_t)| < 1$ when $(w_{t-1}, e_t) \in N_1 \cup N_3$, but $|\lambda_1 (w_{t-1}, e_t)| > 1$ when $(w_{t-1}, e_t) \in N_2$. This system exhibits local stability in neighborhoods N_1 and N_3, but local instability in neighborhood N_2. Local instability in N_2 means that dynamics would tend to move y_t away from N_2. In situations where N_2 is surrounded by N_1 and N_3, this would identify points in N_2 as tipping points, that is, as points where y_t would tend to escape from as they move toward locally stable neighborhoods. In this case, knowing which locally stable neighborhood (N_1 or N_3) is more likely to be visited would be of interest. For example, if being in N_1 is seen as being undesirable, then an escape from N_2 to N_3 would be seen as a better scenario than moving from N_2 to N_1.

These patterns are illustrated in figure 8.1 under four scenarios. Figure 8.1 shows how $|\lambda_1|$ can vary with e_t, where higher (lower) values of e_t are interpreted as favorable (unfavorable) shocks. The first scenario is the case where λ_1 is constant. This occurs when the dynamic is represented by a linear autoregressive (AR) process, in which case the dynamic response to shocks does not depend on the situation considered. Scenarios 2–4 are associated with nonlinear dynamics where λ_1 is not constant. Scenario 2 exhibits a pattern where $|\lambda_1|$ has an inverted U-shape with respect to e_t, with a zone of instability (where $|\lambda_1| > 1$) surrounded by two zones of stability (where $|\lambda_1| < 1$): a favorable zone (where e_t is high) and an unfavorable zone (where e_t is low). It means that the forward path of y_t would tend to escape from the instable zone. And in the case where there is a low probability of escaping from the unfavorable stable zone, this would identify this zone as a trap. Scenario 3 shows a situation where there is a zone of instability, but it occurs only for low values of e_t. This is an example of resilience where the dynamics would move the system away from unfavorable outcomes. Finally, Scenario 4 shows a situation where there is a zone of instability but it occurs only for high values of e_t. This represents a collapse where the dynamics move the system away from favorable outcomes. These examples illustrate that many patterns of dynamics are possible.[2] Note that the dynamics would gain additional complexities when we note that $|\lambda_1 (w_{t-1}, e_t)|$ can vary with both e_t and w_{t-1}. The empirical challenge to evaluating these complexities is addressed in section 8.3.

---

2. Indeed, there are many possible scenarios (e.g., Azariadis and Stachurski 2005). Other possible scenarios (not shown in figure 8.1) are when there is a zone of stability surrounded by zones of instability, or when instability is global (e.g., under chaos).

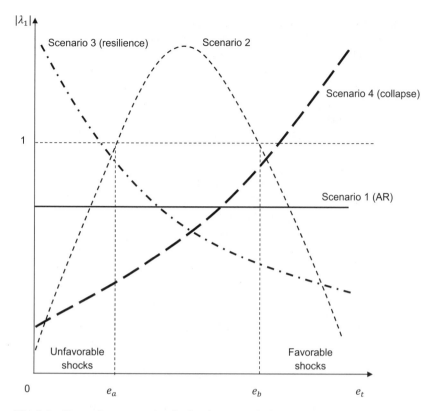

Fig. 8.1   Dynamic patterns for the dominant root $|\lambda_1|$

Under stochastic dynamics, a related issue is: What are the implications of dynamics for the distribution of y_t in the long run? To address this question, note that the dynamics in equation (3) can be alternatively written in terms of a Markov chain (Billingsley 1961; Meyn and Tweedie 1993). Consider partitioning the space $\mathbb{R}$ into K mutually exclusive intervals $\{v_1, \ldots, v_K\}$. To illustrate, consider the case where $m = 1$. Letting $M = \{1, \ldots, K\}$, we have

(5a) $\text{Prob}\,(y_t \in v_i) = \displaystyle\sum_{j \in M} \{\text{Prob}\,[y_t \in v_i \mid y_t = f(y_{t-1}, e_t), y_{t-1} \in v_j]$

$$\text{Prob}[y_{t-1} \in v_j]\}$$

for $i \in M$. Under time invariance, equation (5a) can be written as the Markov chain model

(5b) $$p_t = A p_{t-1}$$

where $p_t = (p_{t,1}, \ldots, p_{t,K})'$ is a $(K \times 1)$ vector with $p_{t,j} = \text{Prob}\,(y_t \in v_j)$, $j \in M$, and A is a $(K \times K)$ matrix of Markov transition probabilities. The

Markov matrix A has a dominant root equal to 1. Under time-invariant transition probabilities, when this dominant root is unique, the dynamic system (5b) has a unique stationary equilibrium given by $p^e = \lim_{t \to \infty} p_t$ for all initial conditions p_0. This provides a basis to evaluate the long-run distribution of y. This long-run distribution will depend on the underlying dynamics. Again, the long-run distribution of y can exhibit many patterns (Azariadis and Stachurski 2005). For example, the long-run probability density of y_t could exhibit a single peak with little skewness (e.g., under Gaussian shocks and a linear AR process). Alternatively, it could be skewed when the dynamics implies an escape from low outcomes (under resilience) or from high outcomes (under collapse). Finally, it could exhibit multiple peaks (e.g., when a system tends to escape from a zone of instability toward surrounding zones of stability, leading to a bimodal density in the long run). Again, these examples indicate that many patterns of long-run distribution are possible, stressing the importance of a flexible approach in the empirical investigation of dynamics.

8.3   Econometric Analysis of Stochastic Dynamics

Consider the case where equation (3) takes the general form $y_t = f(y_{t-1}, \ldots, y_{t-p}, x_t, e_t)$ where x_t is a vector of explanatory variables affecting y_t at time t. Define the conditional distribution function of y_t as $F(v \mid y_{t-1}, \ldots, y_{t-m}, x_t) = \text{Prob}[y_t \leq v \mid y_{t-1}, \ldots, y_{t-m}, x_t] = \text{Prob}[f(y_{t-1}, \ldots, y_{t-m}, x_t, e_t) \leq v]$. The distribution function $F(v \mid y_{t-1}, \ldots, y_{t-m}, x_t)$ is conditional on lagged values $(y_{t-1}, \ldots, y_{t-m})$ and on x_t. Define the associated conditional quantile function as the inverse function $q(r \mid y_{t-1}, \ldots, y_{t-m}, x_t) \equiv \inf_v \{v : F(v \mid y_{t-1}, \ldots, y_{t-m}, x_t) \geq r\}$ where $r \in (0,1)$ is the rth quantile. When $r = 0.5$, this includes as special case the conditional median $q(0.5 \mid y_{t-1}, \ldots, y_{t-m}, x_t)$. Both the distribution function $F(v \mid y_{t-1}, \ldots, y_{t-m}, x_t)$ and the quantile function $q(r \mid y_{t-1}, \ldots, y_{t-m}, x_t)$ are generic: they provide a general characterization of the dynamics of y. In the rest of the chapter, we will make extensive use of the quantile function $q(r \mid y_{t-1}, \ldots, y_{t-m}, x_t)$ in the analysis of the dynamics of y_t.

Relying on the conditional quantile function $q(r \mid y_{t-1}, \ldots, y_{t-m}, x_t)$, we focus our attention on the case where the conditional quantile function takes the form $q(r \mid y_1, \ldots, y_{t-m}, x_t) = X(y_{t-1}, \ldots, y_{t-m}, x_t)\beta(r), r \in (0,1)$, where $X(\cdot)$ is a $(1 \times K)$ vector and $\beta(r) \in \mathbb{R}^K$ is a $(K \times 1)$ vector of parameters. This restricts the analysis to situations where conditional quantiles are linear in the parameters $\beta(r)$. This specification allows the parameters $\beta(r)$ to vary across quantiles, thus providing a flexible representation of the underlying distribution function and its dynamics. In addition, the function $X(y_{t-1}, \ldots, y_{t-m}, x_t)$ can possibly be nonlinear in $(y_{t-1}, \ldots, y_{t-m})$, thus allowing for nonlinear dynamics.

In the analysis presented below, we consider an econometric model specification of the form

(6) $$q(r \mid y_1, \ldots, y_{t-m}, x_t) = \beta_0(r, x_t) + \sum_{j=1}^{m} \beta_j(r, x_t) y_{t-j}.$$

To illustrate the flexibility of this specification, note that it reduces to a standard autoregressive model of order m, AR(m) (e.g., see Enders 2010), when $\beta_j(r, x_t) = \beta_j, j = 1, \ldots, m$, for all $r \in (0, 1)$ and all x_t, that is, when the autoregression parameters β_j's are constant and do not vary across quantiles. When the intercept $\beta_0(r, x_t)$ varies across quantiles r, this provides a flexible representation of the distribution function (e.g., it allows for any variance, skewness, and kurtosis). Also, when $\beta_0(r, x_t)$ varies with x_t, this allows x_t to shift the intercept. But an AR(m) model is restrictive in two important ways: (a) it is restricted to linear dynamics in the mean; and (b) it does not provide a flexible representation of dynamics in variance, skewness, or kurtosis. Such limitations have stimulated more general specifications capturing dynamics in variance (e.g., the generalized autoregressive conditional heteroscedastic [GARCH] model proposed by Bollerslev [1986]) and nonlinear dynamics (e.g., Markov switching models, Hamilton [1989]), threshold autoregressive (TAR) models (Tong 1990), and smooth transition autoregressive (STAR) models (Van Dijk, Teräsvirta, and Franses 2002).

When $\beta_j(r, x_t) = \beta_j(r), j = 1, \ldots, m$, the above specification reduces to the quantile autoregressive model QAR(m) proposed by Koenker and Xiao (2006). Unlike an AR(m), the QAR(m) model allows the autoregression parameters $\beta_j(r)$ to vary across quantiles $r \in (0, 1)$, thus permitting dynamics to differ in different parts of the distribution. In the more general case, $\beta_j(r, x_t)$ can vary with the explanatory variables x_t, allowing economic conditions to affect dynamics.

In addition, considering the case where the state space $\mathbb{R}$ is partitioned into K subsets $\mathbb{R} = \{S_1, \ldots, S_K\}$, define $d_{k,t-j} = \{{}_0^1\}$ when $y_{t-j} {\{{}^{\in S_k}_{\notin S_k}\}}, k = 1, \ldots, K, j = 1, \ldots, m$. Depending on the value taken by the lagged variable y_{t-j}, this identifies K regimes $(S_1, \ldots, S_K)$ with the $d_{k,t-j}$'s being variables capturing the switching between regimes, $j = 1, \ldots, m$. When x_t includes the variables $d_{k,t-j}$'s, this allows the autoregression parameter $\beta_j(r, x_t)$ to vary across the K regimes, $j = 1, \ldots, m$. The general case corresponds to a threshold quantile autoregressive (TQAR[m]) model where, for each lag j, $\beta_j(r, x_t)$ can vary both across quantiles $r \in (0, 1)$ and across regimes (Galvao, Montes-Rojas, and Olmo 2011; Chavas and Di Falco 2017). When $\beta_j(r, x_t) = \beta_j(x_t), j = 1, \ldots, m$ (i.e., when the autoregression parameters do not vary across quantiles), a TQAR(m) reduces to a threshold autoregressive (TAR[m]) model (see Tong 1990). And as noted above, a TQAR(m) model includes as special cases a QAR(m) model (obtained when $\beta_j(r, x_t) = \beta_j(r)$, $j = 1, \ldots, m$), as well as an AR(m) model (obtained when $\beta_j(r, x_t) = \beta_j$,

$j = 1, \ldots, m$). In general, a TQAR(m) model is very flexible at representing nonlinear dynamics. Indeed, in a TQAR(m) model and for each lag j, the autoregression parameter $\beta_j(r, x_t)$ can vary with the value of the current variable y_t (as captured by the quantile r), with the value of the lagged variable y_{t-j} (as captured by the regime-switching variables $d_{k,t-j}$'s), and with the value of other variables in x_t. A TQAR(m) model will be used below in our empirical investigation of dynamics.

Consider a sample of n observations on (y, X), where X is a vector of explanatory variables and $q(r \mid X) = X\beta(r), r \in (0, 1)$. Denote the ith observation by $(y_i, X_i), i \in N \equiv \{1, \ldots, n\}$. For a given quantile $r \in (0, 1)$ and following Koenker (2005), the quantile regression estimate of $\beta(r)$ is

$$(7) \qquad \hat{\beta}(r) \in argmin_{\beta}\{\sum_{i \in N} \rho_r(y_i - X_i\beta)\},$$

where $\rho_r(w) = w[r - I(w < 0)]$ and $I(\cdot)$ is the indicator function. As discussed in Koenker (2005), the quantile estimator $\hat{\beta}(r)$ in equation (7) is a minimum-distance estimator with desirable statistical properties. The quantile estimator (7) applied to the dynamic specification (6) will provide the basis for our empirical analysis presented next.

8.4   An Application to the Dynamics of Wheat Productivity

Our investigation proceeds studying the dynamics of wheat productivity in Kansas. The analysis involves annual wheat yield in Kansas over the period 1885–2012 (USDA 2015). This covers the period of the American Dust Bowl (in the 1930s) when the US Great Plains were affected by a major environmental catastrophe. The Dust Bowl was the joint product of adverse weather shocks (a major drought) and poor agricultural management. The Dust Bowl is remembered by two of its main features: (a) severe drought leading to crop failure and triggering massive migration out of the western Great Plains, and (b) soil and wind erosion (Hornbeck 2012). The Dust Bowl had short-term effects on agricultural production (as drought generated crop failure). But it also had longer effects: soil erosion had lasting adverse effects on land productivity (Hornbeck 2012). Kansas has been the leading wheat producing state in the United States (USDA 2015). As noted in the introduction, this makes studying wheat yield dynamics in Kansas a great case study of the response of productivity to environmental shocks.

The data on wheat yield (t / ha) in Kansas over the period 1885–2012 were obtained from the United States Department of Agriculture (USDA 2015). They are presented in figure 8.2. Figure 8.2 shows three interesting features. First, as expected, the early 1930s (corresponding to the Dust Bowl) is a period exhibiting low yields. Second, wheat yields have been trending upward, especially after 1940, indicating the presence of significant productivity growth and technological progress over the last seventy years. Third,

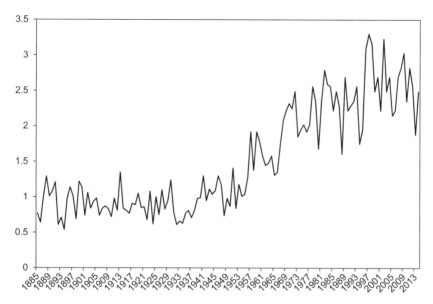

Fig. 8.2   Kansas wheat yield (ton per ha)

there is much variability in yield over time, reflecting the impact of various environmental shocks (including weather shocks).

Our investigation explores the distribution of wheat yield as if we were farmers. Since weather shocks are mostly unpredictable, it means that the distribution of yield is evaluated ex ante at the beginning of the growing season, that is, before weather shocks become observable. In the ex ante assessment, the yield distribution is thus *unconditional* with respect to *all* unobservable factors affecting farm productivity (including weather effects). In this context, the investigation of dynamic adjustments in Kansas wheat yield is presented next.

8.4.1   Preliminary Econometric Analysis

We start with a simple analysis of yield dynamics. With wheat yield y_t as the dependent variable, we first estimate simple autoregressive models. Table 8.1 presents the estimation results for alternative model specifications. Two time-trend variables are included in all models: a general time trend t = year − 2000 and a time trend t_1 = max $\{0, year − T_1\}$ where t_1 captures technological progress after the year T_1. The models include autoregressive models of order m, AR(m), with m = 1, 2. Using a grid search, the value T_1 = 1935 was chosen as it provided the best fit to the data. The AR(1) model shows that lag-1 coefficient is 0.703 and highly significant. This documents the presence of dynamics in yield adjustments. The lagged-2 coefficient in the AR(2) model is not statistically significant. A formal Wald test of the

Table 8.1   **Estimates of autoregressive models**

Parameters	AR(1)	AR(2)	TAR(1)	TAR(2)
Intercept	0.703***	0.706***	0.543***	0.540**
y_{t-1}	0.236***	0.219**	0.409**	0.463**
y_{t-2}		0.034		−0.039
$d_{1,t-1} * y_{t-1}$			0.098*	0.111*
$d_{3,t-1} * y_{t-1}$			−0.010	−0.018
$d_{1,t-2} * y_{t-2}$				−0.020
$d_{3,t-2} * y_{t-2}$				−0.011
t	−0.002	−0.003	−0.002	−0.002
t_1	0.0023***	0.024***	0.017**	0.017**
R^2	0.857	0.856	0.859	0.860

***Significant at the 1 percent level.
**Significant at the 5 percent level.
*Significant at the 10 percent level.

AR(1) model as a null hypothesis against the AR(2) model gave a p-value of 0.709, indicating that there is no significant dynamics going beyond one-period lag.

Table 8.1 also reports threshold autoregressive models (TAR[m]) allowing the autoregression parameters to vary across three regimes (d_1, d_2, d_3). The regimes are defined such that $d_{i,t} = \{{}^{1}_{0}\}$ when $y_t{}^{\in S_{i,t}}_{\notin S_{i,t}}$, i = 1, 2, 3, with $S_{1,t} = [-\infty, b_{1,t}]$, $S_{2,t} = (b_{1,t}, b_{3,t}]$ and $S_{3,t} = (b_{3,t}, \infty]$, $b_{1,t}$, and $b_{3,t}$ being, respectively, the 1/3 and 2/3 quantile of the yield distribution obtained from the AR(1) model reported in table 8.1. Thus, regime 1 means that yield is in the 1/3 lower quantile of the yield distribution, and regime 3 means that yield is in the 1/3 upper quantile of the yield distribution. In this context, having $d_{1,t-1} = 1$ corresponds to situations of low lag-1 yield where y_{t-1} is in regime 1. And having $d_{3,t-1} = 1$ corresponds to situations of high lag-1 yield where y_{t-1} is in regime 3. In TAR(m) models, the autoregression parameters are allowed to shift across the three regimes. For a TAR(1), table 8.1 shows that the lag-1 coefficient is 0.409 in regime 2, 0.507 in regime 1, and 0.407 in regime 3. Importantly, the difference in coefficients between regime 1 and regime 2 (0.098) is statistically significant at the 10 percent level. This provides statistical evidence that yield dynamics differ across regimes. This is our first hint of nonlinear dynamics. We also estimated a TAR(2) model. As reported in table 8.1, the lag-2 coefficients of the TAR(2) model are not statistically significant. A formal Wald test of the TAR(1) model as null hypothesis against a TAR(2) model gave a p-value of 0.959. Again, this indicates no significant dynamics going beyond one-period lag. On that basis, we continue our analysis based on autoregressive models of order 1.

Note that all estimated models reported in table 8.1 show that the overall time trend t is not statistically significant, but the effect of the post-1935

Table 8.2   **Estimates of threshold quantile autoregressive model TQAR(1) for selected quantiles**

Parameters	Quantile				
	$r = 0.1$	$r = 0.3$	$r = 0.5$	$r = 0.7$	$r = 0.9$
Intercept	−0.003	0.481**	0.747***	1.036***	1.409***
y_{t-1}	0.687***	0.407	0.272	−0.036	−0.341
$d_{1,t-1} * y_{t-1}$	0.234***	0.086	−0.015	−0.026	−0.007
$d_{3,t-1} * y_{t-1}$	−0.067***	−0.057	−0.051	0.125	0.156
t	0.000	−0.003	−0.005**	−0.005**	−0.001
t_1	0.003	0.018**	0.027***	0.035***	0.040***

Note: Hypothesis testing is conducted using bootstrapping.
***Significant at the 1 percent level.
**Significant at the 5 percent level.
*Significant at the 10 percent level.

time trend t_1 is always positive and statistically significant. This reflects the presence of significant improvements in agricultural technology over the last seventy years.[3] Interestingly, the coefficient of the t_1 variable is smaller in the TAR(1) model (0.017) compared to the AR(1) model (0.023). This indicates that productivity growth interacts with changing dynamics across regimes.

8.4.2   Quantile Dynamics

Our preliminary analysis found statistical support for a TAR(1) specification. A discussed in section 8.3, while a TAR model allows the autoregression parameters to vary across regimes, it does not allow them to vary across quantiles of the current yield distribution. We now extend the analysis by considering a threshold quantile autoregressive model. As noted, a TQAR model provides a flexible representation of nonlinear dynamics by allowing autoregression parameters to change both across regimes and across quantiles. This section focuses on an ex ante analysis of quantile dynamics. An ex post quantile analysis (conditional on weather shocks) is presented in the next section.

Table 8.2 reports parameter estimates of a TQAR(1) model applied to wheat yield for selected quantiles (0.1, 0.3, 0.5, 0.7, 0.9). The variables are the same as in the TAR(1) model reported in table 8.1. Table 8.2 shows how the dynamics vary across quantiles. We tested the null hypothesis that the regression parameters are the same across quantiles (0.1, 0.5, 0.9). With 10 degrees of freedom, the chi-square test value was 5.703 with a p-value less

---

3. Note that technological progress involves many factors, including improved wheat varieties, increased use of fertilizer, greater reliance on irrigation, and improved farm management practices.

than 0.01. This implies a strong rejection of the TAR(1) model in favor of the TQAR(1) model. Thus, we find statistical evidence that the regression parameters vary across quantiles. Table 8.2 shows that the lag-1 coefficient under regime 2 is 0.687 at the 0.1 quantile. This coefficient is larger than for higher quantiles, indicating the presence of stronger dynamics in the lower tail of the yield distribution. Table 8.2 also reports that, for the 0.1 quantile, the lag-1 coefficient differs between regime 1 (where $d_{1,t-1} = 1$) and regime 2. The difference is 0.234. Using bootstrapping for hypothesis testing, we find this difference to be statistically significant at the 1 percent level. This provides evidence against a QAR model and in favor of a TQAR specification. The lag-1 coefficient for the 0.1 quantile is 0.921 under regime 1 (when lagged yield is low), which is much higher than under the other regimes. This documents the presence of much stronger dynamics in the lower tail of yield distribution *and* when lagged yield is low. This is one of our key findings: dynamic yield adjustments to shocks become quantitatively very different under repeated adverse shocks. As we show below, this is a scenario where adjustments also become qualitatively different.

In addition, table 8.2 shows the effects of the t_1 trend variable are much stronger in the upper tail of the distribution. This indicates that technological progress has contributed to a rapid increase in the upper tail of the yield distribution. But such effects are weaker in the lower tail of the distribution. This reflects significant shifts in the shape of the yield distribution over time (as further discussed below).

To conduct robustness checks, we explored issues related to the number of lags used in our dynamic analysis. While table 8.2 reports estimates for a TQAR(1) model, we also estimated a TQAR(2) model. In a way consistent with the results shown in table 8.1, we found that none of the lag-2 coefficients were statistically significant. This indicates that the TQAR(1) model provides an appropriate representation of dynamics. On that basis, the analysis presented in the rest of the chapter focuses on a model with one-period lag.

8.5   Implications

Our estimated TQAR(1) model provides a refined representation of the nonlinear dynamics of yield. As noted in section 8.3, it allows for flexible patterns of stability and instability. To explore in more detail the nature and implications of these patterns, we estimate our TQAR(1) model for *all* quantiles, thus providing a representation of the whole distribution of wheat yield and its dynamics.

First, we use our TQAR(1) model estimated for all quantiles to evaluate the distribution function of wheat yield at selected sample points. The resulting simulated distribution is presented in figure 8.3 for selected years (1950, 1970, 1990, 2010). As expected, over time, the distribution shifts strongly

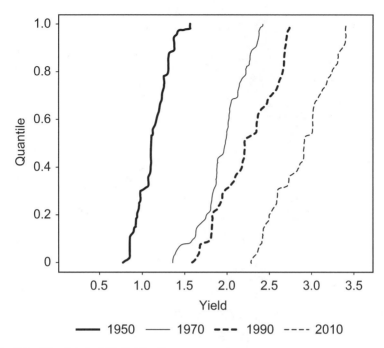

Fig. 8.3 Simulated yield distribution

to the right, reflecting the major effects of technological progress on agricultural productivity. Interestingly, the yield distribution exhibits greater spread (and thus greater risk exposure) in 2010 than in previous years, indicating an increase in the magnitude of unpredictable shocks (possibly due to climate change).

Next, using equation (4), we examine the dynamic properties of our estimated TQAR(1) by evaluating the associated root $\lambda = \partial H / \partial y_{t-1}$. Under nonlinear dynamics, this root varies with the situation considered. As discussed in section 8.2, dynamics is locally stable (unstable) at points where $\lambda < 1 (> 1)$. We calculated the root λ for all quantiles and all three regimes. The results are reported in figure 8.4. Figure 8.4 documents the patterns of nonlinear dynamics associated with our estimated TQAR(1) model. It shows three important results. First, from figure 8.4, the root λ is similar across all three regimes for quantiles greater than 0.3, but it exhibits different dynamics for lower quantiles (less than 0.3). More specifically, compared to other regimes, the root λ is larger under regime 1 (when lagged yield is low) *and* in the lower tail of the distribution. This is consistent with the discussion of table 8.2 presented in the previous section.

Second, figure 8.4 shows that the root λ remains in the unit circle (with $|\lambda| < 1$) in many situations, including regimes 2 and 3 (when lagged yield are *not* low) or the absence of adverse current shock (for quantiles greater than

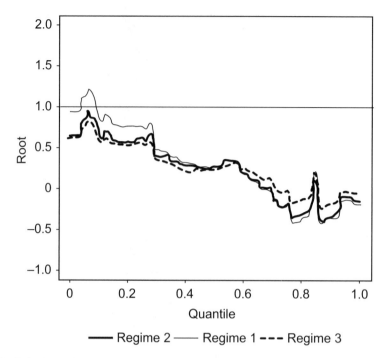

Fig. 8.4   **Root of the dynamic yield equation**

0.2). This implies that the system is locally stable in many situations, especially in situations excluding adverse shocks. This is an important result:
investigating dynamics in situations around or above the median could only
uncover evidence of local stability. As discussed in section 8.2, this would
preclude finding any evidence of traps.

Third, figure 8.4 shows that the root λ can be larger than 1 but only in
situations of successive adverse shocks, that is, when both y_t and y_{t-1} are in
the lower tail of the yield distribution. Associating $\lambda > 1$ with local instability, we thus find evidence of local instability in the presence of adverse
shocks. This has several implications. First, we have identified a zone of
local dynamic instability, that is, a zone of tipping points where the system
tends to escape from. Second, associating a zone of instability with successive adverse shocks is an important finding. This raises the question: Is the
zone of instability associated with resilience? Or is it associated with a trap
or collapse? It depends on the path of escape. As discussed in section 8.2, if
the escape from the zone of instability is toward more favorable situations,
the system would be characterized as resilient (e.g., as represented by Scenario 3 in figure 8.1). Alternatively, if the escape is toward more unfavorable
situations, the system may be experiencing a trap or a collapse (e.g., Scenario
4 in figure 8.1).

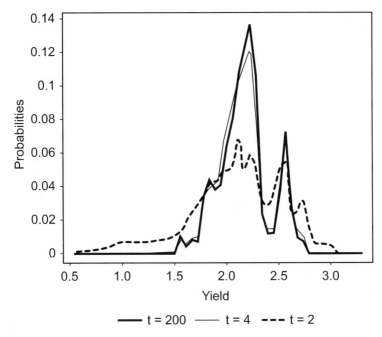

Fig. 8.5   Simulated probability function of wheat yield in the short run ($t = 2$), intermediate run ($t = 4$), and long run ($t = 200$)

In our case, the zone of instability occurs only under successive unfavorable shocks generating very low yields. It suggests that starting in this zone, there is only one place to go: toward higher yields. Thus, the zone of instability can be associated with a resilient system that tends to escape from low productivity toward higher productivity under adverse shocks. Indeed, figure 8.4 exhibits patterns that are similar to Scenario 3 in figure 8.1. To examine this issue in more detail, we consider the Markov chain representation of our TQAR(1) model, as given in equations (5a) and (5b). Using $K = 50$ and evaluated under conditions occurring in 1995, we obtained the Markov matrix A in equation (5b). The matrix A has a unique unit root, indicating that the Markov chain is stationary and has a long-run distribution. The second root of A has modulus 0.37, indicating a fairly fast adjustment toward the long-run distribution. The evolution of the probability function of wheat yield was simulated from equation (5b), starting from a uniform distribution over the range of the data. Starting at $t = 0$, the simulated probabilities are reported in figure 8.5 under three scenarios: in the short run (after 2 periods, $t = 2$), in the intermediate run (after 4 periods, $t = 4$), and in the long run (after 200 periods, $t = 200$). Figure 8.5 shows several important results. First, the adjustments toward the steady-state probability function occurs fairly quickly. Second, the simulated probability functions depart from the normal distribution in two ways: (a) they exhibit multiple peaks, and (b) they are skewed, with a left tail that is much longer than the right tail. Indeed, in all scenarios, Shapiro-Wilk tests of normality have a *p*-value less than 0.01, providing strong evidence of departure from normality. Third, figure 8.5 shows that the probability of being in the left tail of the probability function declines fast as one moves forward in time (as *t* goes from 2 to 4 to 200). This implies a dynamic escape from unfavorable events located in the lower tail of the distribution. Since escaping an unfavorable zone is the essence of resilience, if follows that figure 8.5 documents the presence of resilience. In other words, our estimated TQAR(1) model applied to wheat yield dynamics has two key characteristics: (a) a zone of instability occurs in the presence of successive unfavorable shocks, and (b) resilience arises as the underlying dynamic process tends to escape from this unfavorable zone. The significance of these findings is further discussed in section 8.8 below.

As discussed in section 8.2, the TQAR model reported in table 8.2 is a reduced-form model. While a reduced-form model provides a valid representation of dynamics, it does not provide structural information on the nature of dynamics. In the Kansas agroecosystem, a major source of shocks comes from the weather. Indeed, the Dust Bowl was the result of a major drought that hit the western Great Plains in the 1930s. This suggests evaluating a structural model where weather variables are explicit determinants of Kansas wheat yield. On that basis, we also specified and estimated a dynamic model of wheat yield including the effects of three weather variables: rainfall in the previous fall *rainf*, rainfall in the spring *rains*, and average temperature during the growing season *temp*. Data on these variables were obtained from Burnette, Stahle, and Mock (2010), Burnette and Stahle (2013), and the National Oceanographic and Atmospheric Administration (NOAA 2016).[4] These weather variables were introduced in the model both as intercept shifters and as interactions with lagged yield. These interaction effects allow yield dynamics to vary with weather conditions. Estimates of the associated quantile regression equation is presented in table 8A.1 in the appendix. As expected, table 8A.1 shows that weather has statistically significant effects on yield. Rainfall in the previous fall has a positive effect on yield, especially on the lower tail of the distribution. Temperature has a negative effect on yield through its interaction effect with lagged yield, especially in the upper tail of the distribution. This documents that both drought and high temperature have adverse effects on agricultural productivity. Such results are consistent with previous research (e.g., Tack Harri, and Coble 2012; Tack, Barkley, and Nalley 2015). Table 8A.1 also shows the presence of dynamics. Lagged yield has statistically significant effects on current yield either directly or through its interaction with temperature.

4. Rainfall is measured in millimeters and temperature in degree Celsius.

To evaluate the nature of dynamics in the structural model reported in table 8A.1, we calculated the root of the estimated dynamic process across quantiles. Interestingly, we found that the root varies between -0.2 and $+0.6$ depending on the evaluation point. The root is always in the unit circle for any quantile or any weather condition within the range of data. This implies global stability. Thus, the dynamic model reported in table 8A.1 does not show any evidence of instability. This contrasts with the reduced-form model reported in table 8.2 (which exhibits local instability as discussed above).[5] While this result is somewhat surprising, it has two important implications. First, since controlling for weather effects implies the disappearance of instability, it means that there is close association between instability and weather shocks. In other words, our reduced-form evidence of instability must be linked with weather shocks. Second, weather being mostly unpredictable, we do not expect much dynamics in the determination of weather shocks. This indicates that any linkage between weather and yield dynamics must be because of the dynamic response of management and policy to weather shocks. We expand on this interpretation below.

8.6 Discussion

From our reduced-form model, our first finding is about local dynamic instability arising, but only under unfavorable shocks. This is important. It suggests that a search for local instability is unlikely to be successful if the analysis focuses on "average conditions." This can be problematic in economic research to the extent that most econometric analyses involve estimating means or conditional means. While studying the properties of means and conditional means can be interesting, it neglects key information related to events located in the tails of the distribution. In a stochastic context, our findings indicate a need to expand analyses with a focus on dynamics associated with rare and unfavorable events. This is an intuitive argument. On the positive side, increasing resilience is about improving the odds of escaping the long-term effects of facing adverse shocks. On the negative side, avoiding collapse or traps is about reducing the odds of facing adverse conditions and increasing the odds of escaping toward better outcomes. All escape scenarios are about identifying local instability. Our TQAR model provides a good basis to support such inquiries.

Our second finding is also very interesting: applied to wheat yield dynamics, our analysis uncovered evidence of resilience as local instability tends to create an escape away from unfavorable events toward improved outcomes. But it also raises questions about the process supporting such dynamics. Below, we reflect on this process and the interpretations and implications of our findings.

5. Note that Chavas and Di Falco (2017) obtained a similar result for English wheat.

As noted above, our analysis has relied on an ex ante analysis of yield dynamics and focused on assessing the distribution of yield based on information available at the beginning of each growing season. Since weather conditions are mostly unpredictable, we treated the effects of rainfall and temperature during the growing season as part of the shocks represented by the yield distribution function. This raises the question: What constitutes an adverse shock? Much research has examined the determinants of wheat yield (e.g., Olmstead and Rhode 2011; Tack, Barkley, and Nalley 2015). Both rainfall and temperature are major factors affecting wheat yield (e.g., Tack, Barkley, and Nalley 2015; Chavas and Di Falco 2017). In particular, farming in the western Great Plains faces much rainfall uncertainty as it has experienced repeated periods of severe droughts (Burnette and Stahle 2013). One of the most severe droughts occurred in the 1930s: it led to massive crop failures and to the Dust Bowl. Because of the massive soil erosion it generated, the Dust Bowl is often seen as an environmental catastrophe (Hornbeck 2012). Yet, our evidence of resilience suggests a different interpretation.

First, the Dust Bowl induced significant changes in agricultural management and policy. A major federal policy change was the creation of the Soil Conservation Service (SCS) in 1935. The SCS played a major role in reducing the incidence of wind erosion in the western Great Plains (Hurt 1981). The circumstances under which the SCS was created are of interest. Starting in 1932, severe droughts caused widespread crop failure in the Great Plains, exposing the soil to blowing winds and generating large dust storms. On March 6, 1935, and again on March 21, 1935, dust clouds passed over Washington, DC, and darkened the sky as Congress was having hearings on soil conservation legislation. It motivated policymakers to act: the Soil Conservation Act was signed by President Roosevelt on April 27, 1935, creating the Soil Conservation Service in the USDA. This was an example of a fast policy response to a crisis.

The Dust Bowl also stimulated significant adjustments in agricultural management. The SCS established demonstration projects to persuade farmers to adopt more sustainable tillage and cropping practices (including contour plowing, terracing, strip cropping, planting drought resistant crops, and greater reliance on pasture). For participating farmers, the SCS programs contributed to improving farm practices, increasing land values, and boosting farm income (Hurt 1981). As a result, farmers shifted land from wheat into hay and pasture, and they implemented new soil conservation techniques (Hornbeck 2012, 1480). Such changes helped mitigate the adverse effects of severe droughts.

Second, the Dust Bowl did not start a process of desertification of the western Great Plains. On the contrary, cultivated farmland increased during the 1930s and 1940s (Hornbeck 2012, 1480–90). This indicates that the 1930s droughts stimulated major innovations in agricultural management and policy. To the extent that these changes reduced the adverse effects of droughts, they contributed to creating a more resilient agroecological system.

Thus, we associate our evidence of resilience with induced innovations in both policy and management that followed the Dust Bowl. This interpretation raises the question: What would have been the effects of the Dust Bowl without such innovations? Of course, this is a hypothetical scenario that we have not observed, but we can discuss what might have happened. First, our evidence of resilience would likely disappear. For example, without innovations, continued soil erosion may have led to the desertification of the western Great Plains. Under this scenario, the adverse long-term effects of the Dust Bowl assessed by Hornbeck (2012) would have been much worse. The agroecosystem of the western Great Plains may have collapsed. In this case, the zone of instability identified in figure 8.4 would move to the right. In the context of figure 8.1, this would correspond to a move from Scenario 3 (resilience) toward Scenario 2 or even toward Scenario 4 (collapse). The process of collapse would occur when adverse shocks put the system in the zone of instability with a tendency to move toward lower outcomes (e.g., Scenario 4 in figure 8.1). Figure 8.5 would also change. Under collapse, the lower tail of the yield distribution would become much thicker. And the probability function may exhibit multiple peaks in the lower tail, with a new peak possibly rising in the extreme lower tail (corresponding to collapse). In this case, a key issue would be whether "valleys" exist in between peaks in the probability density function. The presence of valleys would indicate that there are positive probabilities of escaping the lower tail of the distribution. Alternatively, the absence of such valleys would mean any collapse obtained under adverse shocks would be irreversible.

Of course, these hypothetical scenarios differ from the ones reported in figures 8.4 and 8.5. Yet, our discussion has three important implications. First, evaluating resilience/collapse/traps must focus on the nature of dynamics under adverse shocks. As noted above, just knowing what is happening "on average" is not sufficient. Second, the assessment of local instability is crucial. Our TQAR approach provides a great analytical framework to conduct this assessment. Third, in general, the dynamic response to adverse shocks depends on management and policy. Our discussion has pointed out the role of innovations. On the negative side, collapse/traps are more likely to arise in the absence of management and policy response to adverse shocks. On the positive side, induced innovations in management and policy can be a crucial part of designing a more resilient system. Our analysis indicates the important role played by the induced response of management and policy to adverse shocks.

8.7 Conclusion

This chapter has studied the dynamic response to shocks, with an application to agroecosystem productivity. It has proposed a threshold quantile autoregressive model as a flexible representation of stochastic dynamics. It has focused on the identification of zones of local instability and their usefulness in the characterization of resilience and traps. The usefulness of the approach was illustrated in an application to the dynamics of wheat yield in Kansas. The analysis examined the effects of extreme shocks both in the short run and in the long run. It identified a zone of instability in the presence of successive adverse shocks. It also finds evidence of resilience. We associate the resilience with induced innovations in management and policy in response to adverse shocks.

Our approach is generic and can be applied to the analysis of dynamics in any economic system. Our empirical analysis focused on a particular agro-ecosystem. Our findings documented the role of local instability in response adverse shocks. Such findings are expected to vary across situations. This motivates a need to extend our analysis and its applications to other economic systems where traps and resilience issues are of interest.

Appendix

Table 8A.1   **Estimates of quantile autoregressive model of wheat yield including weather shocks, selected quantiles**

	Quantile				
Parameters	$r = 0.1$	$r = 0.3$	$r = 0.5$	$r = 0.7$	$r = 0.9$
Intercept	0.44929	0.02457	0.11511	−0.09011	−0.06440
y_{t-1}	0.22780	0.23496	0.29597**	0.18766	0.19131**
rain_s	−0.00045	−0.00043	0.00055	0.00027	0.00025
rain_f	0.00094*	0.00071	0.00089	0.00119**	0.00074
temp	−0.00081	0.00994	0.00584	0.01346	0.01549
rain_s * y_{t-1}	0.00057	0.00060	−0.00068	−0.00040	−0.00036
temp * y_{t-1}	−0.00395	−0.01454	−0.01458	−0.02326***	−0.02495***
t	−0.00076	−0.00108	−0.00356	−0.00520**	−0.00093
t_1	0.01823***	0.02043***	0.02751***	0.03565***	0.03070***

Note: Hypothesis testing is conducted using bootstrapping.
***Significant at the 1 percent level.
**Significant at the 5 percent level.
*Significant at the 10 percent level.

References

Azariadis, C., and J. Stachurski. 2005. "Poverty Traps." In *Handbook of Economic Growth*, vol. 1, part A, edited by P. Aghion and S. N. Durlauf. Amsterdam: Elsevier.

Barrett, C. B., and M. R. Carter. 2013. "The Economics of Poverty Traps and Persistent Poverty: Empirical and Policy Implications." *Journal of Development Studies* 49:976–90.

Barrett, C. B., and M. A. Constas. 2014. "Toward a Theory of Resilience for International Development Applications." *Proceedings of the National Academy of Sciences* 111:14625–30.

Billingsley, P. 1961. *Statistical Inference for Markov Processes*. Chicago: University of Chicago Press.

Bollerslev, T. 1986. "Generalized Autoregressive Conditional Heteroscedasticity." *Journal of Econometrics* 31:307–27.

Burnette, D. J., and D. W. Stahle. 2013. "Historical Perspective on the Dust Bowl Drought in the Central Unites States." *Climate Change* 116:479–94.

Burnette, D. J., D. W. Stahle, and C. J. Mock. 2010. "Daily-Mean Temperature Reconstructed for Kansas from Early Instrumental and Modern Observations." *Journal of Climate* 23:1308–33.

Chavas, J. P., and S. Di Falco. 2017. "Resilience and Dynamic Adjustments in Agroecosystems: The Case of Wheat Yield in England." *Environmental and Resource Economics* 67 (2): 297–320.

Common, M., and C. Perrings. 1992. "Towards an Ecological Economics of Sustainability." *Ecological Economics* 6:7–34.

Dasgupta, P. 1997. "Nutritional Status, the Capacity for Work and Poverty Traps." *Journal of Econometrics* 77:5–37.

Derissen S., M. F. Quaas, and S. Baumgärtner. 2011. "The Relationship between Resilience and Sustainable Development of Ecological-Economic Systems." *Ecological Economics* 70:1121–28.

Diamond, J. M. 2005. *Collapse: How Societies Choose to Fail or Succeed*. New York: Viking Books.

Di Falco, S., and J. P. Chavas. 2008. "Rainfall Shocks, Resilience and the Effects of Crop Biodiversity on Agroecosystem Productivity." *Land Economics* 64:83–96.

Enders, W. 2010. *Applied Econometric Time Series*, 3rd ed. New York: Wiley.

Folke, C., S. R. Carpenter, B. H. Walker, M. Scheffer, T. Elmqvist, L. H. Gunderson, and C. S. Holling. 2004. "Regime Shifts, Resilience, and Biodiversity in Ecosystem Management." *Annual Review of Ecology, Evolution and Systematics* 35:557–81.

Galvao, A., G. Montes-Rojas, and J. Olmo. 2011. "Threshold Quantile Autoregressive Model." *Journal of Time Series Analysis* 32:253–67.

Gill, R. B. 2000. *The Great Maya Droughts: Water, Life, and Death*. Albuquerque: University of New Mexico Press.

Gunderson, L. H. 2000. "Ecological Resilience in Theory and Application." *Annual Review of Ecological Systems* 31:425–39.

Hamilton, J. D. 1989. "A New Approach to the Economic Analysis of Nonstationary Time Series and the Business Cycle." *Econometrica* 57:357–84.

Hasselblatt, B., and A. Katok. 2003. *A First Course in Dynamics*. New York: Cambridge University Press.

Headey, D. 2011. "Rethinking the Global Food Crisis: The Role of Trade Shocks." *Food Policy* 36:136–46.

Holling, C. S. 1973. "Resilience and Stability of Ecological Systems." *Annual Review of Ecology and Systematics* 4:1–23.

Hornbeck, R. 2012. "The Enduring Impact of the American Dust Bowl: Short- and Long-Run Adjustments to Environmental Catastrophe." *American Economic Review* 102 (1): 1477–507.

Hurt, D. R. 1981. *The Dust Bowl: An Agricultural and Social History*. Chicago: Nelson-Hall.

Kalkuhl, M., J. von Braun, and M. Torero, eds. 2016. *Food Price Volatility and Its Implications for Food Security and Policy*. London: Springer Open.

Koenker, R. 2005. *Quantile Regression*. Cambridge: Cambridge University Press.

Koenker, R., and Z. Xiao. 2006. "Quantile Autoregression." *Journal of the American Statistical Association* 101:980–90.

Kraay, A., and D. McKenzie. 2014. "Do Poverty Traps Exist? Assessing the Evidence." *Journal of Economic Perspectives* 28:127–48.

Marriner, N., C. Flaux, D. Kaniewski, C. Morhange, G. Leduc, V. Moron, Z. Chen, F. Gasse, J.-Y. Empereur, and J.-D. Stanley. 2012. "ITCZ and ENSO-Like Pacing of Nile Delta Hydro-geomorphology during the Holocene." *Quarterly Science Reviews* 45 (29): 73–84.

May, R. M. 1976. "Simple Mathematical Models with Very Complicated Dynamics." *Nature* 261:459–67.

Medina-Elizalde, M., and E. J. Rohling. 2012. "Collapse of Classic Maya Civilization Related to Modest Reduction in Precipitation." *Science* 335:956–59.

Meyn, S. P., and R. L. Tweedie. 1993. *Markov Chains and Stochastic Stability*. London: Springer-Verlag.

National Oceanographic and Atmospheric Administration (NOAA). 2016. Global Historical Climatology Network (GHCN). National Center for Environmental Information. United States Department of Commerce, Washington, DC.

Nelson, G. C., H. Valin, R. D. Sands, P. Havlik, H. Ahammad, D. Derying, J. Elliott, et al. 2014. "Climate Change Effects on Agriculture: Economic Responses to Biophysical Shocks." *Proceedings of the National Academy of Sciences of the United States of America* 111:3274–79.

Olmstead, A. L., and P. W. Rhode. 2011. "Adapting North American Wheat Production to Climatic Challenges, 1839–2009." *Proceedings of the National Academy of Sciences* 108:480–85.

Perrings, C. 1998. "Resilience in the Dynamics of Economy-Environment Systems." *Environmental and Resource Economics* 11:503–20.

Shaw, J. 2000. *The Oxford History of Ancient Egypt*. Oxford: Oxford University Press.

Tack, J., A. Barkley, and L. L. Nalley. 2015. "Effect of Warming Temperatures on US Wheat Yields." *Proceedings of the National Academy of Sciences* 112:6931–36.

Tack, J., A. Harri, and K. Coble. 2012. "More Than Mean Effects: Modeling the Effect of Climate on the Higher Order Moments of Crop Yields." *American Journal of Agricultural Economics* 94:1037–54.

Tainter, J. A. 1990. *The Collapse of Complex Societies*. Cambridge: Cambridge University Press.

Tong, H. 1990. *Non-linear Time Series: A Dynamical System Approach*. Oxford: Clarendon Press.

United States Department of Agriculture (USDA). 2015. "Kansas Wheat History." United States Department of Agriculture, National Agricultural Statistics Service, Northern Plains Regional Field Office, Lincoln, NE.

Van Dijk, D., T. Teräsvirta, and P. H. Franses. 2002. "Smooth Transition Autoregressive Models—A Survey of Recent Developments." *Econometric Reviews* 21:1–47.

Webster, D. L. 2002. *The Fall of the Ancient Maya: Solving the Mystery of the Maya Collapse*. London: Thames and Hudson.

Comment on Chapters 7 and 8

Edward B. Barbier

There is mounting evidence that remote, less favored agricultural lands, which face severe biophysical constraints on production and are in locations with limited market access, are significant *poverty-environment* traps.[1] Such traps occur when the unique environmental and geographic conditions faced by poor households in such regions are important factors determining the dynamics of the poverty trap.[2] For marginal agricultural areas, the key characteristics are that production is subject to low yields and soil degradation, while lack of access to markets and infrastructure limit improvements to farming systems or restrict off-farm employment opportunities. Consequently, "the evidence most consistent with poverty traps comes from poor households in remote rural regions" (Kraay and McKenzie 2014, 143), "the extreme poor in more marginal areas are especially vulnerable," and "one concern is the existence of geographical poverty traps" (World Bank 2008, 49).

These two chapters highlight another characteristic, which is the vulnerability of agroecosystems on marginal lands to withstand, or be resilient, in the face of external environmental shocks such as changes in rainfall, temperature, or drought (Chavas), and the resulting impact of these environmental risks on wealth accumulation of affected households (Santos and Barrett). Thus, the chapters offer important insights to the burgeoning literature on poverty traps in marginal agricultural areas.

Edward B. Barbier is professor of economics and a senior scholar in the School of Global Environmental Sustainability at Colorado State University.

I am grateful for comments provided by Michael Carter. For acknowledgments, sources of research support, and disclosure of the author's material financial relationships, if any, please see http://www.nber.org/chapters/c13950.ack.

1. See Barbier (2010) and Barbier, López, and Hochard (2016) for recent reviews.
2. To my knowledge, the first analysis of this phenomenon is by Jalan and Ravallion (2002).

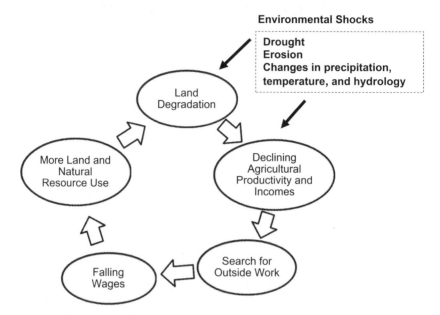

Fig. 7/8C.1 The poverty trap and environmental shocks
Source: Based on Barbier (2010).

Note: In marginal agricultural areas, household responses to land degradation and natural resource dynamics can lead to a downward spiral of poverty. Environmental shocks further tighten the vicious cycle that characterizes this poverty trap.

Figure 7/8C.1 (based on Barbier 2010) illustrates the elements of the poverty trap that can occur in marginal areas, and the threat posed by environmental risks. The vicious cycle depicted in the figure is inherently a dynamic process that can lead to a downward poverty spiral for many households in such areas. Because much of the available land has low productive potential, is located far from markets and discourages investment in land improvement, agriculture is prone to topsoil degradation, biomass loss, and low productivity. As agricultural productivity and incomes decline over time, poor households allocate more labor for outside work to boost or supplement incomes. However, with large numbers of households seeking outside employment in these isolated areas, the supply of labor for paid work could exceed demand, causing the market wage to decrease. If the wage rate falls below the reservation wage of households, they are forced to reallocate household labor back to agricultural production and extracting natural resources from the surrounding environment. The result is the self-perpetuating vicious cycle depicted in figure 7/8C.1. Persistent and periodic environmental risks such as drought, erosion, and changes in precipitation, temperature, and hydrology, are shocks to this cycle that may directly affect poor households in marginal areas through causing declining agricultural productivity and income, or indirectly through affecting land and natural resource use (see figure 7/8C.1). Such shocks further tighten the vicious cycle that characterizes the poverty trap. The result affects not only the livelihoods of households, but also their ability to accumulate and maintain key agricultural and natural resource assets. Over the long term, households caught in this poverty trap either remain destitute or must face the difficult choice of migration to other areas.

The key contributions of these two chapters is to determine the conditions that make vulnerable households in marginal areas more "resilient" to the environmental shocks and poverty trap effects depicted in figure 7/8C.1, and whether policy responses may affect the degree of resilience.

Comments on Chapter 8

Exploring the nonlinear dynamic response of agroecosystems in marginal areas to environmental shocks is the key focus of the chapter by Jean-Paul Chavas. He distinguishes between "resilience," which is the probability of escaping from undesirable zones of instability toward zones that are more desirable and stable, and a "trap," which is the low probability of escaping from zones that are both undesirable and stable. Such zones are analogous to the type of vicious cycle depicted in figure 7/8C.1. Chavas uses threshold quantile autoregression (TQAR) to estimate how the dynamics of a specific agroecosystem, and especially how the resilience of the system and the presence of traps, might vary with both current shocks and past states. This approach is applied to wheat yields in the US Great Plains state of Kansas from 1885 to 2012. Over this period, the Great Plains have experienced many periods of severe drought, including the devastating Dust Bowl of the 1930s.

Chavas's findings are inherently optimistic and encouraging. His analysis suggests that successive adverse shocks will lead to a zone of instability, which could reduce the odds of escaping from a "trap." However, this instability might be local, and thus the odds of falling into a trap may not necessarily be inevitable, as implied by the movement away from unstable equilibria to a low-level, long-run equilibrium in conventional poverty trap models. For example, Chavas suggests that the Dust Bowl of the 1930s was an example of an extreme environmental shock that initially induced profound local instability to wheat-farming systems in Kansas, but ultimately induced significant changes in agricultural management and policy that led to improved resilience over the long run. One policy innovation was the creation of the US Soil Conservation Service in 1935, which improved farm practices, increased land values and boosted farm incomes, as well as facilitated a range of continuous innovations that began in Great Plains wheat farming during the immediate post–World War II era.

Overall, the long-run analysis by Chavas of the dynamic conditions lead-ing to resilience as opposed to traps is compelling. Traps are more likely to arise in the absence of management and policy response to adverse shocks, whereas induced innovations in management and policy can be a crucial part of designing a more resilient system. However, there are two important developments that should also be considered in the long-term analysis of the wheat production in the Great Plains and the United States.

First, over the period of analysis 1885–2012, the United States changed profoundly from being an economy dominated by agricultural land expan-sion through small-scale agricultural smallholdings employing traditional farming methods to an advanced industrialized economy based on mineral wealth exploitation, manufacturing, and commercial services (Barbier 2011, ch. 7). This raises an important question: Can all of the rises in wheat yields in Great Plains agroecosystems be attributed solely to specific policy and management responses to adverse shocks, such as the Dust Bowl, or were economy-wide agricultural innovations leading to total factor productivity increases also relevant? Certainly, there is substantial evidence that from the 1920s onward increased development and use of chemical-based fertilizers, mechanization, and irrigation expansion contributed significantly to the ris-ing productivity and yields of US agriculture (Barbier 2011; Federico 2005; Goklany 2002; Rhodes and Wheeler 1996). The most successful example of such agricultural development occurred in the Great Plains, where begin-ning in the 1930s the expansion of rural electric cooperatives and low-cost, government-supplied electricity made large-scale, groundwater-based irri-gation farming both very productive and profitable, facilitating the remark-able recovery of the region from economic devastation of the Dust Bowl years (Rhodes and Wheeler 1996).

Second, environmental shocks, such as drought and the devastating Dust Bowl of the 1930s, were not the only dislocation faced by farming in the Great Plains in the early half of the twentieth century. The region also suffered from the prolonged economic shock of the massive western "farm failure" that was triggered by the fall in crop prices after World War I (Alston 1983; Hansen and Libecap 2004a, 2004b; Libecap 2007). The combination of drought, especially the Dust Bowl, and declining commodity prices changed profoundly the structure of western farming (Libecap 2007). The immediate effect was a large migration of rural households fleeing drought-prone areas. A longer-term consequence was gradual farm consolidation.

In sum, the wheat-farming systems that emerged in Great Plains states such as Kansas during the second half of the twentieth century may have been more resilient than previously thought. But they were fundamentally different systems that were also transformed by economy-wide agricultural developments. Moreover, the farm foreclosures, widespread out-migration, and farm consolidation meant that farm populations and structures were irrevocably changed by the persistent environmental and economic shocks that occurred during the interwar period. As Hansen and Libecap (2004a, 2004b) have shown, the small farms with limited market access that were prevalent in the region were too inefficient as productive units to escape the pressures of natural resource degradation and the loss of wealth from rising debt that precipitated the vicious poverty trap cycle depicted in figure 7/8C.1. For these destitute farming families, the only escape from widespread collapse of smallholder farming across the Great Plains was through massive migration from the region.

Comments on Chapter 7

Santos and Barrett illustrate the asset-based approach to analyzing poverty traps (Carter and Barrett 2006) with a case study of Boran pastoralists in southern Ethiopia. As the authors point out, for these households their livestock herds are their main, and possibly only, nonhuman asset. Even opportunities for employment locally are severely limited. In the remote, less favored semiarid zones that these pastoralists inhabit, the dynamic poverty trap mechanism may be affected by both environment risk, such as sparse rainfall and drought, and differences in herding ability among the various livestock owners, which includes diverse skills such as treating livestock diseases and injuries, protecting cattle against predators, navigating to grazing and water sites, managing calving, and so on. Moreover, risk and ability may be related. Whereas periods of poor rainfall might drive all pastoralists toward a low-equilibrium poverty trap, those with better herding ability may be able to avoid this outcome through more efficient livestock management. Based on these assumptions, the authors investigate the hypothesis that a herder's ability conditions wealth dynamics, especially when faced with unfavorable environmental conditions such as low rainfall.

Overall, their findings confirm this hypothesis. Regardless of any differences in their ability, all herders expect their herds to grow in good and normal rainfall years, whereas S-shaped dynamics occur for herders in bad rainfall years. However, when adverse rainfall conditions occur, lower-ability herders appear to converge to a unique low-equilibrium herd size (one to two head of cattle over time). Instead, multiple dynamic equilibria can occur for high-ability herders; in addition to the stable poverty trap equilibrium of one to two head, there is an unstable equilibrium at eleven to seventeen cattle, and a relatively wealthier stable steady state at twenty-nine to thirty-five head. Thus, even under adverse environmental conditions, higher-ability herders will be able to avoid a poverty trap and accumulate wealth as long as they can maintain herd size above the eleven to seventeen cattle threshold. Moreover, additional scenario analysis suggests that there should be both an increase in average herd size and a large increase in inequality over time, as low-ability herders are unable to escape poverty and higher-ability herders steadily grow their livestock holdings.

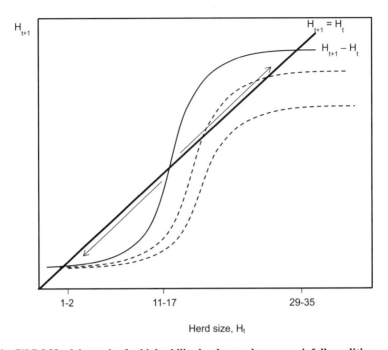

Fig. 7/8C.2 Herd dynamics for high-ability herders under poor rainfall conditions
Note: Prolonged drought and adverse rainfall may also cause the vegetation dynamics of pasture biomass to change, thus causing the herd dynamics curve to shift down (dotted line). Pasture degradation may compound the problem, making high cattle-stocking rates unsustainable. The result over the long run may be a single low-asset stable equilibrium even for high-ability herders.

However, a surprising omission is consideration of another important "natural" asset, which is the pasture biomass that sustains cattle. Since Torell, Lyon, and Godfrey (1991), dynamic economic models of cattle stocking on open rangeland have shown that reduced future forage production, diminished range condition, and reduced performance interact to determine how many cattle can be kept on a given rangeland area, both currently and over time. Such factors are especially relevant for semiarid rangelands that experience uncertain rainfall. For example, Quaas and Baumgärtner (2012, 368) find that "optimal stocking density varies with both reserve biomass and rainfall," although density choices are also affected by the degree of risk aversion of herders.

The impact of poor rainfall on vegetation dynamics, the implications for potential overgrazing in the long run, and the resulting effects on equilibrium herd size could influence the expected herd dynamics portrayed by Santos and Barrett. Not much is likely to change for low-ability herders, who will still converge to the poverty trap herd size of one to two head of cattle when adverse rainfall conditions prevail. However, high-ability herders could be significantly affected, especially if lack of rainfall also leads to changing stocking density and thus greater pasture degradation over the long term as well, as described by Quaas and Baumgärtner (2012). For instance, one possible outcome is for the S-curve for high-ability herders to pivot downward (see figure 7/8C.2). The result is that the unstable equilibrium for herd size is now higher, possibly twenty to twenty-five head of cattle. Higher-ability herders will now only be able to avoid a poverty trap and accumulate wealth if they can maintain herd size above this increased threshold. But if poor rainfall conditions and higher stocking rates on given pasture area also lead to deteriorating vegetation, then the result may be overgrazing. The higher stocking rates above twenty to twenty-five cattle that high-ability herders require to avoid a poverty trap may not be sustainable over long periods of poor rainfall. The ensuing pasture degradation from overgrazing will cause the S-curve to pivot further downward, and the only outcome for all herders is the poverty trap equilibrium of one to two head of cattle (figure 7/8C.2). This is exactly the downward poverty spiral depicted in figure 7/8C.1.

References

Alston, Lee J. 1983. "Farm Foreclosures in the United States during the Interwar Period." *Journal of Economic History* 43 (4): 885–903.

Barbier, Edward B. 2010. "Poverty, Development, and Environment." *Environment and Development Economics* 15 (6): 635–60.

———. 2011. *Scarcity and Frontiers: How Economies Have Developed through Natural Resource Exploitation.* Cambridge: Cambridge University Press.

Barbier, Edward B., Ramón E. López, and Jacob P. Hochard. 2016. "Debt, Poverty and Resource Management in a Smallholder Economy." *Environmental and Resource Economics* 63:411–27.

Carter, M., and C. Barrett. 2006. "The Economics of Poverty Traps and Persistent Poverty: An Asset-Based Approach." *Journal of Development Studies* 42:178–99.

Federico, Giovanni. 2005. *Feeding the World: An Economic History of Agriculture, 1800–2000.* Princeton, NJ: Princeton University Press.

Goklany, Indur M. 2002. "Comparing 20th Century Trends in U.S. and Global Agricultural Water and Land Use." *Water International* 27 (3): 321–29.

Hansen, Zeynep K., and Gary D. Libecap. 2004a. "The Allocation of Property Rights to Land: U.S. Land Policy and Farm Failure in the Northern Great Plains." *Explorations in Economic History* 41:103–29.

———. 2004b. "Small Farms, Externalities, and the Dust Bowl of the 1930s." *Journal of Political Economy* 112 (3): 665–93.

Jalan, J., and M. Ravallion. 2002. "Geographic Poverty Traps? A Micro Model of Consumption Growth in Rural China." *Journal of Applied Econometrics* 17: 329–46.

Kraay, Aart, and David McKenzie. 2014. "Do Poverty Traps Exist? Assessing the Evidence." *Journal of Economic Perspectives* 28:127–48.

Libecap, Gary D. 2007. "The Assignment of Property Rights on the Western Frontier: Lessons for Contemporary Environmental and Resource Policy." *Journal of Economic History* 67 (2): 257–90.

Quaas, Martin F., and Stefan Baumgärtner. 2012. "Optimal Grazing Management Rules in Semi-arid Rangelands with Uncertain Rainfall." *Natural Resource Modeling* 25:364–87.

Rhodes, Stephen L., and Samuel E. Wheeler. 1996. "Rural Electrification and Irrigation in the U.S. High Plains." *Journal of Rural Studies* 12 (3): 311–17.

Torell, L. Allen, Kenneth S. Lyon, and E. Bruce Godfrey. 1991. "Long-Run versus Short-Run Planning Horizons and the Rangeland Stocking Rate Decision." *American Journal of Agricultural Economics* 73:795–807.

World Bank. 2008. *World Development Report 2008: Agricultural Development.* Washington, DC: World Bank.

V

Policy in the Presence of
Poverty Trap Mechanisms

9
Sustaining Impacts When Transfers End
Women Leaders, Aspirations, and Investments in Children

Karen Macours and Renos Vakis

9.1 Introduction

The intergenerational transmission of poverty often occurs through low levels of investment in education and nutrition. Conditional cash transfer (CCT) programs and many other development interventions specifically aim to increase human capital investment by the poor. A large body of evidence shows that CCT programs have been successful in augmenting investment in education and nutrition in many settings (Fiszbein and Schady 2009; Ganimian and Murnane 2014). A key question is whether CCTs can have lasting impacts on investment behavior after households stop receiving transfers. Only a few papers study whether the impacts on households' human capital investments persist after such programs end, and the evidence is mixed (Macours, Schady, and Vakis 2012; Baird, McIntosh, and Özler 2016). Even

Karen Macours is associate professor at the Paris School of Economics and a researcher at Institut National de la Recherche Agronomique (INRA). Renos Vakis is a lead economist with the Poverty and Equity Global Practice at the World Bank.

We are grateful to the program team at the Ministerio de la Familia, and in particular Carold Herrera and Teresa Suazo for their collaboration during the design of the impact evaluation, as well as the Centro de Investigación de Estudios Rurales y Urbanos de Nicaragua (in particular, Veronica Aguilera and Enoe Moncada) for excellent data collection. We are indebted to Ximena Del Carpio, Fernando Galeana, and Patrick Premand for countless contributions to the wider research project. We also would like to thank Caridad Araujo, Mariano Bosch, Karla Hoff, Norbert Schady, and participants of the NBER conference for their suggestions. Financial support for this research has been received from BASIS-AMA (under the USAID Agreement no. EDH-A-00-06-0003-00 awarded to the Assets and Market Access Collaborative Research Support Program) and the World Bank (ESSD trust funds, the RRB grant, as well as the Government of the Netherlands through the BNPP program). The views expressed in this chapter are those of the authors and do not necessarily reflect those of the World Bank or any of its affiliated organizations. All errors and omissions are our own. For acknowledgments, sources of research support, and disclosure of the authors' material financial relationships, if any, please see http://www.nber.org/chapters/c13837.ack.

less is known about the possible mechanisms underlying persistence. A better understanding is needed to derive lessons regarding optimal design of new programs and adjustments to existing ones. More generally, knowing whether and how short-term programs can result in long-term increases in human capital investment is important for policy design.

For programs to have a persistent effect on households' human capital investments, they need either to permanently lift existing liquidity constraints or to change the value households attribute to investments in education and nutrition.[1] The latter may occur if the interventions increase the perceived returns to such investments by reducing information asymmetries or changing preferences. Nguyen (2008) and Jensen (2010) show that changes in the perceived returns to schooling through information can lead to educational gains. Recent evidence also suggests the potential of external interventions to shift preferences by changing parents' aspirations for their children (Beaman et al. 2012; Bernard et al. 2014).[2]

Understanding how to design interventions to maximize such shifts hence becomes an important policy question. Several design features of CCT programs could be contributing to shifts in investment behavior. The CCTs typically include heavy social marketing and conditionalities enforcing attendance at regular meetings in which the nutritional, health, and educational objectives are discussed. To the extent that such messages get internalized, one could expect increased human capital investments to persist. Targeting the transfers to women in the household could shift gender norms regarding decision-making within the household, and this too could persist after the transfers stop. Often programs also assign specific roles to key women in the community to reinforce the messages, but causal evidence on their specific role is rare.[3]

This chapter shows that interactions with local female leaders can contribute to the persistence of a program's impacts by providing evidence for a CCT pilot program in Nicaragua. It builds on Macours and Vakis (2014), where we showed that exposure to successful and motivated female leaders substantially increased impacts on nutritional and educational investments, as well as future-oriented attitudes, while the program was operating. This chapter analyzes whether these shifts were sustained after the program ended. A priori the answer is not obvious. Increasing aspirations in the presence of many other remaining constraints may lead to only

---

1. If some decisions are driven by habits, a program that changes habits can also have a persistent effect.

2. External interventions can also change the aspirations of children themselves (Wydick, Glewwe, and Rutledge 2013) or aspirations of adults for themselves (Lybbert and Wydick 2016).

3. The importance of these local female leaders has been recognized in several qualitative evaluations of CCT programs (Adato 2000; Adato and Roopnaraine 2004). In Colombia, an independent ECD intervention specifically targeted the "madre voluntarias" of the CCT program in recognition of their local leadership role (Attanasio et al. 2014).

short-term gains, and households could revert back to preprogram behavior when the transfers stop. On the other hand, if social interactions during the program changed norms and beliefs regarding human capital investments, the increased investment levels could persist even after the end of the program. Macours, Schady, and Vakis (2012) show that the Nicaraguan CCT indeed had persistent effects on parental investments in early childhood. This chapter helps explain why.

Using data collected two years after the program ended, we show that social interactions with successful and motivated leaders were crucial for the persistence of the educational and nutritional investment. Two years after the transfers stopped, former beneficiaries who live in the proximity of such leaders still show significantly higher investments in both education and nutrition of their children. Random exposure to successful leaders also led to significant shifts in parental aspirations and expectations for their children's future.[4]

We use a two-stage randomized design to identify the social interaction effects. The program combined a regular CCT with interventions aimed at increasing households' productive potential. Because it targeted the vast majority of households in each community and explicitly encouraged group formation, it is a good setting to analyze the role of social interactions. The experiment varied the nature and the size of the benefit packages leaders and other households received, and as such created random variation in whether beneficiaries lived close to leaders that received the largest package. In general all leaders have higher human capital investments and aspirations than other beneficiaries, and hence provide potential examples to follow. The leaders that received the largest package, in addition, outperformed other leaders in terms of economic outcomes and also had higher expectations for their children's future. Earlier findings also showed that leaders with the largest package communicated more with other beneficiaries during the intervention.[5] We analyze whether proximity to these successful and motivated leaders affected human capital investments of other beneficiaries.

We follow Manski (2000) and define social interactions as interactions with agents—in this case leaders with the largest package—that affect actions of other agents through changing constraints, expectations, or preferences. We provide empirical evidence in support of those different channels by

4. We draw on a rich set of questions measuring parental expectations and aspirations. As in Beaman et al. (2012) and Bernard et al. (2014) we measure aspirations by asking parents about what they would like their children to achieve on a number of dimensions, such as the desired education level or occupation. As in the later paper, we also separately measure expectations by asking parents what they think their children realistically will achieve on those same dimensions. Both set of indicators more broadly capture future-oriented attitudes.
5. More specifically, distance between houses generally reduces communication between leaders and beneficiaries (as expected), but this was not the case for leaders with the largest package. The differences between leaders with different packages were significant (Macours and Vakis 2014).

exploiting the random variation in the type of package each of the nonleaders received and the variation in per capita expenditure levels that resulted two years after the intervention. Beneficiaries of the largest package—on average—still had higher per capita expenditures two years after the end of the transfers, and more so when they were exposed to leaders with the same package. Such effects do not exist for beneficiaries of the other packages. Hence while changes for the first group can be driven in part by relaxing spending constraints, changes for the other groups are more likely driven by shifts in expectations or aspirations (and hence preferences).

The chapter contributes to the developing literature in economics and the wider social sciences on the role and the formation of aspirations (Genicot and Ray 2014; Besley 2017). Appadurai (2004) and Ray (2006) argue that upward mobility might be difficult for the poor when they lack the capacity to aspire, that is, when their own experiences and the experiences of those that are close to them suggest that escaping poverty is not a feasible option. Yet learning about the positive experiences of others that are sufficiently "close" may help open their "aspiration window." Hence social interactions may be instrumental in changing aspirations and shaping positive attitudes toward the future, and in turn lead to investments in their children's future.[6] Empirical evidence of such mechanisms is rare due to the "reflection problem." This chapter addresses the problem through the randomized assignment of leaders and other beneficiaries to different benefit packages.

More broadly, this chapter relates to recent work on the potential of social interactions to shift norms and behavior (Paluck and Shepherd 2012; Feigenberg, Field, and Pande 2013) and to the emerging literature about mental models and attitudinal changes (Jensen and Oster 2009; La Ferrara, Chong, and Duryea 2012; World Bank 2015; Hoff and Stiglitz 2016). By focusing on local female leaders, the chapter also relates to the literature on female reservations for local leadership positions in India (Chattopadhyay and Duflo 2004; Beaman et al. 2009), and in particular to Beaman et al. (2012), who show that a law reserving leadership positions for women affected girls' educational aspirations.

Finally, this study relates to the growing literature on longer-term impacts of CCT programs (see Molina-Millan et al. [2016] for a review). We contribute by studying the impacts of a one-year randomized pilot program after it ended, and for which the experimental control group was never phased in. This allows providing clean evidence of the sustainability of impacts on human capital investments after only a few years, avoiding selection (attrition) concerns that often hamper long-term studies. That said, because the intervention only lasted one year, it differs from many of the large CCT programs

---

6. Appadurai (2004) describes how mobilization by social movements can expand the capacity to aspire, in part through regular social gatherings and sharing ideas and experiences about future-oriented activities among the poor.

in Latin America, where beneficiaries often receive transfers for many years.[7] We return to this point in the conclusion. By focusing on the impact on human capital investment, we complement other studies that analyze whether the impacts on human capital outcomes (as opposed to investments) or other welfare outcomes persist on the longer run. While some studies analyze long-term impacts of ongoing programs (Behrman, Parker, and Todd 2009, 2011; Gertler, Martinez, and Rubio-Codina 2012; Araujo, Bosch, and Schady 2016), others, like us, provide evidence on programs with short duration (Barham, Macours, and Maluccio 2013a, 2013b; Macours, Premand, and Vakis 2012; Barrera-Osorio, Linden, and Saavedra 2015; Filmer and Schady 2014).

The chapter is organized as follows: in the next section we discuss the program and the relevance of social interactions. Section 9.3 discusses the data and the empirical strategy. Section 9.4 shows that social interactions with successful leaders had persistent impacts on other beneficiaries' human capital investments. Section 9.5 shows results for per capita expenditures, parental expectations, and aspirations; section 9.6 concludes.

9.2   Program Information and Design

9.2.1   Program Description and Treatment Packages[8]

The Atención a Crisis program was a one-year pilot program implemented in 2006 by the Ministry of the Family in Nicaragua. In the treatment communities, three different treatments were randomly allocated among 3,000 eligible households. All selected households were eligible for the basic CCT, which included cash transfers conditional on children's primary school attendance and health center visits. The transfers came with a strong social marketing message reinforcing the importance of investing in children's education and in a diversified diet. Take-up of the CCT was 95 percent. In addition to the CCT, one-third of the eligible households received a scholarship for a vocational training for one adult (with take-up of 89 percent). Another third of eligible households received, in addition to the basic CCT, a US$200 lump-sum grant to invest in a small nonagricultural business (with take-up of 99 percent). This last treatment was perceived by the beneficiaries as the most attractive and involved the largest cash amount. We call it the "largest package." Given the high take-up rates, we henceforth refer to eligible households in treatment communities as beneficiaries.

The program design aimed to change households' investment behavior through several mechanisms. The level of cash transfers was substantial, rang-

7. In the large national CCT programs in Colombia or Mexico, for instance, beneficiaries only exit when their children reach a certain age or after households reach a higher income level.

8. More details about the program are provided in the online appendixes of Macours, Schady, and Vakis (2012) and Macours and Vakis (2014), as well as the following website: http://go.worldbank.org/VUYJAQ3UN0.

ing from 18 percent of average annual household income for those receiving the basic CCT package to 34 percent for those receiving the productive investment package. The conditionalities and social marketing on education, health, and nutrition aimed at changing households' perspectives about investment in long-term human capital. The program design also created many opportunities for enhanced communication between beneficiaries. More than 90 percent of the households in treatment communities were eligible for the program, increasing the opportunities for information sharing, possibly resulting in higher motivation and program ownership. Beneficiaries were also required to participate in local events ranging from discussions on nutrition and health practices to workshops on the importance of education, business development, and labor market skills. The program put in place a system of volunteer local *promotoras* to enhance information flows and compliance with program requirements. The *promotoras* met frequently with small groups of beneficiary women to talk about these requirements and the program's objectives. As such, the program created a lot of new leadership positions for women.[9] Women self-selected into these positions and then subsequently were randomly allocated to one of the three program packages (see below). Interviews during and after the intervention showed that most of the *promotoras* had taken strong ownership of the messages and objectives of the program, and were committed to reminding other beneficiaries that the purpose of the cash transfers was to invest in the nutrition and education of their children. During payment days, for instance, *promotoras* would often organize with the beneficiaries in their group to collectively buy food products and material for their children. Among other things, this allowed beneficiaries to directly observe investments by their *promotoras*. Qualitative evidence further confirms that beneficiaries were very aware of investments by others, with plenty of stories about children in the village going to school well fed, with new cloths and material.

9.2.2   Program Randomization

The program targeted six municipalities in the northwest of Nicaragua, and a first lottery randomly selected fifty-six intervention and fifty control communities. Baseline data were used to define household program eligibility using proxy means methods for both treatment and control.[10] In the treatment communities, the main female caregiver from each eligible household was invited to a registration assembly. If there were more than thirty eligible households in a community, several assemblies were organized at the same time, and households were assigned to one of the assemblies based on the geographic location of their house. In total, there were 134 assemblies (hence, on average, 2.4 per community).

9. Before the program, leadership positions for women were limited mostly to positions as teachers and health coordinators.
10. As more than 90 percent of all households were eligible, the analysis in this chapter is limited to the eligible households.

During the assemblies, the program objectives and its various components were explained and women were asked to volunteer for the *promotora* positions. Volunteers were approved by the assembly and each *promotora* became responsible for a group of approximately ten beneficiaries living close to her, with *promotoras* and beneficiaries mutually agreeing on the compositions of the group. After the groups were formed, and at the very end of each assembly, all the beneficiaries—including the *promotoras*—participated in a second lottery process through which the three packages described above were randomly allocated among the beneficiaries, with each of the three packages assigned to one-third of households in the treatment communities. As a result of the two lotteries, households were randomly assigned to the control group (in the control communities), or to one of three packages: the CCT, the CCT plus training, or the CCT plus productive investment grant (the largest package). Since *promotoras* and existing female leaders in the treatment communities were randomly allocated to one of the three treatment groups, beneficiary households were randomly exposed to leaders with a treatment package that could be different from theirs. In particular, as there are on average four leaders in each assembly, some beneficiaries will randomly live close to several leaders that got the largest package, while others may not have any leaders with that package in their registration assembly.[11] This is the main exogenous variation that we exploit.

9.3   Data and Empirical Strategy

9.3.1   Data

In treatment communities, data were collected from all households. In control communities, a random sample of households was selected at baseline so that the control group was of equal size as each of the three intervention groups (1,000 households). The data analyzed in this chapter was collected between August 2008 and May 2009, approximately two years after the last transfer. Individuals who had migrated out of the area were tracked to different locations in Nicaragua, resulting in a very low attrition rate (3 percent at the household level), which is uncorrelated with treatment.

The survey instrument was modeled after the Nicaraguan Living Standard Measurement Survey (LSMS), with modules on education, health, and detailed household expenditures, among others. For the main set of results, we use the same education and nutrition investment indicators as those used in Macours and Vakis (2014). Specifically, for child-level education

---

11. While the meetings of the *promotoras* with their groups were, by design, more frequent than meetings with the larger group of beneficiaries of an assembly, we use the larger assemblies as the reference group in part because the administrative information on the composition of the small groups is less precise than the information on who participated in which assemblies. In addition, it is possible that beneficiaries reorganized the groups after the assemblies, so that the effective groups may not correspond to the administrative data on groups.

outcomes, we consider all children between seven and eighteen years old, and use an indicator of whether the child was attending school, the number of days the child has been absent from school in the last month, and the amount spent on school expenditures since the start of the academic year. Nutrition investment is measured at the household level and is measured by the shares of food expenditures for animal products and for vegetables and fruits, reflecting the emphasis of the program's messaging on the importance of such nutrients for children. To account for multiple hypotheses testing, we also combine the education and nutrition variables in two aggregate indices, by first calculating z-scores for each variable using the mean and standard deviation of the control group, and then averaging over these z-scores, following Kling, Liebman, and Katz (2007).

We complement this analysis with indicators of investments in children from birth to seven years old, using the same indicators of investment in early childhood as Macours, Schady, and Vakis (2012). We analyze impacts on three families of outcomes by calculating average z-scores of a set of indicators for nutrition, education, and health.[12] These are the three early childhood risk factors for which investments on average were still higher in the treatment than in the control, two years after the end of the transfers. As this is an age group that is not yet in primary school, the stimulation index can be seen as the equivalent of the education index for the older children. We use these indices to specifically analyze social multiplier effects on investment in children born after the end of the transfer (and hence approximately from birth to two years old). This allows testing whether the change in investment behavior is also observed for children not directly affected by the intervention, which provides a strong test of a more permanent shift in investment behavior.

A specific module was added in 2008 to ask mothers about expectations and aspirations for all their children between seven and fifteen years old.[13] Mothers were asked both what they desired (to measure aspirations) and what they realistically expected for their children in terms of final educational attainment, occupation, future monthly earnings, and living standards. To proxy for future living standards, we also asked mothers for the number of rooms they desired and expected for the house their children would live in in thirty years' time. For occupation, we consider two possible definitions. The first is a dummy indicating whether the mother expected or desired a professional

12. The nutrition index is the average of the z-scores for the share of food in total expenditures, the shares of animal proteins and of fruit and vegetables in total food expenditures, and the reverse of the share of staples in total food expenditures; the stimulation index is the average of the z-scores for variables indicating whether the household has pen and paper, has a toy, somebody tells stories or sings to the child, and the number of hours reading to the child per week; and the health index is the average of the z-scores for variables indicating whether the child was weighed, got vitamins or iron, got deworming drugs, and the number of days sick in bed. See Macours, Schady, and Vakis (2012) for detailed definitions.

13. The module was not asked for children younger than seven, as mothers demonstrated difficulties answering such questions for their young children during piloting.

job for her child, that is, a job for which university education is required. The second is a dummy indicating whether she expected or desired a professional or skilled salary job, that is, a job for which at least secondary education would be required. For monthly earnings, and taking into account the highly skewed nature of the distribution of this variable, we follow Athey and Imbens (2016) and use an indicator of the rank in the earnings distribution.[14] Finally, to account for multiple hypotheses testing, we use an aggregate indicator for both aspirations and expectations, which is the average of the standardized measures for educational attainment, occupation, monthly earnings, and living standard (number of rooms in the house), following Kling, Liebman, and Katz (2007).[15] All standardized measures were obtained by subtracting the mean and dividing by the standard deviation of the control group.

9.3.2   Outcomes for Leaders

Identification relies on the random allocation of beneficiaries to one of the three program packages or the control, and the random allocation of these same packages among leaders. We consider both the leadership positions created in the treatment communities by the program (the *promotoras*) and other women with leadership positions, since they are not mutually exclusive (many health coordinators and teachers volunteered to be *promotoras*). Female leaders tend to be younger and more educated than the average female beneficiary. While beneficiaries on average have completed three years of education, leaders have completed, on average, five years. Other indicators of socioeconomic status at baseline are similar between leaders and nonleaders.

In Macours and Vakis (2014) we show that the randomization worked well and that the short-term returns to the largest package for the leaders were higher than for the other beneficiaries. During the intervention, leaders with the largest package also had higher nonagricultural and total income than leaders with other packages, reflecting the additional cash they had received to start new activities. As the income level and the income sources of these leaders at baseline were similar to those of the other beneficiaries, it seems plausible that beneficiaries could identify with their success during the program and that this might have motivated and inspired them.

The largest package is also the only intervention that led to gains in average income and consumption levels two years after the end of the program (Macours, Schady, and Vakis 2012; Macours, Premand, and Vakis 2012). Table 9.1 shows that leaders who received this package continue to

14. Results are qualitatively similar when using the absolute value of earnings, winsorized at the 95th percentile.

15. As an important share of parents desire professional jobs for their children, but few expect their children to get such jobs, we use the variable for professional job in the aggregate index for aspirations, and the variable for professional or skilled wage job in the aggregate index for expectations.

Table 9.1   Comparison of follow-up outcomes of leaders with largest package with other leaders and nonleaders

	Leader T1	Leader T2	Leader T3	Nonleader T3	P-value leaders T3–T1	P-value leaders T3–T2	P-value leaders T3–nonleader T3
Economic activities (in córdoba, per capita)							
Income from nonagricultural self-employment	489.1	546	810	557	0.04**	0.09*	0.04**
Income from commercial activities	190.9	156	404	222	0.05**	0.02***	0.05**
Income from agricultural wages	602.8	749	679	973	0.51	0.55	0.01**
Value animal stock	1,630	2,104	2,191	1,631	0.14	0.84	0.13
Total income	11,707	12,049	12,272	10,925	0.51	0.78	0.05*
Expectations for children's future							
Average index	0.15	0.17	0.37	0.00	0.01***	0.02**	0.00***
Expected years of education attained	9.72	9.82	10.39	8.64	0.06*	0.07*	0.00***
Expected occupation: professional	0.03	0.04	0.04	0.05	0.43	0.77	0.90
Expected occupation: professional or skilled empl.	0.35	0.36	0.47	0.26	0.04**	0.06*	0.00***
Expected number of rooms in house	2.64	2.76	2.87	2.74	0.05*	0.40	0.28
Expected monthly earnings	2,132	2,047	2,332	1,976	0.12	0.02**	0.00***
Expected monthly earnings (winsorized 95%)	1,703	1,637	1,898	1,593	0.13	0.04**	0.00***
Aspirations for children's future							
Average index	0.06	0.19	0.17	0.02	0.15	0.83	0.06*
Desired years of education attained	14.05	14.39	14.49	13.56	0.12	0.78	0.00***

Desired occupation: professional	0.53	0.63	0.60	0.53	0.13	0.62	0.16
Desired occupation: professional or skilled empl.	0.90	0.94	0.92	0.88	0.49	0.56	0.09*
Desired number of rooms in house	5.18	5.35	5.221	5.25	0.83	0.49	0.88
Desired monthly earnings: rank	2,140	2,239	2,273	2,037	0.30	0.79	0.06*
Desired monthly earnings (winsorized 95%)	4,532	4,655	4,831	4,274	0.38	0.64	0.10*
Human capital investment							
Attending school	0.863	0.84	0.82	0.77	0.49	0.96	0.00***
Number of days absent from school	4.329	5.16	5.71	6.35	0.44	0.70	0.02**
School expenditures	767	683	636	518	0.51	0.67	0.00***
Share of food expenditures for animal products	0.17	0.17	0.18	0.16	0.37	0.97	0.07*
Share of food expenditures for vegetables and fruit	0.07	0.07	0.08	0.07	0.47	0.51	0.16

Note: Sample includes intent-to-treat households in treatment communities. Economic outcomes and food expenditures are household-level data. Data on education, expectations, and aspirations are child-level data. Highest and lowest 0.5 percent outliers of income and expenditures data trimmed. Expectation and aspirations questions refer to children nine to fifteen years old. Education questions refer to children seven to eighteen years old. Average expectation index is average of standardized outcomes for expected years of education, professional or skilled employment, number of rooms in the house, and monthly earnings rank. Average aspiration index is average of standardized outcomes for expected years of education, professional employment, number of rooms in the house, and monthly earnings rank. Earnings ranks are calculated by converting the absolute monthly earnings to the rank in the earnings distribution, combining answers of leaders and nonleaders. All monetary values are in córdoba (1 US$ = ~ 20 córdobas). *P*-values account for clustering at the community level.

***Significant at the 1 percent level.

**Significant at the 5 percent level.

*Significant at the 10 percent level.

stand out. Two years after the end of the intervention, leaders who had the largest package still have higher incomes from nonagricultural self-employment than other leaders. And their nonagricultural income and total income is significantly higher than for other beneficiaries who received the same package, even if their income from agricultural wages is lower. This suggests they may have been better in maintaining their new commercial activities and likely continue to be seen as successful leaders in the community.

We observe the same patterns with respect to parents' expectations for their children's future. For leaders who received the largest package, expectations are significantly higher than for other leaders. They expect their children to achieve higher schooling levels and earn higher wages, and are 11 percentage points more likely to expect their children to become a professional or skilled salary earner (table 9.1). There are also large differences in the expectations of these leaders and those of other beneficiaries who received the same package, with leaders expecting their children to obtain 1.5 years more education, and 21 percentage points more likely to become a professional or skilled salary earner. These latter differences are consistent with the program identifying natural leaders through self-selection. The differences mean that these leaders may be seen as local success stories—in both current achievement and their attitudes toward the future—that others could aspire to emulate.

A similar pattern is found for differences between leaders and others in their reported aspirations for their children, although differences in aspirations are smaller than differences in expectations. Comparing mean values of aspirations and expectations shows large gaps between the two sets of outcomes, with expectations for educational attainment, for instance, five years less than aspirations and similarly large differences for earnings, occupation, and living standards. Interestingly, these gaps are smaller for leaders than nonleaders. The pattern suggests that both leaders and other households internalize their constraints when reporting their expectations, but they also suggest a capacity to aspire to a much better lives for their children.[16]

In line with the other results, leaders' investments in the education and nutrition of their children are higher than those of others beneficiaries. The significant differences in human capital investment between leaders and nonleaders in table 9.1 mirror similar findings from the baseline and the midline survey (Macours and Vakis 2014). Leaders with the largest package hence provided positive examples for others, in line with the program objectives, both during the program and two years after the transfers ended.

16. The questions for expectations specifically asked: "Taking into account your current situation, what do you expect . . . ?"

9.3.3   Empirical Specification

To analyze whether higher exposure to leaders with the largest package changed education and nutrition investments of other beneficiaries, we calculate the share of leaders randomly allocated to the largest package in each registration assembly, including—as before—both *promotoras* and other women with leadership positions in the community. The average number of leaders in an assembly is four so that there is substantial variation in the share of leaders that got the largest package in an assembly. There is much less variation in the share of other beneficiaries who got the largest package since the number of households in each assembly was relatively large and thus the share of nonleaders with the largest package in each assembly is close to one-third in all assemblies.[17]

Our general specification is

$$(1) \qquad Y_{ia} = \delta_0 + \delta_1 T_{ia} + \delta_2 (T_{ia} * S_a) + \delta_3 S_a + \varepsilon_{ia}$$

where Y_{ia} is an outcome indicator for eligible household i (or a child of household i) who was invited to assembly a, T_{ia} is assignment of i to any of the three treatment groups, and S_a is the share of leaders in the assembly that randomly received the largest package in i's registration assembly. Given that households were invited to particular assemblies based on geographic proximity, S_a will capture the share of leaders with the largest package that live in the proximity of i.[18] Since S_a is always 0 in the control communities, and since all eligible households in the treatment communities receive one of the three intervention packages, the term $\delta_3 S_a$ cancels out of the estimation. The coefficients of interest are δ_1 and δ_2. A finding, for example, that δ_1 and δ_2 are both positive would imply that while assignment to the treatment group increases the outcome of interest (δ_1), there is an additional impact of the program that comes from the social interactions (δ_2). We also explore how the share of leaders with the largest package affects impacts for beneficiaries of each of the three packages separately. All regressions are estimated on the sample of eligible households (or their children) that are not leaders themselves.

9.4   Social Interaction Effects on Human Capital Investments

9.4.1   Main Results

We first pool households across treatment packages and investigate whether there is a general relationship between program impacts and proximity to

17. The shares of peers at the 10th and 90th percentiles of the distribution are 21 and 39 percent, respectively. In contrast, for the leaders, the shares at the 10th and 90th percentiles of the distribution are 0 and 67 percent.

18. Location of one's house might be endogenous, and people living in the proximity of leaders might also be more likely to be their family members, or otherwise have similar characteristics. The identification in this chapter does not depend, however, on the proximity to the leader per se, but instead it depends on the random allocation of certain packages to those leaders.

leaders who received the largest package. Table 9.2 presents in the top panel the results for 2008, the main focus of this chapter, and in the bottom panel, the findings for 2006 from our earlier work for comparison. The interaction terms in the top panel suggest that social interactions are crucial to sustain program impacts on education and nutrition investments after the end of the intervention. Indeed, the findings indicate no significant sustained impacts on human capital investments when no leader was assigned the largest package, in contrast to the findings during program implementation.

The interaction terms suggest that the higher the share of leaders with the largest package, the less likely children are absent in school and the more households invest in education, in animal proteins, and in fruit and vegetables. The social multiplier effects are not only statistically significant but also large. For example, school expenditures increase 49 percent when all the leaders in one's assembly got the largest package, while school absences decline by 21 percent. Strikingly, the magnitude of the social multiplier effects two years after the end of the program are similar, if not larger, than those while the intervention was in place. The coefficients of the z-scores in table 9.2 also imply that, two years after the transfers, the impact on nutrition, respectively educational, investment was only significantly different from zero if at least 33 percent, respectively 75 percent, of leaders in one's registration assembly received the largest package.

Table 9.3 shows the social interaction impacts on human capital investments by treatment group. The effects are strongest for beneficiaries of the largest package. For instance, school expenditures more than double for beneficiaries of the largest package in the extreme case that the share of female leaders with the same package changes from 0 to 1. The impacts are about half the size for the beneficiaries of the training packages (and even smaller for those with the basic package) for most outcomes and the interaction effects for education investments are not significant. Nevertheless, as for the 2006 findings, the p-values indicate that we cannot reject that the social effects are the same for the three groups for most variables. And when pooling the basic and the training packages, the interaction effects for school expenditures, the nutrition index, expenditures for animal proteins, and fruit and vegetables are all significant (not shown). This suggests that the results are not only driven by complementarities between the extra cash received by beneficiaries and the leaders' package.

Note that while the coefficients of the interaction effects are large, there are on average about four leaders in a registration assembly. The estimates hence indicate that having one additional leader with the largest package in one's assembly reduces school absences by 0.4 days per month and increases school expenditures by about 16 percent. For households that have the largest package, one additional leader with the same package increases school attendance by 2.5 percentage points and increases school expenditures by 25 percent. These are not only large effects, but are similar or even larger than

Table 9.2 Social interaction effects on human capital investments

	Education				Nutrition		
	Z-score education investment	Attending school (7–18-year-olds)	Number of days absent from school (7–18-year-olds)	School expenditures (7–18-year-olds)	Z-score nutrition investment	Share of food expenditures for animal products	Share of food expenditures for fruit and vegetables
	2008 (two years after program ended)						
Intent-to-treat × % leaders	0.116**	0.045	−1.506*	310.9***	0.353***	0.039**	0.022***
with largest package	(0.050)	(0.040)	(0.88)	(118)	(0.12)	(0.017)	(0.008)
Intent-to-treat	−0.031	−0.008	0.197	−68.80	−0.013	−0.005	0.001
	(0.027)	(0.026)	(0.58)	(62.5)	(0.066)	(0.010)	(0.004)
Mean dep. variable in control	0.001	0.777	6.341	493.4	−0.002	0.154	0.0581
Observations	5,231	5,228	5,228	5,205	3,230	3,214	3,214
	2006 (during implementation)						
Intent-to-treat × % leaders	0.127**	0.062*	−1.760***	191.7***	0.201**	0.022	0.014**
with largest package	(0.054)	(0.032)	(0.669)	(70.9)	(0.093)	(0.017)	(0.006)
Intent-to-treat	0.134***	0.050***	−1.352***	188.6***	0.381***	0.055***	0.019***
	(0.028)	(0.019)	(0.405)	(34.8)	(0.058)	(0.010)	(0.004)
Mean dep. variable in control	0.001	0.761	6.209	300.9	−0.003	0.152	0.066
Observations	5,181	5,176	5,169	5,153	3,294	3,278	3,279

Note: Coefficients for index of family of outcomes calculated following Kling, Liebman, and Katz (2007). The share of leaders measures the share of female leaders with the productive investment package over all female leaders in a beneficiary's registration assembly. Individual-level data for education and household-level data for food expenditures. Excluding households with female leaders. Intent-to-treat estimators. Highest and lowest 0.5 percent of outliers in expenditures trimmed. Robust standard errors in parentheses, corrected for clustering at the community level.

***Significant at the 1 percent level.
**Significant at the 5 percent level.
*Significant at the 10 percent level.

Table 9.3 Social interaction effects on human capital investments by intervention group

	Education				Nutrition		
	Z-score education investment	Attending school (7–18-year-olds)	Number of days absent from school (7–18-year-olds)	School expenditures (7–18-year-olds)	Z-score nutrition investment	Share of food expenditures for animal products	Share of food expenditures for fruit and vegetables
	2008 (two years after program ended)						
Productive investment package × % leaders with largest package	0.188** (0.091)	0.093* (0.050)	−2.676** (1.09)	485.4** (200)	0.498*** (0.13)	0.050** (0.019)	0.034*** (0.011)
Training package × % leaders with largest package	0.096 (0.071)	0.029 (0.061)	−1.017 (1.38)	246.2 (165)	0.364** (0.15)	0.038* (0.021)	0.023** (0.011)
Basic package × % leaders with largest package	0.062 (0.060)	−0.001 (0.053)	−0.538 (1.15)	192.8 (154)	0.222 (0.15)	0.032 (0.020)	0.011 (0.012)
Productive investment package	−0.050 (0.032)	−0.034 (0.032)	0.764 (0.69)	−114.0 (72.0)	−0.022 (0.062)	−0.004 (0.001)	−0.001 (0.005)
Training package	−0.014 (0.034)	0.007 (0.030)	−0.041 (0.69)	−36.92 (77.2)	−0.072 (0.082)	−0.012 (0.013)	−0.002 (0.006)
Basic package	−0.024 (0.029)	0.011 (0.031)	−0.299 (0.69)	−46.06 (69.4)	0.051 (0.079)	0.001 (0.011)	0.005 (0.005)
P-value test social effect on T3 vs. T2	0.413	0.360	0.291	0.348	0.350	0.575	0.373
P-value test social effect on T3 vs. T1	0.196	0.109	0.116	0.193	0.035**	0.252	0.069*
P-value test social effect on T1 vs. T2	0.668	0.671	0.744	0.779	0.350	0.743	0.350
Mean dependent variable in control	0.001	0.777	6.341	493.4	−0.002	0.154	0.0581
Observations	5,231	5,228	5,228	5,205	3,230	3,214	3,214

2006 (during implementation)

	(1)	(2)	(3)	(4)	(5)	(6)	(7)
Productive investment package × % leaders with largest package	0.192** (0.076)	0.097** (0.047)	-2.579*** (0.975)	291.6*** (102.5)	0.328** (0.13)	0.044** (0.019)	0.019* (0.011)
Training package × % leaders with largest package	0.097 (0.066)	0.047 (0.041)	-1.356 (0.844)	145.6* (81.9)	0.139 (0.11)	0.017 (0.021)	0.008 (0.007)
Basic package × % leaders with largest package	0.102 (0.062)	0.045 (0.052)	-1.293 (1.128)	149.3* (82.8)	0.158 (0.13)	0.006 (0.021)	0.016 (0.010)
Productive investment package	0.129*** (0.031)	0.045** (0.022)	-1.107** (0.458)	174.3*** (39.5)	0.368*** (0.067)	0.049*** (0.011)	0.020*** (0.005)
Training package	0.125*** (0.032)	0.049** (0.023)	-1.438*** (0.479)	181.4*** (39.4)	0.379*** (0.059)	0.057*** (0.011)	0.018*** (0.004)
Basic package	0.149*** (0.033)	0.057** (0.026)	-1.574*** (0.584)	211.8*** (42.2)	0.393*** (0.070)	0.058*** (0.011)	0.020*** (0.005)
P-value test social effect on T3 vs. T2	0.226	0.434	0.360	0.151	0.170	0.174	0.327
P-value test social effect on T3 vs. T1	0.192	0.306	0.238	0.124	0.208	0.0325**	0.810
P-value test social effect on T1 vs. T2	0.934	0.964	0.959	0.964	0.889	0.603	0.518
Mean dependent variable in control	0.001	0.761	6.209	300.9	-0.003	0.152	0.066
Observations	5,181	5,176	5,169	5,153	3,294	3,278	3,279

Note: Coefficients for index of family of outcomes calculated following Kling, Liebman, and Katz (2007). The share of leaders measures the share of female leaders with the productive investment package over all female leaders in a beneficiary's registration assembly. Individual-level data for education and household-level data for food expenditures. Excluding households with female leaders. Intent-to-treat estimators. Highest and lowest 0.5 percent of outliers in expenditures trimmed. Robust standard errors in parentheses, corrected for clustering at the community level.

***Significant at the 1 percent level.

**Significant at the 5 percent level.

*Significant at the 10 percent level.

the effects found in 2006. Hence, interactions with leaders had a remarkably persistent impact on other households' investment behavior, and the impact is particularly important for households that themselves received the largest package.

In contrast to the impacts during the intervention, however, none of the packages had positive impacts on investments for beneficiaries that were not exposed to any leader with the largest package, and indeed the point estimates are negative for a number of indicators. Hence positive significant effects are only found for the subset of the beneficiaries with high exposure to successful leaders.

9.4.2   Robustness

The results are robust to several alternative specifications.[19] A first concern could be that the results are driven by extreme values in the independent variable. While the average share of leaders with the largest package is 0.33, for 95 percent of the observations, the range is between 0 and 0.67. The first robustness check in table 9.4 excludes observations with values above 0.67. This does not substantially alter any of the results, even if, as expected, the standard errors increase. The results are also robust to clustering the standard errors at the level of the registration assembly, as opposed to the community level, and to not excluding outliers. The next two specifications show that the results are further robust to controls for the total number of people in an assembly, or the total number of peers (defined as beneficiaries that are not leaders) in an assembly. Finally, the results remain generally robust when including a community fixed effect, with the exception of the food expenditures for animal products, even if the variation in the independent variable is reduced.

Table 9.4 also shows alternative specifications using the number of leaders with the largest package instead of the share. These specifications separately control for the total number of leaders in the registration assembly. The coefficient on the number of leaders with the largest package is consistent with the main results in terms of sign, size, and magnitude. We can then also compare the coefficient of the number of leaders with the largest package and with the coefficient of the number of peers with the largest package (last specification in table 9.4). The results suggest that social interaction effects from peers might be more limited: the coefficients are generally not significant and smaller than the coefficients for the number of leaders, with the exception of the expenditures for animal products. The coefficients for leaders and peers are significantly different for school attendance, absences, and spending on fruit and vegetables. Note, however, that these results should be interpreted with caution, given that they could be

19. Table 9.4 presents robustness checks for the beneficiaries with the productive investment package. Results pooling all beneficiaries are similarly robust.

Table 9.4   Robustness checks and alternative specifications: beneficiaries of largest package two years after program

	Attending school (7–18-year-olds)	Number of days absent from school (7–18-year-olds)	School expenditures (7–18-year-olds)	Share of food expenditures for animal products	Share of food expenditures for fruit and vegetables
Base specification	0.093*	−2.676**	485.4**	0.050**	0.034***
	(0.050)	(1.09)	(200)	(0.019)	(0.011)
Robustness checks					
Excluding extreme values independent variable	0.064	−2.087*	319.5*	0.061***	0.037***
	(0.057)	(1.25)	(186)	(0.022)	(0.012)
SE clustered at level of assembly	0.093	−2.676**	485.4***	0.050***	0.034***
	(0.061)	(1.29)	(177)	(0.022)	(0.010)
Not excluding outliers			726.0**	0.051**	0.040***
			(325)	(0.020)	(0.012)
Controlling for number of people in assembly	0.093*	−2.681**	485.8**	0.051***	0.034***
	(0.049)	(1.06)	(201)	(0.019)	(0.011)
Controlling for number of peers in assembly	0.095*	−2.745**	495.4**	0.051***	0.034***
	(0.048)	(1.05)	(203)	(0.019)	(0.011)
With community fixed effects	0.096*	−2.668**	350.2	0.009	0.022**
	(0.051)	(1.16)	(226)	(0.019)	(0.010)
Alternative specifications with number of leaders					
No. leaders with largest package controlling for total no. leaders	0.019	−0.599*	94.64**	0.013**	0.009***
	(0.015)	(0.33)	(47.2)	(0.005)	(0.003)
No. leaders with largest package controlling for total no. leaders and community f.e.	0.033**	−0.855**	72.98	0.001	0.006**
	(0.016)	(0.36)	(53.8)	(0.005)	(0.003)
Alternative specifications with number of leaders and number of peers					
No. leaders with largest package controlling for total no. leaders	0.031	−0.833*	100.3*	0.009	0.007**
	(0.019)	(0.42)	(55.2)	(0.007)	(0.003)
No. peers with largest package controlling for total no. peers and community f.e.	−0.003	0.028	32.76	0.012**	0.001
	(0.020)	(0.45)	(36.9)	(0.005)	(0.003)
P-value test social effect leader = social effect peer	0.064*	0.046**	0.265	0.567	0.100*

Note: See notes to table 9.3. Every line corresponds to a separate specification, with the exception of the last specification where the number of leaders and peers are included in the same specification. Peers are defined as all beneficiaries with the same package that are not leaders. Specification with extreme values of independent variable excluded: excludes observations for which the value of the share is in the upper 5 percent of the distribution.

***Significant at the 1 percent level.

**Significant at the 5 percent level.

*Significant at the 10 percent level.

driven by the fact that there is less variation to identify the social effects of peers.

9.4.3   Results for Investments in Early Childhood

Table 9.5 shows estimates of the social multiplier effects for investments during early childhood, showing estimates for all children from birth to seven years old, and separately for the cohort of children born after the end of the transfers (i.e., children approximately from birth to two years old). The results show relatively large social multiplier effects for both age groups for both nutrition and stimulation. In contrast, we do not observe a similar pattern for health investments. This result is interesting, as the health conditionalities in Atención a Crisis were never monitored due to coordination problems between the ministry of health and the ministry of the family. It seems plausible that the health component was seen as less salient by leaders and less emphasized during discussions about the program. For nutrition and stimulation, the coefficients are positive and significantly different from zero for almost all beneficiaries, except those that were not exposed to any leader with the largest package. Impacts are larger for beneficiaries with higher exposure to such leaders.

Importantly, we find similar strong and significant social multiplier effects for investments in nutrition and stimulation for children born after the end of the transfers. This is true even if the statistical power is reduced as the cohort is much smaller. There are no significant differences in the coefficient of the multiplier effects for beneficiaries with different packages. Overall, these results point to a permanent shift in investment behavior among families exposed to successful leaders that goes beyond the impacts on the children that directly benefited from the intervention. This result suggests that the results in this chapter are not only driven by lasting impacts on children directly exposed to the positive CCT shock.

9.5   Social Interaction Effects on Per Capita Expenditures, Expectations, and Aspirations

While the identification strategy allows to clearly demonstrate the importance of the social interaction effects, it does not necessarily help to understand how exactly leaders might be influencing other households' investments. Indeed, one can wonder whether interaction with leaders with the largest package may have lifted economic constraints of other households, whether the interaction effects are driven by other households mimicking the behavior of these leaders, or whether they capture actual shifts in aspirations and expectations of nonleader households for the future of their children.

We investigate this question by analyzing the data regarding mothers' expectations and aspirations for children's final educational levels, future occupation, and earnings and living standards. Table 9.6 shows results of

Table 9.5   Social interaction effects on human capital investments in early childhood two years after program (2008)

Z-scores	Children 0–7 years old			Children born after end of transfers (0–2 years old)		
	Nutrition	Stimulation	Health	Nutrition	Stimulation	Health
Intent-to-treat × % leaders with largest package	0.323***	0.143*	0.004	0.383**	0.243**	0.087
	(0.11)	(0.078)	(0.076)	(0.18)	(0.11)	(0.089)
Intent-to-treat	−0.001	0.048	0.083**	0.067	0.033	−0.010
	(0.047)	(0.051)	(0.035)	(0.072)	(0.059)	(0.045)
Observations	3,410	3,405	3,410	660	641	660

Note: Coefficients for index of family of outcomes calculated following Kling, Liebman, and Katz (2007). Nutrition index includes share of food in total expenditures and shares of staples, animal proteins, and fruit and vegetables in total food expenditures; stimulation index includes whether household has pen and paper, has toy, somebody tells stories/sings to child, and number of hours reading to child per week; health index includes whether child was weighed, got vitamins or iron, got deworming drugs, and number of days sick in bed. See Macours, Schady, and Vakis (2012) for detailed definitions. The share of leaders measures the share of female leaders with the productive investment package over all female leaders in a beneficiary's registration assembly. Excluding households with female leaders. Intent-to-treat estimators. Robust standard errors in parentheses, corrected for clustering at the community level.

***Significant at the 1 percent level.

**Significant at the 5 percent level.

*Significant at the 10 percent level.

Table 9.6   Social interaction effects on parental expectations and aspirations, educational attainment, and per capita expenditures two years after program

	Average expectation index	Expected years of education attained	Expected occupation: professional	Expected occupation: professional or skilled empl.	Expected number of rooms in house	Expected monthly earnings: rank	Years of education attained	Log (per capita expenditures)
Intent-to-treat × % leaders with largest package	0.267***	0.805	0.035**	0.137***	0.304**	315.1**	0.700***	0.126
	(0.095)	(0.50)	(0.017)	(0.048)	(0.12)	(147)	(0.22)	(0.096)
Intent-to-treat	−0.052	−0.132	0.002	−0.033	−0.032	−79.30	−0.171	0.008
	(0.056)	(0.27)	(0.008)	(0.030)	(0.076)	(93.4)	(0.15)	(0.049)
Mean dependent variable in the control	0.00	8.41	0.023	0.25	2.62	2,543	3.12	9.11
Observations	4,304	4,300	4,291	4,291	4,299	4,242	4,086	3,230

	Average aspiration index	Desired years of education attained	Desired occupation: professional	Desired occupation: professional or skilled empl.	Desired number of rooms in house	Desired monthly earnings: rank
Intent-to-treat × % leaders with largest package	0.205*	0.946**	0.115*	0.028	0.146	342.2*
	(0.10)	(0.42)	(0.065)	(0.026)	(0.37)	(185)
Intent-to-treat	−0.018	−0.090	−0.015	0.015	−0.063	26.48
	(0.067)	(0.26)	(0.048)	(0.019)	(0.15)	(124)
Mean dependent variable in the control	−0.001	13.29	0.50	0.872	5.19	2.485
Observations	4,302	4,300	4,299	4,299	4,300	4,289

Note: The share of leaders measures the share of female leaders with the productive investment package over all female leaders in a beneficiary's registration assembly. Individual-level data for children seven to fifteen years old in 2008. Per capita expenditure measured at the household level. Excluding households with female leaders. Intent-to-treat estimators. Robust standard errors in parentheses, corrected for clustering at the community level. Average expectation index is average of standardized outcomes for expected years of education, professional or skilled employment, number of rooms in the house, and monthly earnings rank. Average aspiration index is average of standardized outcomes for expected years of education, professional employment, number of rooms in the house, and monthly earnings rank. Earnings ranks are calculated by converting the absolute monthly earnings to the rank in the earnings distribution, and combining answers of leaders and nonleaders.

***Significant at the 1 percent level.

**Significant at the 5 percent level.

*Significant at the 10 percent level.

the main specification for these outcomes, and also shows the spillovers on the educational level attained by 2008 and on per capita expenditures levels. These questions were only asked for children less than fifteen years old, as older children are more likely to already have reached their final education levels.[20] The top panel shows the impacts on the expectations mothers reported for their children, while the lower panel shows impacts on their aspirations.

Table 9.6 shows that parents' expectations about their children obtaining professional jobs or skilled salary jobs are strongly affected by exposure to leaders with the largest package. Having one more such leader in one's registration assembly increases expectations of parents for their children to become (white-collar) professionals by almost 50 percent (starting from a very low level in the control group). Strong social multiplier effects are also found for expectations regarding children's future earnings and living standards. The social interaction effects for mothers' aspirations follow a similar pattern.

Averaging over the different indicators, we find that the difference between no exposure and full exposure to leaders with the largest package increases expectations regarding children's future with 0.27 standard deviations, while it increases aspirations with 0.21 standard deviations.[21] The coefficients of the z-scores in table 9.6 also imply that, two years after the transfers, the impact on expectations and aspirations was only significantly different from zero if at least 60 percent of leaders in one's registration assembly received the largest package. Overall, these findings show that interactions with successful female leaders changed beneficiaries' expectations and aspirations for their children's educational and occupational future, consistent with the sustained higher levels of human capital investments.

The table further shows that the large spillover effects in investments are reflected in spillovers in educational attainment by 2008. Indeed, two years after the end of the intervention, being exposed to one additional leader with the largest package increases children's school attainment with 0.18 years of schooling. A comparison of this coefficient with the estimate on expectations suggests that parents expect the educational gains to persist and possibly slightly increase in the future. The estimates also imply, however, that the one-year CCT program did not significantly increase educational attainment for more than half of the children in the sample. Finally, the table shows that there is no significant social multiplier for per capita expenditures.

---

20. In an alternative specification, we excluded children below nine years old from the analysis, as the younger children did not directly benefit from the educational component of the CCT during the intervention. Results are broadly similar, but social multipliers on expected years of education, attained years of education, and expected earnings are slightly larger for the beneficiaries of the largest package.

21. Increases in aspirations (expectations) reflect a change toward more ambitious aspirations (expectations).

To further understand the potential role of relaxing economic constraints, table 9.7A shows social multiplier effects separately for each of the three types of beneficiaries. The last column in table 9.7A shows a significant social multiplier effect on per capita expenditures for households who got the largest package, but no such effects exist for the two other packages. Hence, beneficiaries who got the largest package are still better off two years after the intervention when a sufficiently large share of leaders in their proximity received the same package. This result is in line with findings on similar spillovers for productive investments during the intervention (Macours and Vakis 2014). In contrast, the coefficients of the interaction effects of per capita expenditures for beneficiaries with the basic and training package are very small, not significantly different from zero, and significantly different from the interaction effect for the largest package. Hence for the two other groups, economic spillovers cannot explain the change in education and nutrition investment.[22]

Considering then the impacts on expectations (table 9.7A), we see that social multiplier effects are significant for all three interventions, and are not significantly different from each other. Hence beneficiaries of the three packages expect a better future for their children, as long as they have sufficiently high exposure to leaders with the largest package. This is so even if only beneficiaries with the largest package are economically better off two years after the interventions. This mirrors the findings for investments, where we also found no significant differences between groups, even if the point estimates are higher for beneficiaries of the largest package. Hence the social multiplier effects do not just come from changes in economic constraints, as expectations and investments change also for the groups for whom economic constraints were not relaxed.

The results on aspirations (table 9.7B) complete the picture, as the social multiplier effects for aspirations are concentrated on beneficiaries who received the training package (and to a lesser extent those with the basic package). Possibly, for beneficiaries of the productive package, their own experience of trying to develop a nonagricultural activity may have dampened the impact of leaders' experiences on aspirations, in particular, given that average aspiration levels were already high. One could also hypothesize that the focus of this package on nonagricultural self-employment led these beneficiaries to put less weight on professional occupations or high levels of education for their children. In contrast, the results for beneficiaries of the training package are driven in particular by the aspirations for education and professional occupation, which may suggest training led to a higher

---

22. One could have thought such economic spillovers could arrive from leaders employing other beneficiaries in their new business, or otherwise transferring economic benefits from their increased income to other beneficiaries.

Table 9.7A   Social interaction effects on parental expectations, educational attainment, and per capita expenditures two years after program

	Average expectation index	Expected years of education attained	Expected occupation: professional	Expected occupation: professional or skilled employment	Expected number of rooms in house	Expected monthly earnings: rank	Years of education attained	Log (per capita expenditures)
Productive investment package × % leaders with largest package	0.270**	0.658	0.105***	0.158***	0.315*	343.3	0.521	0.277***
	(0.12)	(0.74)	(0.036)	(0.058)	(0.17)	(207)	(0.44)	(0.083)
Training package × % leaders with largest package	0.306**	0.991	−0.010	0.157**	0.385**	267.7	0.931***	0.070
	(0.14)	(0.73)	(0.028)	(0.076)	(0.16)	(223)	(0.32)	(0.10)
Basic package × % leaders with largest package	0.220*	0.761	0.016	0.092	0.217	310.4	0.596*	0.051
	(0.12)	(0.53)	(0.027)	(0.070)	(0.19)	(237)	(0.35)	(0.15)
Productive investment package	−0.055	−0.087	−0.010	−0.041	−0.020	−112.5	−0.169	−0.010
	(0.057)	(0.28)	(0.011)	(0.033)	(0.079)	(102)	(0.18)	(0.045)
Training package	−0.068	−0.225	0.010	−0.036	−0.065	−87.8	−0.265	0.011
	(0.072)	(0.38)	(0.014)	(0.037)	(0.10)	(108)	(0.19)	(0.057)
Basic package	−0.029	−0.086	0.006	−0.021	−0.013	−22.2	−0.061	0.022
	(0.066)	(0.30)	(0.010)	(0.035)	(0.10)	(119)	(0.17)	(0.064)
P-value test social effect on T3 vs. T2	0.830	0.737	0.004***	0.996	0.757	0.743	0.490	0.026**
P-value test social effect on T3 vs. T1	0.693	0.863	0.088*	0.428	0.629	0.911	0.885	0.061*
P-value test social effect on T1 vs. T2	0.550	0.725	0.527	0.476	0.452	0.899	0.430	0.860
Mean dependent variable in the control	0.00	8.41	0.023	0.25	2.62	2.543	3.12	9.11
Observations	4,304	4,300	4,291	4,291	4,299	4,242	4,086	3,230

Note: The share of leaders measures the share of female leaders with the productive investment package over all female leaders in a beneficiary's registration assembly. Individual-level data for children seven to fifteen years old in 2008. Per capita expenditure measured at the household level. Excluding households with female leaders. Intent-to-treat estimators. Robust standard errors in parentheses, corrected for clustering at the community level. Average expectation index is average of standardized outcomes for expected years of education, professional or skilled employment, number of rooms in the house, and monthly earnings rank. Earnings ranks are calculated by converting the absolute monthly earnings to the rank in the earnings distribution, and combining answers of leaders and nonleaders.

***Significant at the 1 percent level.

**Significant at the 5 percent level.

*Significant at the 10 percent level.

Table 9.7B   Social interaction effects on parental aspirations by intervention group two years after program ended

	Average aspiration index	Desired years of education attained	Desired occupation: professional	Desired occupation: professional or skilled empl.	Desired number of rooms in house	Desired monthly earnings: rank
Productive investment package × % leaders with largest package	-0.008	0.338	-0.032	-0.038	-0.481	331.0
	(0.12)	(0.57)	(0.091)	(0.042)	(0.34)	(304)
Training package × % leaders with largest package	0.406***	2.114***	0.297***	0.084**	0.378	266.3
	(0.13)	(0.70)	(0.097)	(0.042)	(0.24)	(236)
Basic package × % leaders with largest package	0.233	0.379	0.081	0.039	0.603	470.6*
	(0.18)	(0.52)	(0.078)	(0.046)	(0.89)	(276)
Productive investment package	0.068	0.169	0.039	0.034	0.163	68.1
	(0.072)	(0.29)	(0.051)	(0.023)	(0.17)	(154)
Training package	-0.147**	-0.661*	-0.119**	-0.016	-0.300**	26.5
	(0.074)	(0.36)	(0.059)	(0.027)	(0.15)	(125)
Basic package	0.015	0.212	0.033	0.025	-0.087	-32.3
	(0.079)	(0.29)	(0.051)	(0.026)	(0.22)	(151)
P-value test social effect on T3 vs. T2	0.006***	0.027**	0.007***	0.290	0.033**	0.853
P-value test social effect on T3 vs. T1	0.206	0.958	0.309	0.832	0.211	0.701
P-value test social effect on T1 vs. T2	0.319	0.016**	0.017**	0.375	0.784	0.548
Mean dependent variable in the control	-0.001	13.29	0.50	0.872	5.19	2,485
Observations	4,302	4,300	4,299	4,299	4,300	4,289

Note: The share of leaders measures the share of female leaders with the productive investment package over all female leaders in a beneficiary's registration assembly. Individual-level data for children seven to fifteen years old in 2008. Excluding households with female leaders. Intent-to-treat estimators. Robust standard errors in parentheses, corrected for clustering at the community level. Average aspiration index is average of standardized outcomes for expected years of education, professional employment, number of rooms in the house, and monthly earnings rank. Earnings ranks are calculated by converting the absolute monthly earnings to the rank in the earnings distribution, and combining answers of leaders and nonleaders.

***Significant at the 1 percent level.

**Significant at the 5 percent level.

*Significant at the 10 percent level.

orientation toward education.[23] Yet the results show these increased aspirations only materialized if they were exposed to a large share of leaders with the largest package. Indeed, there even is a significant negative impact on aspirations if none of the leaders in their proximity got the largest package, suggesting that some training beneficiaries in fact got demotivated.[24]

While the differences in findings for expectations and aspirations are intriguing, they could in part be driven by measurement errors. Parents may find hypothetical questions regarding the desired future for their children hard to answer and the difference between expectations and aspirations, while theoretically important for economists, are not necessarily accurately captured by the answers mothers gave to the respective questions. A more cautious interpretation of the results in tables 9.6 and 9.7A and B, therefore, is that there was a significant social multiplier effect on parents' attitudes regarding their children's future for the three types of beneficiaries. This attitudinal change in turn is consistent with the social multiplier effect on investment behavior, and helps explain the increased investment by beneficiaries for whom per capita expenditure levels did not increase.

Finally, one can wonder whether the results after the end of the program result because leaders with the largest package are still communicating more with other beneficiaries than leaders with other packages. This does not appear to be the case, as we find no significant social multiplier effects on the probability of talking to a leader, a teacher, or health coordinators two years after the intervention (not reported). This is in line with qualitative interviews after the end of the program, which suggested that some *promotoras* may have continued to meet with beneficiaries, but that this was rather limited. Nevertheless, increased communication during the program may have played a role in shifting the local social norms toward more investment in children on the short term, which in turn may have led to persistent changes in investment behavior.

9.6 Conclusions

Many development interventions aim, through a variety of mechanisms, to shift the investment behavior of beneficiary households. Conditional cash transfer programs have an implicit or explicit objective to change households' attitudes and the social norms toward investment in the education, health, and nutrition of their children. When programs are designed to last for only a limited period, the sustainability of the impacts might crucially

23. The vocational training may have made beneficiaries more aware of the potential gains to formal education through a number of channels: exposure to the professional staff conducting the training, increased awareness of the benefits of skilled wage employment, or awareness of the importance of education to increase returns to other training (as illiterate beneficiaries in particular were very limited in their choice of courses).

24. As training did not lead to significant increases in income, this does not seem implausible.

depend on whether changes in investment behavior persist after the end of the program. Yet, the mechanisms through which such change can be reached and reinforced are not always clear.

This chapter shows that social interactions with successful and motivated local leaders can change the way parents think about their children's future and result in sustainable changes in educational and nutritional investment. The evidence in this chapter hence draws attention to the positive role local leaders can play, which contrasts with the focus in many policy discussions of the negative role of leaders through elite capture. The results suggest that natural leaders living in people's close proximity can be important vehicles for change by motivating and encouraging others and by providing examples that people aspire to follow. We find these effects when both leaders and other beneficiaries received sizable transfers, and social effects are particularly large when leaders and beneficiaries received the same package. Hence the results do not suggest that interventions should be primarily targeted to leaders. Instead, it points to the importance of assuring that development program designs take into account the presence of local natural leaders and enhance their ownership of a program's objectives to help shift beneficiaries' attitudes.

The large social interactions effects found in this chapter are suggestive of the existence of multiple equilibria and can hence be interpreted in the context of dynamic poverty trap models (Barrett, Carter, and Chavas, introduction, this volume). Interventions such as the program studied in this chapter may not only affect external constraints, but also shift internal potential constraints, potentially breaking existing poverty traps, in line with Lybbert and Wydick (chapter 4, this volume). If internal constraints are partly driven by beliefs or social norms, local leaders can have an important role in helping shift these social norms and help tip communities toward the high equilibrium.

The results also have implications for the debate on the sustainability of using cash or asset transfer programs in low- and middle-income countries. The evidence in this chapter suggests that designing such programs in ways that facilitate and encourage social interactions may be important to create sustainable change. An important caveat for the interpretation of the findings is that we provide evidence of program persistence for a pilot program that only lasted one year. As such it differs from many other CCT programs in Latin America, where beneficiaries often receive transfers for many years. This could have implications for the external validity of the findings, as households do not necessarily react similarly to a one-year transitory shock than to a longer-term transfer program. The chapter hence should primarily be seen as a proof-of-concept for the role local leaders can play in sustainably shifting poor households' educational and nutritional investments. More generally, the findings highlight the potential importance for careful attention to social dynamics in the design and implementation of programs targeting human capital investments.

References

Adato, Michele. 2000. *Final Report: The Impact of Progresa on Community Social Relationships*. Washington, DC: International Food Policy Research Institute.

Adato, Michelle, and Terry Roopnaraine. 2004. *Final Report: A Social Analysis of the Red de Proteccion Social (RPS) in Nicaragua*. Washington, DC: International Food Policy Research Institute.

Appadurai, Arjun. 2004. "The Capacity to Aspire." In *Culture and Public Action*, edited by V. Rao and M. Walton. Palo Alto, CA: Stanford University Press.

Araujo, Caridad, Mariano Bosch, and Norbert Schady, 2016. "Can Cash Transfers Help Households Escape an Inter-generational Poverty Trap?" NBER Working Paper no. 22670, Cambridge, MA.

Athey, Susan, and Guido W. Imbens. 2016. "The Econometrics of Randomized Experiments." In *Handbook of Economic Field Experiments*, vol. 1, edited by A. Banerjee and E. Duflo. Amsterdam: Elsevier.

Attanasio, Orazio, Camila Fernandez, Emla Fitzsimons, Sally Grantham-McGregor, Costas Meghir, and Marta Rubio-Codina. 2014. "Using the Infrastructure of a Conditional Cash Transfer Program to Deliver a Scalable Integrated Early Child Development Program in Colombia: Cluster Randomised Controlled Trial." *British Medical Journal* 349:5785. https://doi.org/10.1136/bmj.g5785.

Baird, Sarah, Craig McIntosh, and Berk Özler. 2016. "When the Money Runs Out: Do Cash Transfers Have Sustained Effects?" Policy Research Working Paper no. 7901, World Bank.

Barham, Tania, Karen Macours, and John A. Maluccio. 2013a. "Boys' Cognitive Skill Formation and Physical Growth: Long-Term Experimental Evidence on Critical Ages for Early Childhood Interventions." *American Economic Review Papers and Proceedings* 103 (3): 467–71.

———. 2013b. "More Schooling and More Learning? Effects of a Three-Year Conditional Cash Transfer Program in Nicaragua after 10 Years." IADB Working Paper no. IDB-WP-432, Inter-American Development Bank.

Barrera-Osorio, Felipe, Leigh L. Linden, and Juan E. Saavedra. 2015. "Long-Term Educational Consequences of Alternative Conditional Cash Transfer Designs: Experimental Evidence from Colombia." Unpublished manuscript.

Beaman, Lori, Raghabendra Chattopadhyay, Esther Duflo, Rohini Pande, and Petia Topalova. 2009. "Powerful Women: Does Exposure Reduce Bias?" *Quarterly Journal of Economics* 124 (4): 1497–540.

Beaman, Lori, Esther Duflo, Rohini Pande, and Petia Topalova. 2012. "Female Leadership Raises Aspirations and Educational Attainment for Girls: A Policy Experiment in India." *Science* 355:582–86.

Behrman, Jere R., Susan W. Parker, and Petra E. Todd. 2009. "Schooling Impacts of Conditional Cash Transfers on Young Children: Evidence from Mexico." *Economic Development and Cultural Change* 57 (3): 439–77.

———. 2011. "Do Conditional Cash Transfers for Schooling Generate Lasting Benefits? Five-Year Follow-Up of PROGRESA/Oportunidades." *Journal of Human Resources* 46 (1): 93–122.

Bernard, Tanguy, Stefan Dercon, Kate Orkin, and Alemayehu Seyoum Taffesse. 2014. "The Future in Mind: Aspirations and Forward-Looking Behaviour in Rural Ethiopia." CSAE Working Paper no. WPS/2014-16, Centre for the Study of African Economies, University of Oxford.

Besley, Timothy. 2017. "Aspirations and the Political Economy of Inequality." *Oxford Economic Papers* 69 (1): 1–35.

Chattopadhyay, Raghabendra, and Esther Duflo. 2004. "Women as Policy Makers: Evidence from a Randomized Policy Experiment in India." *Econometrica* 72 (5): 1409–43.

Feigenberg, Benjamin, Erica Field, and Rohini Pande. 2013. "The Economic Returns to Social Interaction: Experimental Evidence from Microfinance." *Review of Economic Studies* 80 (4): 1459–83.

Filmer, Deon, and Norbert R. Schady. 2014. "The Medium-Term Effects of Scholarships in a Low-Income Country." *Journal of Human Resources* 49 (3): 663–94.

Fiszbein, Ariel, and Norbert R. Schady, 2009. "Conditional Cash Transfers: Reducing Present and Future Poverty." World Bank Policy Research Report, Washington, DC, World Bank.

Ganimian, Alejandro J., and Richard J. Murnane, 2014. "Improving Educational Outcomes in Developing Countries: Lessons from Rigorous Evaluations." NBER Working Paper no. 20284, Cambridge, MA.

Genicot, Garance, and Debraj Ray. 2014. "Aspirations and Inequality." NBER Working Paper no. 19976, Cambridge, MA.

Gertler, Paul, Sebastian Martinez, and Marta Rubio-Codina. 2012. "Investing Cash Transfers to Raise Long-Term Living Standards." *American Economic Journal: Applied Economics* 4 (1): 164–92.

Hoff, Karla, and Joseph E. Stiglitz. 2016. "Striving for Balance in Economics: Towards a Theory of the Social Determination of Behavior." *Journal of Economic Behavior & Organization* 126 (PB): 25–57.

Jensen, Robert. 2010. "Impact of Information on the Returns to Education on the Demand for Schooling in the Dominican Republic." *Quarterly Journal of Economics* 125:515–48.

Jensen, Robert, and Emily Oster. 2009. "The Power of TV: Cable Television and Women's Status in India." *Quarterly Journal of Economics* 124 (3): 1057–94.

Kling, Jeffrey, R., Jeffrey B. Liebman, and Lawrence F. Katz. 2007. "Experimental Analysis of Neighborhood Effects." *Econometrica* 75 (1): 83–119.

La Ferrara, Eliana, Alberto Chong, and Suzanne Duryea. 2012. "Soap Operas and Fertility: Evidence from Brazil." *American Economic Journal: Applied Economics* 4 (4): 1–31.

Lybbert, Travis, and Bruce Wydick. 2016. "Poverty, Aspirations, and the Economics of Hope: A Framework for Study with Preliminary Results from the Oaxaca Hope Project." Paper presented at NBER conference "The Economics of Asset Dynamics and Poverty Traps," Washington, DC, June 28. https://basis.ucdavis.edu/sites/g/files/dgvnsk466/files/inline-files/NBER-Conference-DC_6-28-16.pdf.

Macours, Karen, Patrick Premand, and Renos Vakis. 2012. "Transfers, Diversification and Household Risk Strategies: Experimental Evidence with Lessons for Climate Change Adaptation." CEPR Discussion Paper no. 8940, London, Center for Economic Policy Research.

Macours, Karen, Norbert R. Schady, and Renos Vakis. 2012. "Cash Transfers, Behavioral Changes, and Cognitive Development in Early Childhood: Evidence from a Randomized Experiment." *American Economic Journal: Applied Economics* 4 (2): 247–73.

Macours, Karen, and Renos Vakis. 2014. "Changing Households' Investment Behaviour through Social Interactions with Local Leaders: Evidence from a Randomized Transfer Program." *Economic Journal* 124:607–33.

Manski, Charles F. 2000. "Economic Analysis of Social Interactions." *Journal of Economic Perspectives* 14 (3): 115–36.

Molina-Millan, Teresa, Tania Barham, Karen Macours, John A. Maluccio, and Marco Stampini. 2016. "Long-Term Impacts of Conditional Cash Transfers in Latin America: Review of the Evidence." IAB Technical Note no. IDB-N-923, Inter-American Development Bank.

Nguyen, Trang. 2008. "Information, Role Models and Perceived Returns to Education: Experimental Evidence from Madagascar." Working paper, Massachusetts Institute of Technology.

Paluck, Elizabeth Levy, and Hana Shepherd. 2012. "The Salience of Social Referents: A Field Experiment on Collective Norms and Harassment Behavior in a School Social Network." *Journal of Personality and Social Psychology* 103 (6): 899–915.

Ray, Debraj. 2006. "Aspirations, Poverty, and Economic Change." In *Understanding Poverty*, edited by Abhijit V. Banerjee, Roland Bénabou, and Dilip Mookherjee. Oxford: Oxford University Press.

World Bank. 2015. *World Development Report 2015: Mind, Society and Behavior.* Washington, DC: World Bank.

Wydick, Bruce, Paul Glewwe, and Laine Rutledge. 2013. "Does International Child Sponsorship Work? A Six-Country Study of Impacts on Adult Life Outcomes." *Journal of Political Economy* 121 (2): 393–436.

Can Cash Transfers Help Households Escape an Intergenerational Poverty Trap?

M. Caridad Araujo, Mariano Bosch,
and Norbert Schady

10.1 Introduction

A substantial proportion of households in developing countries are poor.[1] These households suffer from multiple deprivations—low income, poor health, low education levels, poor housing conditions, and inadequate access to a variety of services like potable water and sanitation. Many poor households are also liquidity constrained, and are not able to borrow to invest in the human capital of their children, even if the returns to these investments are high.[2] This, in turn, could result in an intergenerational poverty trap: the children of poor households are more likely to be poor in adulthood in part because of failures in credit and other markets. Programs that directly transfer cash to households are one way of attempting to break the cycle whereby poverty is transmitted from one generation to the next.

Cash transfer programs have become very popular in many developing countries. In Latin America, the largest programs have budgets close to one-

M. Caridad Araujo is Principal Social Protection Economist in the Social Protection and Health Division of the Inter-American Development Bank. Mariano Bosch is Principal Economist and Pensions Coordinator at the Labor Market and Social Security Unit of the Inter-American Development Bank. Norbert Schady is the Principal Economic Advisor for the Social Sector of the Inter-American Development Bank.

We are grateful to Jere Behrman, Karen Macours, and participants at the NBER conference for their comments. For acknowledgments, sources of research support, and disclosure of the authors' material financial relationships, if any, please see http://www.nber.org/chapters /c13838.ack.

1. The World Bank estimates that in 2012, 12.7 percent of the world's population was extremely poor (living below a poverty line of US$1.90 per capita per day), while 35 percent lived below a poverty line of US$3.10 (World Bank 2016).

2. There are other reasons why poor parents may underinvest in the human capital of their children, including incomplete altruism or mistaken beliefs about the returns to investments in children.

half point of gross domestic product (GDP) (Levy and Schady 2013). Do cash transfers reduce current poverty? And do they reduce the likelihood that the children of currently poor households will be poor in the future, thus helping households escape an intergenerational poverty trap?

Whether cash transfers reduce *current* poverty depends primarily on the magnitude of the transfer, and on the extent to which households offset transfer income by working less. In practice, a number of evaluations and simulations suggest that cash transfers reduce current income or consumption poverty, especially when the amount transferred is large (Fiszbein and Schady 2009). Separate evidence shows that cash transfers do not reduce work effort in the short run (Banerjee et al. 2017) or medium run (Araujo, Bosch, and Schady 2017).[3]

The extent to which cash transfers reduce *future* poverty hinges largely on whether the children of households that received transfers accumulate more human capital.[4] There is considerable evidence that cash transfers increase school enrollment.[5] Having children enroll in school, however, may not be enough to improve their life chances in adulthood if these children do not complete more years of schooling, or learn little while they are in school.

To credibly assess whether cash transfers can help children escape an intergenerational poverty trap, one needs panel data that follow children from the period in which their parents received cash transfers into adolescence or adulthood. Such data are very infrequent (Molina-Millan et al. [2016] is a review).

Barham, Macours, and Maluccio (2013, 2016) study the long-term effects of cash transfers made in Nicaragua. In one paper (Barham, Macours, and Maluccio 2013) they compare outcomes for children whose families received cash transfers during the potentially critical "first 1,000 days" window (while the child was in utero and in the first two years of life) with children in families that received transfers somewhat later. They find that receiving cash transfers earlier in life raised performance on tests of cognition of boys by 0.15 standard deviations ten years later. Barham, Macours, and Maluccio (2016) focus on transfers received in late childhood. They find that boys who

3. Cash transfers do reduce child labor, as intended. See Attanasio et al. (2010) on Colombia, Edmonds and Schady (2012) on Ecuador, and Maluccio and Flores (2005) on Nicaragua. However, the reductions in child labor are not large enough to offset the effect of the transfer on total household income. A separate question is whether transfer income is spent in the same way as other sources of income. There is some evidence from developing countries that this is not the case. For example, a disproportionate proportion of the transfer appears to be spent on food and on goods that benefit children (see Angelucci and Attanasio [2013] and Attanasio and Lechene [2014] on Mexico; Attanasio et al. [2010] on Colombia; Macours, Schady, and Vakis [2012] on Nicaragua; and Schady and Rosero [2008] on Ecuador). It is unclear whether this is a result of the fact that transfers are made to women, who are likely to have different preferences than men, or the fact that transfers are frequently conditional or "labeled." Conversely, there is no evidence that cash transfers are disproportionately spent on "sin goods" like alcohol and tobacco (Evans and Popova 2014).

4. Cash transfers could also reduce future poverty if households invest the transfer in a productive asset that yields a stream of income in the future. The evidence on this is mixed. See Gertler, Martínez, and Rubio-Codina (2012) on Mexico, and Maluccio (2010) on Nicaragua.

5. Baird et al. (2014) and Fiszbein and Schady (2009) review the evidence.

benefited from cash transfers complete 0.5 more years of schooling, have test scores that are 0.2 standard deviations higher, and have 10–30 percent higher monthly off-farm income ten years later.

However, the results from other evaluations have been less encouraging. In Mexico, Behrman, Parker, and Todd (2009, 2011) conclude that three years of cash transfers (relative to no transfers) resulted in approximately 0.3 more grades of completed schooling, but did not increase performance on tests of reading, writing, and math. In Cambodia, a program that made transfers to families of girls in middle school increased school attainment by 0.6 years, but did not improve test scores or labor market outcomes (employment and earnings) three years after the program had ended (Filmer and Schady 2014).

In this chapter, we study the long-term (ten-year) effects of transfers made by what at the time of our analysis was the largest (in proportional terms) cash transfer program in Latin America, the Bono de Desarrollo Humano (BDH; Human Development Bond) in Ecuador. The BDH made generous transfers—by 2010 transfers accounted for 20 percent of pretransfer income of recipient households, on average. At its peak, the program covered 40 percent of households in the country, and had a budget of 0.7 percent of GDP. Unlike some of the better-known programs in Latin America (like the PROGRESA program in Mexico or the Bolsa Familia program in Brazil), BDH transfers were not explicitly conditional on prespecified behaviors like school enrollment, although households were encouraged to spend transfer income on children (Schady and Araujo 2008).

We present results from two different data sources, two identification strategies, and corresponding to two critical stages in the accumulation of human capital over the life cycle. The first set of results focuses on children who became eligible for transfers in early childhood. Many authors in a number of disciplines have stressed the importance of health and development in the first years of life.[6] Our results are based on data from an evaluation that randomly assigned households to an "early" and "late" treatment group in 2003. All households in the evaluation sample had at least one child under the age of six years at baseline. The early treatment group began to receive BDH transfers in 2004, while the late treatment group only became eligible for transfers three years later. We use data collected in a household survey in 2014 to test whether children in the early treatment group outperform those in the late treatment group in various dimensions. By 2011, the last year in which we have administrative data on BDH payments, the early treatment group had received about twice as much in total transfers as the late treatment group. Despite this, we find no difference between children in the two groups in performance on tests of language, math, attention, working memory, fluency of recovery, and in behavioral outcomes.

---

6. See, among many important references, Almond and Currie (2010), Cunha and Heckman (2007), and Shonkoff and Phillips (2000).

In Ecuador, like many other middle-income countries, elementary school completion rates are essentially universal. The first critical decision point that determines how much schooling a child attains occurs in secondary school. For this reason, in our second set of results we focus on children in households that were eligible for transfers when these children were of an age at which they were making decisions about secondary school enrollment and completion. We make use of the fact that the BDH program has used a poverty score to determine eligibility for transfers since 2003. This poverty score creates a sharp cutoff in eligibility. We compare the school attainment and employment status of young adults, ages nineteen to twenty-five in 2013/14, in households that were just-eligible and just-ineligible for cash transfers between 2003 and 2009.

We find that young adults in households that were just-eligible for transfers are more likely to have completed secondary school. However, the magnitude of the effect is modest, between 1 and 2 percentage points (from a counterfactual of 75 percent). Program impacts appear to be somewhat larger (and are only significant) among women than men. On the other hand, we do not find that BDH transfers increased employment among young adults. This does *not* appear to be because transfer recipients are more likely to continue on to tertiary education—there is no effect of the transfer on the probability that a young adult is enrolled in an educational institution in 2013/14. Rather, it appears that cash transfers prevented a small fraction of women from dropping out of school before completing secondary school, but did not have a measurable effect on their later education or work choices.

In sum, our analysis shows that children in households that received larger cash transfers in early childhood do not have better outcomes in late childhood than those who received substantially smaller transfers, while cash transfers received in late childhood had small effects on the school attainment of young adults. We conclude that, although our results are not definitive, it is likely that cash transfers will have at most a modest effect on the probability that the children of poor households in Ecuador will escape poverty in the future.

The rest of the chapter proceeds as follows. In section 10.2, we describe the BDH program, earlier evaluations, and education in Ecuador. Section 10.3 discusses our identification strategy, and section 10.4 presents results. We conclude in section 10.5.

10.2   Context

10.2.1   Cash Transfers in Ecuador

The current welfare system in Ecuador, which includes the BDH program, dates back to the late 1990s. In 1999 the country suffered from a severe banking crisis, GDP per capita fell by 32 percent in a single year, and unemployment increased from 9 to 17 percent. In this context, the Ecuadorean government created a cash transfer program, the Bono Solidario (Solidarity Bond). Payments were intended to go to poor households. However, because the program did not have clear selection criteria, many recipients were non-poor, and many poor households did not receive transfers.

In 2000/02, the government carried out a "poverty census" known as the Selben; the Selben covered about 90 percent of households in rural areas, and about the same fraction of households in select urban areas that were judged to have a high incidence of poverty. It gathered information on household composition, education levels, work, dwelling characteristics, and access to services. This information was aggregated into a poverty score by principal components. Beginning in March 2003, this poverty score was used to determine eligibility for transfers. The name of the program was also changed from Bono Solidario to Bono de Desarrollo Humano.

New poverty censuses were carried out in 2007/08 and 2013/14. Once again, the information was aggregated by principal components, and new poverty scores were calculated in 2009 and 2015. In both cases, the change in the poverty score resulted in considerable reshuffling of households in and out of eligibility.[7]

Transfer payments in Ecuador have grown in magnitude over time. Bono Solidario began with a seven dollar transfer per household. With the creation of the BDH in 2003, the transfer increased to fifteen dollars, was revised upward in 2009 (to thirty-five dollars), and increased again in 2014 (to fifty dollars). Payments have also grown as a proportion of household income of the poor—from 13 percent of the pretransfer income of the poorest 40 percent of the population in 1999 to 20 percent a decade later.

10.2.2 Earlier Evaluations of the BDH Program

There are numerous evaluations of the impact of BDH transfers on a variety of outcomes. These are based on different samples and different identification strategies. Paxson and Schady (2010) use a randomized experiment to evaluate the short-term effects of transfers on the development of young children. They find no effects of the transfers, on average. However, among the poorest households, BDH transfers improved child physical development (by 0.16 standard deviations) and cognitive and socioemotional development (by 0.18 standard deviations).[8] Using data from the same

---

7. For example, 36 percent of all households in the first poverty census had scores that placed them within 5 points of the cutoff that determined eligibility for transfers. Among these households, 46 percent of those eligible for transfers by the first poverty census became ineligible, and 42 percent of households who were ineligible became eligible.

8. The measure of child physical development is based on three outcomes: child height, elevation-adjusted hemoglobin, and a measure of fine motor control. The measure of child cognitive and behavioral development is based on five outcomes: language development, tests of short- and long-term memory, a test in which a child is asked to find patterns in pictures, and the Behavioral Problems Index (BPI), a commonly used scale that is based on the frequency that a child displays each of twenty-nine behaviors, as reported by her mother. Within a composite, each individual outcome receives the same weight.

experiment, Fernald and Hidrobo (2011) show that the program improved outcomes of infants and toddlers, while Hidrobo and Fernald (2013) argue that the intervention reduced domestic violence. Schady (2012a) shows that BDH transfers reduced the proportion of adult women who were anemic. In our chapter, we use panel data from this evaluation. Specifically, we follow children who were five years of age or younger at baseline into late childhood to test for program effects ten years later.

A second randomized experiment of the BDH focused on households with school-age children at baseline. With these data, Schady and Araujo (2008) find that BDH transfers substantially increased school enrollment, especially among households who (erroneously) believed that the transfers were conditional on enrollment. Positive effects of transfers on school enrollment are also reported by Oosterbeek, Ponce, and Schady (2008). Edmonds and Schady (2012) show that BDH transfers substantially reduced child labor. Schady and Rosero (2008) find that transfers resulted in an upward shift of the food Engel curve—households who were eligible for transfers spent a higher fraction of income on food.

Others have exploited the fact that the BDH program used a poverty score to determine eligibility as a source of identification. Ponce and Bedi (2010) report positive program effects on tests of language and math achievement. An important limitation of their paper, however, is that they do not have data on the actual poverty score of households. Rather, they attempt to recreate poverty scores with data from a household survey. Araujo, Bosch, and Schady (2017) analyze whether transfers affected the work decisions of adults. The data they use include the household poverty scores that the BDH program used to determine eligibility for transfers. Their analysis, which is similar in spirit to that which we carry out in this chapter, finds that the BDH did not reduce work effort. However, transfers appear to have shifted some women from formal to informal employment as a way of hiding income.

In sum, there are a number of earlier evaluations of the BDH program, including on schooling outcomes. However, with the exception of Araujo, Bosch, and Schady (2017), all of these evaluations have focused on short-term impacts. The most important contribution of our chapter is that we study the effects of cash transfers on young children (birth to five years of age) and somewhat older children (nine to fifteen years of age) after ten years.

10.2.3   Schooling in Ecuador

Schooling in Ecuador is compulsory from five to fourteen years of age. The elementary school cycle runs from kindergarten to 6th grade, and secondary school from 7th through 12th grades. Eighty percent of school-age children are enrolled in public schools, with the remainder in private schools. After secondary school, there are a large number of vocational colleges, technical schools, and universities, both public and private.

Ecuador has made considerable progress expanding the coverage of the education system, as can be seen in figure 10.1.[9] Panel A shows that school enrollment of children of elementary school age is close to universal—over 99 percent of children age six to eleven are enrolled in school. Panel B shows there have been substantial increases in elementary school completion over time. Averaging across men and women, the proportion who graduated from elementary school increased from 65 percent for the cohort born in 1950–1954 to 94 percent for the cohort born in 1985–1989. Importantly, this suggests that there is little room for a cash transfer program like the BDH (or any other program) to affect the school enrollment of young children or elementary school completion rates.

Turning to somewhat older children, figure 10.1, panel A, shows that, after age eleven, school enrollment declines gradually: at age fifteen, 92 percent of children are enrolled in school, and at age eighteen, only 49 percent of individuals are enrolled in some educational institution. Panel C, finally, shows that secondary school completion rates have gone up sharply over time—from 24 percent for the cohort born in 1950–1954 to 58 percent for the cohort born in 1985–1989. However, even in the most recent cohorts, a substantial proportion of adults dropped out before completing secondary school. It follows that cash transfers could, in principle, increase school enrollment and attainment for this age group.[10]

Finally, figure 10.1 shows that educational gaps between men and women have closed over time. As is the case in other Latin American countries, there are now no substantive differences in enrollment rates of boys and girls. For the most recent cohorts, there are no differences by gender in graduation rates from elementary or secondary school, either.

Although school enrollment rates in Ecuador have gone up, the quality of education is a serious challenge. Ecuador does not participate in the international PISA (Programme for International Student Assessment) tests, so it is hard to benchmark the performance of children in high school in Ecuador relative to other countries. However, Ecuador was one of fifteen countries in Latin America that participated in TERCE, a test of 3rd and 6th grade children carried out in 2013. In 3rd grade math, 47.8 percent of children in Ecuador had the lowest of the four levels of performance on the test, very similar to the average for Latin America (47.2 percent), but substantially more than higher-performing countries like Costa Rica (23.1 percent) or Chile (15.4 percent) (UNESCO 2015). Results are very similar for 6th graders.

9. To carry out these calculations, we used the 2015 Encuesta Nacional de Empleo, Desempleo y Subempleo (ENEMDU), a nationally representative household survey in Ecuador.

10. Evidence from a number of evaluations shows that, unsurprisingly, cash transfers have the biggest effects on school enrollment for children in grades where dropout is high. See Barrera-Osorio et al. (2011) on Colombia, de Janvry and Sadoulet (2006) and Schultz (2004) on Mexico, Filmer and Schady (2008, 2014) on Cambodia, and Schady and Araujo (2008) on Ecuador.

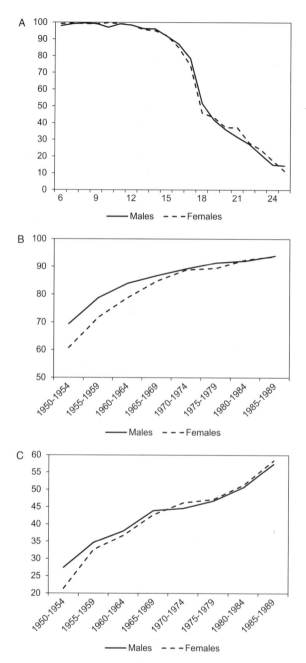

Fig. 10.1 **Schooling outcomes in Ecuador by gender.** *A*, **school enrollment by age;** *B*, **elementary school completion by birth cohort;** *C*, **secondary school completion by birth cohort.**

Note: Own calculations based on the 2016 ENEMDU household survey.

There are steep socioeconomic gradients in test scores of school-age children in Ecuador (Berlinski and Schady 2015). To a large extent, these gradients are already apparent before children enter school (Paxson and Schady 2007; Schady et al. 2015). The deep deficits in cognitive development, and the low test scores of poor children in Ecuador, suggest that cash transfers could in principle improve learning outcomes if transfer income were spent in a way that benefits children.

10.3   Data and Identification Strategy

10.3.1   Experimental Analysis

As discussed above, one set of estimates we report is based on data from a panel of households that have been followed since 2003. Households in this panel were part of a randomized evaluation of the impact of cash transfers on child health and development (see Paxson and Schady [2010] for a discussion). One group of households was randomly assigned to an early treatment group, and another to a late treatment group.[11] At baseline, all households in both groups had at least one child under the age of six years.[12] The baseline survey was collected between October 2003 and March 2004; follow-up surveys have been carried out regularly since then, most recently in 2014.[13]

Figure 10.2 shows that the proportion of households in the early treatment group that received transfers rose sharply after June 2004, when they were first made eligible; by March 2005, roughly 50 percent of households in this group received transfers in any given month. The figure also shows that the proportion of households in the late treatment group that received transfers increased steadily after March 2007, when they in turn were first made eligible; however, the take-up of the BDH increased more slowly in this group, and never fully caught up with the early treatment group. It is likely that this occurred because some households in the late treatment group never realized that their eligibility status had, in fact, changed. In any event, by the end of 2011 (the last point at which we have payment data for this sample) households

11. Random assignment was done at the parish level. Parishes are the smallest administrative units in Ecuador. Fifty-one parishes were assigned to the early treatment and twenty-six to the late treatment group. Within these parishes, a sample of households who were in principle eligible for transfers given their poverty score, but had never received payments, was selected.

12. An additional requirement was that households in the sample did not have any children six years of age or older. Payments made by the BDH are not conditional on any prespecified household behaviors. At an early stage, however, program administrators considered making the program conditional on regular health checkups for households with young children, and on school attendance for households with older children. It was not clear which condition would apply to households that had both younger and older children. For this reason, the evaluation design required that households in the sample have young children, but not older children.

13. The original sample included households in urban and rural areas. Since 2005, however, only households in rural areas have been followed. For this reason, our analysis is restricted to households in the rural sample.

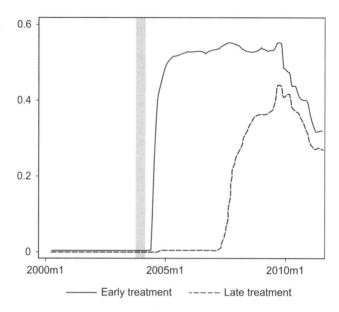

Fig. 10.2   Cash transfers received by the early and late treatment groups, experimental sample

Note: Sample size is 1,338 children, 898 in the early treatment and 440 in the late treatment group. These sample sizes are somewhat smaller than those in the estimation sample in figure 10.5 and table 10.2 because we could not merge all of the households in the survey with the monthly payment data from the BDH. The discrepancy is likely due to errors in reporting, collecting, or inputting the data on national identifiers (*cédulas*) during the household survey.

in the early treatment group had received approximately twice as much in transfers as those in the late treatment group (US$1,200, compared to $625, on average).[14]

Paxson and Schady (2010) show that the characteristics of the early and late treatment groups were balanced at baseline. Attrition between the base-line survey and the 2014 follow-up ten years later was modest, 19 percent, and is uncorrelated with assignment to the early or late treatment groups. Moreover, the characteristics of attritors in the early and late treatment groups are similar. The 2014 survey, which is the basis of the analysis we carry out in this chapter, administered a particularly rich set of tests, includ-

14. Figure 10.2 also shows that, beginning in December 2009, the proportion of households in the evaluation sample that received payments began to decline, and by September 2011 had fallen by roughly 20 percentage points in the early treatment group (15 percentage points in the late treatment group, where take-up was lower). This decline is a result of the change in the poverty score from the first to the second poverty census. The change in the score meant that a substantial proportion of households in the sample were no longer eligible for payments (because their score on the second poverty census placed them above the cutoff for eligibility); no new households entered the evaluation sample.

ing three language tests; four math tests; tests of attention and working memory; and two other tests that measure fluency of recovery and the incidence of behavior problems, respectively. Details of the tests we use in our analysis are given in the data appendix.

We transform the raw scores on each test into a z-score with zero mean and unit standard deviation. We then construct three test aggregates (for language, math, and "other tests"). Each test within an aggregate receives the same weight, and the aggregate, in turn, is standardized so it too has a mean of zero and a standard deviation of one. We also construct an overall aggregate, which equally weights the three groups of tests.

Given random assignment, identification is straightforward. We report the results of intent-to-treat regressions that take the following form:

$$(1) \qquad Y_{ihp} = \alpha_c + Z_{ihp}\beta_1 + X_{ihp}\beta_2 + \varepsilon_{ihp}$$

where the i, h, and p subscripts refer to individuals, households, and parishes; Y_{ihp} is one of the four test aggregates; α_c is a set of canton fixed effects;[15] Z_{ihp} is a dummy variable for whether the child in question is in a household that was assigned to early or late treatment groups; X_{ihp} is a vector of baseline characteristics, which we include to correct for any possible imbalance between early and late treatment groups and to increase precision; and ε_{ihp} is the error term. We run regressions by ordinary least squares (OLS), and cluster standard errors at the parish level. The parameter of interest is β_1, the intent-to-treat estimate of the effect of being assigned to the early treatment group on test scores.

10.3.2   Regression Discontinuity (RD) Analysis

To generate the data set for the second set of estimates, we merged data from three different sources:[16] data on a household's poverty score calculated from the 2000/02 poverty census; monthly data on welfare payments (from BDH administrative records); and data on education and work outcomes, as reported in the 2013/14 poverty census.[17]

The approach we take is straightforward. We compare outcomes for households who were just-eligible or just-ineligible for transfers between

---

15. Cantons are administrative units at a higher level than parishes, comparable to municipalities.

16. All of these data are confidential. The process of merging the various data sets was carried out by staff of the BDH program and the Ministry of Social Development in Ecuador. The data set we use has been made anonymous by removing the *cédula*, the unique individual identifier that is present in all these data sets and is used to merge them.

17. An advantage of the RD sample is the large number of observations. The disadvantage, on the other hand, is the small number of outcomes. To define school enrollment we use a single question on the poverty census: "Are you currently attending some educational institution?"; similarly, to define "work" we use a single question: "In the last week, did you work at least one hour, with or without pay?" Both questions are asked of all household members ages five and older.

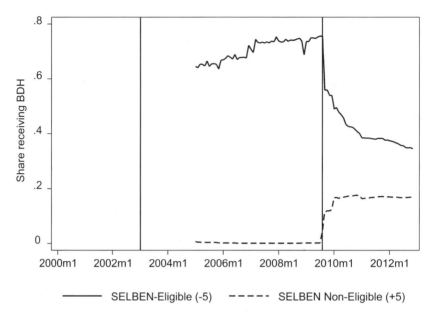

SELBEN-Eligible (-5)   SELBEN Non-Eligible (+5)

Fig. 10.3   Cash transfers received by eligible and ineligible households, regression discontinuity sample

Note: The figure depicts the share of eligible and ineligible households (within 5 points of the eligibility cutoff, as determined by the 2000/02 poverty census) receiving BDH cash transfers. Sample size is 249,846 households (41,530 transfer-ineligible and 208,316 transfer-eligible). Calculations are based on the administrative data on payments kept by the BDH.

2003 and 2009 (based on their poverty score, calculated with the 2000/02 poverty census). To assess program impacts on school enrollment, educational attainment, and work, we use the responses on the 2013/14 poverty census.

We begin by verifying that the 2000/02 poverty score was in fact used to determine eligibility for cash transfers in the 2005–2009 period (data on payments for this sample are not available before 2005). Figure 10.3 clearly indicates that this was the case. The proportion of eligible households who received transfers in any given month is between 70 and 80 percent, while the proportion of ineligible households who received transfers is essentially zero. On the other hand, the differences in transfers between the two groups are much smaller after 2009 (when a new poverty score, based on the 2007/08 poverty census, was used to determine eligibility).

The regressions we run to estimate BDH program impacts take the following form:

$$(2) \qquad Y_{ihc} = \alpha_c + S_{ihc}\beta_1 + I(S_{ihc} < C)\beta_2 + I(S_{ihc} < C) * S_{ihc}\beta_3 + \varepsilon_{ihc}$$

where Y_{ihc} is an outcome for young adult i in household h and canton c; α_c is a set of canton fixed effects; S_{ihc} is a parametrization of the control function, the poverty score calculated on the basis of the 2000/02 poverty census; $I(S_{ihc} < C)$ is an indicator variable that takes on the value of one for individuals whose 2000/02 poverty score placed them below the cutoff for eligibility; $I(S_{ihc} < C) * S_{ihc}$ is an interaction term between the control function and the eligibility dummy; and ε_{ihc} is the error term. We run regressions by OLS, and cluster standard errors at the parish level. The parameter of interest is β_2, the intent-to-treat effect of cash transfers on enrollment, educational attainment, and employment in young adulthood.

As in other applications of RD, it is important to ensure that results are not driven by a particular parametrization of the control function. In our preferred specification, we run local linear regressions (LLRs) and determine the optimal bandwidth using the approach recommended in Imbens and Kalyanaraman (2012). To check for robustness, we also report results with different bandwidths, as well as estimates that use the full sample of young adults and control for a quartic (rather than just a linear term) in the control function. Also, as in other applications of RD, it is important to note that the results we present are local in the sense that they only apply to individuals at the 2000/02 eligibility cutoff.

We report the results from two standard RD checks. First, panel A of figure 10.4 shows that there is no unusual heaping of households on one or the other side of the eligibility cutoff. Second, we test for differences in the observable baseline characteristics of households who are just-eligible and just-ineligible for transfers. Table 10.1 shows that the differences at the cutoff are generally small, and are only significant at conventional levels for one out of sixteen characteristics (two if we include differences that are borderline significant).

In interpreting our RD estimates, two additional considerations should be kept in mind. First, if there are positive spillovers from eligible to ineligible households, as has been suggested for secondary education by Bobonis and Finan (2009) and Lalive and Cattaneo (2009) using data from the PROGRESA cash transfer program in Mexico, then our estimates would be a lower bound on the true underlying effect of transfers on enrollment and secondary school completion. If, on the other hand, there are negative spillovers, as might occur because of crowding of classrooms, then the estimates we report would be an upper bound on the effects of BDH transfers.

Second, an additional concern arises because of the way we merge the different data sets we use in our analysis. In each household covered by the 2000/02 poverty census, the BDH recorded at least one *cédula* (national ID number), generally of one adult woman (who would then become the recipient of BDH transfers if her poverty score placed her below the eligibility cutoff). We use the *cédula* to merge data from the two poverty censuses. In our analysis, we then test whether young adults in households of adults for whom we have the *cédula*, as recorded in 2000/02, have different schooling

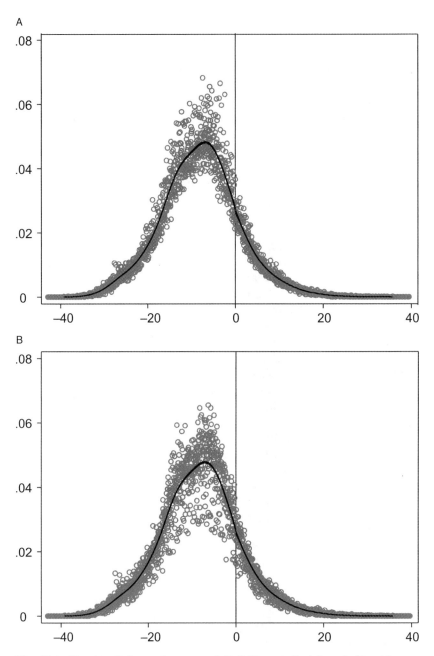

Fig. 10.4 Density of observations around eligibility cutoff. *A*, households with at least one young adult age nineteen to twenty-five; *B*, young adults age nineteen to twenty-five.

Note: This graph includes all young adults age nineteen to twenty-five in 2013/14 in the merged sample. Sample size is 307,394 observations (B) in 249,846 households (A). The McCrary test is −0.020 (0.019) in A and −0.023 (0.017) in B.

Table 10.1   Balance in the regression discontinuity sample

	Eligible households	Ineligible households	Difference
Data from 2000/02 poverty census			
Urban	0.784	0.748	0.020***
Dwelling is house or apartment	0.852	0.777	−0.011*
Has unfinished floors	0.242	0.383	0.004
Has toilet indoors	0.573	0.387	0.002
Has shower indoors	0.304	0.145	0.005
Has gas stove	0.983	0.964	0.002
Has electricity	0.998	0.992	−0.001
Owns lands	0.173	0.167	−0.002
Number of rooms	2.563	2.189	0.010
Individual-level data (for those with *cédula*)			
Age	0.41	0.47	0.025
Years of schooling	5.26	6.51	0.203
Household head	0.47	0.50	0.022
Working	0.45	0.47	0.024
Data from 2013/14 poverty census			
Household size	4.099	4.154	−0.015
Number of children ages 0–15	0.777	0.878	−0.007
Number of young adults ages 19–25	1.444	1.481	0.013

Note: Sample size for all calculations is 249,846 households. The values for the columns labeled "eligible households" and "ineligible households" are means for all households below and above the eligibility cutoff, respectively. The value for the column labeled "difference" is the coefficient on the eligibility dummy, based on our preferred LLR as discussed in the text. These regressions also include the poverty score, the interaction between the poverty score and the eligibility dummy, and canton fixed effects. Standard errors are clustered at the parish level.
***Significant at the 1 percent level.
*Significant at the 10 percent level.

and work outcomes, as recorded in the 2013/14 poverty census, depending on eligibility for transfers during the 2003–2009 period.[18]

The fact that we merge observations in the two censuses using a woman's *cédula* is potentially important. It means that our estimates are only based

18. We were able to merge 55 percent of all households in the 2000/02 poverty census into the 2013/14 census. There are many reasons why one would not expect a perfect merge: First, the geographic coverage of the 2013/14 poverty census was smaller than that of the 2000/02 poverty census. Second, participation in the two poverty censuses was not mandatory. Households that reasoned that, given their socioeconomic status, they would be unlikely to be eligible for BDH transfers may simply have chosen not to participate in the 2013/14 census. (In actual fact we do find that relatively wealthier households in 2000/02 are less likely to be found in 2013/14, although there are no differences at the cutoff.) Third, there may have been keying errors in the *cédula* in either census. Fourth, some household members may have died, or "aged out" of being the household head or his spouse (in which case, enumerators may have registered the *cédula* of some other household member). We do not believe that the less-than-perfect merge of households across the two censuses affects the internal consistency of our results because there is no unusual heaping of mass on one or the other side of the cutoff, and because the characteristics of individuals on both sides of the cutoff are very similar, as discussed in the main body of the

on, and are potentially only relevant for, the behavior of young adults who continue to live in the household they were in as children (and not for those who start their own household or move into a different one). This may limit the generalizability of our results.[19]

Moreover, if eligibility for transfers in 2003–2009 made it more (or less) likely that a young adult left home, our estimates could in part pick up these compositional changes. To test for this, we plot the number of young adults (as opposed to households) in panel B of figure 10.4. The panel shows there is no evidence of heaping of young adults on one or the other side of the cutoff.[20] We conclude that, while we cannot definitively rule out that there are compositional changes in households that are correlated with eligibility for transfers ten years earlier, these are unlikely to be a first-order concern.

10.4   Results

10.4.1   Results from Randomized Evaluation

The main results on the impact of BDH transfers using the randomized evaluation are in table 10.2 and figure 10.5. Table 10.2 reports ten-year program effects for the sample as a whole; separately for children who were younger than three years of age (including children who were in utero) at baseline and children who were older; for girls and boys; and for children whose mothers had at most completed elementary school and those whose mothers had higher school attainment. In each case, we report the results from regressions in which the outcome variable is total scores and, separately, language, math, or "other scores," respectively.

Table 10.2 shows that, for no sample and for no test aggregate, are there positive and significant program effects. In fact, the coefficients are overwhelmingly *negative* (albeit, they are close to zero and are not significant with one exception, corresponding to the impact of transfers on language outcomes for younger children).

---

chapter. In a small number of cases, 5.6 percent of the total, there is a household in the 2013/14 for whom we can merge the *cédula* of more than one individual, and where these individuals were found in two or more households in the 2000/02 census. This raises a complication because the household in which these individuals live in 2013/14 could in principle be assigned one of two or more poverty scores from the 2000/02 census. In these cases, we assign households the lowest of the relevant poverty scores. However, our results are very similar when we simply exclude these households, and the young adults in them, from our calculations.

19. We used the dates in which the two poverty censuses were carried out and the age of individuals in both censuses to see if children in the 2000/02 poverty census could be matched with young adults in the same households in 2013/14. Among households we could match, we were able to find 46 percent of children in the 2000/02 poverty census as equivalently aged young adults in the same households in the 2013/14 census.

20. It is of course possible that different kinds of young adults left just-eligible and just-ineligible households. We cannot test for this in a convincing manner because the only information we have for children at baseline is their age, gender, whether they were enrolled in school, and whether they worked. However, in the age range we consider, essentially all children were enrolled in school, and virtually none of them worked.

Table 10.2   **Experimental estimates of BDH effects on test scores after ten years**

	Total scores	Language scores	Math scores	"Other" scores
Full sample (n = 1,707)	−0.071	−0.060	−0.090	−0.023
	(0.083)	(0.068)	(0.094)	(0.064)
Children −9 to 35 months at baseline	−0.081	−0.170*	−0.039	−0.017
(n = 612)	(0.078)	(0.088)	(0.087)	(0.065)
Children 36 months or older at	−0.068	−0.001	−0.125	−0.022
baseline (n = 1,095)	(0.107)	(0.084)	(0.119)	(0.089)
Females (n = 858)	−0.050	−0.009	−0.110	0.014
	(0.078)	(0.061)	(0.093)	(0.082)
Males (n = 849)	−0.070	−0.094	−0.052	−0.041
	(0.108)	(0.102)	(0.118)	(0.079)
"Low" education mothers (n = 1,123)	−0.026	−0.021	−0.071	0.041
	(0.088)	(0.081)	(0.086)	(0.083)
"High" education mothers (n = 584)	−0.178	−0.165	−0.137	−0.167
	(0.140)	(0.120)	(0.170)	(0.102)

Note: All regressions include canton fixed effects and the following controls: gender of the child, age at baseline in months, maternal years of education, household size, and the number of durables owned by household. Standard errors are clustered at the parish level.
*Significant at the 10 percent level.

Figure 10.5 presents results by cumulative ventile of the distribution of per capita expenditures at baseline.[21] We do this in part because Paxson and Schady (2010) found that BDH transfers did not have significant effects on child development for the sample as a whole, but substantially improved outcomes for children in the lowest quartile of the distribution of per capita expenditures. Figure 10.5 shows that the estimates become more precise as we move from left to right in each panel, as expected given the larger sample sizes. However, there is no evidence that receiving transfers earlier in life, or receiving more in total transfers, improved test scores anywhere in the distribution of per capita expenditures.

21. The first (leftmost) value in each panel of figure 10.5 corresponds to coefficients and confidence intervals for regressions that limit the sample to the 5 percent poorest households, the next corresponds to the 10 percent poorest households, and so on. The rightmost value in each panel corresponds to the sample as a whole, and is equivalent to the estimates in table 10.2. Log per capita expenditures is "imputed." As Paxson and Schady (2010) discuss, the baseline 2003/04 survey collected information on housing characteristics and ownership of a list of household durables, but did not include an expenditure module. A companion study collected the same information on housing and durables and included an expenditure module. (These data are the basis for the analysis in Schady and Araujo [2008], Schady and Rosero [2008], and Edmonds and Schady [2012].) Paxson and Schady (2010) used data from this companion study to estimate a regression of the logarithm of monthly expenditure on measures of housing quality and access to services, durable goods ownership, and several household characteristics such as the household head's age and education level and household size, and used the resulting coefficients to impute the logarithm of expenditure at baseline for the sample of households in the panel. We use the same measure in the analysis in this chapter.

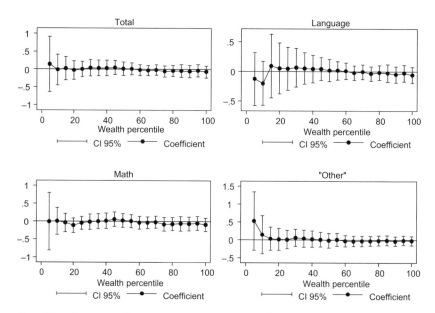

Fig. 10.5 Program effects on test score aggregates, by ventile of baseline per capita consumption, experimental sample

Note: Each figure depicts coefficients and 95 percent confidence intervals from regressions of outcomes on a dummy variable for children in the early treatment group, and by cumulative ventile of the distribution of per capita expenditures at baseline. The first (leftmost) value in each figure corresponds to coefficients and confidence intervals for regressions that limit the sample to the 5 percent poorest households, the next corresponds to the 10 percent poorest households, and so on. The rightmost value in each figure corresponds to the sample as a whole, and is equivalent to the estimates in table 10.2. All regressions include canton fixed effects and the following controls: gender of the child, age at baseline in months, maternal years of education, household size, and the number of durables owned by the household. Standard errors are clustered at the parish level.

In sum, table 10.2 and figure 10.5 indicate that, ten years after children randomly assigned to the early treatment group began to receive transfers, children in this group did not have higher scores on any of a large number of tests taken in late childhood than children in the late treatment group.[22]

22. Given an attrition rate of 19 percent, it is in principle possible that the fact that we observe BDH effects in the short run (as in Paxson and Schady 2010) but not in the long run (as in table 10.2 in this chapter) could be explained by the change in the sample. Specifically, it could be that program effects are particularly large among children who attrit from the sample between 2004 and 2014. To test whether this is the case, we went back to the sample of children in Paxson and Schady (2010) and reestimated short-run program effects, limiting the sample of children to those that could be found in the 2014 survey. For their sample of 2,069 children, Paxson and Schady (2010) report a program effect of 0.052 standard deviations for the sample as a whole (with a standard error of 0.052), and 0.170 standard deviations for children in the poorest quartile (with a standard error of 0.074). When we reestimate these regressions for the smaller sample of children who could be found in 2014 (1,734 children), we find a program effect of 0.055 standard deviations for the sample as a whole (with a standard error of 0.053) and 0.199 standard deviations for children in the poorest quartile (with a standard error of

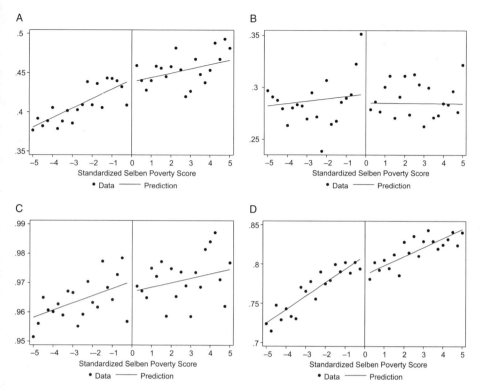

Fig. 10.6   BDH program effects, women. *A***, enrollment at any educational institution;** *B***, work;** *C***, elementary school completion;** *D***, secondary school completion.**

Note: The figure shows estimates of the effect of BDH eligibility (according to the 2000/02 poverty census) on the probability of being enrolled at any educational institution (A), working (B), having completed primary education (C), and having completed secondary education (D) in 2013/14 for women. Each panel also plots the LLR estimate, estimated separately on each side of the cutoff, with bandwidth of 5. Sample size is 34,672.

10.4.2   Results from Regression Discontinuity Analysis

We report the results from our RD estimates in figure 10.6 (for women), figure 10.7 (for men), and table 10.3. Figures 10.6 and 10.7 show no evidence of jumps at the eligibility cutoff in the probability of enrollment in an educational institution (panel A) or work (panel B), for women or men. Panels C in both figures suggest that the BDH had at most a very modest effect on the probability that young adults have completed elementary school, which is not surprising given the very high counterfactual completion rates. Finally,

0.080). These comparisons suggest that the fade-out of BDH program effects between 2004 and 2014 is unlikely to be driven by sample attrition. We thank Karen Macours for suggesting this exercise to us.

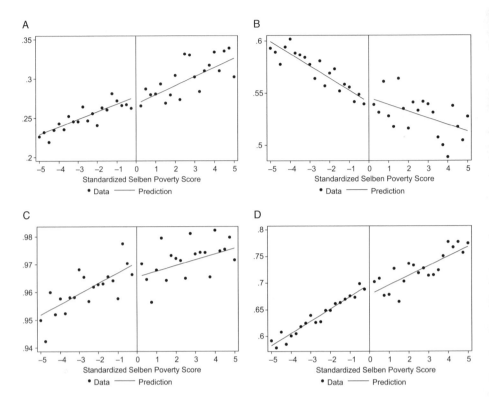

Fig. 10.7   BDH program effects, men. *A*, **enrollment at any educational institution;** *B*, **work;** *C*, **elementary school completion;** *D*, **secondary school completion.**

Note: The figure shows estimates of the effect of BDH eligibility (according to the 2000/02 poverty census) on the probability of being enrolled at any educational institution (A), working (B), having completed primary education (C), and having completed secondary education (D) in 2013/14 for men. Each panel also plots the LLR estimate, estimated separately on each side of the cutoff, with bandwidth of 5. Sample size is 53,442.

panels D suggest somewhat larger effects on the probability of completing secondary school, especially for women, where there is a jump at the cutoff in completion rates of roughly 2 percentage points.

Regression results for various samples and specifications are reported in table 10.3. The table confirms that young women in households that were eligible for transfers when they were in late childhood are 2–3 percentage points more likely to have graduated from secondary school ten years later. These results are stable across specifications. Results on secondary school completion for men are smaller in magnitude and are generally not significant. There is no evidence that young men or women who were eligible for transfers are more or less likely to be enrolled in some tertiary educational institution in 2013/14. In the case of work, some of the coefficients

	Mean, ineligibles	(1)	(2)	(3)	(4)	(5)
Enrolled in school						
All	0.34	0.005	0.007	0.005	0.002	0.005
		(0.005)	(0.007)	(0.006)	(0.004)	(0.007)
Males	0.27	0.004	0.012	0.008	0.005	0.010
		(0.007)	(0.009)	(0.007)	(0.006)	(0.011)
Females	0.44	0.001	−0.009	−0.001	−0.002	−0.004
		(0.010)	(0.012)	(0.009)	(0.007)	(0.013)
Working						
All	0.43	−0.005	0.009	0.001	−0.006	0.004
		(0.005)	(0.008)	(0.006)	(0.005)	(0.008)
Males	0.53	−0.008	−0.009	−0.003	−0.009	−0.004
		(0.006)	(0.010)	(0.008)	(0.006)	(0.010)
Females	0.28	0.006	0.044***	0.008	−0.003	0.022*
		(0.008)	(0.012)	(0.010)	(0.008)	(0.011)
Completed elementary school						
All	0.96	0.002	0.004	0.004*	0.003	0.003
		(0.002)	(0.004)	(0.002)	(0.002)	(0.003)
Males	0.96	0.002	0.005	0.005	0.003	0.006
		(0.002)	(0.005)	(0.004)	(0.002)	(0.005)
Females	0.96	0.000	0.002	0.003	0.001	−0.001
		(0.002)	(0.005)	(0.004)	(0.002)	(0.005)
Completed secondary school						
All	0.73	0.015***	0.018**	0.016***	0.012***	0.019**
		(0.006)	(0.008)	(0.006)	(0.004)	(0.008)
Males	0.69	0.013*	0.013	0.014*	0.009	0.013
		(0.007)	(0.010)	(0.007)	(0.006)	(0.008)
Females	0.79	0.019***	0.024**	0.019**	0.017***	0.028**
		(0.007)	(0.012)	(0.009)	(0.006)	(0.013)

Table 10.3 Regression discontinuity estimates of BDH effects on schooling and work outcomes after ten years

Note: "Mean, ineligibles" refers to the value of the outcome in question at the eligibility cutoff. Specification (1) corresponds to LLR with an optimal bandwidth; specifications (2), (3), and (4) correspond to LLRs with bandwidth = 2.5, 5, and 10, respectively; specification (5) uses the full sample and includes a quartic in the control function (the 2000/02 poverty score). All regressions include canton fixed effects. Standard errors clustered at the parish level. In the regression for "All," sample sizes are approximately 100,000 in specification (1) (with the exact number varying by outcome), 43,227 in specification (2), 88,114 in specification (3), 174,148 in specification (4), and 307,394 in specification (5). Females represent approximately 40 percent of the sample.

***Significant at the 1 percent level.

**Significant at the 5 percent level.

*Significant at the 10 percent level.

for women in table 10.3 are significant, but these results are sensitive to how the control function is parametrized.

In sum, our RD results show that ten years after one group of households became eligible for transfers and another one did not, young women in transfer-eligible households had modestly higher secondary school completion rates than those in transfer-ineligible households. However, this did not translate into a higher probability of continuing on to university or some other tertiary institution. Moreover, there is no clear effect on the probability that these women work. The broad pattern of results suggests that cash transfers prevented a small fraction of women from dropping out of secondary school, but did not have a measurable effect on their subsequent education and work choices.

10.5 Conclusion

In this chapter, we use two different data sets and two identification strategies to assess the long-term (ten-year) effects of the BDH cash transfer program in Ecuador on various measures of human capital accumulation. We note that ours is one of only two evaluations that look at the effects of cash transfers after a decade. (Barham, Macours, and Maluccio [2013, 2016] look at the ten-year effects of a conditional cash transfer program in Nicaragua.)

Our experimental estimates show that children in households that received transfers earlier, and received substantially more in total transfers, did not have better learning outcomes in late childhood. Our regression discontinuity estimates show that cash transfers received in late childhood modestly increased the proportion of young women who completed secondary school but did not affect their education and work choices after graduation. It may be that larger program effects on educational attainment and achievement, or on labor market outcomes like employment rates or wages, will become apparent as individuals in the sample age. It is simply too early to tell. Nevertheless, based on the evidence that is available to date, we cautiously conclude that cash transfers will likely have only a modest effect on the intergenerational transmission of poverty in Ecuador.

Data Appendix

This data appendix provides additional details on the tests applied in the 2014 household survey. The survey included three language tests. The first test, the Test de Vocabulario en Imágenes Peabody (TVIP), is the Spanish-speaking version of the much-used Peabody Picture Vocabulary Test (PPVT) (Dunn et al. 1986). The TVIP has been used in a number of surveys in Ecuador

(Araujo, Bosch, and Schady 2017; Paxson and Schady 2007, 2010; Schady 2011) as well as in other countries in Latin America (Macours, Schady, and Vakis 2012; Schady et al. 2015). The test has been shown to be highly predictive of future outcomes, including in the United States (Case and Paxson 2008; Cunha and Heckman 2007) and in Ecuador (Schady 2012b). The other two language tests are a test of verbal comprehension, which evaluates knowledge of synonyms, antonyms, and analogies, and a test of reading comprehension, in which a child is asked to read two short texts and is then asked simple questions about their contents. These tests were drawn from the Woodcock-Johnson-Muñoz battery of achievement tests (Muñoz-Sandoval et al. 2005).

The 2014 survey included four math tests, all of which are part of the Woodcock-Johnson-Muñoz battery of achievement tests. One test, numeric series, asks the child to complete a series of numbers where one is missing; the test measures mathematical content and reasoning. A second test, math fluency, assesses the ability of children to rapidly solve basic addition, subtraction, and multiplication problems. A third test, calculations, focuses on more complex mathematical problems. The final test, applied problems, asks a child to solve a number of word problems.

In addition to the language and math tests, the survey collected data on tests of attention and working memory. Attention and working memory are two domains in what is referred to as "executive function" (EF).[23] Executive function includes a set of basic self-regulatory skills that involve various parts of the brain, but in particular the prefrontal cortex. It is an important determinant of how well young children adapt to and learn in school. Low levels of EF in childhood carry over to adulthood. A longitudinal study that followed a birth cohort in New Zealand to age thirty-two years found that low levels of self-control in early childhood are associated with lower school achievement, worse health, lower incomes, and a higher likelihood of being involved in criminal activity in adulthood, even after controlling for IQ and socioeconomic status in childhood (Moffitt et al. 2011).

Finally, the 2014 survey included a test of fluency of recovery and a test of behavioral problems. The test of fluency of recovery was drawn from the Woodcock-Johnson-Muñoz battery of cognitive tests; it measures the capacity to recover cumulative knowledge. The behavioral test is the Strengths and Difficulties Questionnaire (Goodman 1997, 2001), which is based on direct report from the children who were interviewed. The test has five scales measuring emotional symptoms, conduct problems, hyperactivity, peer relationship problems, and prosocial behavior.

All tests were extensively piloted in Ecuador, and adjustments were made so they would be appropriate for the sample of children as needed.

---

23. The other two domains of executive function are inhibitory control and cognitive flexibility.

References

Almond, Douglas, and Janet Currie. 2010. "Human Capital Development before Age Five." In *Handbook of Labor Economics*, edited by David Card and Orley Ashenfelter, 1315–486. New York: North Holland.

Angelucci, Manuela, and Orazio Attanasio. 2013. "The Demand for Food of Poor Urban Mexican Households: Understanding Policy Impacts Using Structural Models." *American Economic Journal: Economic Policy* 5 (1): 146–78.

Araujo, M. Caridad, Mariano Bosch, and Norbert Schady. 2017. "The Effect of Welfare Payments on Work in a Middle-Income Country." IADB Working Paper no. 8509, Inter-American Development Bank.

Attanasio, Orazio, Emla Fitzsimons, Ana Gómez, Martha Isabel Gutiérrez, Costas Meghir, and Alice Mesnard. 2010. "Children's Schooling and Work in the Presence of a Conditional Cash Transfer Program in Rural Colombia." *Economic Development and Cultural Change* 58 (2): 181–210.

Attanasio, Orazio, and Valérie Lechene. 2014. "Efficient Responses to Targeted Cash Transfers." *Journal of Political Economy* 122 (1): 178–222.

Baird, Sarah, Francisco Ferreira, Berk Özler, and Michael Woolcock. 2014. "Conditional, Unconditional, and Everything in Between: A Systematic Review of the Effects of Cash Transfer Programmes on Schooling Outcomes." *Journal of Development Effectiveness* 6 (1): 1–43.

Banerjee, Abhijit, Rema Hanna, Gabriel Kreindler, and Benjamin A. Olken. 2017. "Debunking the Myth of the Lazy Welfare Recipient: Evidence from Cash Transfer Programs Worldwide." *World Bank Research Observer* 32 (2): 155–84.

Barham, Tania, Karen Macours, and John A. Maluccio. 2013. "Boys' Cognitive Skill Formation and Physical Growth: Long-Term Experimental Evidence on Critical Ages for Early Childhood Interventions." *American Economic Review Papers and Proceedings* 103 (3): 467–71.

———. 2016. "More Schooling, More Learning, More Earnings: Effects of a Three-Year Conditional Cash Transfer Program in Nicaragua after 10 Years." Unpublished manuscript, Inter-American Development Bank.

Barrera-Osorio, Felipe, Marianne Bertrand, Leigh L. Linden, and Francisco Pérez. 2011. "Improving the Design of Conditional Cash Transfer Programs: Evidence from a Randomized Experiment in Colombia." *American Economic Journal: Applied Economics* 3 (2): 167–95.

Behrman, Jere R., Susan W. Parker, and Petra E. Todd. 2009. "Medium-Term Impacts of the *Oportunidades* Conditional Cash Transfer Program on Rural Youth in Mexico." In *Poverty, Inequality, and Policy in Latin America*, edited by Stephan Klasen and Felicity Nowak-Lehmann, 219–70. Cambridge, MA: MIT Press.

———. 2011. "Do Conditional Cash Transfers for Schooling Generate Lasting Benefits? Five-Year Follow-Up of PROGRESA/Oportunidades." *Journal of Human Resources* 46 (1): 93–122.

Berlinski, Samuel, and Norbert Schady. 2015. *The Early Years: Child Well-Being and the Role of Public Policy*. New York: Palgrave Macmillan.

Bobonis, Gustavo, and Frederico Finan. 2009. "Neighborhood Peer Effects in Secondary School Enrollment Decisions." *Review of Economics and Statistics* 91 (4): 695–716.

Case, A., and C. Paxson. 2008. "Stature and Status: Height, Ability, and Labor Market Outcomes." *Journal of Political Economy* 116 (3): 499–532.

Cunha, Flavio, and James Heckman. 2007. "The Technology of Skill Formation." *American Economic Review* 97 (2): 31–47.

De Janvry, Alain, and Elisabeth Sadoulet. 2006. "Making Conditional Cash Transfer Programs More Efficient: Designing for Maximum Effects of the Conditionality." *World Bank Economic Review* 20 (1): 1–29.

Dunn, Lloyd M., Delia E. Lugo, Eligio R. Padilla, and Leota M. Dunn. 1986. *Test de Vocabulario en Imágenes Peabody.* Circle Pines, MN: American Guidance Service.

Edmonds, Eric, and Norbert Schady. 2012. "Poverty Alleviation and Child Labor." *American Economic Journal: Economic Policy* 4 (4): 100–124.

Evans, David K., and Anna Popova. 2014. "Cash Transfers and Temptation Goods: A Review of Global Evidence." World Bank Policy Research Working Paper no. 6886, World Bank.

Fernald, Lia C. H., and Melissa Hidrobo. 2011. "Effect of Ecuador's Cash Transfer Program (Bono de Desarrollo Humano) on Child Development in Infants and Toddlers: A Randomized Effectiveness Trial." *Social Science and Medicine* 72 (9): 1437–46.

Filmer, Deon, and Norbert Schady. 2008. "Getting Girls into School: Evidence from a Scholarship Program in Cambodia." *Economic Development and Cultural Change* 56 (2): 581–617.

———. 2014. "The Medium-Term Effects of Scholarships in a Low-Income Country." *Journal of Human Resources* 49 (3): 663–94.

Fiszbein, Ariel, and Norbert Schady. 2009. *Conditional Cash Transfers: Reducing Present and Future Poverty.* Washington, DC: World Bank.

Gertler, Paul J., Sebastian Martinez, and Marta Rubio-Codina. 2012. "Investing Cash Transfers to Raise Long-Term Living Standards." *American Economic Journal: Applied Economics* 4 (1): 164–92.

Goodman, Robert. 1997. "The Strengths and Difficulties Questionnaire: A Research Note." *Journal of Child Psychology and Psychiatry* 38 (5): 581–86.

———. 2001. "Psychometric Properties of the Strengths and Difficulties Questionnaire." *Journal of the American Academy of Child & Adolescent Psychiatry* 40 (11): 1337–45.

Hidrobo, Melissa, and Lia C. H. Fernald. 2013. "Cash Transfers and Domestic Violence." *Journal of Health Economics* 32 (1): 304–19.

Imbens, Guido, and Karthik Kalyanaraman. 2012. "Optimal Bandwidth Choice for the Regression Discontinuity Estimator." *Review of Economic Studies* 79 (3): 933–59.

Lalive, Rafael, and Alejandra Cattaneo. 2009. "Social Interactions and Schooling Decisions." *Review of Economics and Statistics* 91 (3): 457–77.

Levy, Santiago, and Norbert Schady. 2013. "Latin America's Social Policy Challenge: Education, Social Insurance, Redistribution." *Journal of Economic Perspectives* 27 (2): 193–218.

Macours, Karen, Norbert Schady, and Renos Vakis. 2012. "Cash Transfers, Behavioral Changes, and Cognitive Development in Early Childhood: Evidence from a Randomized Experiment." *American Economic Journal: Applied Economics* 4 (2): 247–73.

Maluccio, John A. 2010. "The Impact of Conditional Cash Transfers on Consumption and Investment in Nicaragua." *Journal of Development Studies* 46 (1): 14–38.

Maluccio, John A., and Rafael Flores. 2005. "Impact Evaluation of a Conditional Cash Transfer Program: The Nicaraguan Red de Protección Social." Research Report no. 141, International Food Policy Research Institute.

McCrary, Justin. 2008. "Manipulation of the Running Variable in the Regression Discontinuity Design: A Density Test." *Journal of Econometrics* 142 (2): 698–714.

Moffitt, Terrie, Louise Arseneault, Daniel Belsky, Nigel Dickson, Robert Hancox, HonaLee Harrington, Renate Houts, et al. 2011. "A Gradient of Childhood Self-Control Predicts Health, Wealth, and Public Safety." *Proceedings of the National Academy of Sciences* 108 (7): 2693–98.

Molina-Millan, Teresa, Tania Barham, Karen Macours, John A. Maluccio, and Marco Stampini. 2016. "Long-Term Impacts of Conditional Cash Transfers in Latin America: Review of the Evidence." Social Protection Division Technical Note no. IDB-TN-923, Inter-American Development Bank.

Muñoz-Sandoval, Ana, Richard W. Woodcock, Kevin S. McGrew, and Nancy Mather. 2005. *Batería III Woodcock-Muñoz*. Itasca, IL: Riverside Publishing.

Oosterbeek, Hessel, Juan Ponce, and Norbert Schady. 2008. "The Impact of Cash Transfers on School Enrollment: Evidence from Ecuador." World Bank Policy Research Working Paper no. 4645, World Bank.

Paxson, Christina, and Norbert Schady. 2007. "Cognitive Development among Young Children in Ecuador: The Roles of Wealth, Health, and Parenting." *Journal of Human Resources* 42 (1): 49–84.

———. 2010. "Does Money Matter? The Effects of Cash Transfers on Child Health and Development in Rural Ecuador." *Economic Development and Cultural Change* 59 (1): 187–229.

Ponce, Juan, and Arjun S. Bedi. 2010. "The Impact of a Cash Transfer Program on Cognitive Achievement: The Bono de Desarrollo Humano of Ecuador." *Economics of Education Review* 29 (1): 116–25.

Schady, Norbert. 2011. "Parental Education, Vocabulary, and Cognitive Development in Early Childhood: Longitudinal Evidence from Ecuador." *American Journal of Public Health* 101 (12): 2299–307.

———. 2012a. "Cash Transfers and Anemia among Women of Reproductive Age." *Economics Letters* 117 (3): 887–90.

———. 2012b. "El Desarrollo Infantil Temprano en América Latina y el Caribe: Acceso, Resultados y Evidencia Longitudinal de Ecuador." In *Educación para la Transformación*, edited by Marcelo Cabrol and Miguel Székely. Washington, DC: Inter-American Development Bank.

Schady, Norbert, and M. Caridad Araujo. 2008. "Cash Transfers, Conditions, and School Enrollment in Ecuador." *Journal of the Latin American and Caribbean Economic Association* 8 (2): 43–70.

Schady, Norbert, Jere Behrman, M. Caridad Araujo, Rodrigo Azuero, Raquel Bernal, David Bravo, Florencia López-Boo, Karen Macours, Daniela Marshall, Christina Paxson, and Renos Vakis. 2015. "Wealth Gradients in Early Childhood Cognitive Development in Five Latin American Countries." *Journal of Human Resources* 50 (2): 446–63.

Schady, Norbert, and José Rosero. 2008. "Are Cash Transfers Made to Women Spent Like Other Sources of Income?" *Economics Letters* 101 (3): 246–48.

Schultz, T. Paul. 2004. "School Subsidies for the Poor: Evaluating the Mexican PRO-GRESA Poverty Program." *Journal of Development Economics* 74 (1): 199–250.

Shonkoff, Jack P., and Deborah A. Phillips, eds. 2000. *From Neurons to Neighborhoods: The Science of Early Childhood Development*. Washington, DC: National Academies Press.

United Nations Educational, Scientific and Cultural Organization (UNESCO). 2015. "Informe de Resultados: TERCE-Tercer Estudio Regional Comparativo y Explicativo." Accessed September 9, 2016. http://unesdoc.unesco.org/images/0024/002435/243532S.pdf.

World Bank. 2016. "Poverty: Overview." Accessed September 9, 2016. http://www.worldbank.org/en/topic/poverty/overview.

Comment on Chapters 9 and 10

Maitreesh Ghatak

A common premise underlying many antipoverty policies is that current interventions can have long-run effects, outlasting the duration of the policy. This in turn reflects the fact that a notion of persistence of poverty underlies much of development economics. This means there is some underlying positive feedback mechanism—with a suitable push, the poor will be on a self-sustaining trajectory of development. If poverty was a transitional and a largely self-correcting phenomenon, such as life cycle poverty, then the effect of these policies would not be long lasting unless they are permanently in place. This is as we would expect from standard growth models (e.g., the Solow model) that feature convergence of an individual to a unique steady state within a reasonable time frame.

If poverty is persistent, then the scope for policies to have outcomes beyond their duration becomes possible. There are two broad class of mechanisms for it. The first relates to poverty traps where two individuals who, except for income or wealth, are identical can end up with very different steady-state income and wealth levels.[1] The second class of mechanisms relates to what in the growth literature is known as the notion of conditional convergence, namely, the poor face unfavorable productivity parameters and so while they converge to a unique steady state, that involves income and wealth levels that

Maitreesh Ghatak is professor of economics at London School of Economics.

I thank conference participants for helpful feedback, and Christopher Barrett for helpful comments on the first draft of this comment. For acknowledgments, sources of research support, and disclosure of the author's material financial relationships, if any, please see http://www.nber.org/chapters/c13951.ack.

1. See Azariadis (1996), Barrett and Carter (2013), Ghatak (2015), and Kraay and McKenzie (2014) for reviews of the literature on poverty traps.

are below the poverty line.[2] In this world, two individuals who are identical in all respects except initial income and wealth will converge to the same income and wealth levels in the long run, and so they are not trapped in poverty in a narrow sense, but poverty can be persistent as the steady-state income or wealth levels are below the poverty line since their productivity is low (e.g., with geographic poverty traps).

I will discuss three recent empirical papers on the long-run impact of specific transfer policies aimed at the poor. The nature of the transfer programs, the settings, and the time horizons are quite different, which is very helpful in trying to absorb the lessons of these kinds of programs. Two of these papers are included in this volume—Araujo, Bosch, and Schady (chapter 10) and Macours and Vakis (chapter 9). The third one was presented in the conference that preceded the publication of this volume (Bandiera et al. 2017).

The plan of this comment is as follows. In the next section I will sketch a conceptual framework used to interpret the findings based on Ghatak (2015). In the third section I will discuss the three individual papers and draw out the general lessons from them. In my concluding remarks I offer some thoughts about how to combine theory and empirical work to provide a better understanding of "what works best where" in terms of the effectiveness of alternative strategies aimed at overcoming the persistence of poverty.

Conceptual Framework

Suppose that the current income of an individual, y_t, depends on the existing stock of capital (or wealth) k_t via a production function $y_t = Af(k_t)$ where A is a productivity parameter that depends on other factors, for example, the quality of institutions, infrastructure, and availability of complementary inputs. The capital stock evolves over time through investments the individual makes, i_t (say, investment), but that in turn depends on y_t or k_t via the budget constraint of the individual and his or her ability to borrow or save. For simplicity assume, as in the textbook Solow model, that individuals save a constant fraction s of their incomes and capital depreciates completely. Therefore, the transition equation is $k_{t+1} = sAf(k_t)$.

If capital markets are perfect, then an individual can borrow or lend k at a given (gross) interest rate r (which stays constant for this individual, for simplicity, because, say, interest rates are fixed by the international capital market), and will choose the efficient level of k defined by $Af'(k) = r$ irrespec-

---

2. Yet another mechanism for persistence of poverty could be that there is convergence to a unique steady state, but it is slow. Typically, this would happen under similar parameters that would also cause convergence to a steady state involving low levels of income and wealth, such as low productivity parameters and low saving rates.

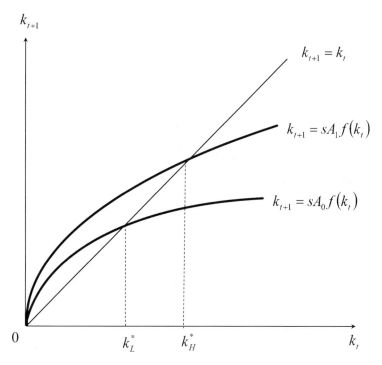

Fig. 9/10C.1   Conditional convergence in the Solow model

tive of how much k he owns. Let $\pi = Af(k^*) - rk^*$ be the maximized value of profit. Then the transition equation is $k_{t+1} = s(\pi + rk_t)$.

If either the production technology is convex, in which case the transition equation will be a concave function, or if capital markets are perfect, so that the transition equation is effectively linear (and hence, a concave function), the individual would converge to a unique stable steady state. However, even if there is a unique and stable steady state, but the actual A is much lower than the potential A (say, A'), poverty can be persistent, which is the notion of conditional convergence. In figure 9/10C.1 the production technology is convex, but depending on the value of A (with $A_0 < A_1$), the individual reaches steady-state levels of wealth k_L^* and k_H^* that are quite different. Any policy that can change A from A_0 to A_1 can have a permanent effect on the steady-state income and wealth levels of the individual.

If, however, the production technology is subject to nonconvexities, then poverty traps can arise. Suppose there is a threshold level of capital, $\underline{k}$, such that $y_t = A_1 f(k_t)$ for $k \geq \underline{k}$ and $y_t = A_0 f(k_t)$ for $k \leq \underline{k}$, where $A_0 < A_1$. If individuals could borrow from a competitive credit market, they could overcome the indivisibility by directly borrowing the amount k_H^*. But if capital markets are imperfect in addition to the nonconvexity, then multiple stable

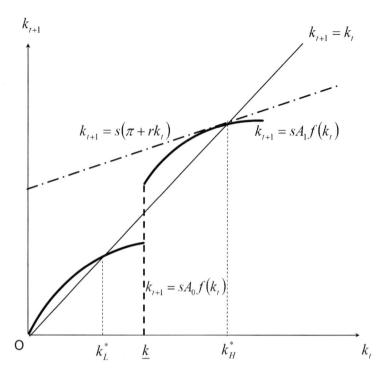

Fig. 9/10C.2   External frictions and poverty traps

steady states can arise as captured in figure 9/10C.2. In Ghatak (2015) I refer
to this as an example of an "external frictions"–driven poverty trap. The
poor here are just like the nonpoor in terms of their potential (that includes
ability and preferences), but they operate with a tighter choice set, which is
exacerbated by various frictions such as market failures as well as technological nonconvexities that make it disadvantageous to be operating at very
low scales.

However, even if there are no frictions in the external environment (in
particular, the technology is convex and credit markets are perfect in the
current setting), poverty traps can arise if preferences display strong income
effects. For example, in the current setting, the poor can have a saving rate s
that is significantly lower than the nonpoor in a way that can generate multiple steady states. This is illustrated in figure 9/10C.3, where there is a threshold level of capital, $\underline{k}$ (kept the same as in the previous case for comparabil-
ity), such that the rate of saving is s_0 or s_1 with $s_0 < s_1$ and this affects the
transition equation under autarchy as well as the one with perfect credit
markets. The dichotomous savings rate is merely meant to convey the idea
simply. In Ghatak (2015), there is a simple model that illustrates this more
formally. Clearly, a more realistic framework with savings as a continuous

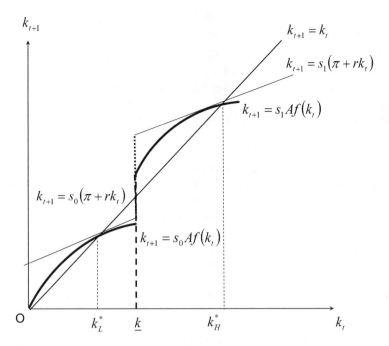

Fig. 9/10C.3   Choice under scarcity and poverty traps

function of income (or capital) will have a similar positive feedback feature that gives rise to a poverty trap.

In this view of poverty traps, even if there are no frictions in the external environment that policy can potentially try to "fix," the poor make choices that are very different from the nonpoor in a way that can reinforce poverty. This can happen for a number alternative reasons: subsistence needs may rule out the feasibility of saving and investing money in health and education at high rates for low levels of income, the poor can discount the future more, or put less weight on the welfare of their children.

The advantage of this framework is that it helps us see that different mechanisms could be at work to find similar effects of a policy in reducing poverty in the long run, but at the same time, it provides some structure to offer ways to try to interpret the evidence and try to disentangle these alternative mechanisms. We use this framework because it connects directly with the classic growth models and helps us see clearly what kind of departures from these models could lead to poverty traps. It should be noted that there are many other potential mechanisms that could lead to poverty traps that are not directly captured in theoretical framework developed here. For example, poverty may make individuals more risk averse, thereby choosing projects that are low variance but also low mean. Also, it is possible that some behavioral biases are accentuated with poverty (see, e.g., Banerjee and Mullainathan 2010).

Evidence

I now turn to the discussion of the three recent empirical papers that study medium- to long-term effects of transfer programs to the poor mentioned in the introduction. All three papers study some form of cash/wealth transfer to the poor: a pure cash transfer (Araujo, Bosch, and Schady), a combination of transfer of livestock assets and skills (Bandiera et al.), and a conditional cash transfer (CCT) combined with exposure to social interaction with local leaders (Macours and Vakis). The first study has one of the longest horizons—they study the effect of cash transfers in Ecuador after a decade. The other two studies have shorter time horizons, but both look at effects of these programs even after the direct resource transfer was withdrawn. Therefore, all three studies are particularly well placed to study the effect on such policies on persistence of poverty.

Araujo, Bosch, and Schady study whether cash transfers can help households escape poverty traps, that is, the long-term effects of cash transfers. The key mechanism they have in mind is whether transfers had positive effects on various measures of human capital accumulation by relaxing the budget constraints of liquidity constrained households, enabling them to invest in their children's human capital. They use two data sets and empirical strategies to look at the medium- and long-term effects of this cash transfer program in Ecuador on human capital that started in 2003. They provide experimental evidence that used the fact that children under the age of six years were assigned to early and late treatment groups. Although the early treatment group received twice as much in total transfers, the long-term enrollment rates, grade attainment, and test scores are not significantly different between these two groups. They also note the fact that a poverty index was used to determine the eligibility for transfers. Using a regression discontinuity approach comparing children who were in the just-eligible and just-ineligible households in late childhood in terms of school attainment ten years later, the authors find that the transfers did increase secondary school completion but the effects are relatively small. Overall, the authors conclude that the effect of this cash transfer program on intergenerational persistence of poverty is likely to be modest.

Macours and Vakis analyze the medium-term impacts of a short-term CCT program in Nicaragua and, in particular, the role of social interactions of beneficiaries with local female leaders for sustaining the impact of this program. They build on their earlier work (Macours and Vakis 2014) that showed that social interactions with successful leaders substantially increased program impacts on nutritional and educational investments while the program was operating. In this chapter, they use data collected two years after the program ended to show that these social multiplier effects persisted to a remarkable degree. Two years after the transfers stopped, households who live in the proximity of successful leaders still show significantly higher investments in both education and nutrition of their children. The earlier work showed social interactions with nearby leaders positively affected human capital and productive investments as well as the future-oriented attitudes of other beneficiaries during the program, but the worry was whether these shifts are sustainable—households might well quickly revert back to preprogram behavior when the transfers stop. The new results suggest that interactions with leaders may have affected other households' aspirations by setting good examples and sharing their experiences. They further show that interactions with leaders changed parents' beliefs or expectations about their children's educational and occupational potential, which can help explain the sustained higher levels of human capital investments.

The paper by Bandiera et al. (2017) provides experimental evidence on a nationwide one-off combination of transfer of livestock assets and skills transfer in Bangladesh to poor women in rural areas. They study the medium- to long-term effects of this program and, in particular, focus on the impact even after the direct resource transfer is withdrawn. Therefore, this study is particularly well suited to study the effect of antipoverty policies that involve income or asset transfers with or without some other "missing input" (in this case, training) on the persistence of poverty. Their study covers around 1,300 villages in rural Bangladesh and 21,000 households surveyed four times over a period of seven years. Poor women in their sample mostly engage in supplying casual labor, while wealthier women specialize in livestock rearing, which has higher hourly returns and more regular labor demand. Their study focused on the question of whether a one-off transfer set the poor women on a sustainable trajectory out of poverty by allowing them to switch from supplying labor to the more remunerative activity of livestock rearing. They found that the treatment group saved more (a ninefold increase after two and four years) and accumulated more assets over time, leading to larger gains, which is consistent with the mechanism of poverty traps. These gains are not at the expense of reduction in overall labor supply. Rather, the program leverages idle capacity with the average beneficiary working 22 percent more hours and earning 37 percent more.

The key question that arises in the Araujo, Bosch, and Schady study is why this transfer program, one of the largest cash transfer programs in proportional terms in Latin America, was not very effective. There are several possible explanations. It could be because the sums were small relative to need (e.g., private schools), or the lack of conditionality (even though the households were encouraged to spend transfer income on children), or the lack of combination of this program with other complementary interventions (e.g., improvement in schools). Another possible explanation of the results of Araujo, Bosch, and Schady is that they lack a true control group. If any intervention yielded an effect, whether early or late, then the difference *between* the two treatment groups would be insignificant even if the difference between either treatment group with a *no-treatment* group might be large.[3]

What the paper by Macours and Vakis shows is that the combination of shifting beliefs and resources can be effective, and the effects long lasting. Ideally, we would like to see the marginal contribution of individual inputs, that is, beliefs and resources. In particular, in their study shifting aspirations is like shifting expected returns, and is equivalent to a one-shot change in the productivity parameter A. This alone can be effective to reduce the persistence of poverty as in the conditional-convergence-like argument discussed earlier. It is similar in spirit to Jensen (2010), who found school completion rates improved in the Dominican Republic when 8th grade boys were provided a correct measure of returns to secondary school, which was higher than the perceived rate of returns in the baseline population. Therefore, while the study cannot separate out a poverty trap mechanism from one that involves a one-time shift in the productivity parameter, it provides strong evidence on the ability of temporary policies to have long-term effects in reducing the persistence of poverty, and also suggests (though cannot demonstrate) that a combination of different interventions is likely to be particularly effective compared to individual policies.

While Bandiera et al. provides strongly suggestive evidence on poverty traps, several questions remain. Since they study the effect of the combination of asset transfer and training, we cannot answer the question whether an equivalent transfer of cash or access to credit in suitable terms might have worked as well. Like the Macours and Vakis study, it is possible that training shifted the productivity parameter, and that itself would be enough to push these women out of poverty. This seems unlikely in this context, as McKenzie and Woodruff (2014) review training business owners from a dozen randomized experiments and find little lasting impact on profits or sales. Still, having a sense of the marginal contributions of the asset transfer and the training would help us calibrate the design of the policy in contexts where the relative scarcity of these two inputs vary.

All three studies provide evidence on the ability of specific policies or their combinations to reduce the persistence of poverty in the long run. There are several common elements that these studies offer in terms of what we learn about the effectiveness of antipoverty policies.

First, a combination of policies seems to work well. Is it the case of classic complementarities that we are well familiar with from standard economic models, where $y = Af(x_1, x_2)$ and $f_{12} > 0$ where y is the outcome variable of interest and x_1 and x_2 are two different policies? Or do they reflect a multiple-friction or distortion view of the world and so just a big enough cash transfer or making credit available is not enough? For example, certain critical markets other than credit could be imperfect (e.g., training), individuals may not possess the best information about themselves or the external

---

3. I thank Christopher Barrett for this observation.

world (aspirations, self-belief), and given all of this, simply providing cash or capital may not be sufficient.

Second, together they make some progress toward disentangling different mechanisms that could lead to the persistence of poverty—namely, whether it is poverty traps or conditional convergence, and if it is poverty traps, whether it is due to external frictions or strong income effects that cause the poor to insufficiently save and invest in their own or their children's future. However, a lot remains to be understood as the findings are consistent with several mechanisms. For example, the evidence provided by the Bandiera et al. (2017) paper supports all three mechanisms: these women were credit constrained, they (presumably) needed training, and their saving rates increased significantly as result of the program. They support other mechanisms too that are not directly captured by theoretical framework here. For example, the training component of this program not only involved initial training, but also regular visits by livestock specialists and program officers of the nongovernmental organization that undertook the program over a two-year period after the transfer to cover the life cycle of livestock. One could argue that to the extent the poor are subject to behavioral biases, these visits may have helped them overcome these in addition to the stated goal of helping them overcome their limited experience of dealing with livestock.

Third, they highlight the need to have a clear theoretical framework that helps us understand better the relationship between specific antipoverty policies and particular mechanisms for persistence of poverty. For example, if strong income effects are the main culprit, then cash transfers are the best (unless there are supply-side delivery constraints, such as markets being inaccessible in remote rural areas or strong grounds for paternalistic concerns). Otherwise, cash transfers may not have much of an effect beyond current consumption. That may be the reason behind the findings of Araujo, Bosch, and Schady in Nicaragua. In contrast, if capital market frictions are the main problem, then direct provision of credit or facilitating borrowing and savings may be better and more cost-effective than income or wealth transfer. However, if training or some other input is depressing overall productivity in the area, then without addressing that constraint, none of these interventions will be particularly effective.

Conclusion

As we know, what a given policy evaluation provides is the marginal effect of changing an instrument (or, a combination of instruments) given a certain vector of individual and local characteristics. What it does not tell us (interactions do a partial job) is what would be the effect of the same policy in other settings. This is partly a point about external validity that is well known. But a related and more subtle implication of this point is, given those characteristics, what would be the effect of alternative policies?

The choice of a given policy reflects a researcher's implicit priors about what is the binding constraint or scarce input in a given setting. For example, a village that lacks a road that connects it to the market will not benefit much from other interventions. This highlights the importance of having a method of diagnosing what are the key frictions in a given setting, and in particular, what is the most binding constraint. For that, baseline surveys and some basic diagnostic theoretical framework is needed. Otherwise, there is a real risk of throwing darts in the dark, or to draw a closer analogy, applying a treatment on a patient without checking the symptoms.

Theory helps us in this endeavor in three distinct ways. First, it helps us ask the right questions: what are the causes of the persistence of poverty, what are the consequences or symptoms, and which one is likely to be salient under what parameter conditions? This helps us formulate empirical tests and design experiments. Second, theory allows us to do counterfactual analysis. What happened in the context of evaluating a specific policy is one of many possibilities. Having different arms of treatments is costly in terms of the required sample size to have statistical power. Also, external validity requires many experiments in different settings, which while essential, is not feasible in the short to medium run. A theoretical framework allows us to generate alternative hypothetical scenarios, and coupled with quantitative analysis with existing data, can help tell us what alternative policies could have done, thereby helping suggest new directions for empirical research. Finally, theory allows us to do welfare analysis. Once we know a particular program leads to a specific outcome, we need a normative framework where the cost of funds and the benefits to the target group are all taken into account to do a proper social cost-benefit analysis.

This feeds into a broader policy lesson that there is no unique policy that will help remove poverty or achieve development. Even when overall average treatment effects are not impressive, we cannot abandon a particular policy as a policy tool because of the potential importance of heterogeneous treatment effects. Otherwise, it would be the same as abandoning a particular medication for the population at large, and not those subject to certain health conditions. What works presupposes that we know the problems of a given individual or an area well, and are simply trying to figure out which method works best. As much as different ailments require different treatments, rather than ask "what works," it is best to ask "what works for a particular problem for a given individual?"

References

Azariadis, C. 1996. "The Economics of Poverty Traps Part One: Complete Markets." *Journal of Economic Growth* 1:449–86.

Bandiera, Oriana, Robin Burgess, Narayan Das, Selim Gulesci, Imran Rasul, and Munshi Sulaiman. 2017. "Labor Markets and Poverty in Village Economies." *Quarterly Journal of Economics* 132 (2): 811–70.

Banerjee, Abhijit, and Sendhil Mullainathan. 2010. "The Shape of Temptation: Implications for the Economic Lives of the Poor." NBER Working Paper no. 15973, Cambridge, MA.

Barrett, Christopher B., and Michael R. Carter. 2013. "The Economics of Poverty Traps and Persistent Poverty: An Asset-Based Approach." *Journal of Development Studies* 49 (7): 976–90.

Ghatak, Maitreesh. 2015. "Theories of Poverty Traps and Anti-poverty Policies." *World Bank Economic Review* 29 (Suppl. 1): S77–105.

Jensen, Robert. 2010. "The (Perceived) Returns to Education and the Demand for Schooling." *Quarterly Journal of Economics* 125 (2): 515–48.

Kraay, Aart, and David McKenzie. 2014. "Do Poverty Traps Exist? Assessing the Evidence." *Journal of Economic Perspectives* 28 (3): 127–48.

Macours, Karen, and Renos Vakis. 2014. "Changing Households' Investment Behaviour through Social Interactions with Local Leaders: Evidence from a Randomized Transfer Program." *Economic Journal* 124:607–33.

McKenzie, D., and C. Woodruff. 2014. "What Are We Learning from Business Training and Entrepreneurship Evaluations around the Developing World?" *World Bank Research Observer* 29 (1): 48–82.

Contributors

M. Caridad Araujo
Inter-American Development Bank
1300 New York Avenue, NW
Washington, DC 20577

Edward B. Barbier
Department of Economics
Colorado State University
1771 Campus Delivery
Fort Collins, CO 80523-1771

Christopher B. Barrett
Charles H. Dyson School of Applied
    Economics and Management
301G Warren Hall
Cornell University
Ithaca, NY 14853-7801

Mariano Bosch
Inter-American Development Bank
1300 New York Avenue, NW
Washington, DC 20577

Francisco J. Buera
Department of Economics
Washington University in St. Louis
One Brookings Drive
St. Louis, MO 63130-4899

Michael R. Carter
Department of Agricultural and
    Resource Economics
University of California, Davis
One Shields Avenue
Davis, CA 95616

Jean-Paul Chavas
Department of Agriculture and
    Applied Economics
University of Wisconsin
Taylor Hall, 427 Lorch Street
Madison, WI 53706

Emma Boswell Dean
Department of Health Management
    and Policy
5250 University Drive
Miami Business School
University of Miami
Coral Gables, FL 33146

Jonathan de Quidt
Institute for International Economic
    Studies
Stockholm University
106 91 Stockholm Sweden

Elizabeth Frankenberg
Carolina Population Center and
  Department of Sociology
University of North Carolina, Chapel
  Hill
123 West Franklin Street
Chapel Hill, NC 27514

Maitreesh Ghatak
London School of Economics
Department of Economics
Houghton Street
London WC2A 2AE United Kingdom

Johannes Haushofer
Woodrow Wilson School
427 Peretsman-Scully Hall
Princeton University
Princeton, NJ 08540

John Hoddinott
Division of Nutritional Sciences
Savage Hall, Room 305
Cornell University
Ithaca, NY 14853

Munenobu Ikegami
Faculty of Economics
Hosei University
4342 Aiharamachi, Machidashi
Tokyo 194-0298 Japan

Sarah Janzen
Department of Agricultural
  Economics
Kansas State University
342 Waters Hall
Manhattan, KS 66506

Joseph P. Kaboski
Department of Economics
434 Flanner Hall
University of Notre Dame
Notre Dame, IN 46556

Rachid Laajaj
Department of Economics
Universidad de los Andes
Calle 19A No. 1-37 Este, Edificio W
Bogota, Colombia

Travis J. Lybbert
Agricultural and Resources Economics
University of California, Davis
1 Shields Avenue
Davis, CA 95616

Karen Macours
Paris School of Economics
Campus Jourdan
48 Boulevard Jourdan
75014 Paris France

Paulo Santos
Department of Economics
Monash University
900 Dandenong Road, Caulfield
Victoria 3145 Australia

Norbert Schady
Inter-American Development Bank
1300 New York Avenue, NW
Washington, DC 20577

Frank Schilbach
Department of Economics, E52-560
Massachusetts Institute of Technology
77 Massachusetts Avenue
Cambridge, MA 02139

Heather Schofield
Perelman School of Medicine and
  The Wharton School
University of Pennsylvania
Blockley Hall 11th floor
423 Guardian Drive
Philadelphia, PA 19104

Yongseok Shin
Department of Economics
Washington University in St. Louis
One Brookings Drive
St. Louis, MO 63130

Stephen C. Smith
Department of Economics
Monroe Hall 340
The George Washington University
2115 G Street, NW
Washington, DC 20052

Duncan Thomas
Department of Economics
Duke University
Box 90097
Durham, NC 27708

Renos Vakis
The World Bank
1818 H Street, NW
Washington, DC 20043

Bruce Wydick
Department of Economics
University of San Francisco
San Francisco, CA 94117

Author Index

Hasselblatt, B., 294, 295
Haushofer, J., 58, 82, 83, 88, 90, 133, 136, 149, 199
Haynes, R. B., 91
Headey, D., 292
Heckman, J. J., 27, 94, 103, 359n6, 379
Henrion, M., 270
Herculano-Houzel, S., 76
Hermalin, B. E., 138
Hermes, R., 45
Hidrobo, M., 362
Hinson, J. M., 92
Hirschi, T., 90
Hitch, G., 68
Hochard, J. P., 315n1
Hochberg, Y., 44n3
Hockey, G. R., 81
Hoddinott, J., 3n3, 14, 32
Hoff, K., 265n1, 328
Hofmann, W., 65
Holling, C. S., 292, 295
Holmer, I., 81
Hommel, G., 44n3
Horn, J. L., 61, 71
Hornbeck, R., 293, 299, 310, 311
Horwood, L. J., 134
Howieson, D. B., 61
Hsiang, S. M., 82
Huang, L. T., 121
Hubbard, R. G., 245n28
Hulme, D., 17
Hurd, M. D., 269
Hurrell, A., 223n1, 224
Hurst, C., 94
Hurt, D. R., 310
Hygge, S., 81

Ikegami, M., 11, 12, 225, 232n13, 235, 250, 250n33
Imbens, G. W., 333, 369
Inzlicht, M., 65
Irgens-Hansen, K., 81
Isen, A. M., 138

Jaeggi, S. M., 70
Jagnani, M., 9
Jalan, J., 57, 315n2
James, W., 68
Jameson, T. L., 92
Jamir, L., 80
Jamison, J. C., 90
Jamrah, A., 80

Jang, C., 83
Janzen, S. A., 13, 13n14, 225, 227, 250, 250n33
Jaušovec, N., 93
Jensen, R., 159, 250, 326, 328, 390
Jessell, T., 67
Ji, Y.-B., 280n16
Jiang, N. H., 209, 210, 227n5
Johansen, S. N., 63
Johnson, K., 200, 203
Jones, B. F., 82
Josephs, R. A., 58, 76
Judge, T. A., 94, 156n1
Jurado, M. B., 60
Just, R. E., 268n3

Kaboski, J. P., 191, 192n2, 202, 203, 203n8, 204, 206, 207, 207n10, 208, 208n11, 210, 212, 213, 214, 215
Kala, N., 82
Kalkuhl, M., 292
Kalyanaraman, K., 369
Kamara, A., 272n9
Kandasamya, N., 83
Kandel, E., 67
Kane, M. J., 65, 70
Kaplan, S., 65
Kar, B. R., 121
Karkowski, L. M., 130n2
Karlan, D., 21, 87, 88, 91, 194, 200, 200n6, 202, 202n7, 203
Katok, A., 294, 295
Katz, L. F., 148, 149, 170, 332, 333
Kaufman, A. S., 73
Kendler, K. S., 130n2
Kessler, R. C., 127
Keswell, M., 199n5
Khantzian, E. J., 139
Kilby, A., 78
Killgore, W. D. S., 79
Kim, C., 82
Kimberg, D. Y., 60
King, J., 91n9
Kinnan, E., 215
Kinsey, B., 32, 227
Kirchner, W. K., 70
Kirk, M., 272n9
Kjellstrom, T., 81
Kling, J. R., 148, 149, 170, 332, 333
Knight, R., 194
Knox, A. B., 72
Knutson, B., 78

Subject Index

Page numbers followed by "f" or "t" refer to figures or tables, respectively.

accidents: traffic, 86–87; workplace, 86–87
air pollution, 82
alcohol consumption, excessive, impact of poverty on, 77
Appadurai, Arjun, 157–58
aspirations: Appadurai's conception of, 157; impact of augmented, 159–60; impact of television and its effect on women's, in India, 158; Ray's concepts of, 157–58; role modeling and, 158. *See also* hope
aspirations failure, 157–58
aspirations gap, 157
aspirations window, 157
aspire, capacity to, 157
asset accumulation, 1–2
asset dynamics, model of, 227–30
asset grants: assessment of role of programs for, 212–14; to microentrepreneurs, 192–99; studies of, 193t, 196t; to ultrapoor, 195–99
asset shocks, ex post and ex ante effects of, 233–36
associativeness, 90
Atención a Crisis program (Nicaragua): data for study, 331–33; described, 329–30; outcomes for leaders, 333–36; randomization in, 330–31. *See also* conditional cash transfer (CCT) programs

attention: defined, 61, 62; described, 62; empirical evidence for, 85–86; impact of economic conditions on, 83–87; internal vs. external, 62–63; measuring, 63–65; narrow vs. broad, 63; potential pathways for, 86–87; simple vs. complex, 63; theories of, in shaping economic behavior, 84–85
attributional style, 156

Backward Digit Span Task, 98t
BDH. *See* Bono de Desarrollo Humano (BDH) (Ecuador); conditional cash transfer (CCT) programs
Beck, Aaron, 140
belief-driven depression, model of, 136–37
Bono de Desarrollo Humano (BDH) (Ecuador), 359–61. *See also* conditional cash transfer (CCT) programs
Boran (Ethiopia) pastoralist households: ability and expected herd dynamics, 279–84; data for, 268–74; expected herd dynamics in stochastic environment, 274–79; policy challenges, 284–87
broad attention, vs. narrow, 63

Cambodia, cash transfer programs in, 359
capacity to aspire, 157
capital. *See* human capital
CBT (cognitive behavioral therapy), 140